OCTOBER FACTION

OPEN SEASON

Facebook: **facebook.com/idwpublishing**
Twitter: **@idwpublishing**
YouTube: **youtube.com/idwpublishing**
Tumblr: **tumblr.idwpublishing.com**
Instagram: **instagram.com/idwpublishing**

ISBN: 978-1-68405-527-2   22 21 20 19   1 2 3 4

Originally published as THE OCTOBER FACTION issues #1–12.

Chris Ryall, President, Publisher, & CCO
John Barber, Editor-In-Chief
Cara Morrison, Chief Financial Officer
Matt Ruzicka, Chief Accounting Officer
David Hedgecock, Associate Publisher
Jerry Bennington, VP of New Product Development
Lorelei Bunjes, VP of Digital Services
Justin Eisinger, Editorial Director, Graphic Novels & Collections
Eric Moss, Senior Director, Licensing and Business Development

Ted Adams and Robbie Robbins, IDW Founders

Created by
Steve Niles & **Damien Worm**

Written by **Steve Niles**
Illustrated by **Damien Worm**
Color Assist by **Alyzia Zherno**
Letters by **Shawn Lee** and **Robbie Robbins**

Series Edits by **Chris Ryall** and **Michael Benedetto**

Cover Art by **Damien Worm**
Collection Edits by **Justin Eisinger** and **Alonzo Simon**
Collection Design by **Ron Estevez**

I'm going to hijack this introduction.

Right away. Before it even gets started. Two reasons: 1) Who reads introductions? They tend to be full of pretentious bullshit. And 2) Book introductions always feel like extra homework to me. So the hell with pithy, erudite thoughts on the nature of fiction and art. I love *October Faction* because of Steve Niles, the musician. That dude is a total legend in the DC punk——Hold it. I can hear some of you protesting already. "I bought this new cover art version of the graphic novel, and dammit, I want–nay, DESERVE– some pithy insights into why Kindler felt HE was the one with the vision to adapt it to television/streaming/kinescope, etc..!" Fine. I took the job because the comic was incredible. Simple. Elegant. Human. Evolved. A zero-fucks, ass-kicking world about family. The amazing visuals created by Damien Worm were indelible and gorgeous, pulling me in like a blood-splattered magnet by way of Tim Burton.

I usually have a massive allergy to most (not all) pre-existing "intellectual properties" (worst. term. ever.). Meaning half the time someone sends you a graphic novel/book/ video game/toy concept to consider adapting there's usually a good reason it's on your desk and not one belonging to the Russo brothers or someone whose name begins with J.J., Joss, or Damon. And that reason is that said "intellectual property" either shouldn't be or can't decently be converted into moving images.

But this time, I got lucky. This time I got the Glengarry leads. I got *October Faction*. I won the IP lottery. Only one problem: What if the genius who initially thought up all this cool stuff hates how I adapt it? What then?? Again: lucky. Steve came into the writers' room and sat quietly among the very talented group assembled and listened and ate lunch and was polite and then proceeded to blow our minds by telling us how much he loved what we were doing with the world he'd created. You could hear me exhale from miles away. You see, I love and respect Steve so much that if he'd hated what I was doing with *OF* it would have crushed me. Not just because he's a brilliant writer, but because he's also a PUNK ROCK LEGEND.

Steve played bass in Gray Matter, a legendary post-hardcore punk band out of Washington D.C. To me, that made him someone I needed to know. Adapting *October Faction* for Netflix was just the door in. Months later, in November 2018, I'm in Toronto, my home town. The city is gripped in a cold snap of epically cliche proportions.

Publicity people from Netflix as well as the good folks from IDW have descended on the snowy Canadian metropolis for a day-long photography session with the series' cast, as well as interviews with actors, directors, and producers. It's a Saturday and a rare day off from the 24/7 relentlessness of making the show. But fuck that, my mind is on one thing and one thing only: Interviewing Steve Niles. I point blank abuse my power as Showrunner to "ask" (read as "demand") that I interview Steve for the behind-the-scenes media kit. Baffled, frightened by my intensity, and likely in shock from the sub-arctic temperatures, the publicity people allow me to sit with Steve and conduct an intimate one-on-one interview. The idea was we'd discuss how he came up with the idea for *October Faction* and what it was like for him to see that world brought to life.

As you can guess, that's not how it went down.

Instead, I basically tried to pull off my best Lester Bangs impersonation and drilled down deep into the mid-'80s, east coast punk scene. I played drums in a high school band myself, but never went as far and as high as Steve and Gray Matter did. So I had questions, lots of them. None of them were about *October Faction*. Gentleman that he is, Steve answered every question thoughtfully and intelligently. But lurking just below the surface was the bassist for Gray Matter, ready to shred and sweat and pound out an aggressive song that moves your ass and your brain all at once. This is why *October Faction* is so cool. It comes from the same dude.

Enjoy the book. I hope you enjoy the series too. I took a few liberties but, hand to God, nothing without Steve's say-so.

The guy was in Gray Matter. If you pay close attention to the vibe of this book, you'll realize that only a punk legend could have made something this cool.

So prepare for Damien Worm's mind-melting images to grab you, put on some Gray Matter, and dive in.

Damian Kindler
Venice, CA

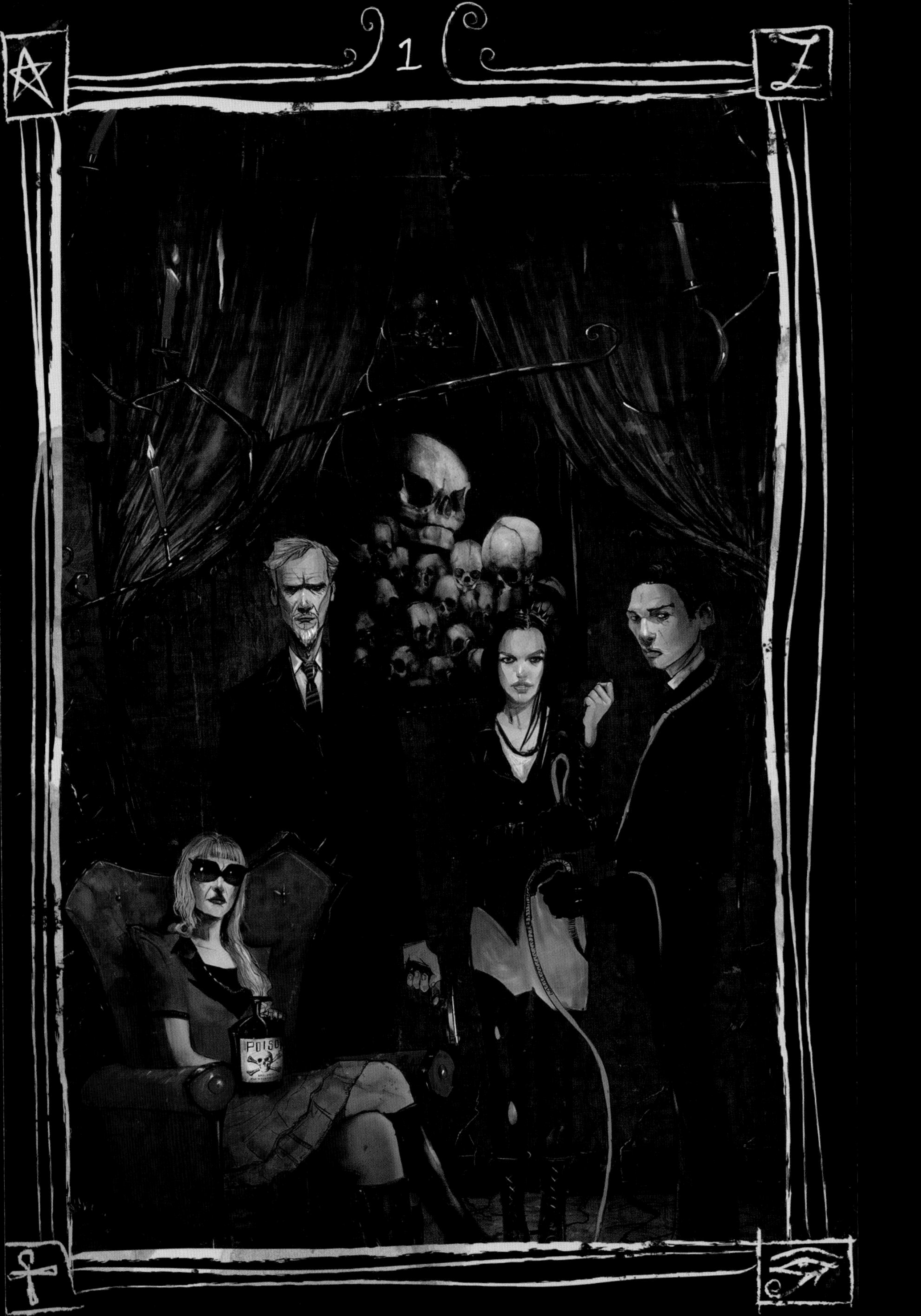
1
POISO

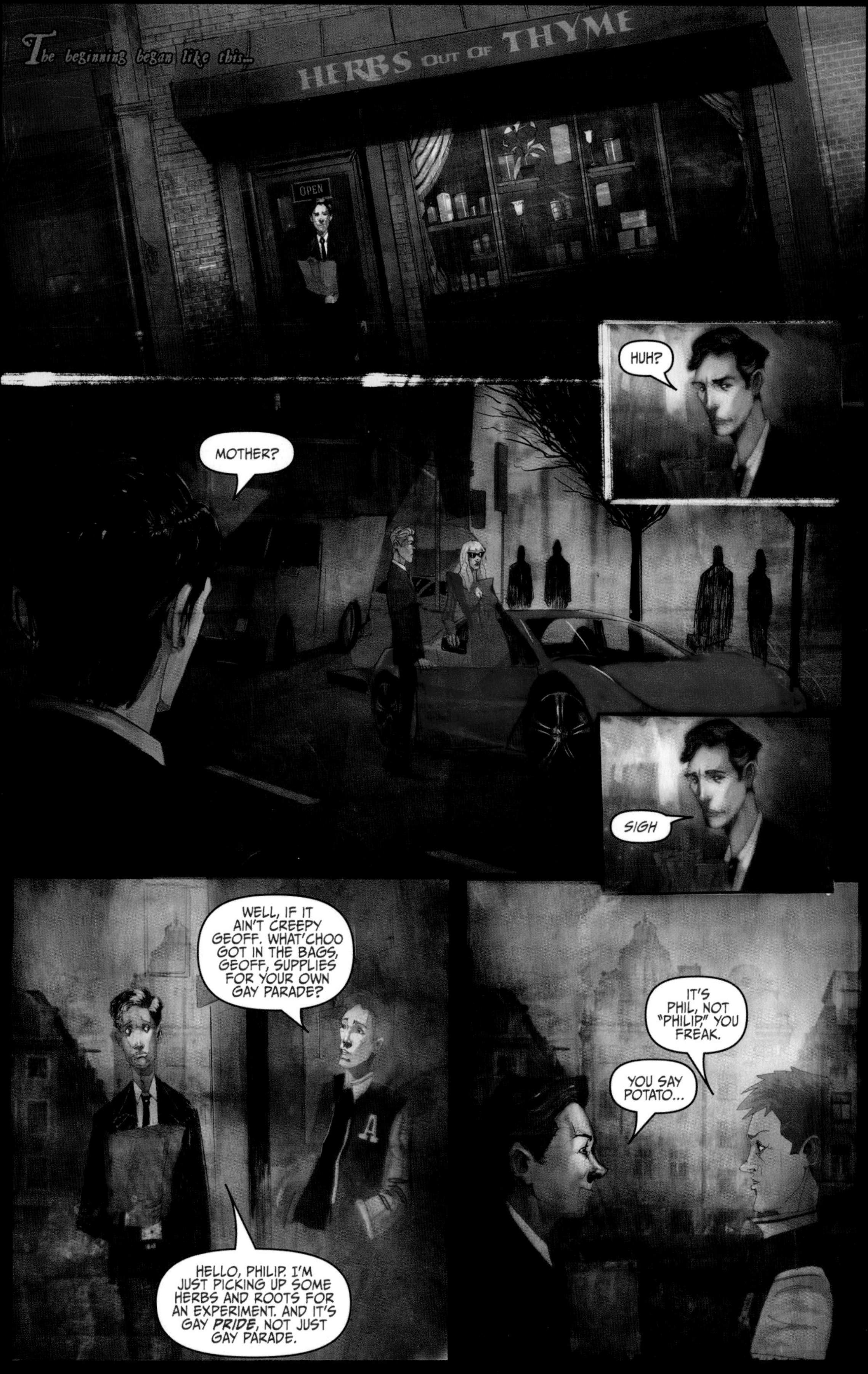

The beginning began like this...
HERBS OUT OF THYME
OPEN
HUH?
MOTHER?
SIGH
WELL, IF IT AIN'T CREEPY GEOFF. WHAT'CHOO GOT IN THE BAGS, GEOFF, SUPPLIES FOR YOUR OWN GAY PARADE?
HELLO, PHILIP. I'M JUST PICKING UP SOME HERBS AND ROOTS FOR AN EXPERIMENT. AND IT'S GAY PRIDE, NOT JUST GAY PARADE.
IT'S PHIL, NOT "PHILIP," YOU FREAK.
YOU SAY POTATO...

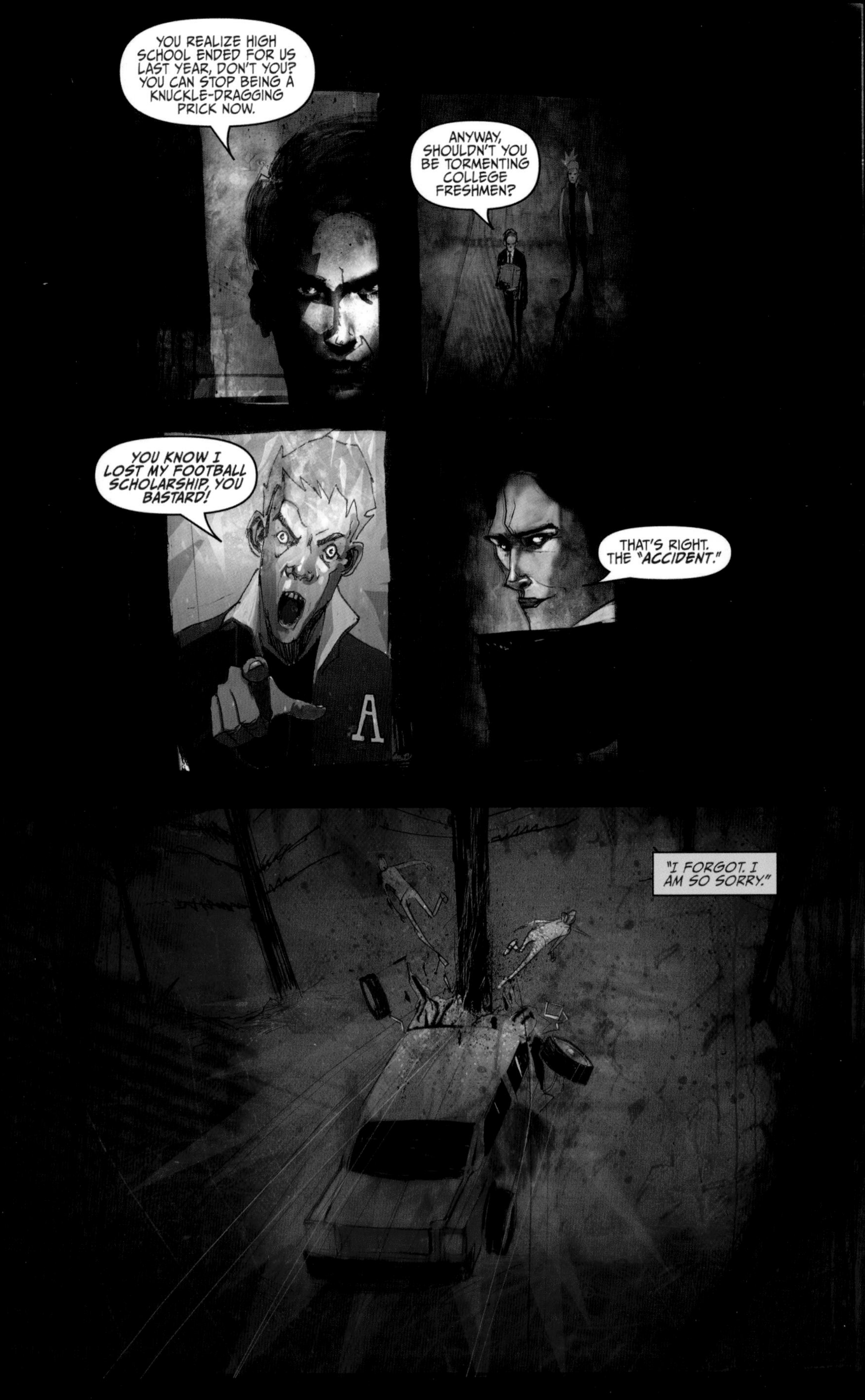

YOU REALIZE HIGH SCHOOL ENDED FOR US LAST YEAR, DON'T YOU? YOU CAN STOP BEING A KNUCKLE-DRAGGING PRICK NOW.
ANYWAY, SHOULDN'T YOU BE TORMENTING COLLEGE FRESHMEN?
YOU KNOW I LOST MY FOOTBALL SCHOLARSHIP, YOU BASTARD!
THAT'S RIGHT. THE "ACCIDENT."
"I FORGOT. I AM SO SORRY."

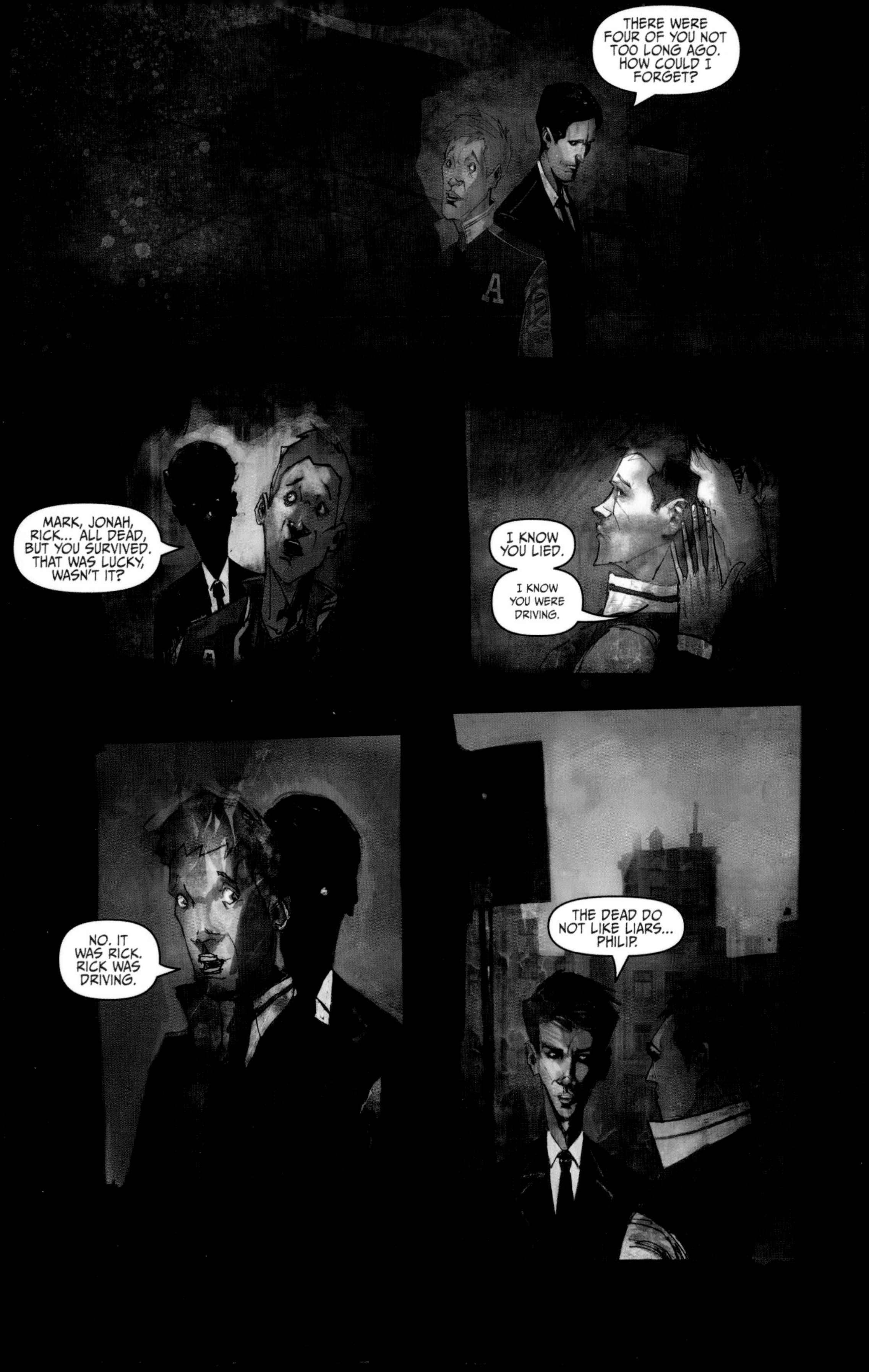
THERE WERE FOUR OF YOU NOT TOO LONG AGO. HOW COULD I FORGET?
MARK, JONAH, RICK... ALL DEAD, BUT YOU SURVIVED. THAT WAS LUCKY, WASN'T IT?
I KNOW YOU LIED.
I KNOW YOU WERE DRIVING.
NO. IT WAS RICK. RICK WAS DRIVING.
THE DEAD DO NOT LIKE LIARS... PHILIP.

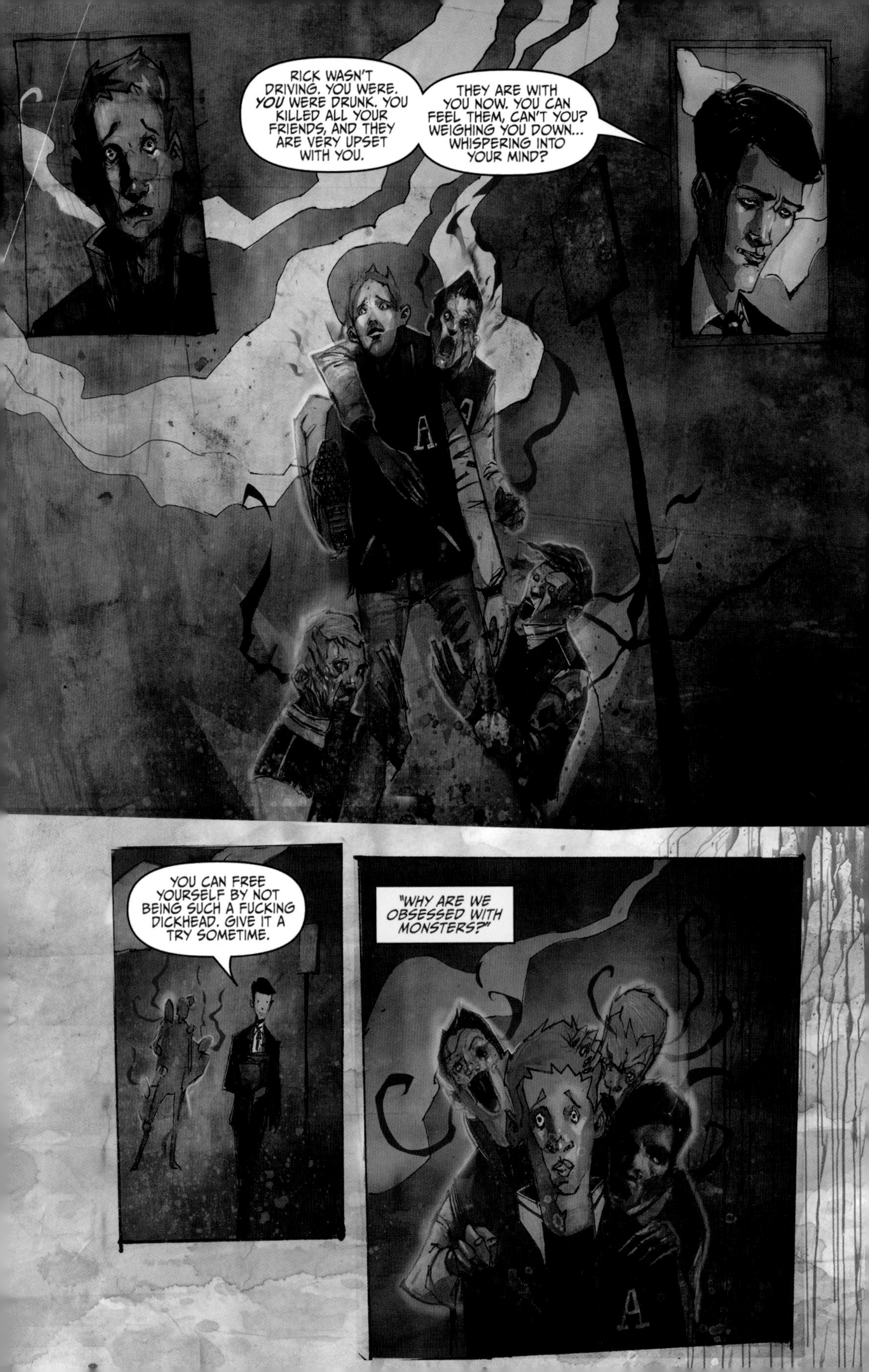
RICK WASN'T DRIVING. YOU WERE. YOU WERE DRUNK. YOU KILLED ALL YOUR FRIENDS, AND THEY ARE VERY UPSET WITH YOU.
THEY ARE WITH YOU NOW. YOU CAN FEEL THEM, CAN'T YOU? WEIGHING YOU DOWN... WHISPERING INTO YOUR MIND?
YOU CAN FREE YOURSELF BY NOT BEING SUCH A FUCKING DICKHEAD. GIVE IT A TRY SOMETIME.
"WHY ARE WE OBSESSED WITH MONSTERS?"

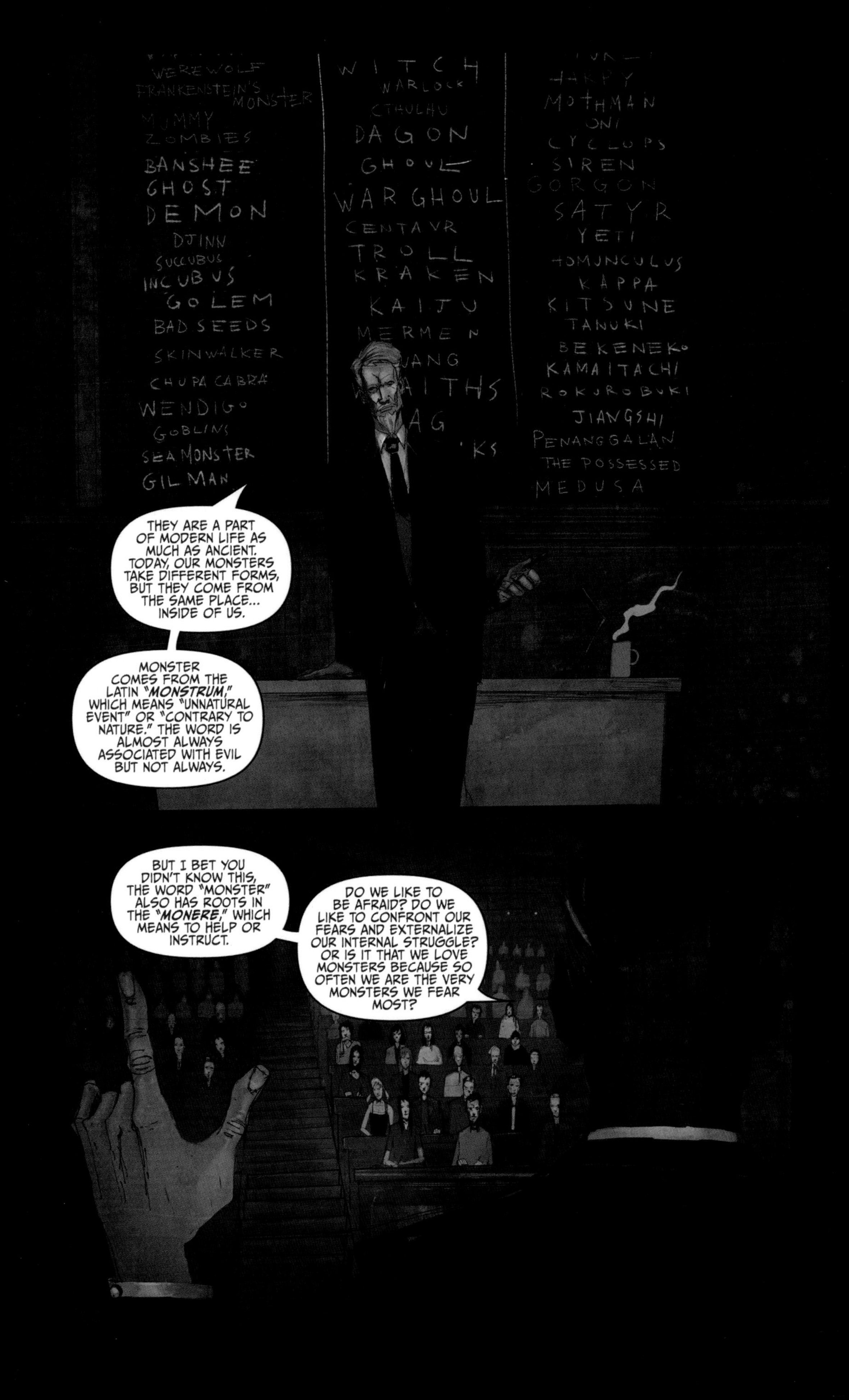
WEREWOLF
FRANKENSTEIN'S MONSTER
MUMMY
ZOMBIES
BANSHEE
GHOST
DEMON
DJINN
SUCCUBUS
INCUBUS
GOLEM
BAD SEEDS
SKINWALKER
CHUPA CABRA
WENDIGO
GOBLINS
SEA MONSTER
GIL MAN
WITCH
WARLOCK
CTHULHU
DAGON
GHOUL
WAR GHOUL
CENTAVR
TROLL
KRAKEN
KAIJU
MERMEN
HARPY
MOTHMAN
ONI
CYCLOPS
SIREN
GORGON
SATYR
YETI
HOMUNCULUS
KAPPA
KITSUNE
TANUKI
BEKENEKO
KAMAITACHI
ROKUROBUKI
JIANGSHI
PENANGGALAN
THE POSSESSED
MEDUSA
THEY ARE A PART OF MODERN LIFE AS MUCH AS ANCIENT. TODAY, OUR MONSTERS TAKE DIFFERENT FORMS, BUT THEY COME FROM THE SAME PLACE... INSIDE OF US.
MONSTER COMES FROM THE LATIN "*MONSTRUM*," WHICH MEANS "UNNATURAL EVENT" OR "CONTRARY TO NATURE." THE WORD IS ALMOST ALWAYS ASSOCIATED WITH EVIL BUT NOT ALWAYS.
BUT I BET YOU DIDN'T KNOW THIS, THE WORD "MONSTER" ALSO HAS ROOTS IN THE "*MONERE*," WHICH MEANS TO HELP OR INSTRUCT.
DO WE LIKE TO BE AFRAID? DO WE LIKE TO CONFRONT OUR FEARS AND EXTERNALIZE OUR INTERNAL STRUGGLE? OR IS IT THAT WE LOVE MONSTERS BECAUSE SO OFTEN WE ARE THE VERY MONSTERS WE FEAR MOST?

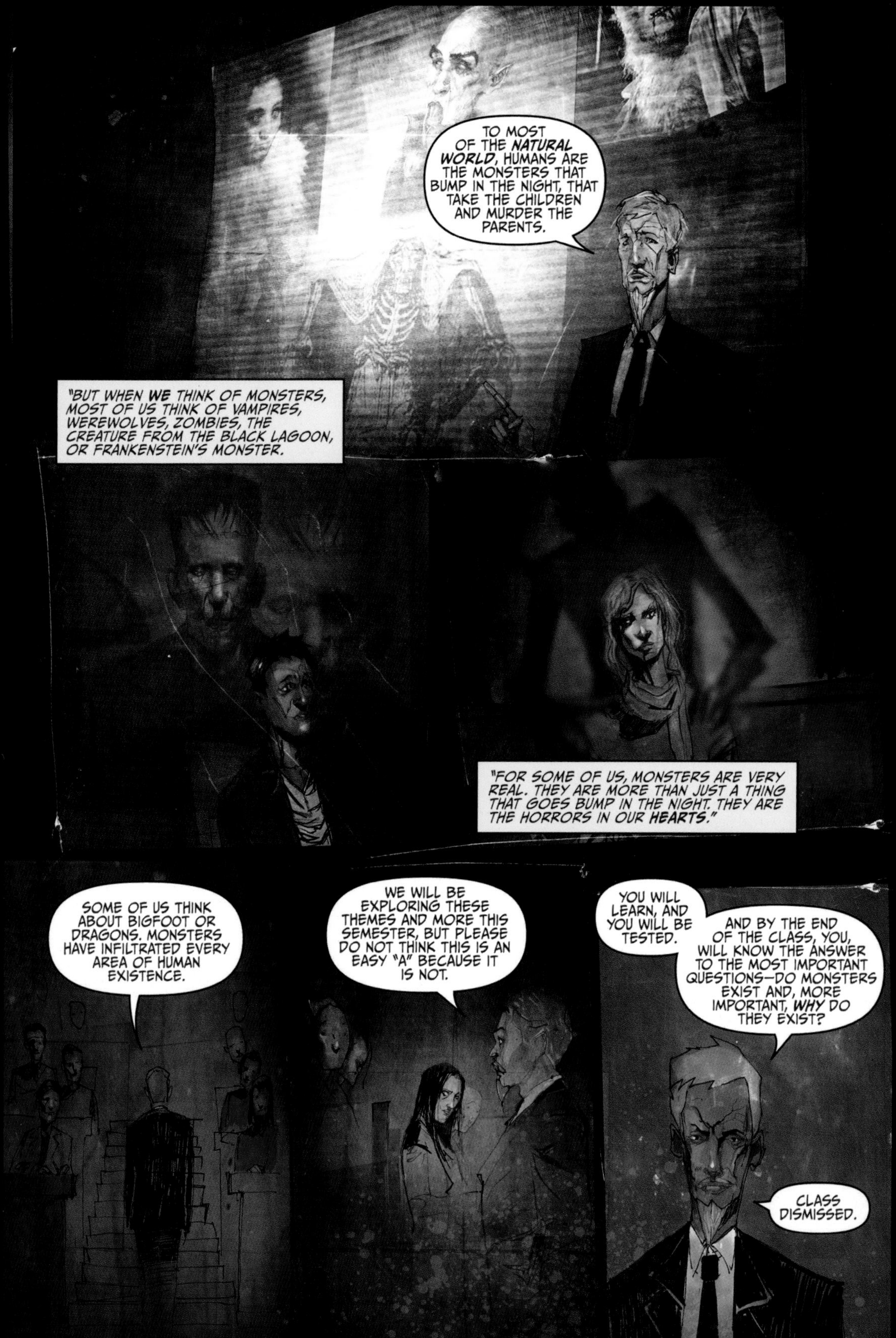
TO MOST OF THE ***NATURAL WORLD***, HUMANS ARE THE MONSTERS THAT BUMP IN THE NIGHT, THAT TAKE THE CHILDREN AND MURDER THE PARENTS.
"BUT WHEN **WE** THINK OF MONSTERS, MOST OF US THINK OF VAMPIRES, WEREWOLVES, ZOMBIES, THE CREATURE FROM THE BLACK LAGOON, OR FRANKENSTEIN'S MONSTER.
"FOR SOME OF US, MONSTERS ARE VERY REAL. THEY ARE MORE THAN JUST A THING THAT GOES BUMP IN THE NIGHT. THEY ARE THE HORRORS IN OUR **HEARTS**."
SOME OF US THINK ABOUT BIGFOOT OR DRAGONS. MONSTERS HAVE INFILTRATED EVERY AREA OF HUMAN EXISTENCE.
WE WILL BE EXPLORING THESE THEMES AND MORE THIS SEMESTER, BUT PLEASE DO NOT THINK THIS IS AN EASY "A" BECAUSE IT IS NOT.
YOU WILL LEARN, AND YOU WILL BE TESTED.
AND BY THE END OF THE CLASS, YOU, WILL KNOW THE ANSWER TO THE MOST IMPORTANT QUESTIONS—DO MONSTERS EXIST AND, MORE IMPORTANT, ***WHY*** DO THEY EXIST?
CLASS DISMISSED.

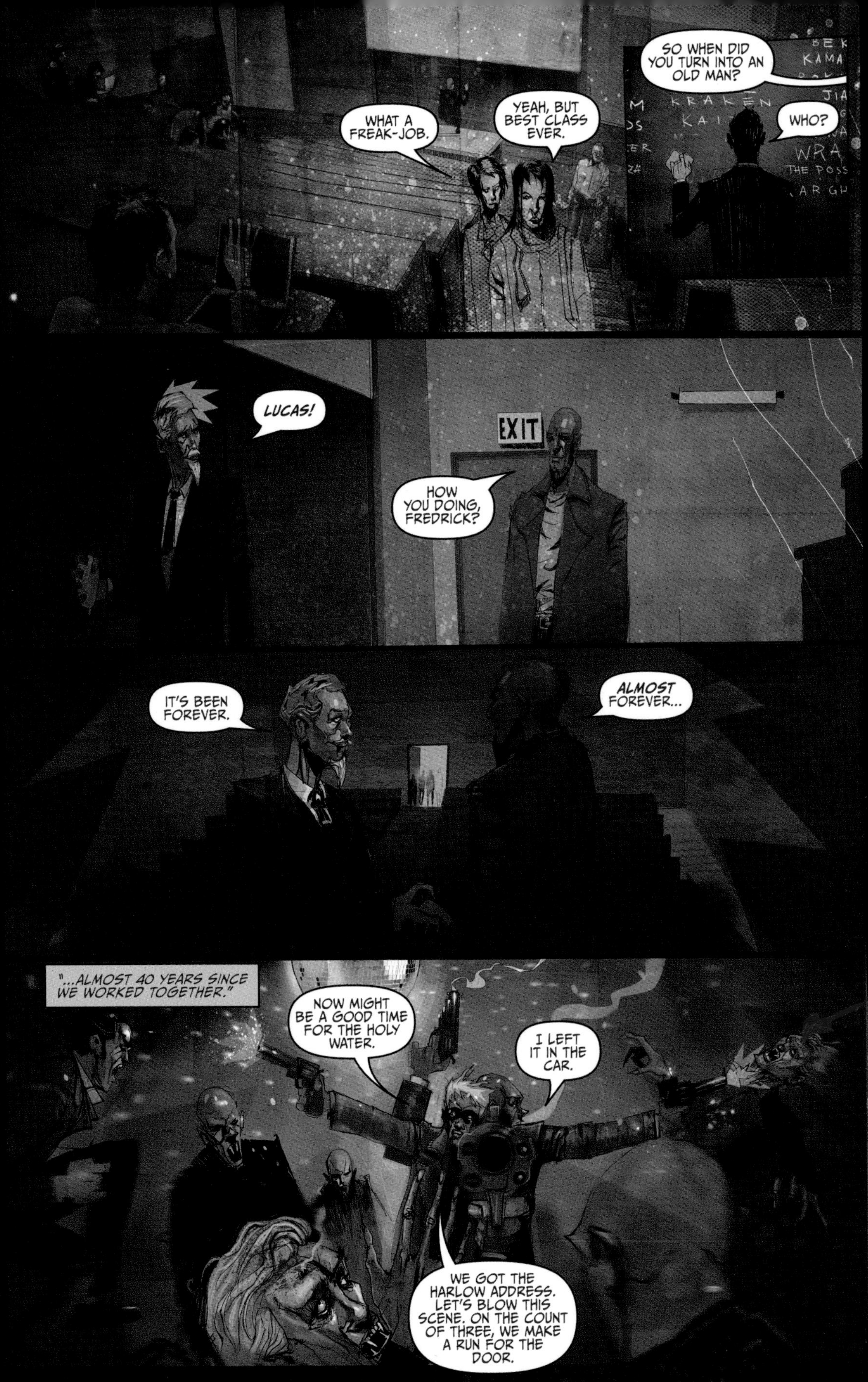
WHAT A FREAK-JOB.
YEAH, BUT BEST CLASS EVER.
SO WHEN DID YOU TURN INTO AN OLD MAN?
WHO?
KRAKEN
WRA
THE POSS
LUCAS!
EXIT
HOW YOU DOING, FREDRICK?
IT'S BEEN FOREVER.
ALMOST FOREVER...
"...ALMOST 40 YEARS SINCE WE WORKED TOGETHER."
NOW MIGHT BE A GOOD TIME FOR THE HOLY WATER.
I LEFT IT IN THE CAR.
WE GOT THE HARLOW ADDRESS. LET'S BLOW THIS SCENE. ON THE COUNT OF THREE, WE MAKE A RUN FOR THE DOOR.

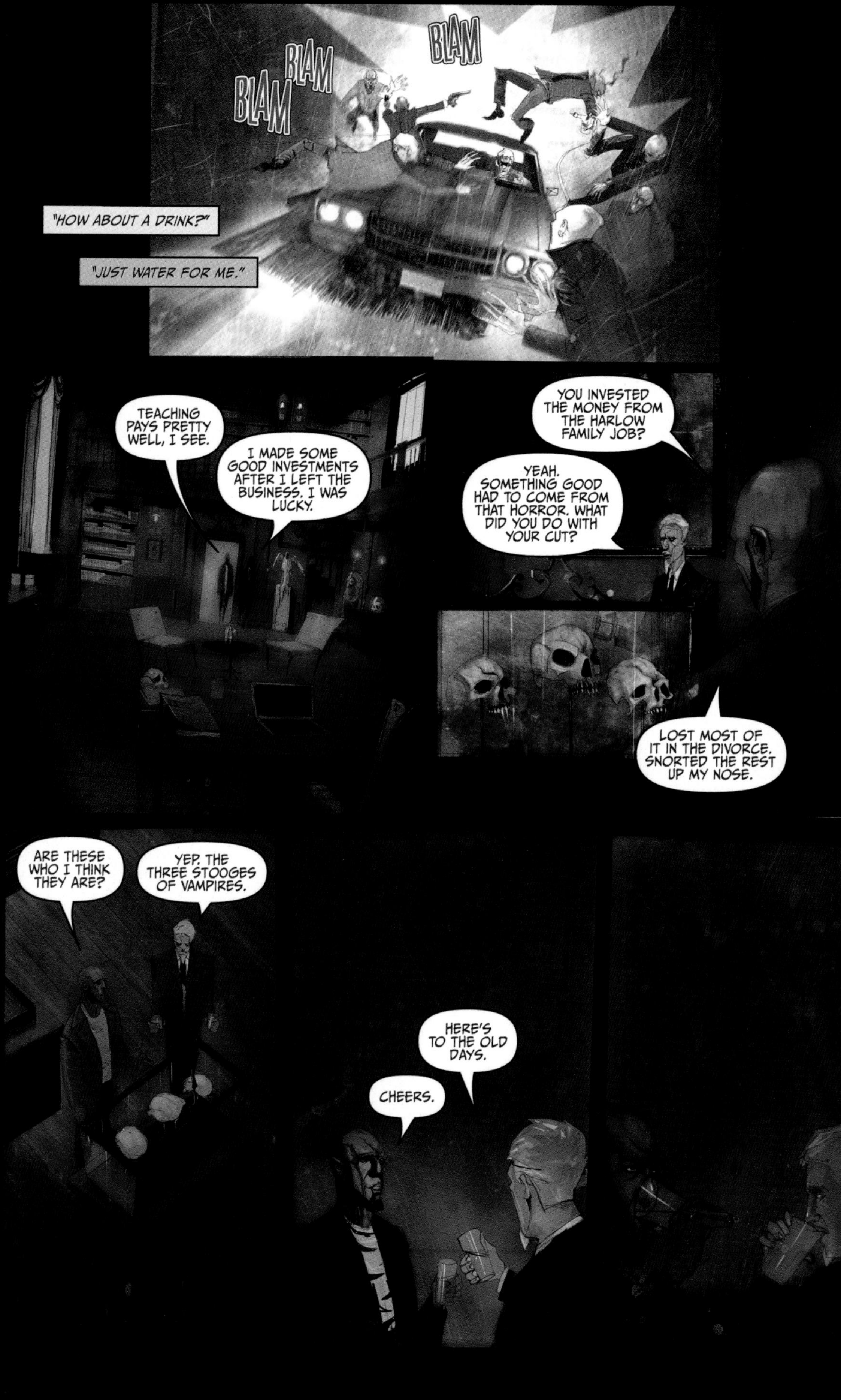
BLAM
BLAM
BLAM
"HOW ABOUT A DRINK?"
"JUST WATER FOR ME."
TEACHING PAYS PRETTY WELL, I SEE.
I MADE SOME GOOD INVESTMENTS AFTER I LEFT THE BUSINESS. I WAS LUCKY.
YOU INVESTED THE MONEY FROM THE HARLOW FAMILY JOB?
YEAH. SOMETHING GOOD HAD TO COME FROM THAT HORROR. WHAT DID YOU DO WITH YOUR CUT?
LOST MOST OF IT IN THE DIVORCE. SNORTED THE REST UP MY NOSE.
ARE THESE WHO I THINK THEY ARE?
YEP. THE THREE STOOGES OF VAMPIRES.
HERE'S TO THE OLD DAYS.
CHEERS.

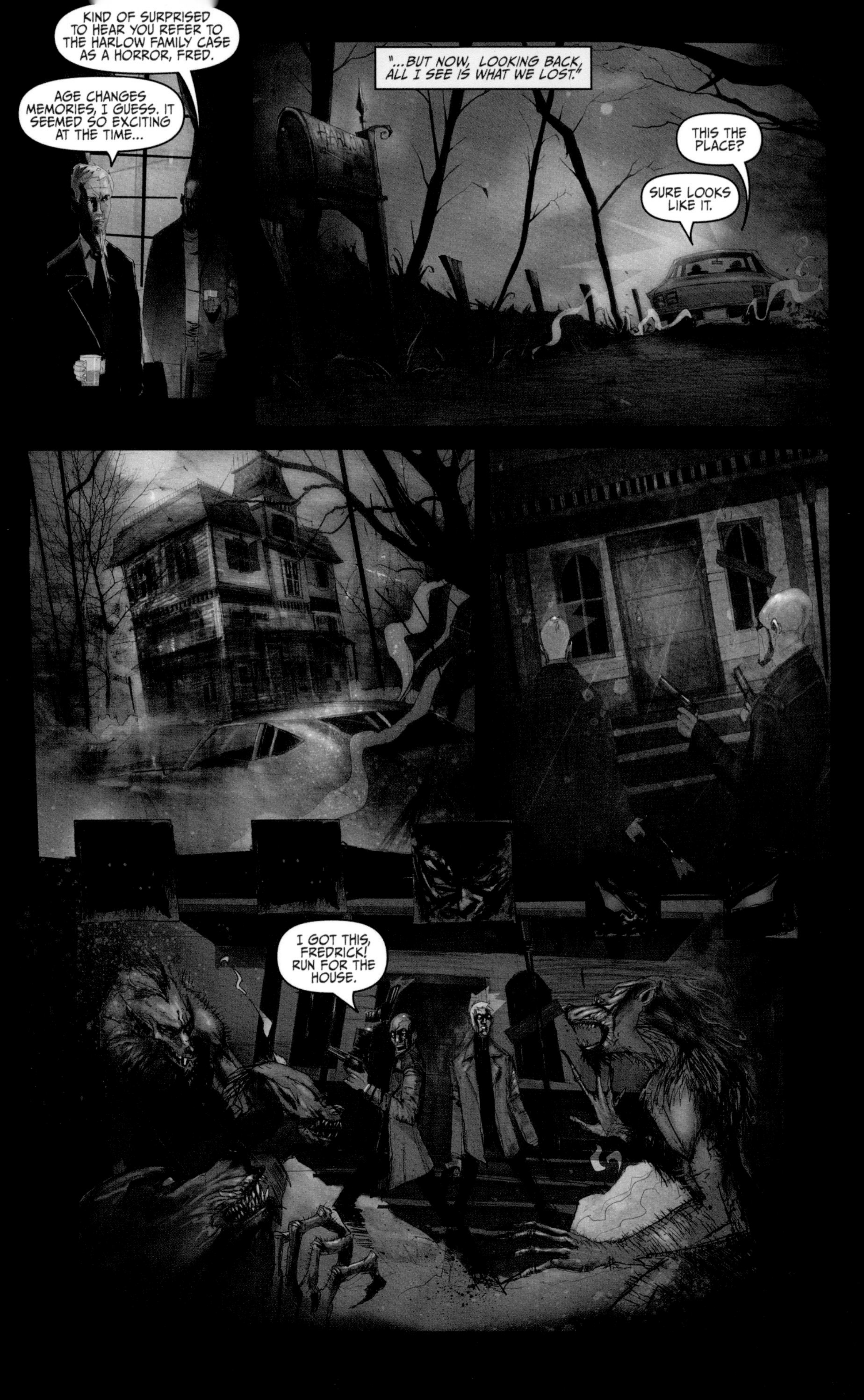
KIND OF SURPRISED TO HEAR YOU REFER TO THE HARLOW FAMILY CASE AS A HORROR, FRED.
AGE CHANGES MEMORIES, I GUESS. IT SEEMED SO EXCITING AT THE TIME...
"...BUT NOW, LOOKING BACK, ALL I SEE IS WHAT WE LOST."
THIS THE PLACE?
SURE LOOKS LIKE IT.
I GOT THIS, FREDRICK! RUN FOR THE HOUSE.

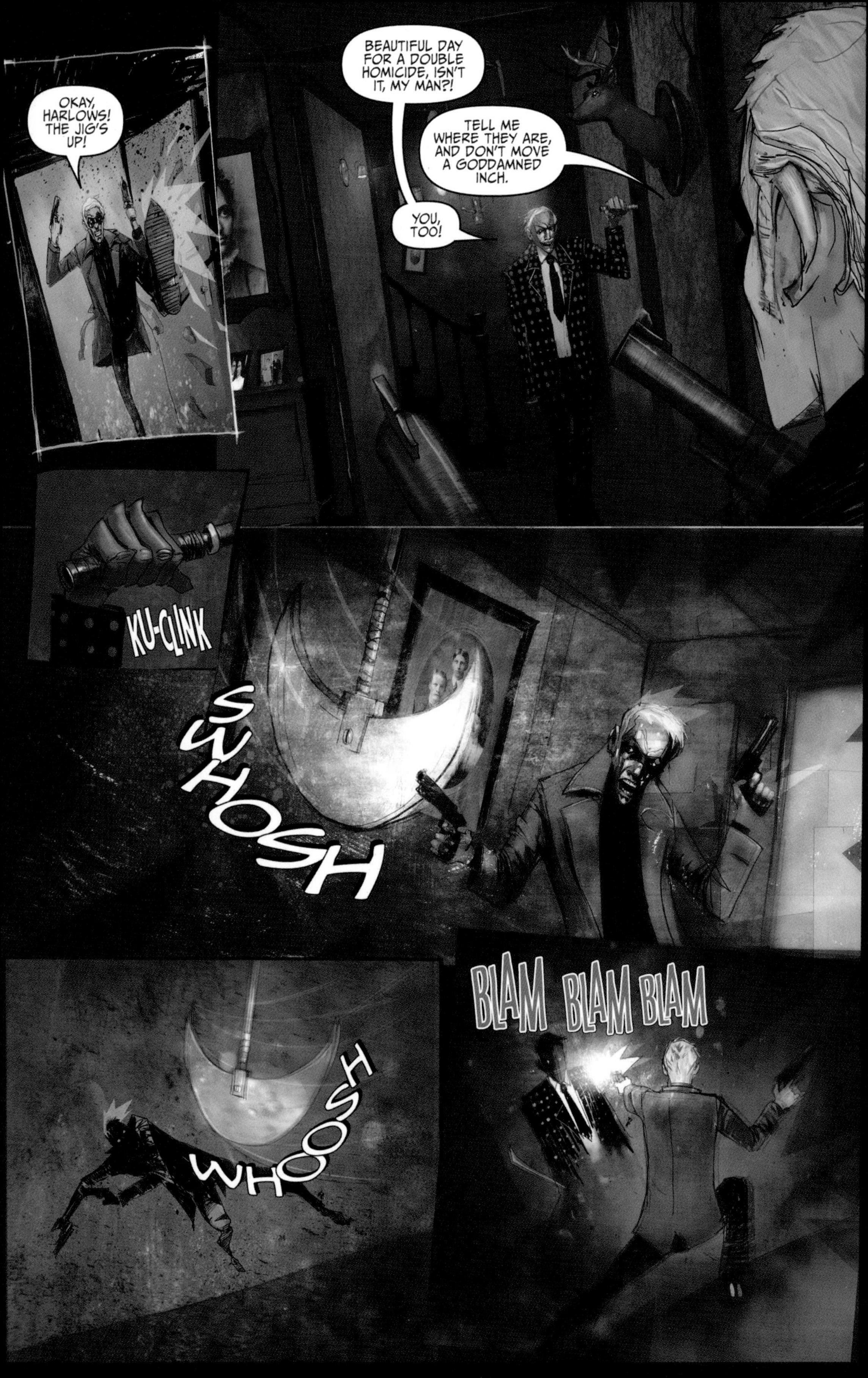
OKAY, HARLOWS! THE JIG'S UP!
BEAUTIFUL DAY FOR A DOUBLE HOMICIDE, ISN'T IT, MY MAN?!
YOU, TOO!
TELL ME WHERE THEY ARE, AND DON'T MOVE A GODDAMNED INCH.
KU-CLINK
SWHOSH
WHOOSH
BLAM BLAM BLAM

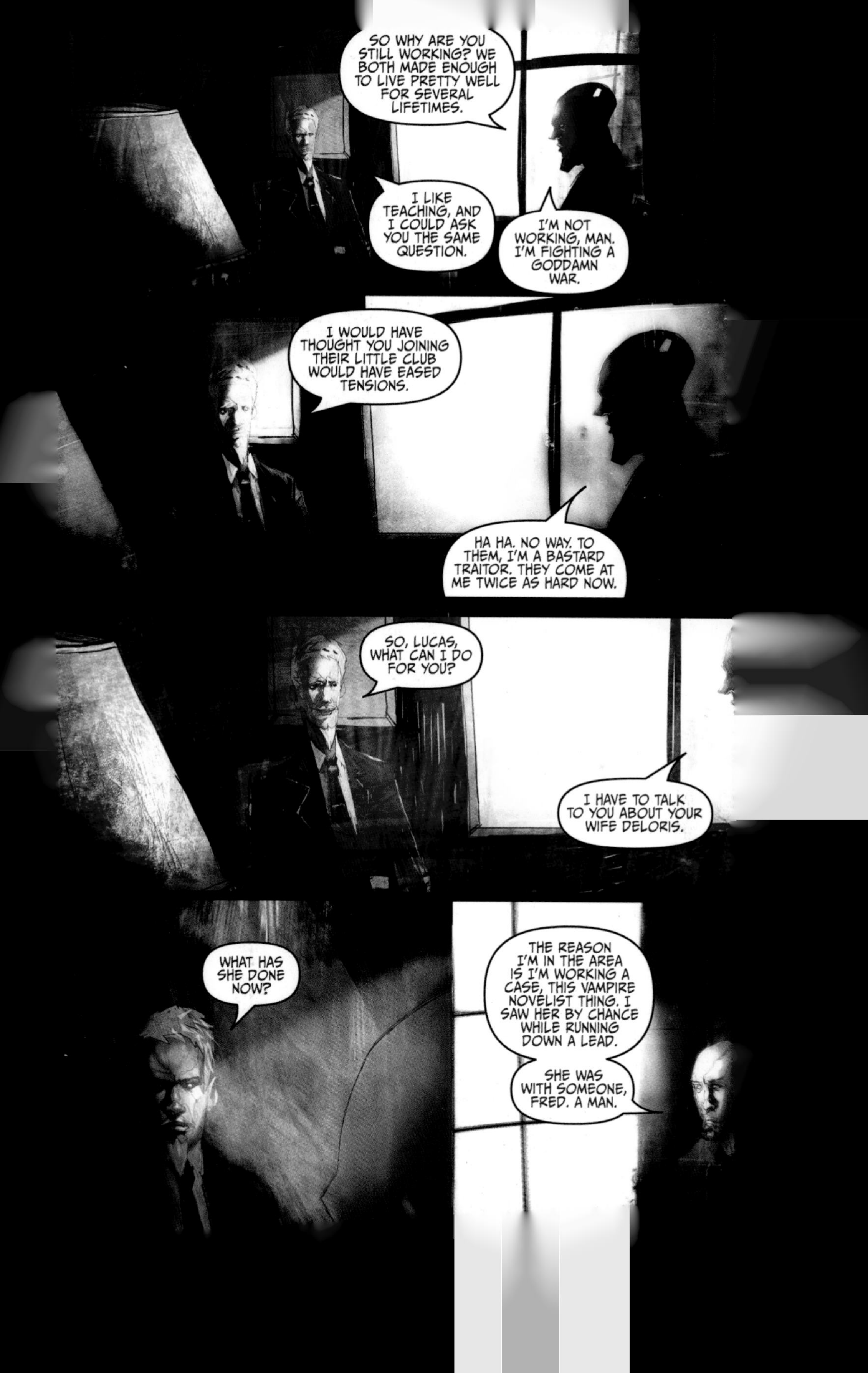

SO WHY ARE YOU STILL WORKING? WE BOTH MADE ENOUGH TO LIVE PRETTY WELL FOR SEVERAL LIFETIMES.
I LIKE TEACHING, AND I COULD ASK YOU THE SAME QUESTION.
I'M NOT WORKING, MAN. I'M FIGHTING A GODDAMN WAR.
I WOULD HAVE THOUGHT YOU JOINING THEIR LITTLE CLUB WOULD HAVE EASED TENSIONS.
HA HA. NO WAY. TO THEM, I'M A BASTARD TRAITOR. THEY COME AT ME TWICE AS HARD NOW.
SO, LUCAS, WHAT CAN I DO FOR YOU?
I HAVE TO TALK TO YOU ABOUT YOUR WIFE DELORIS.
WHAT HAS SHE DONE NOW?
THE REASON I'M IN THE AREA IS I'M WORKING A CASE, THIS VAMPIRE NOVELIST THING. I SAW HER BY CHANCE WHILE RUNNING DOWN A LEAD.
SHE WAS WITH SOMEONE, FRED. A MAN.

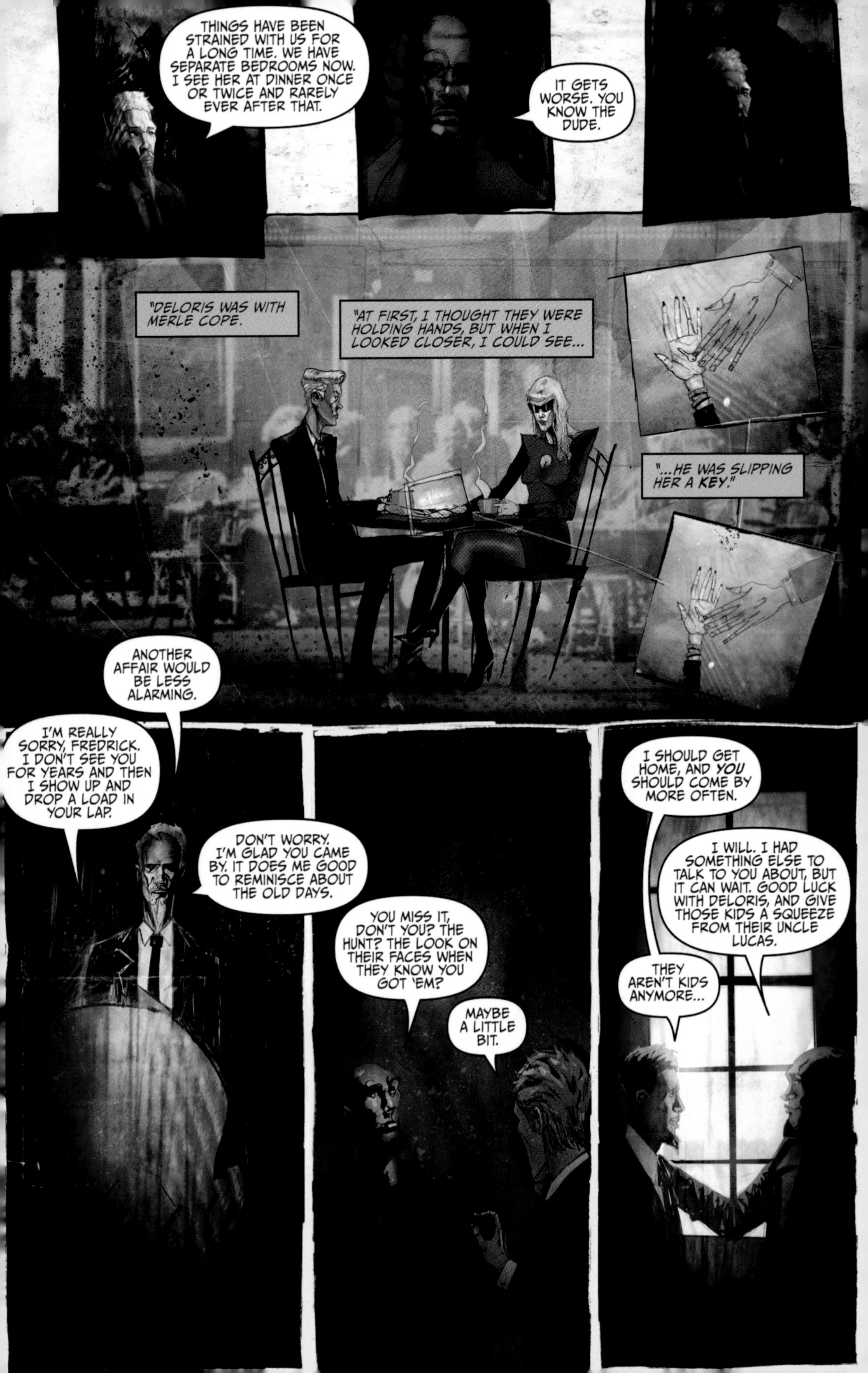
THINGS HAVE BEEN STRAINED WITH US FOR A LONG TIME. WE HAVE SEPARATE BEDROOMS NOW. I SEE HER AT DINNER ONCE OR TWICE AND RARELY EVER AFTER THAT.
IT GETS WORSE. YOU KNOW THE DUDE.
"DELORIS WAS WITH MERLE COPE.
"AT FIRST, I THOUGHT THEY WERE HOLDING HANDS, BUT WHEN I LOOKED CLOSER, I COULD SEE...
"...HE WAS SLIPPING HER A KEY."
ANOTHER AFFAIR WOULD BE LESS ALARMING.
I'M REALLY SORRY, FREDRICK. I DON'T SEE YOU FOR YEARS AND THEN I SHOW UP AND DROP A LOAD IN YOUR LAP.
DON'T WORRY. I'M GLAD YOU CAME BY. IT DOES ME GOOD TO REMINISCE ABOUT THE OLD DAYS.
YOU MISS IT, DON'T YOU? THE HUNT? THE LOOK ON THEIR FACES WHEN THEY KNOW YOU GOT 'EM?
MAYBE A LITTLE BIT.
I SHOULD GET HOME, AND YOU SHOULD COME BY MORE OFTEN.
I WILL. I HAD SOMETHING ELSE TO TALK TO YOU ABOUT, BUT IT CAN WAIT. GOOD LUCK WITH DELORIS, AND GIVE THOSE KIDS A SQUEEZE FROM THEIR UNCLE LUCAS.
THEY AREN'T KIDS ANYMORE...

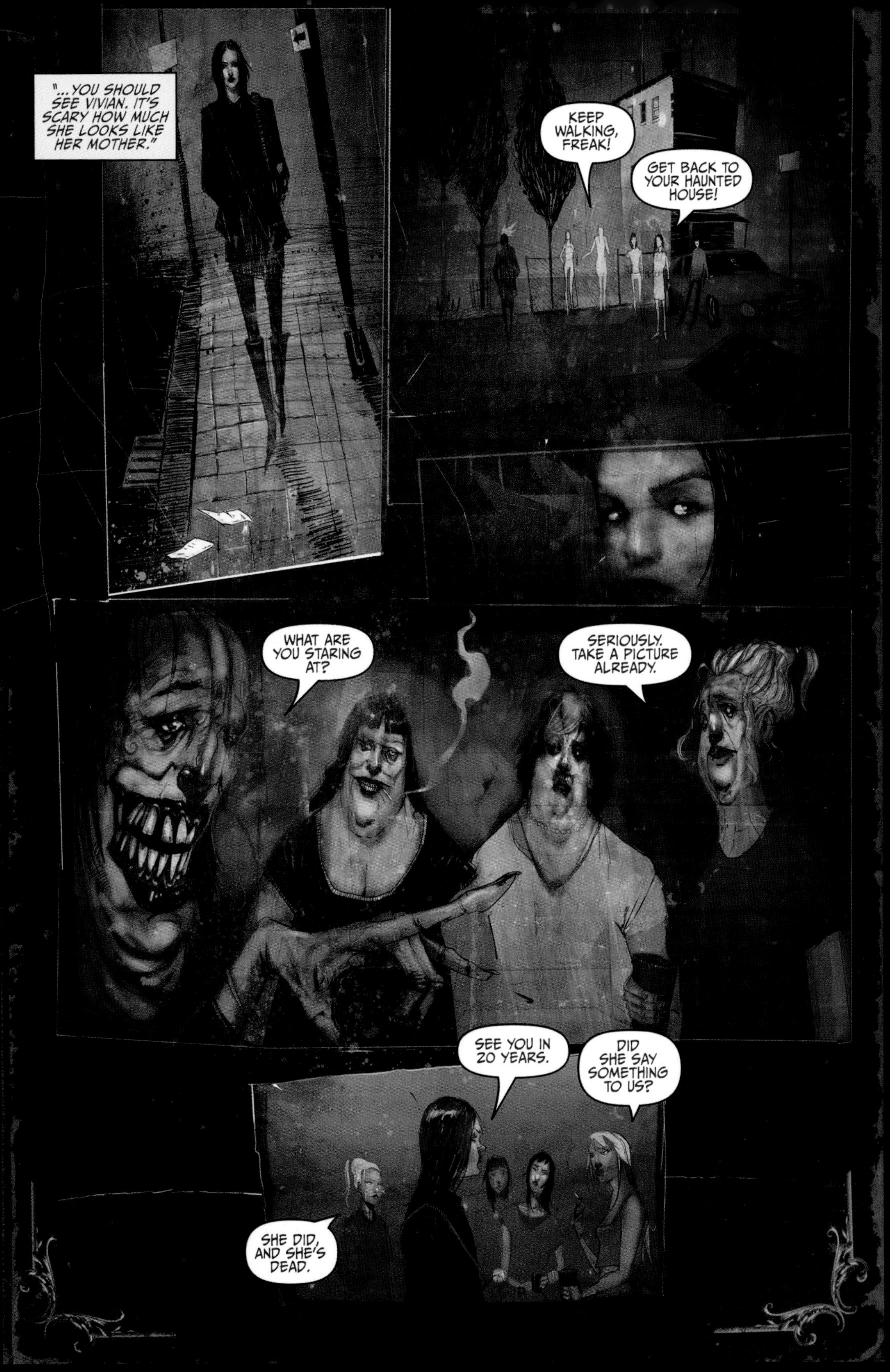
"...YOU SHOULD SEE VIVIAN. IT'S SCARY HOW MUCH SHE LOOKS LIKE HER MOTHER."
KEEP WALKING, FREAK!
GET BACK TO YOUR HAUNTED HOUSE!
WHAT ARE YOU STARING AT?
SERIOUSLY. TAKE A PICTURE ALREADY.
SEE YOU IN 20 YEARS.
DID SHE SAY SOMETHING TO US?
SHE DID, AND SHE'S DEAD.

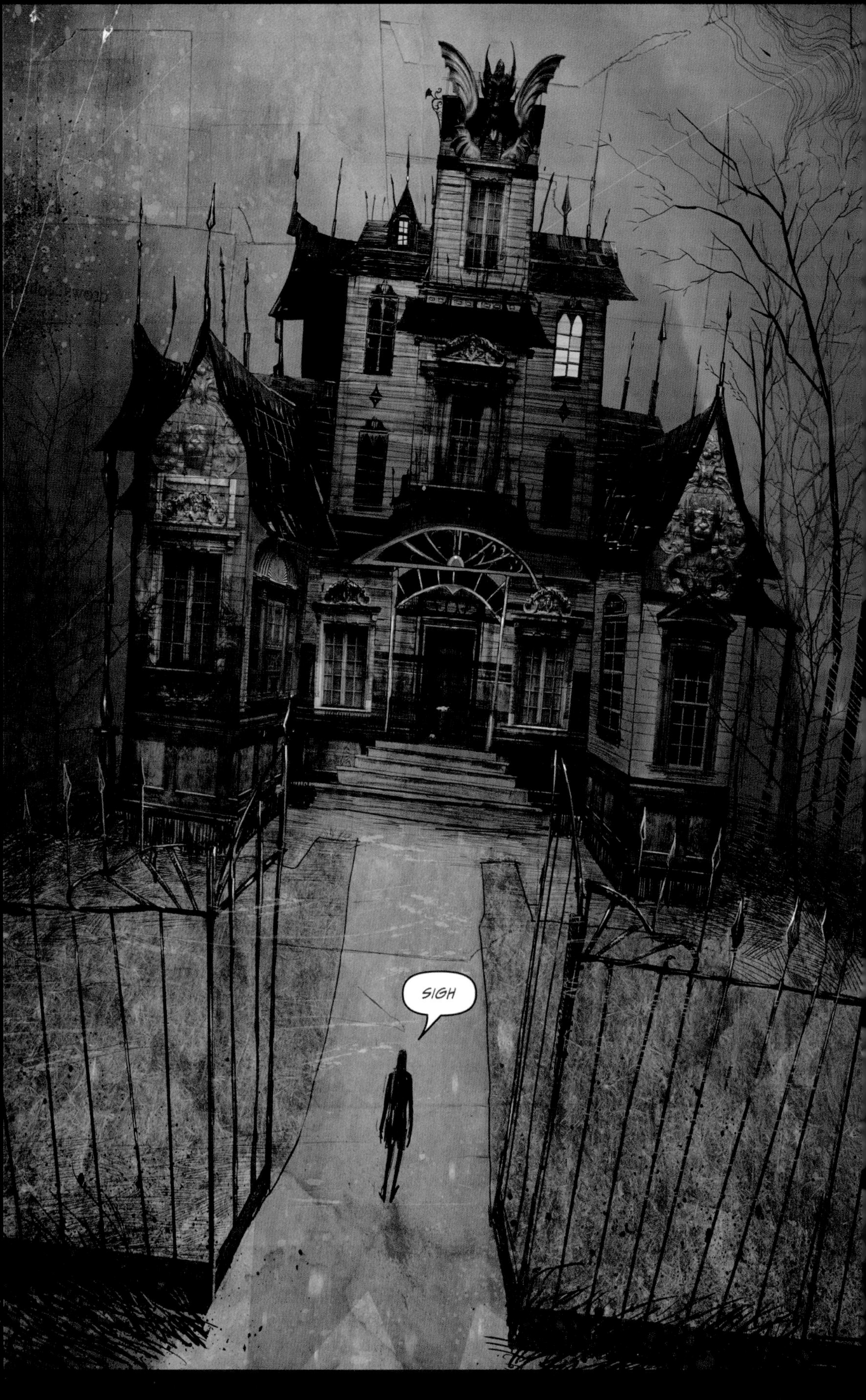
SIGH

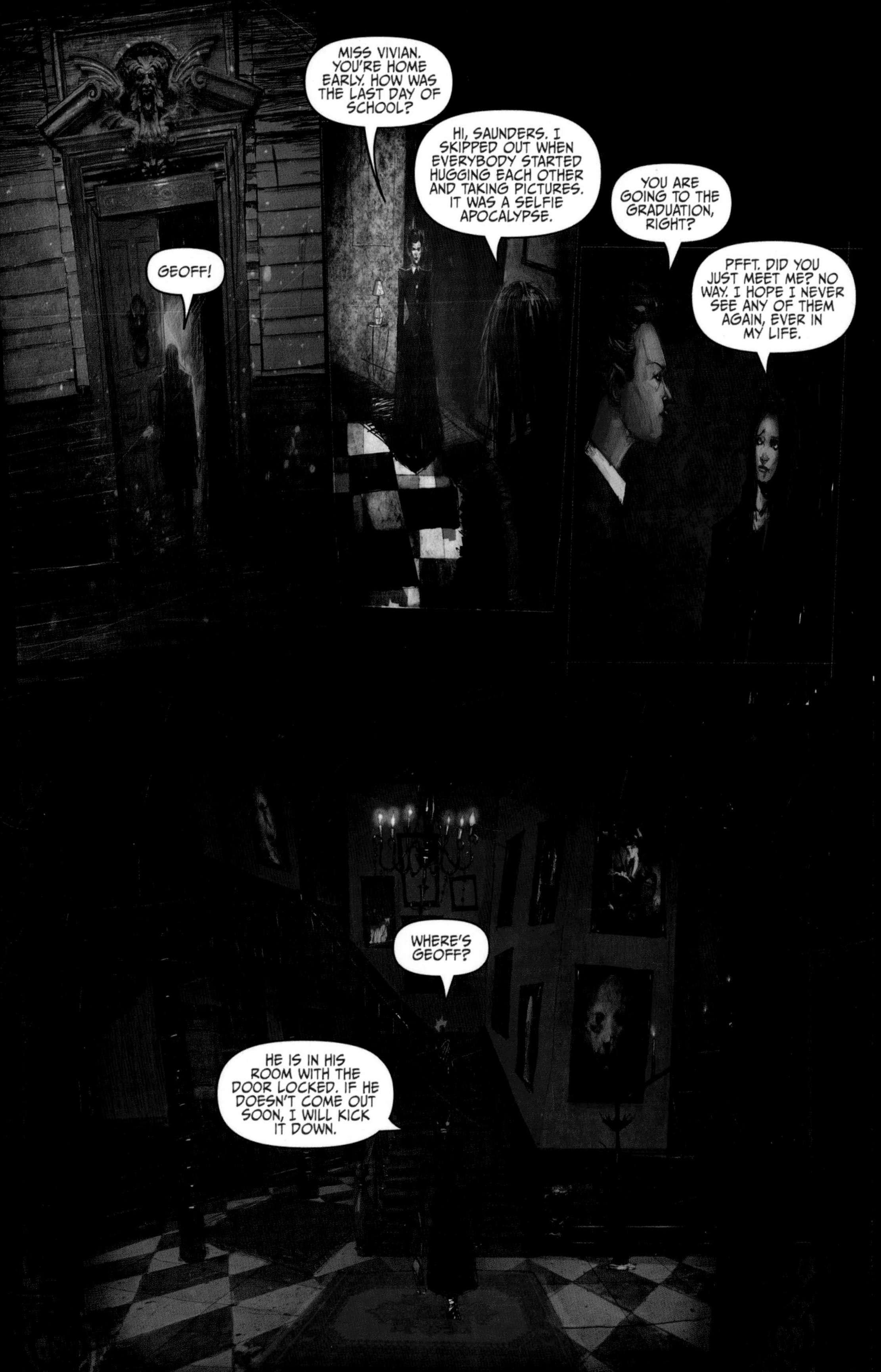
GEOFF!
MISS VIVIAN. YOU'RE HOME EARLY. HOW WAS THE LAST DAY OF SCHOOL?
HI, SAUNDERS. I SKIPPED OUT WHEN EVERYBODY STARTED HUGGING EACH OTHER AND TAKING PICTURES. IT WAS A SELFIE APOCALYPSE.
YOU ARE GOING TO THE GRADUATION, RIGHT?
PFFT. DID YOU JUST MEET ME? NO WAY. I HOPE I NEVER SEE ANY OF THEM AGAIN, EVER IN MY LIFE.
WHERE'S GEOFF?
HE IS IN HIS ROOM WITH THE DOOR LOCKED. IF HE DOESN'T COME OUT SOON, I WILL KICK IT DOWN.

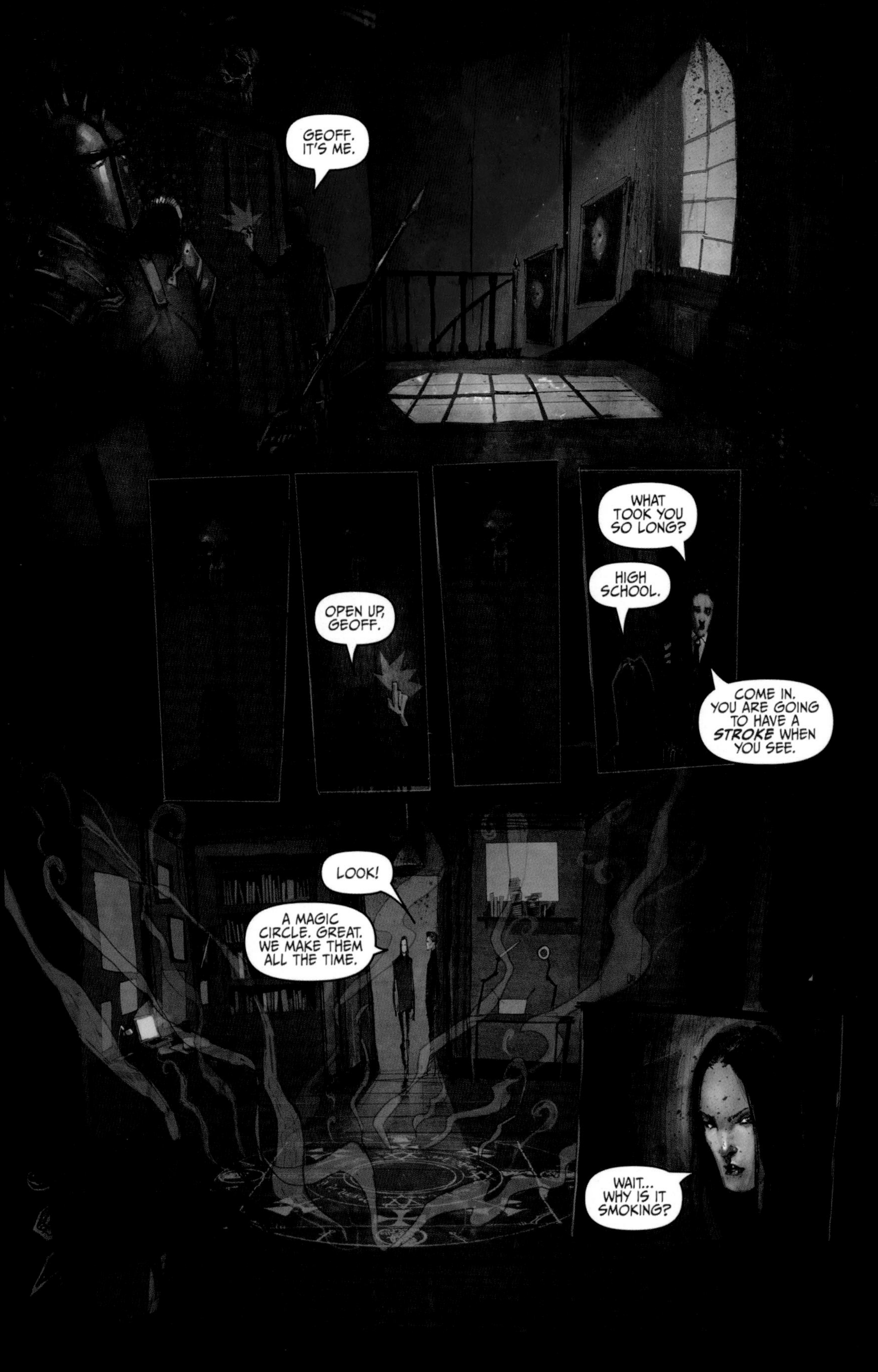
GEOFF. IT'S ME.
OPEN UP, GEOFF.
WHAT TOOK YOU SO LONG?
HIGH SCHOOL.
COME IN. YOU ARE GOING TO HAVE A *STROKE* WHEN YOU SEE.
LOOK!
A MAGIC CIRCLE. GREAT. WE MAKE THEM ALL THE TIME.
WAIT... WHY IS IT SMOKING?

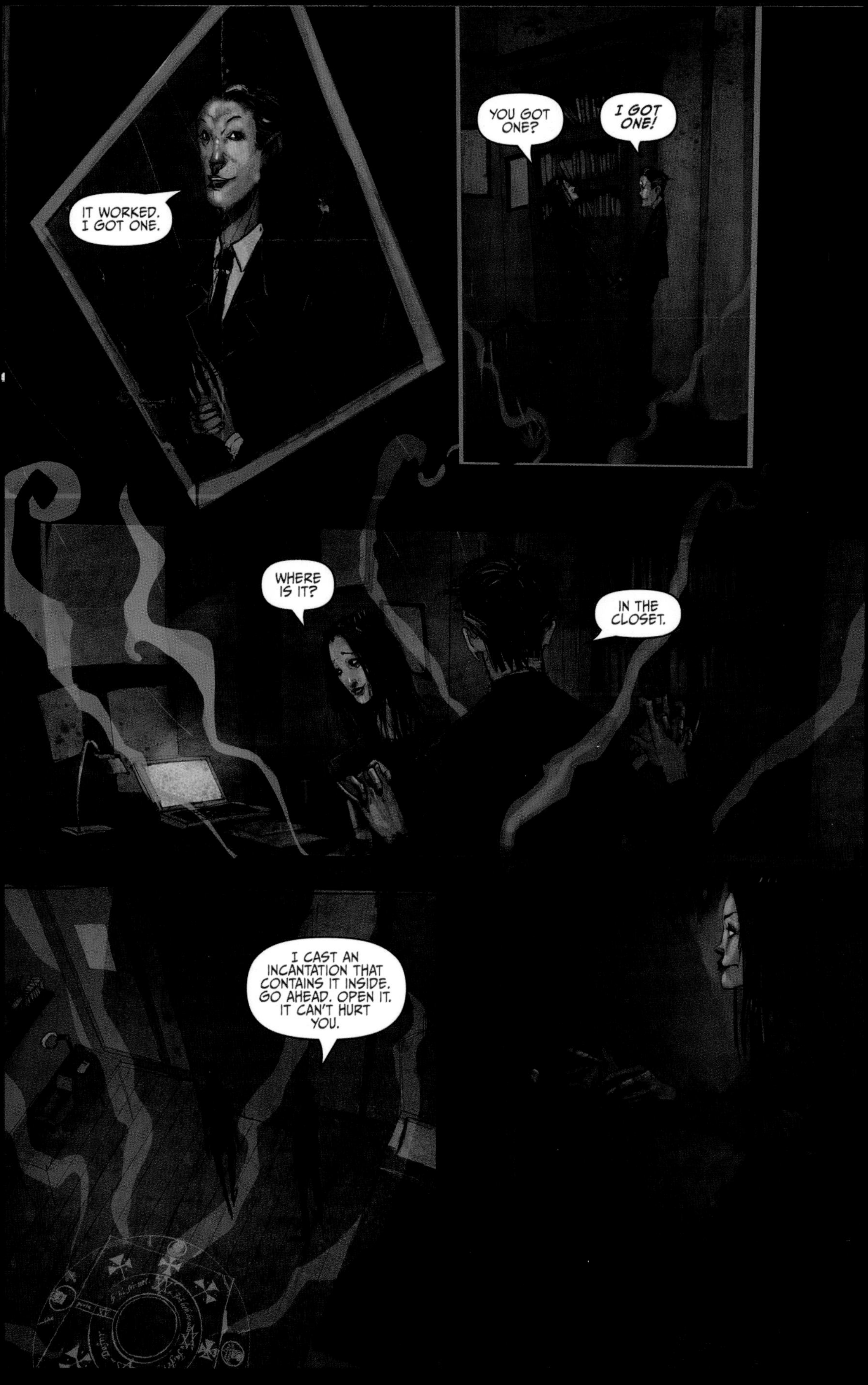
IT WORKED. I GOT ONE.
YOU GOT ONE?
I GOT ONE!
WHERE IS IT?
IN THE CLOSET.
I CAST AN INCANTATION THAT CONTAINS IT INSIDE. GO AHEAD. OPEN IT. IT CAN'T HURT YOU.

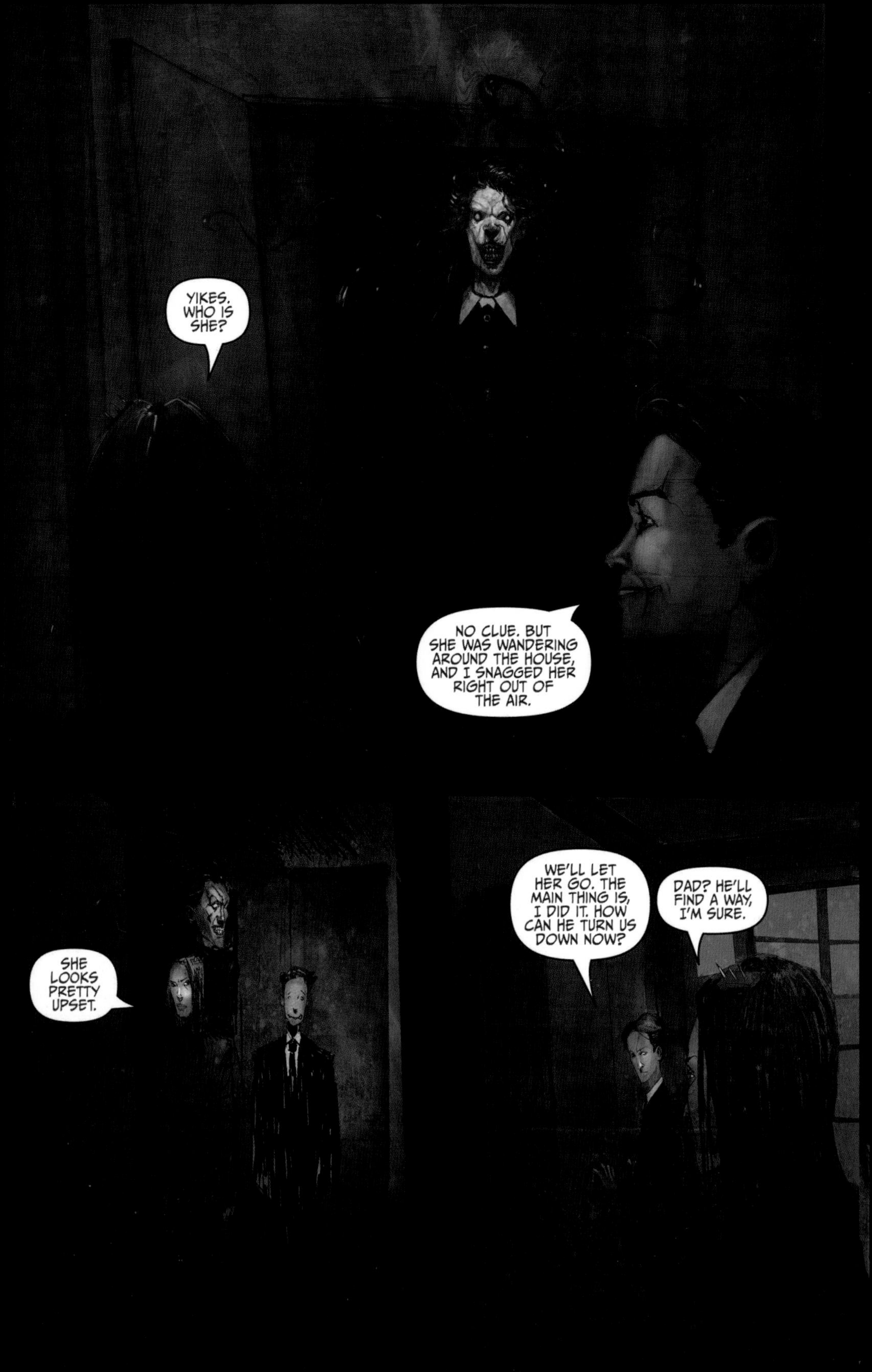
YIKES. WHO IS SHE?
NO CLUE. BUT SHE WAS WANDERING AROUND THE HOUSE, AND I SNAGGED HER RIGHT OUT OF THE AIR.
SHE LOOKS PRETTY UPSET.
WE'LL LET HER GO. THE MAIN THING IS, I DID IT. HOW CAN HE TURN US DOWN NOW?
DAD? HE'LL FIND A WAY, I'M SURE.

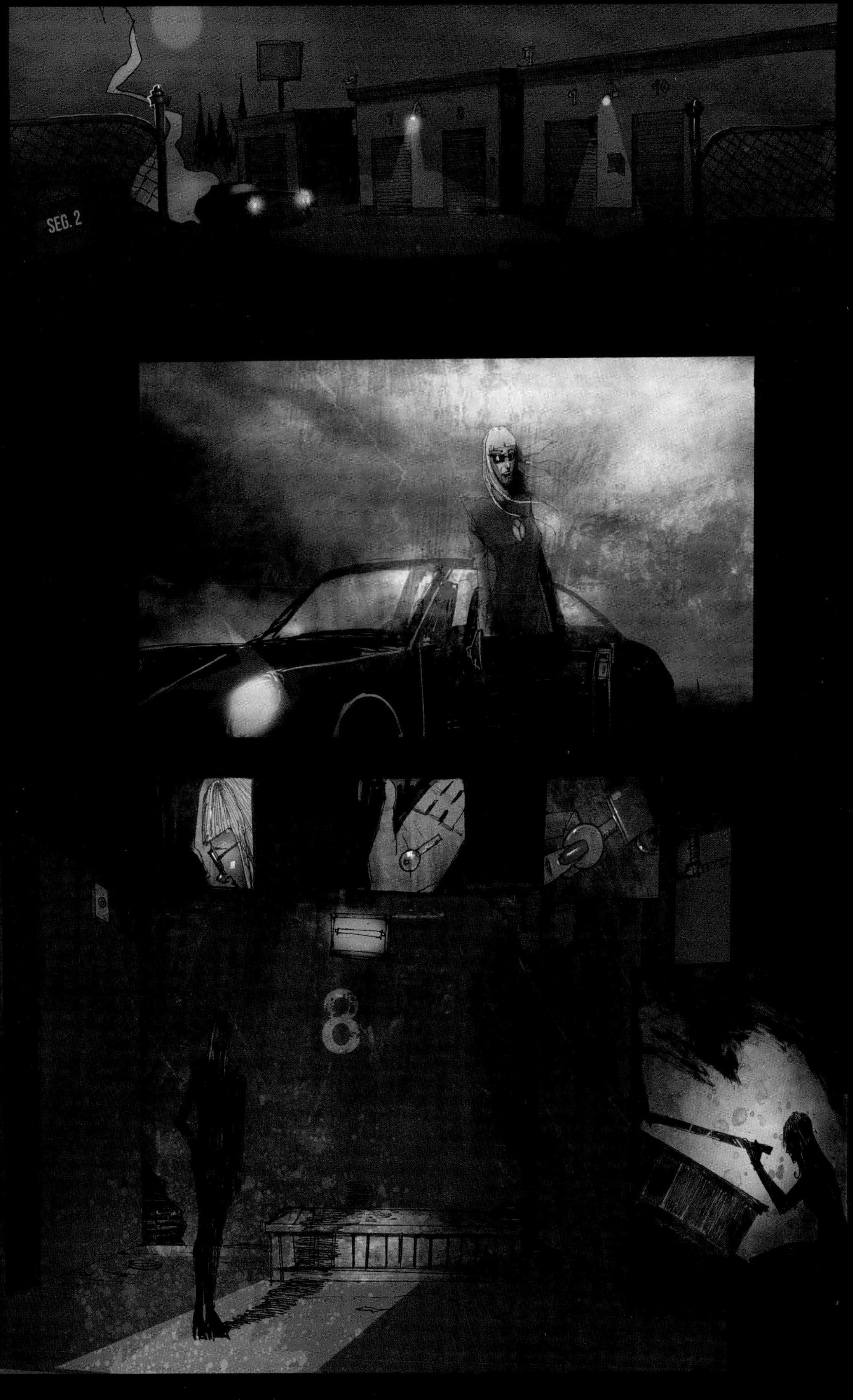
SEG. 2
8

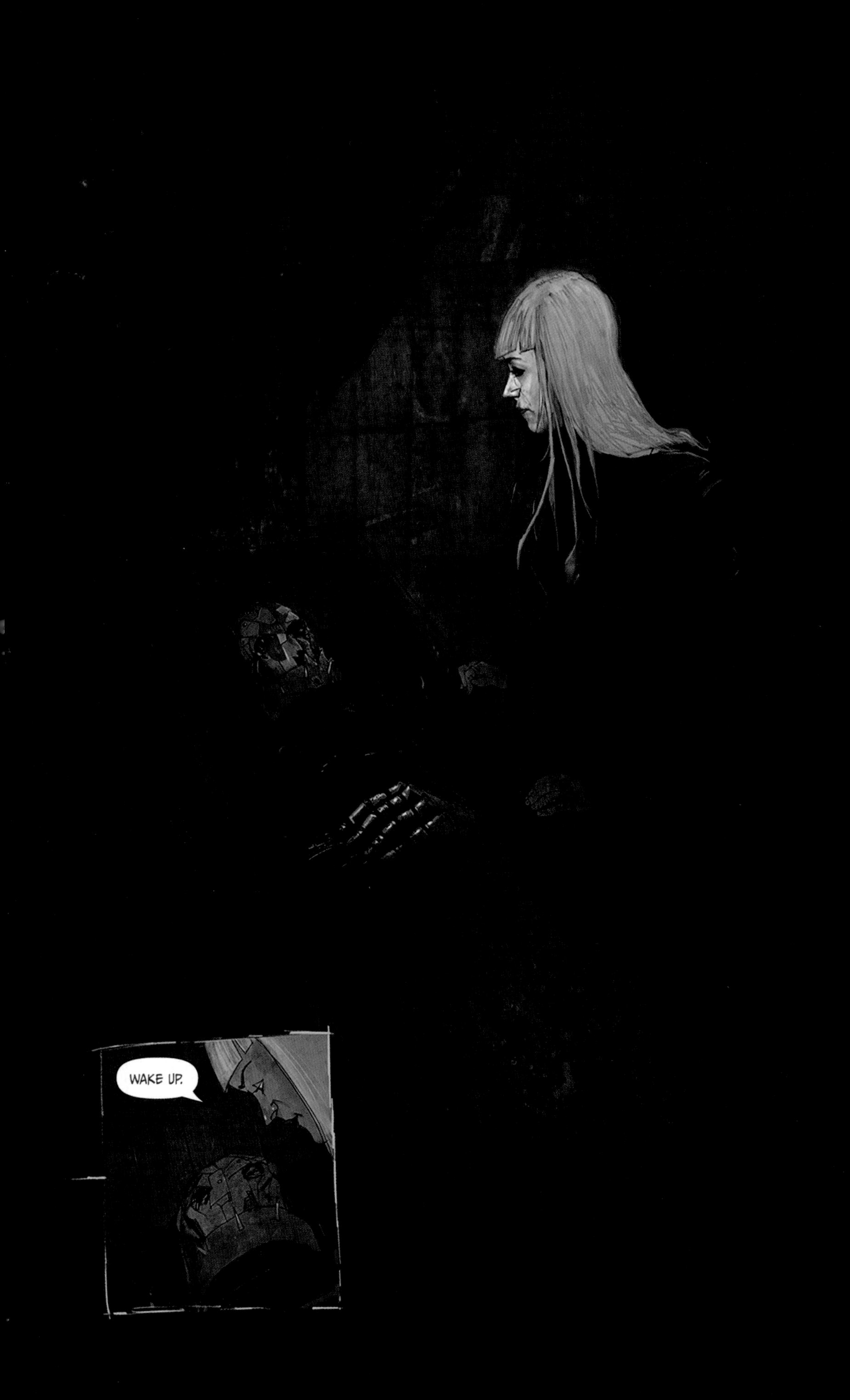
WAKE UP.

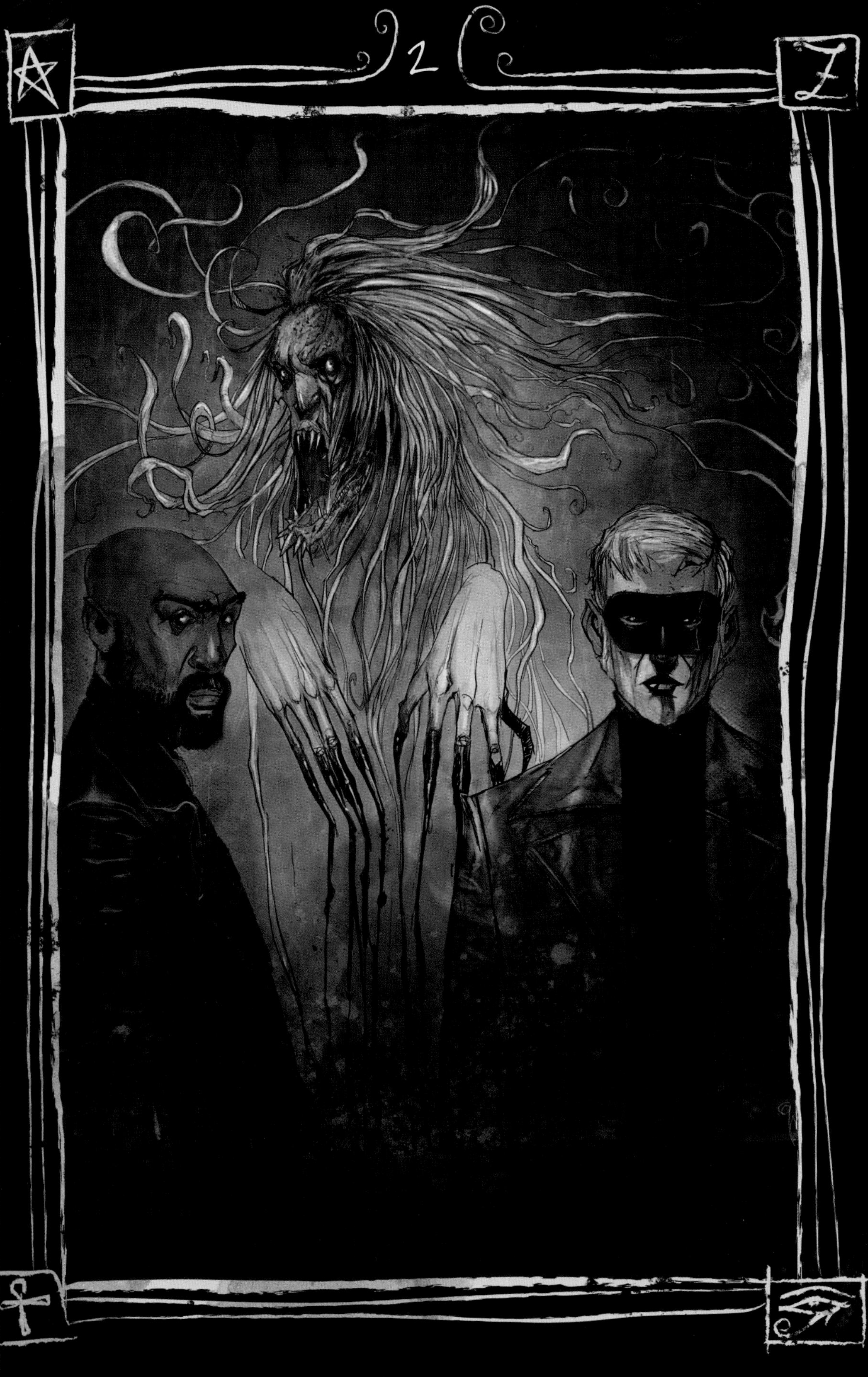
2

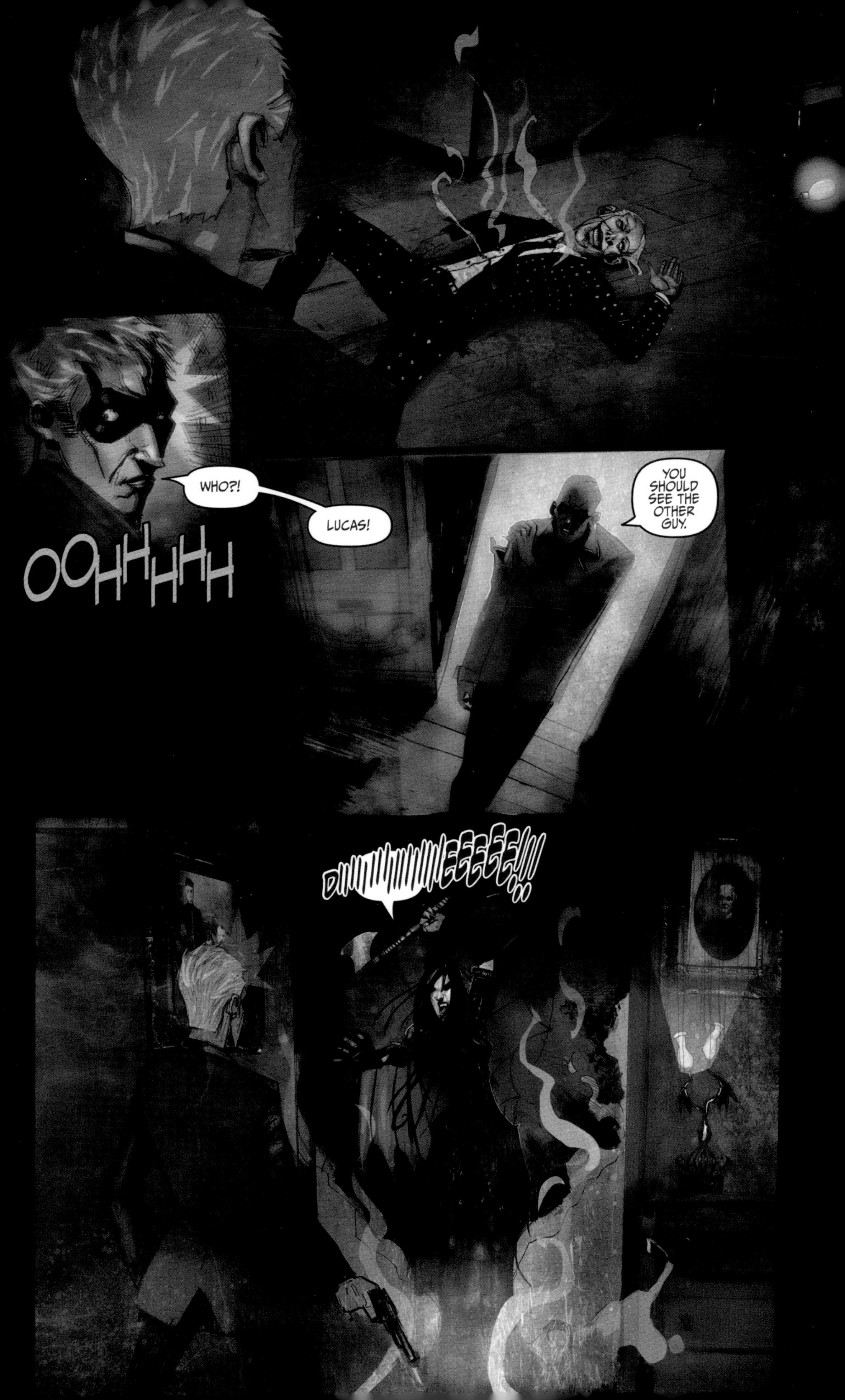
WHO?!
LUCAS!
YOU SHOULD SEE THE OTHER GUY.
OOHHHHHH
DIIIIIIIIIIIIIIIEEEEEE!!!

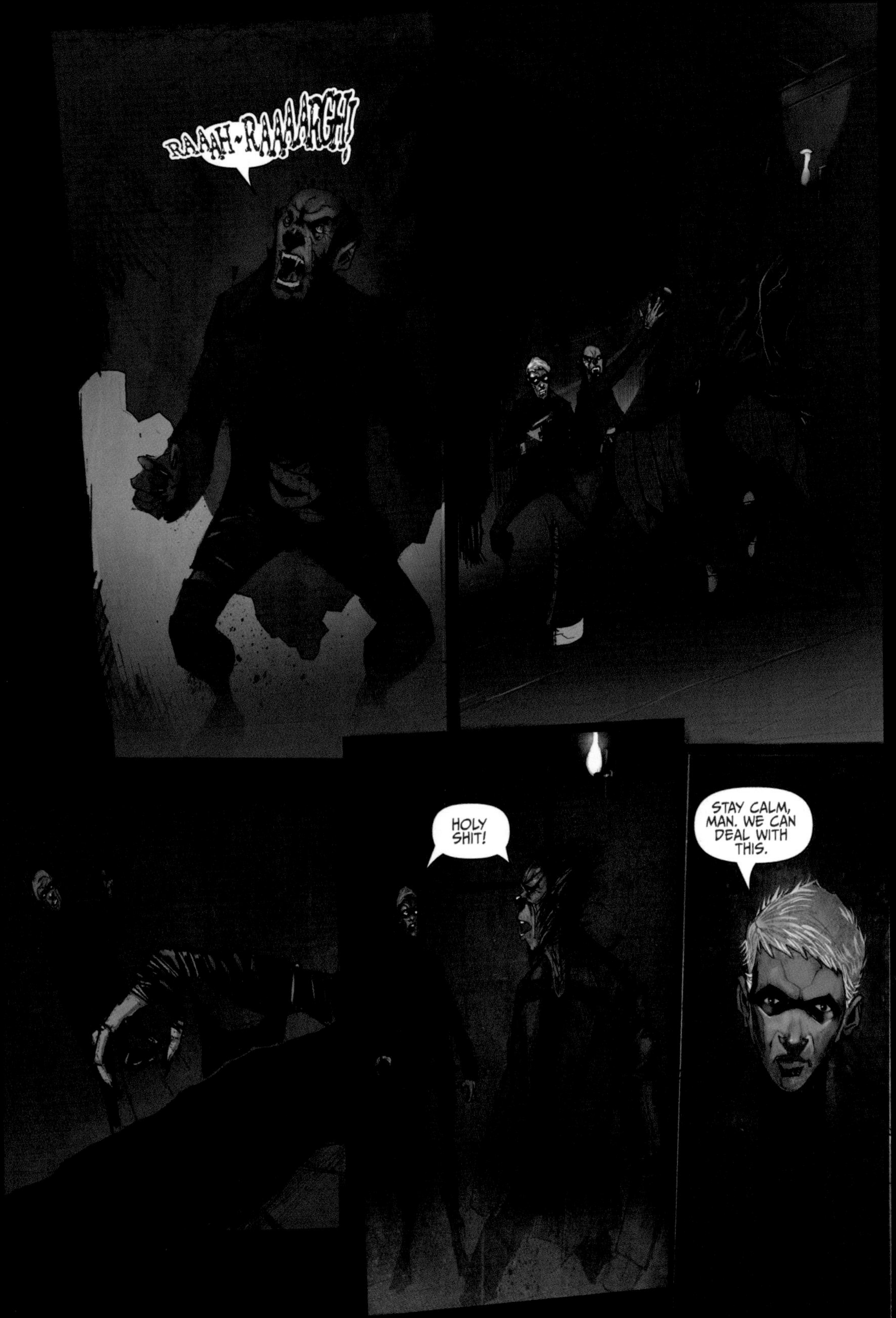
RAAAH-RAAAAAGH!
HOLY SHIT!
STAY CALM, MAN. WE CAN DEAL WITH THIS.

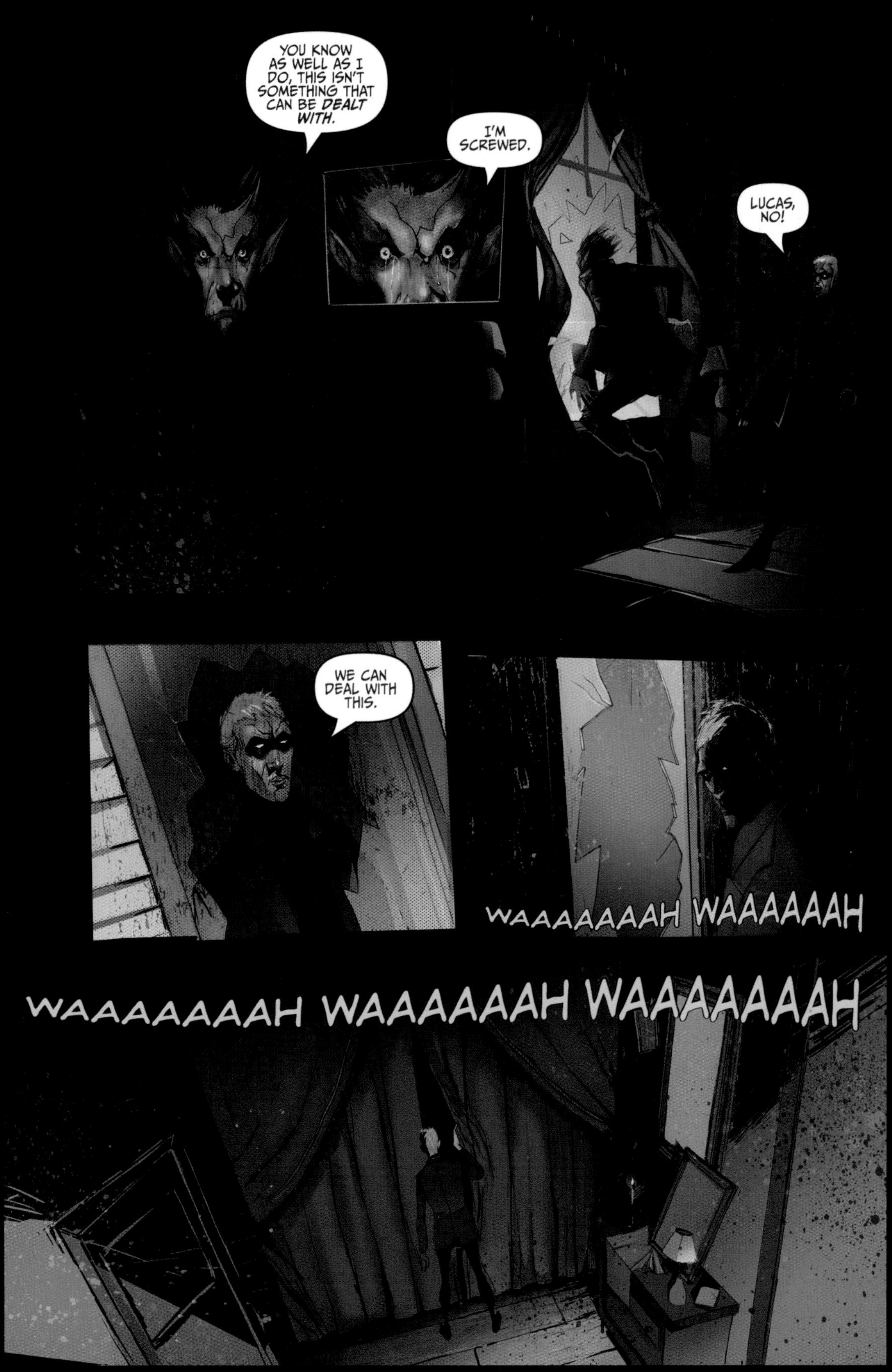
YOU KNOW AS WELL AS I DO, THIS ISN'T SOMETHING THAT CAN BE *DEALT WITH*.
I'M SCREWED.
LUCAS, NO!
WE CAN DEAL WITH THIS.
WAAAAAAAH WAAAAAAH
WAAAAAAAH WAAAAAAH WAAAAAAAH

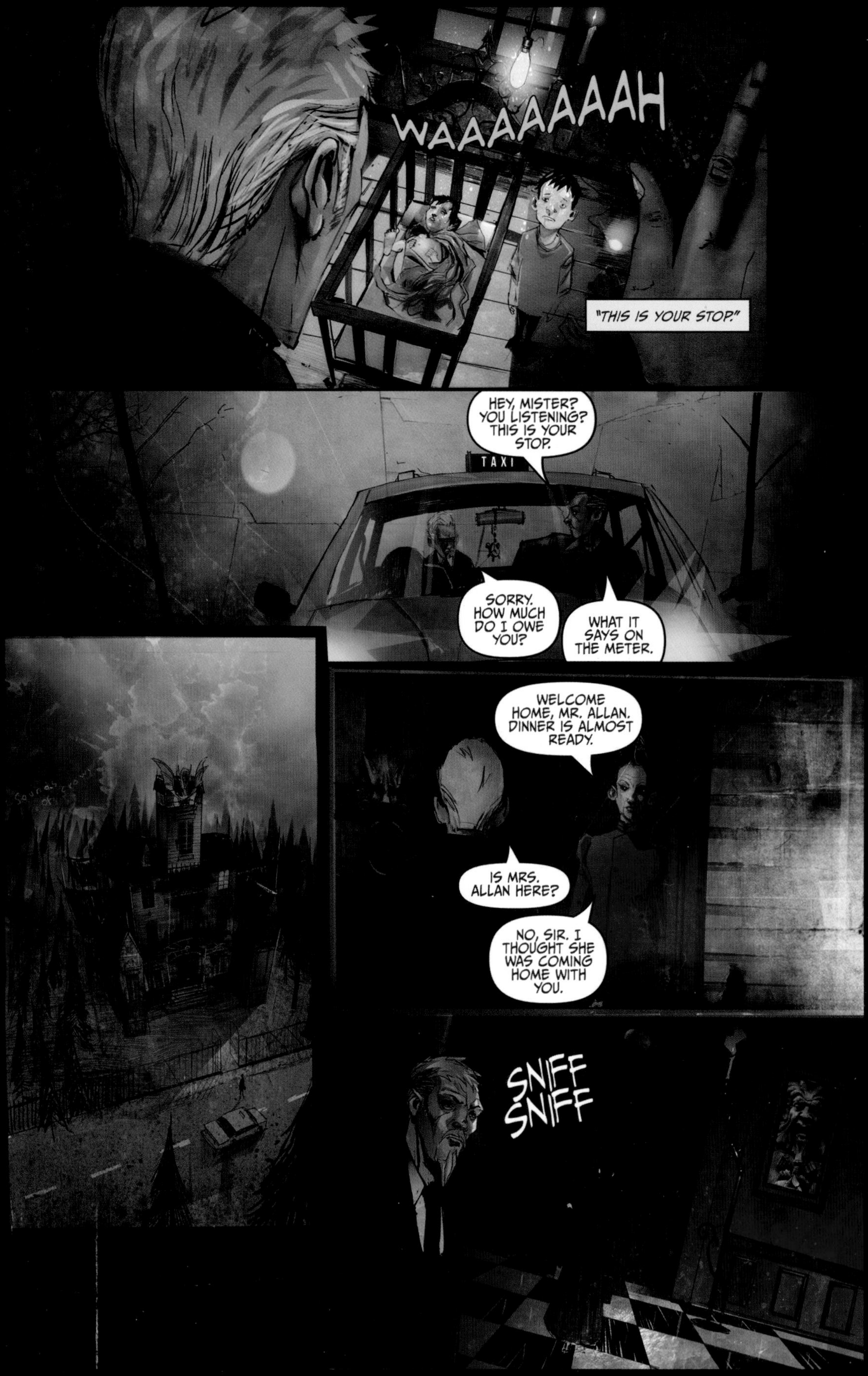
WAAAAAAAAH
"THIS IS YOUR STOP."
HEY, MISTER? YOU LISTENING? THIS IS YOUR STOP.
TAXI
SORRY. HOW MUCH DO I OWE YOU?
WHAT IT SAYS ON THE METER.
WELCOME HOME, MR. ALLAN. DINNER IS ALMOST READY.
IS MRS. ALLAN HERE?
NO, SIR. I THOUGHT SHE WAS COMING HOME WITH YOU.
SNIFF SNIFF

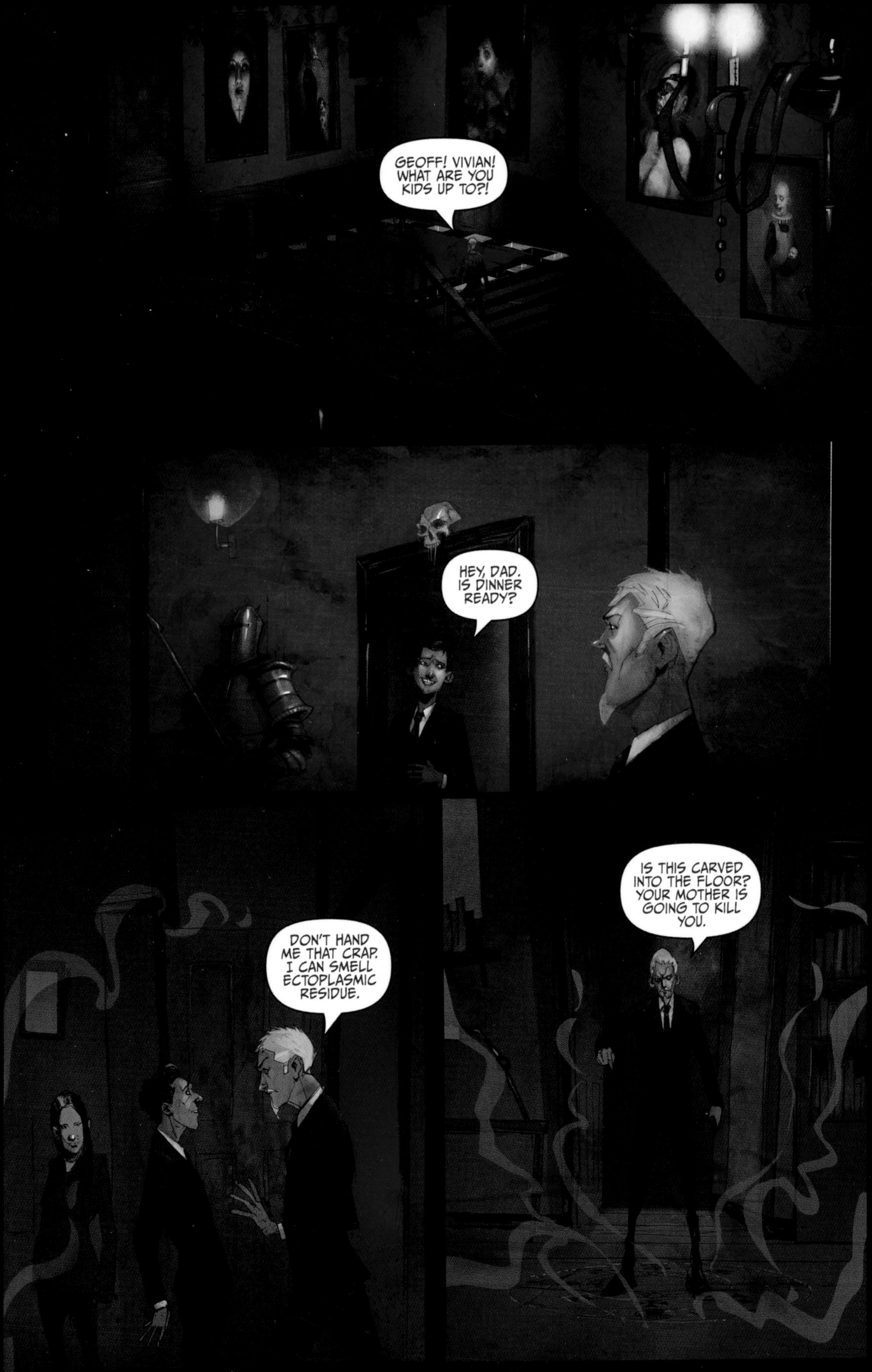
GEOFF! VIVIAN! WHAT ARE YOU KIDS UP TO?!
HEY, DAD. IS DINNER READY?
DON'T HAND ME THAT CRAP. I CAN SMELL ECTOPLASMIC RESIDUE.
IS THIS CARVED INTO THE FLOOR? YOUR MOTHER IS GOING TO KILL YOU.

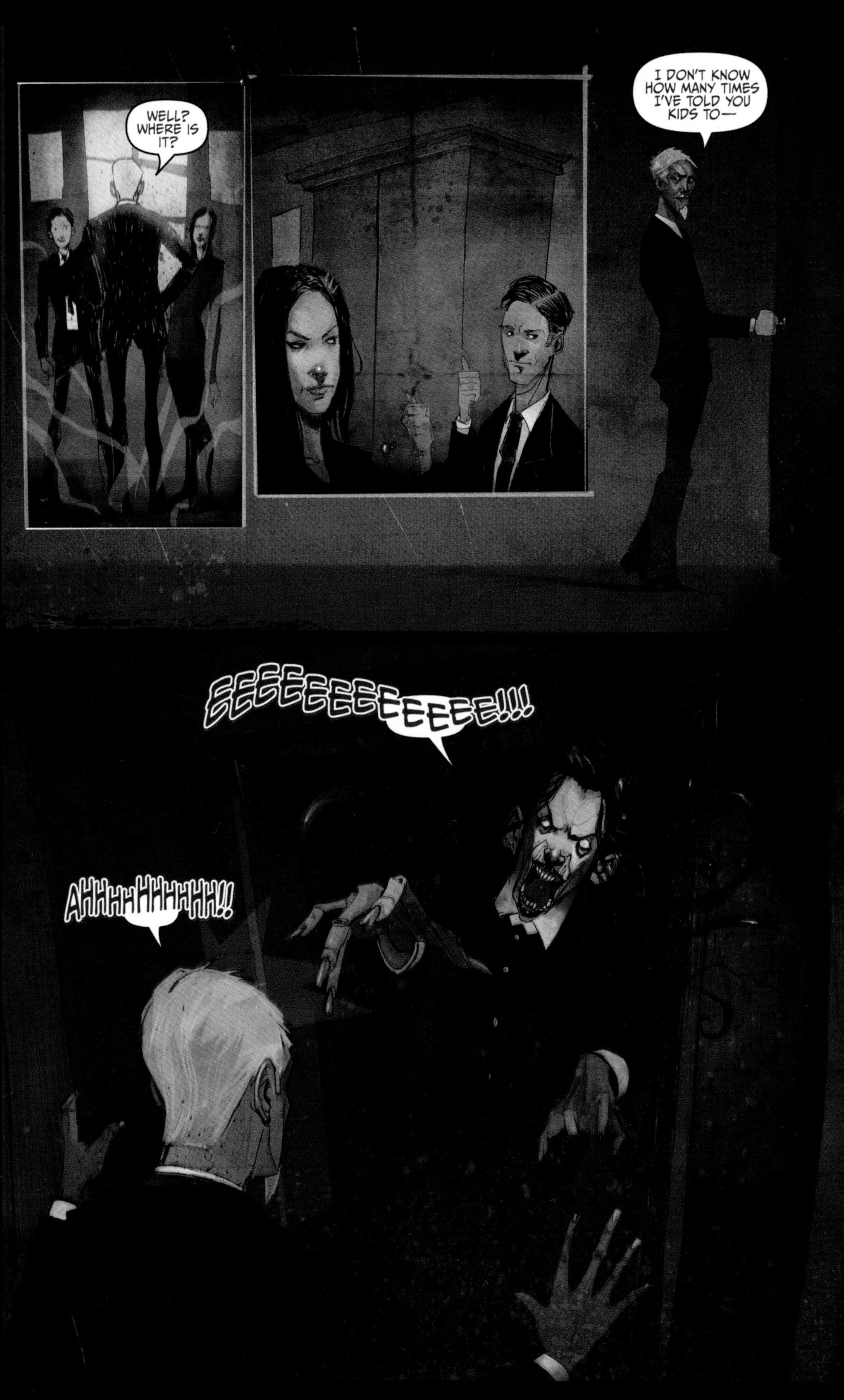
WELL? WHERE IS IT?
I DON'T KNOW HOW MANY TIMES I'VE TOLD YOU KIDS TO—
EEEEEEEEEEEEEEE!!!
AHHHHHHHHH!!

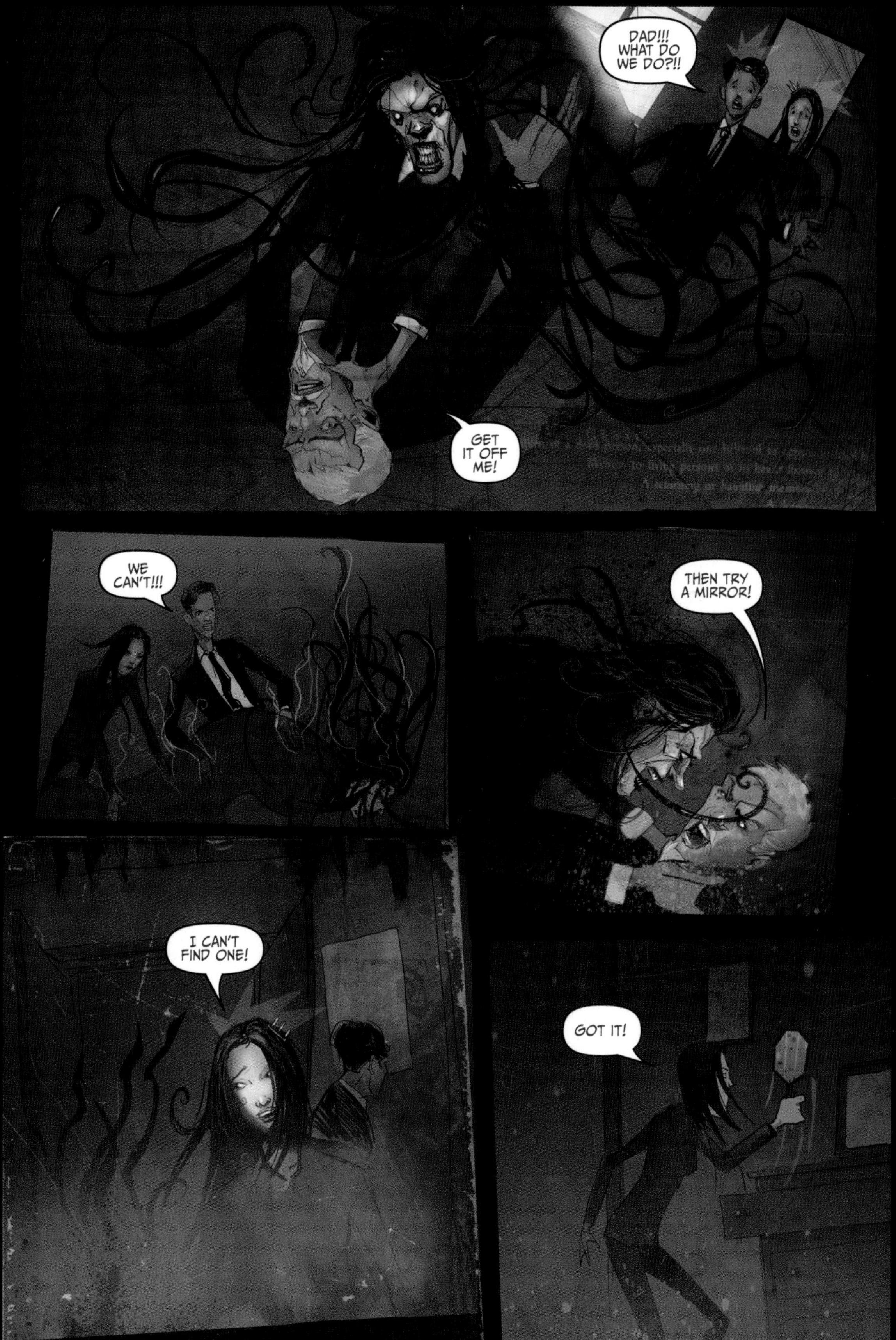
DAD!!! WHAT DO WE DO?!!
GET IT OFF ME!
WE CAN'T!!!
THEN TRY A MIRROR!
I CAN'T FIND ONE!
GOT IT!

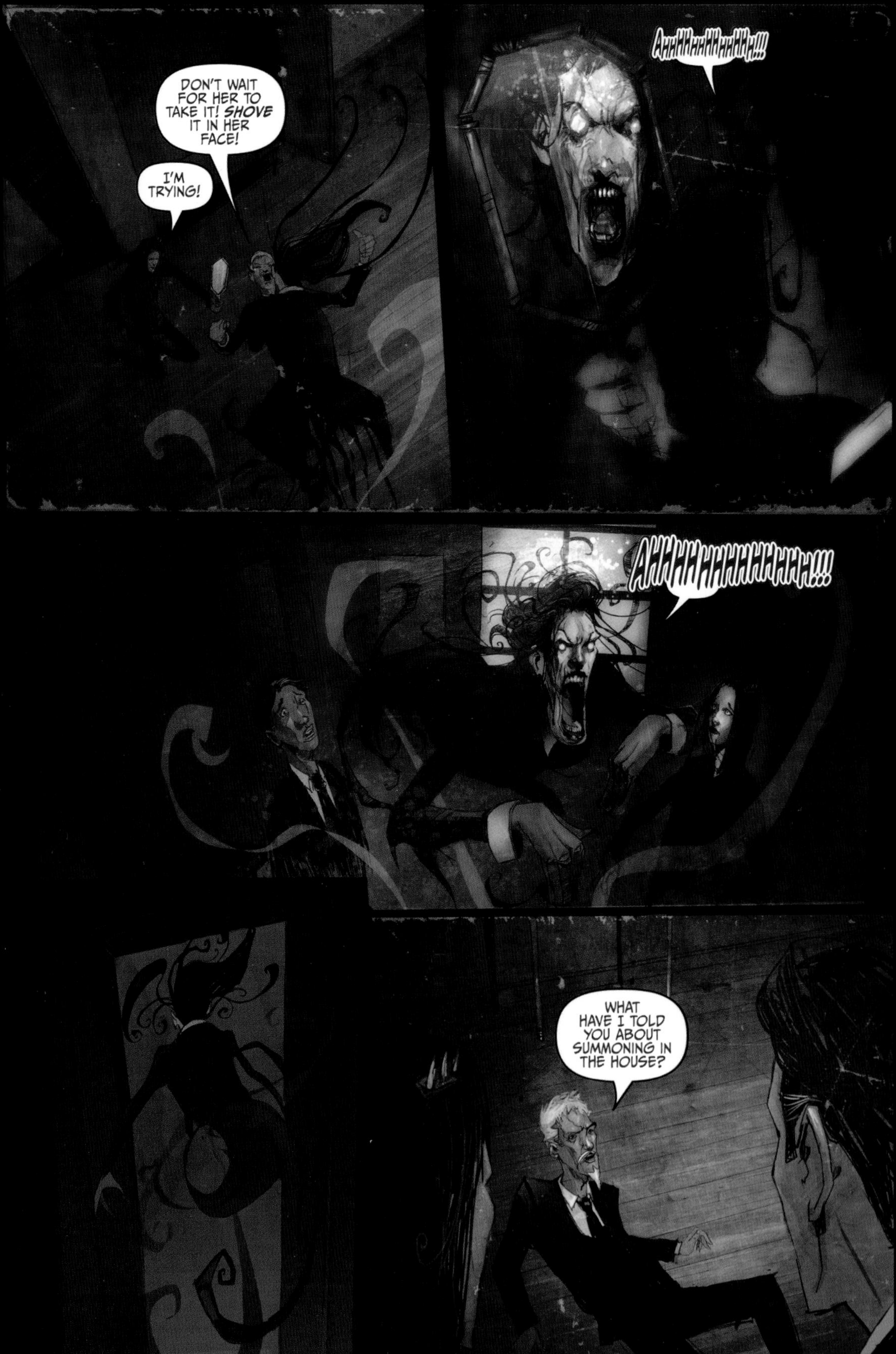
DON'T WAIT FOR HER TO TAKE IT! *SHOVE* IT IN HER FACE!
I'M TRYING!
AHHHHHHHHHHH!!!
AHHHHHHHHHHHHH!!!
WHAT HAVE I TOLD YOU ABOUT SUMMONING IN THE HOUSE?

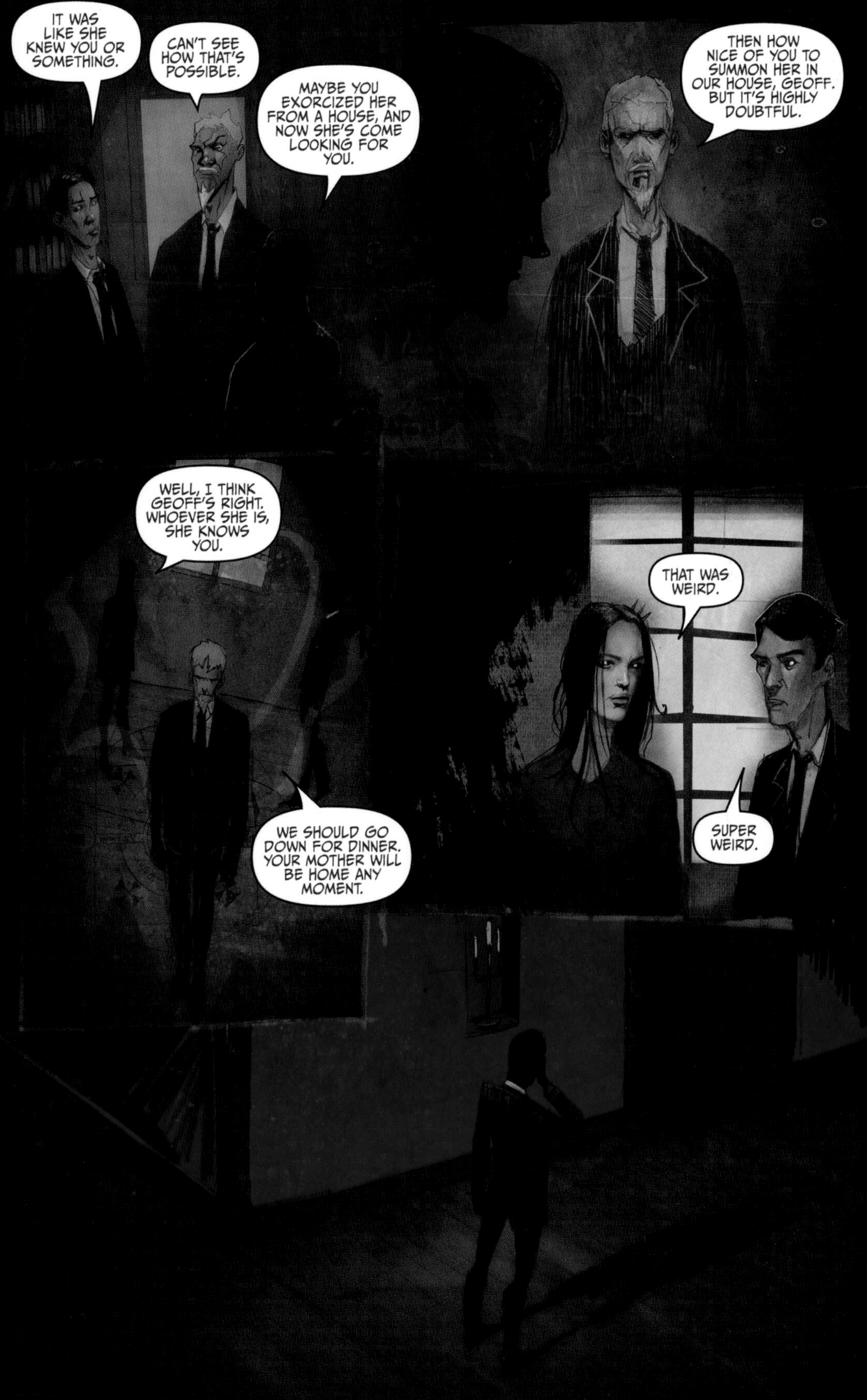

IT WAS LIKE SHE KNEW YOU OR SOMETHING.
CAN'T SEE HOW THAT'S POSSIBLE.
MAYBE YOU EXORCIZED HER FROM A HOUSE, AND NOW SHE'S COME LOOKING FOR YOU.
THEN HOW NICE OF YOU TO SUMMON HER IN OUR HOUSE, GEOFF. BUT IT'S HIGHLY DOUBTFUL.
WELL, I THINK GEOFF'S RIGHT. WHOEVER SHE IS, SHE KNOWS YOU.
WE SHOULD GO DOWN FOR DINNER. YOUR MOTHER WILL BE HOME ANY MOMENT.
THAT WAS WEIRD.
SUPER WEIRD.

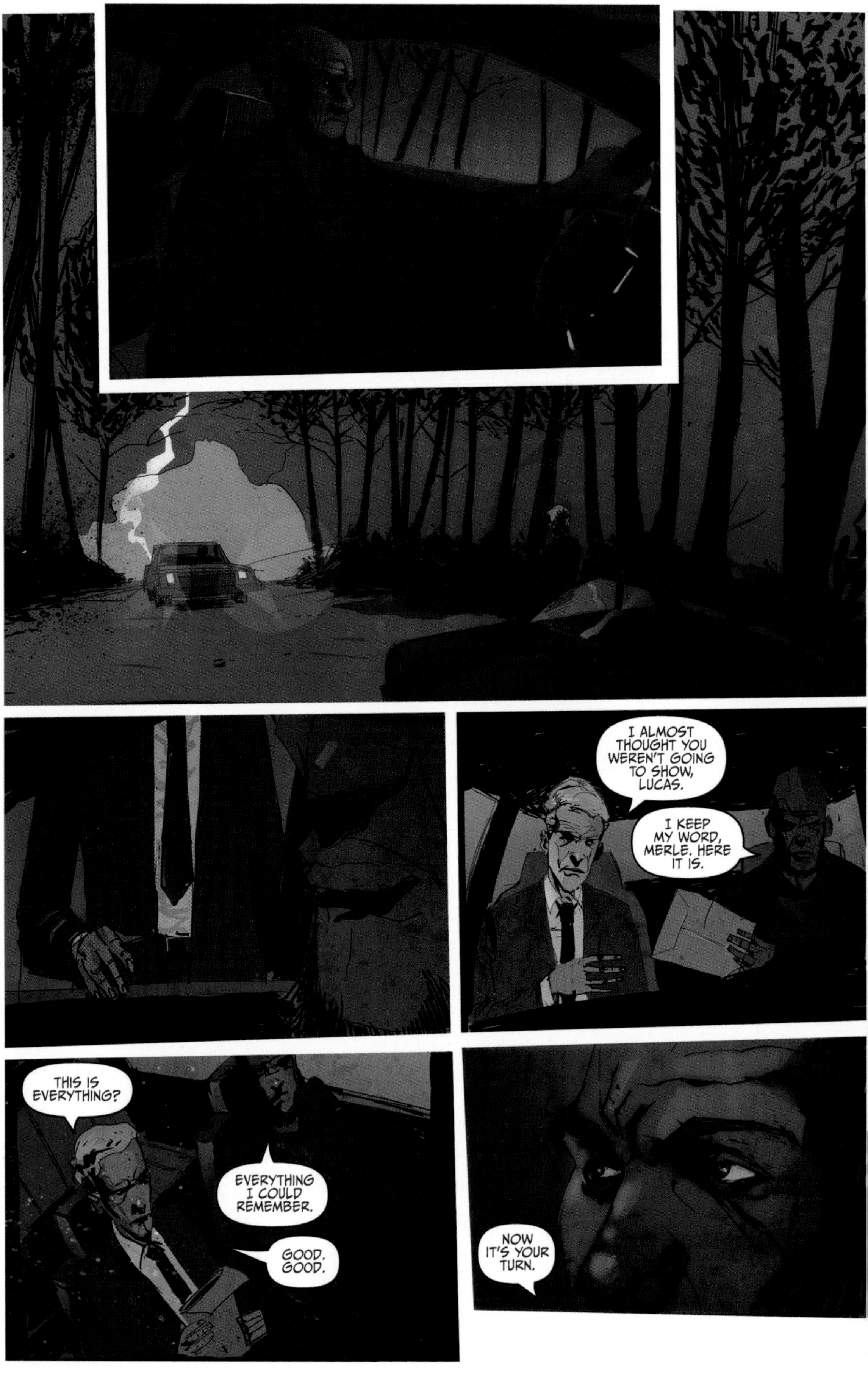
I ALMOST THOUGHT YOU WEREN'T GOING TO SHOW, LUCAS.
I KEEP MY WORD, MERLE. HERE IT IS.
THIS IS EVERYTHING?
EVERYTHING I COULD REMEMBER.
GOOD. GOOD.
NOW IT'S YOUR TURN.

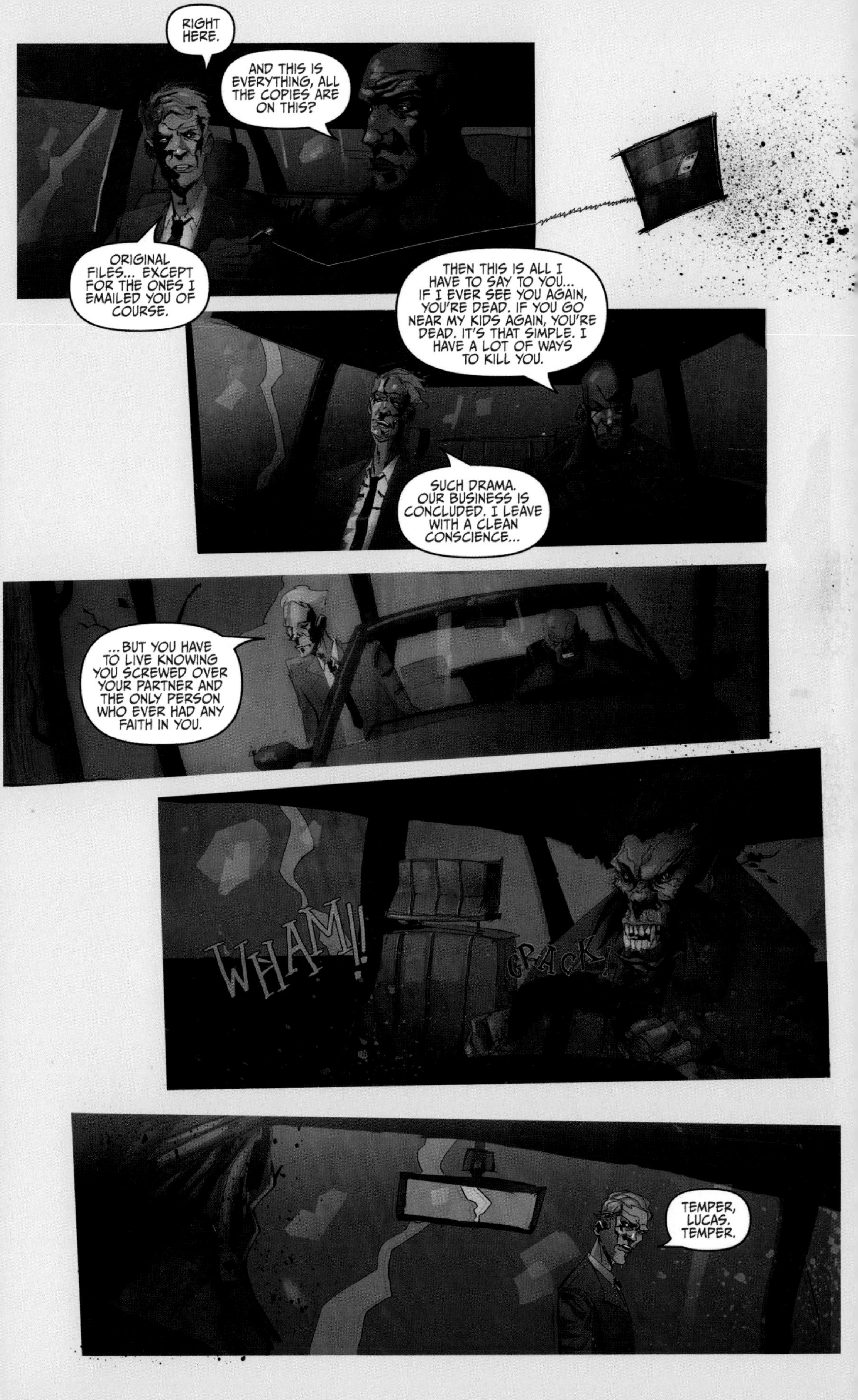
RIGHT HERE.
AND THIS IS EVERYTHING, ALL THE COPIES ARE ON THIS?
ORIGINAL FILES... EXCEPT FOR THE ONES I EMAILED YOU OF COURSE.
THEN THIS IS ALL I HAVE TO SAY TO YOU... IF I EVER SEE YOU AGAIN, YOU'RE DEAD. IF YOU GO NEAR MY KIDS AGAIN, YOU'RE DEAD. IT'S THAT SIMPLE. I HAVE A LOT OF WAYS TO KILL YOU.
SUCH DRAMA. OUR BUSINESS IS CONCLUDED. I LEAVE WITH A CLEAN CONSCIENCE...
...BUT YOU HAVE TO LIVE KNOWING YOU SCREWED OVER YOUR PARTNER AND THE ONLY PERSON WHO EVER HAD ANY FAITH IN YOU.
WHAM!!
CRACK!
TEMPER, LUCAS. TEMPER.

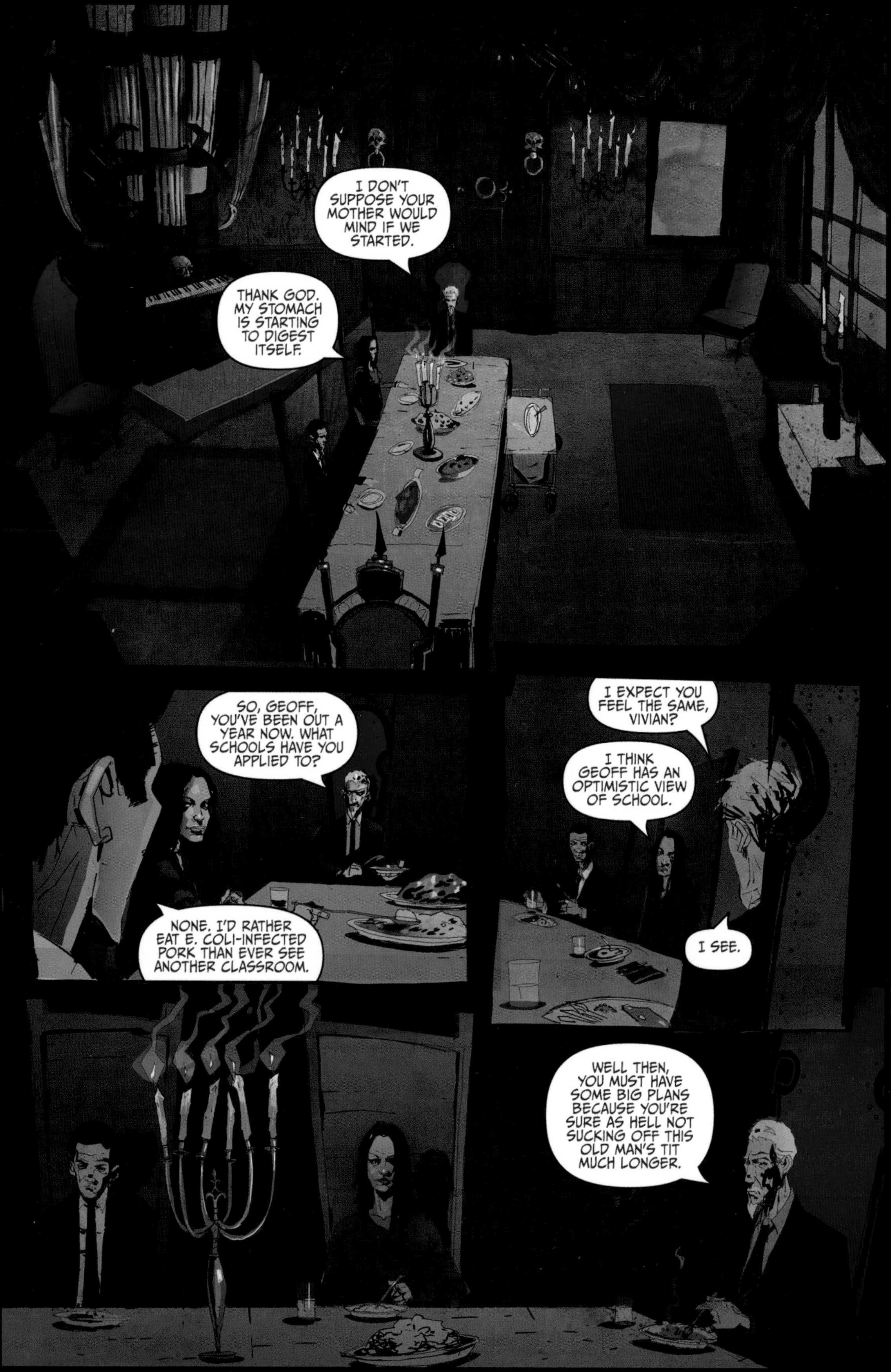
I DON'T SUPPOSE YOUR MOTHER WOULD MIND IF WE STARTED.
THANK GOD. MY STOMACH IS STARTING TO DIGEST ITSELF.
SO, GEOFF, YOU'VE BEEN OUT A YEAR NOW. WHAT SCHOOLS HAVE YOU APPLIED TO?
NONE. I'D RATHER EAT E. COLI-INFECTED PORK THAN EVER SEE ANOTHER CLASSROOM.
I EXPECT YOU FEEL THE SAME, VIVIAN?
I THINK GEOFF HAS AN OPTIMISTIC VIEW OF SCHOOL.
I SEE.
WELL THEN, YOU MUST HAVE SOME BIG PLANS BECAUSE YOU'RE SURE AS HELL NOT SUCKING OFF THIS OLD MAN'S TIT MUCH LONGER.

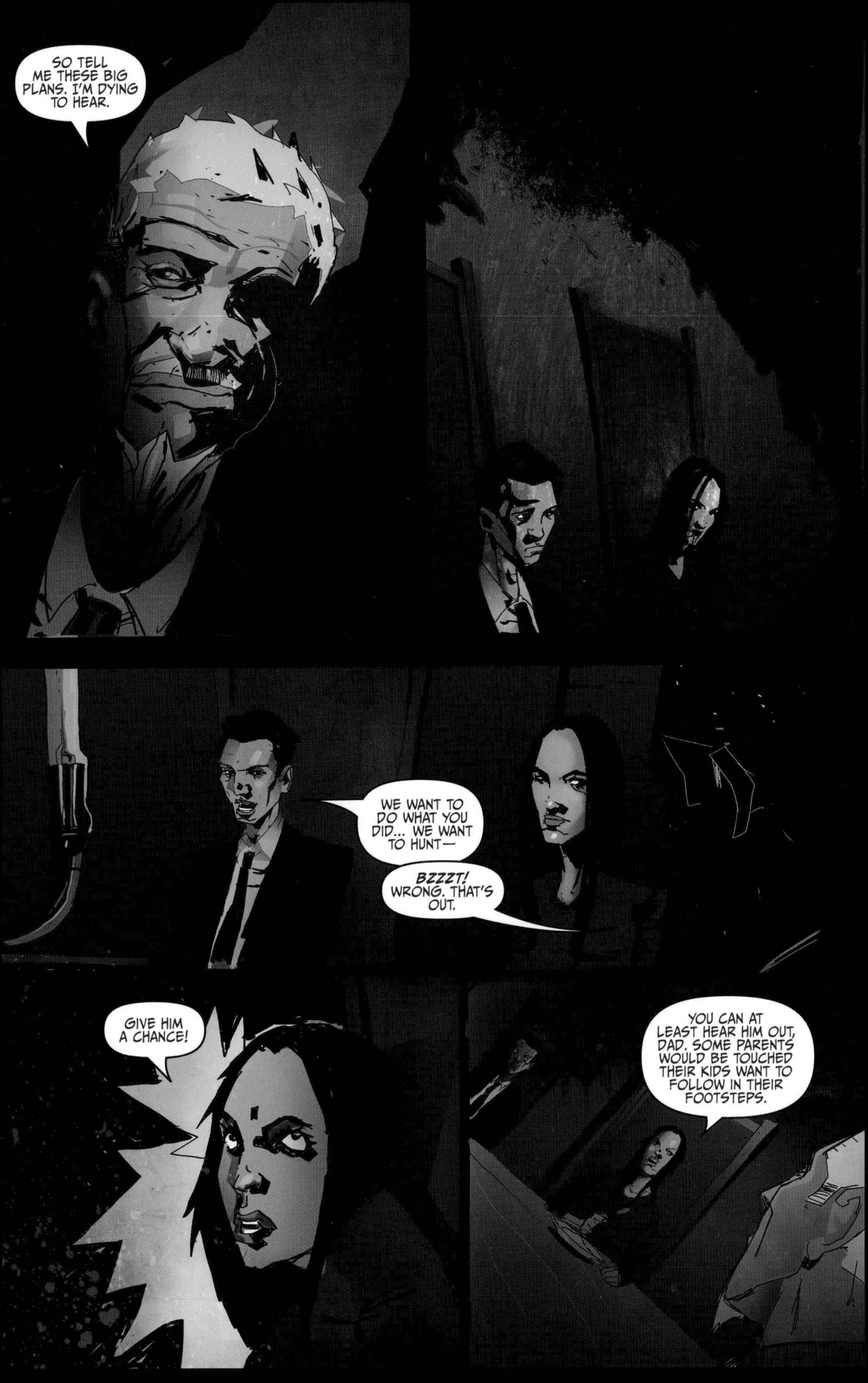
SO TELL ME THESE BIG PLANS. I'M DYING TO HEAR.
WE WANT TO DO WHAT YOU DID... WE WANT TO HUNT—
BZZZT! WRONG. THAT'S OUT.
GIVE HIM A CHANCE!
YOU CAN AT LEAST HEAR HIM OUT, DAD. SOME PARENTS WOULD BE TOUCHED THEIR KIDS WANT TO FOLLOW IN THEIR FOOTSTEPS.

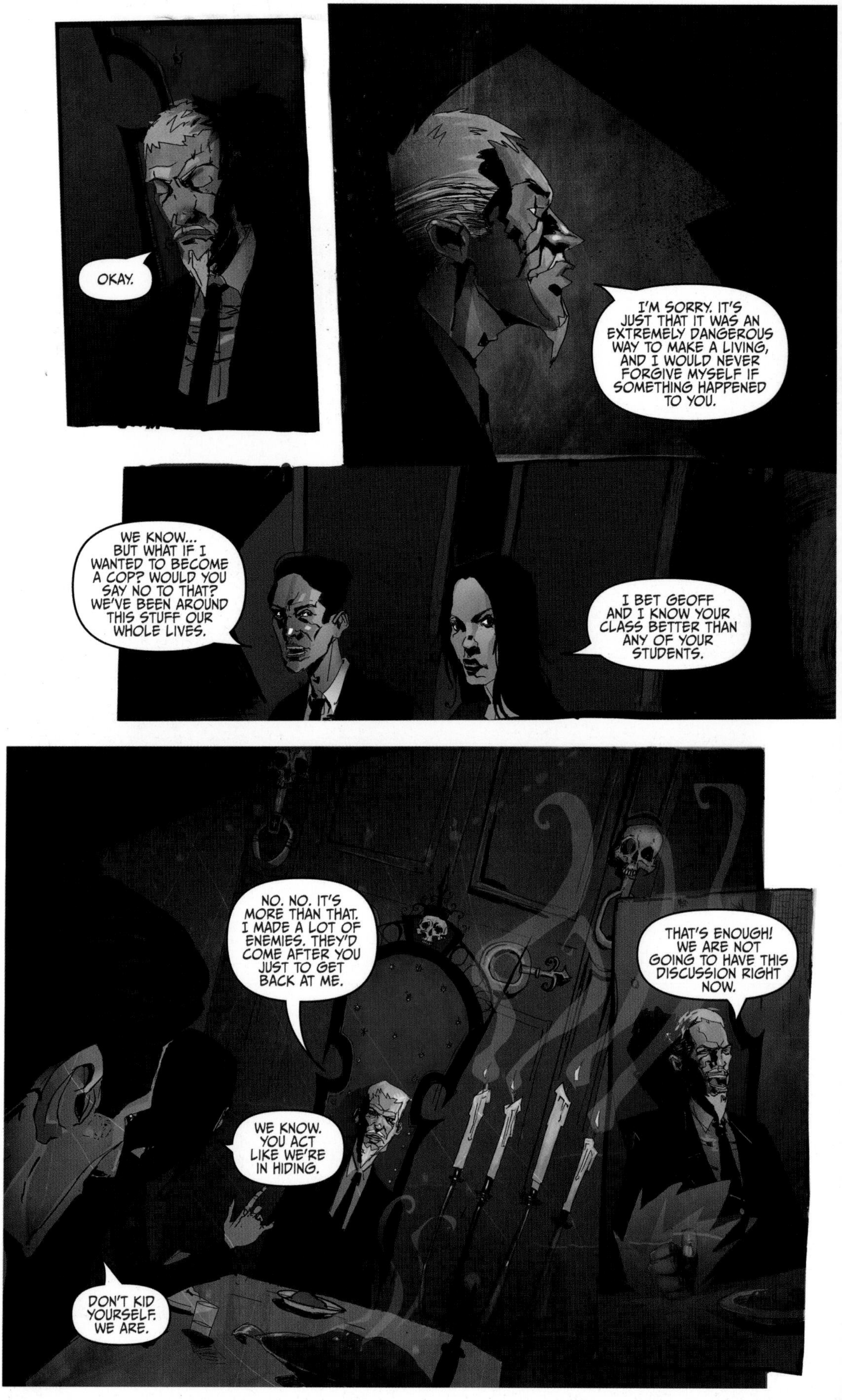
OKAY.
I'M SORRY. IT'S JUST THAT IT WAS AN EXTREMELY DANGEROUS WAY TO MAKE A LIVING, AND I WOULD NEVER FORGIVE MYSELF IF SOMETHING HAPPENED TO YOU.
WE KNOW... BUT WHAT IF I WANTED TO BECOME A COP? WOULD YOU SAY NO TO THAT? WE'VE BEEN AROUND THIS STUFF OUR WHOLE LIVES.
I BET GEOFF AND I KNOW YOUR CLASS BETTER THAN ANY OF YOUR STUDENTS.
NO. NO. IT'S MORE THAN THAT. I MADE A LOT OF ENEMIES. THEY'D COME AFTER YOU JUST TO GET BACK AT ME.
WE KNOW. YOU ACT LIKE WE'RE IN HIDING.
DON'T KID YOURSELF. WE ARE.
THAT'S ENOUGH! WE ARE NOT GOING TO HAVE THIS DISCUSSION RIGHT NOW.

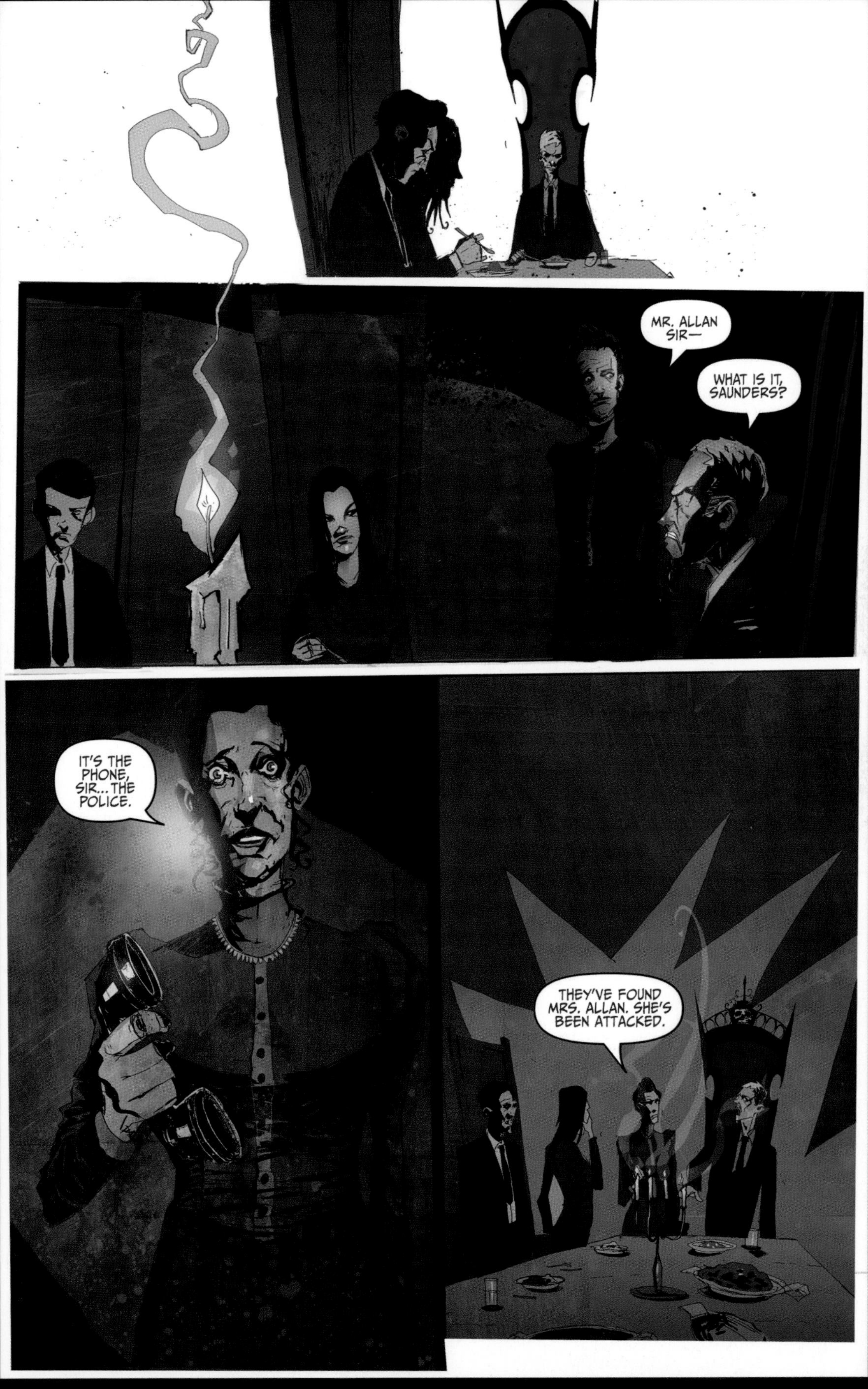
MR. ALLAN SIR—
WHAT IS IT, SAUNDERS?
IT'S THE PHONE, SIR...THE POLICE.
THEY'VE FOUND MRS. ALLAN. SHE'S BEEN ATTACKED.

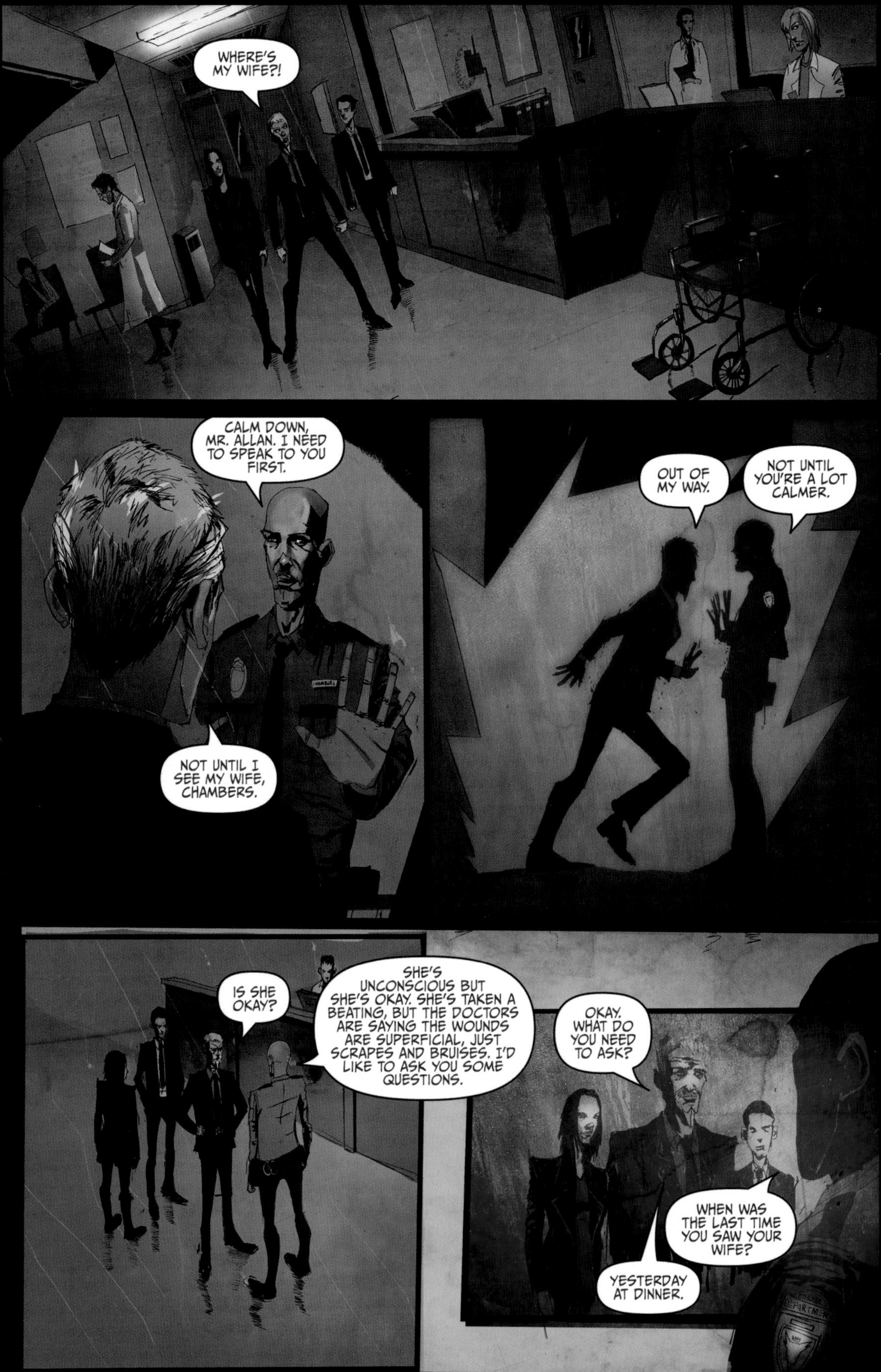
WHERE'S MY WIFE?!
CALM DOWN, MR. ALLAN. I NEED TO SPEAK TO YOU FIRST.
NOT UNTIL I SEE MY WIFE, CHAMBERS.
OUT OF MY WAY.
NOT UNTIL YOU'RE A LOT CALMER.
IS SHE OKAY?
SHE'S UNCONSCIOUS BUT SHE'S OKAY. SHE'S TAKEN A BEATING, BUT THE DOCTORS ARE SAYING THE WOUNDS ARE SUPERFICIAL, JUST SCRAPES AND BRUISES. I'D LIKE TO ASK YOU SOME QUESTIONS.
OKAY. WHAT DO YOU NEED TO ASK?
WHEN WAS THE LAST TIME YOU SAW YOUR WIFE?
YESTERDAY AT DINNER.

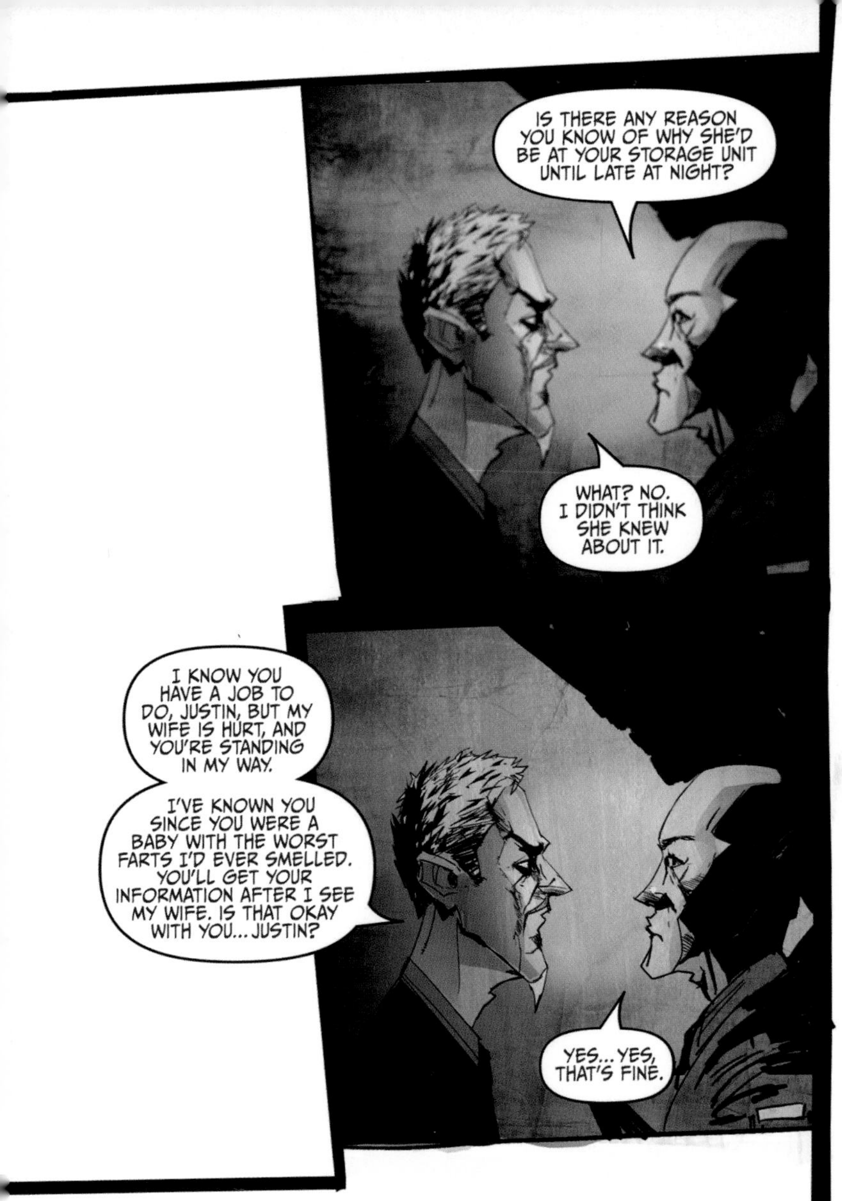
IS THERE ANY REASON YOU KNOW OF WHY SHE'D BE AT YOUR STORAGE UNIT UNTIL LATE AT NIGHT?
WHAT? NO. I DIDN'T THINK SHE KNEW ABOUT IT.
I KNOW YOU HAVE A JOB TO DO, JUSTIN, BUT MY WIFE IS HURT, AND YOU'RE STANDING IN MY WAY.
I'VE KNOWN YOU SINCE YOU WERE A BABY WITH THE WORST FARTS I'D EVER SMELLED. YOU'LL GET YOUR INFORMATION AFTER I SEE MY WIFE. IS THAT OKAY WITH YOU... JUSTIN?
YES... YES, THAT'S FINE.
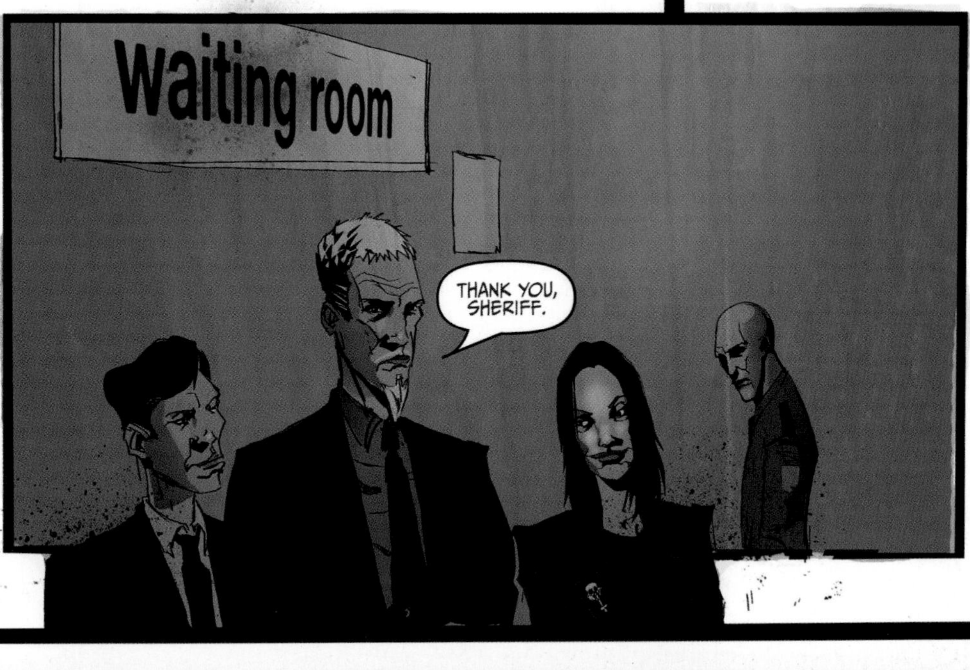
Waiting room
THANK YOU, SHERIFF.

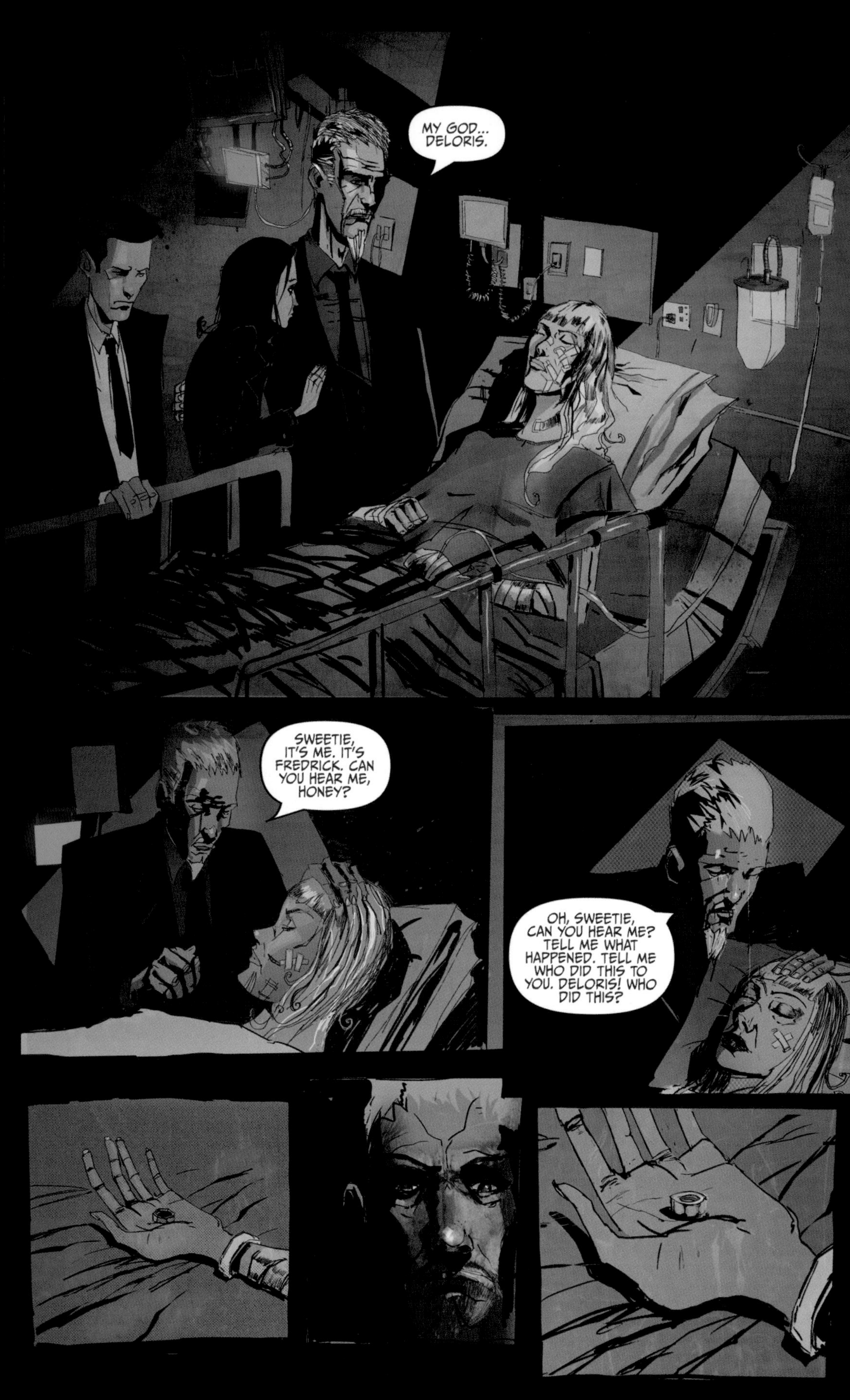
MY GOD... DELORIS.
SWEETIE, IT'S ME. IT'S FREDRICK. CAN YOU HEAR ME, HONEY?
OH, SWEETIE, CAN YOU HEAR ME? TELL ME WHAT HAPPENED. TELL ME WHO DID THIS TO YOU. DELORIS! WHO DID THIS?

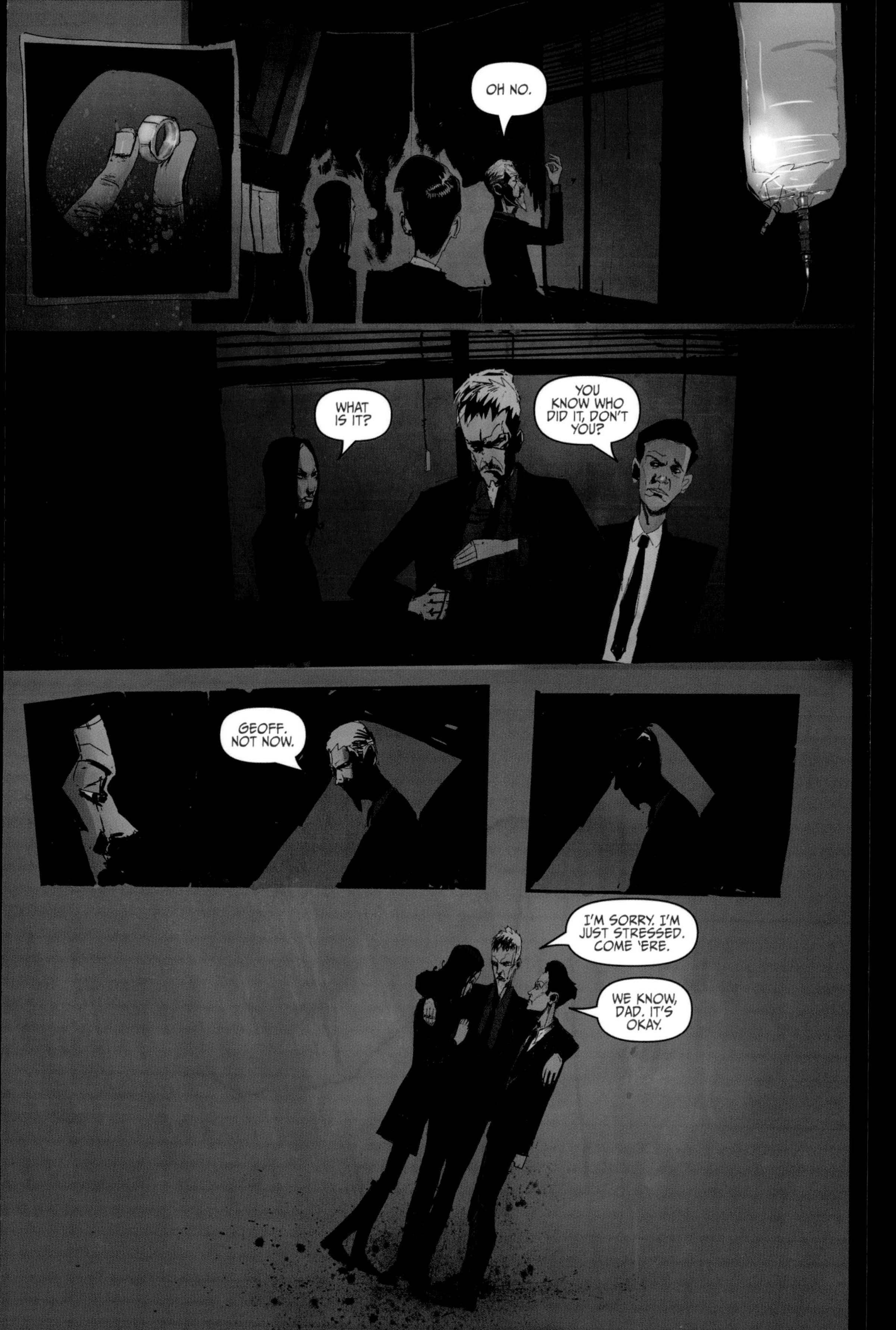
OH NO.
WHAT IS IT?
YOU KNOW WHO DID IT, DON'T YOU?
GEOFF. NOT NOW.
I'M SORRY. I'M JUST STRESSED. COME 'ERE.
WE KNOW, DAD. IT'S OKAY.

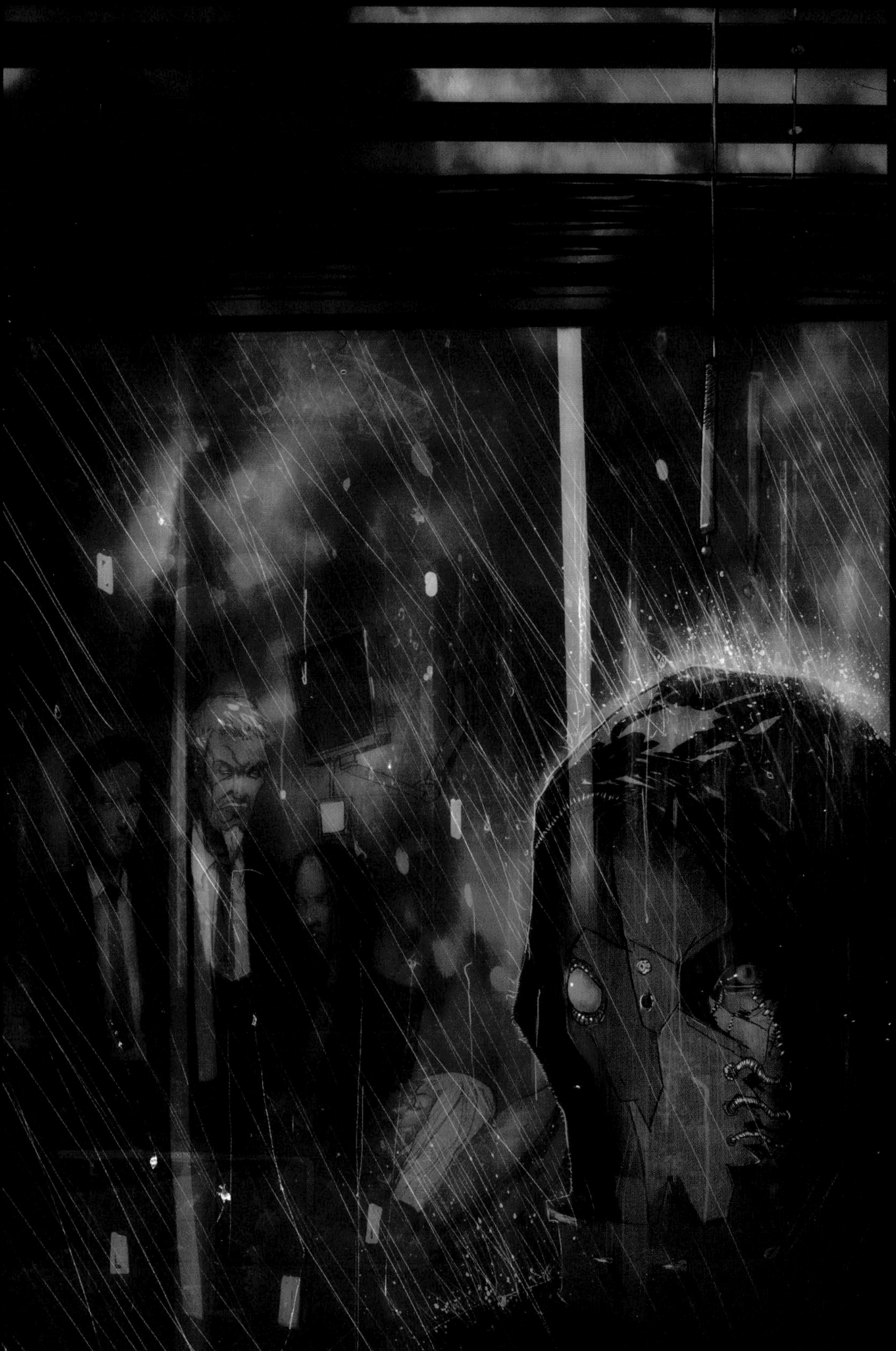

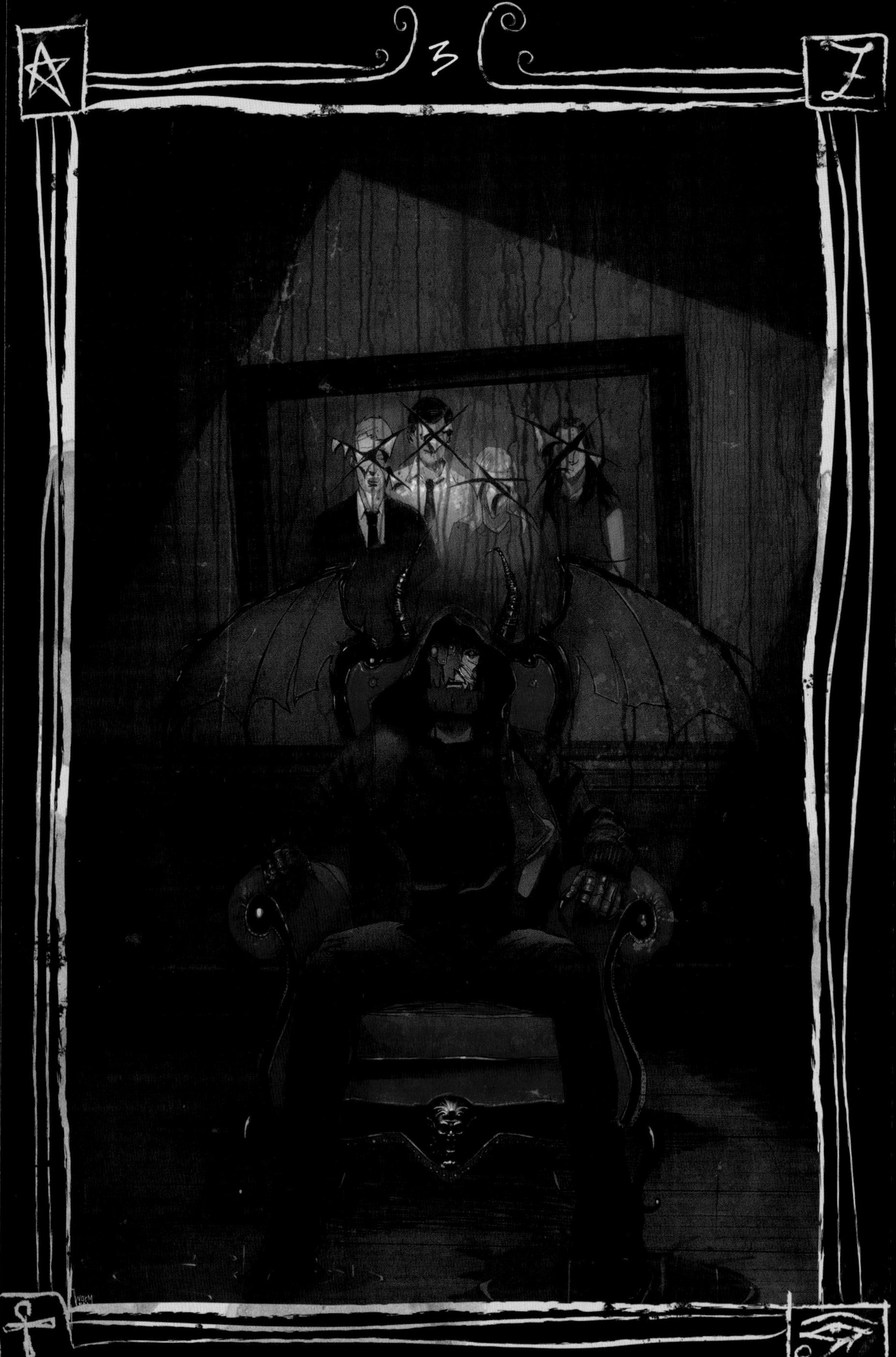
3

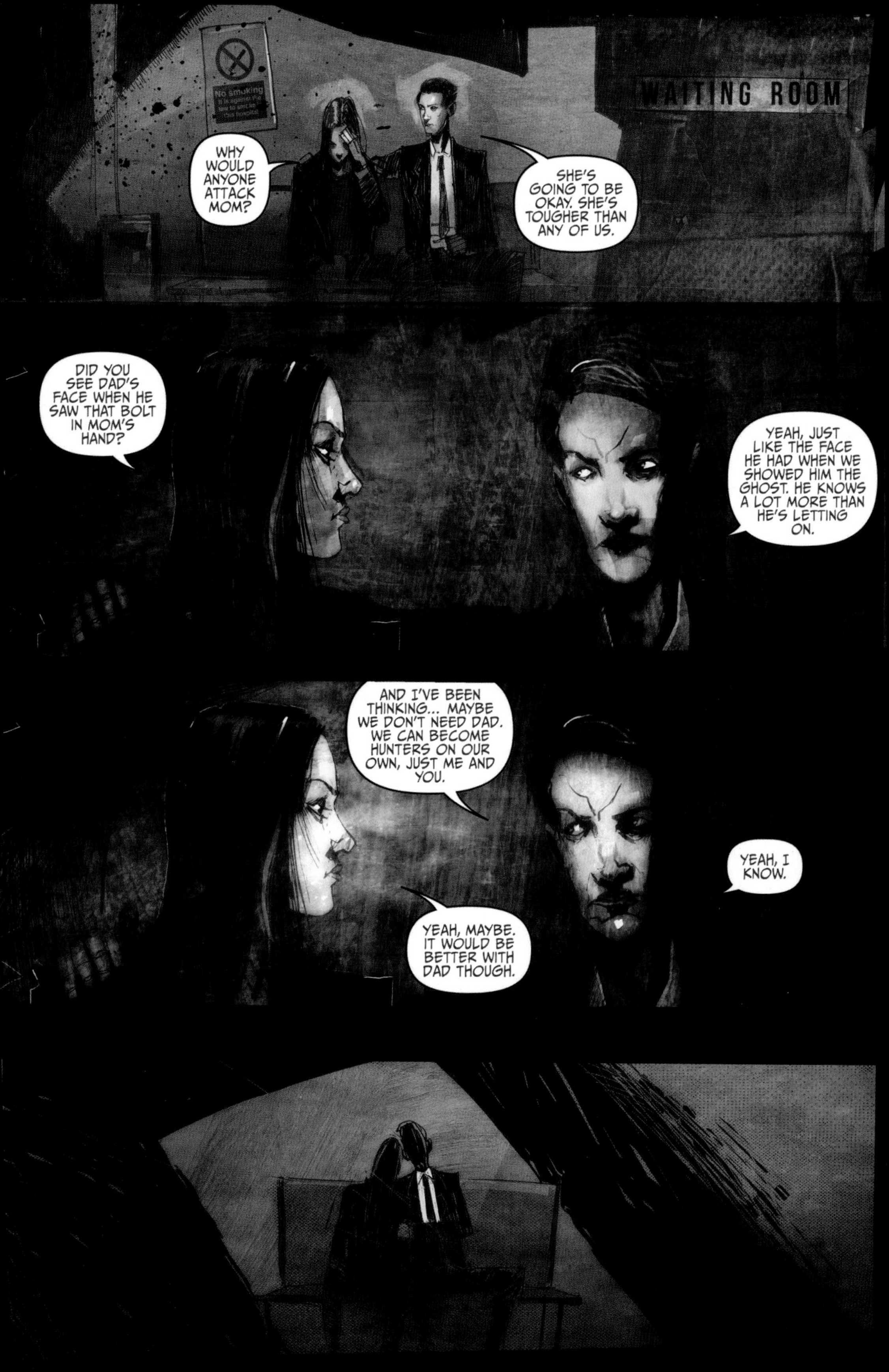
No smoking
WAITING ROOM
WHY WOULD ANYONE ATTACK MOM?
SHE'S GOING TO BE OKAY. SHE'S TOUGHER THAN ANY OF US.
DID YOU SEE DAD'S FACE WHEN HE SAW THAT BOLT IN MOM'S HAND?
YEAH, JUST LIKE THE FACE HE HAD WHEN WE SHOWED HIM THE GHOST. HE KNOWS A LOT MORE THAN HE'S LETTING ON.
AND I'VE BEEN THINKING... MAYBE WE DON'T NEED DAD. WE CAN BECOME HUNTERS ON OUR OWN, JUST ME AND YOU.
YEAH, MAYBE. IT WOULD BE BETTER WITH DAD THOUGH.
YEAH, I KNOW.

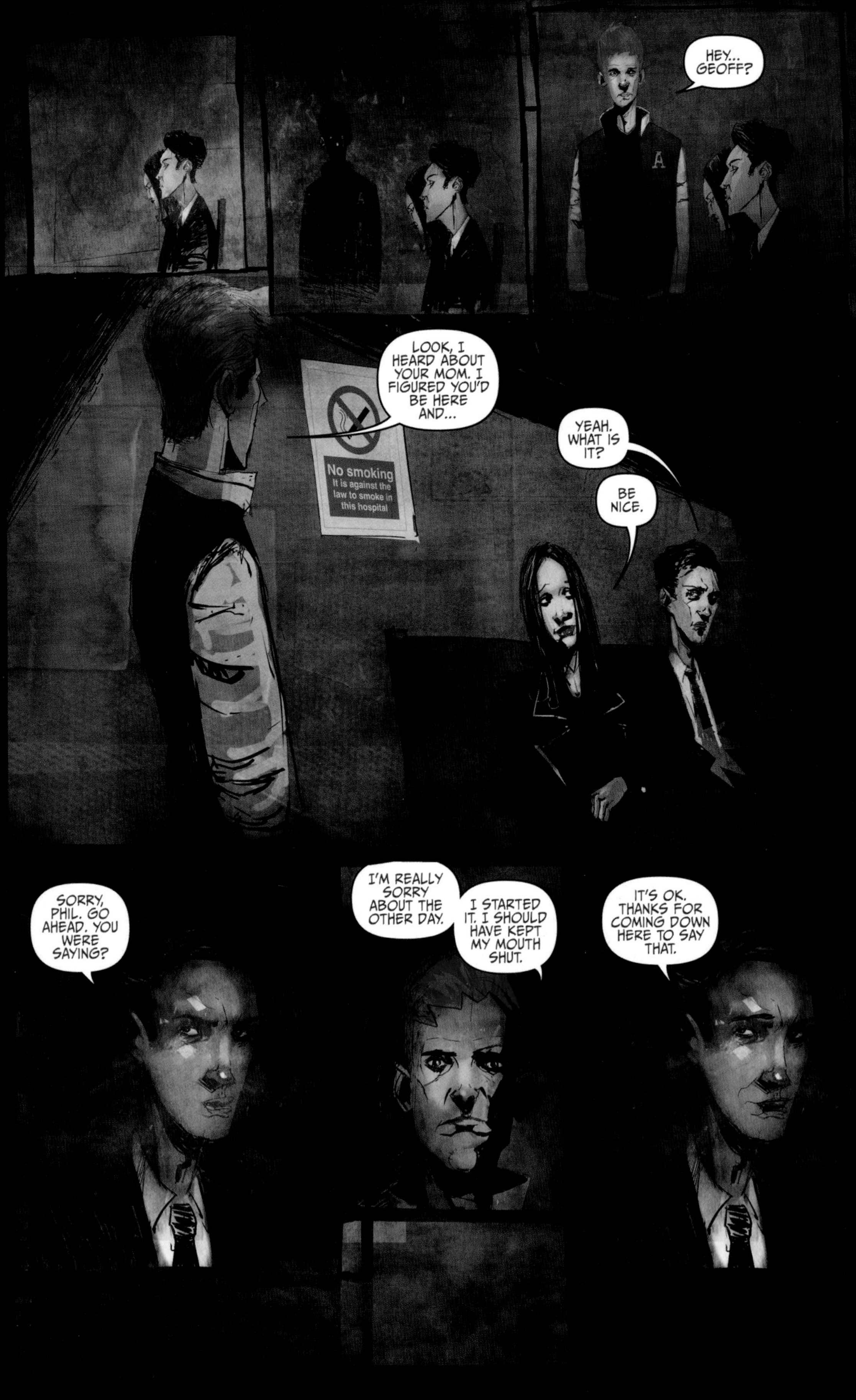
HEY... GEOFF?
LOOK, I HEARD ABOUT YOUR MOM. I FIGURED YOU'D BE HERE AND...
No smoking
It is against the law to smoke in this hospital
YEAH. WHAT IS IT?
BE NICE.
SORRY, PHIL. GO AHEAD. YOU WERE SAYING?
I'M REALLY SORRY ABOUT THE OTHER DAY.
I STARTED IT. I SHOULD HAVE KEPT MY MOUTH SHUT.
IT'S OK. THANKS FOR COMING DOWN HERE TO SAY THAT.

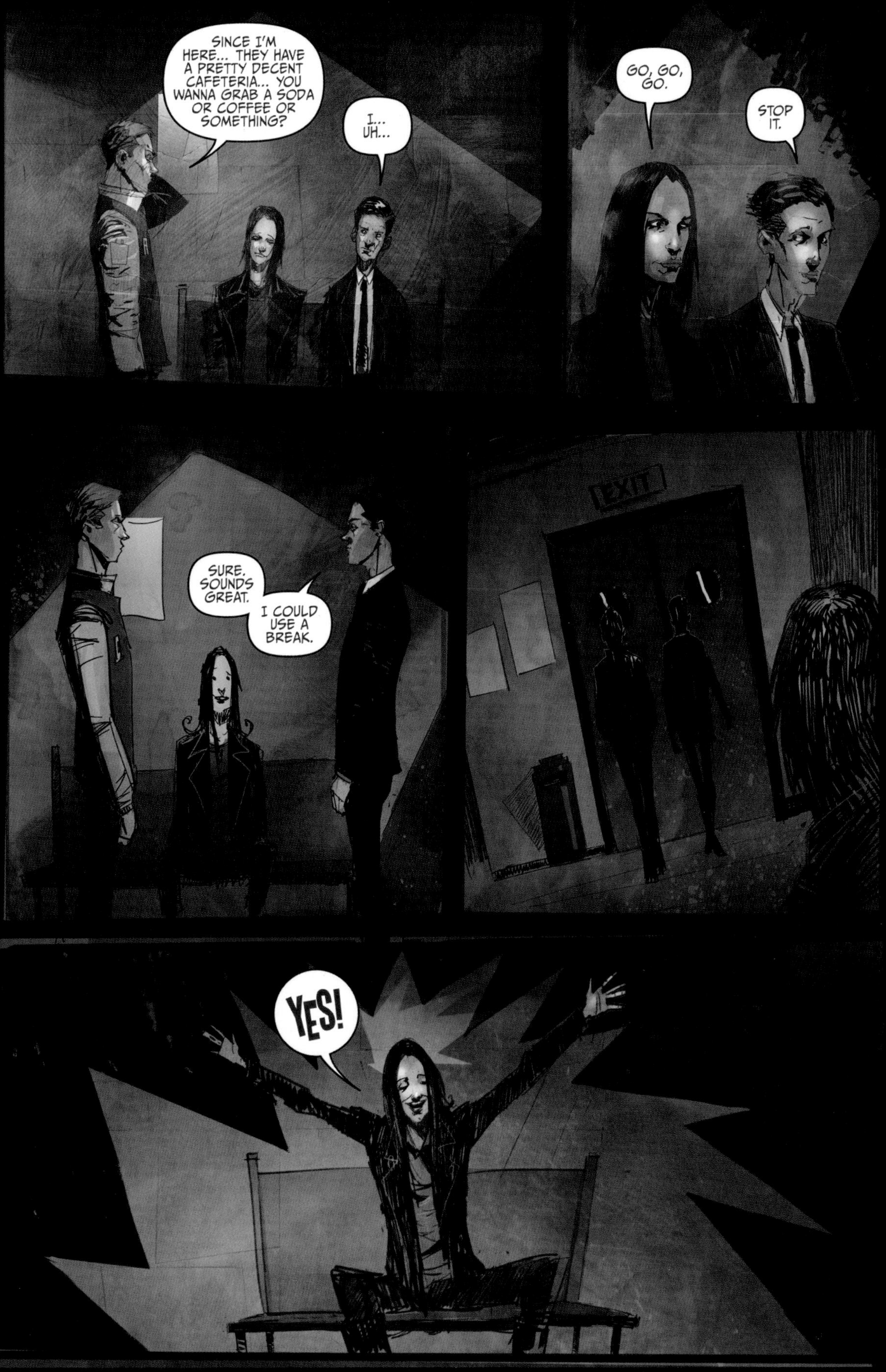

SINCE I'M HERE... THEY HAVE A PRETTY DECENT CAFETERIA... YOU WANNA GRAB A SODA OR COFFEE OR SOMETHING?
I... UH...
GO, GO, GO.
STOP IT.
SURE. SOUNDS GREAT.
I COULD USE A BREAK.
EXIT
YES!

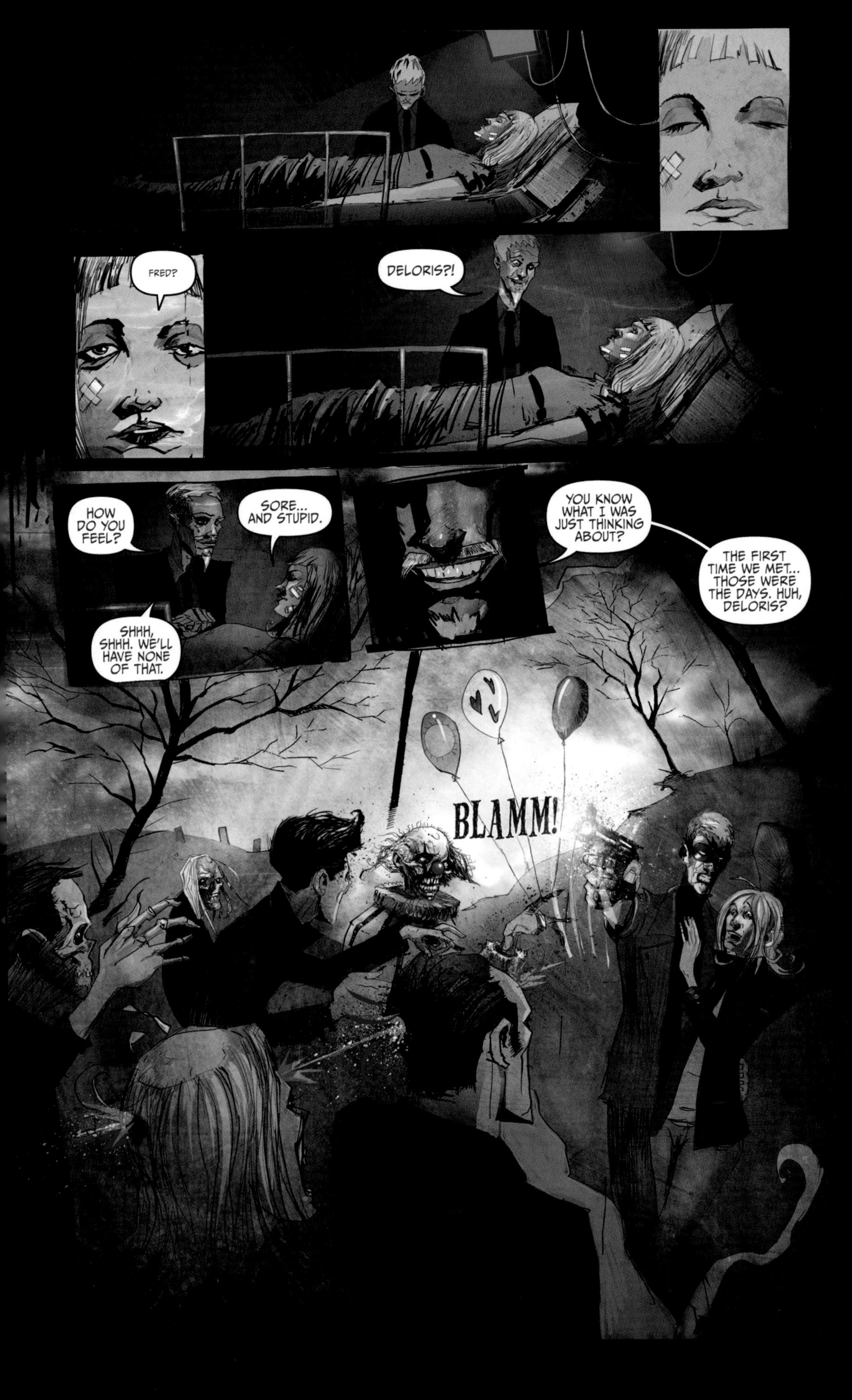
FRED?
DELORIS?!
HOW DO YOU FEEL?
SORE... AND STUPID.
SHHH, SHHH. WE'LL HAVE NONE OF THAT.
YOU KNOW WHAT I WAS JUST THINKING ABOUT?
THE FIRST TIME WE MET... THOSE WERE THE DAYS. HUH, DELORIS?
BLAMM!

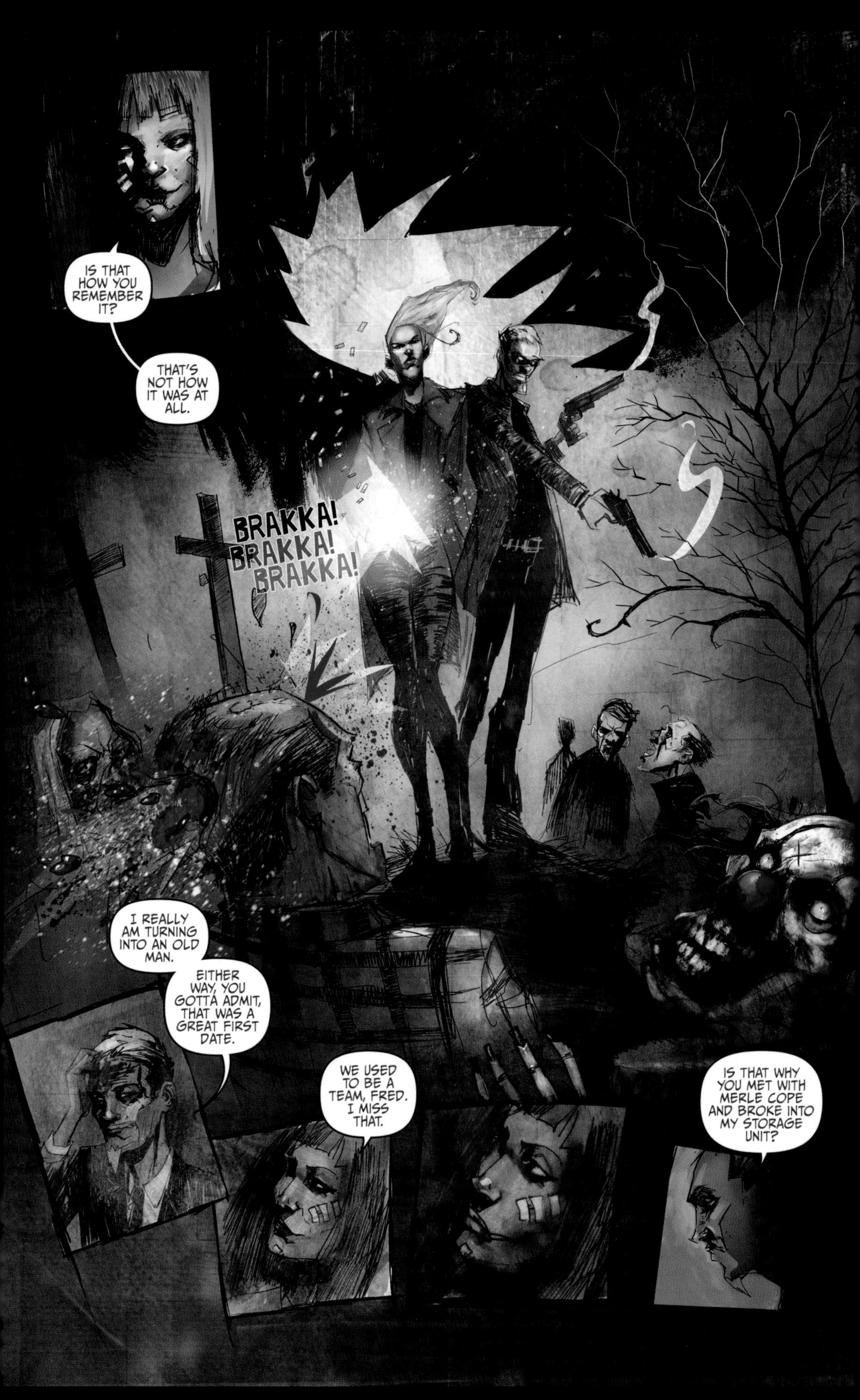
IS THAT HOW YOU REMEMBER IT?
THAT'S NOT HOW IT WAS AT ALL.
BRAKKA! BRAKKA! BRAKKA!
I REALLY AM TURNING INTO AN OLD MAN.
EITHER WAY, YOU GOTTA ADMIT, THAT WAS A GREAT FIRST DATE.
WE USED TO BE A TEAM, FRED. I MISS THAT.
IS THAT WHY YOU MET WITH MERLE COPE AND BROKE INTO MY STORAGE UNIT?

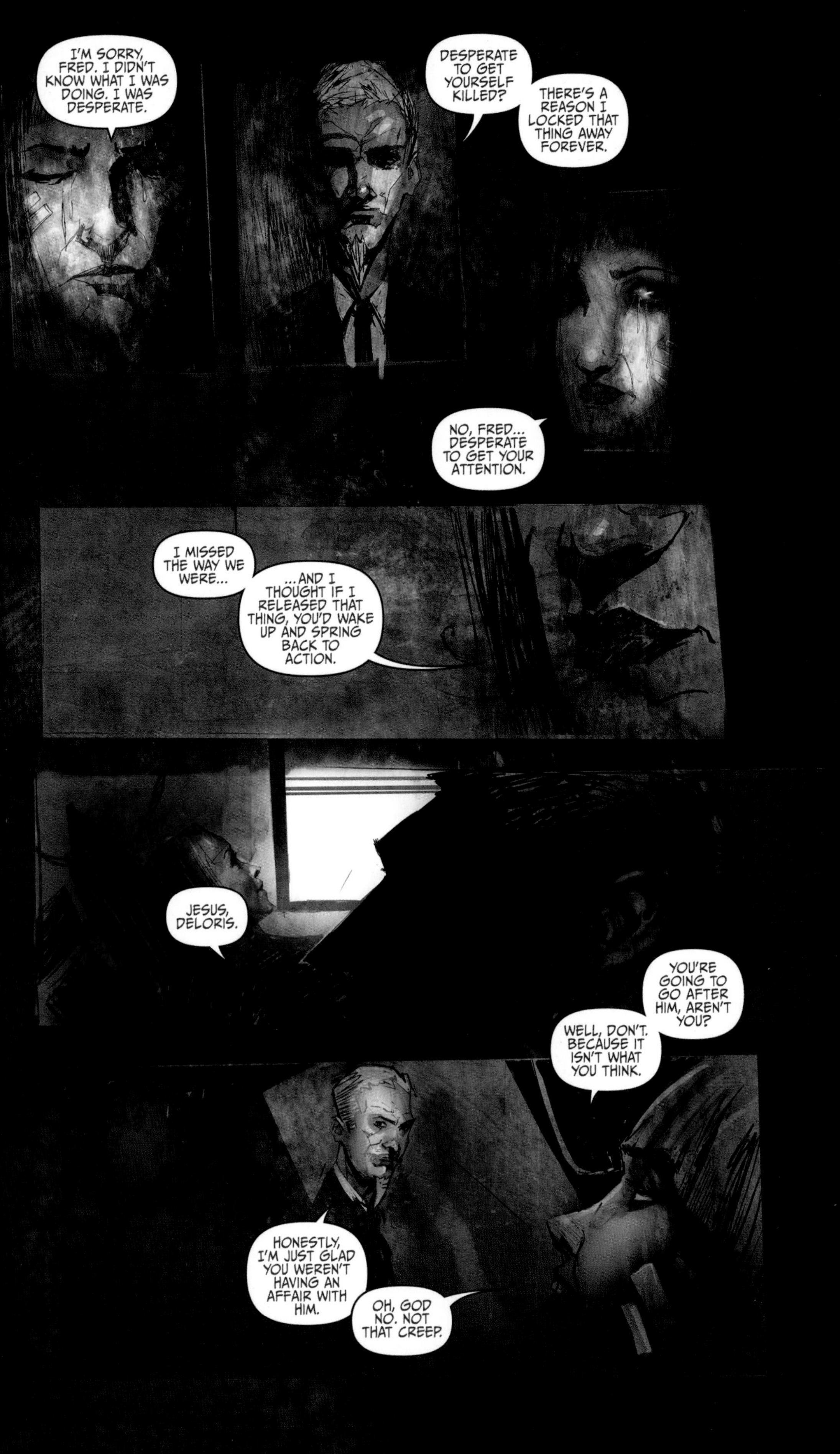
I'M SORRY, FRED. I DIDN'T KNOW WHAT I WAS DOING. I WAS DESPERATE.
DESPERATE TO GET YOURSELF KILLED?
THERE'S A REASON I LOCKED THAT THING AWAY FOREVER.
NO, FRED... DESPERATE TO GET YOUR ATTENTION.
I MISSED THE WAY WE WERE...
...AND I THOUGHT IF I RELEASED THAT THING, YOU'D WAKE UP AND SPRING BACK TO ACTION.
JESUS, DELORIS.
YOU'RE GOING TO GO AFTER HIM, AREN'T YOU?
WELL, DON'T. BECAUSE IT ISN'T WHAT YOU THINK.
HONESTLY, I'M JUST GLAD YOU WEREN'T HAVING AN AFFAIR WITH HIM.
OH, GOD NO. NOT THAT CREEP.

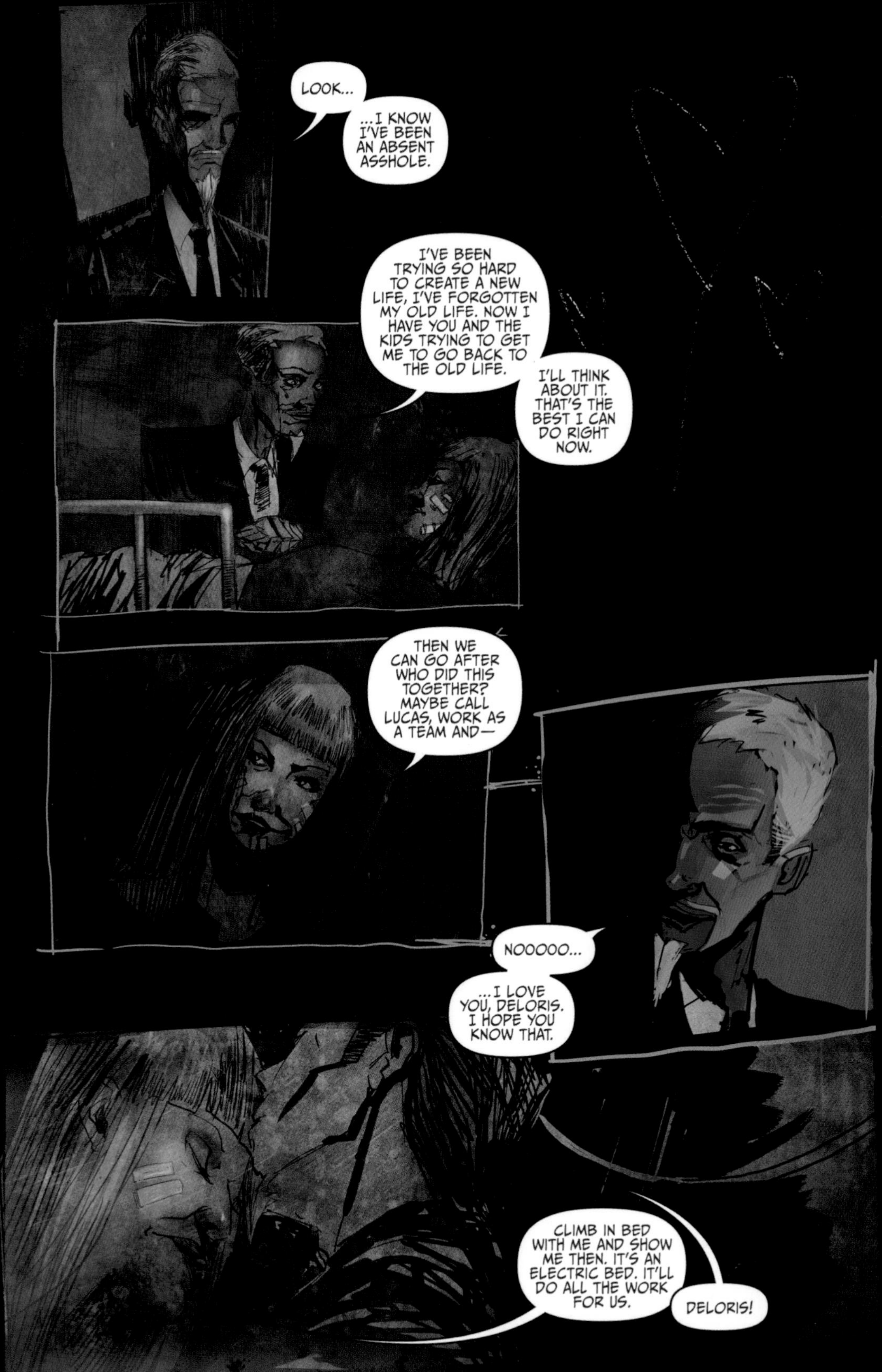
LOOK...
...I KNOW I'VE BEEN AN ABSENT ASSHOLE.
I'VE BEEN TRYING SO HARD TO CREATE A NEW LIFE, I'VE FORGOTTEN MY OLD LIFE. NOW I HAVE YOU AND THE KIDS TRYING TO GET ME TO GO BACK TO THE OLD LIFE.
I'LL THINK ABOUT IT. THAT'S THE BEST I CAN DO RIGHT NOW.
THEN WE CAN GO AFTER WHO DID THIS TOGETHER? MAYBE CALL LUCAS, WORK AS A TEAM AND—
NOOOOO...
...I LOVE YOU, DELORIS. I HOPE YOU KNOW THAT.
CLIMB IN BED WITH ME AND SHOW ME THEN. IT'S AN ELECTRIC BED. IT'LL DO ALL THE WORK FOR US.
DELORIS!

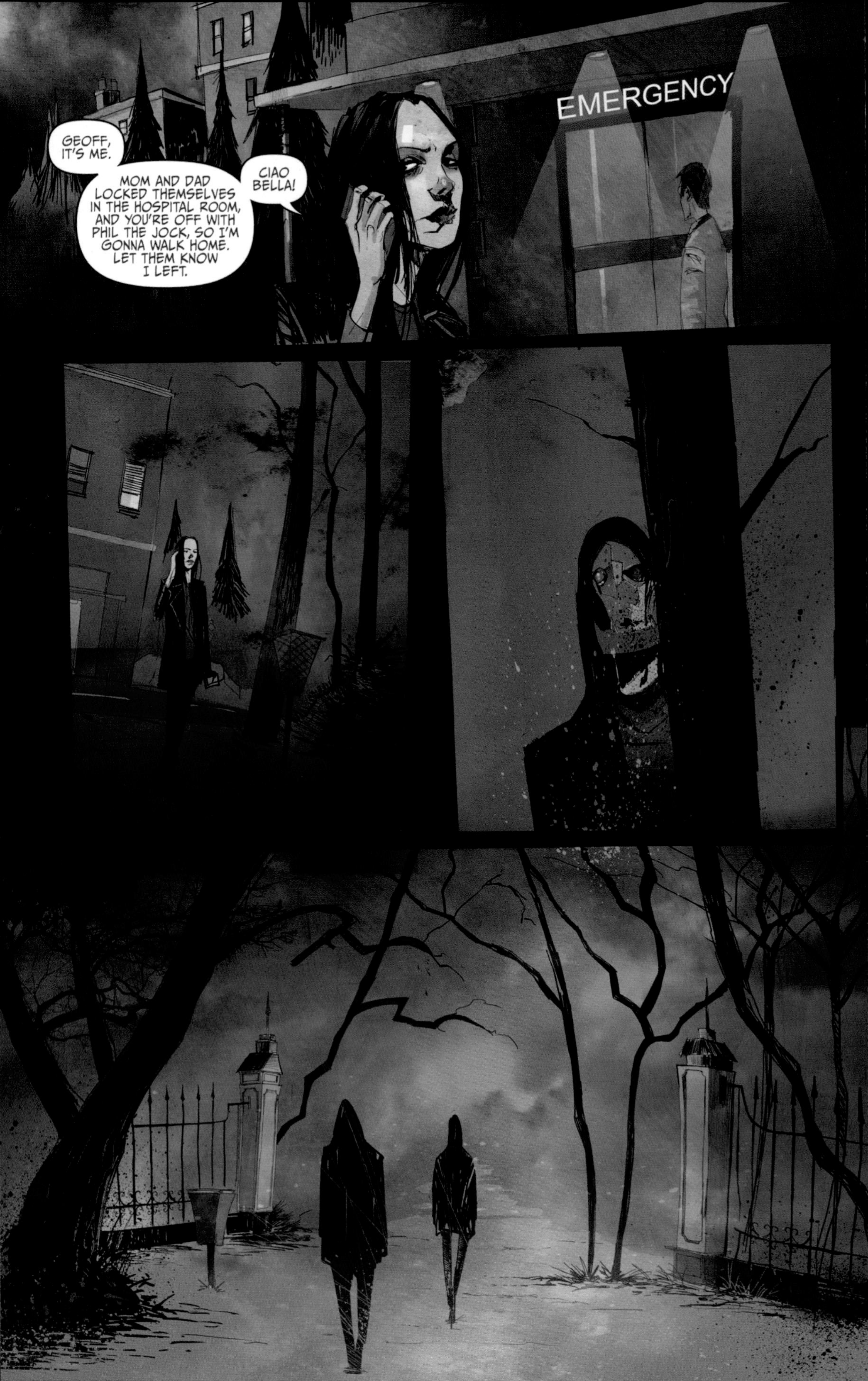
EMERGENCY
GEOFF, IT'S ME.
MOM AND DAD LOCKED THEMSELVES IN THE HOSPITAL ROOM, AND YOU'RE OFF WITH PHIL THE JOCK, SO I'M GONNA WALK HOME. LET THEM KNOW I LEFT.
CIAO BELLA!

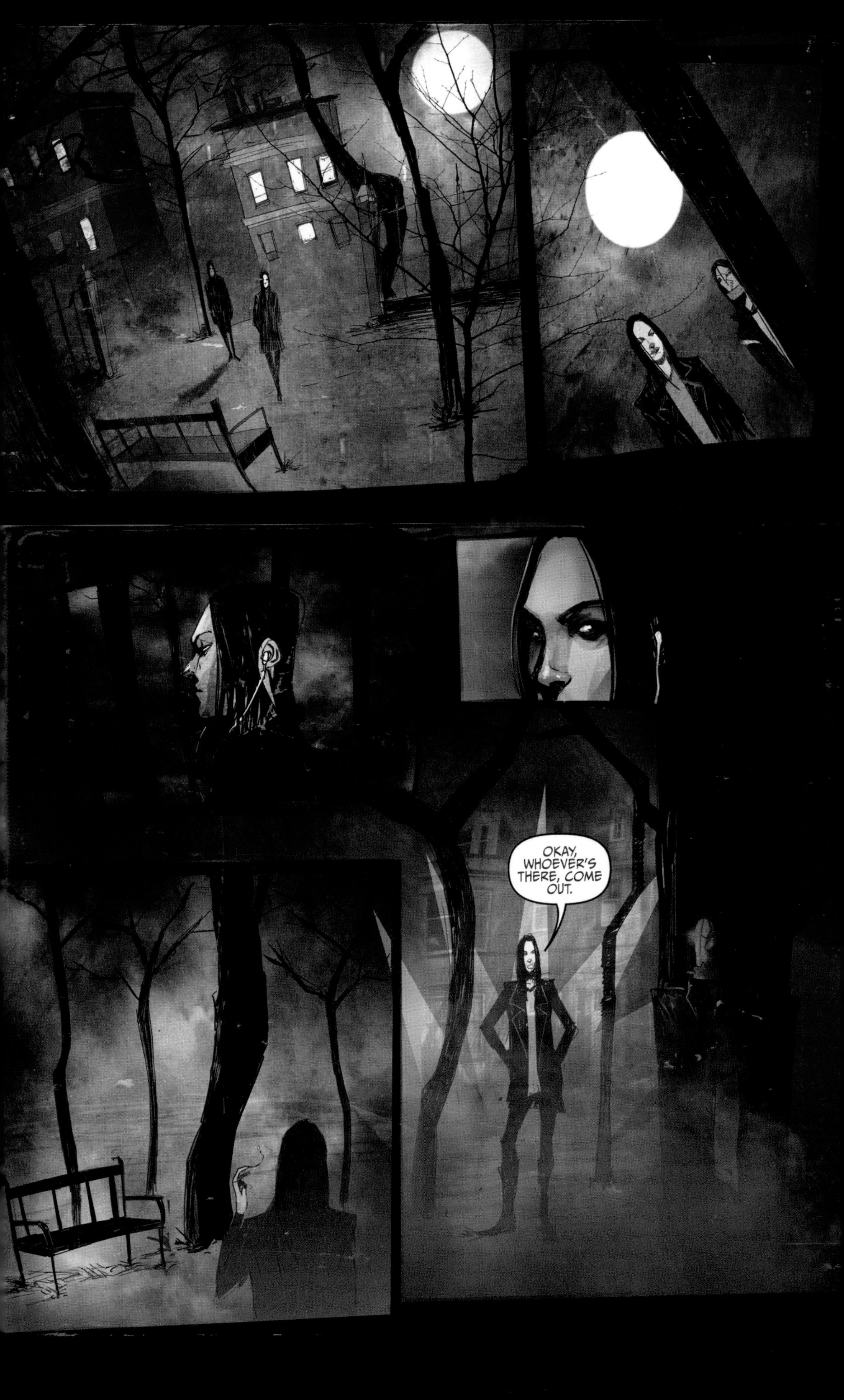
OKAY, WHOEVER'S THERE, COME OUT.

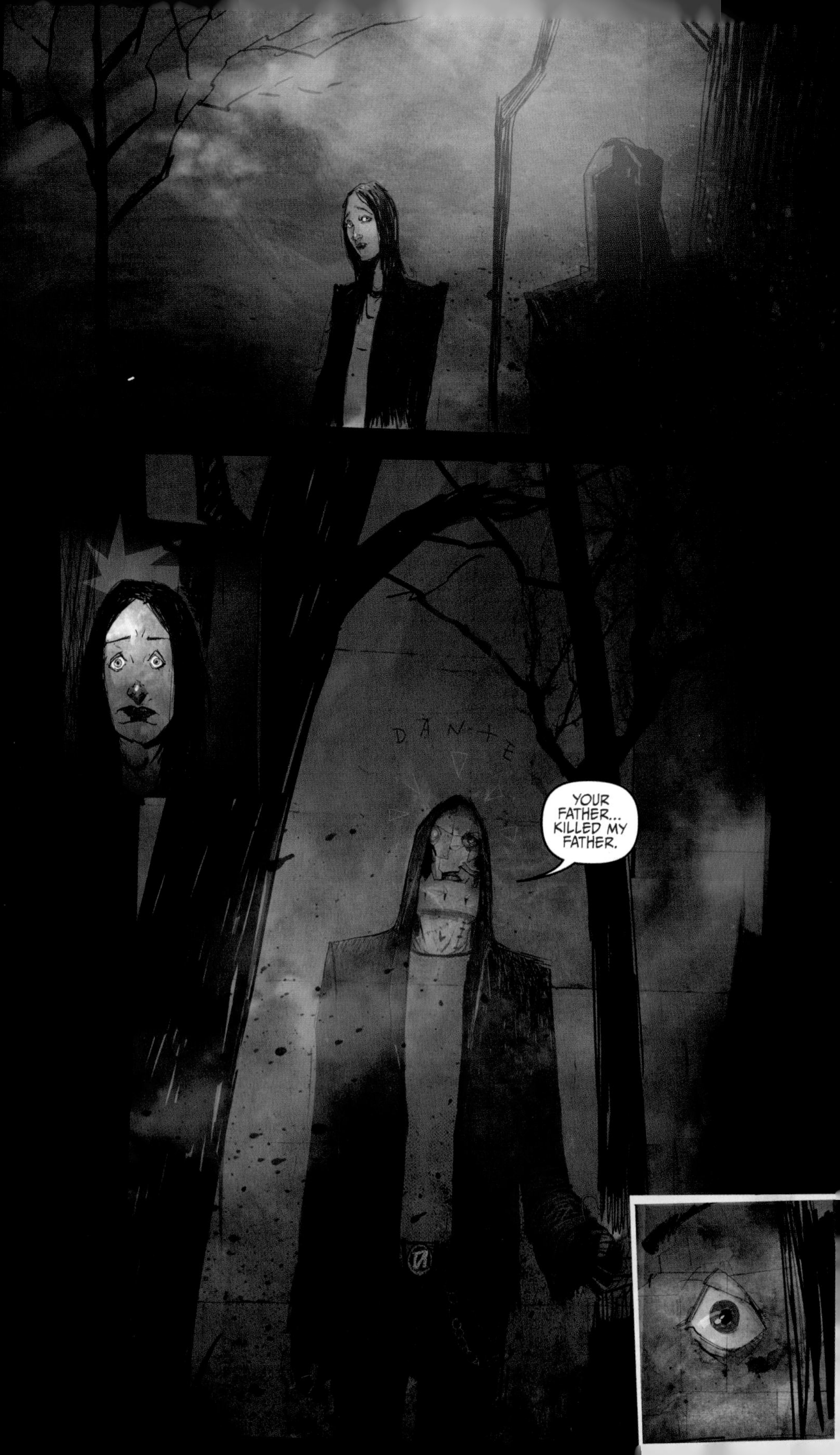
DANTE
YOUR FATHER... KILLED MY FATHER.

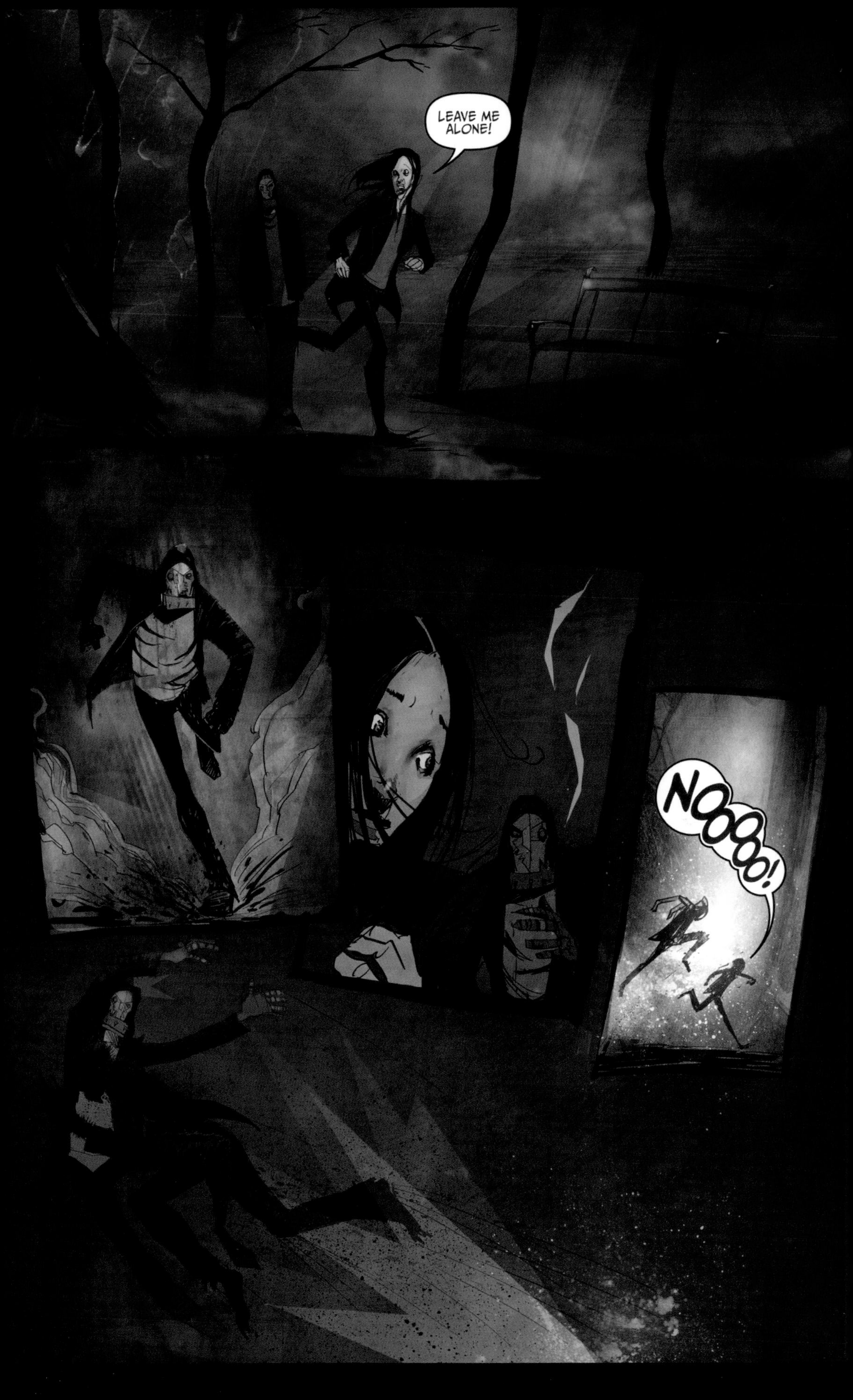
LEAVE ME ALONE!
NOOOOO!

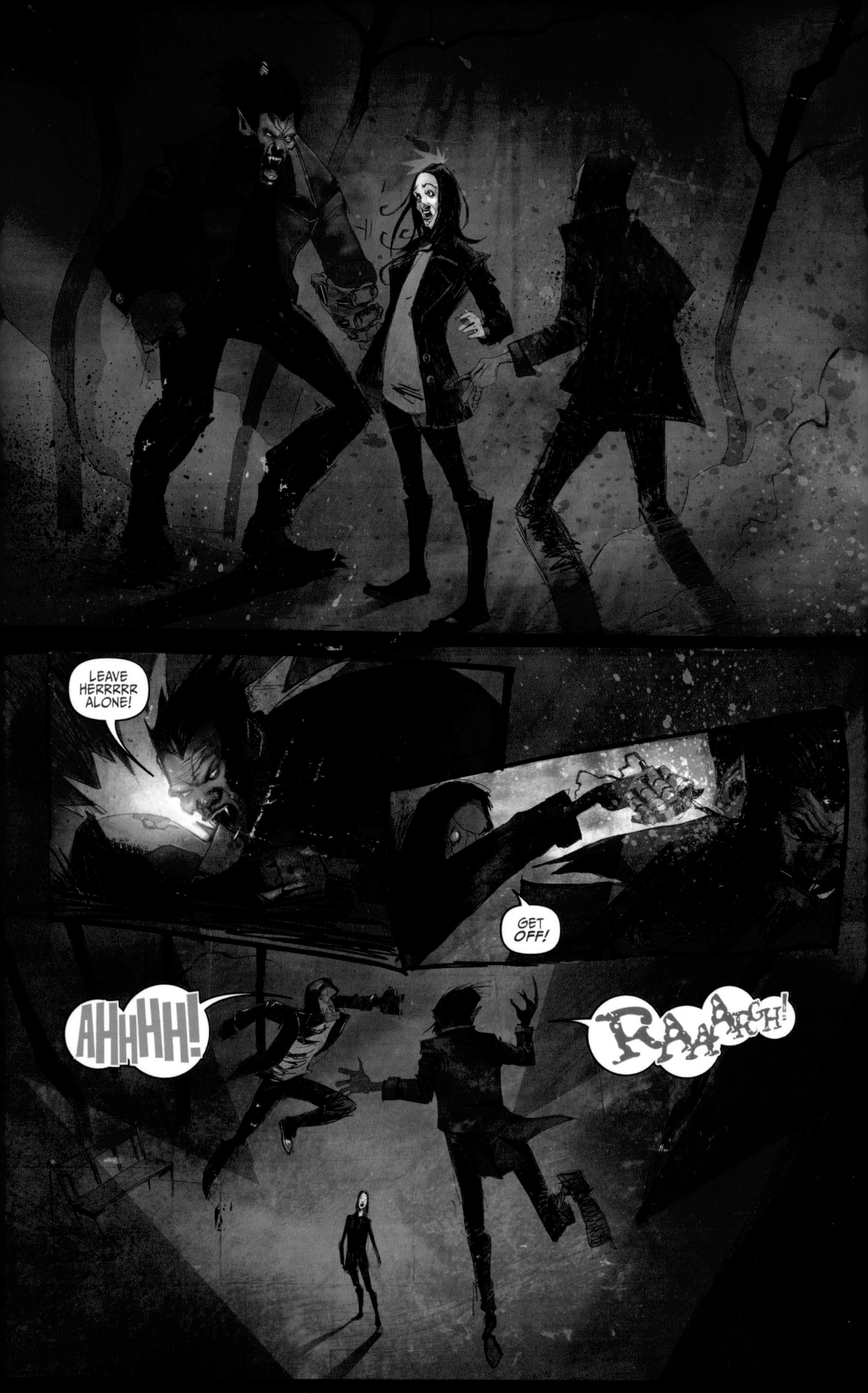
LEAVE HERRRRR ALONE!
GET OFF!
AHHHH!
RAAARGH!

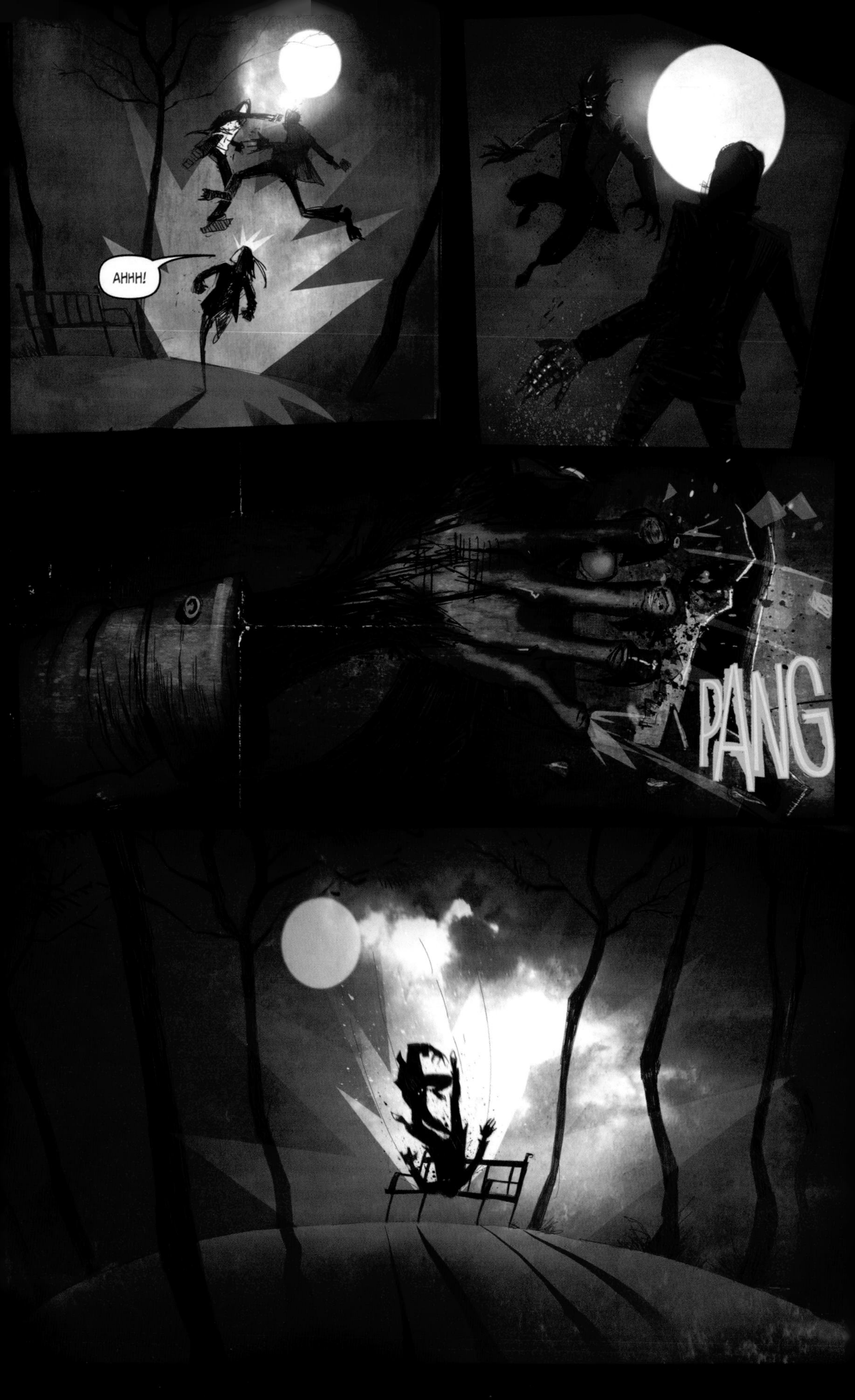
AHHH!
PANG

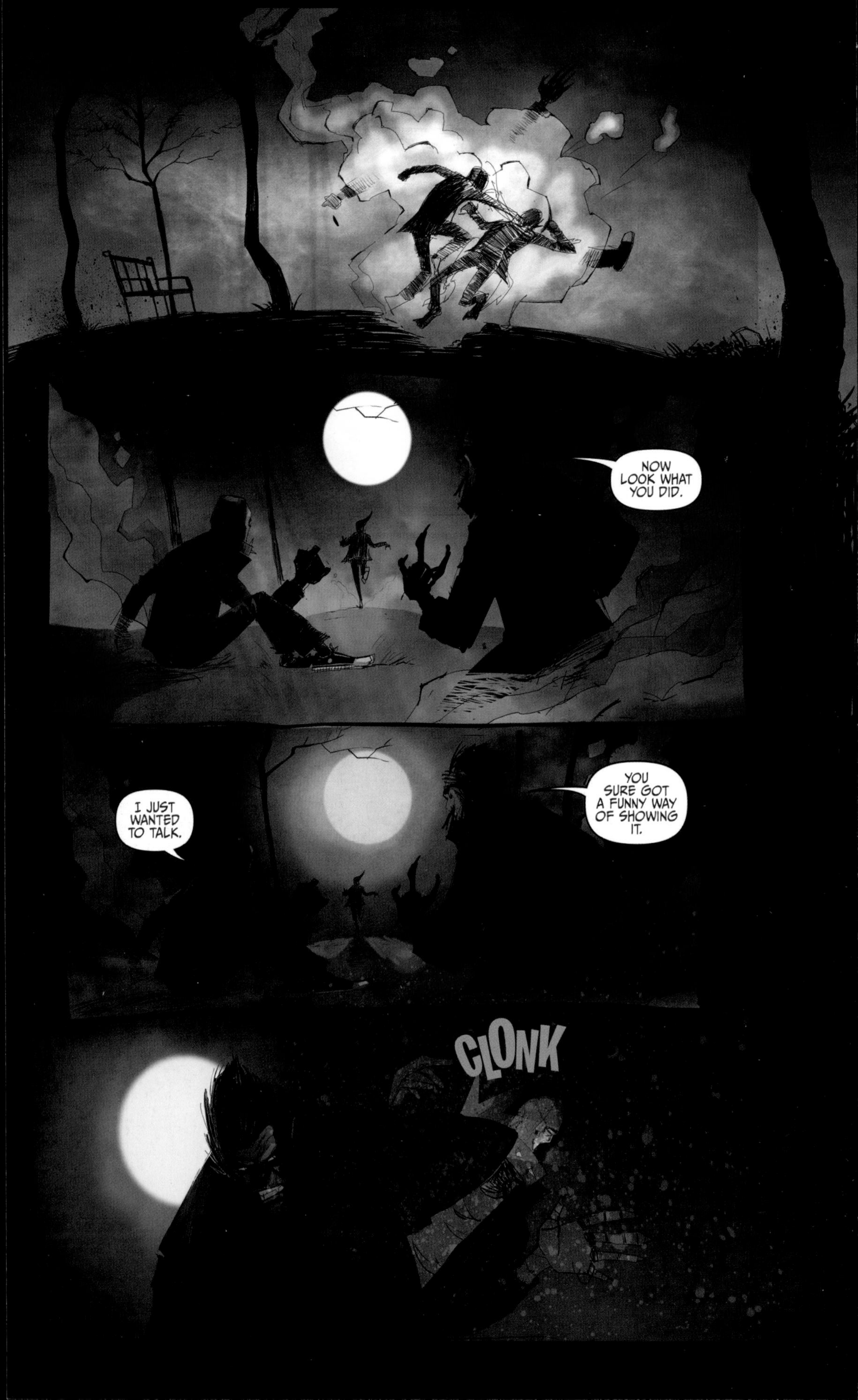
NOW LOOK WHAT YOU DID.
I JUST WANTED TO TALK.
YOU SURE GOT A FUNNY WAY OF SHOWING IT.
CLONK

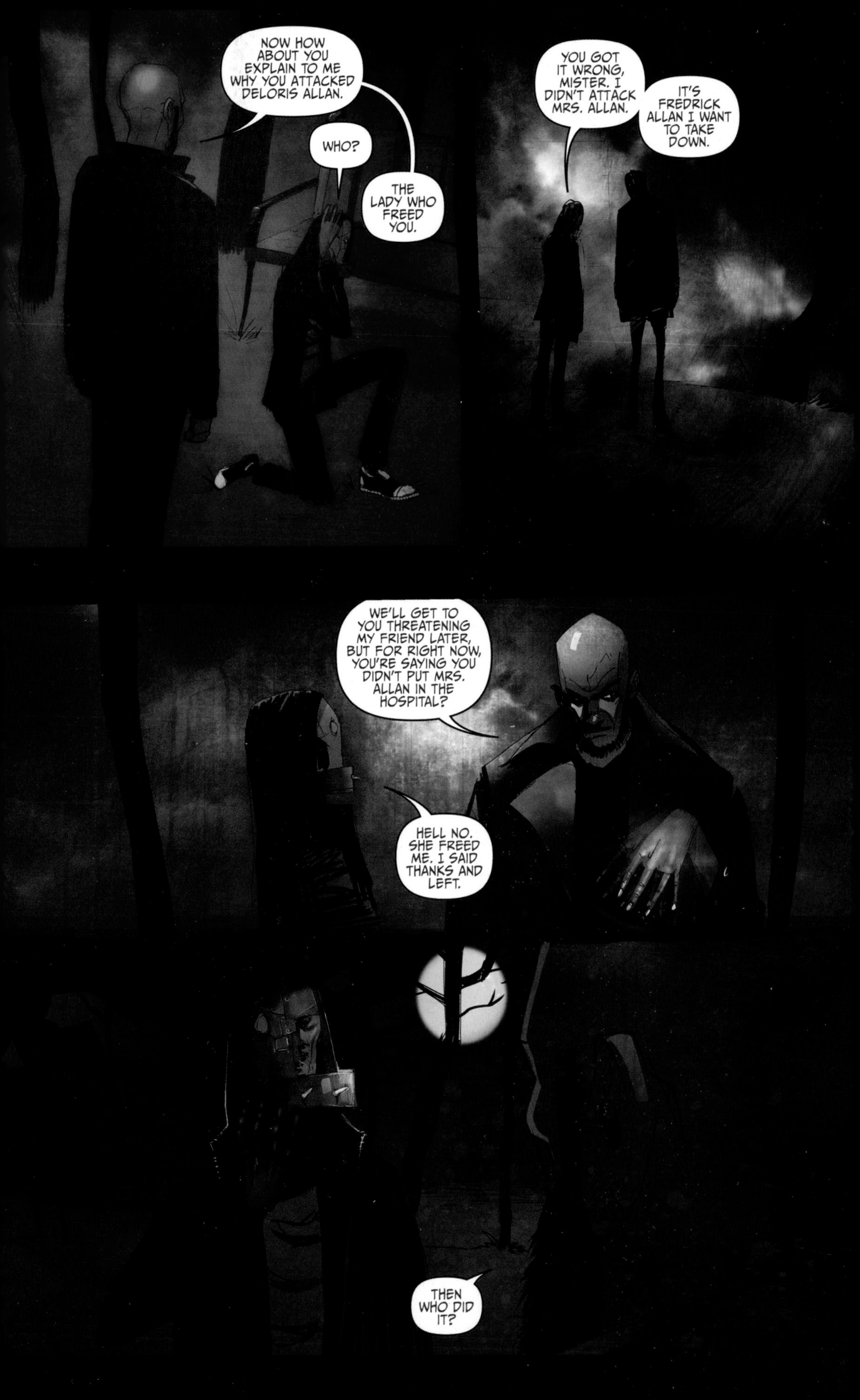
NOW HOW ABOUT YOU EXPLAIN TO ME WHY YOU ATTACKED DELORIS ALLAN.
WHO?
THE LADY WHO FREED YOU.
YOU GOT IT WRONG, MISTER. I DIDN'T ATTACK MRS. ALLAN.
IT'S FREDRICK ALLAN I WANT TO TAKE DOWN.
WE'LL GET TO YOU THREATENING MY FRIEND LATER, BUT FOR RIGHT NOW, YOU'RE SAYING YOU DIDN'T PUT MRS. ALLAN IN THE HOSPITAL?
HELL NO. SHE FREED ME. I SAID THANKS AND LEFT.
THEN WHO DID IT?

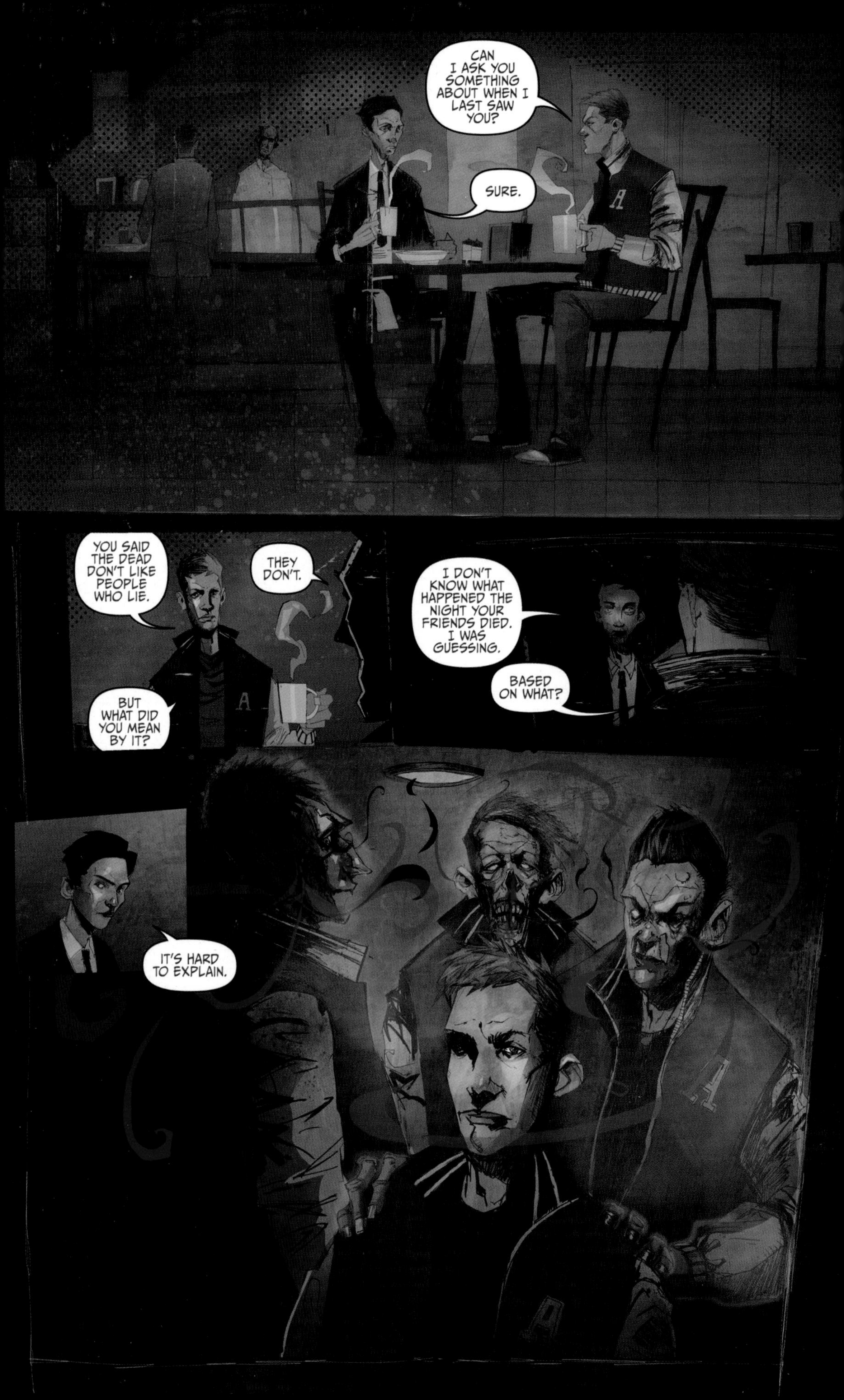
CAN I ASK YOU SOMETHING ABOUT WHEN I LAST SAW YOU?
SURE.
YOU SAID THE DEAD DON'T LIKE PEOPLE WHO LIE.
THEY DON'T.
BUT WHAT DID YOU MEAN BY IT?
I DON'T KNOW WHAT HAPPENED THE NIGHT YOUR FRIENDS DIED. I WAS GUESSING.
BASED ON WHAT?
IT'S HARD TO EXPLAIN.

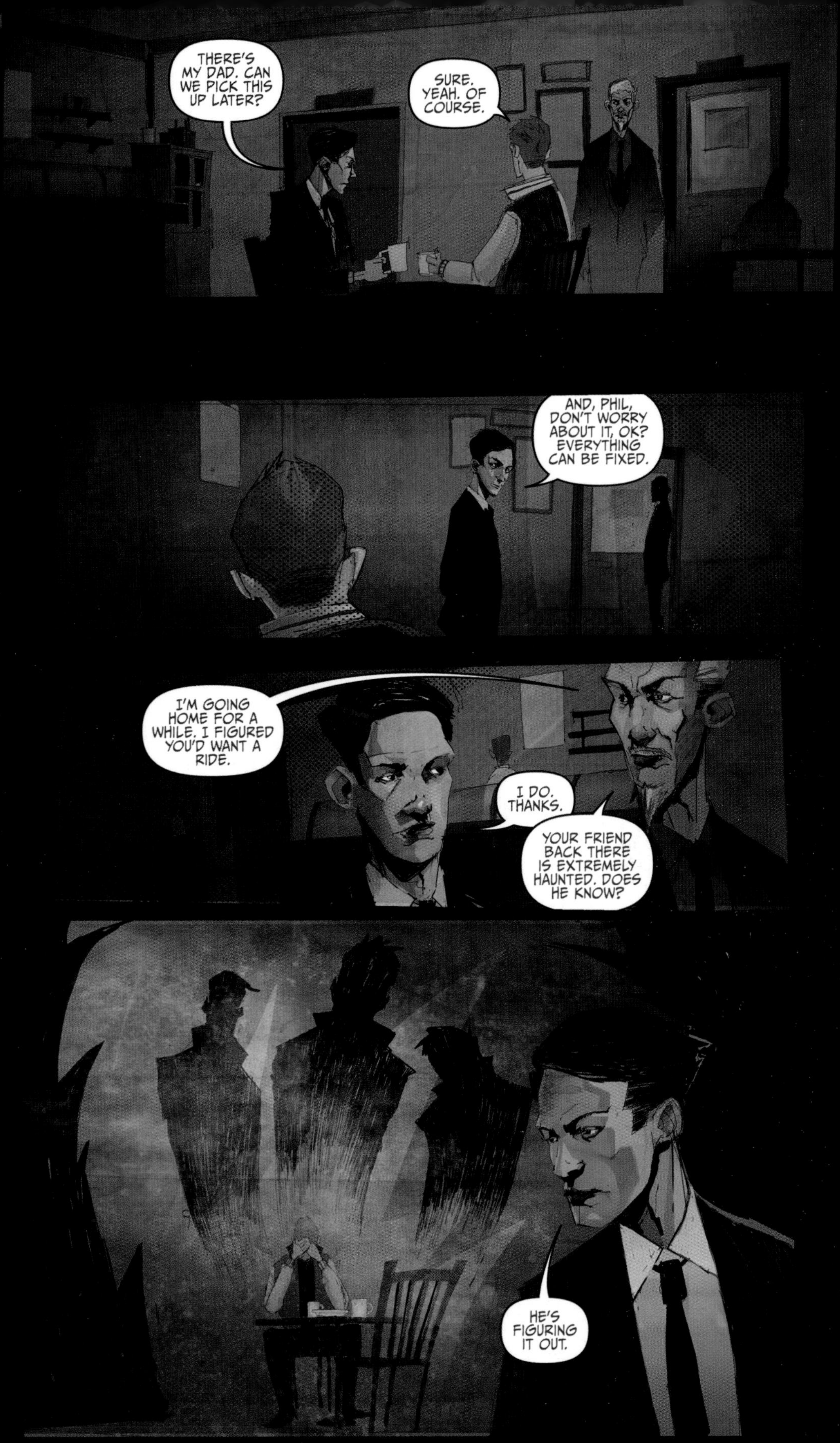
THERE'S MY DAD. CAN WE PICK THIS UP LATER?
SURE. YEAH. OF COURSE.
AND, PHIL, DON'T WORRY ABOUT IT, OK? EVERYTHING CAN BE FIXED.
I'M GOING HOME FOR A WHILE. I FIGURED YOU'D WANT A RIDE.
I DO. THANKS.
YOUR FRIEND BACK THERE IS EXTREMELY HAUNTED. DOES HE KNOW?
HE'S FIGURING IT OUT.

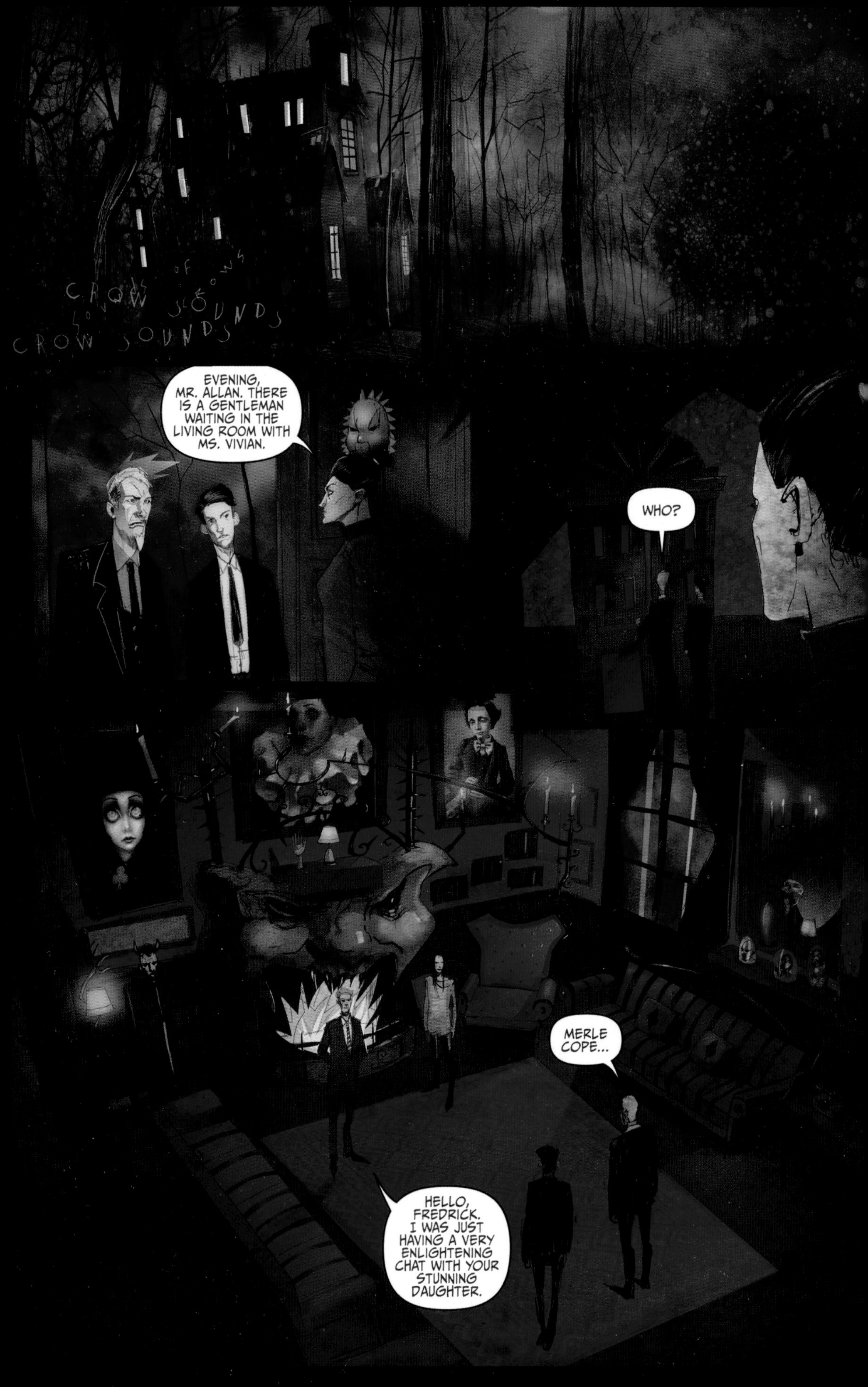
CROW SOUNDS
CROW SOUNDS
EVENING, MR. ALLAN. THERE IS A GENTLEMAN WAITING IN THE LIVING ROOM WITH MS. VIVIAN.
WHO?
MERLE COPE...
HELLO, FREDRICK. I WAS JUST HAVING A VERY ENLIGHTENING CHAT WITH YOUR STUNNING DAUGHTER.

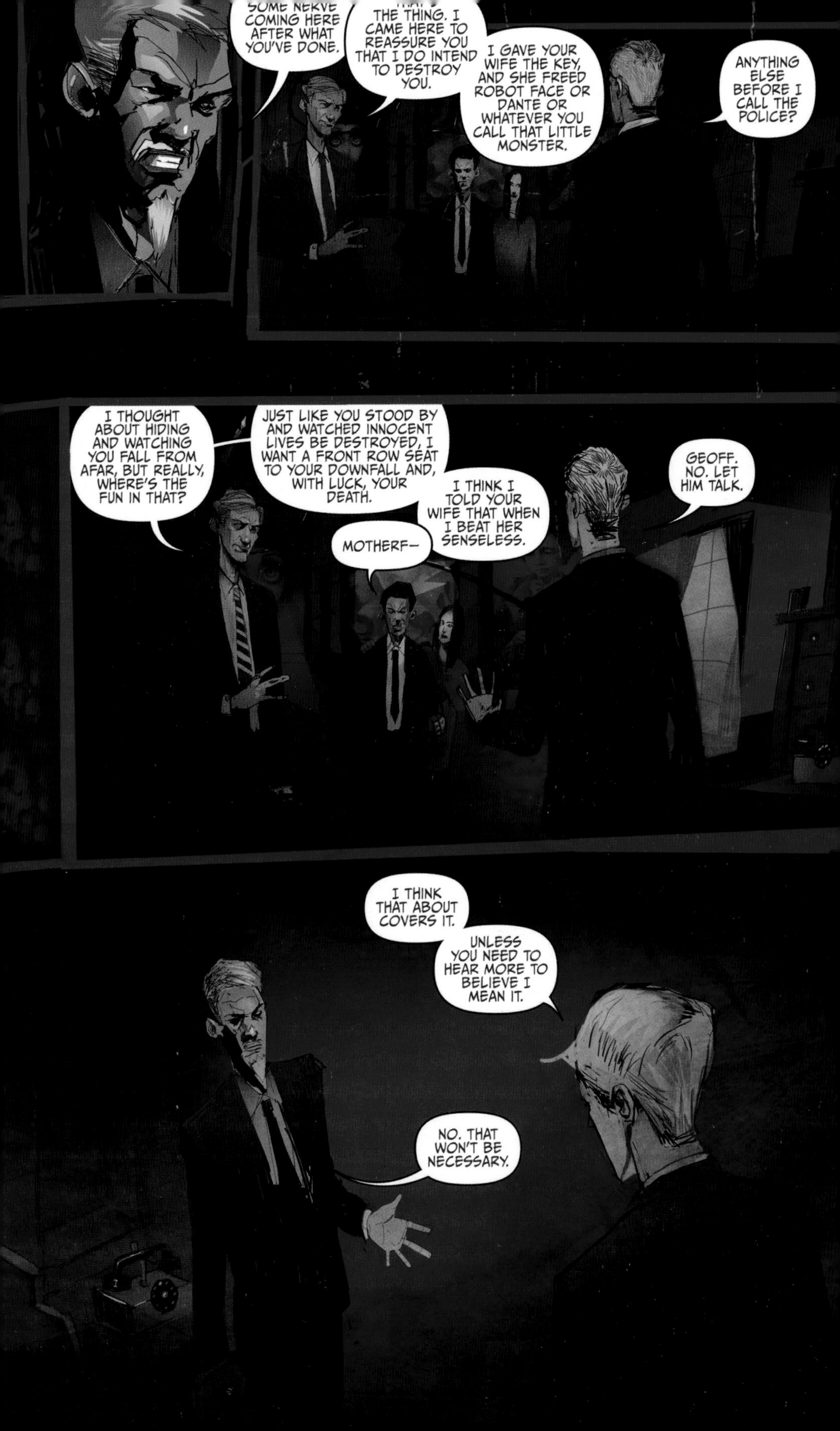
SOME NERVE COMING HERE AFTER WHAT YOU'VE DONE.
THE THING. I CAME HERE TO REASSURE YOU THAT I DO INTEND TO DESTROY YOU.
I GAVE YOUR WIFE THE KEY, AND SHE FREED ROBOT FACE OR DANTE OR WHATEVER YOU CALL THAT LITTLE MONSTER.
ANYTHING ELSE BEFORE I CALL THE POLICE?
I THOUGHT ABOUT HIDING AND WATCHING YOU FALL FROM AFAR, BUT REALLY, WHERE'S THE FUN IN THAT?
JUST LIKE YOU STOOD BY AND WATCHED INNOCENT LIVES BE DESTROYED, I WANT A FRONT ROW SEAT TO YOUR DOWNFALL AND, WITH LUCK, YOUR DEATH.
I THINK I TOLD YOUR WIFE THAT WHEN I BEAT HER SENSELESS.
MOTHERF—
GEOFF. NO. LET HIM TALK.
I THINK THAT ABOUT COVERS IT.
UNLESS YOU NEED TO HEAR MORE TO BELIEVE I MEAN IT.
NO. THAT WON'T BE NECESSARY.

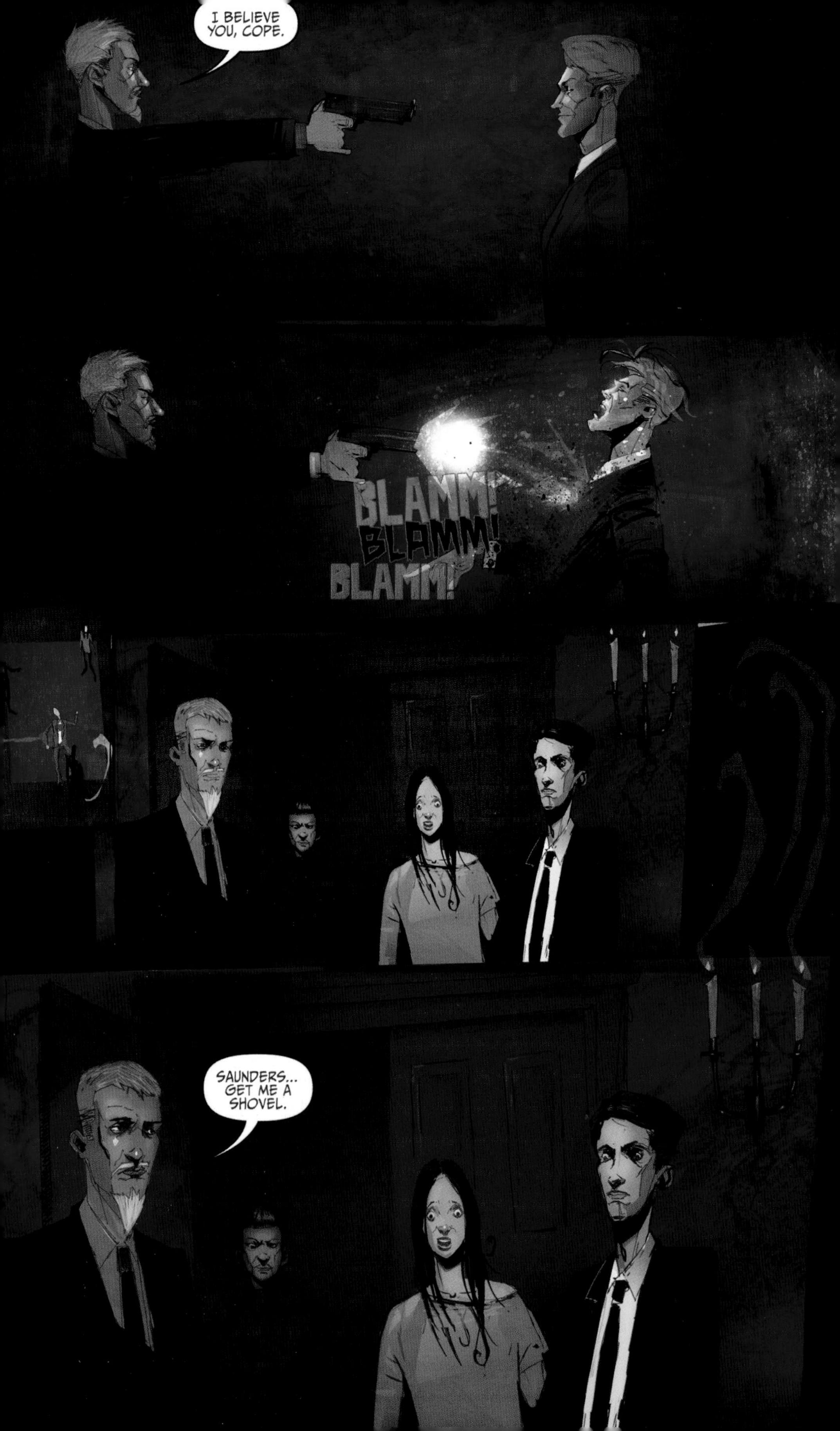
I BELIEVE YOU, COPE.
BLAMM!
BLAMM!
BLAMM!
SAUNDERS... GET ME A SHOVEL.

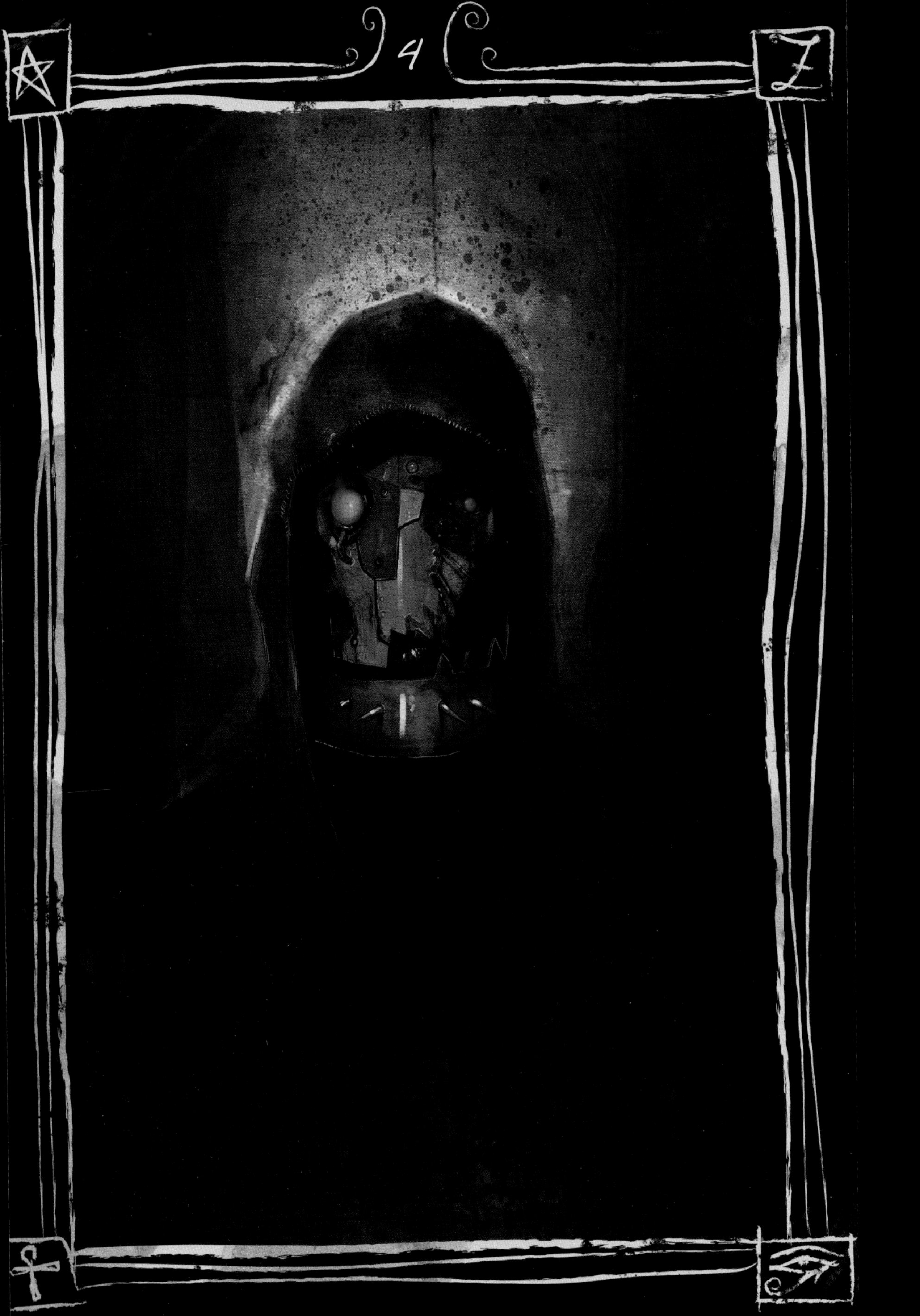
4

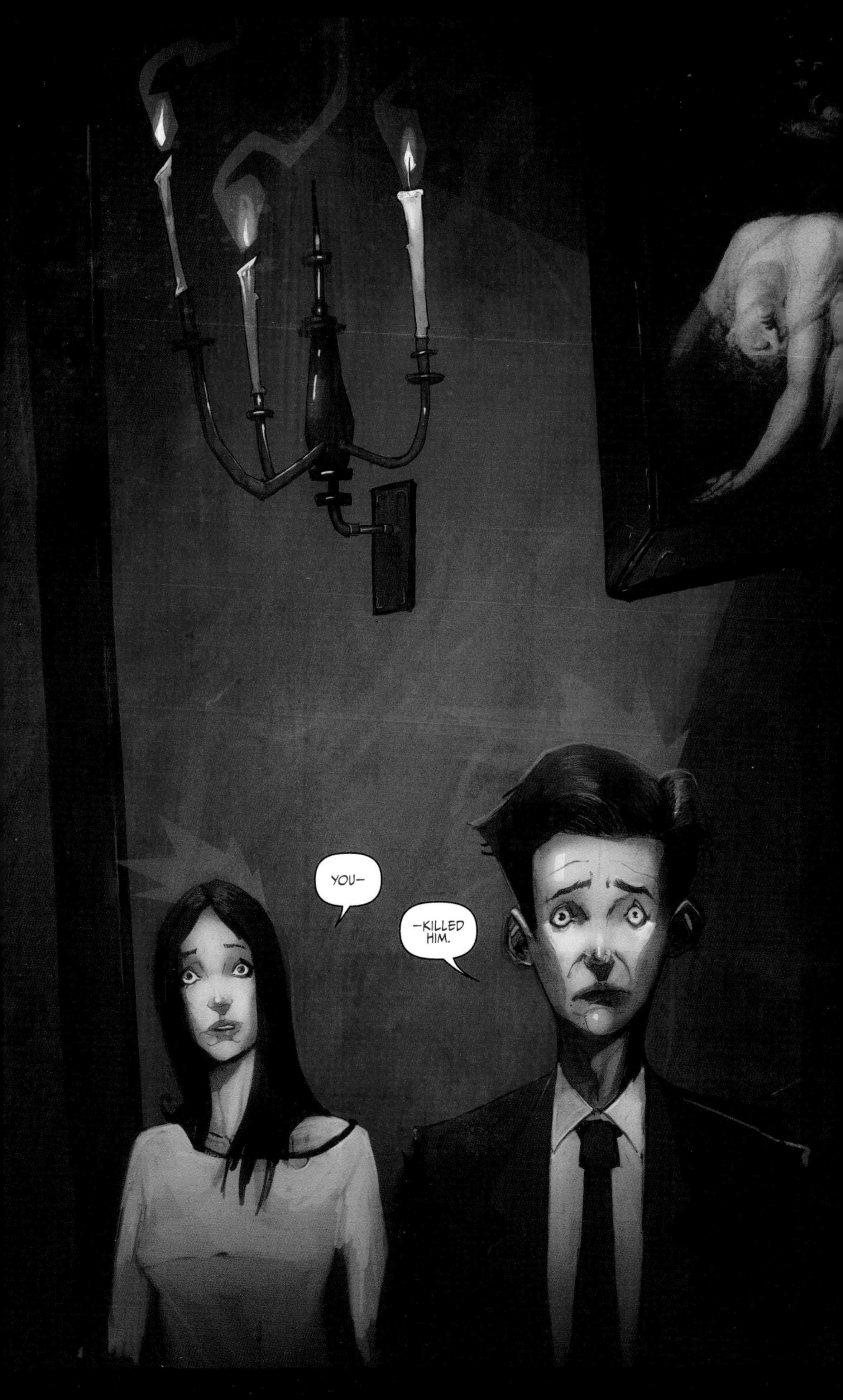
YOU–
–KILLED HIM.

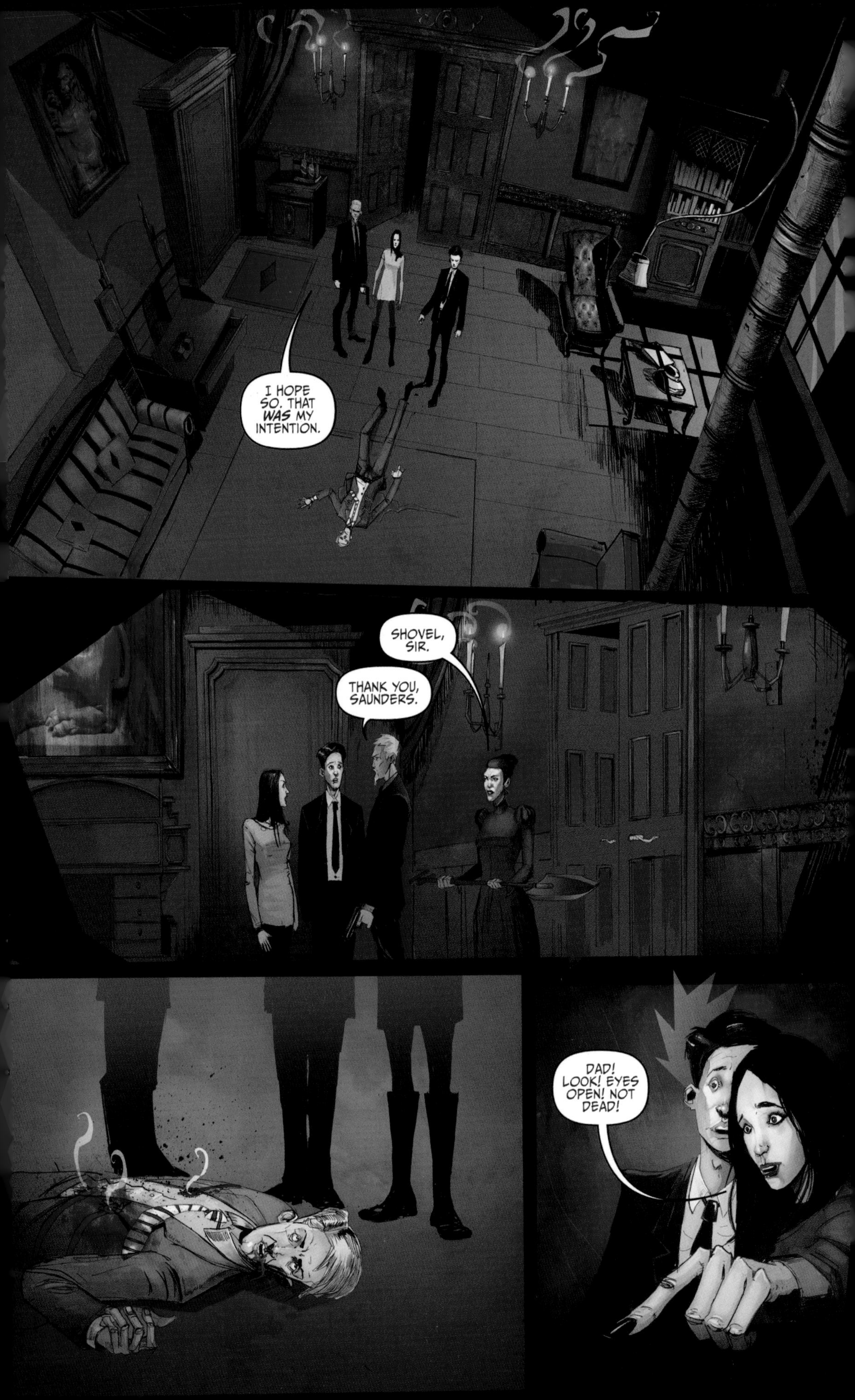
I HOPE SO. THAT *WAS* MY INTENTION.
SHOVEL, SIR.
THANK YOU, SAUNDERS.
DAD! LOOK! EYES OPEN! NOT DEAD!

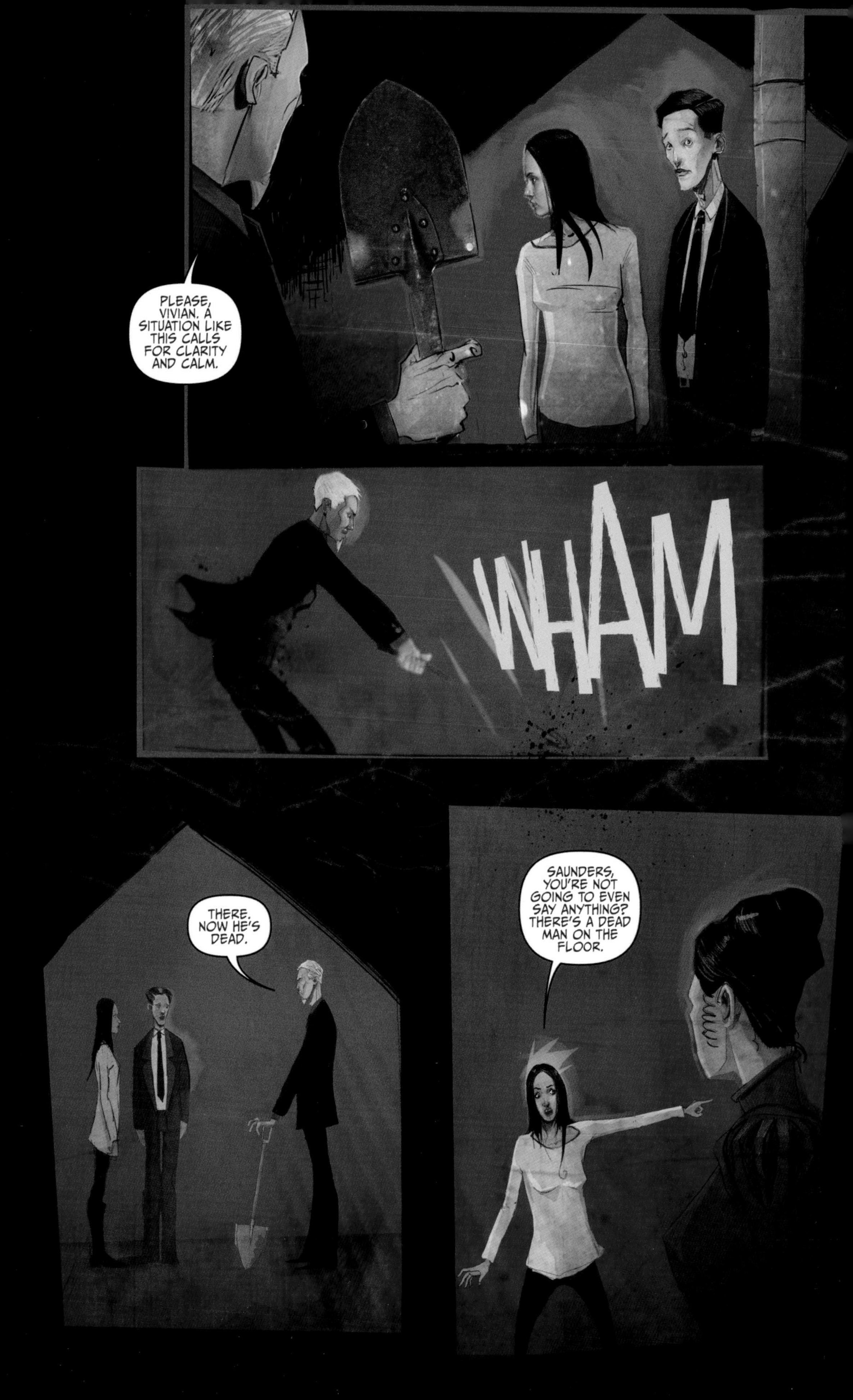
PLEASE, VIVIAN. A SITUATION LIKE THIS CALLS FOR CLARITY AND CALM.
WHAM
THERE. NOW HE'S DEAD.
SAUNDERS, YOU'RE NOT GOING TO EVEN SAY ANYTHING? THERE'S A DEAD MAN ON THE FLOOR.

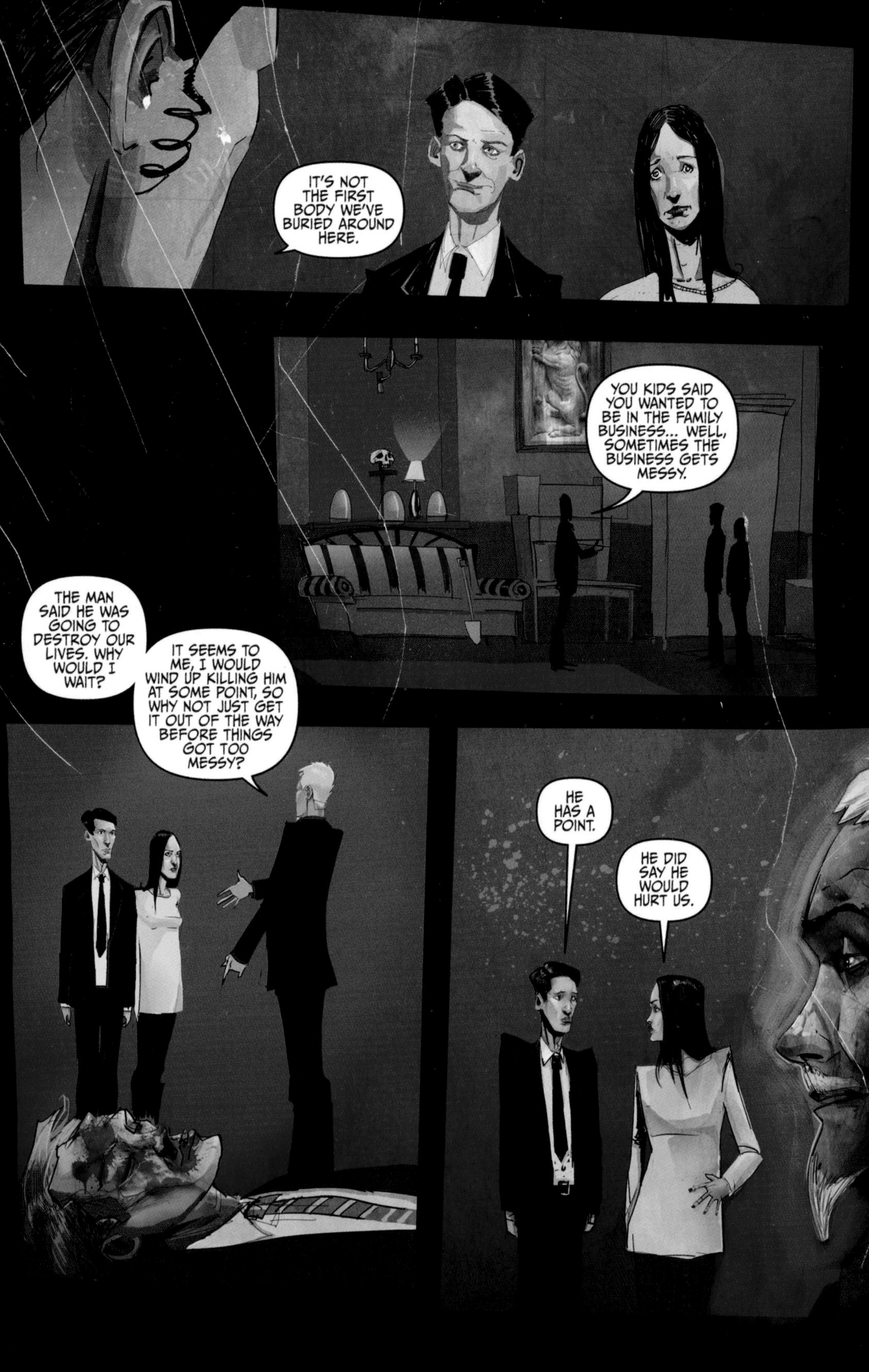
IT'S NOT THE FIRST BODY WE'VE BURIED AROUND HERE.
YOU KIDS SAID YOU WANTED TO BE IN THE FAMILY BUSINESS... WELL, SOMETIMES THE BUSINESS GETS MESSY.
THE MAN SAID HE WAS GOING TO DESTROY OUR LIVES. WHY WOULD I WAIT?
IT SEEMS TO ME, I WOULD WIND UP KILLING HIM AT SOME POINT, SO WHY NOT JUST GET IT OUT OF THE WAY BEFORE THINGS GOT TOO MESSY?
HE HAS A POINT.
HE DID SAY HE WOULD HURT US.

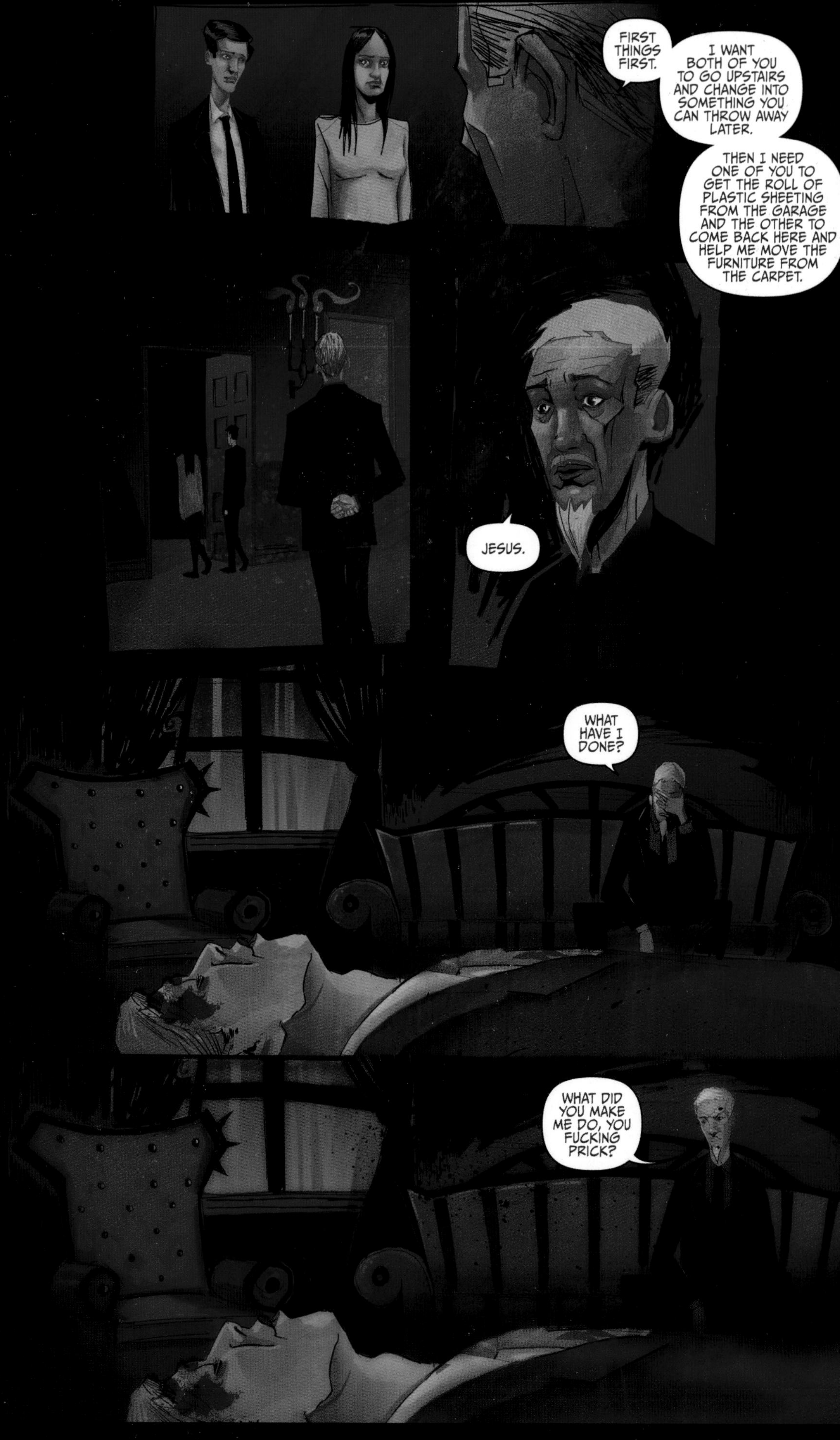
FIRST THINGS FIRST.
I WANT BOTH OF YOU TO GO UPSTAIRS AND CHANGE INTO SOMETHING YOU CAN THROW AWAY LATER.
THEN I NEED ONE OF YOU TO GET THE ROLL OF PLASTIC SHEETING FROM THE GARAGE AND THE OTHER TO COME BACK HERE AND HELP ME MOVE THE FURNITURE FROM THE CARPET.
JESUS.
WHAT HAVE I DONE?
WHAT DID YOU MAKE ME DO, YOU FUCKING PRICK?

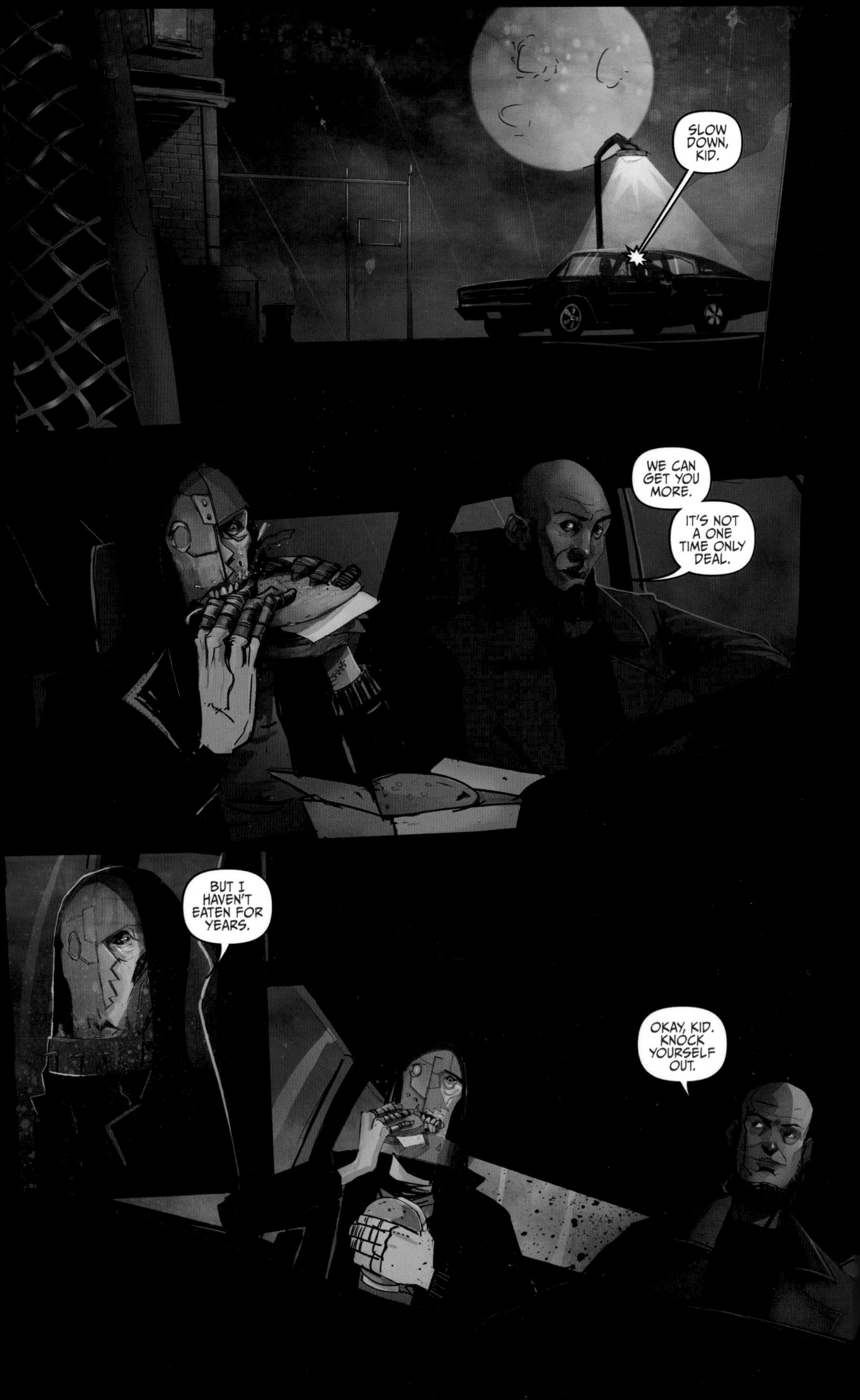
SLOW DOWN, KID.
WE CAN GET YOU MORE.
IT'S NOT A ONE TIME ONLY DEAL.
BUT I HAVEN'T EATEN FOR YEARS.
OKAY, KID. KNOCK YOURSELF OUT.

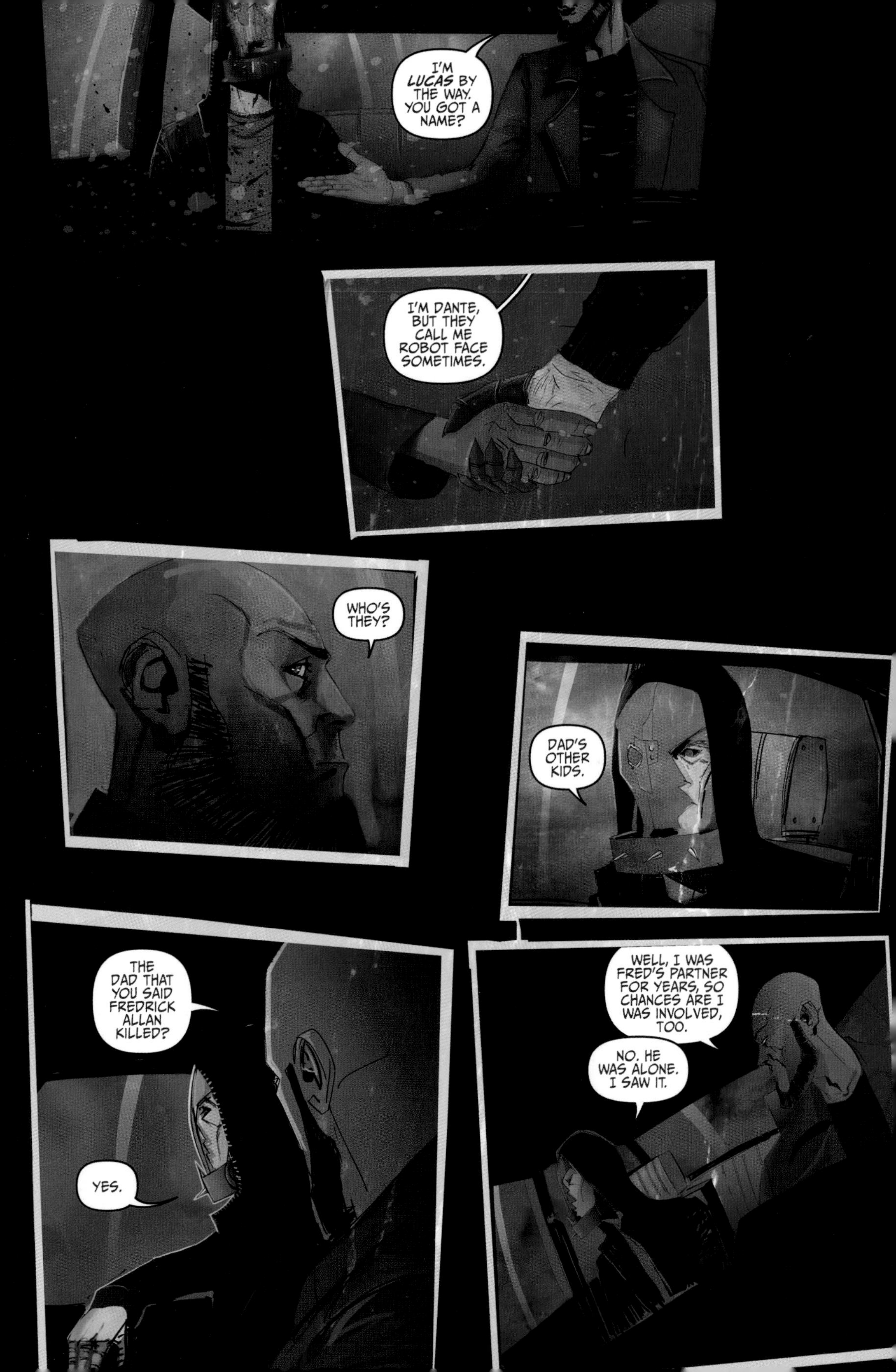
I'M *LUCAS* BY THE WAY. YOU GOT A NAME?
I'M DANTE, BUT THEY CALL ME ROBOT FACE SOMETIMES.
WHO'S THEY?
DAD'S OTHER KIDS.
THE DAD THAT YOU SAID FREDRICK ALLAN KILLED?
YES.
WELL, I WAS FRED'S PARTNER FOR YEARS, SO CHANCES ARE I WAS INVOLVED, TOO.
NO. HE WAS ALONE. I SAW IT.

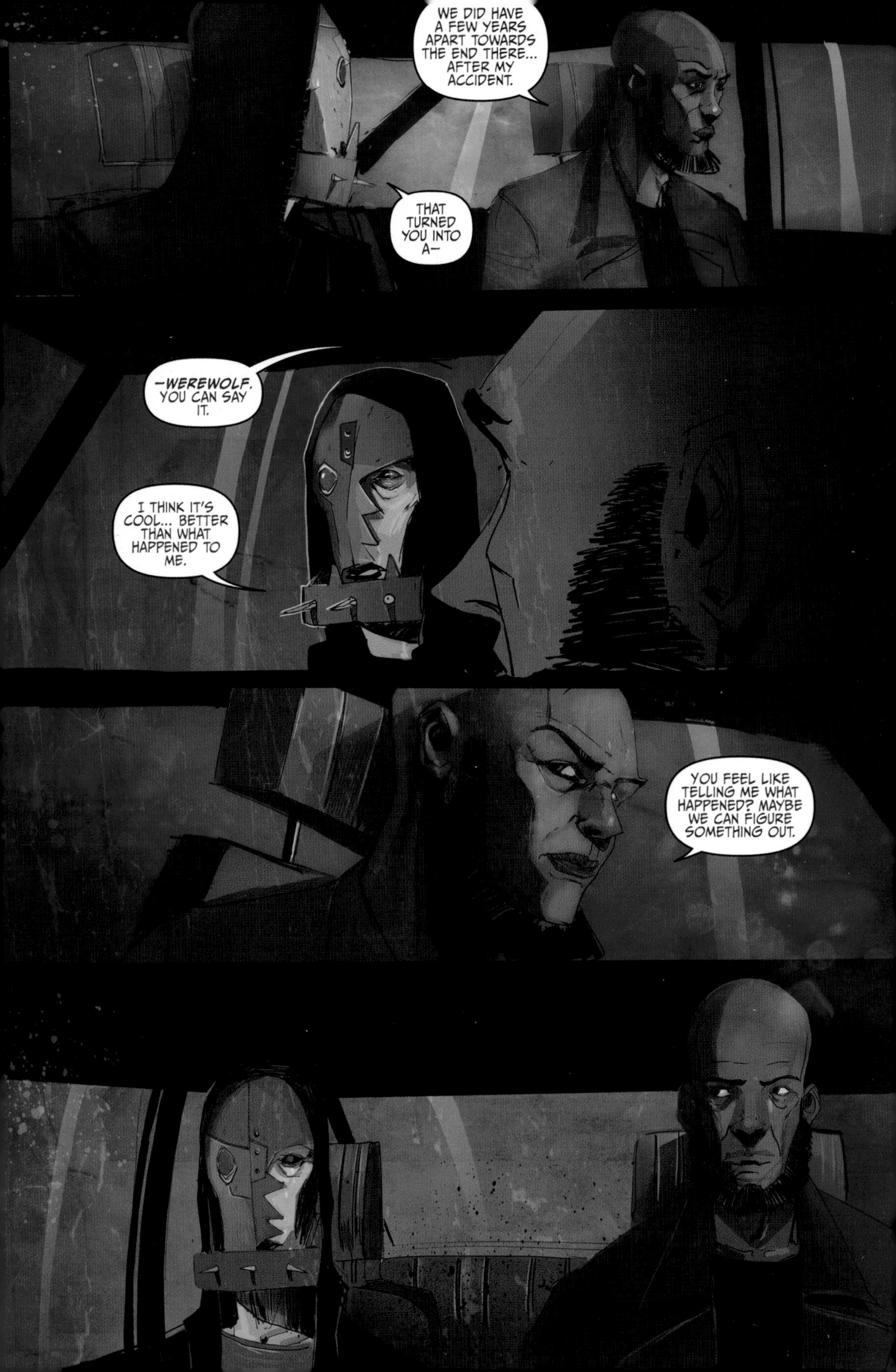
WE DID HAVE A FEW YEARS APART TOWARDS THE END THERE... AFTER MY ACCIDENT.
THAT TURNED YOU INTO A—
—WEREWOLF. YOU CAN SAY IT.
I THINK IT'S COOL... BETTER THAN WHAT HAPPENED TO ME.
YOU FEEL LIKE TELLING ME WHAT HAPPENED? MAYBE WE CAN FIGURE SOMETHING OUT.

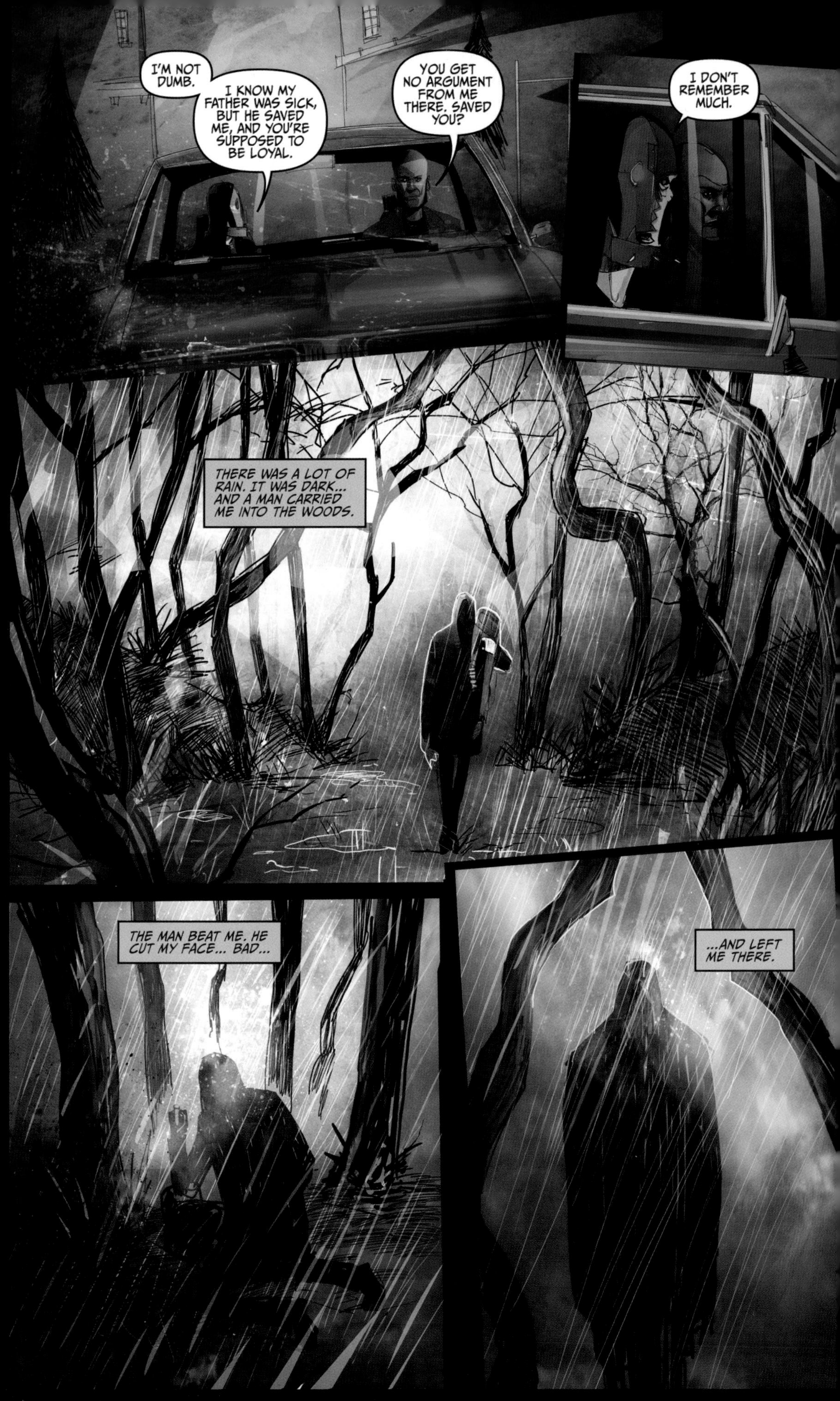
I'M NOT DUMB.
I KNOW MY FATHER WAS SICK, BUT HE SAVED ME, AND YOU'RE SUPPOSED TO BE LOYAL.
YOU GET NO ARGUMENT FROM ME THERE. SAVED YOU?
I DON'T REMEMBER MUCH.
THERE WAS A LOT OF RAIN. IT WAS DARK... AND A MAN CARRIED ME INTO THE WOODS.
THE MAN BEAT ME. HE CUT MY FACE... BAD...
...AND LEFT ME THERE.

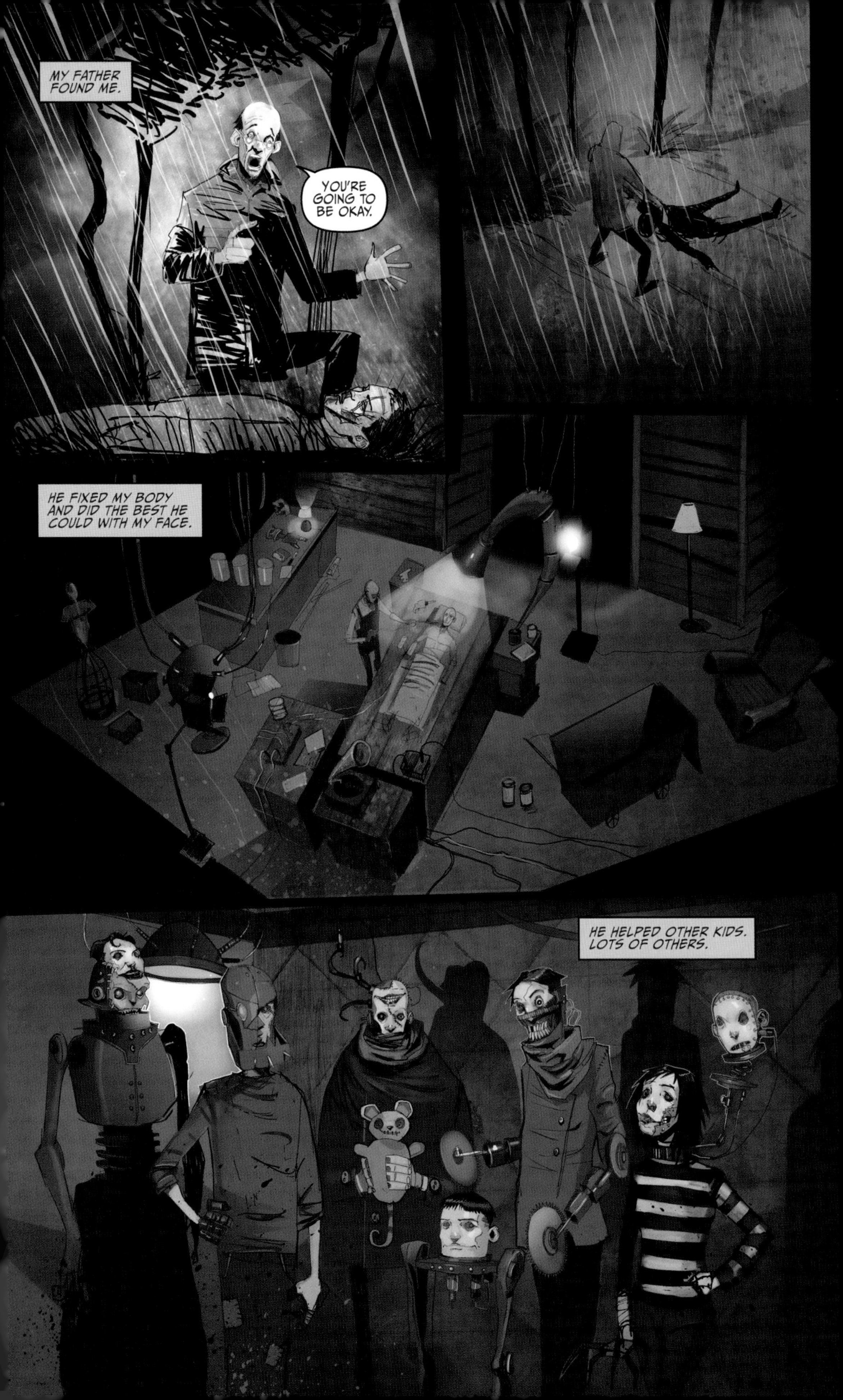
MY FATHER FOUND ME.
YOU'RE GOING TO BE OKAY.
HE FIXED MY BODY AND DID THE BEST HE COULD WITH MY FACE.
HE HELPED OTHER KIDS. LOTS OF OTHERS.

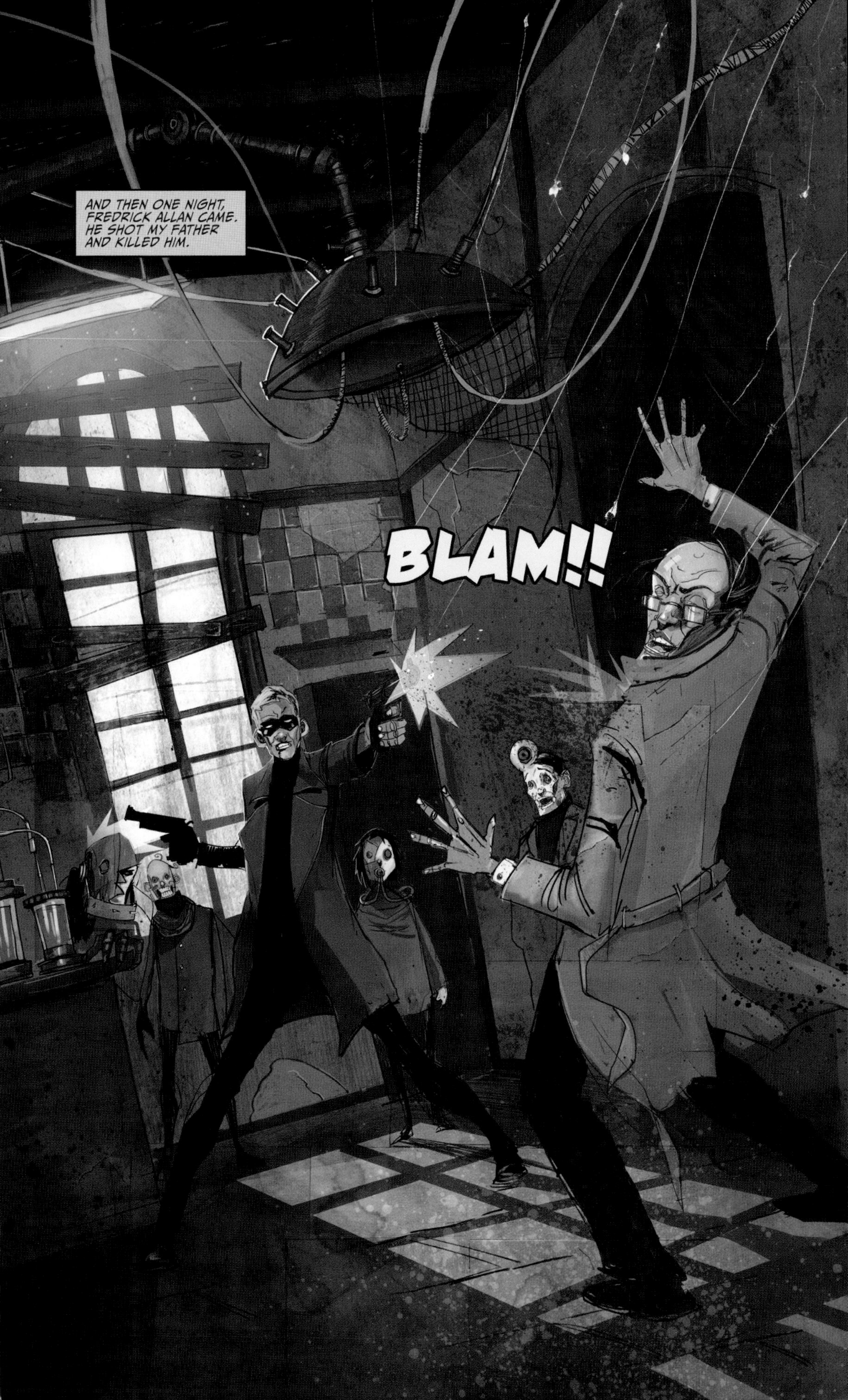
AND THEN ONE NIGHT, FREDRICK ALLAN CAME. HE SHOT MY FATHER AND KILLED HIM.
BLAM!!

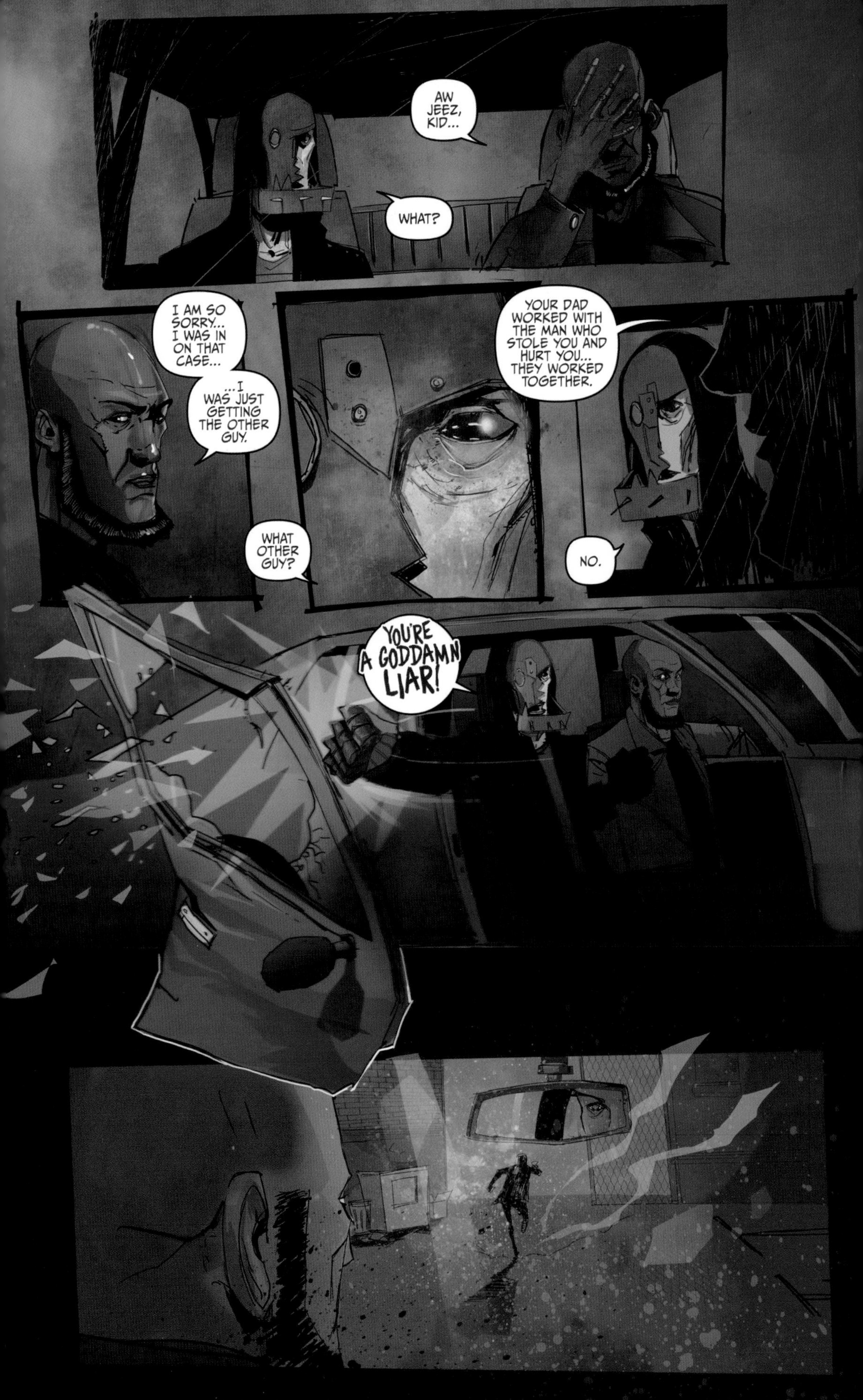
AW JEEZ, KID...
WHAT?
I AM SO SORRY... I WAS IN ON THAT CASE...
...I WAS JUST GETTING THE OTHER GUY.
WHAT OTHER GUY?
YOUR DAD WORKED WITH THE MAN WHO STOLE YOU AND HURT YOU... THEY WORKED TOGETHER.
NO.
YOU'RE A GODDAMN LIAR!

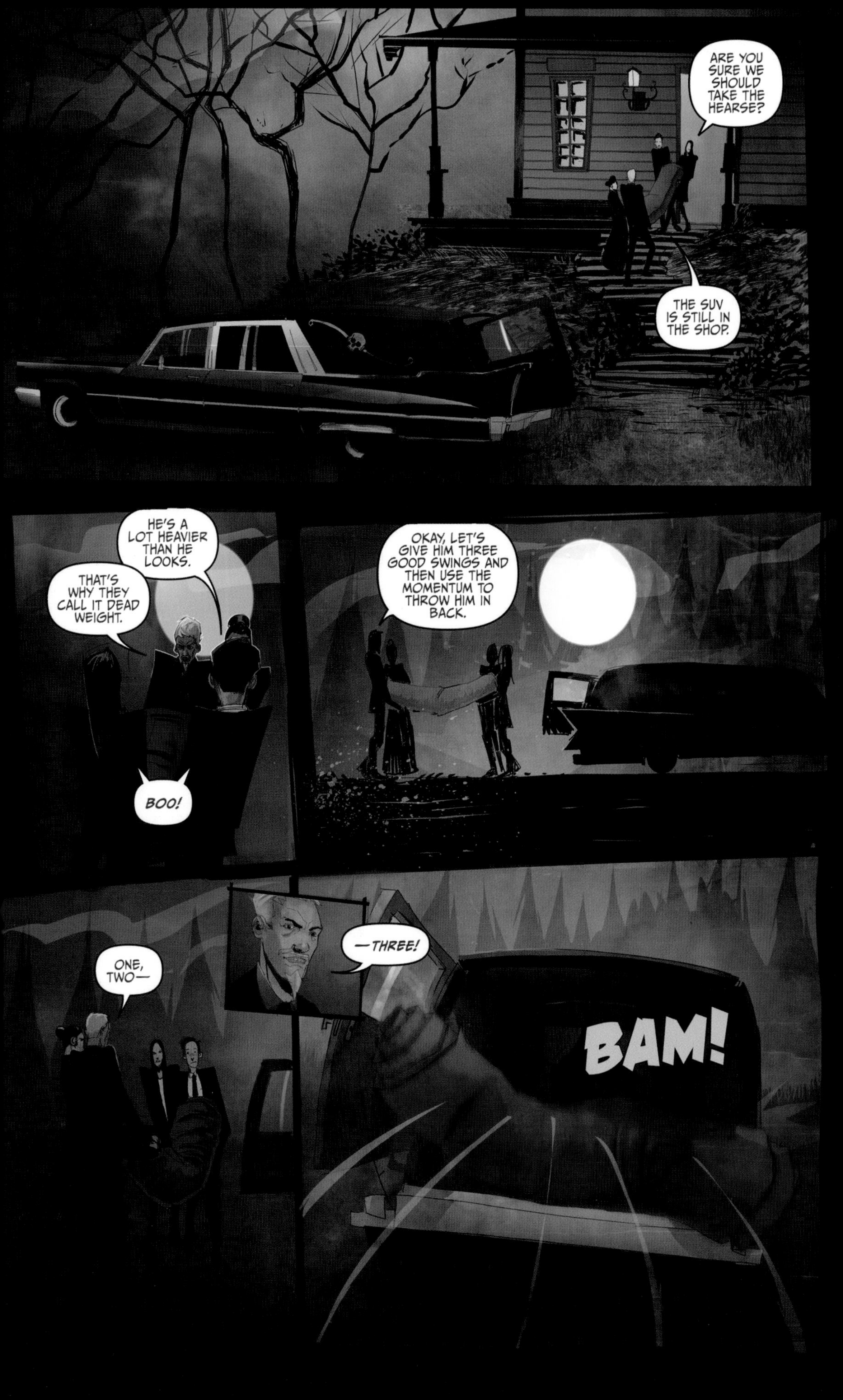
ARE YOU SURE WE SHOULD TAKE THE HEARSE?
THE SUV IS STILL IN THE SHOP.
HE'S A LOT HEAVIER THAN HE LOOKS.
THAT'S WHY THEY CALL IT DEAD WEIGHT.
BOO!
OKAY, LET'S GIVE HIM THREE GOOD SWINGS AND THEN USE THE MOMENTUM TO THROW HIM IN BACK.
ONE, TWO—
—THREE!
BAM!

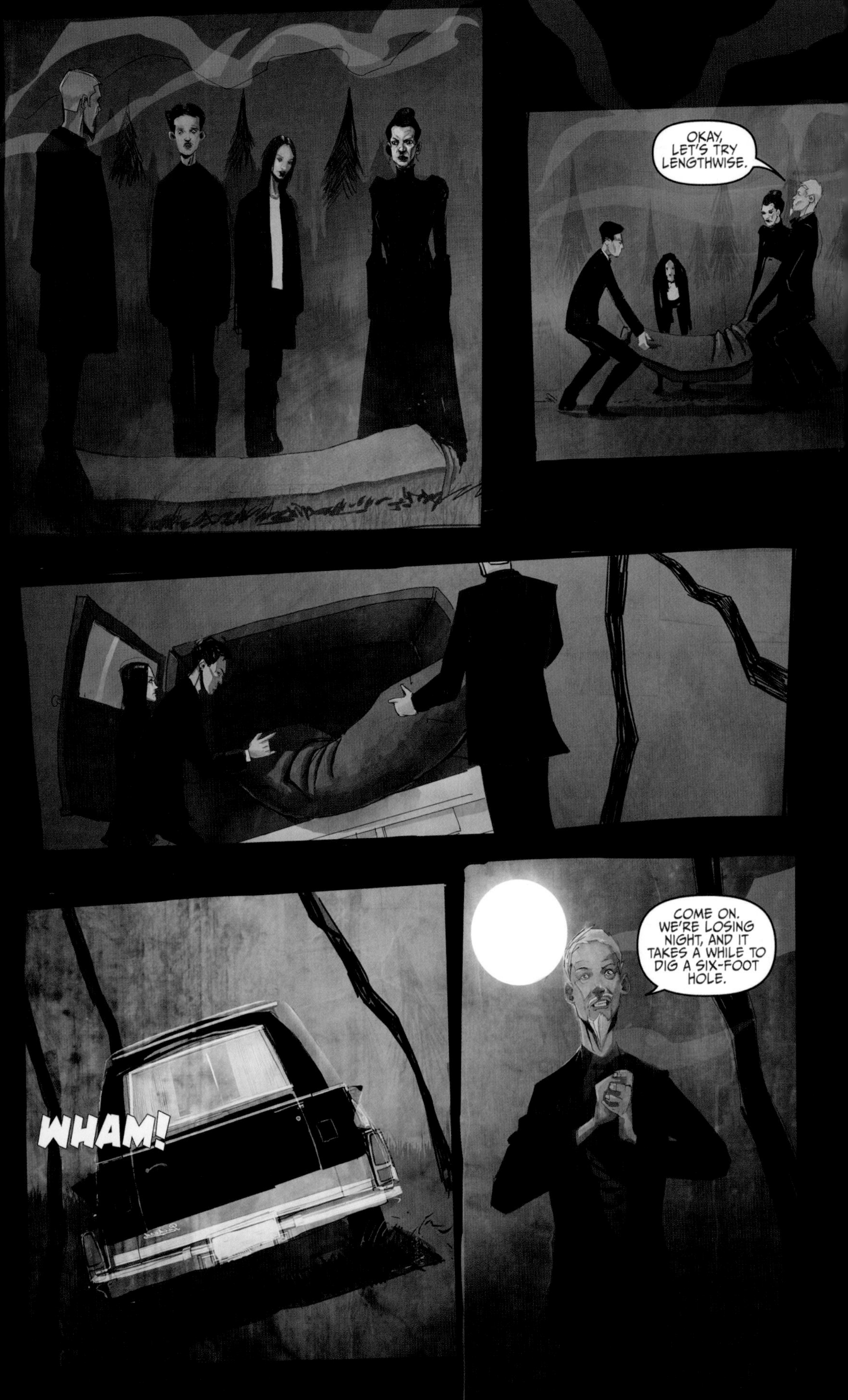
OKAY, LET'S TRY LENGTHWISE.
WHAM!
COME ON. WE'RE LOSING NIGHT, AND IT TAKES A WHILE TO DIG A SIX-FOOT HOLE.

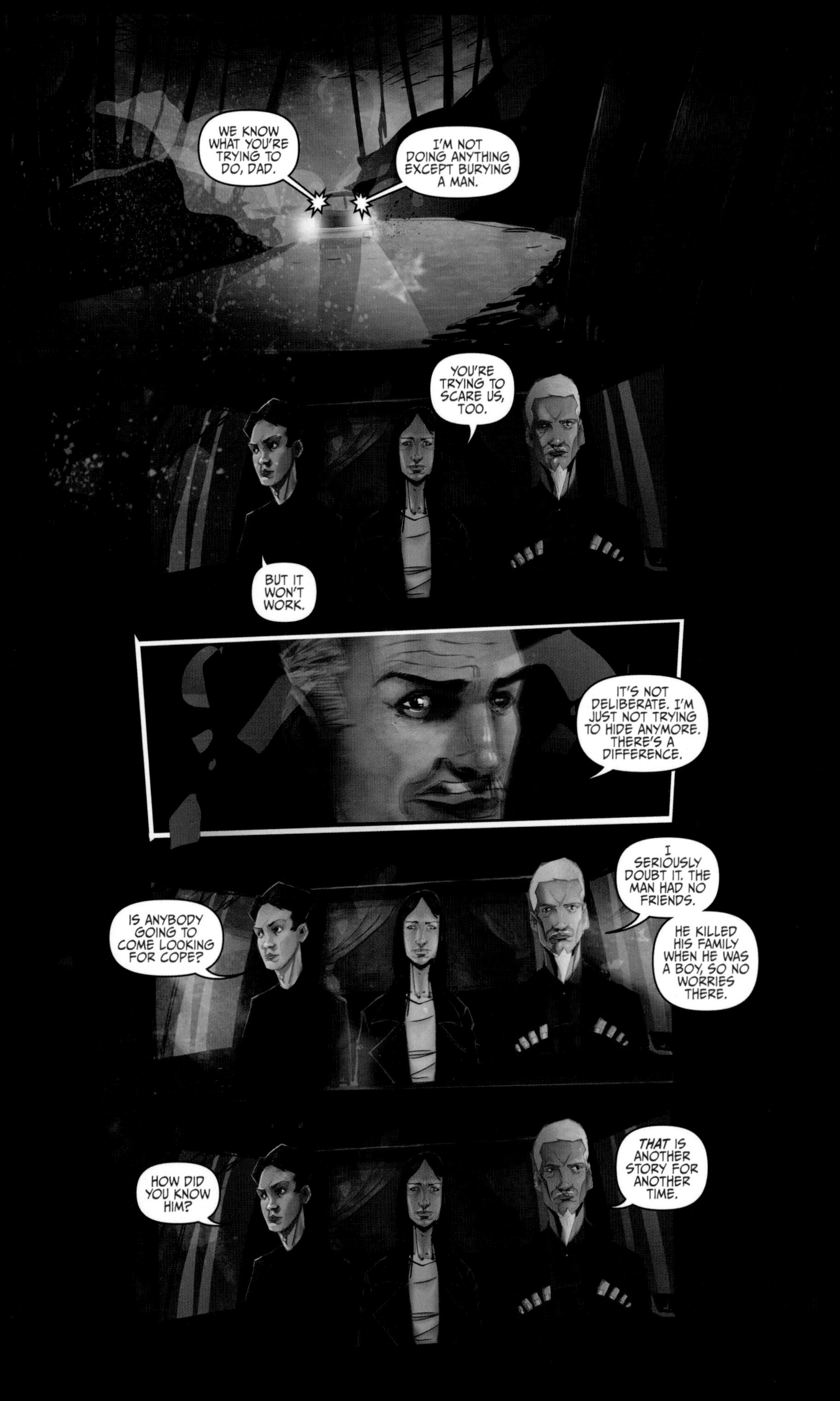
WE KNOW WHAT YOU'RE TRYING TO DO, DAD.
I'M NOT DOING ANYTHING EXCEPT BURYING A MAN.
YOU'RE TRYING TO SCARE US, TOO.
BUT IT WON'T WORK.
IT'S NOT DELIBERATE. I'M JUST NOT TRYING TO HIDE ANYMORE. THERE'S A DIFFERENCE.
IS ANYBODY GOING TO COME LOOKING FOR COPE?
I SERIOUSLY DOUBT IT. THE MAN HAD NO FRIENDS.
HE KILLED HIS FAMILY WHEN HE WAS A BOY, SO NO WORRIES THERE.
HOW DID YOU KNOW HIM?
THAT IS ANOTHER STORY FOR ANOTHER TIME.

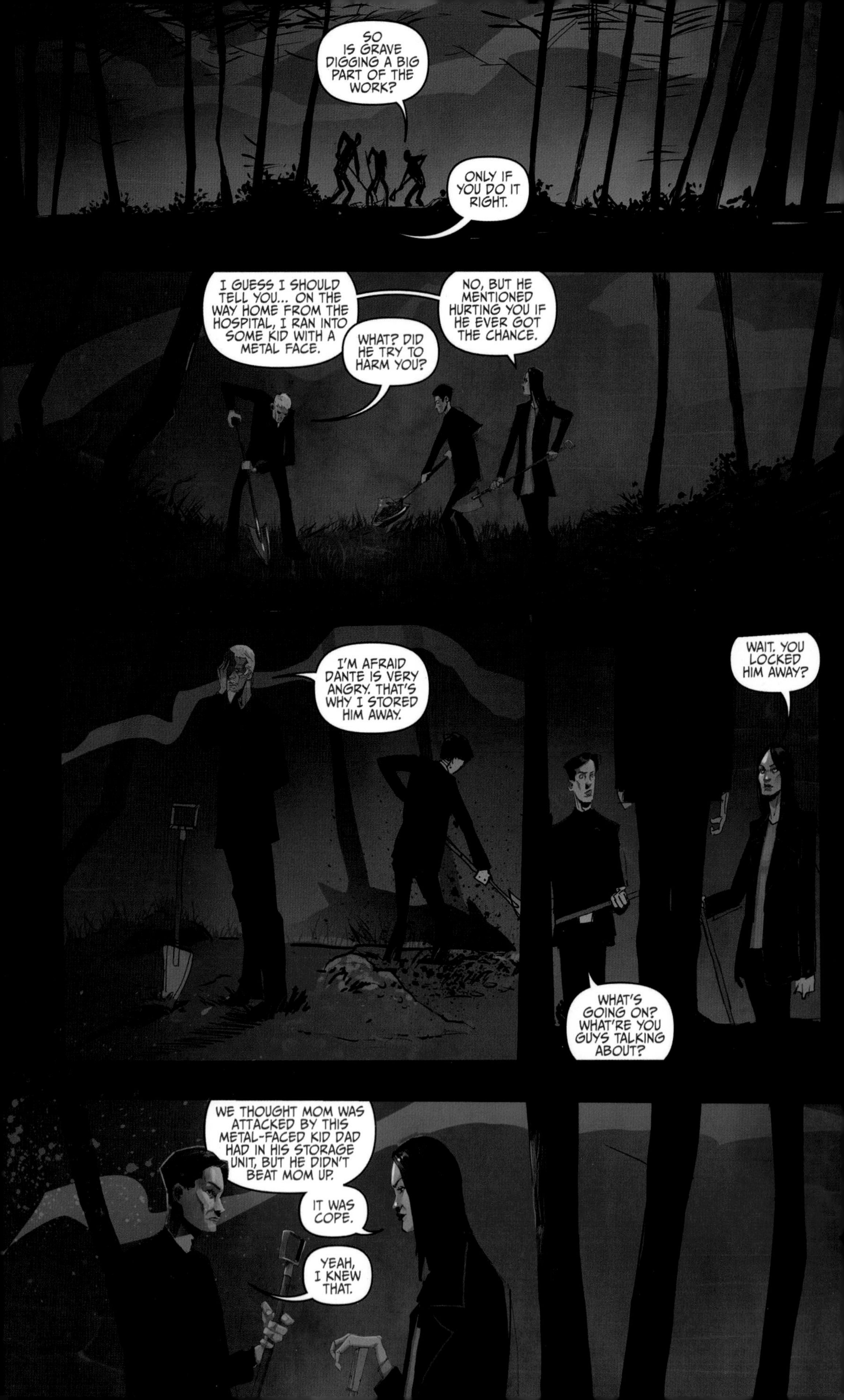
SO IS GRAVE DIGGING A BIG PART OF THE WORK?
ONLY IF YOU DO IT RIGHT.
I GUESS I SHOULD TELL YOU... ON THE WAY HOME FROM THE HOSPITAL, I RAN INTO SOME KID WITH A METAL FACE.
WHAT? DID HE TRY TO HARM YOU?
NO, BUT HE MENTIONED HURTING YOU IF HE EVER GOT THE CHANCE.
I'M AFRAID DANTE IS VERY ANGRY. THAT'S WHY I STORED HIM AWAY.
WAIT. YOU LOCKED HIM AWAY?
WHAT'S GOING ON? WHAT'RE YOU GUYS TALKING ABOUT?
WE THOUGHT MOM WAS ATTACKED BY THIS METAL-FACED KID DAD HAD IN HIS STORAGE UNIT, BUT HE DIDN'T BEAT MOM UP.
IT WAS COPE.
YEAH, I KNEW THAT.

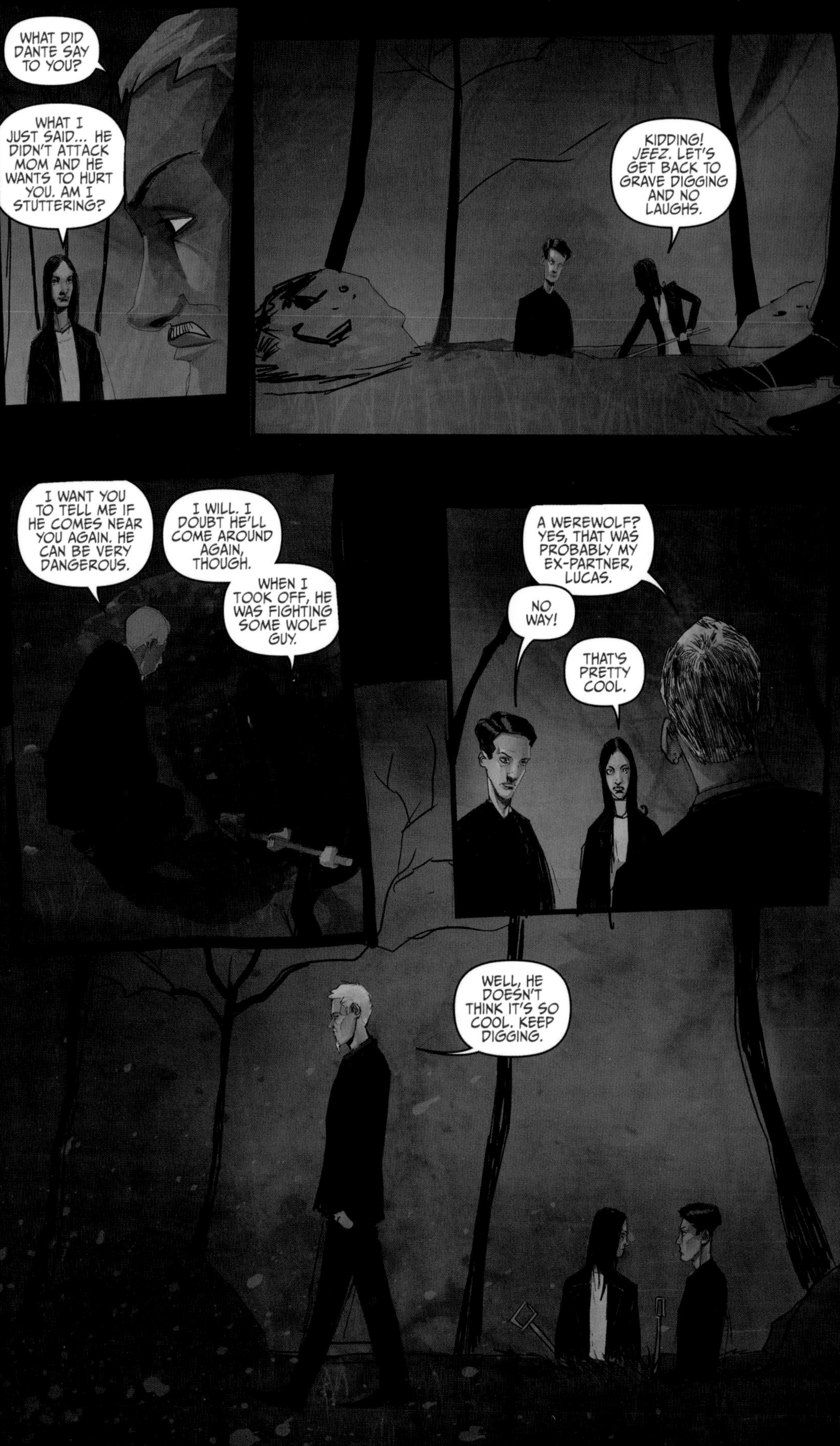
WHAT DID DANTE SAY TO YOU?
WHAT I JUST SAID... HE DIDN'T ATTACK MOM AND HE WANTS TO HURT YOU. AM I STUTTERING?
KIDDING! JEEZ. LET'S GET BACK TO GRAVE DIGGING AND NO LAUGHS.
I WANT YOU TO TELL ME IF HE COMES NEAR YOU AGAIN. HE CAN BE VERY DANGEROUS.
I WILL. I DOUBT HE'LL COME AROUND AGAIN, THOUGH.
WHEN I TOOK OFF, HE WAS FIGHTING SOME WOLF GUY.
A WEREWOLF? YES, THAT WAS PROBABLY MY EX-PARTNER, LUCAS.
NO WAY!
THAT'S PRETTY COOL.
WELL, HE DOESN'T THINK IT'S SO COOL. KEEP DIGGING.

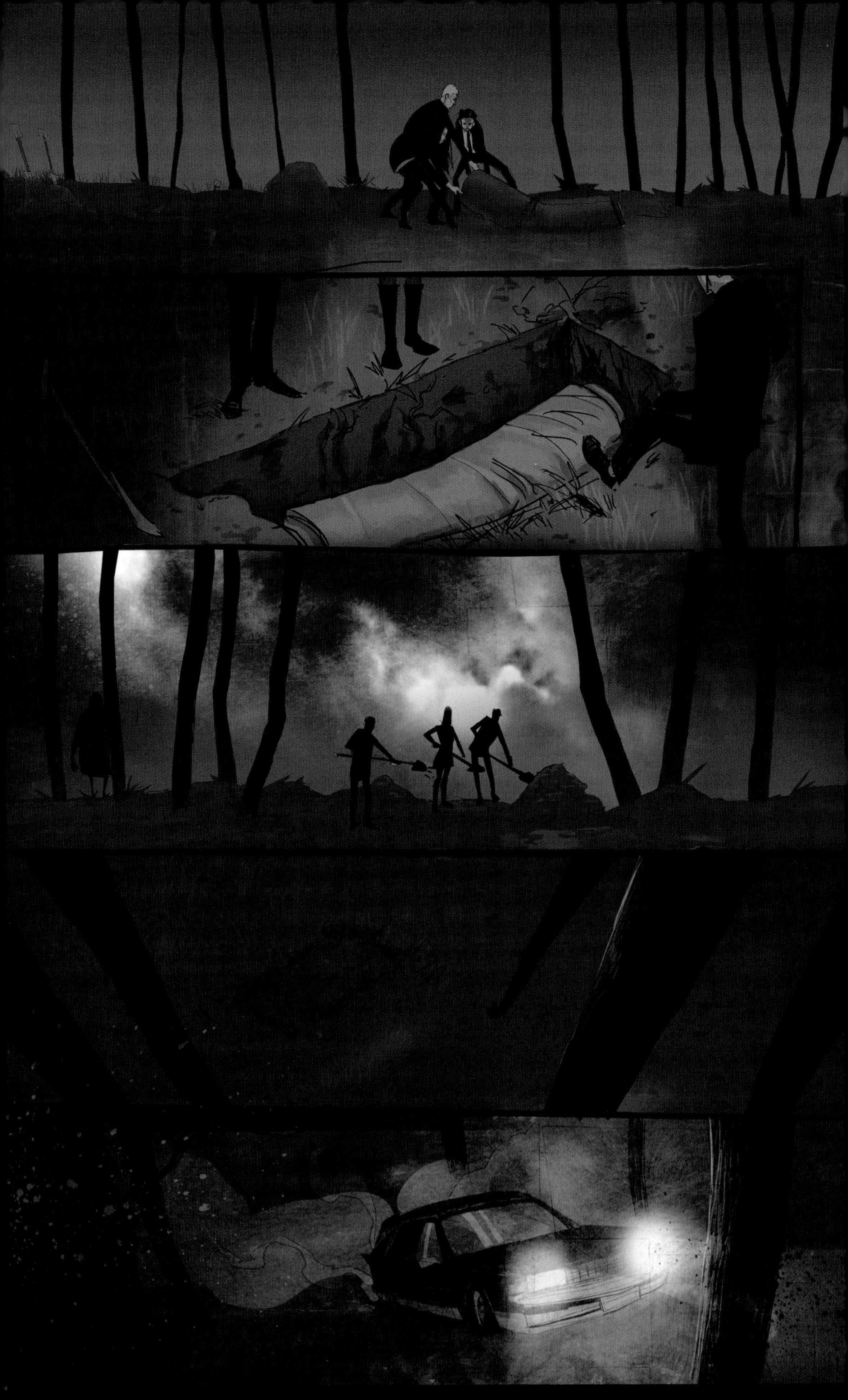

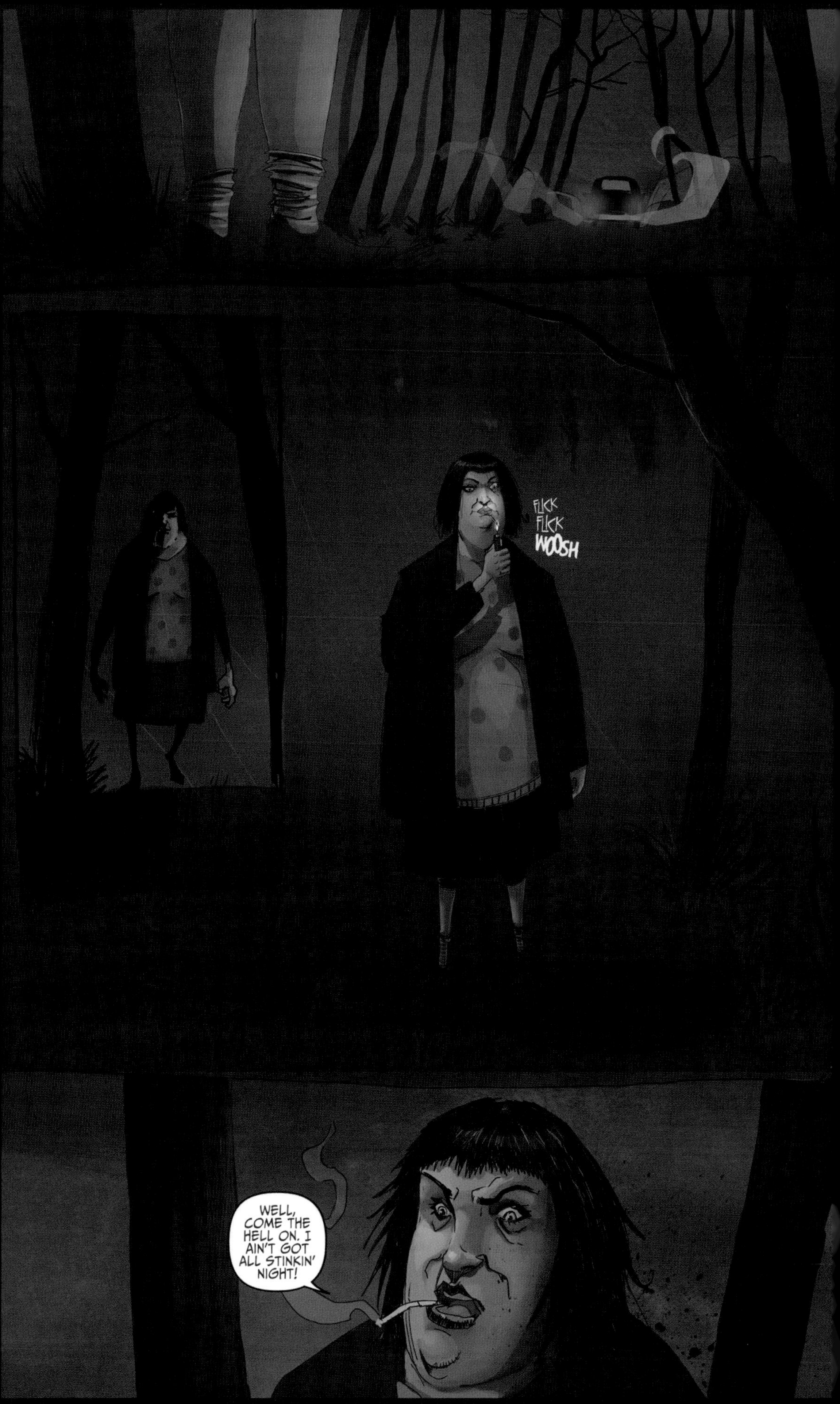
FLICK
FLICK
WOOSH
WELL, COME THE HELL ON. I AIN'T GOT ALL STINKIN' NIGHT!

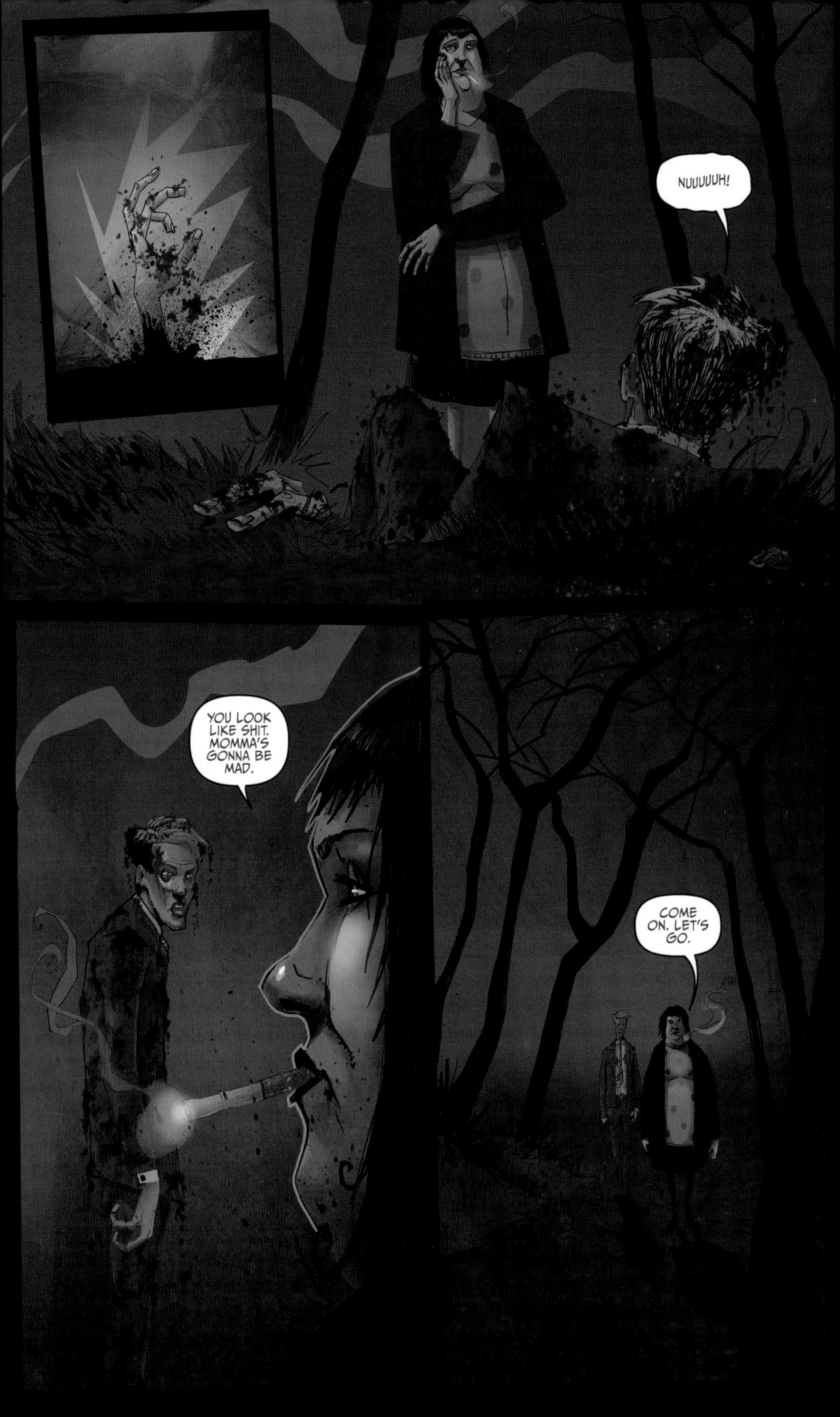
NUUUUUH!
YOU LOOK LIKE SHIT. MOMMA'S GONNA BE MAD.
COME ON. LET'S GO.

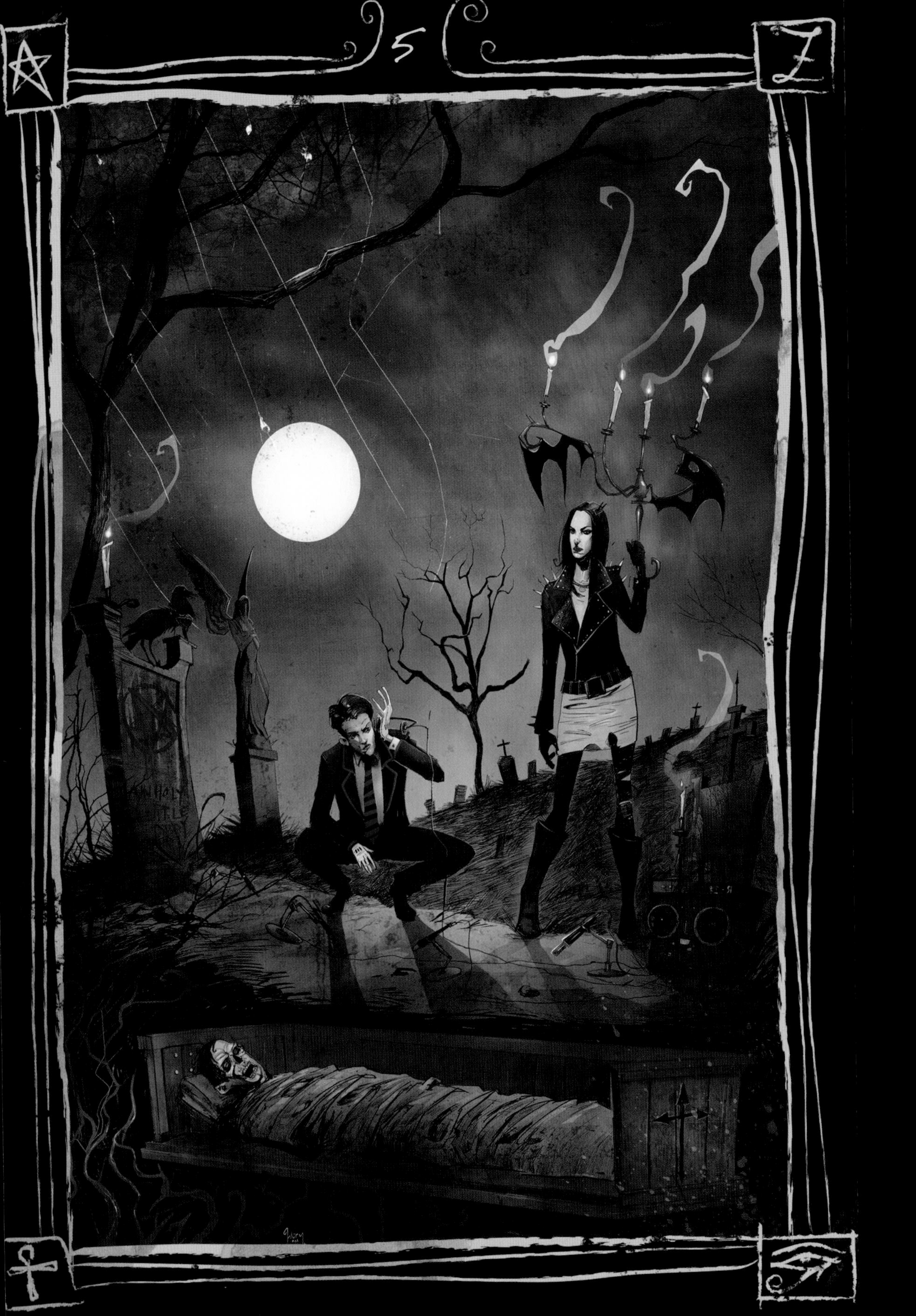
5

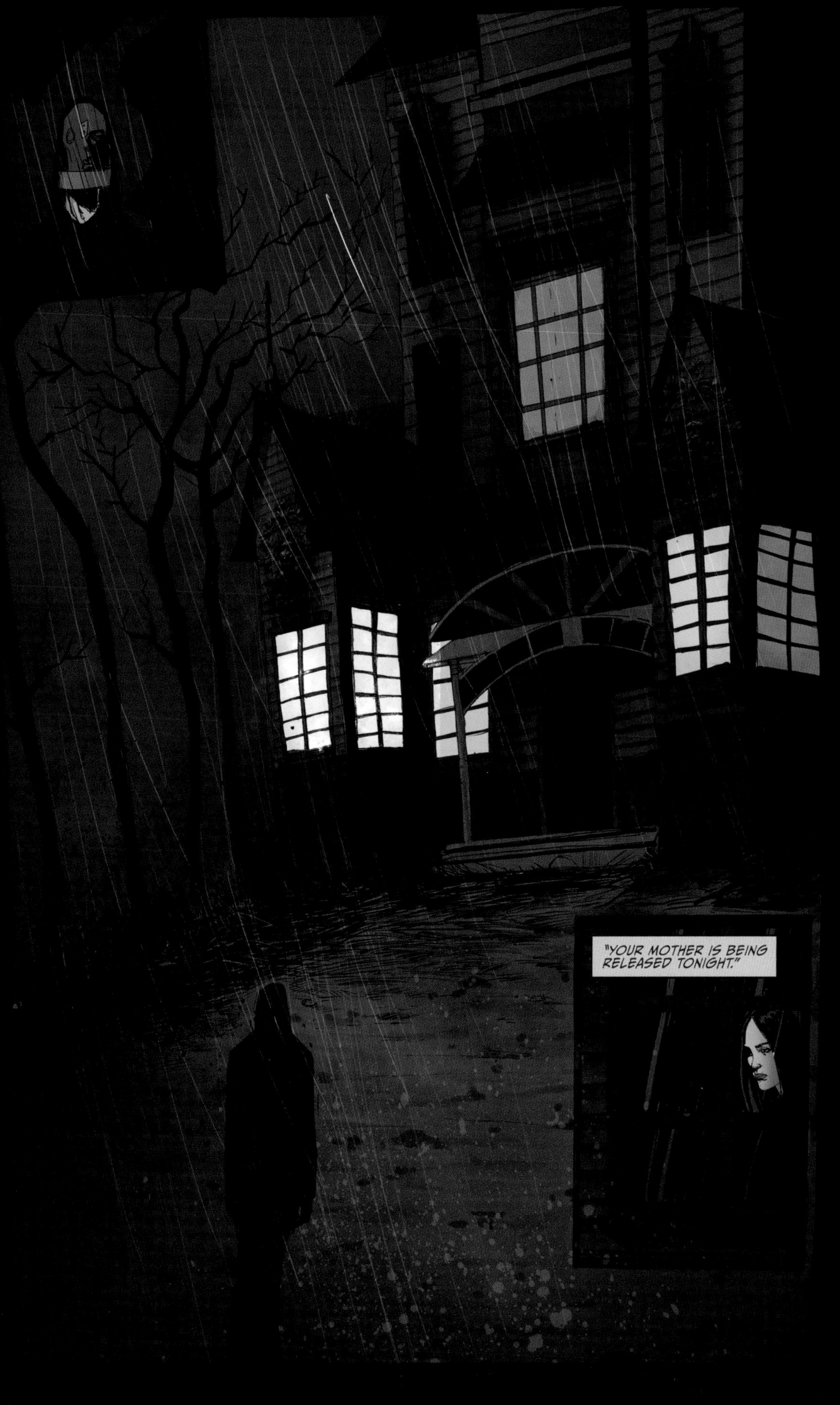
"YOUR MOTHER IS BEING RELEASED TONIGHT."

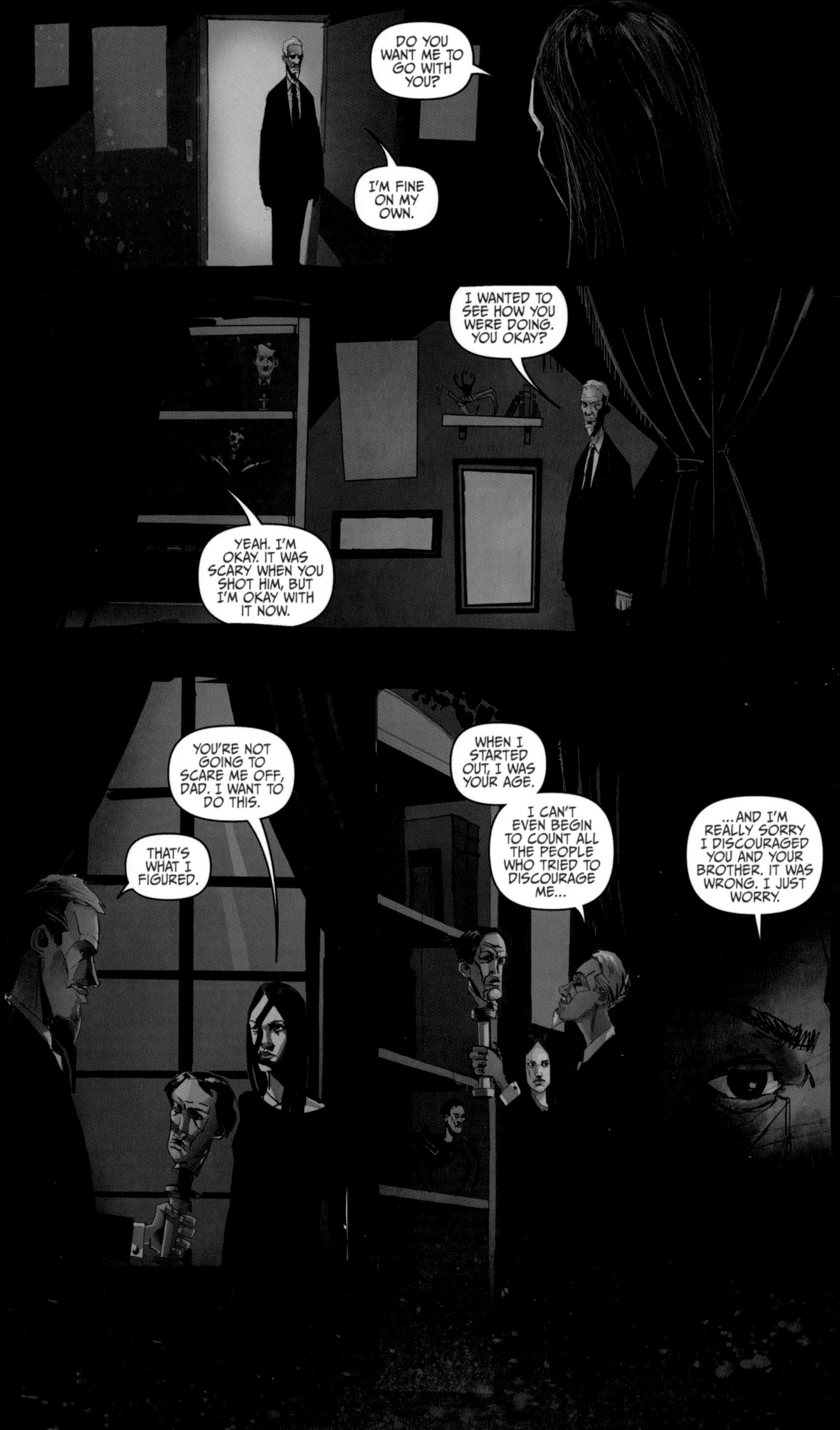
DO YOU WANT ME TO GO WITH YOU?
I'M FINE ON MY OWN.
I WANTED TO SEE HOW YOU WERE DOING. YOU OKAY?
YEAH. I'M OKAY. IT WAS SCARY WHEN YOU SHOT HIM, BUT I'M OKAY WITH IT NOW.
YOU'RE NOT GOING TO SCARE ME OFF, DAD. I WANT TO DO THIS.
THAT'S WHAT I FIGURED.
WHEN I STARTED OUT, I WAS YOUR AGE.
I CAN'T EVEN BEGIN TO COUNT ALL THE PEOPLE WHO TRIED TO DISCOURAGE ME...
...AND I'M REALLY SORRY I DISCOURAGED YOU AND YOUR BROTHER. IT WAS WRONG. I JUST WORRY.

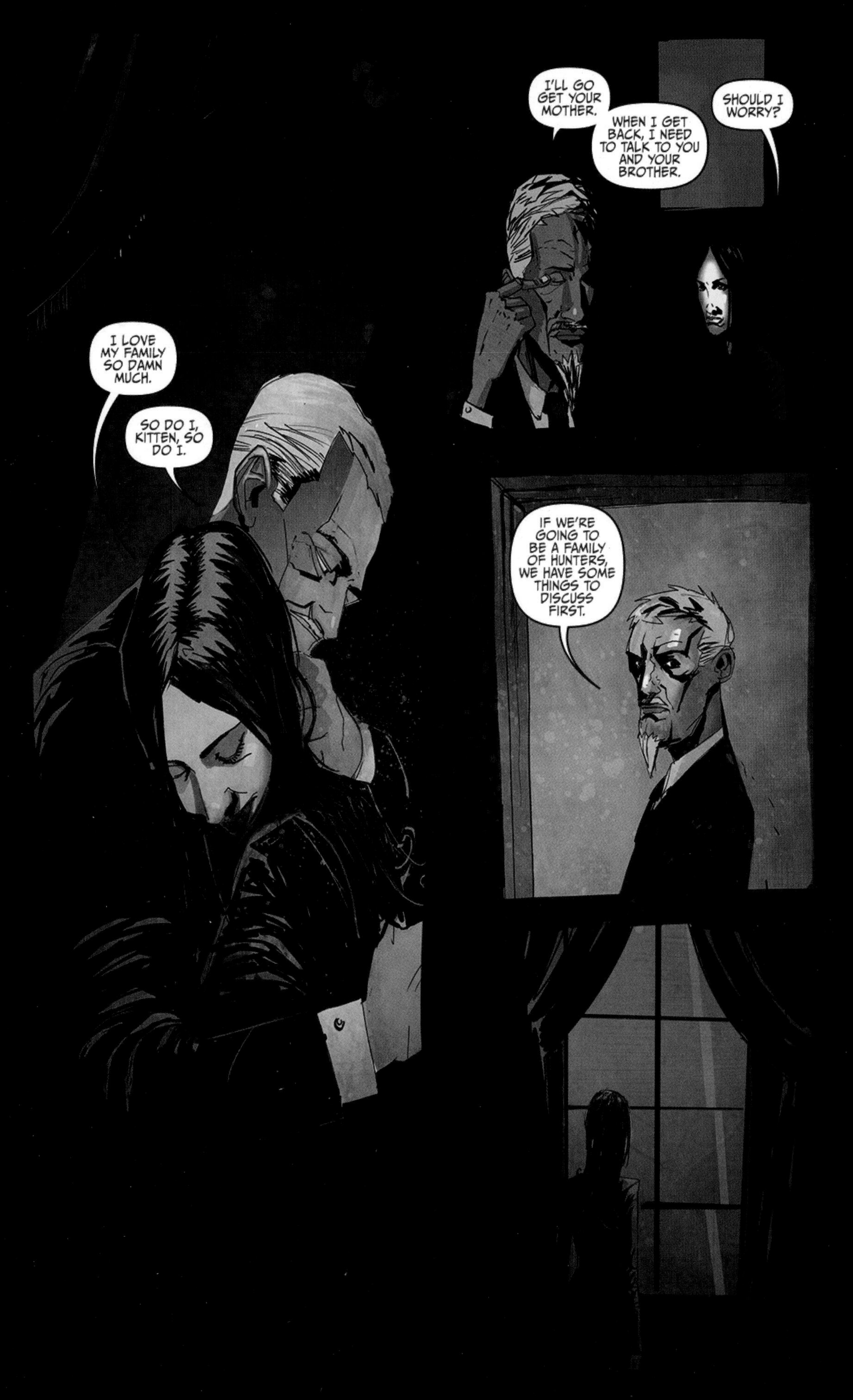
I LOVE MY FAMILY SO DAMN MUCH.
SO DO I, KITTEN, SO DO I.
I'LL GO GET YOUR MOTHER.
WHEN I GET BACK, I NEED TO TALK TO YOU AND YOUR BROTHER.
SHOULD I WORRY?
IF WE'RE GOING TO BE A FAMILY OF HUNTERS, WE HAVE SOME THINGS TO DISCUSS FIRST.

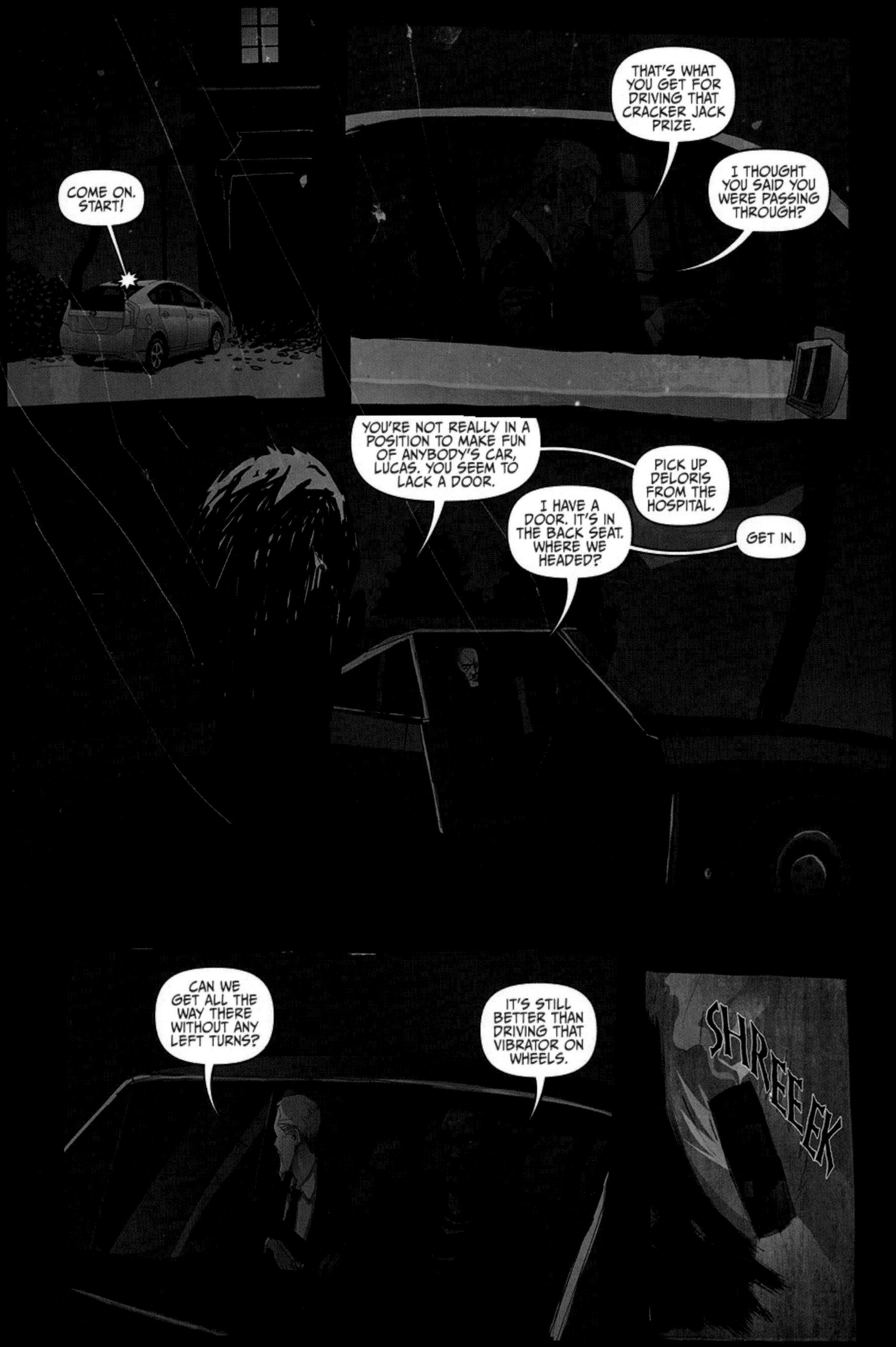
COME ON. START!
THAT'S WHAT YOU GET FOR DRIVING THAT CRACKER JACK PRIZE.
I THOUGHT YOU SAID YOU WERE PASSING THROUGH?
YOU'RE NOT REALLY IN A POSITION TO MAKE FUN OF ANYBODY'S CAR, LUCAS. YOU SEEM TO LACK A DOOR.
I HAVE A DOOR. IT'S IN THE BACK SEAT. WHERE WE HEADED?
PICK UP DELORIS FROM THE HOSPITAL.
GET IN.
CAN WE GET ALL THE WAY THERE WITHOUT ANY LEFT TURNS?
IT'S STILL BETTER THAN DRIVING THAT VIBRATOR ON WHEELS.
SHREEEK

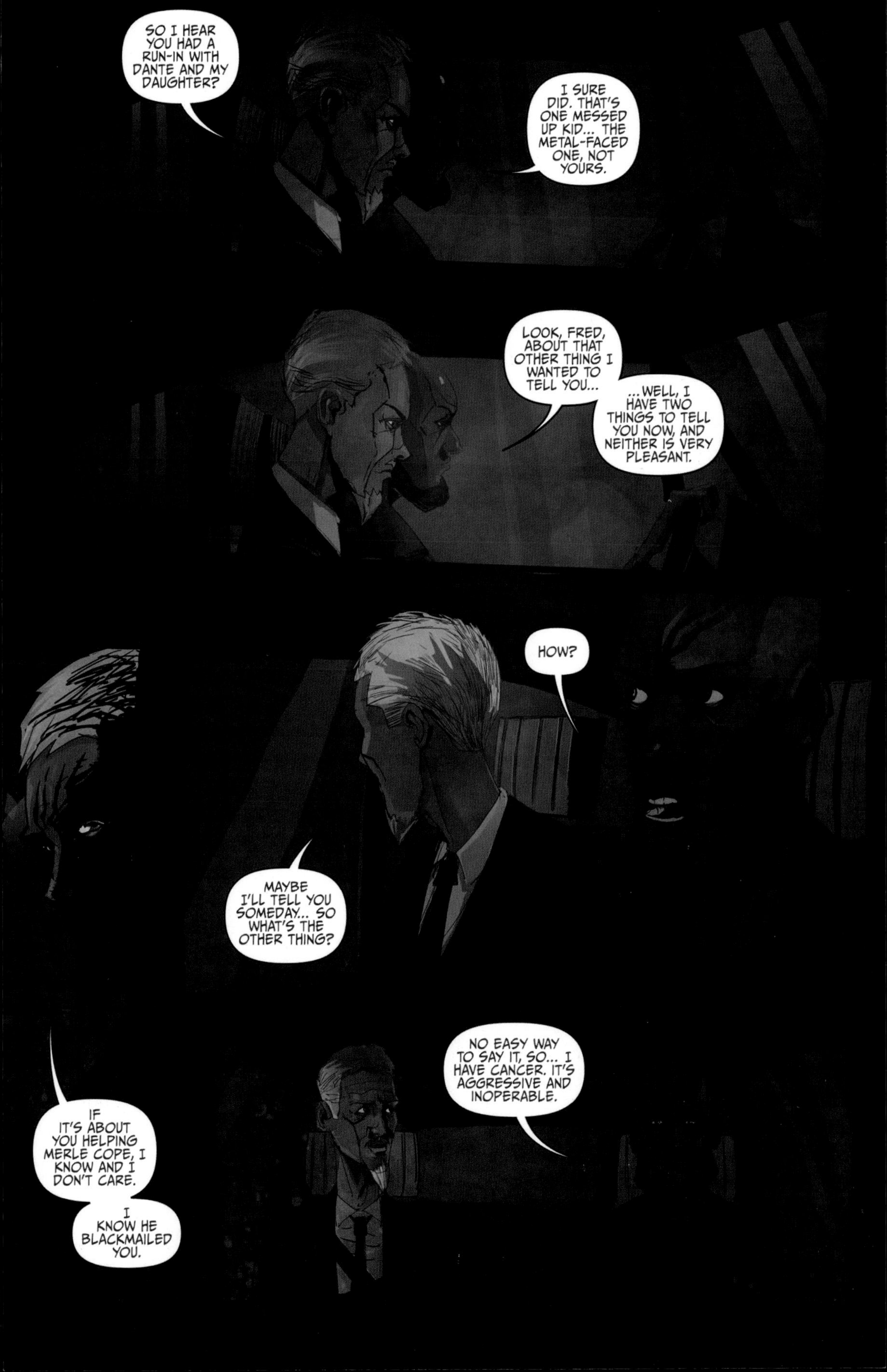
SO I HEAR YOU HAD A RUN-IN WITH DANTE AND MY DAUGHTER?
I SURE DID. THAT'S ONE MESSED UP KID... THE METAL-FACED ONE, NOT YOURS.
LOOK, FRED, ABOUT THAT OTHER THING I WANTED TO TELL YOU...
...WELL, I HAVE TWO THINGS TO TELL YOU NOW, AND NEITHER IS VERY PLEASANT.
HOW?
MAYBE I'LL TELL YOU SOMEDAY... SO WHAT'S THE OTHER THING?
NO EASY WAY TO SAY IT, SO... I HAVE CANCER. IT'S AGGRESSIVE AND INOPERABLE.
IF IT'S ABOUT YOU HELPING MERLE COPE, I KNOW AND I DON'T CARE.
I KNOW HE BLACKMAILED YOU.

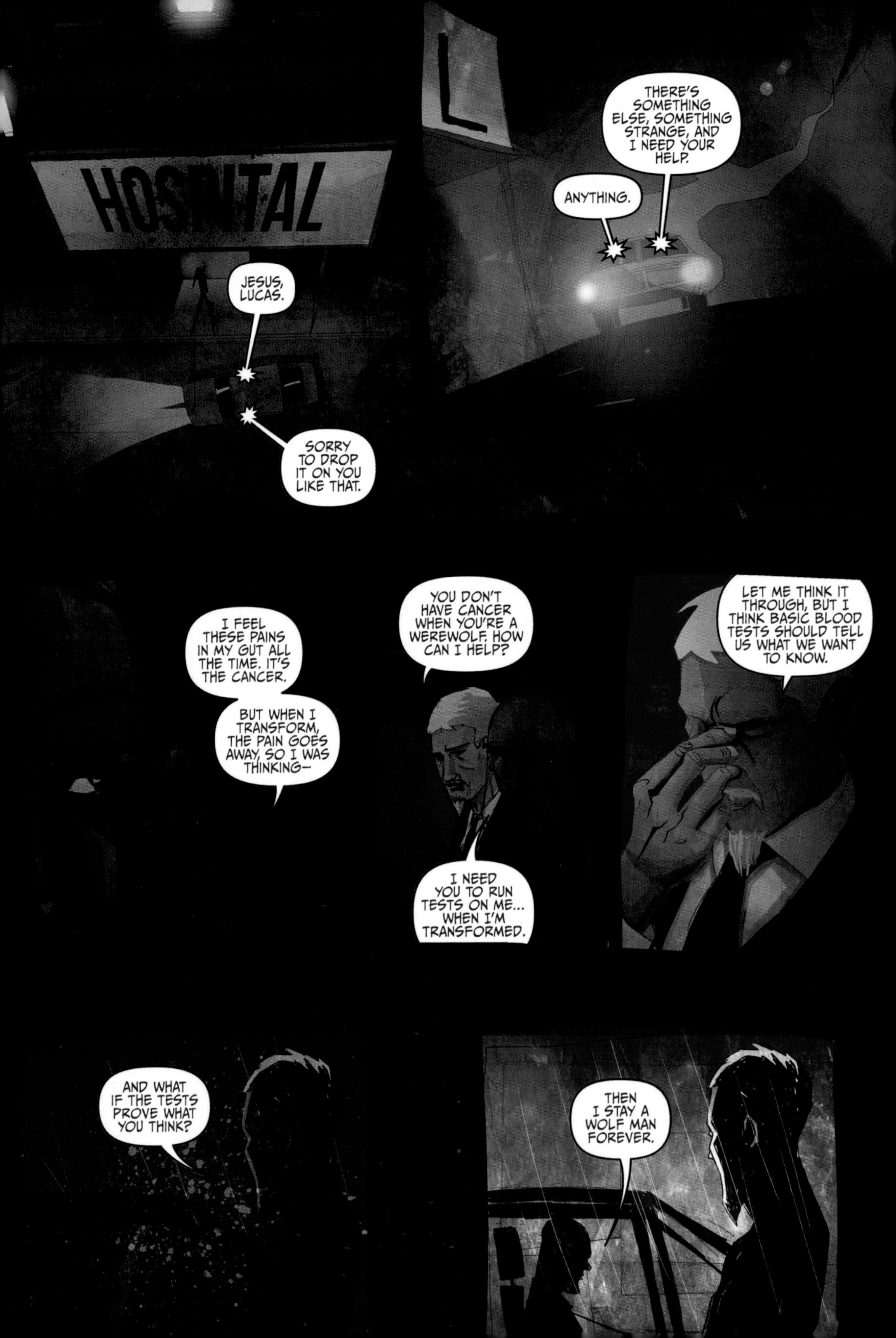
HOSPITAL
JESUS, LUCAS.
SORRY TO DROP IT ON YOU LIKE THAT.
THERE'S SOMETHING ELSE, SOMETHING STRANGE, AND I NEED YOUR HELP.
ANYTHING.
I FEEL THESE PAINS IN MY GUT ALL THE TIME. IT'S THE CANCER.
BUT WHEN I TRANSFORM, THE PAIN GOES AWAY, SO I WAS THINKING—
YOU DON'T HAVE CANCER WHEN YOU'RE A WEREWOLF. HOW CAN I HELP?
I NEED YOU TO RUN TESTS ON ME... WHEN I'M TRANSFORMED.
LET ME THINK IT THROUGH, BUT I THINK BASIC BLOOD TESTS SHOULD TELL US WHAT WE WANT TO KNOW.
AND WHAT IF THE TESTS PROVE WHAT YOU THINK?
THEN I STAY A WOLF MAN FOREVER.

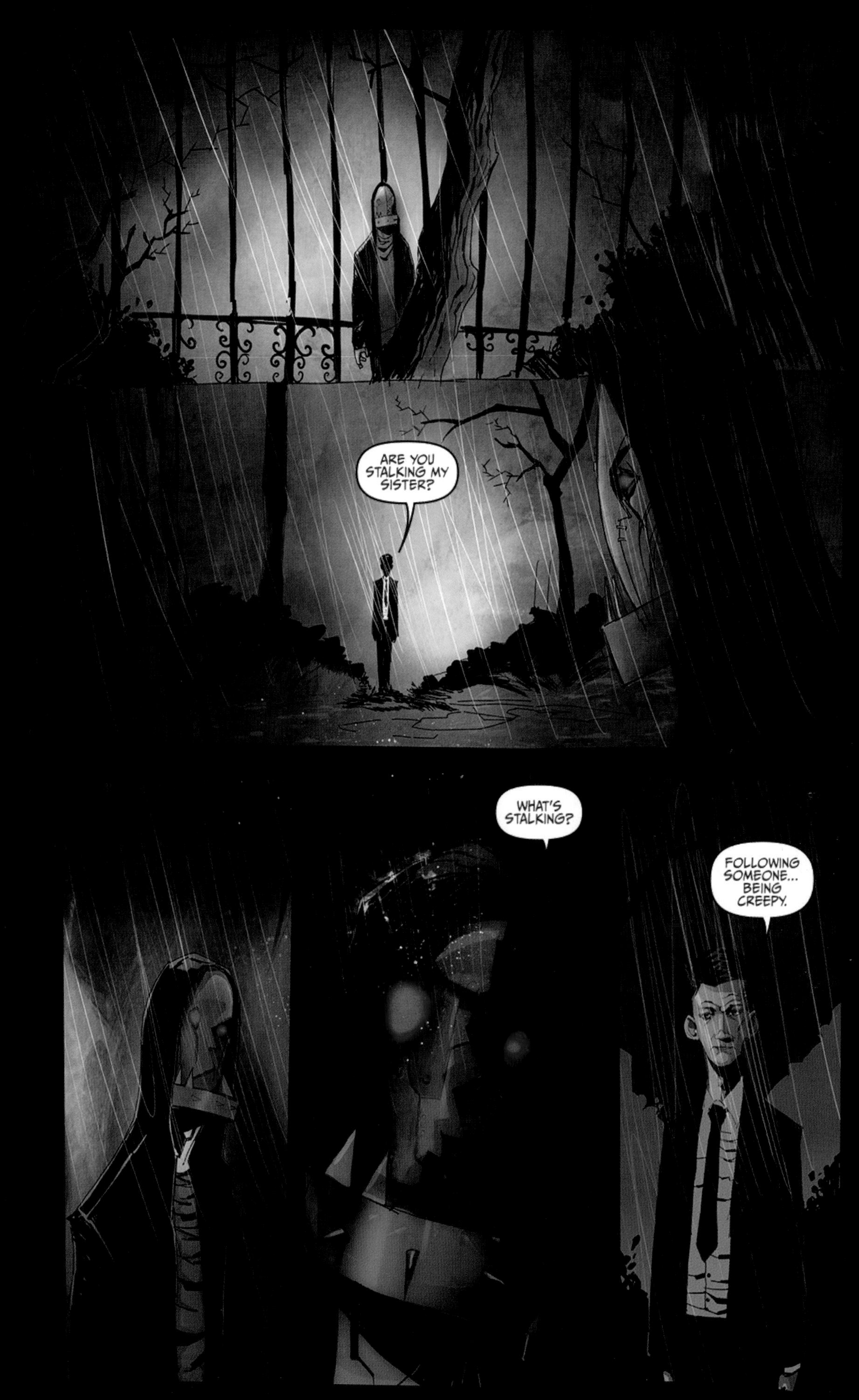
ARE YOU STALKING MY SISTER?
WHAT'S STALKING?
FOLLOWING SOMEONE... BEING CREEPY.

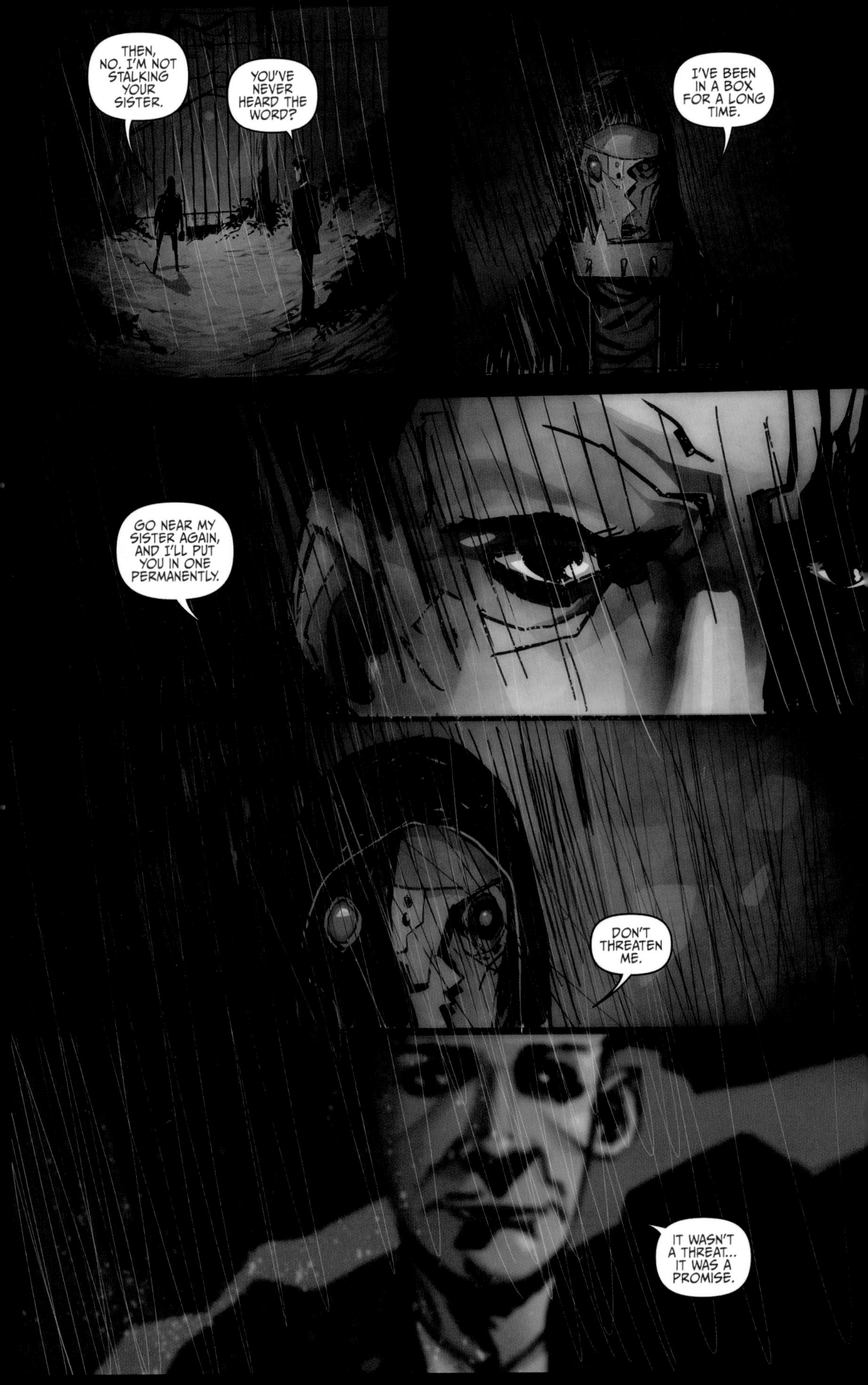
THEN, NO. I'M NOT STALKING YOUR SISTER.
YOU'VE NEVER HEARD THE WORD?
I'VE BEEN IN A BOX FOR A LONG TIME.
GO NEAR MY SISTER AGAIN, AND I'LL PUT YOU IN ONE PERMANENTLY.
DON'T THREATEN ME.
IT WASN'T A THREAT... IT WAS A PROMISE.

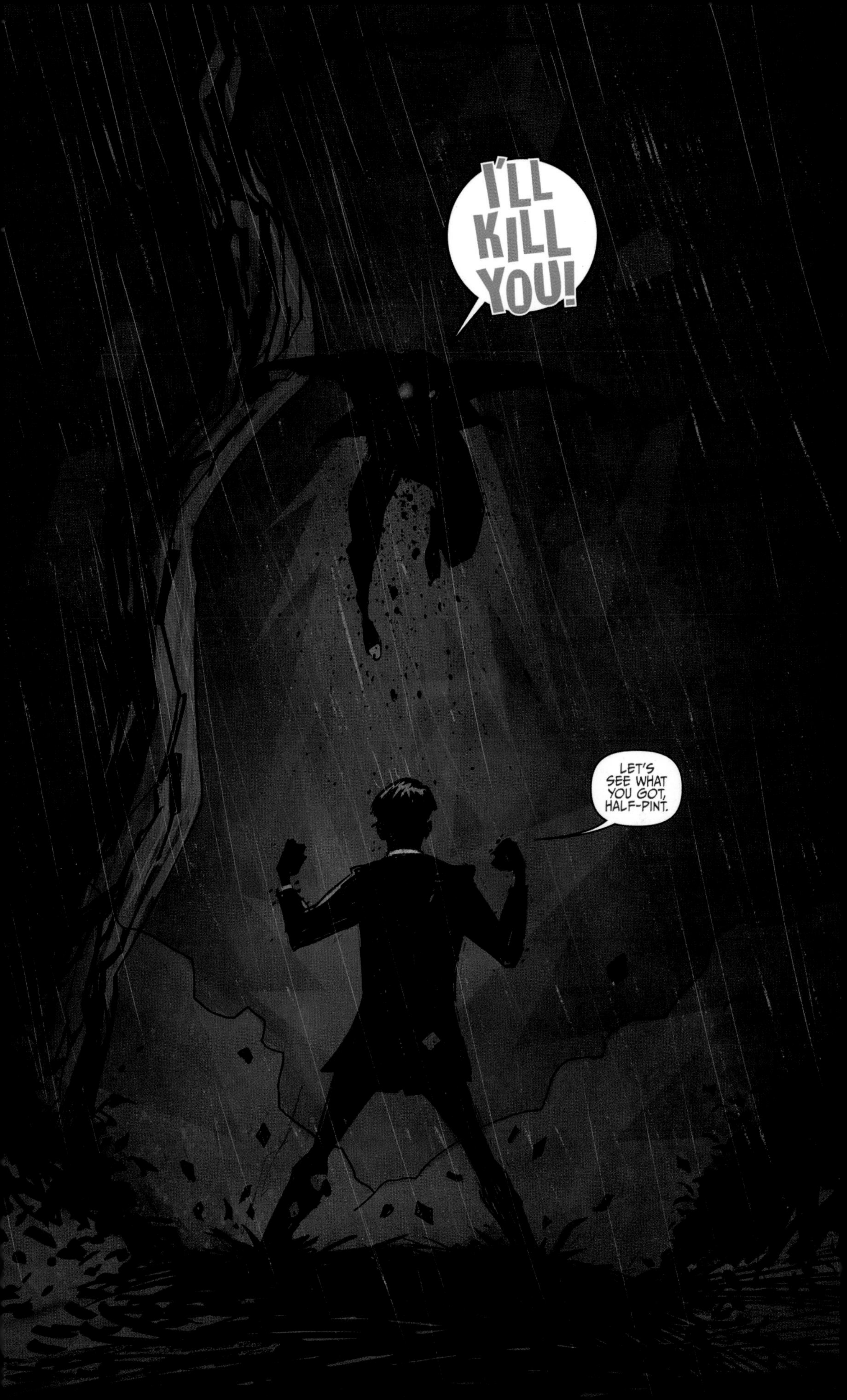
I'LL KILL YOU!
LET'S SEE WHAT YOU GOT, HALF-PINT.

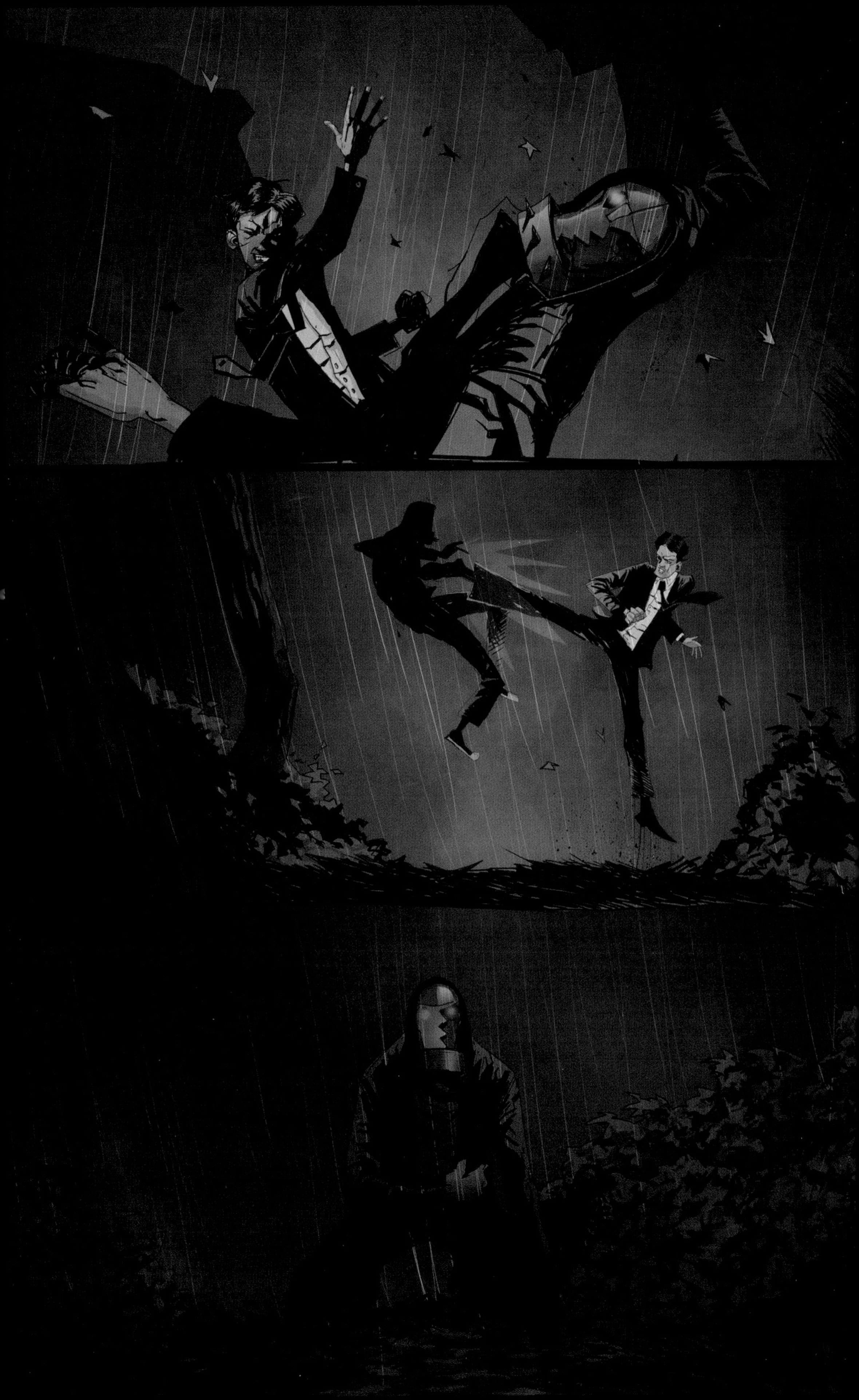

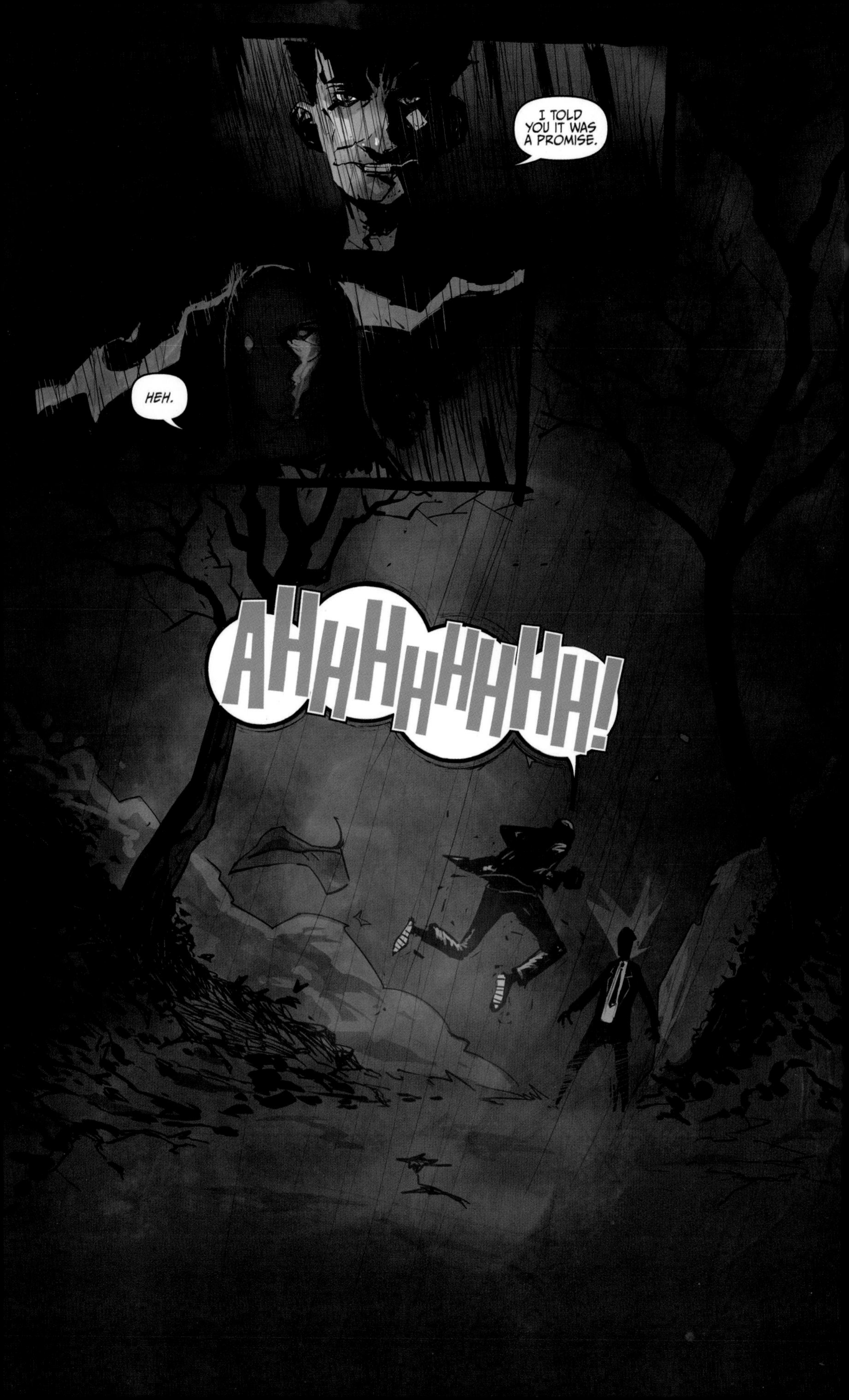
I TOLD YOU IT WAS A PROMISE.
HEH.
AHHHHHHHHH!

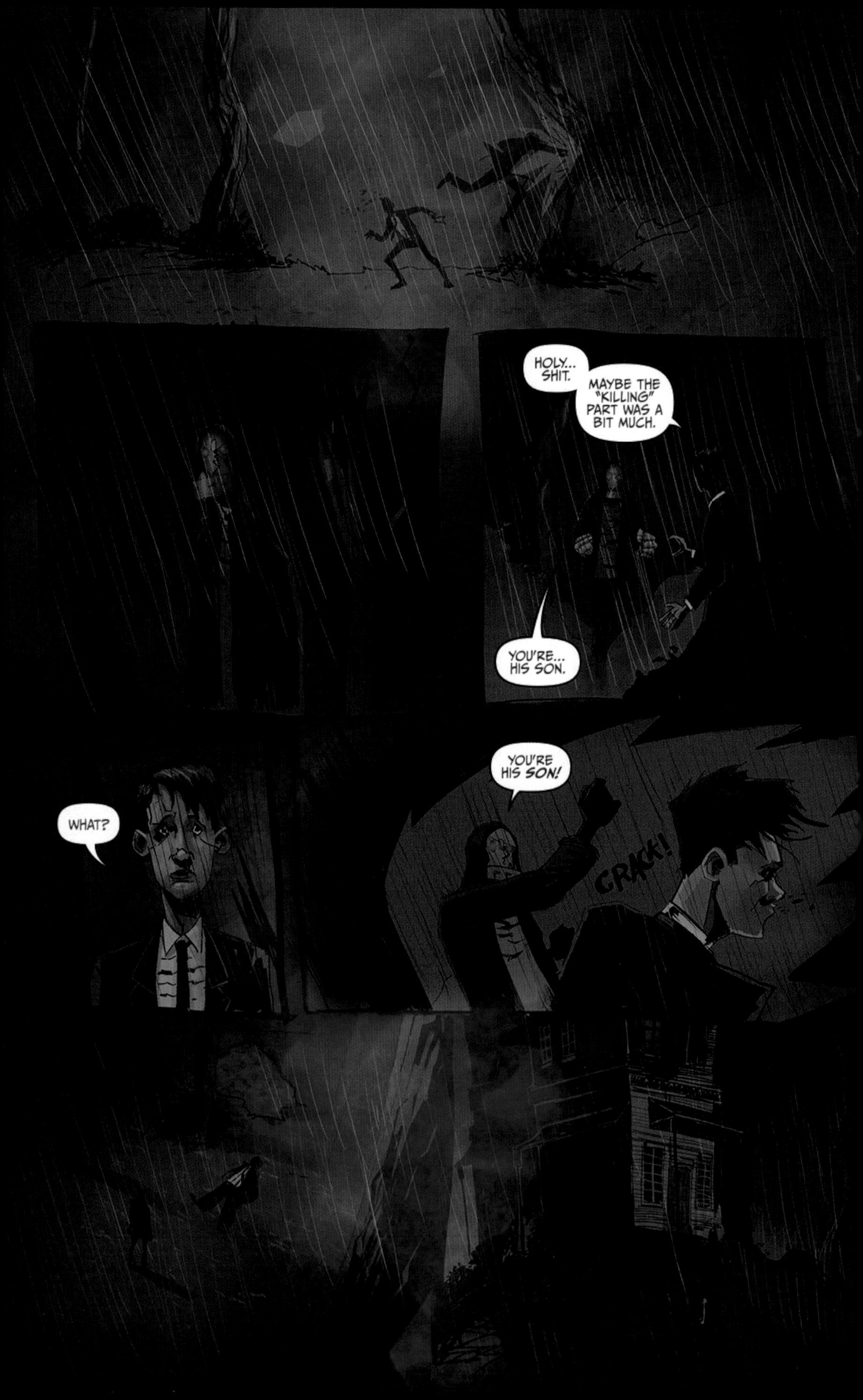
HOLY... SHIT.
MAYBE THE "KILLING" PART WAS A BIT MUCH.
YOU'RE... HIS SON.
WHAT?
YOU'RE HIS SON!
CRACK!

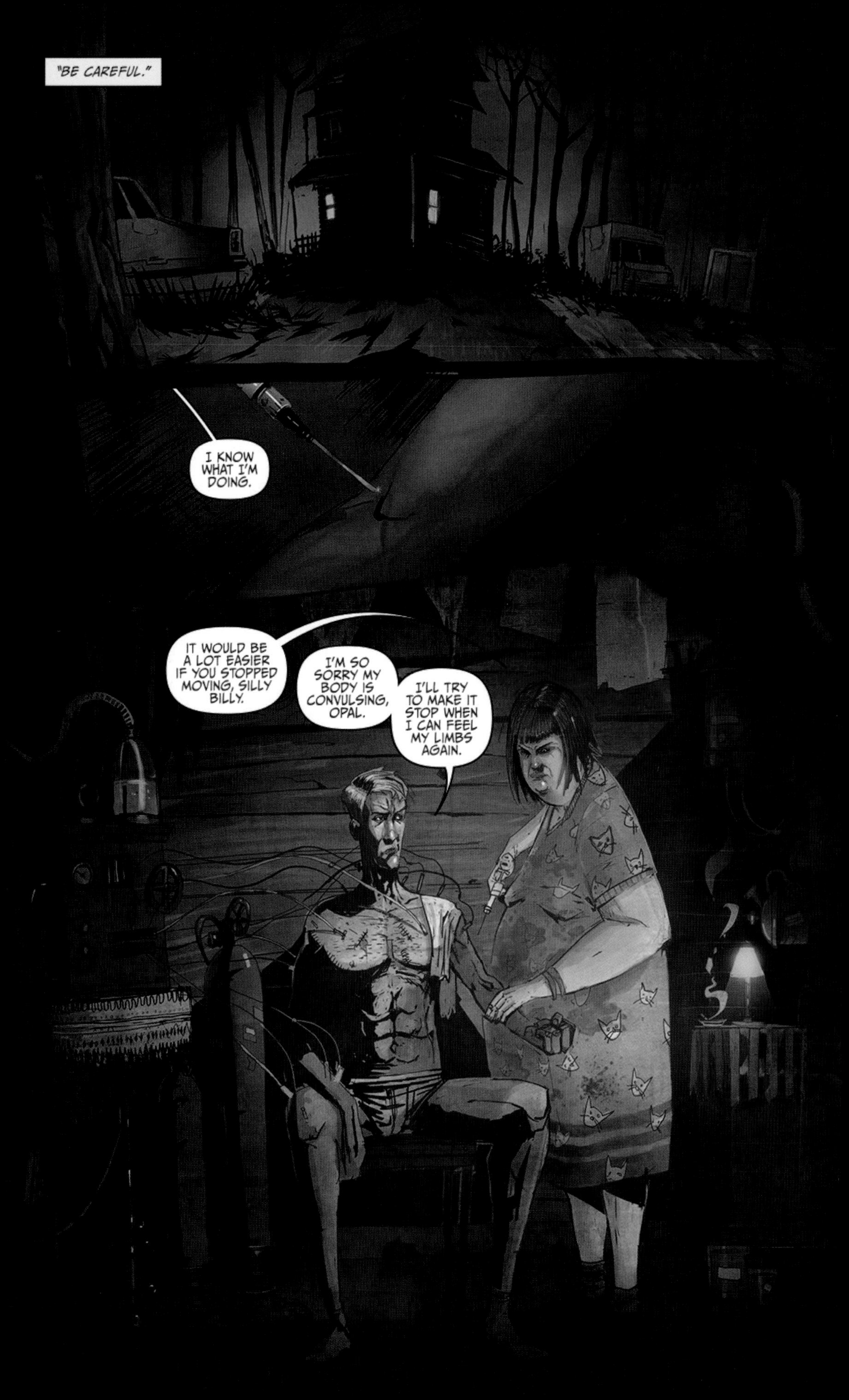
"BE CAREFUL."
I KNOW WHAT I'M DOING.
IT WOULD BE A LOT EASIER IF YOU STOPPED MOVING, SILLY BILLY.
I'M SO SORRY MY BODY IS CONVULSING, OPAL.
I'LL TRY TO MAKE IT STOP WHEN I CAN FEEL MY LIMBS AGAIN.

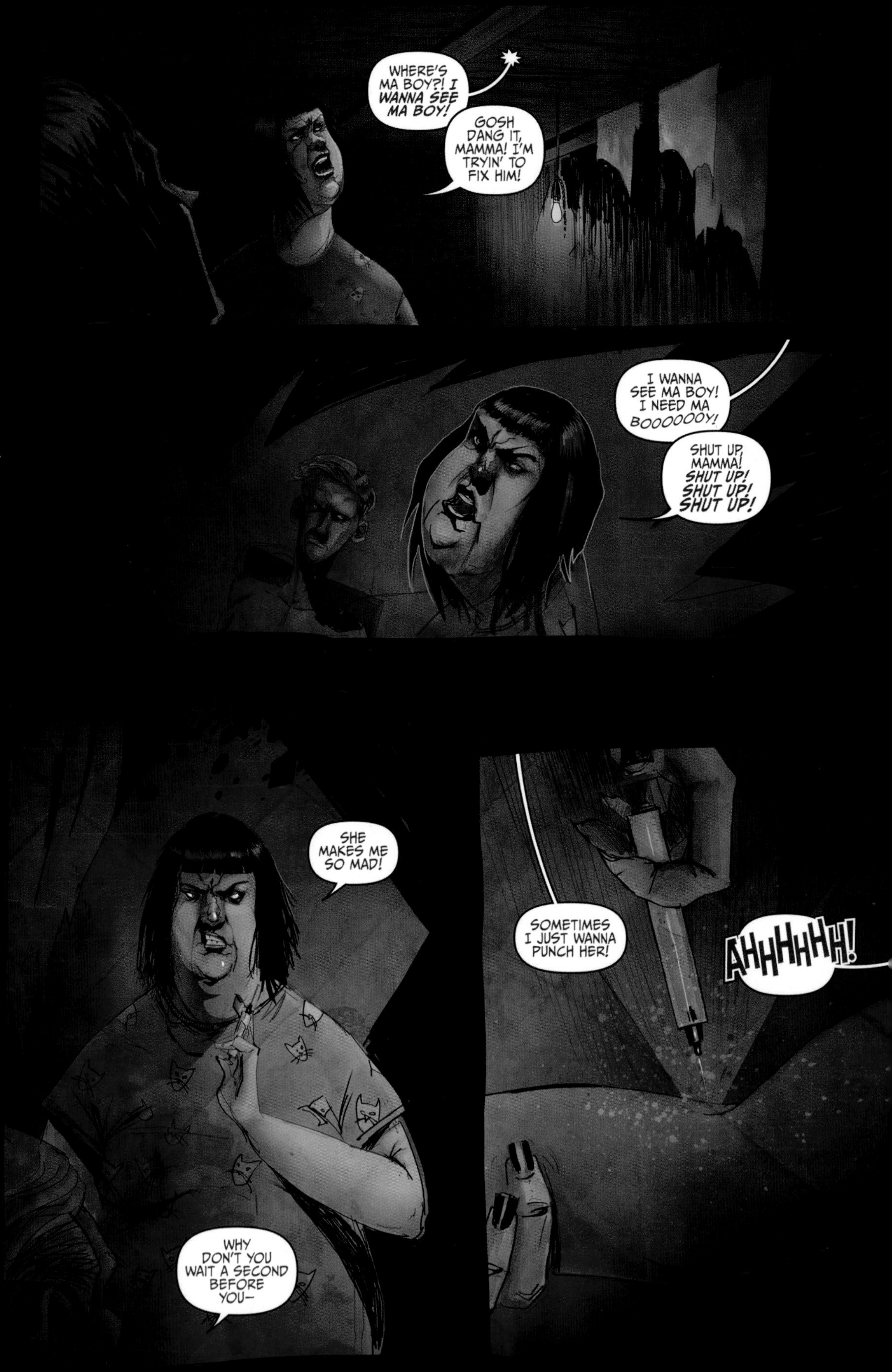

WHERE'S MA BOY?! I *WANNA SEE MA BOY!*
GOSH DANG IT, MAMMA! I'M TRYIN' TO FIX HIM!
I WANNA SEE MA BOY! I NEED MA *BOOOOOOY!*
SHUT UP, MAMMA! *SHUT UP! SHUT UP! SHUT UP!*
SHE MAKES ME SO MAD!
WHY DON'T YOU WAIT A SECOND BEFORE YOU–
SOMETIMES I JUST WANNA PUNCH HER!
AHHHHHH!

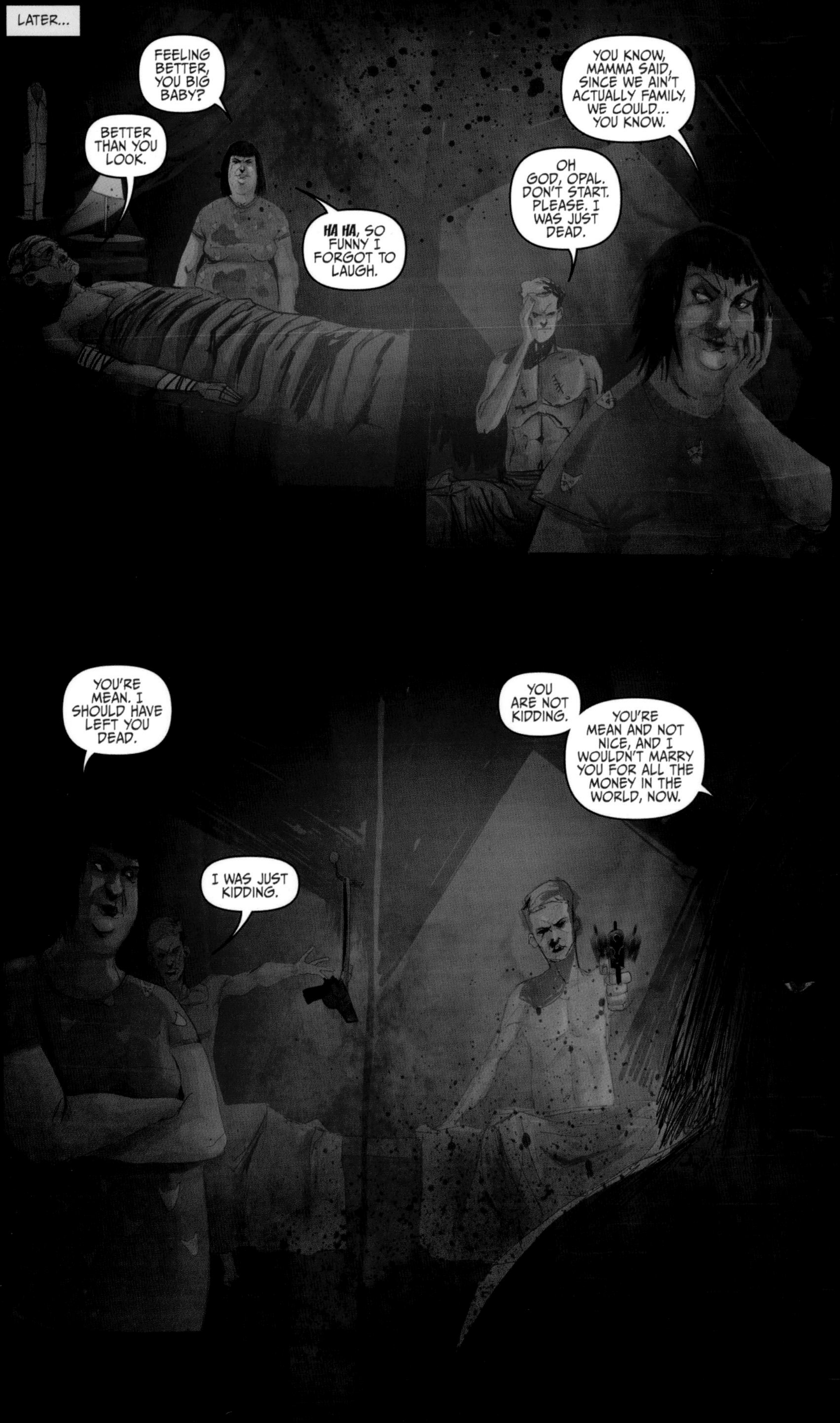
LATER...
FEELING BETTER, YOU BIG BABY?
BETTER THAN YOU LOOK.
HA HA, SO FUNNY I FORGOT TO LAUGH.
YOU KNOW, MAMMA SAID, SINCE WE AIN'T ACTUALLY FAMILY, WE COULD... YOU KNOW.
OH GOD, OPAL. DON'T START. PLEASE. I WAS JUST DEAD.
YOU'RE MEAN. I SHOULD HAVE LEFT YOU DEAD.
I WAS JUST KIDDING.
YOU ARE NOT KIDDING.
YOU'RE MEAN AND NOT NICE, AND I WOULDN'T MARRY YOU FOR ALL THE MONEY IN THE WORLD, NOW.

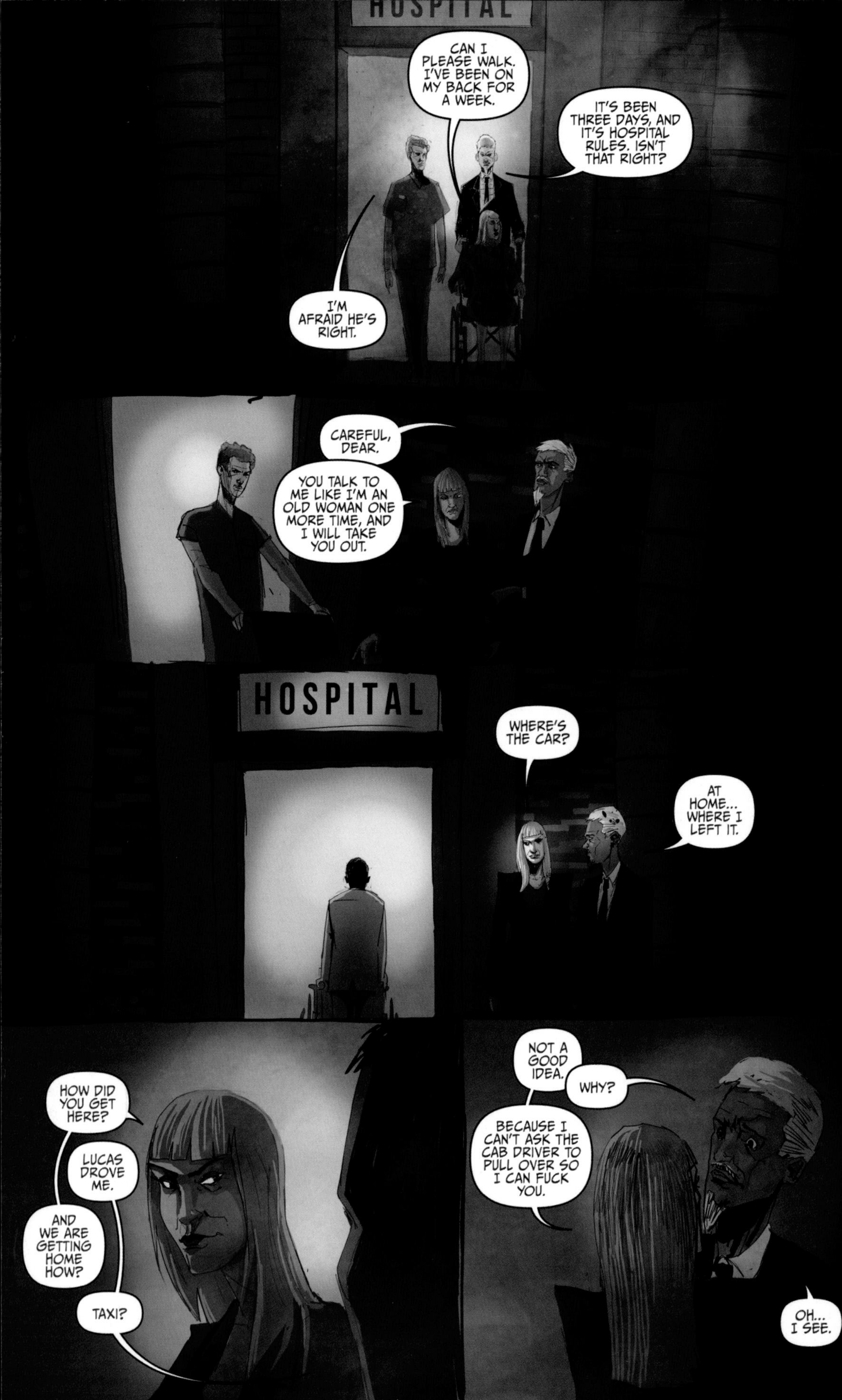
HOSPITAL
CAN I PLEASE WALK. I'VE BEEN ON MY BACK FOR A WEEK.
IT'S BEEN THREE DAYS, AND IT'S HOSPITAL RULES. ISN'T THAT RIGHT?
I'M AFRAID HE'S RIGHT.
CAREFUL, DEAR.
YOU TALK TO ME LIKE I'M AN OLD WOMAN ONE MORE TIME, AND I WILL TAKE YOU OUT.
HOSPITAL
WHERE'S THE CAR?
AT HOME... WHERE I LEFT IT.
HOW DID YOU GET HERE?
LUCAS DROVE ME.
AND WE ARE GETTING HOME HOW?
TAXI?
NOT A GOOD IDEA.
WHY?
BECAUSE I CAN'T ASK THE CAB DRIVER TO PULL OVER SO I CAN FUCK YOU.
OH... I SEE.

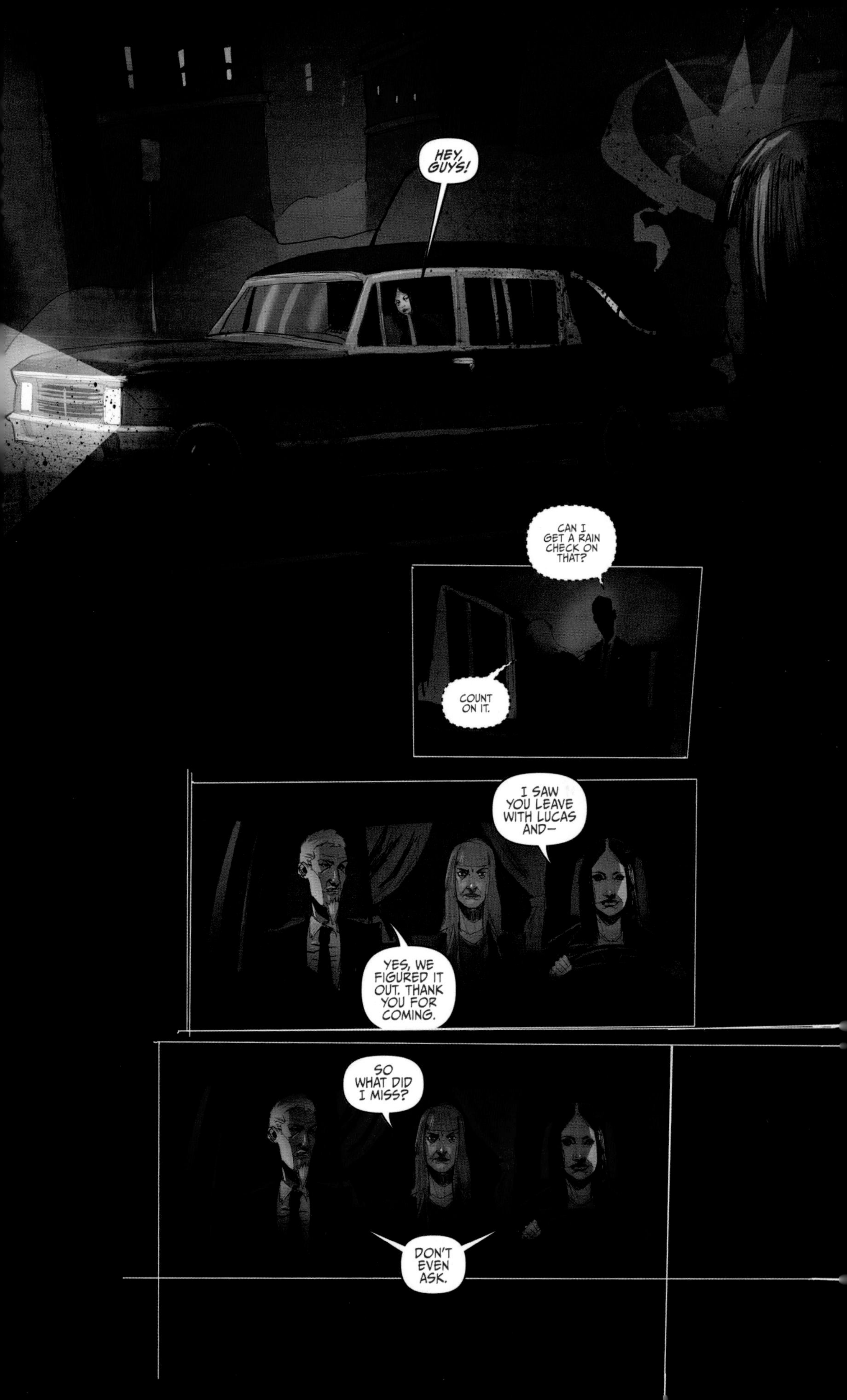
HEY, GUYS!
CAN I GET A RAIN CHECK ON THAT?
COUNT ON IT.
I SAW YOU LEAVE WITH LUCAS AND—
YES, WE FIGURED IT OUT. THANK YOU FOR COMING.
SO WHAT DID I MISS?
DON'T EVEN ASK.

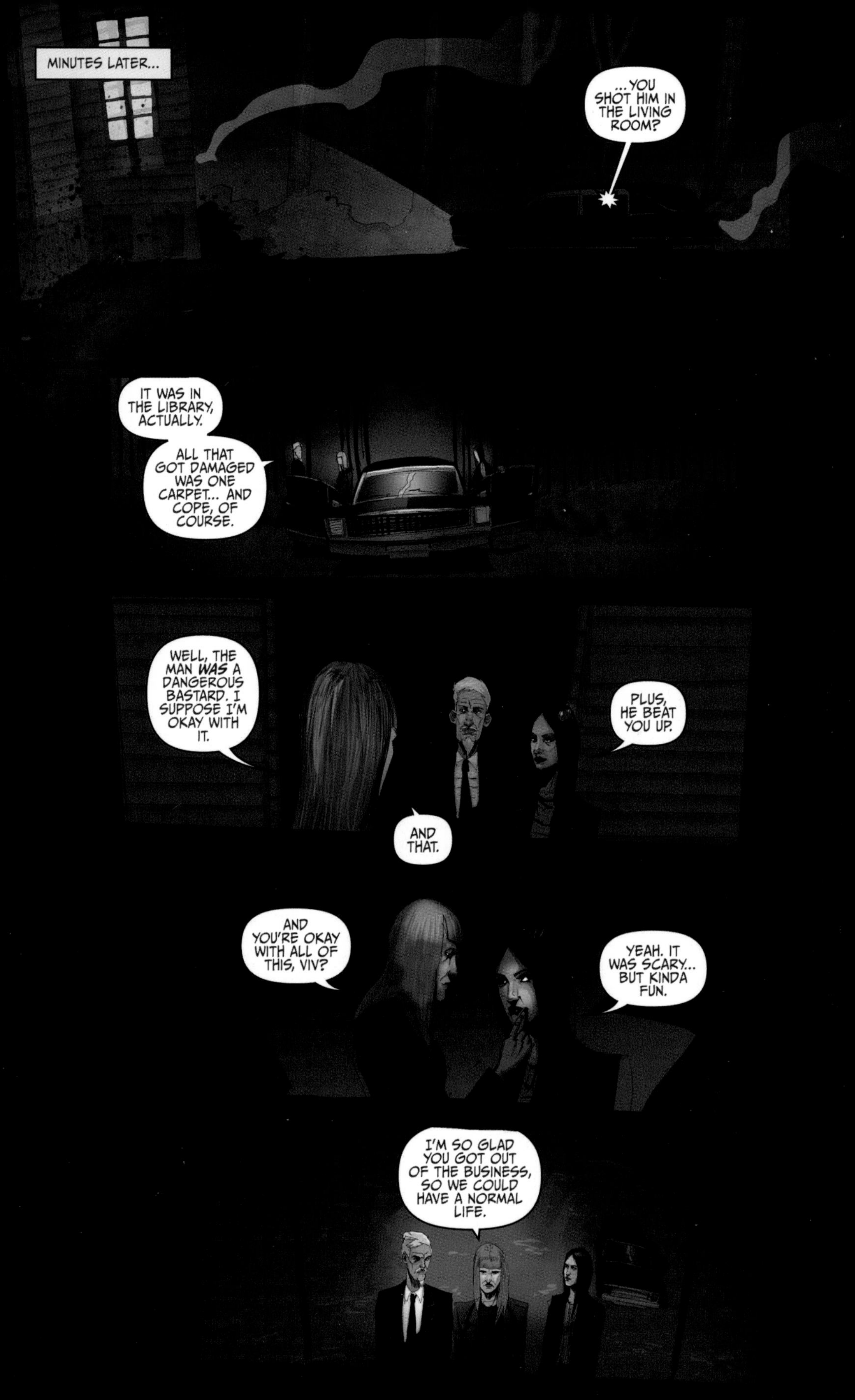
MINUTES LATER...
...YOU SHOT HIM IN THE LIVING ROOM?
IT WAS IN THE LIBRARY, ACTUALLY.
ALL THAT GOT DAMAGED WAS ONE CARPET... AND COPE, OF COURSE.
WELL, THE MAN WAS A DANGEROUS BASTARD. I SUPPOSE I'M OKAY WITH IT.
PLUS, HE BEAT YOU UP.
AND THAT.
AND YOU'RE OKAY WITH ALL OF THIS, VIV?
YEAH. IT WAS SCARY... BUT KINDA FUN.
I'M SO GLAD YOU GOT OUT OF THE BUSINESS, SO WE COULD HAVE A NORMAL LIFE.

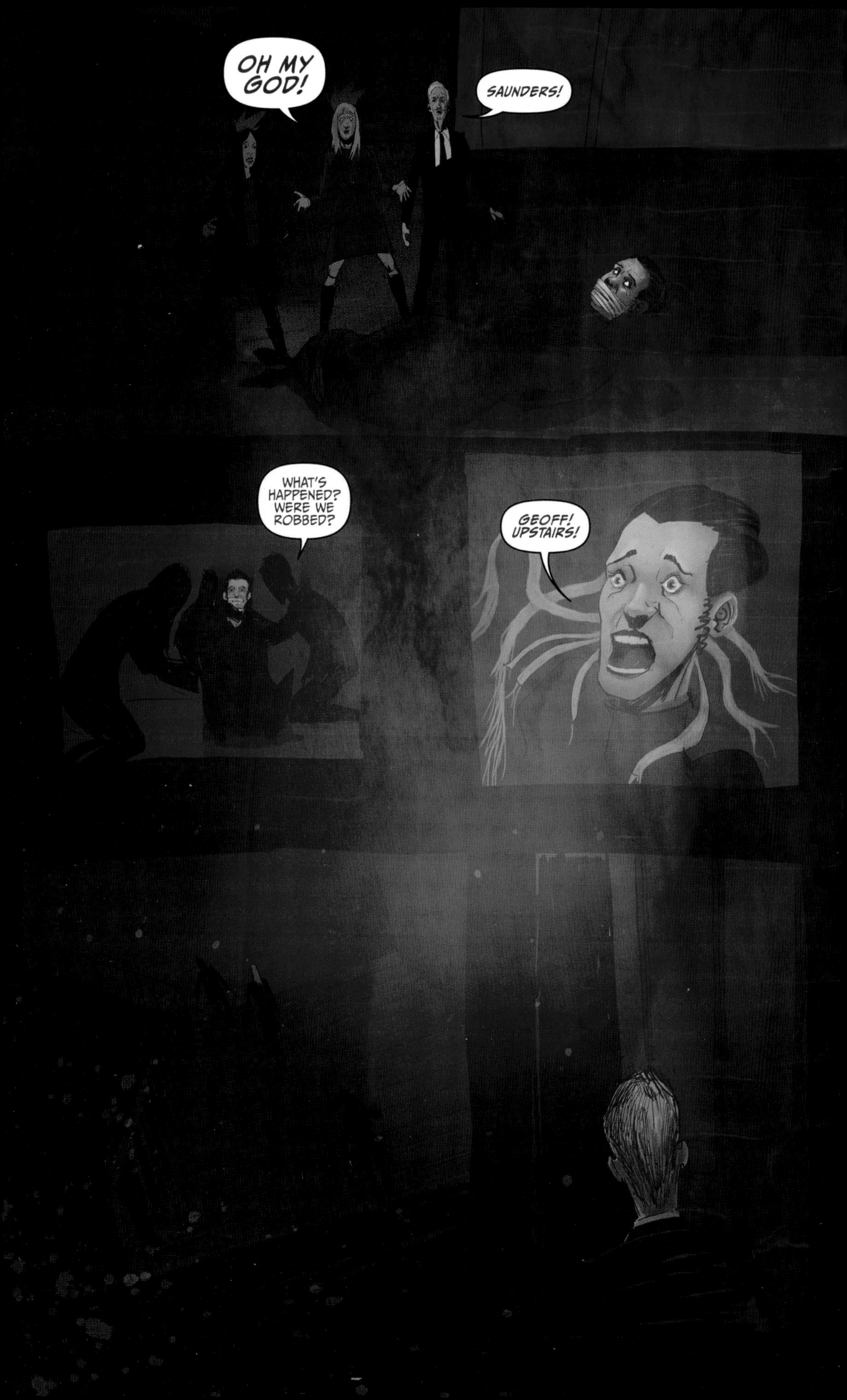
OH MY GOD!
SAUNDERS!
WHAT'S HAPPENED? WERE WE ROBBED?
GEOFF! UPSTAIRS!

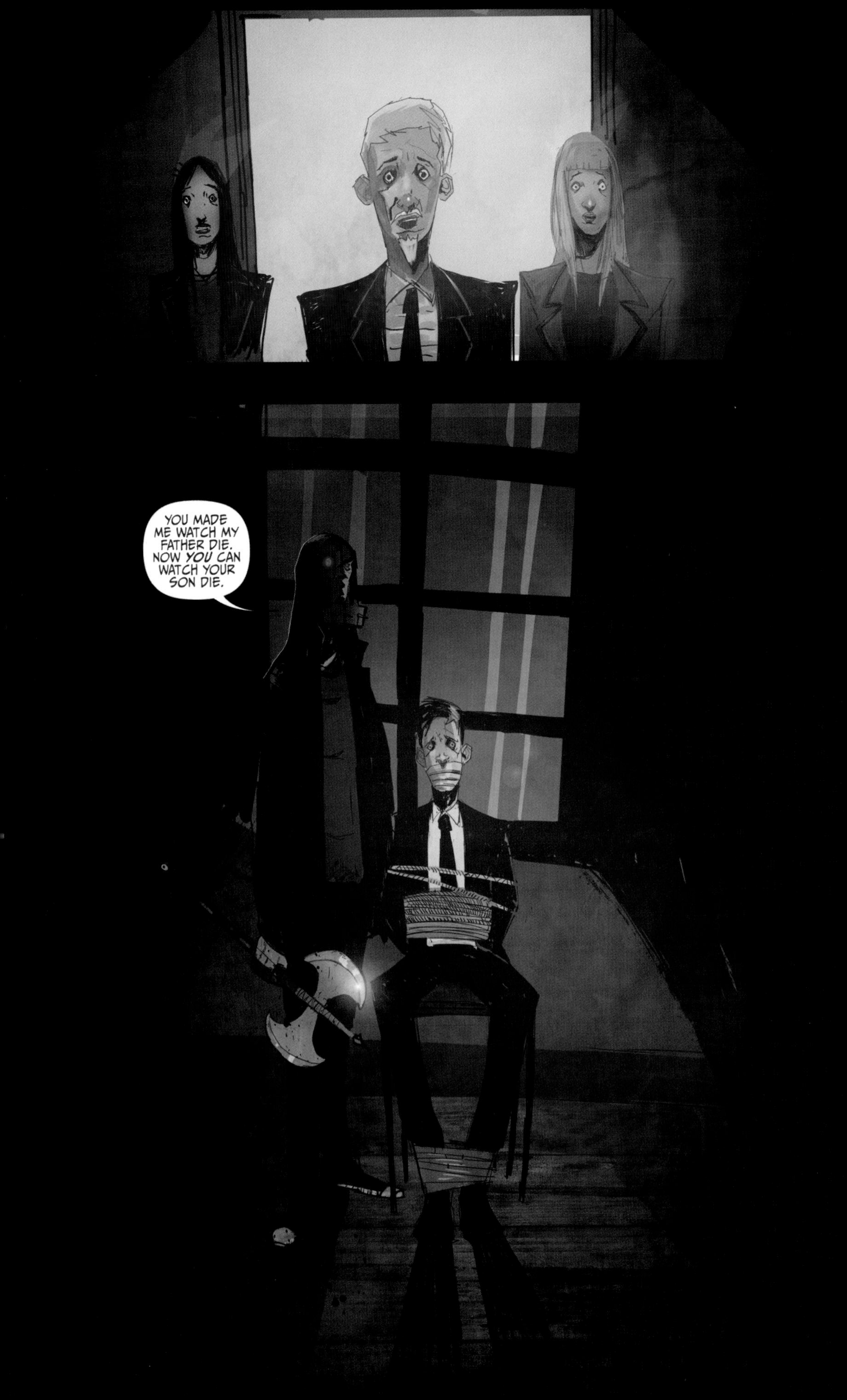
YOU MADE ME WATCH MY FATHER DIE. NOW *YOU* CAN WATCH YOUR SON DIE.

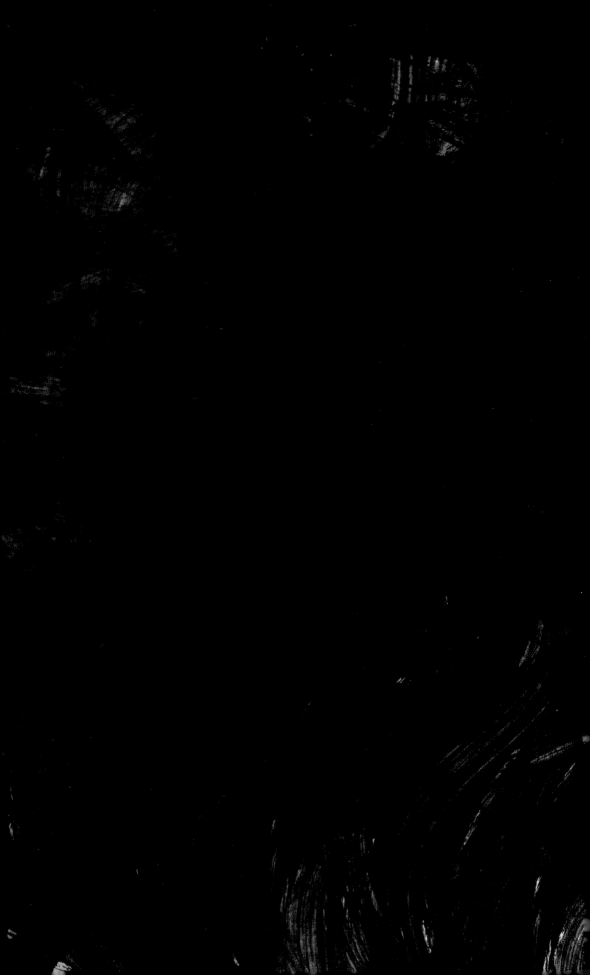

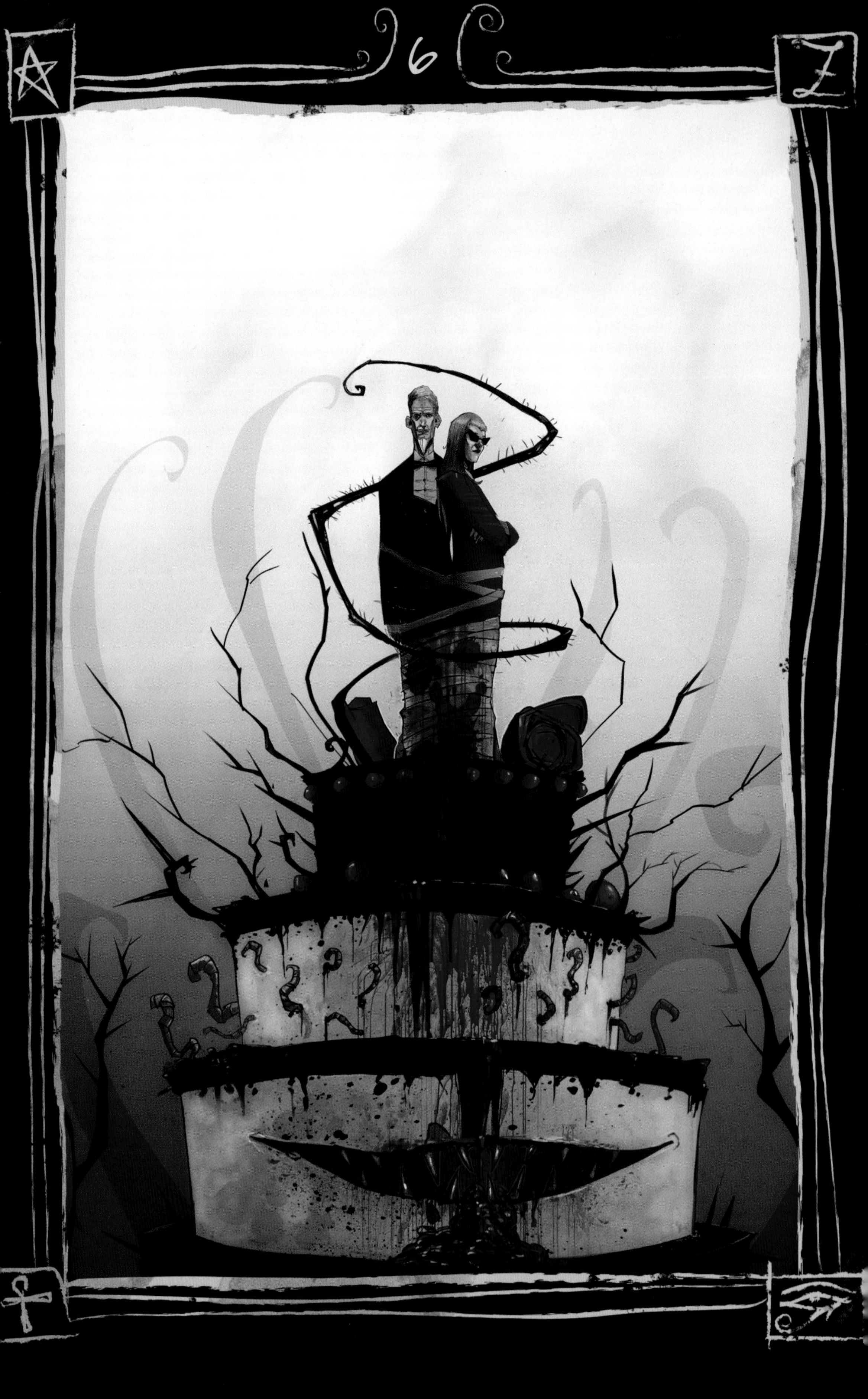
6

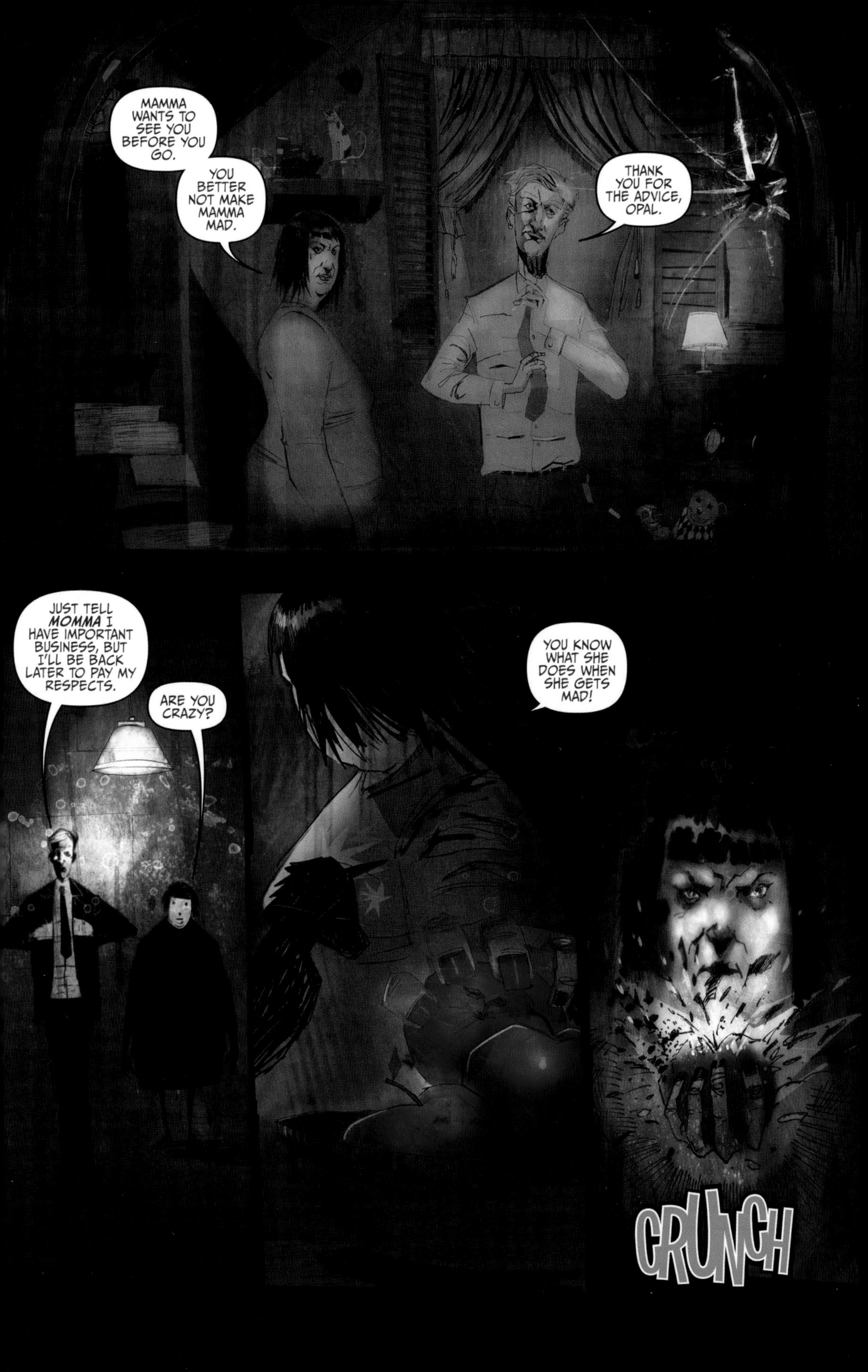
MAMMA WANTS TO SEE YOU BEFORE YOU GO.
YOU BETTER NOT MAKE MAMMA MAD.
THANK YOU FOR THE ADVICE, OPAL.
JUST TELL *MOMMA* I HAVE IMPORTANT BUSINESS, BUT I'LL BE BACK LATER TO PAY MY RESPECTS.
ARE YOU CRAZY?
YOU KNOW WHAT SHE DOES WHEN SHE GETS MAD!
CRUNCH

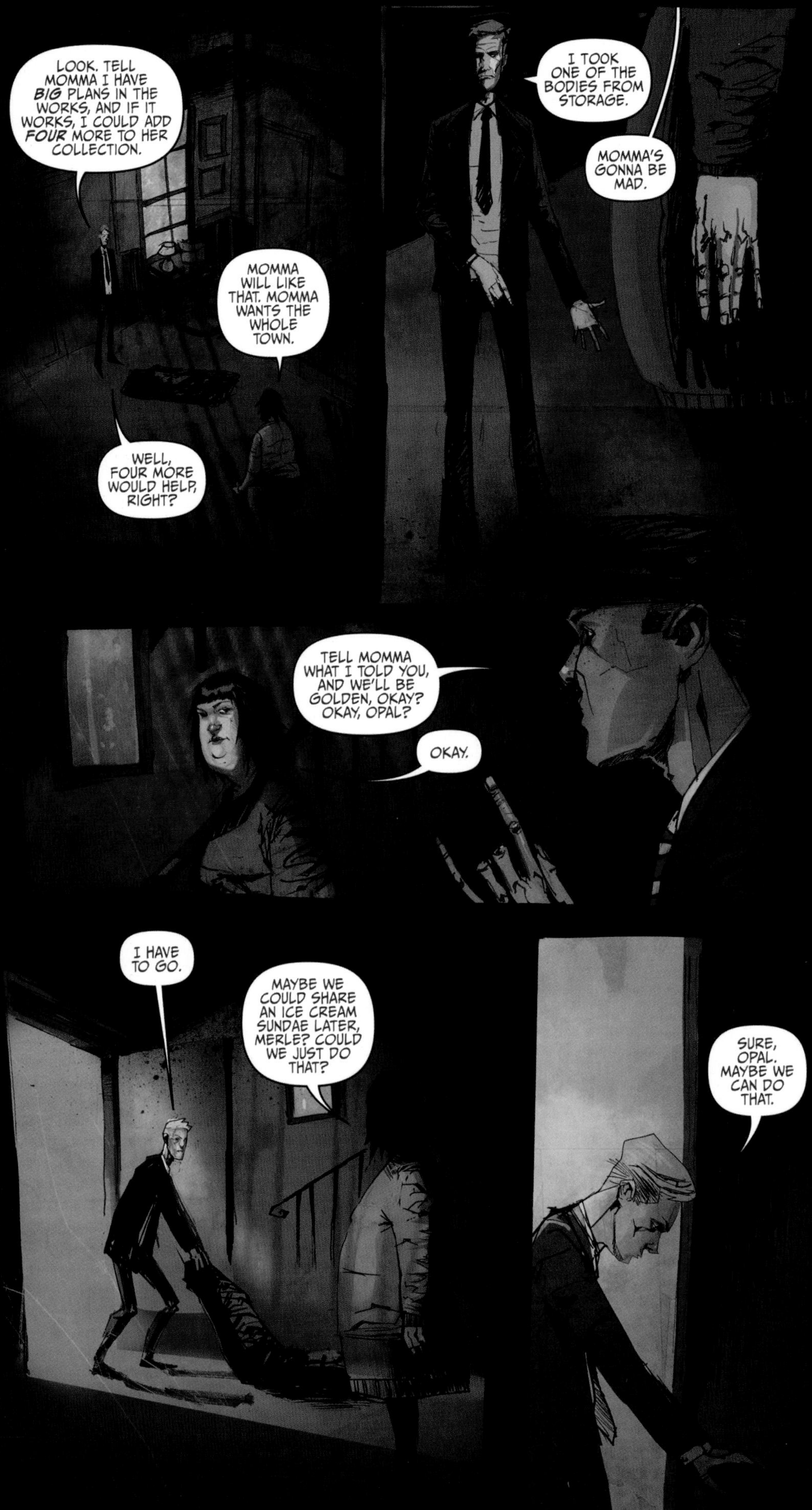

LOOK. TELL MOMMA I HAVE *BIG* PLANS IN THE WORKS, AND IF IT WORKS, I COULD ADD *FOUR* MORE TO HER COLLECTION.
MOMMA WILL LIKE THAT. MOMMA WANTS THE WHOLE TOWN.
WELL, FOUR MORE WOULD HELP, RIGHT?
I TOOK ONE OF THE BODIES FROM STORAGE.
MOMMA'S GONNA BE MAD.
TELL MOMMA WHAT I TOLD YOU, AND WE'LL BE GOLDEN, OKAY? OKAY, OPAL?
OKAY.
I HAVE TO GO.
MAYBE WE COULD SHARE AN ICE CREAM SUNDAE LATER, MERLE? COULD WE JUST DO THAT?
SURE, OPAL. MAYBE WE CAN DO THAT.

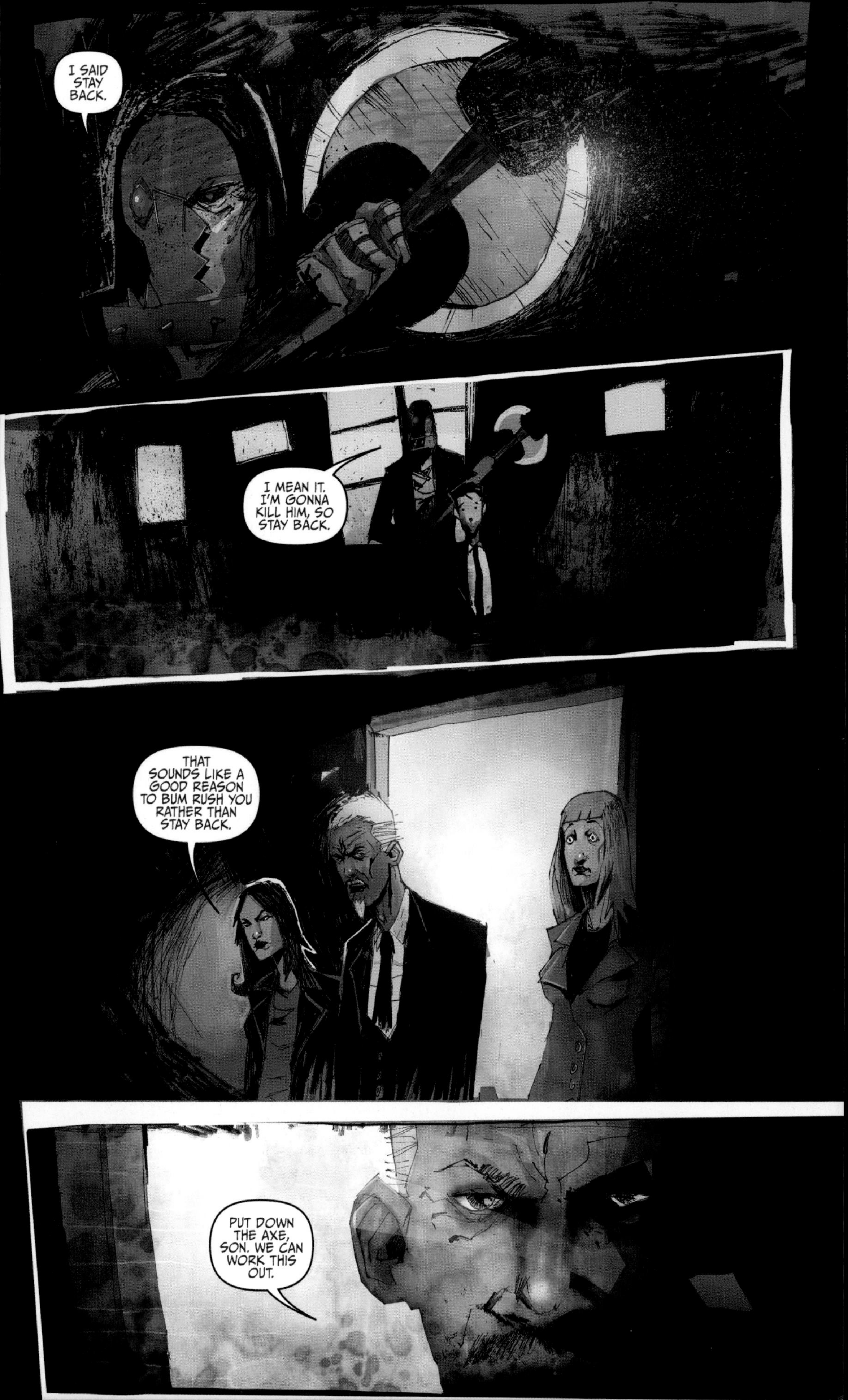
I SAID STAY BACK.
I MEAN IT. I'M GONNA KILL HIM, SO STAY BACK.
THAT SOUNDS LIKE A GOOD REASON TO BUM RUSH YOU RATHER THAN STAY BACK.
PUT DOWN THE AXE, SON. WE CAN WORK THIS OUT.

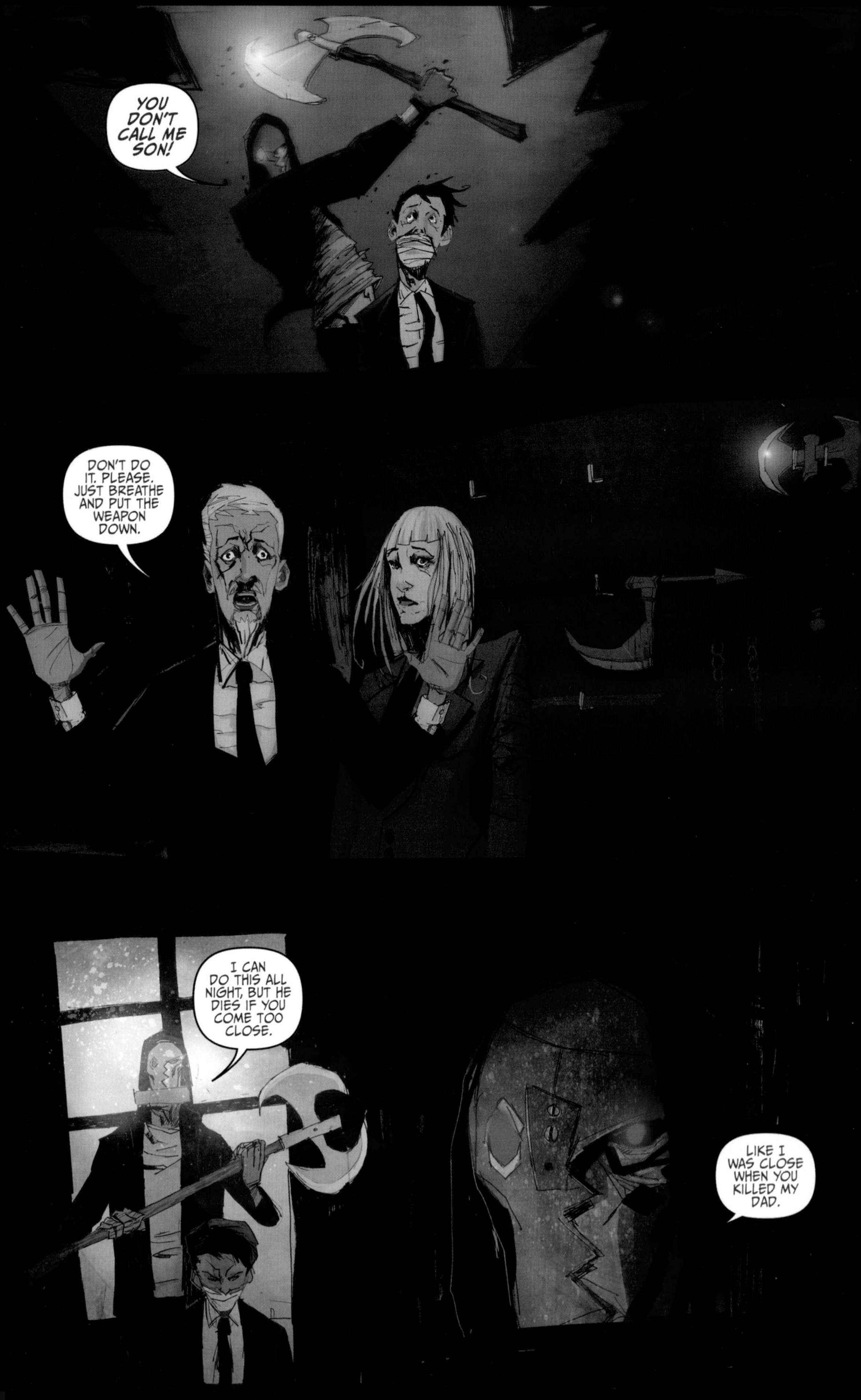
YOU DON'T CALL ME SON!
DON'T DO IT. PLEASE. JUST BREATHE AND PUT THE WEAPON DOWN.
I CAN DO THIS ALL NIGHT, BUT HE DIES IF YOU COME TOO CLOSE.
LIKE I WAS CLOSE WHEN YOU KILLED MY DAD.

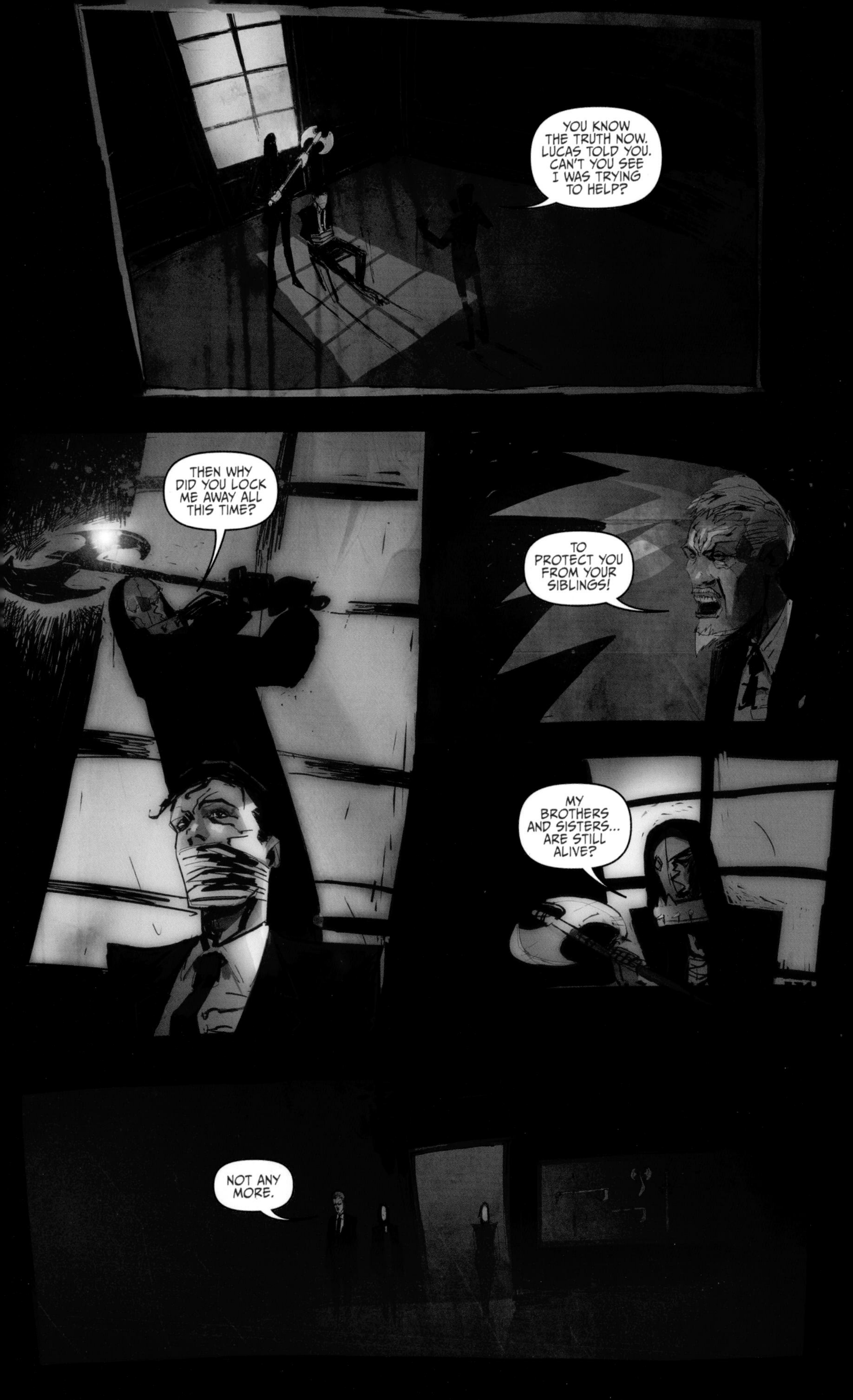
YOU KNOW THE TRUTH NOW. LUCAS TOLD YOU. CAN'T YOU SEE I WAS TRYING TO HELP?
THEN WHY DID YOU LOCK ME AWAY ALL THIS TIME?
TO PROTECT YOU FROM YOUR SIBLINGS!
MY BROTHERS AND SISTERS... ARE STILL ALIVE?
NOT ANY MORE.

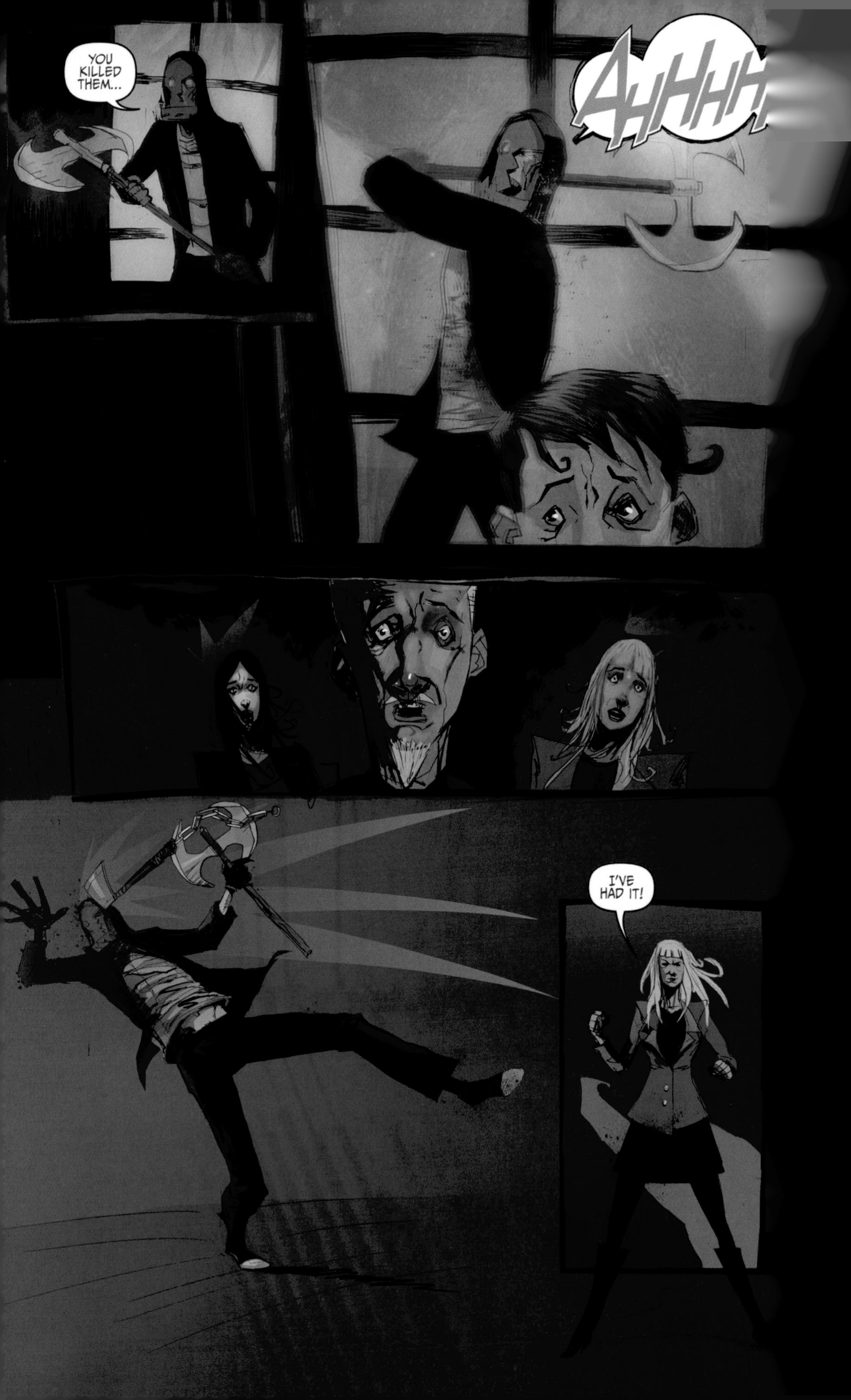
YOU KILLED THEM...
AHHHH
I'VE HAD IT!

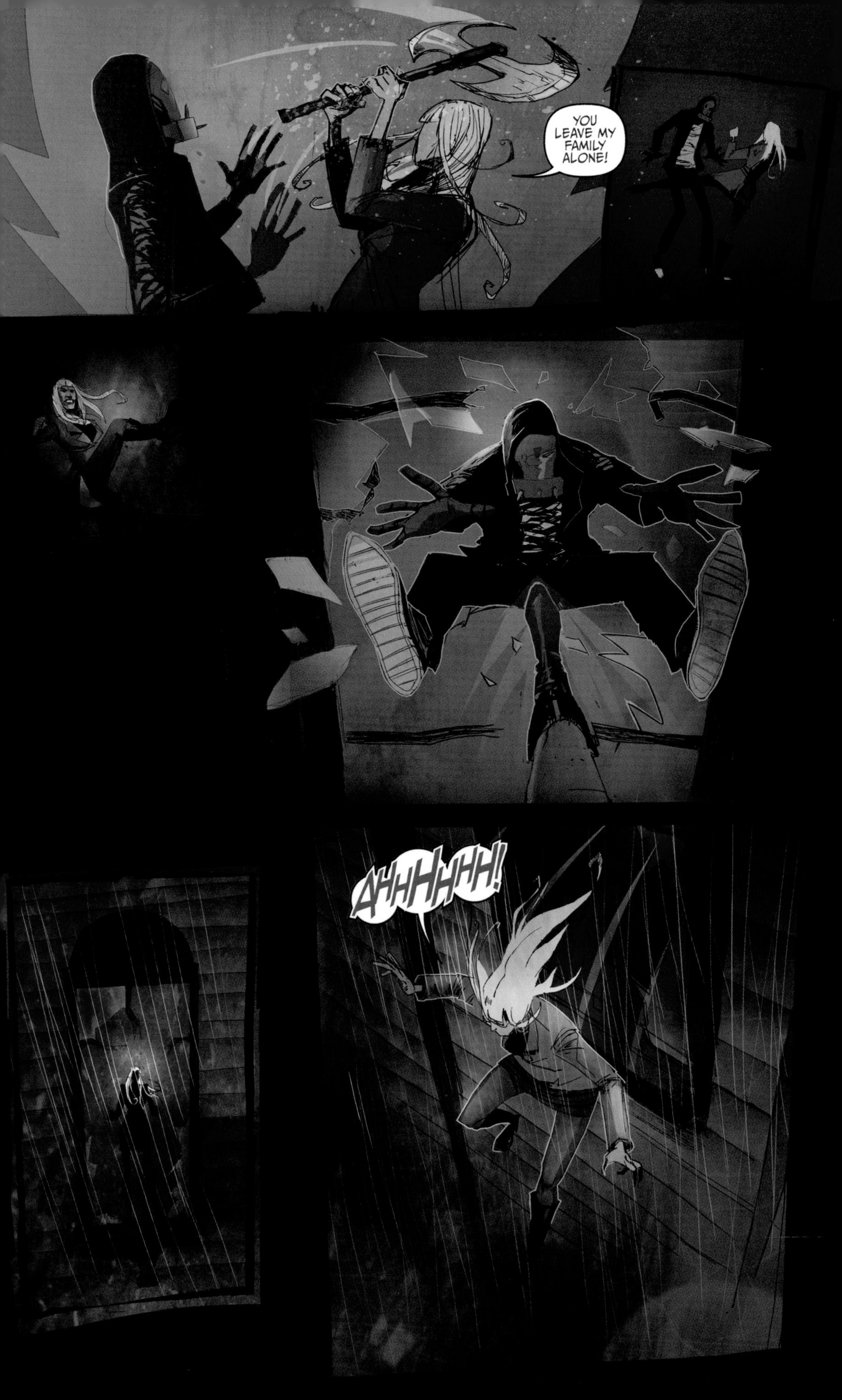
YOU LEAVE MY FAMILY ALONE!
AHHHHH!

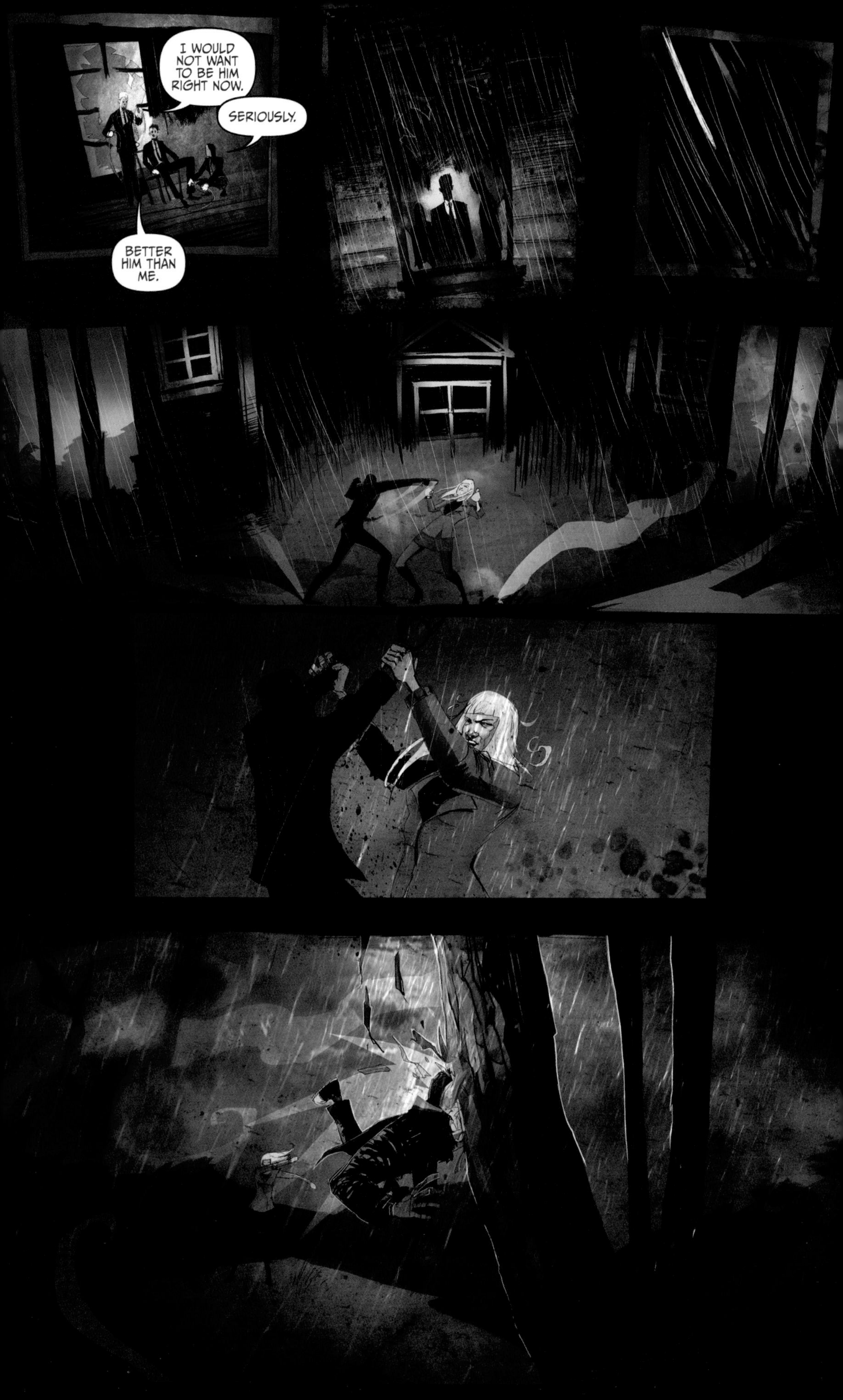
I WOULD NOT WANT TO BE HIM RIGHT NOW.
SERIOUSLY.
BETTER HIM THAN ME.

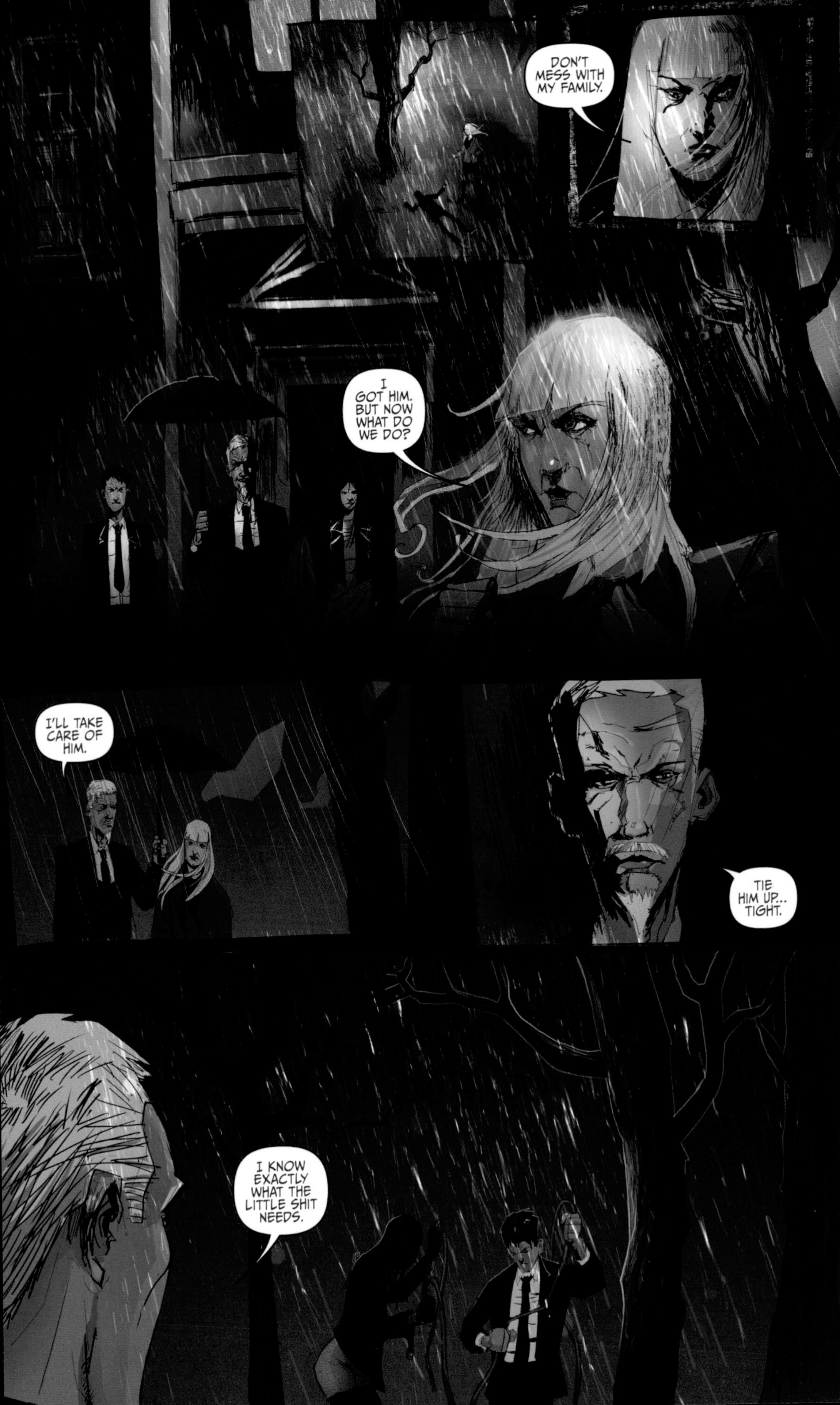
DON'T MESS WITH MY FAMILY.
I GOT HIM. BUT NOW WHAT DO WE DO?
I'LL TAKE CARE OF HIM.
TIE HIM UP... TIGHT.
I KNOW EXACTLY WHAT THE LITTLE SHIT NEEDS.

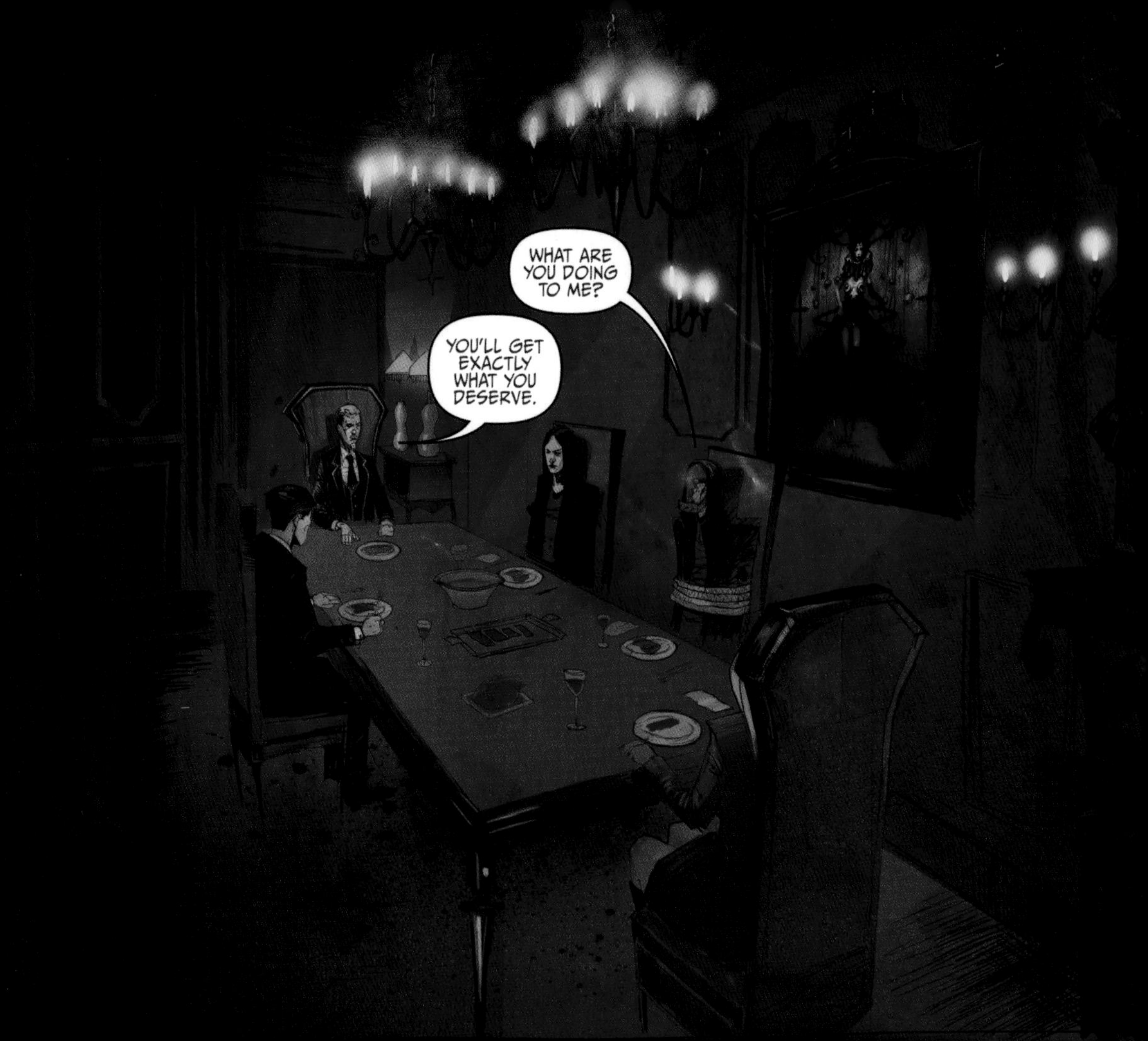
WHAT ARE YOU DOING TO ME?
YOU'LL GET EXACTLY WHAT YOU DESERVE.

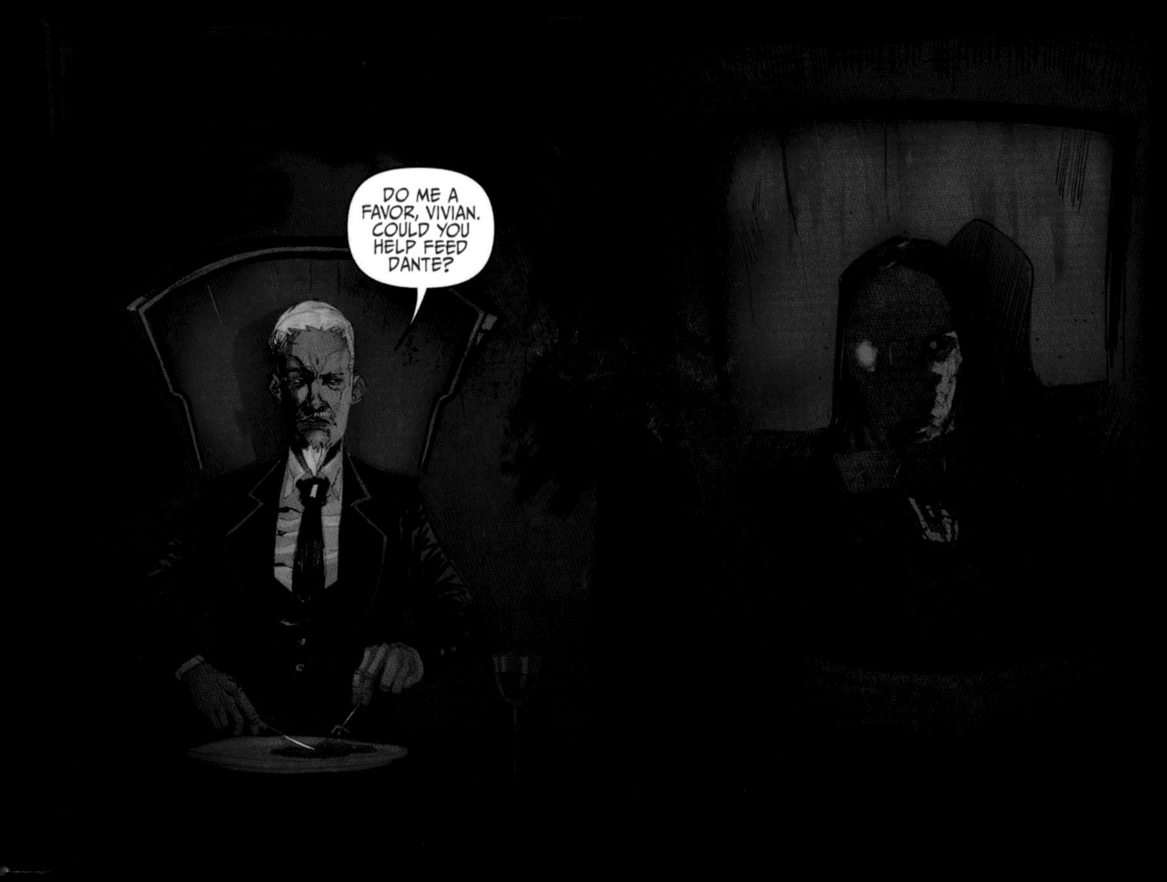
DO ME A FAVOR, VIVIAN. COULD YOU HELP FEED DANTE?

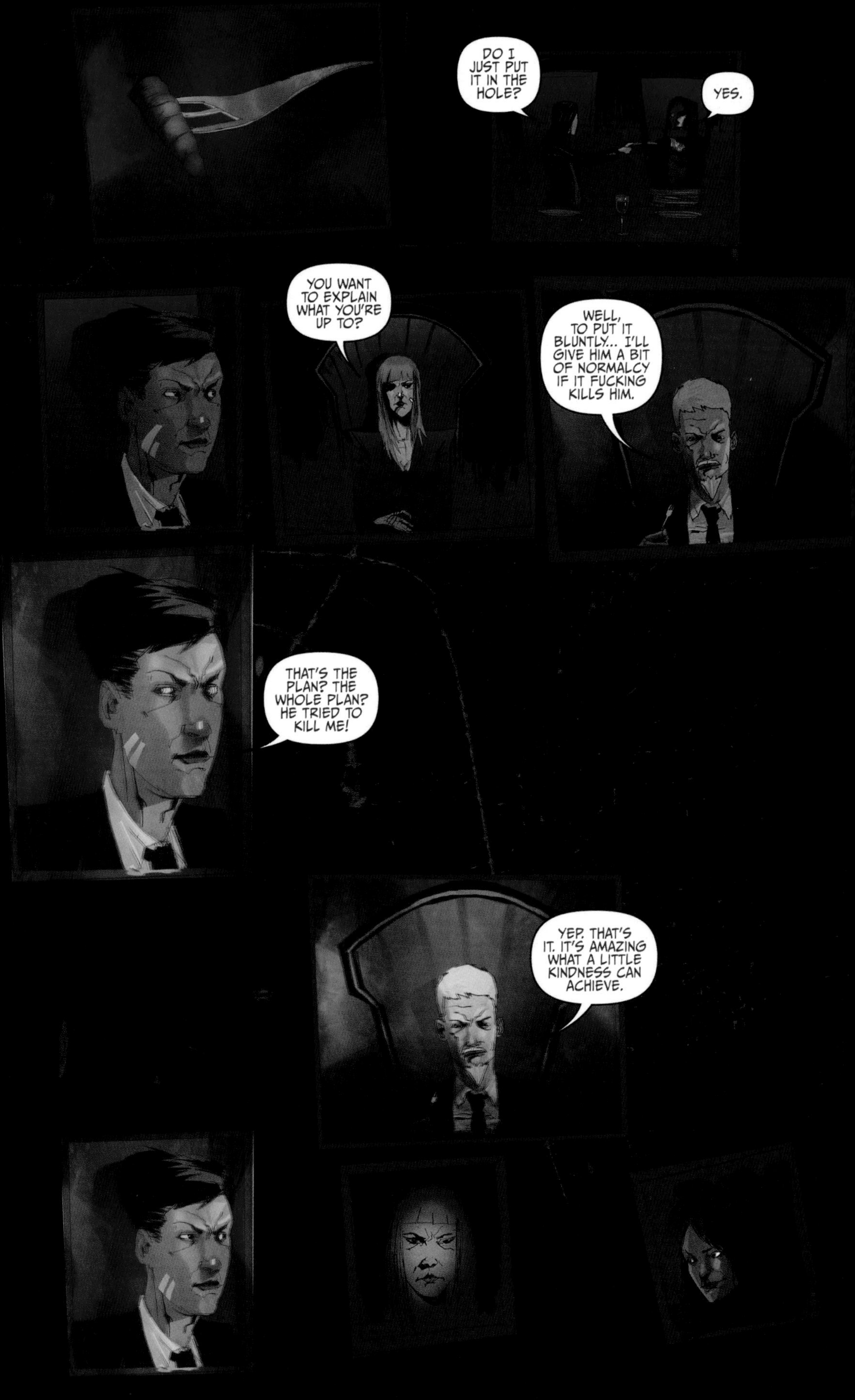
DO I JUST PUT IT IN THE HOLE?
YES.
YOU WANT TO EXPLAIN WHAT YOU'RE UP TO?
WELL, TO PUT IT BLUNTLY... I'LL GIVE HIM A BIT OF NORMALCY IF IT FUCKING KILLS HIM.
THAT'S THE PLAN? THE WHOLE PLAN? HE TRIED TO KILL ME!
YEP. THAT'S IT. IT'S AMAZING WHAT A LITTLE KINDNESS CAN ACHIEVE.

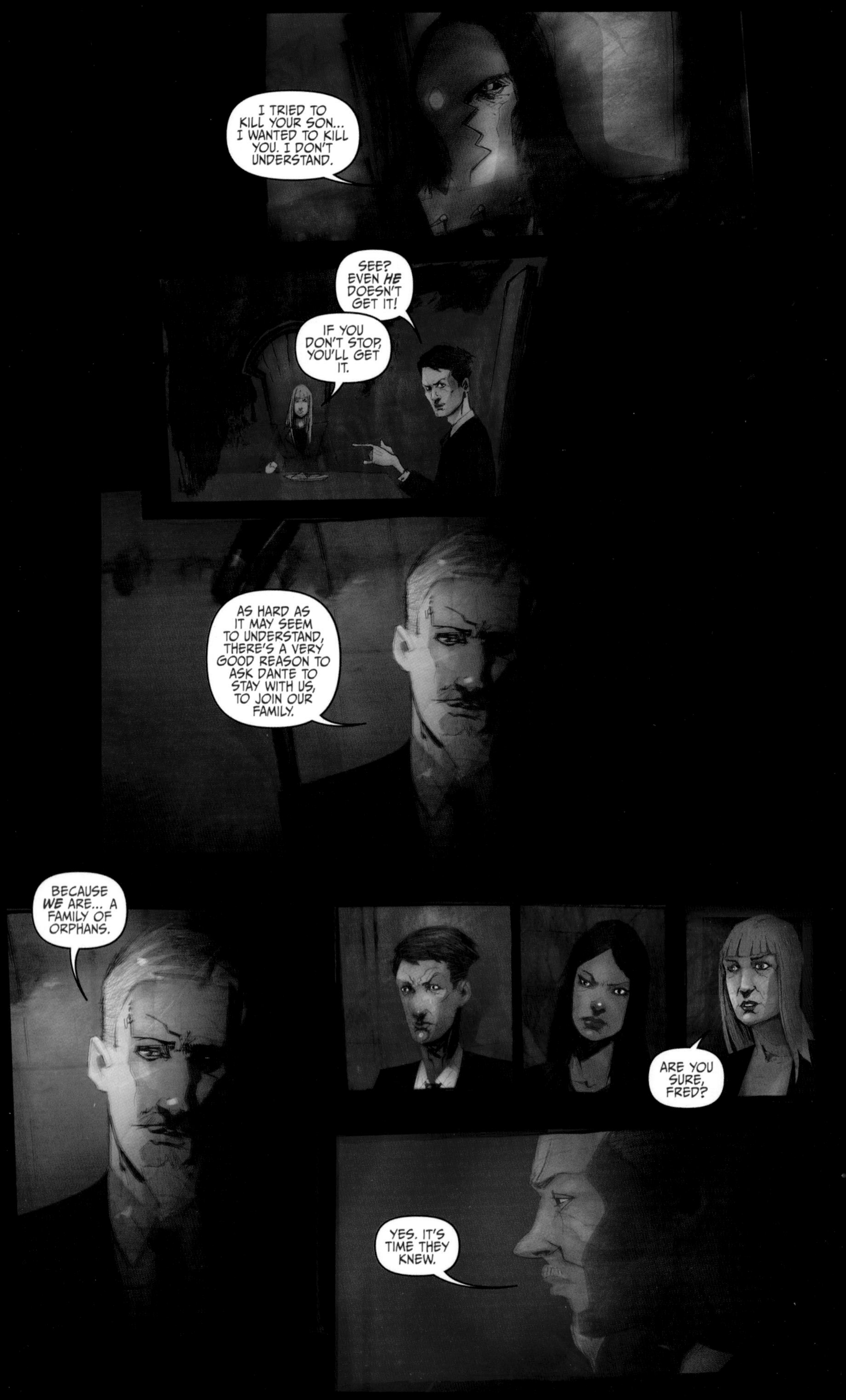
I TRIED TO KILL YOUR SON... I WANTED TO KILL YOU. I DON'T UNDERSTAND.
SEE? EVEN HE DOESN'T GET IT!
IF YOU DON'T STOP, YOU'LL GET IT.
AS HARD AS IT MAY SEEM TO UNDERSTAND, THERE'S A VERY GOOD REASON TO ASK DANTE TO STAY WITH US, TO JOIN OUR FAMILY.
BECAUSE WE ARE... A FAMILY OF ORPHANS.
ARE YOU SURE, FRED?
YES. IT'S TIME THEY KNEW.

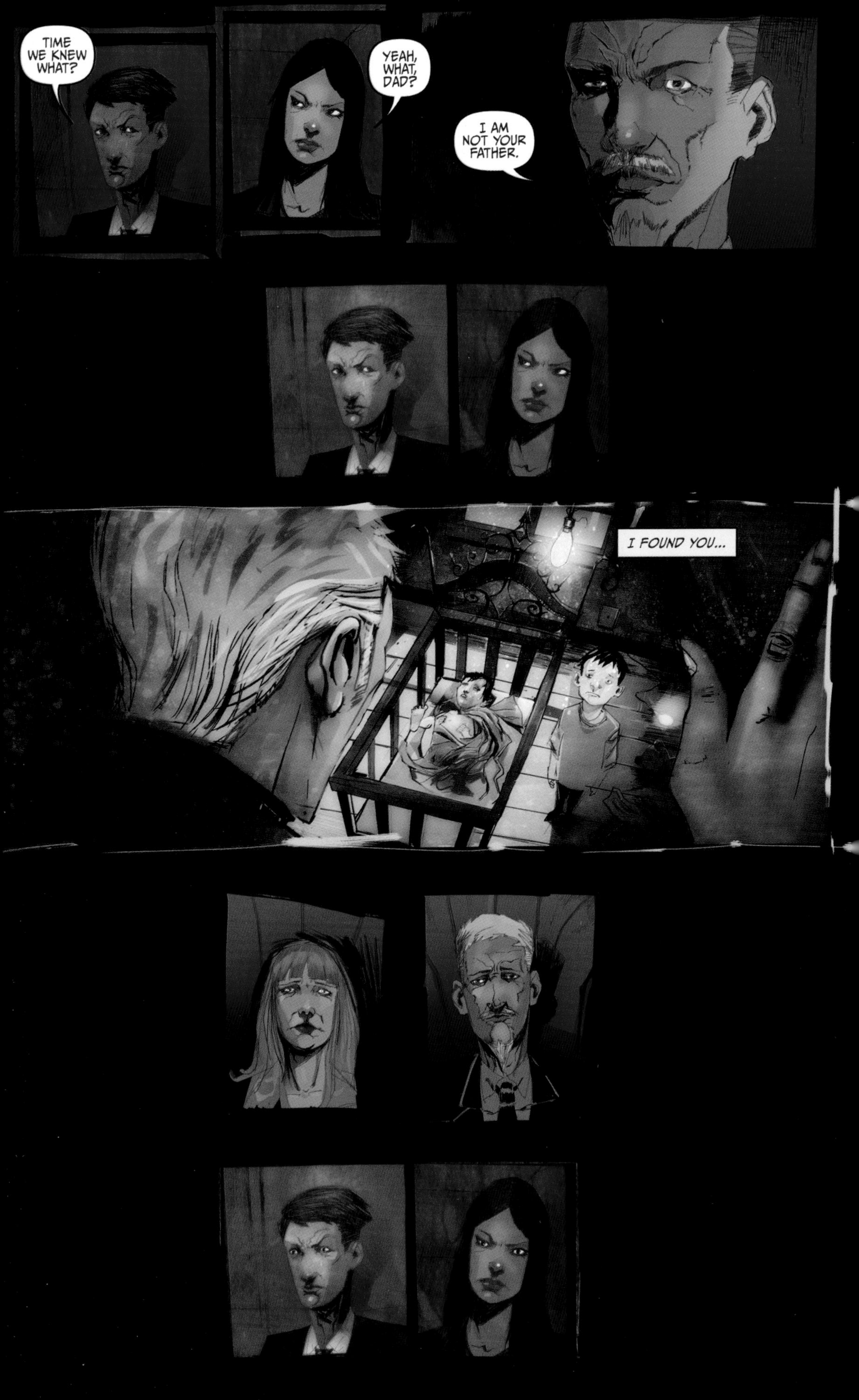
TIME WE KNEW WHAT?
YEAH, WHAT, DAD?
I AM NOT YOUR FATHER.
I FOUND YOU...

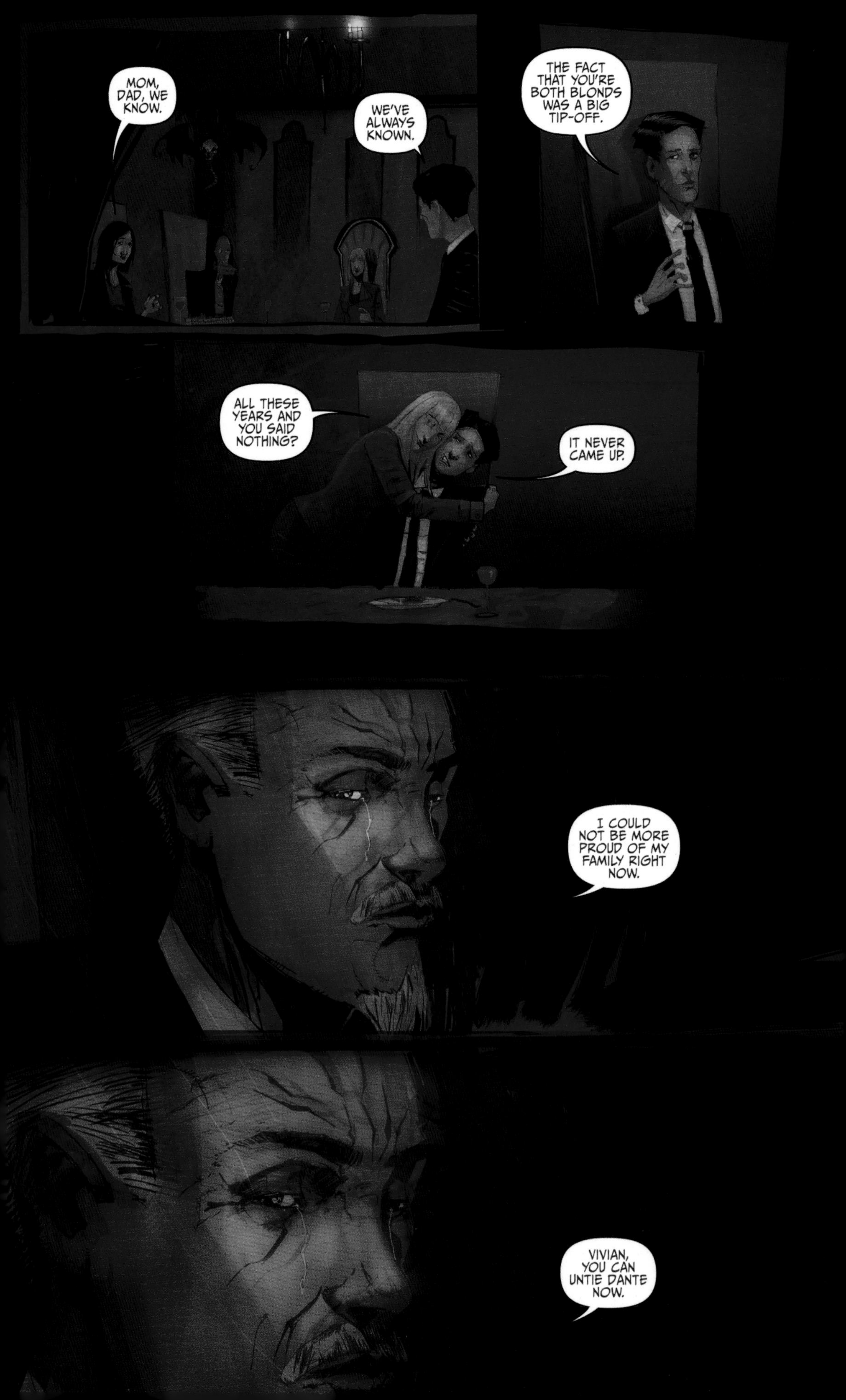
MOM, DAD, WE KNOW.
WE'VE ALWAYS KNOWN.
THE FACT THAT YOU'RE BOTH BLONDS WAS A BIG TIP-OFF.
ALL THESE YEARS AND YOU SAID NOTHING?
IT NEVER CAME UP.
I COULD NOT BE MORE PROUD OF MY FAMILY RIGHT NOW.
VIVIAN, YOU CAN UNTIE DANTE NOW.

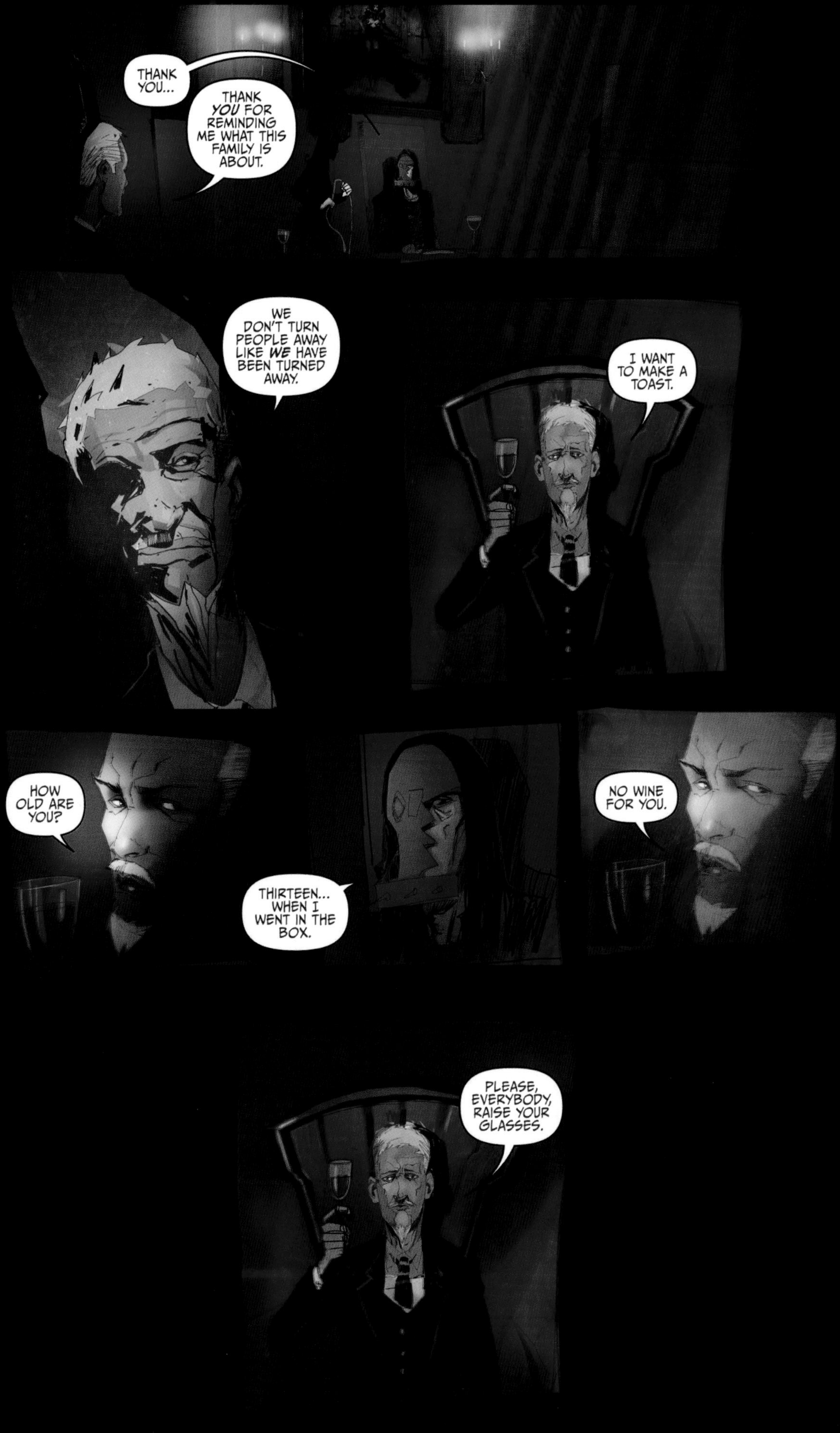
THANK YOU...
THANK YOU FOR REMINDING ME WHAT THIS FAMILY IS ABOUT.
WE DON'T TURN PEOPLE AWAY LIKE WE HAVE BEEN TURNED AWAY.
I WANT TO MAKE A TOAST.
HOW OLD ARE YOU?
THIRTEEN... WHEN I WENT IN THE BOX.
NO WINE FOR YOU.
PLEASE, EVERYBODY, RAISE YOUR GLASSES.

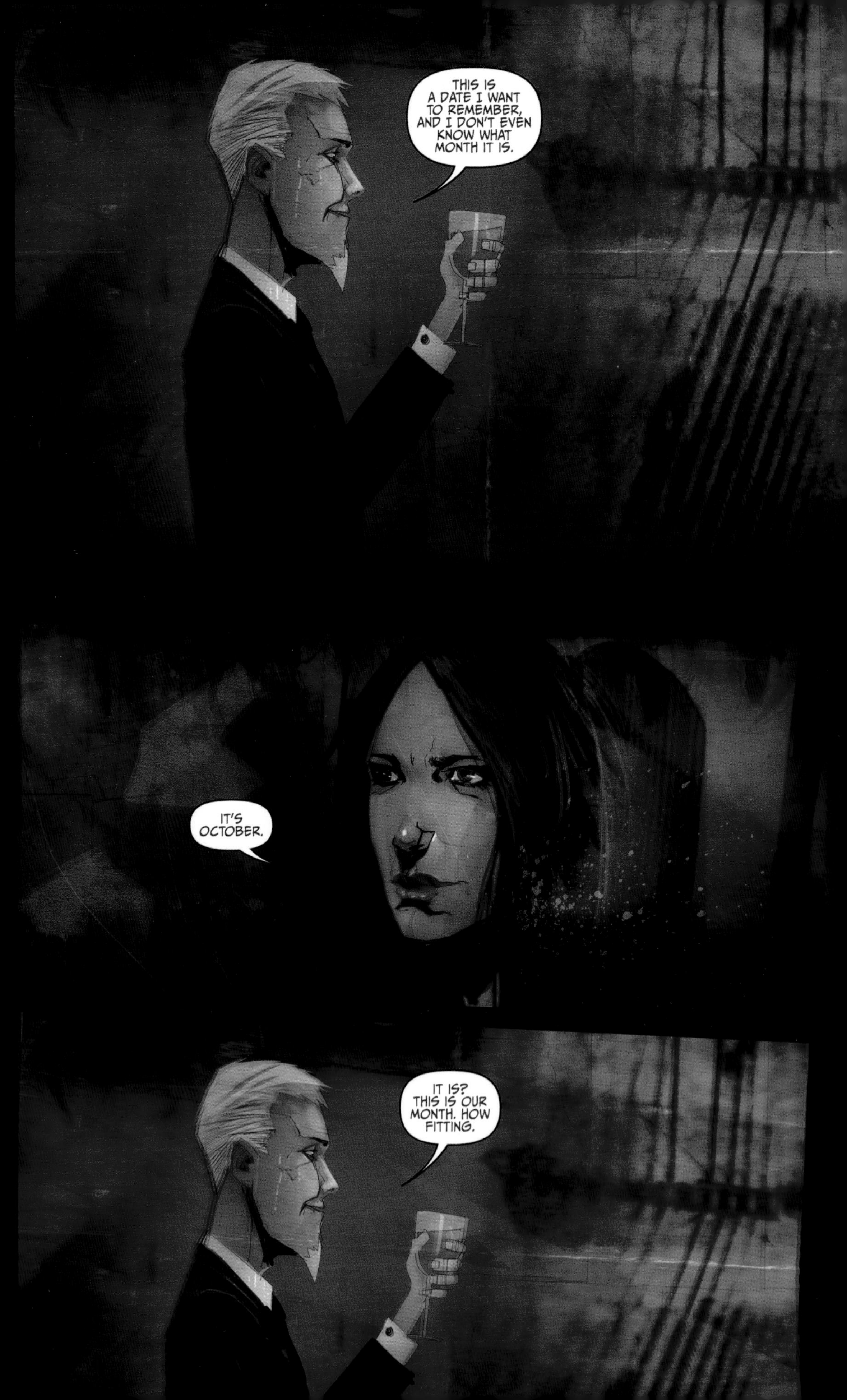
THIS IS A DATE I WANT TO REMEMBER, AND I DON'T EVEN KNOW WHAT MONTH IT IS.
IT'S OCTOBER.
IT IS? THIS IS OUR MONTH. HOW FITTING.

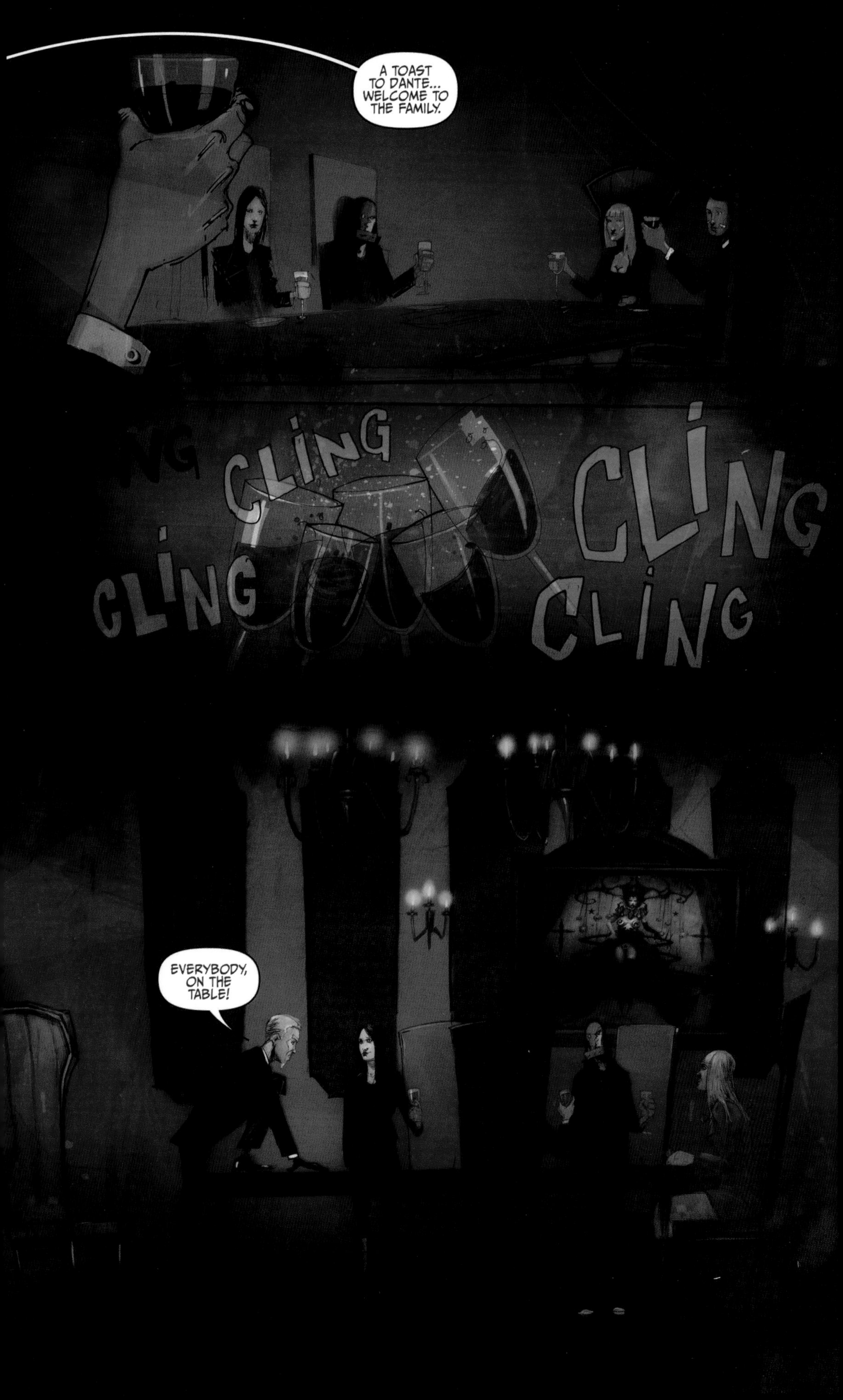
A TOAST TO DANTE... WELCOME TO THE FAMILY.
CLING
CLING
CLING
CLING
EVERYBODY, ON THE TABLE!

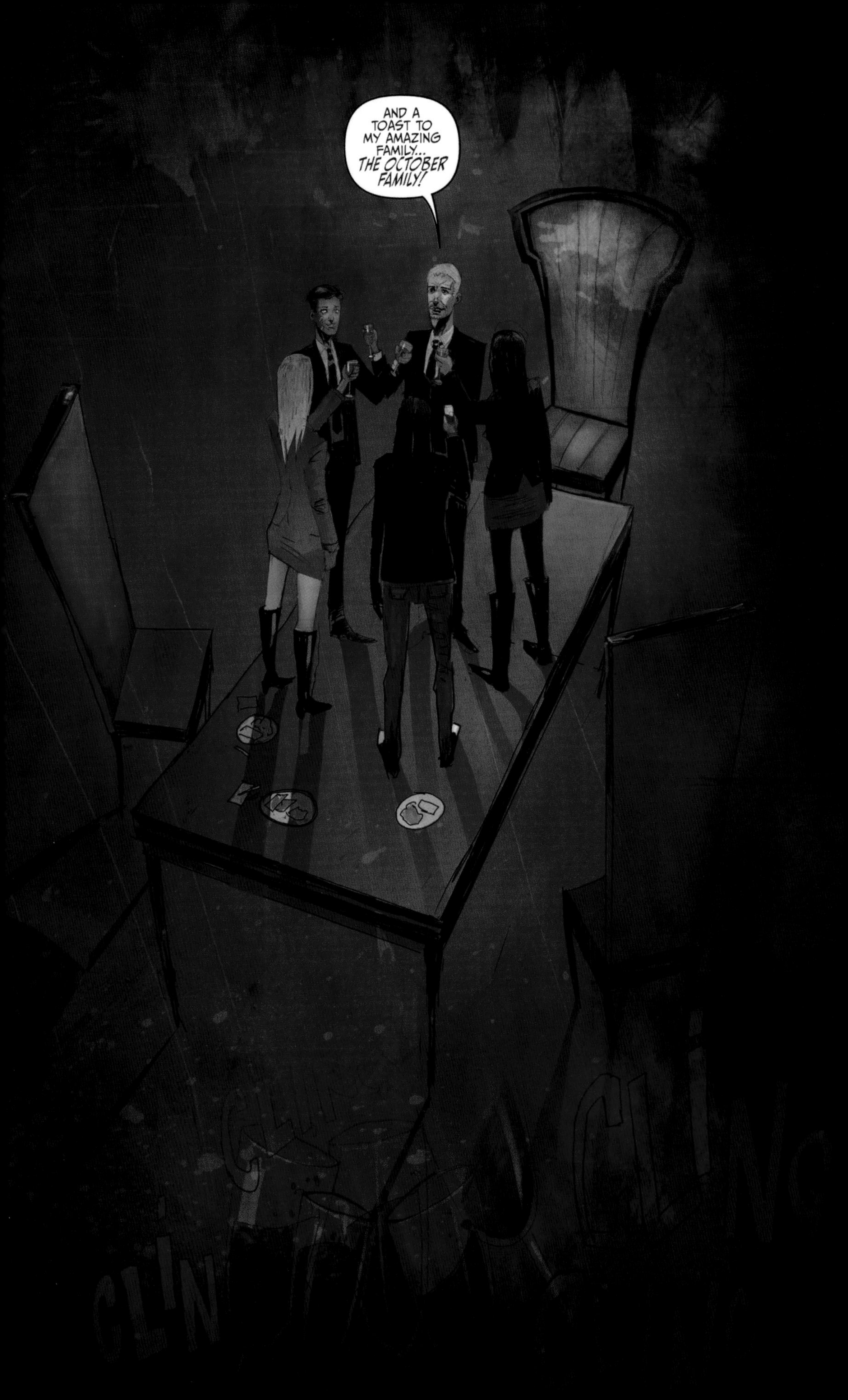
AND A TOAST TO MY AMAZING FAMILY... THE OCTOBER FAMILY!

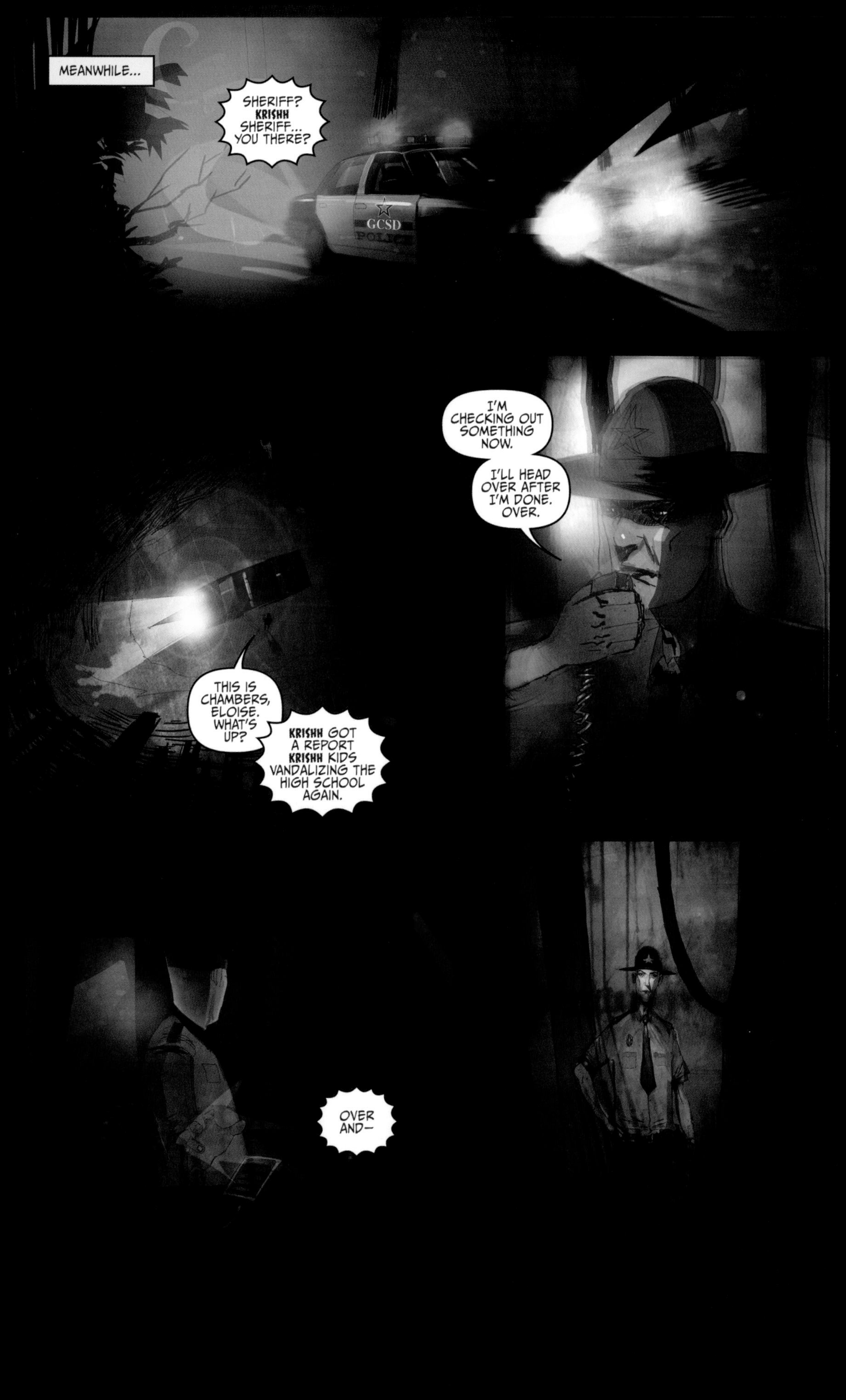
MEANWHILE...
SHERIFF? KRISHH SHERIFF... YOU THERE?
I'M CHECKING OUT SOMETHING NOW.
I'LL HEAD OVER AFTER I'M DONE. OVER.
THIS IS CHAMBERS, ELOISE. WHAT'S UP?
KRISHH GOT A REPORT KRISHH KIDS VANDALIZING THE HIGH SCHOOL AGAIN.
OVER AND—

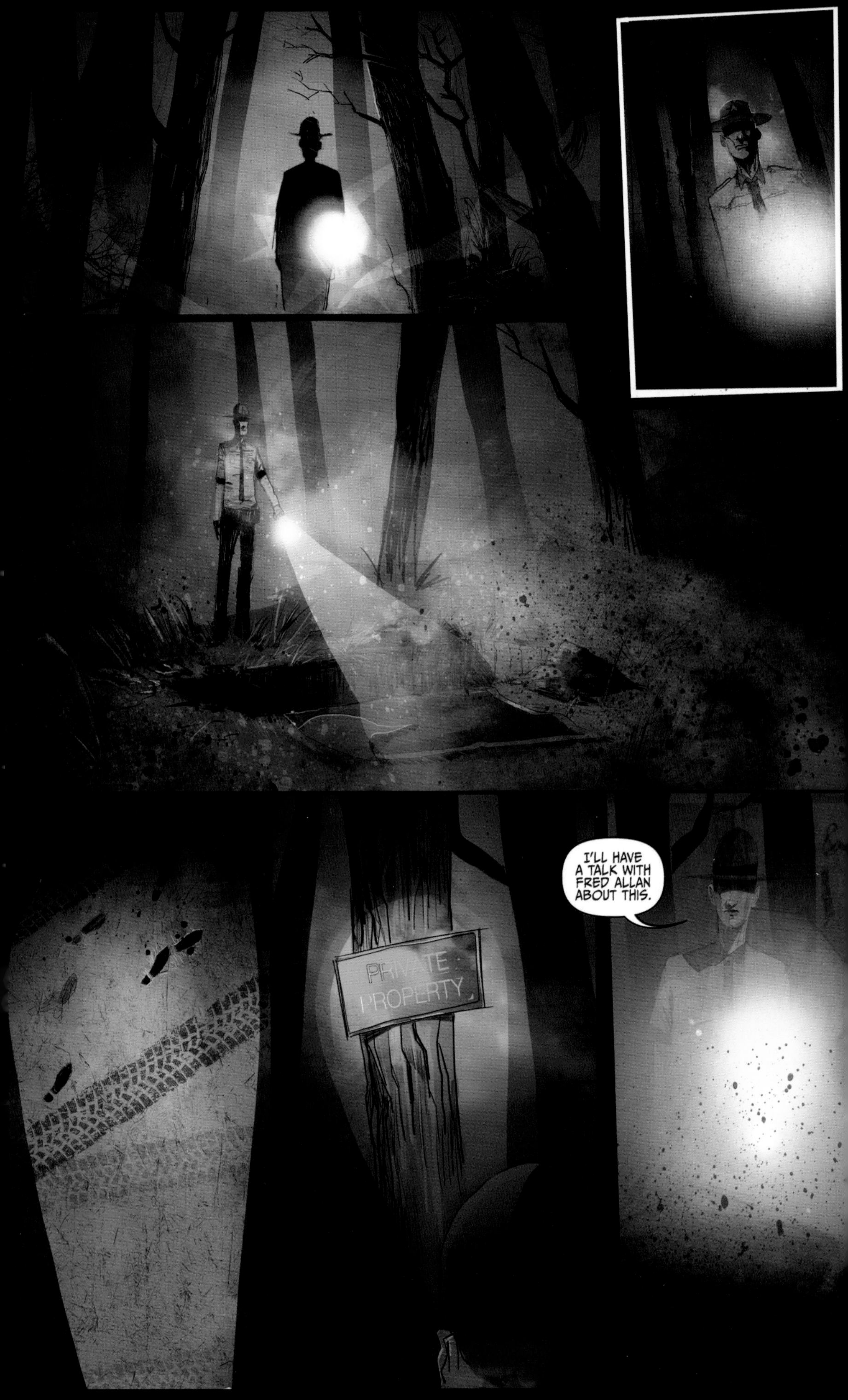
PRIVATE PROPERTY
I'LL HAVE A TALK WITH FRED ALLAN ABOUT THIS.

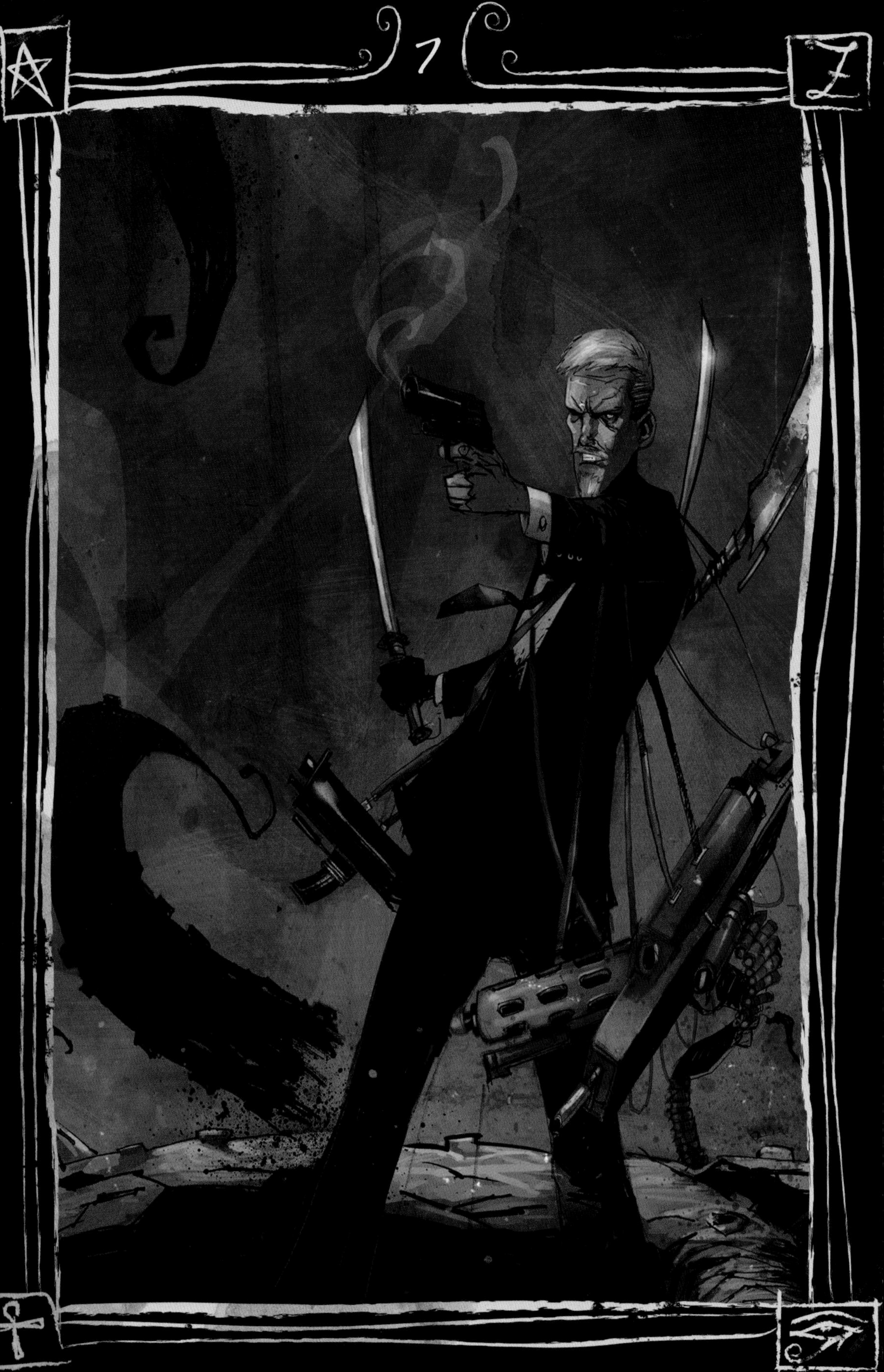
7

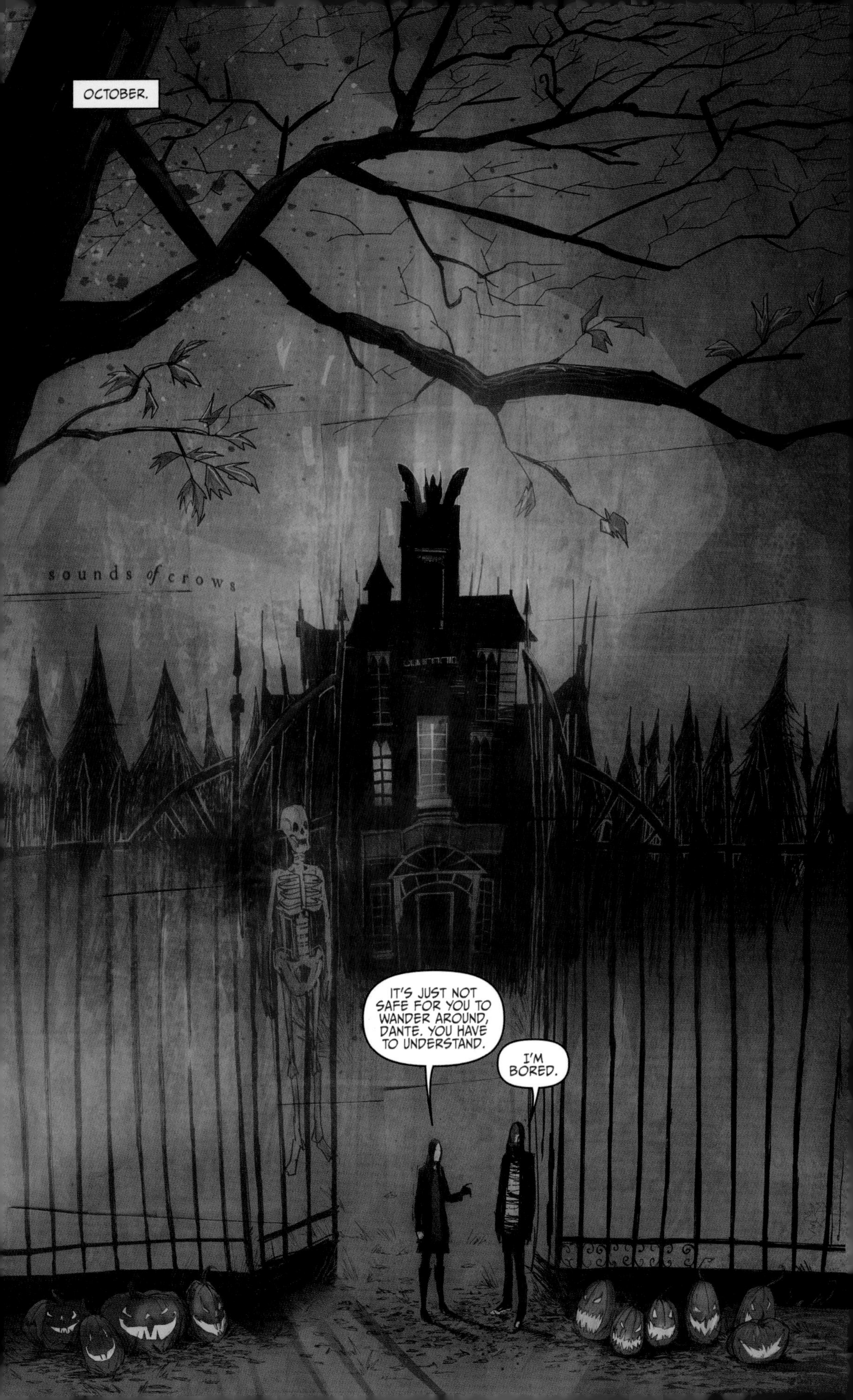
OCTOBER.
sounds of crows
IT'S JUST NOT SAFE FOR YOU TO WANDER AROUND, DANTE. YOU HAVE TO UNDERSTAND.
I'M BORED.

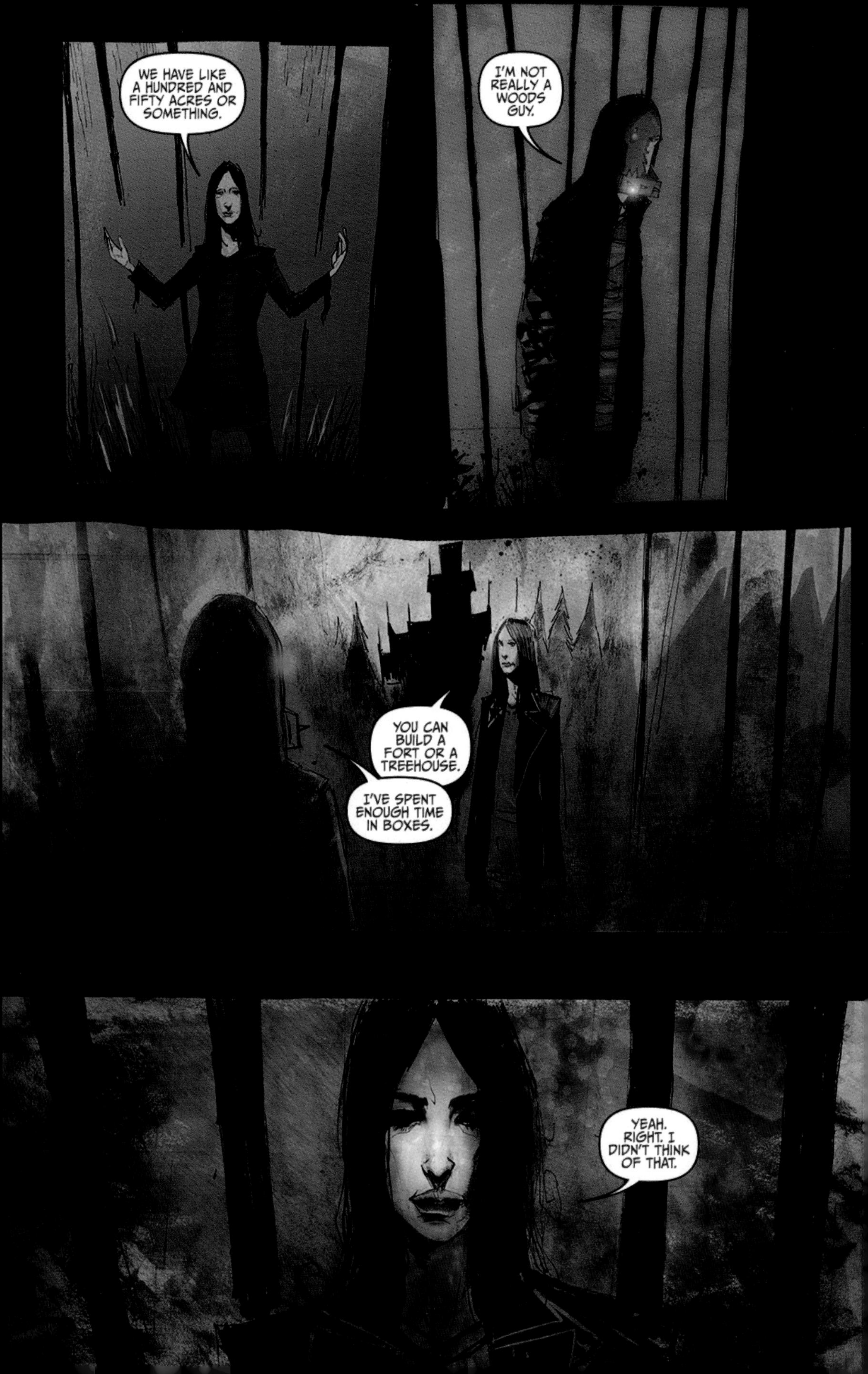
WE HAVE LIKE A HUNDRED AND FIFTY ACRES OR SOMETHING.
I'M NOT REALLY A WOODS GUY.
YOU CAN BUILD A FORT OR A TREEHOUSE.
I'VE SPENT ENOUGH TIME IN BOXES.
YEAH. RIGHT. I DIDN'T THINK OF THAT.

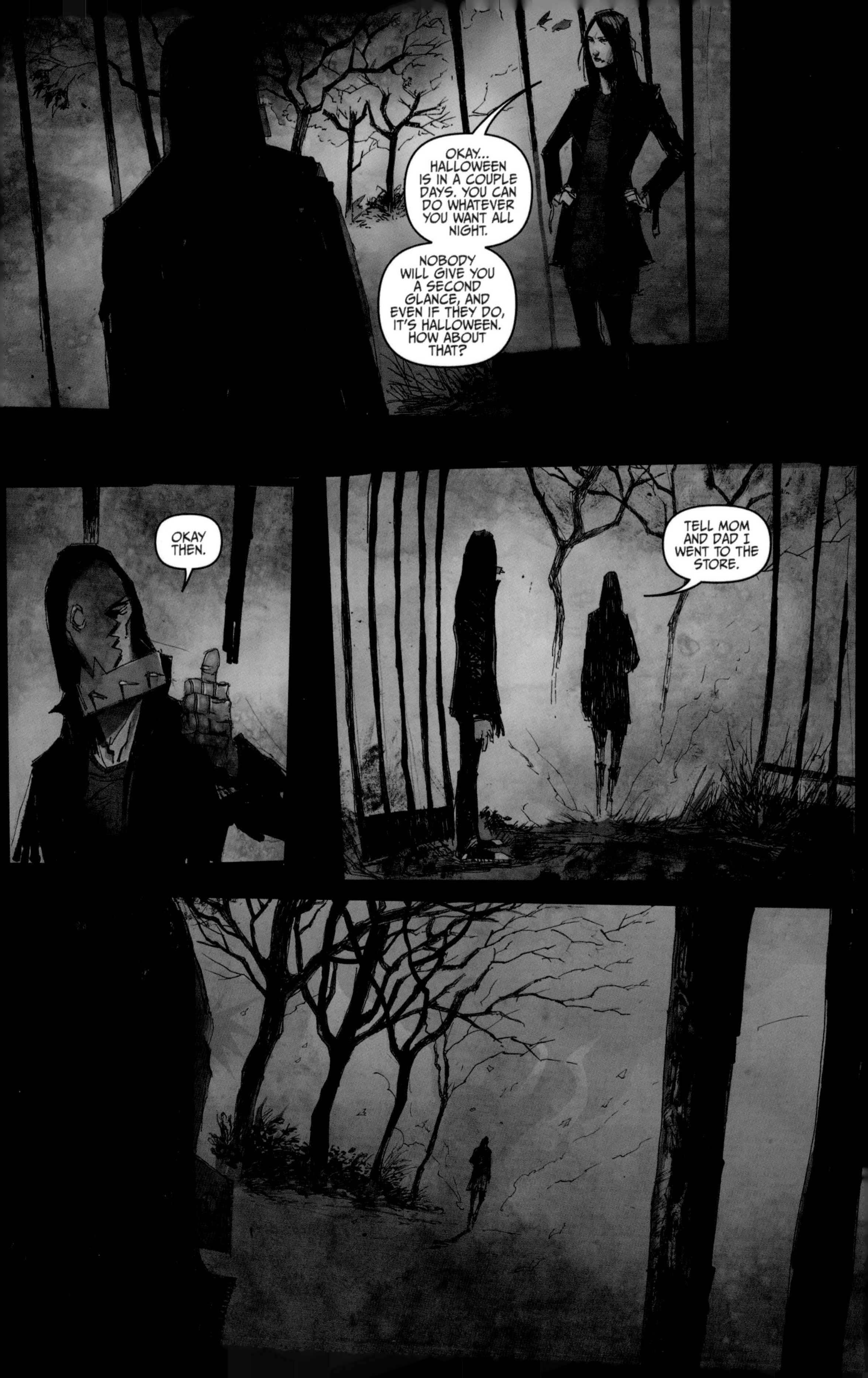
OKAY... HALLOWEEN IS IN A COUPLE DAYS. YOU CAN DO WHATEVER YOU WANT ALL NIGHT.
NOBODY WILL GIVE YOU A SECOND GLANCE, AND EVEN IF THEY DO, IT'S HALLOWEEN. HOW ABOUT THAT?
OKAY THEN.
TELL MOM AND DAD I WENT TO THE STORE.

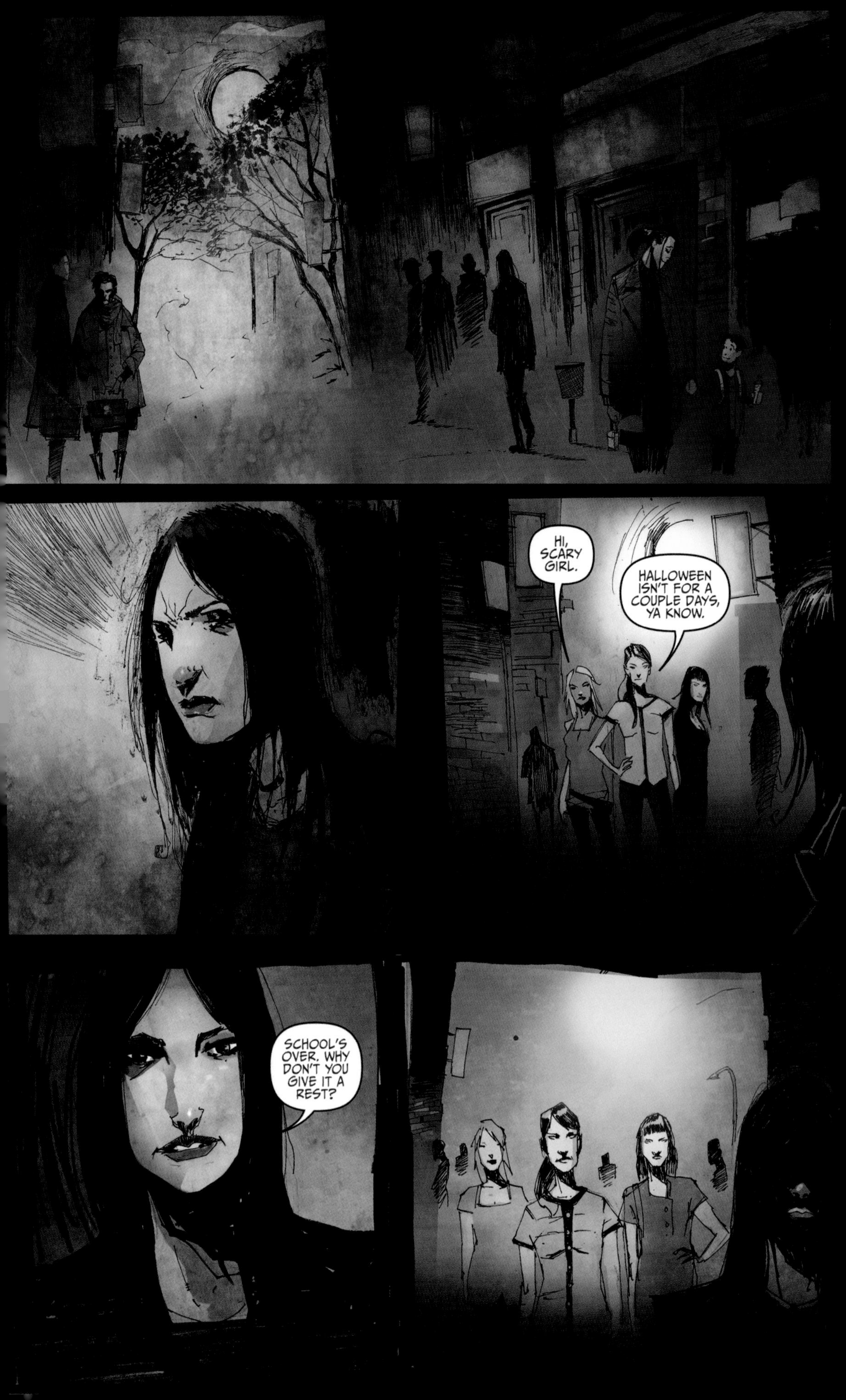
HI, SCARY GIRL.
HALLOWEEN ISN'T FOR A COUPLE DAYS, YA KNOW.
SCHOOL'S OVER. WHY DON'T YOU GIVE IT A REST?

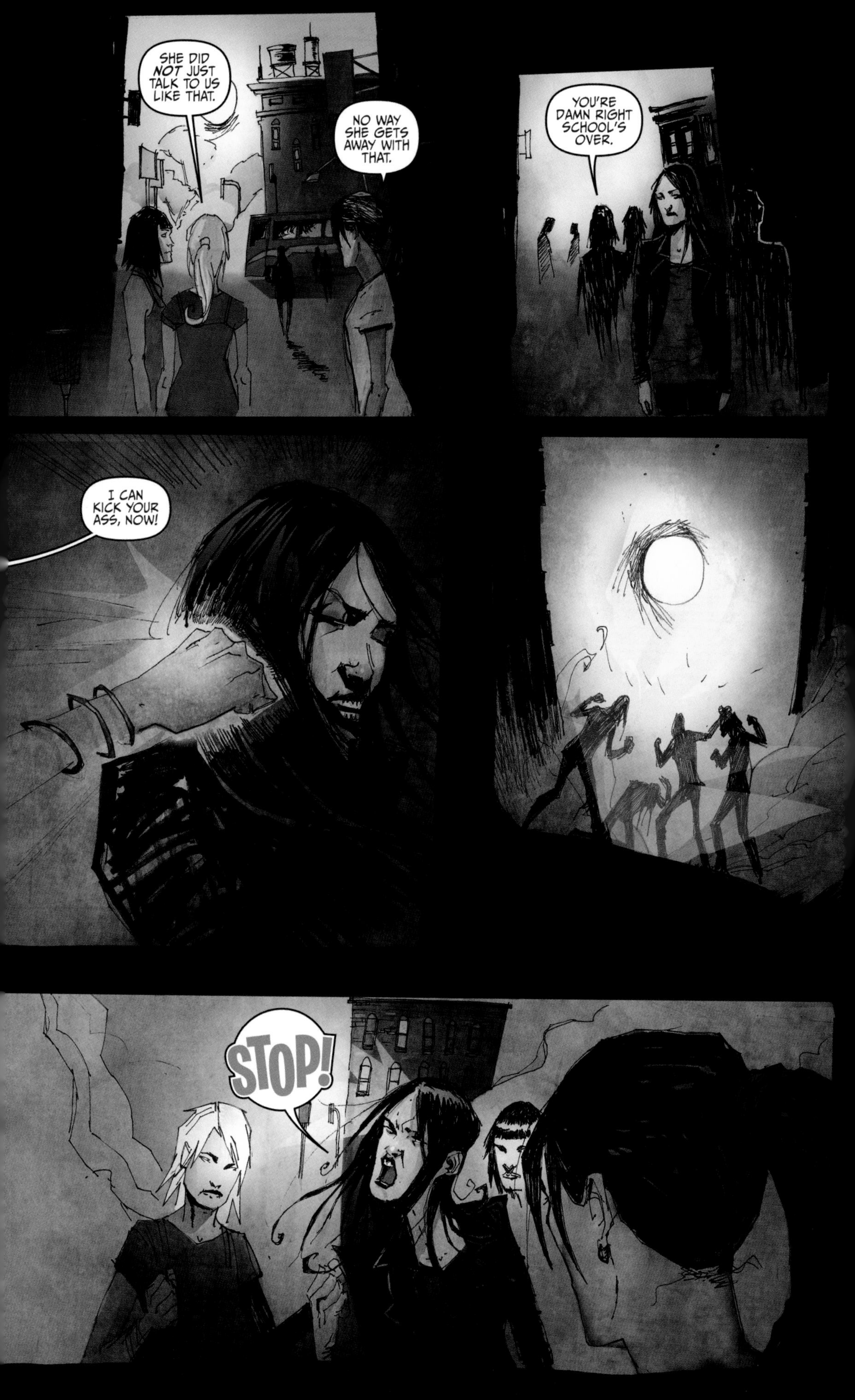

SHE DID *NOT* JUST TALK TO US LIKE THAT.
NO WAY SHE GETS AWAY WITH THAT.
YOU'RE DAMN RIGHT SCHOOL'S OVER.
I CAN KICK YOUR ASS, NOW!
STOP!

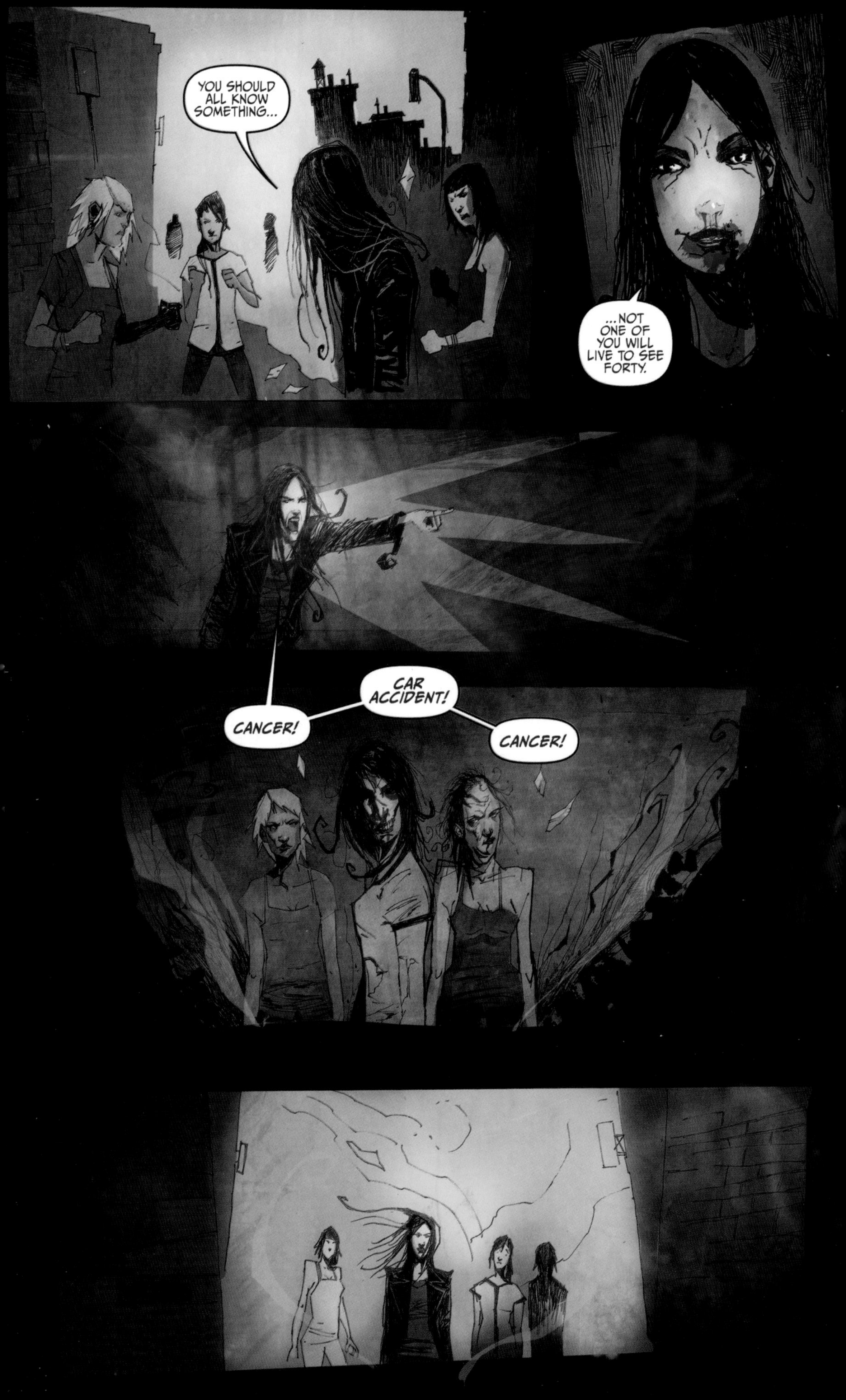
YOU SHOULD ALL KNOW SOMETHING...
...NOT ONE OF YOU WILL LIVE TO SEE FORTY.
CANCER!
CAR ACCIDENT!
CANCER!

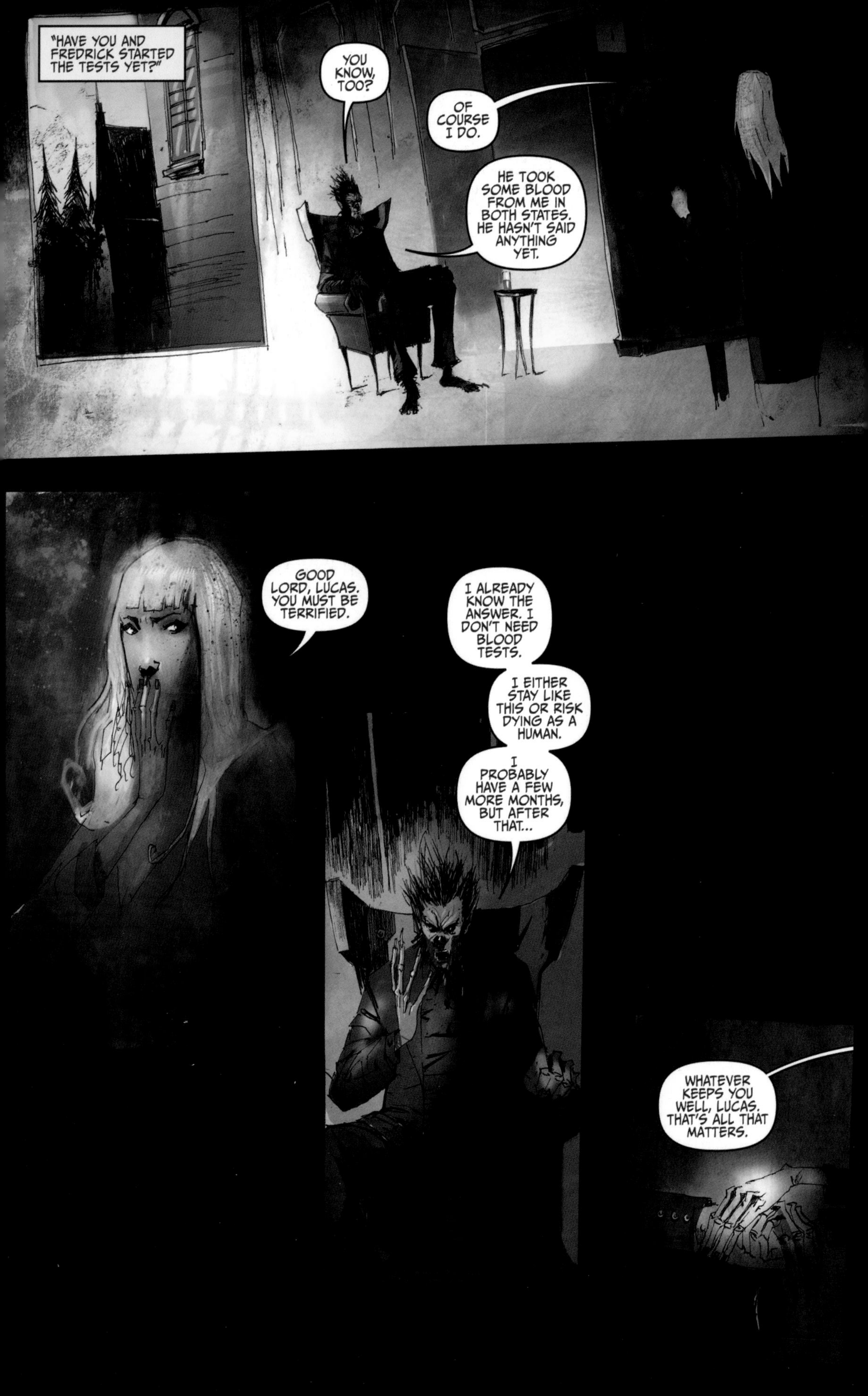
"HAVE YOU AND FREDRICK STARTED THE TESTS YET?"
YOU KNOW, TOO?
OF COURSE I DO.
HE TOOK SOME BLOOD FROM ME IN BOTH STATES. HE HASN'T SAID ANYTHING YET.
GOOD LORD, LUCAS. YOU MUST BE TERRIFIED.
I ALREADY KNOW THE ANSWER. I DON'T NEED BLOOD TESTS.
I EITHER STAY LIKE THIS OR RISK DYING AS A HUMAN.
I PROBABLY HAVE A FEW MORE MONTHS, BUT AFTER THAT...
WHATEVER KEEPS YOU WELL, LUCAS. THAT'S ALL THAT MATTERS.

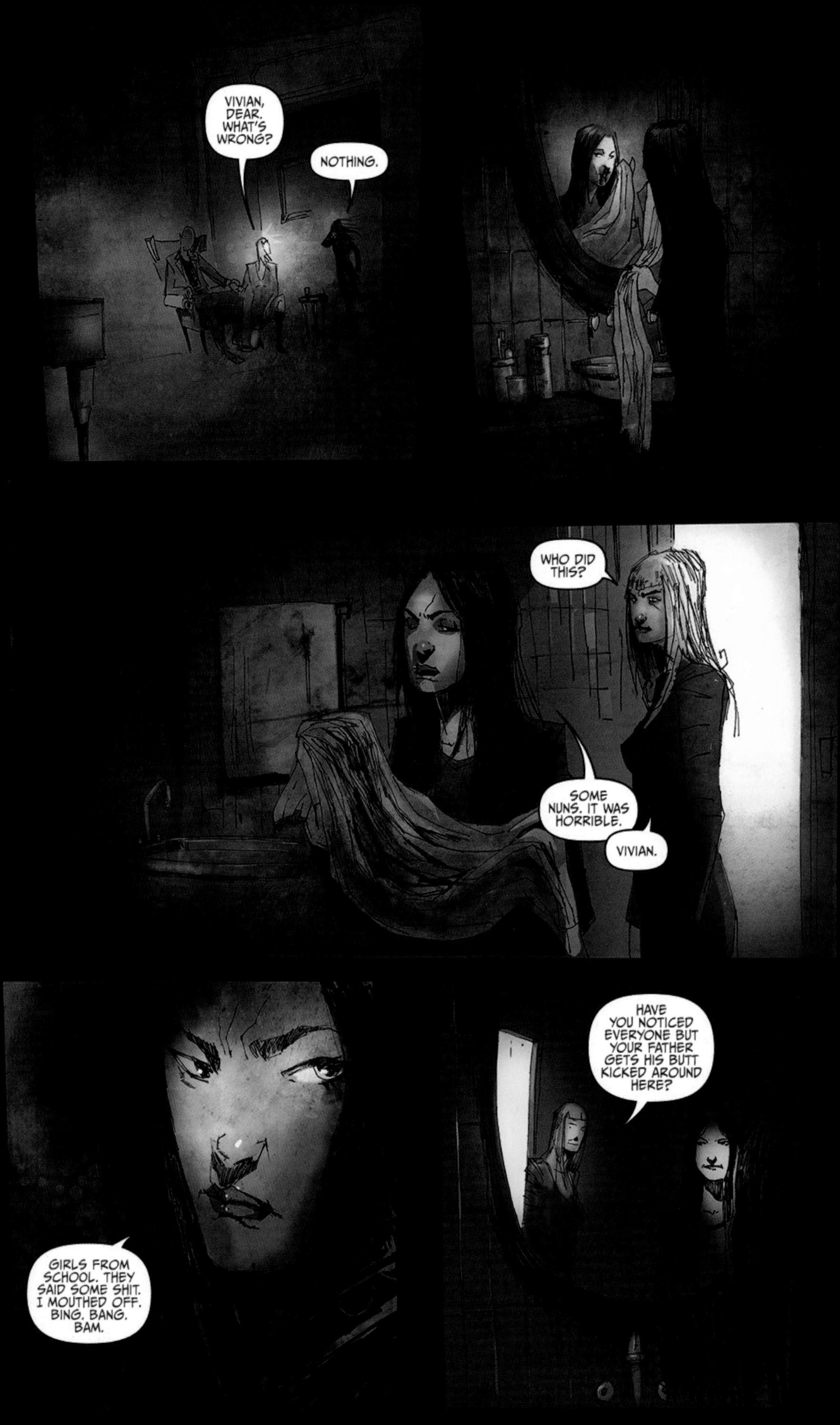
VIVIAN, DEAR. WHAT'S WRONG?
NOTHING.
WHO DID THIS?
SOME NUNS. IT WAS HORRIBLE.
VIVIAN.
GIRLS FROM SCHOOL. THEY SAID SOME SHIT. I MOUTHED OFF. BING. BANG. BAM.
HAVE YOU NOTICED EVERYONE BUT YOUR FATHER GETS HIS BUTT KICKED AROUND HERE?

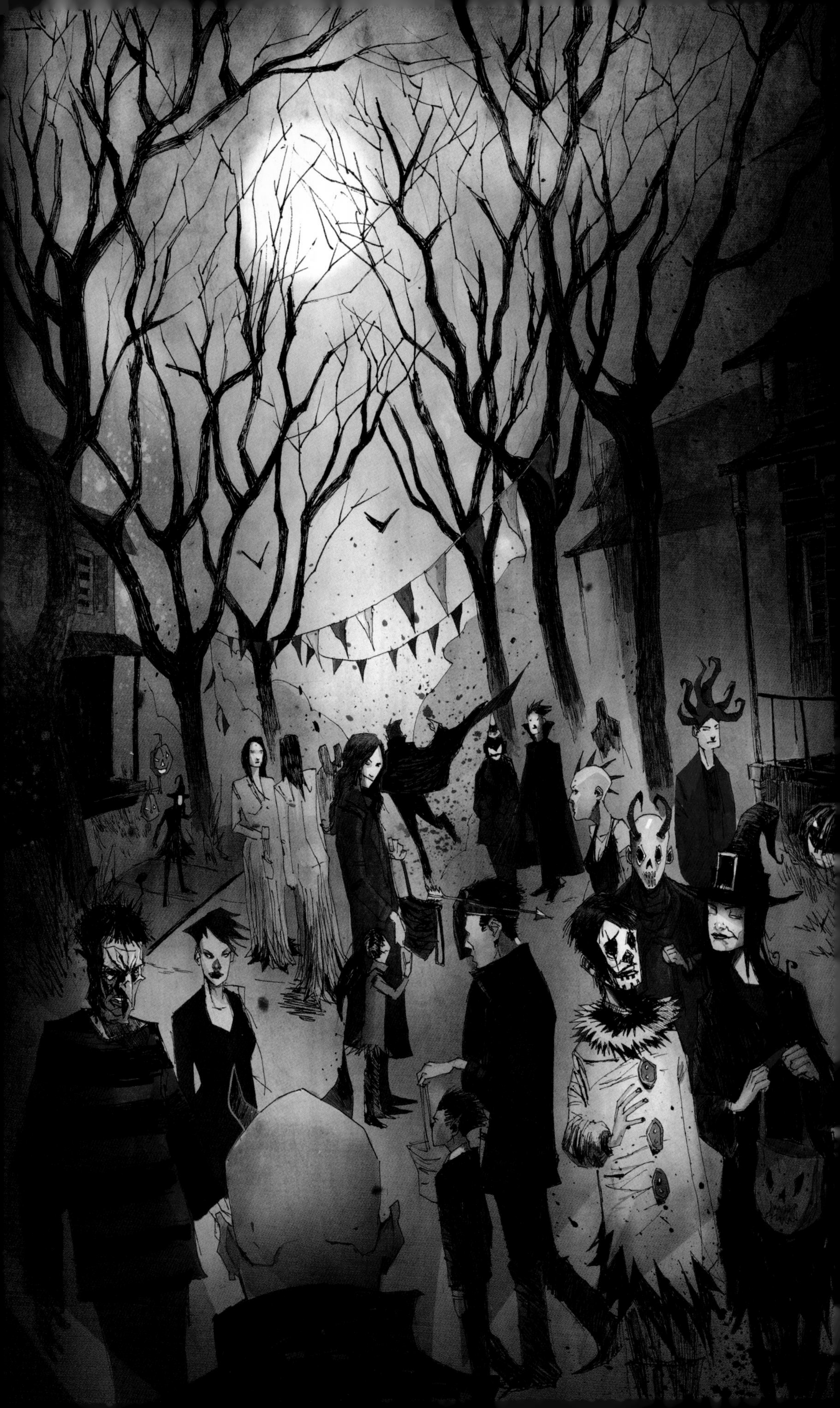

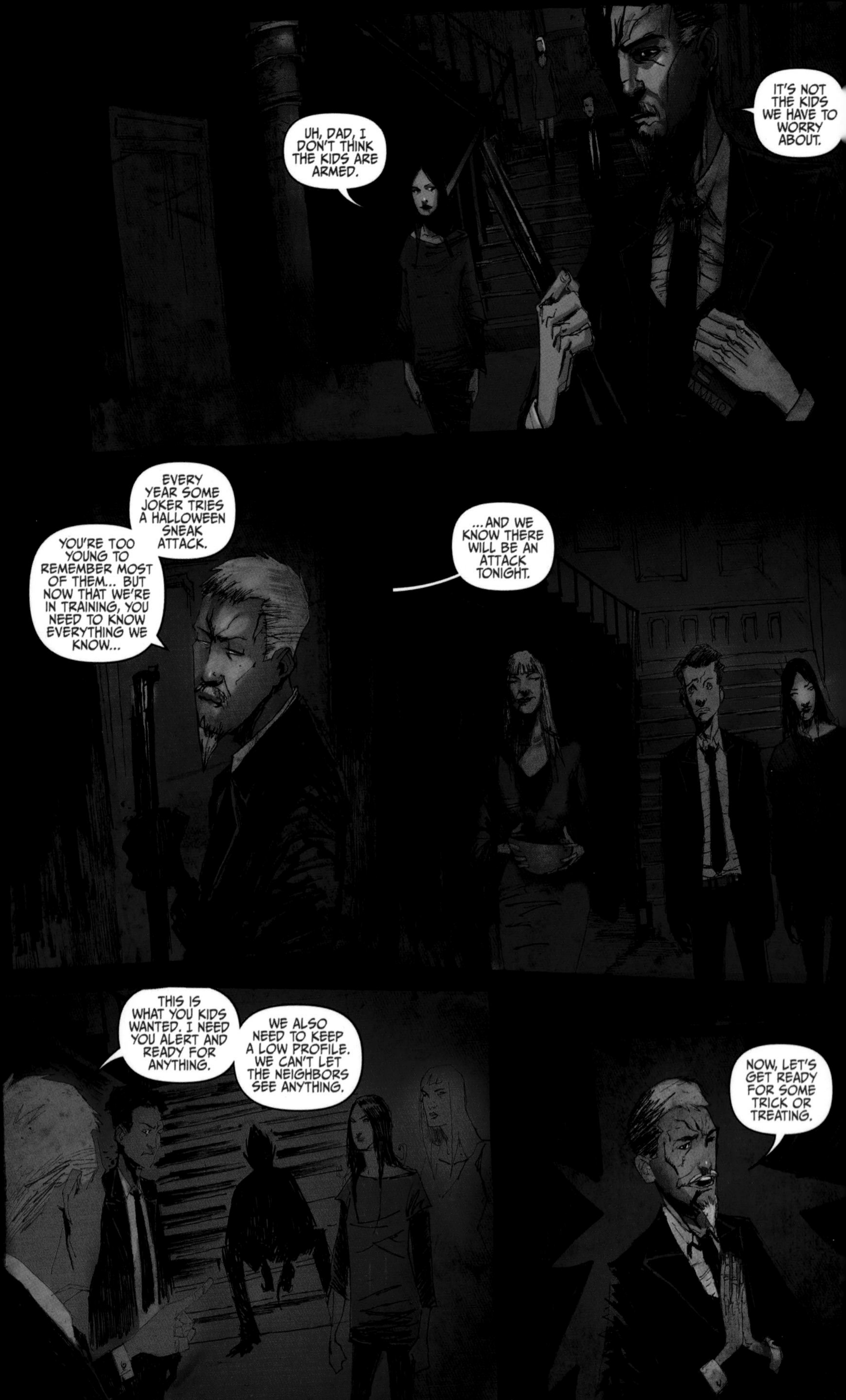
UH, DAD, I DON'T THINK THE KIDS ARE ARMED.
IT'S NOT THE KIDS WE HAVE TO WORRY ABOUT.
EVERY YEAR SOME JOKER TRIES A HALLOWEEN SNEAK ATTACK.
YOU'RE TOO YOUNG TO REMEMBER MOST OF THEM... BUT NOW THAT WE'RE IN TRAINING, YOU NEED TO KNOW EVERYTHING WE KNOW...
...AND WE KNOW THERE WILL BE AN ATTACK TONIGHT.
THIS IS WHAT YOU KIDS WANTED. I NEED YOU ALERT AND READY FOR ANYTHING.
WE ALSO NEED TO KEEP A LOW PROFILE. WE CAN'T LET THE NEIGHBORS SEE ANYTHING.
NOW, LET'S GET READY FOR SOME TRICK OR TREATING.

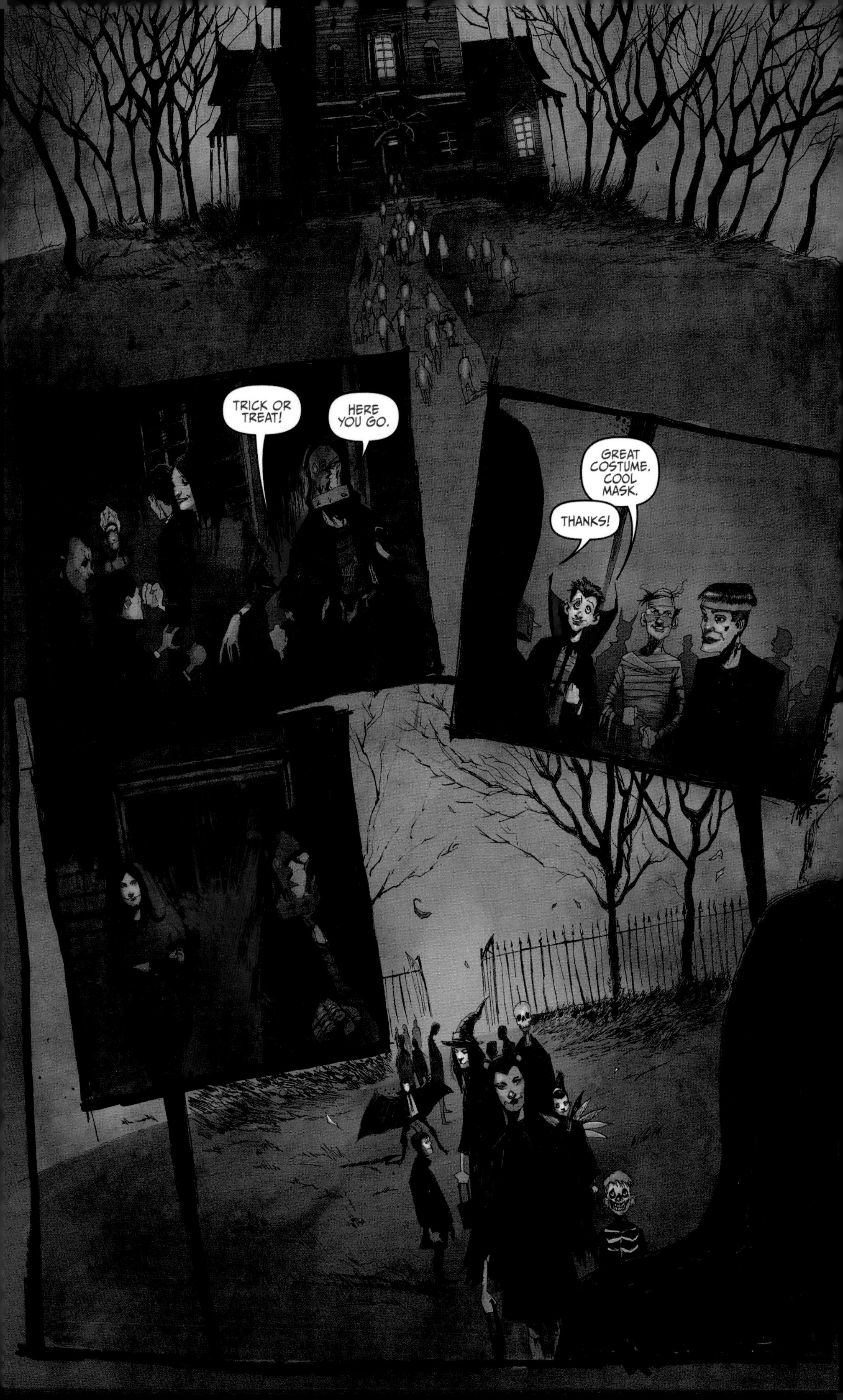
TRICK OR TREAT!
HERE YOU GO.
GREAT COSTUME. COOL MASK.
THANKS!

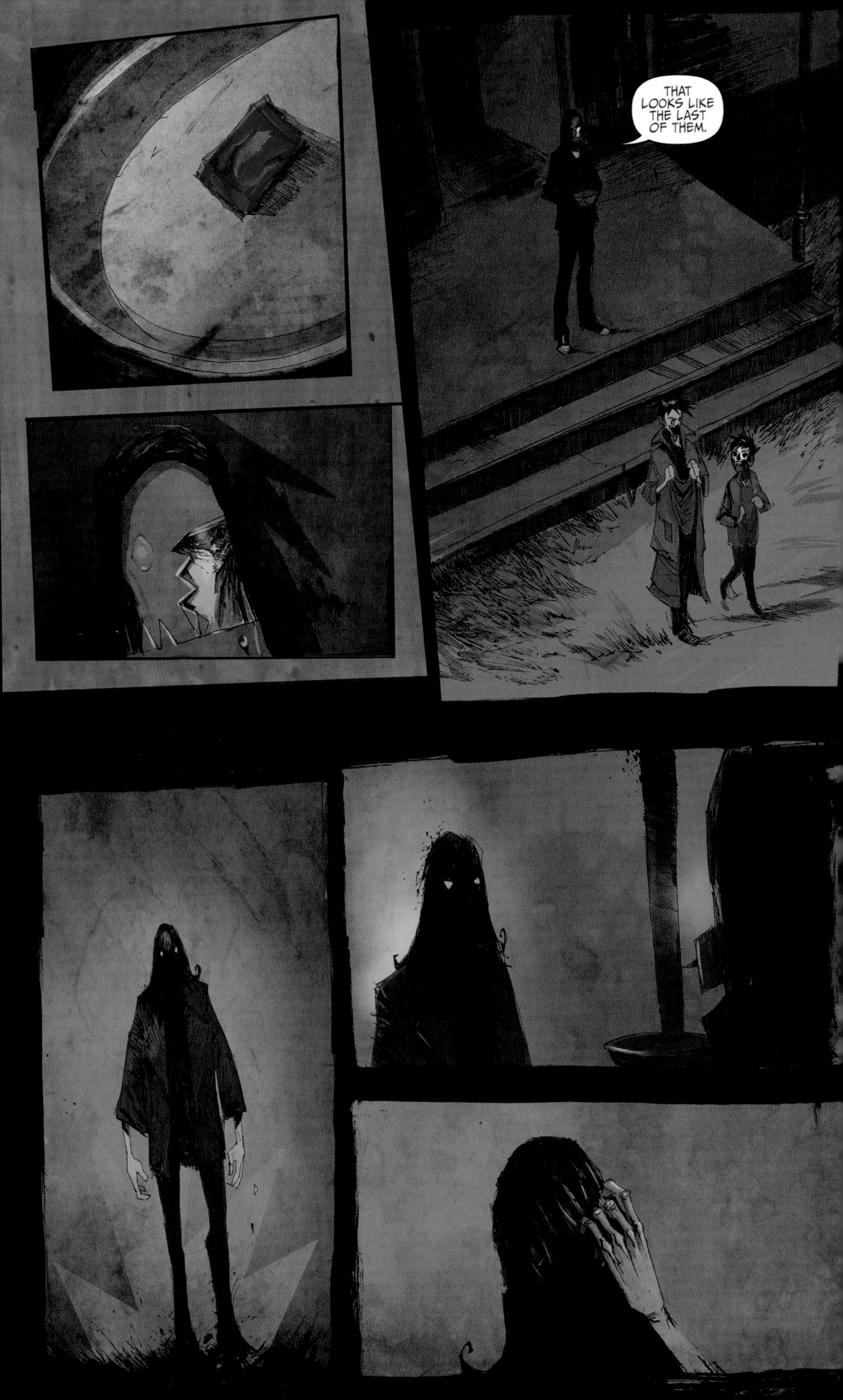
THAT LOOKS LIKE THE LAST OF THEM.

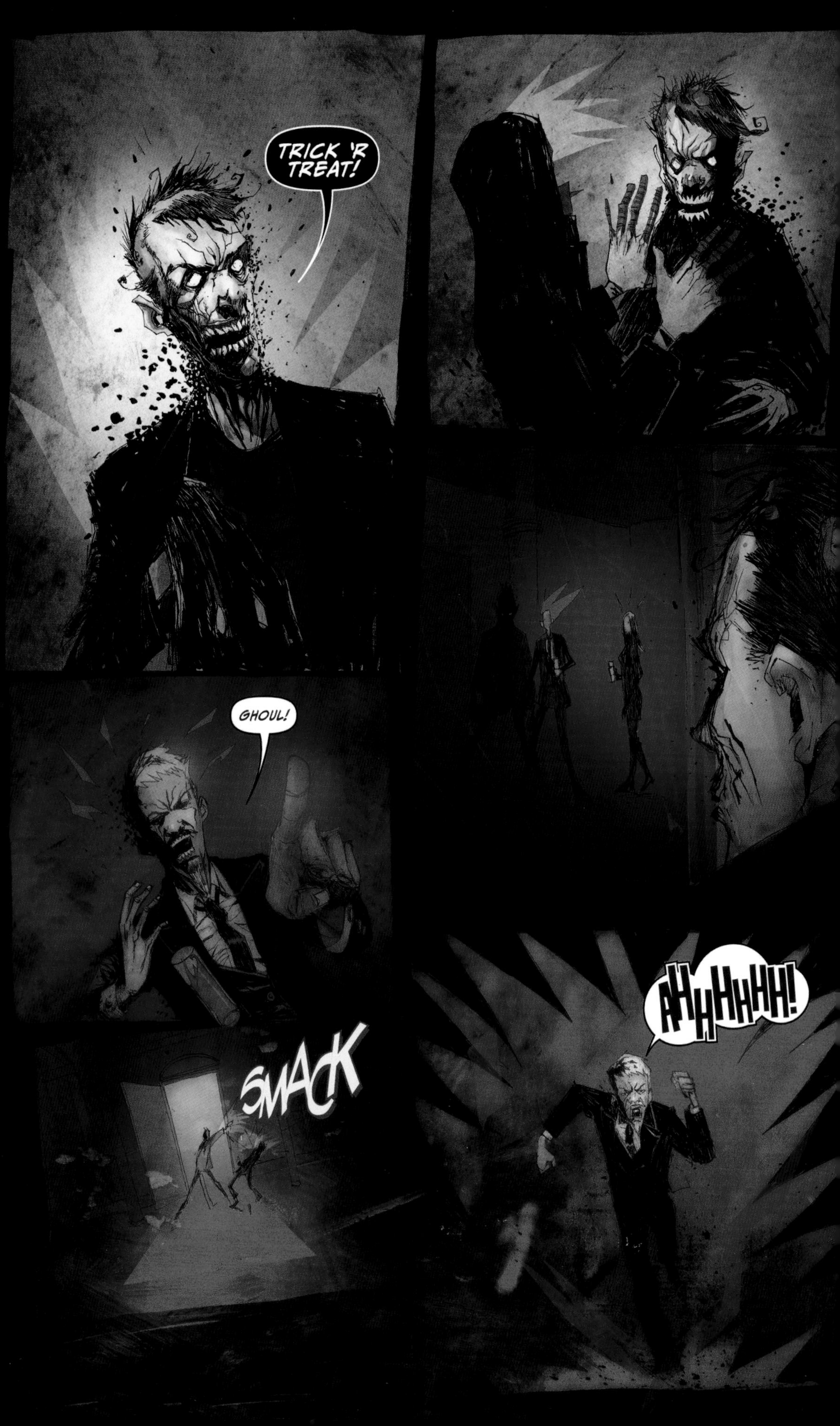
TRICK 'R TREAT!
GHOUL!
SMACK
AHHHHHH!

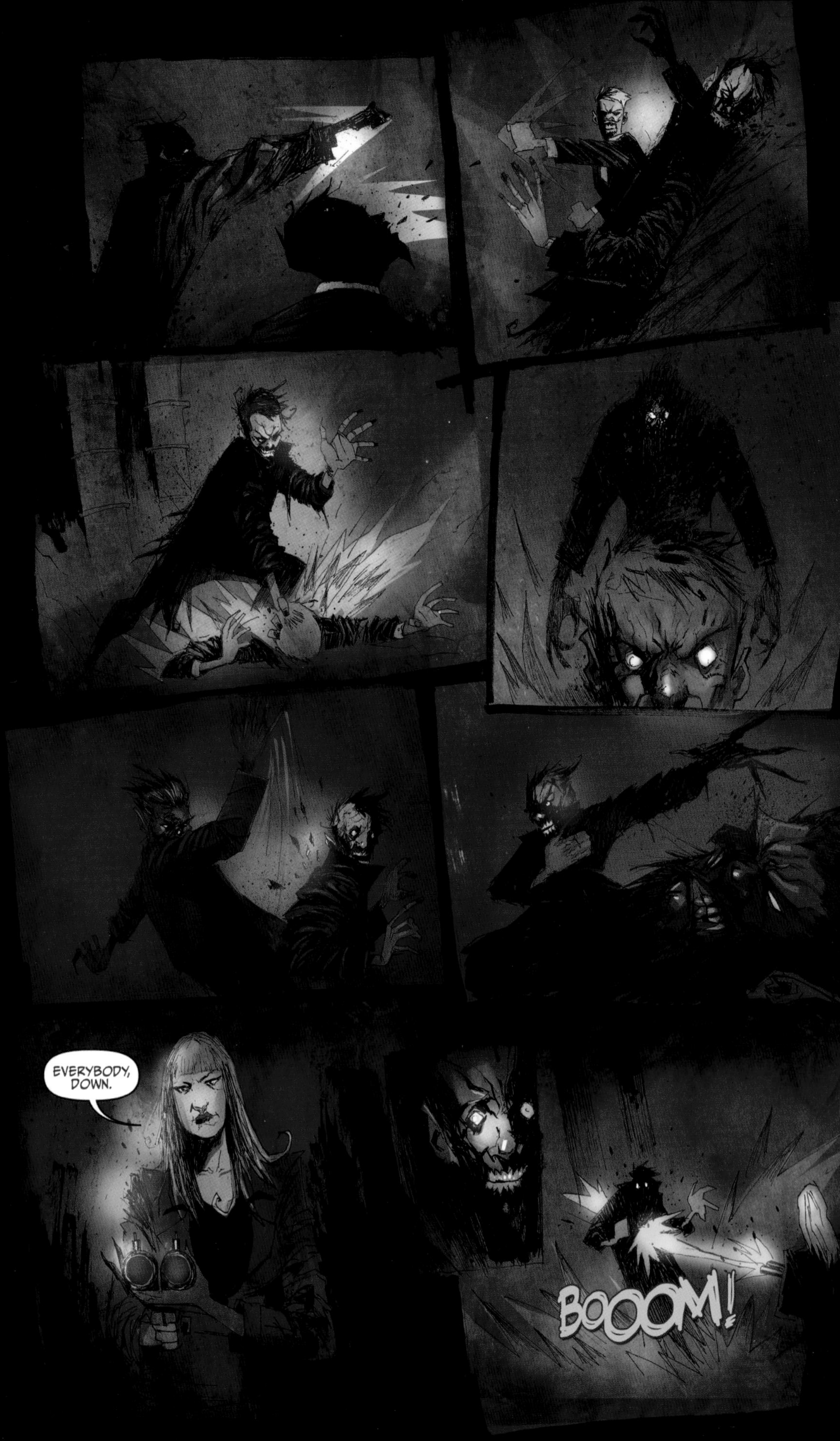
EVERYBODY, DOWN.
BOOOM!

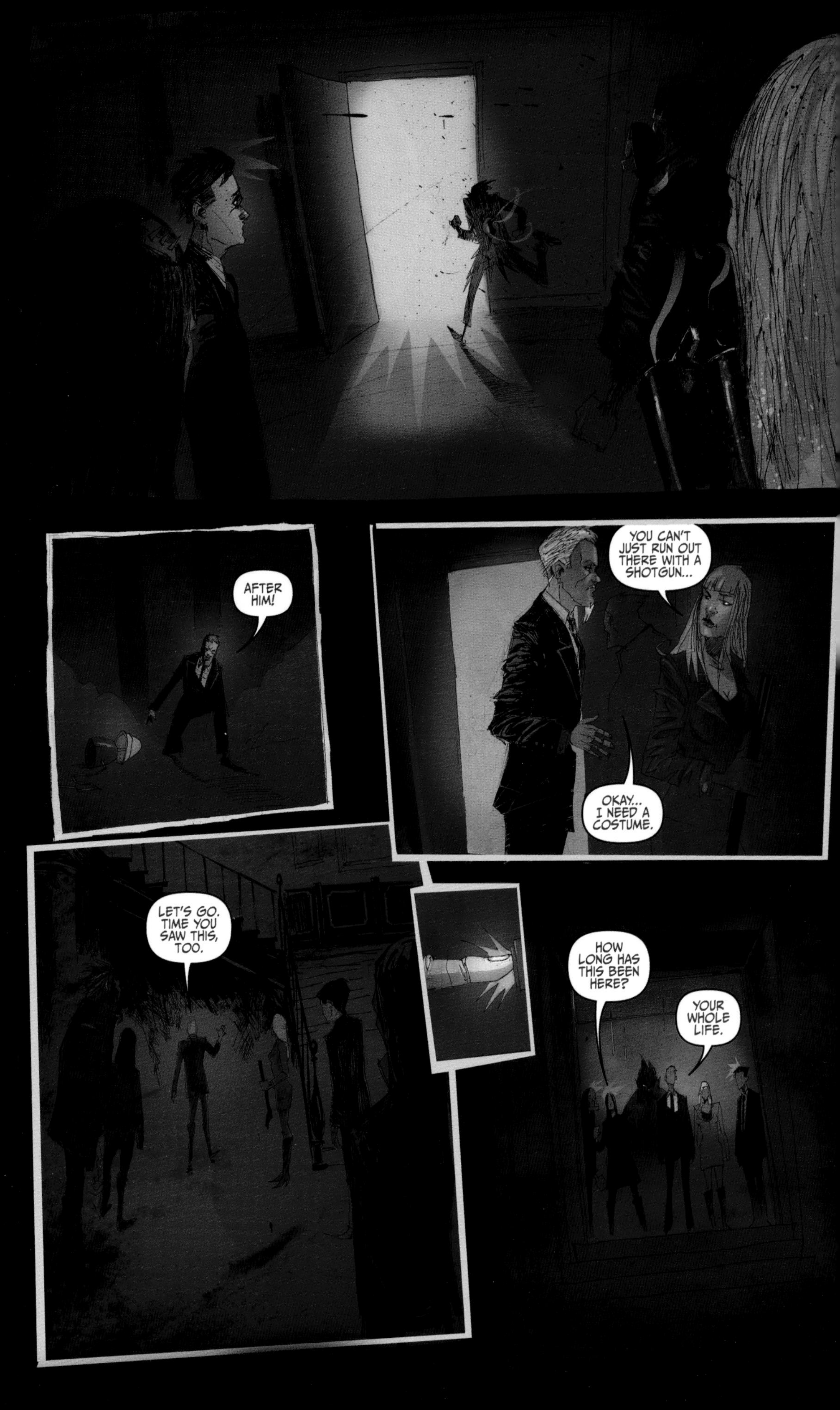
AFTER HIM!
YOU CAN'T JUST RUN OUT THERE WITH A SHOTGUN...
OKAY... I NEED A COSTUME.
LET'S GO. TIME YOU SAW THIS, TOO.
HOW LONG HAS THIS BEEN HERE?
YOUR WHOLE LIFE.

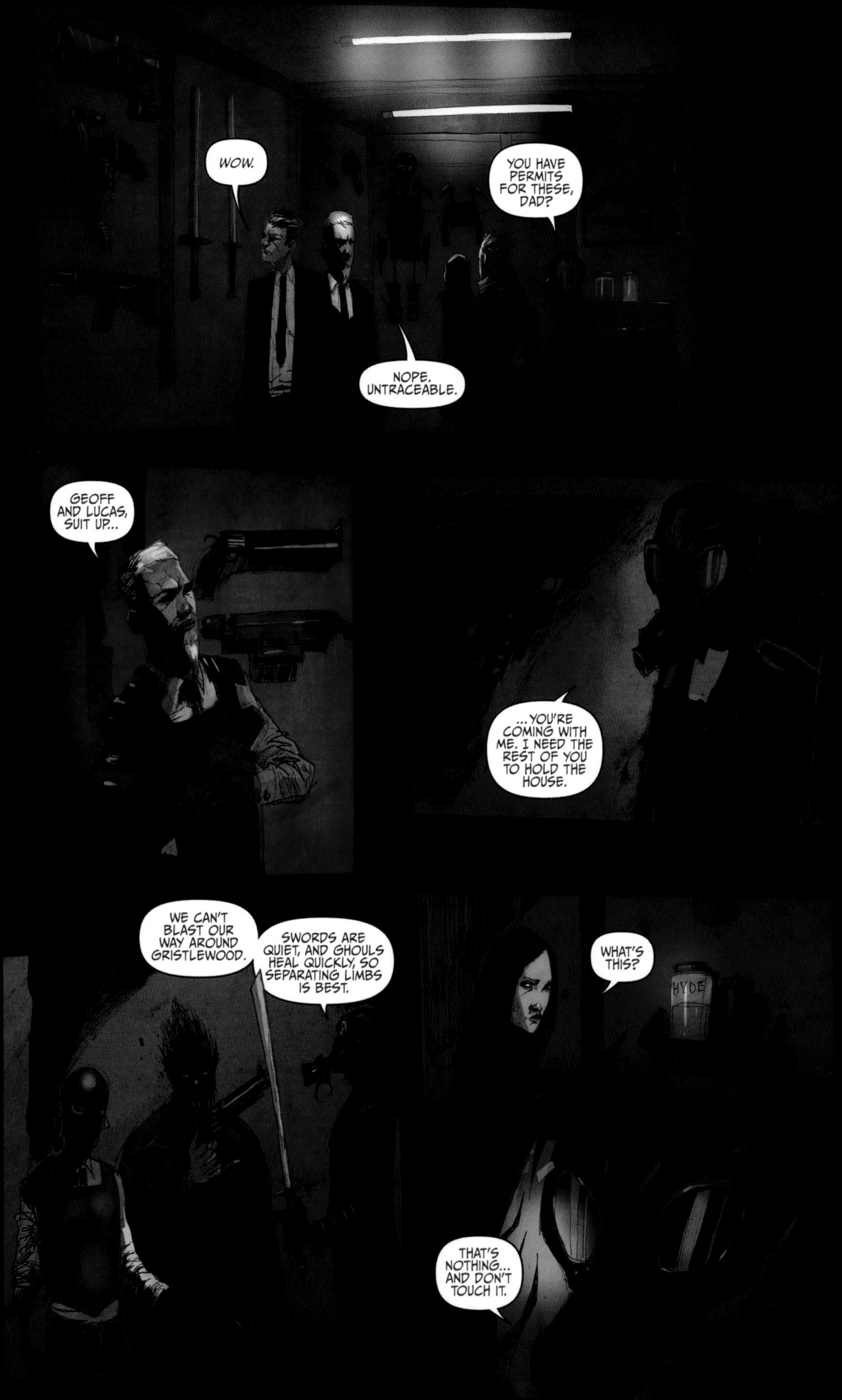
WOW.
YOU HAVE PERMITS FOR THESE, DAD?
NOPE. UNTRACEABLE.
GEOFF AND LUCAS, SUIT UP...
...YOU'RE COMING WITH ME. I NEED THE REST OF YOU TO HOLD THE HOUSE.
WE CAN'T BLAST OUR WAY AROUND GRISTLEWOOD.
SWORDS ARE QUIET, AND GHOULS HEAL QUICKLY, SO SEPARATING LIMBS IS BEST.
WHAT'S THIS?
HYDE
THAT'S NOTHING... AND DON'T TOUCH IT.

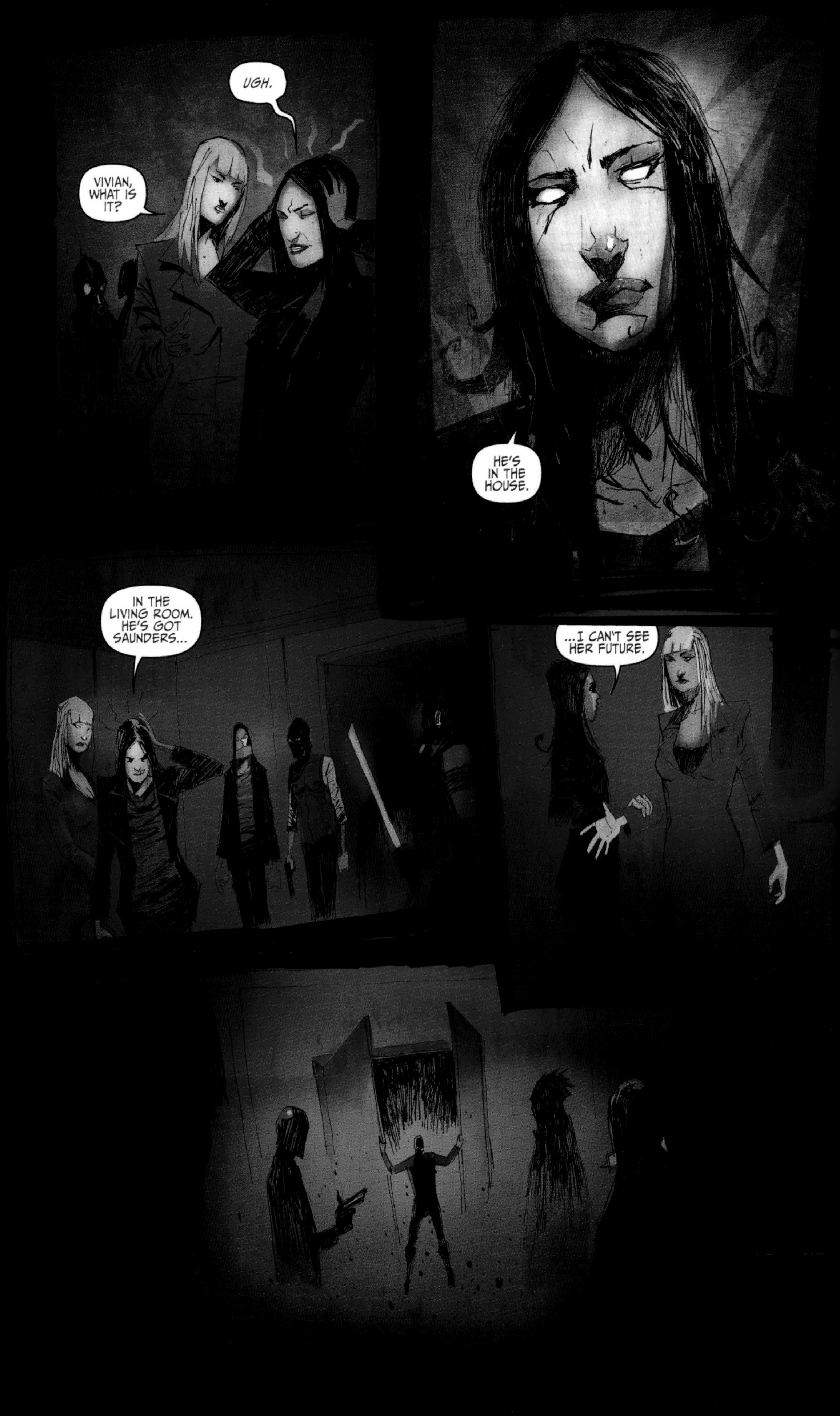
UGH.
VIVIAN, WHAT IS IT?
HE'S IN THE HOUSE.
IN THE LIVING ROOM. HE'S GOT SAUNDERS...
...I CAN'T SEE HER FUTURE.

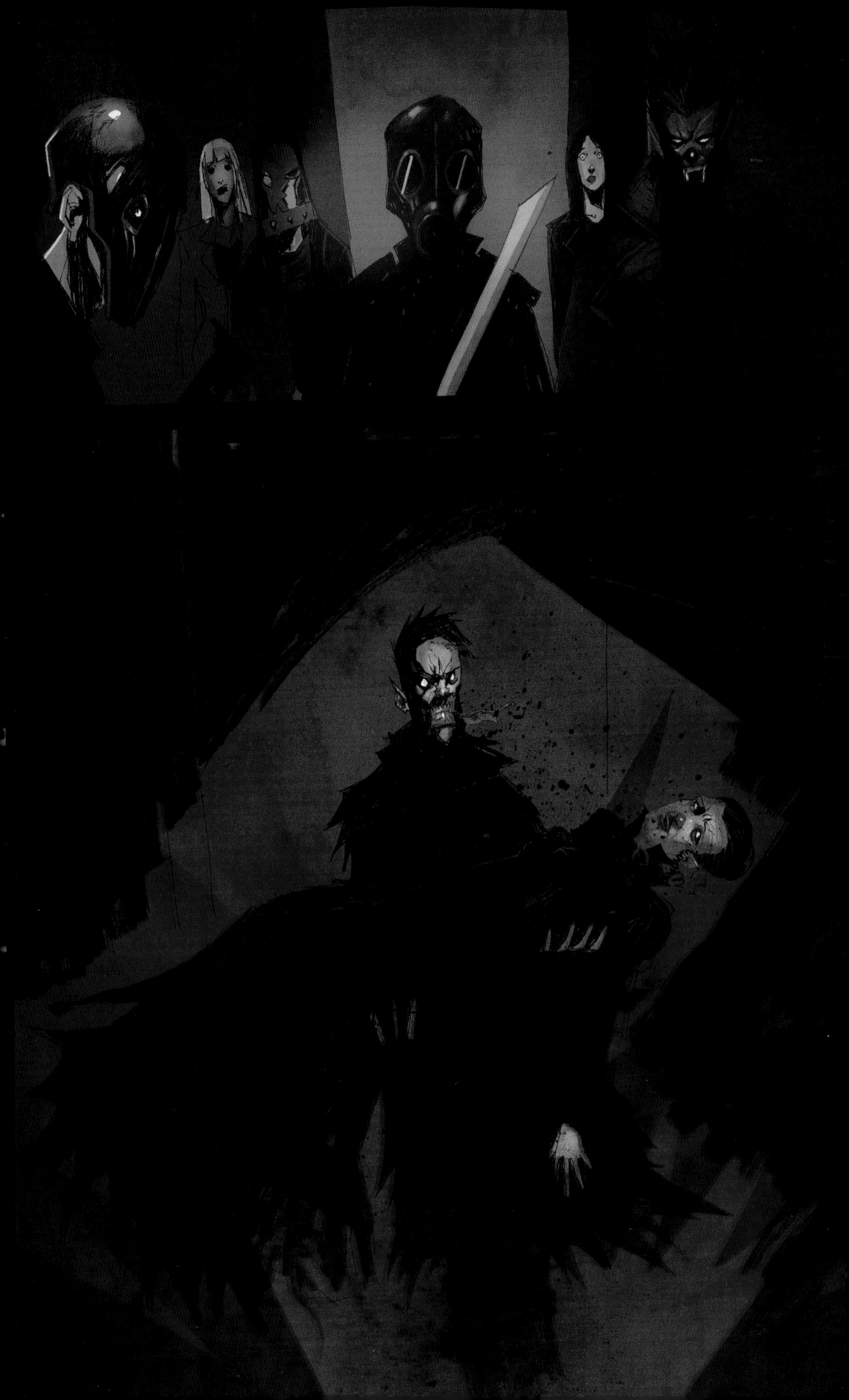

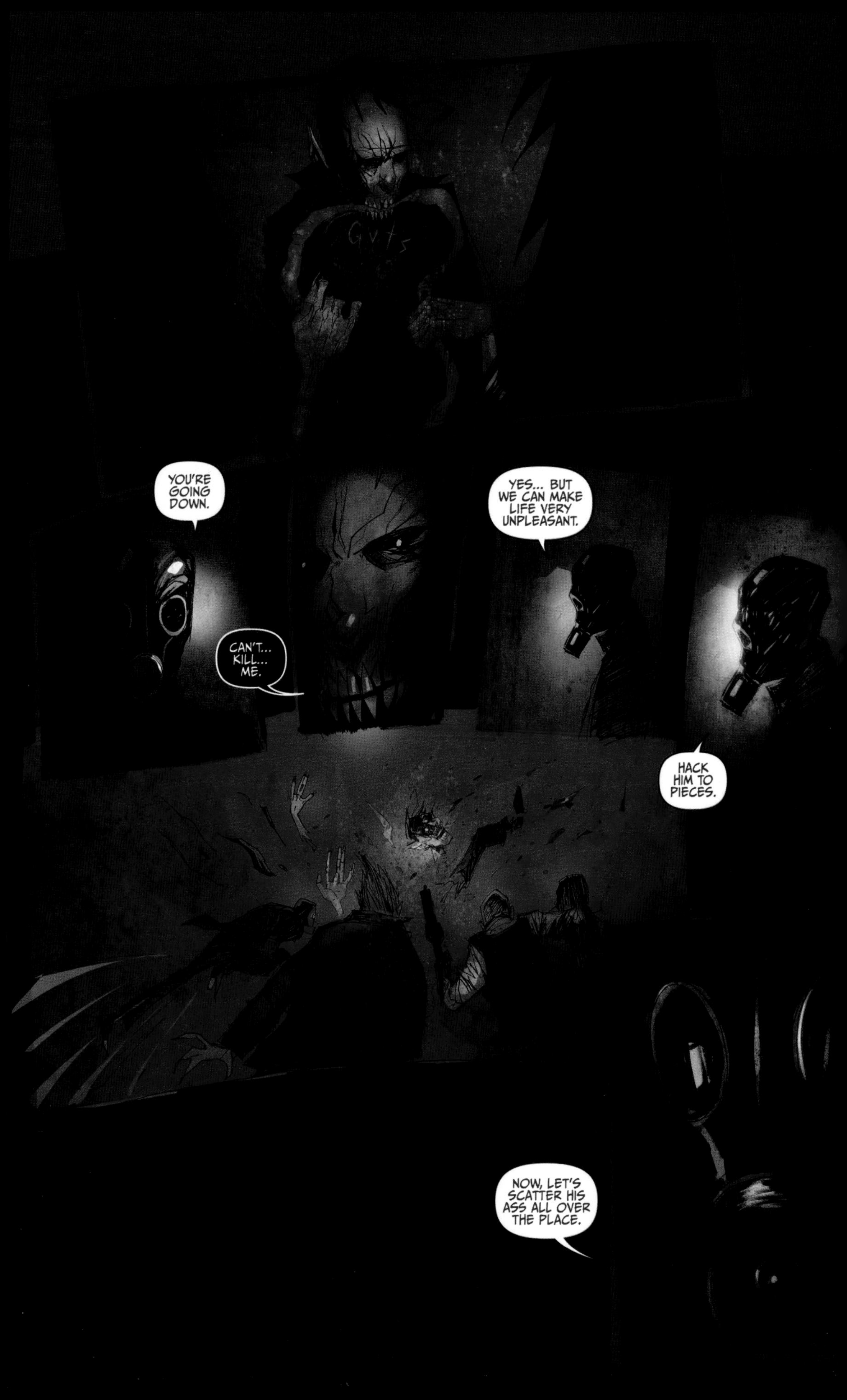
YOU'RE GOING DOWN.
CAN'T... KILL... ME.
YES... BUT WE CAN MAKE LIFE VERY UNPLEASANT.
HACK HIM TO PIECES.
NOW, LET'S SCATTER HIS ASS ALL OVER THE PLACE.

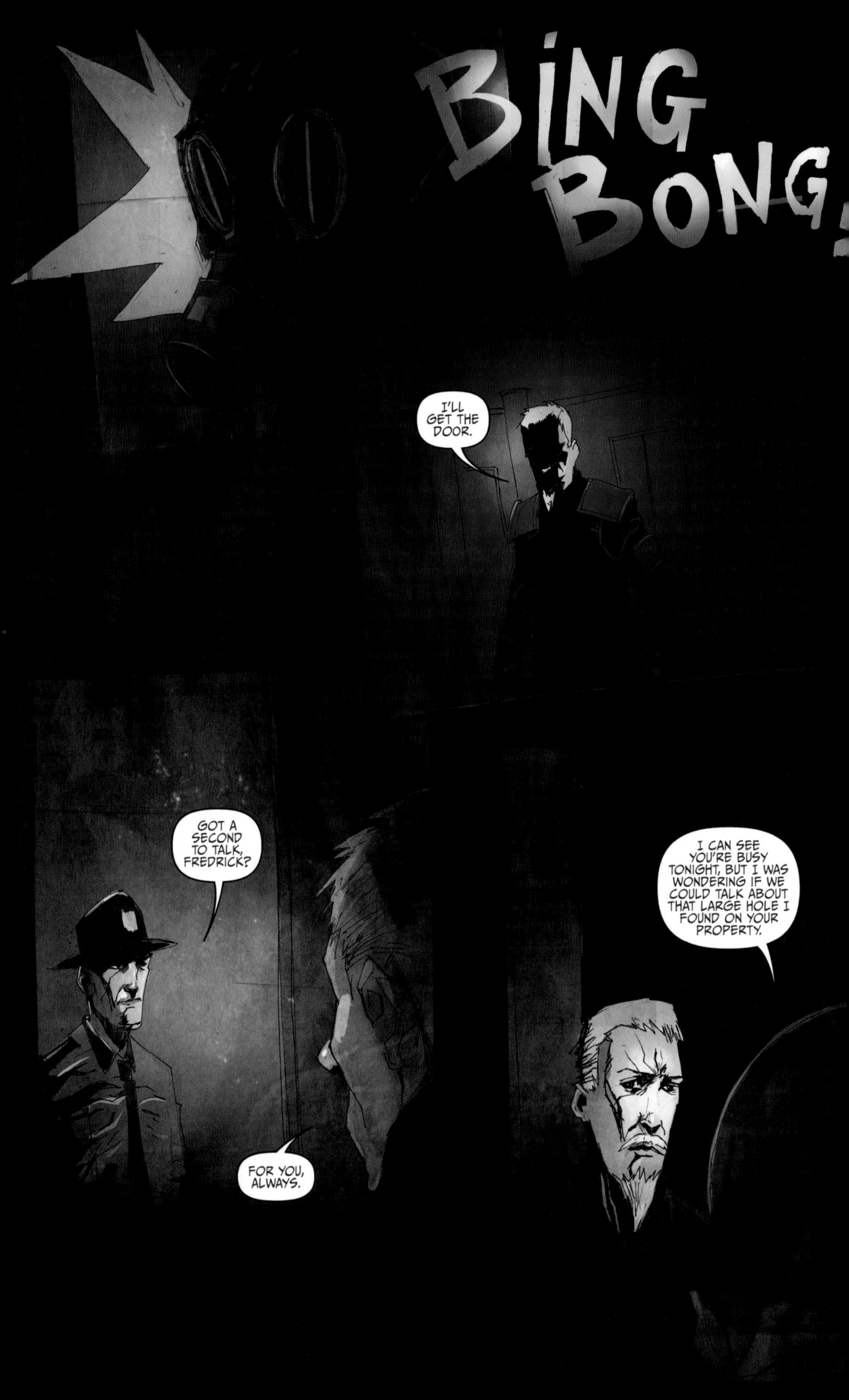
BING BONG!
I'LL GET THE DOOR.
GOT A SECOND TO TALK, FREDRICK?
FOR YOU, ALWAYS.
I CAN SEE YOU'RE BUSY TONIGHT, BUT I WAS WONDERING IF WE COULD TALK ABOUT THAT LARGE HOLE I FOUND ON YOUR PROPERTY.

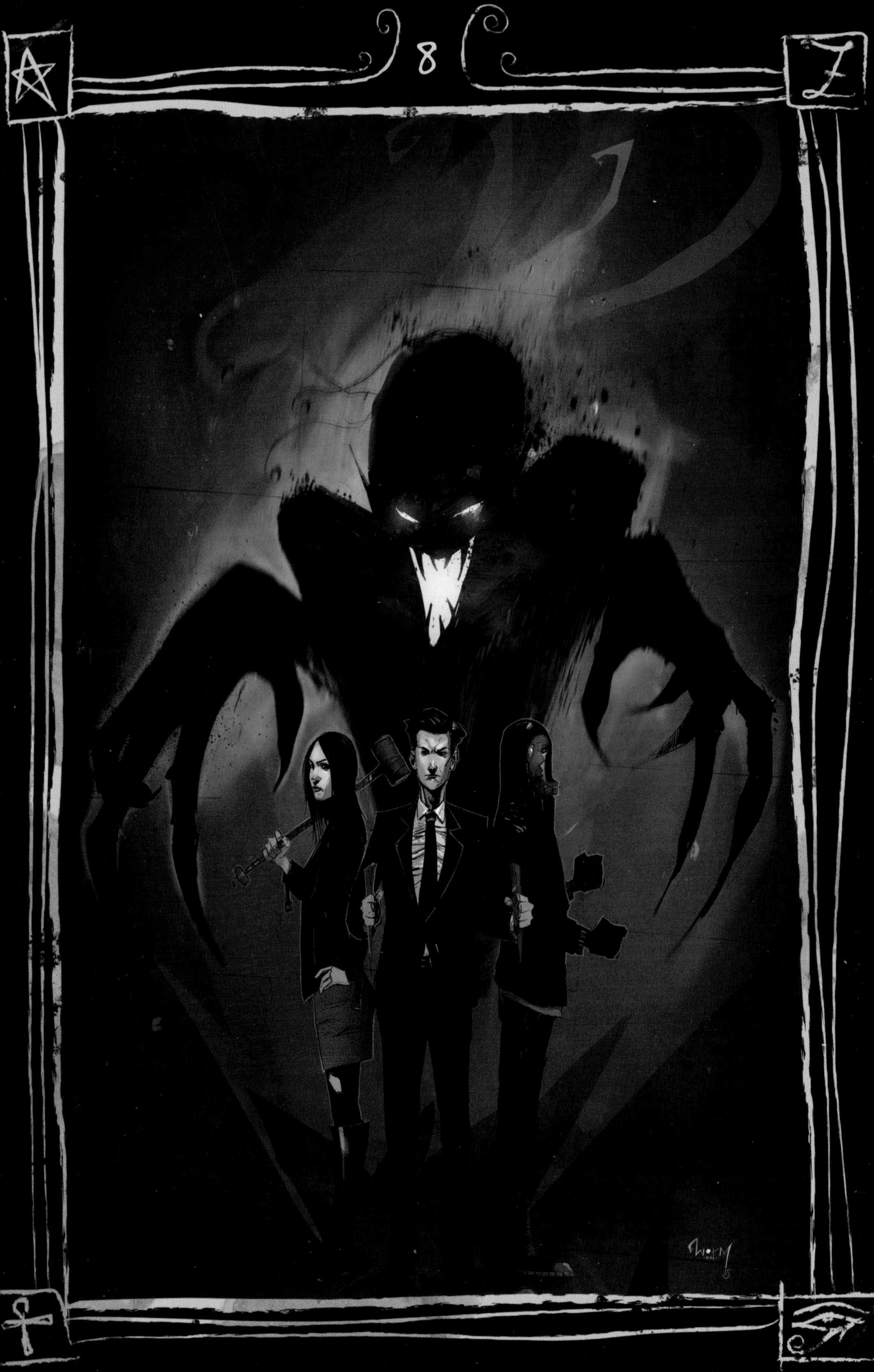
8

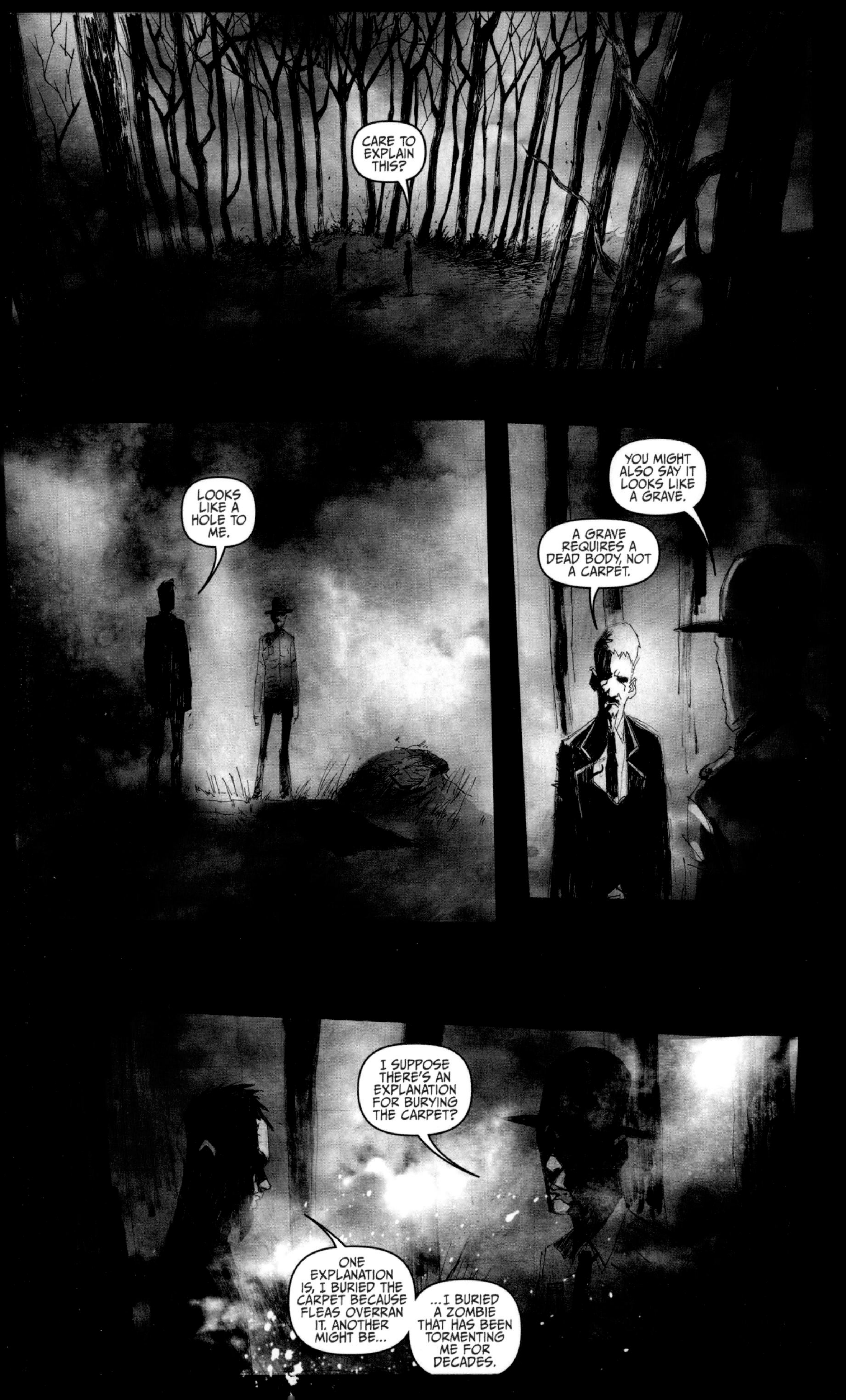
CARE TO EXPLAIN THIS?
LOOKS LIKE A HOLE TO ME.
YOU MIGHT ALSO SAY IT LOOKS LIKE A GRAVE.
A GRAVE REQUIRES A DEAD BODY, NOT A CARPET.
I SUPPOSE THERE'S AN EXPLANATION FOR BURYING THE CARPET?
ONE EXPLANATION IS, I BURIED THE CARPET BECAUSE FLEAS OVERRAN IT. ANOTHER MIGHT BE...
...I BURIED A ZOMBIE THAT HAS BEEN TORMENTING ME FOR DECADES.

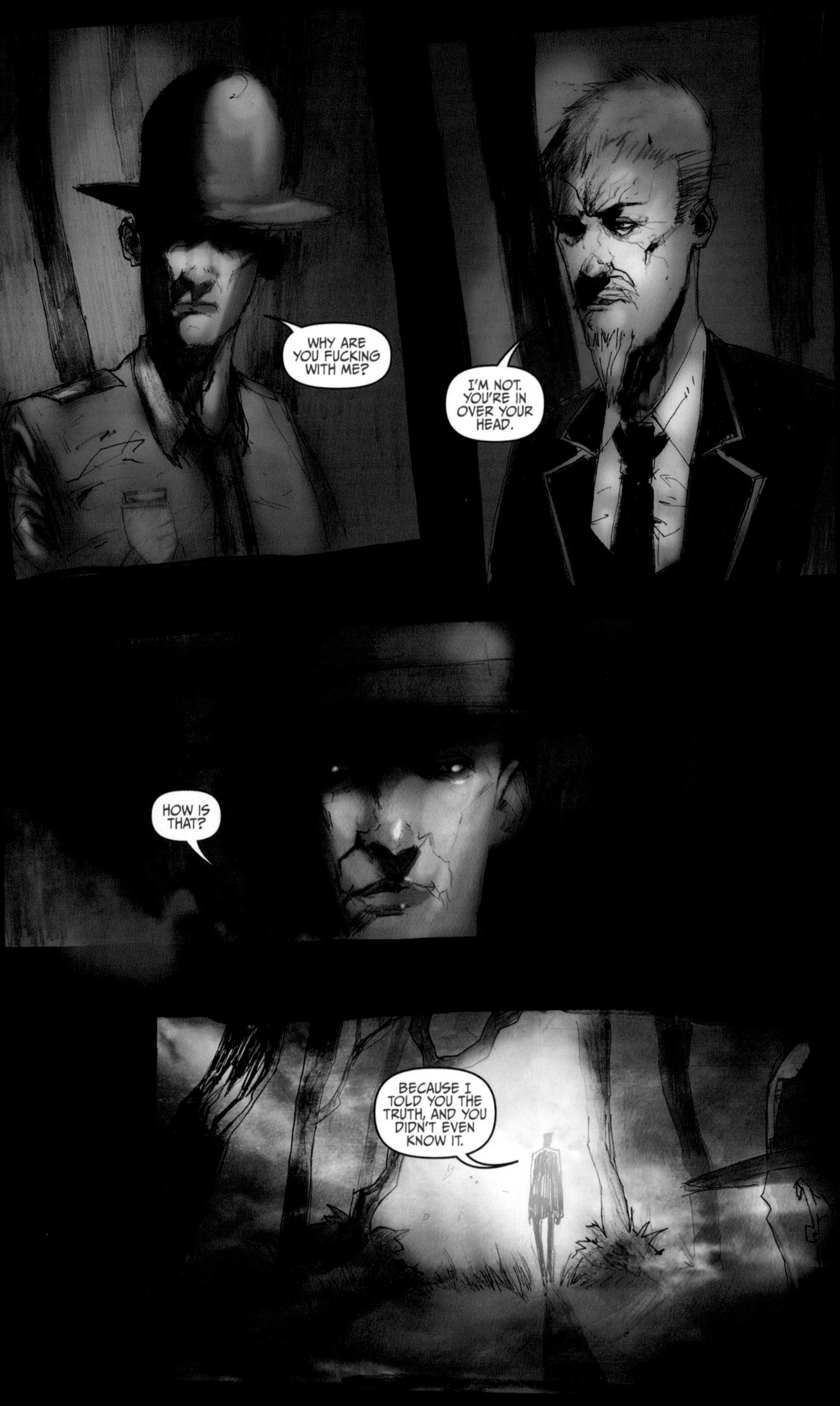
WHY ARE YOU FUCKING WITH ME?
I'M NOT. YOU'RE IN OVER YOUR HEAD.
HOW IS THAT?
BECAUSE I TOLD YOU THE TRUTH, AND YOU DIDN'T EVEN KNOW IT.

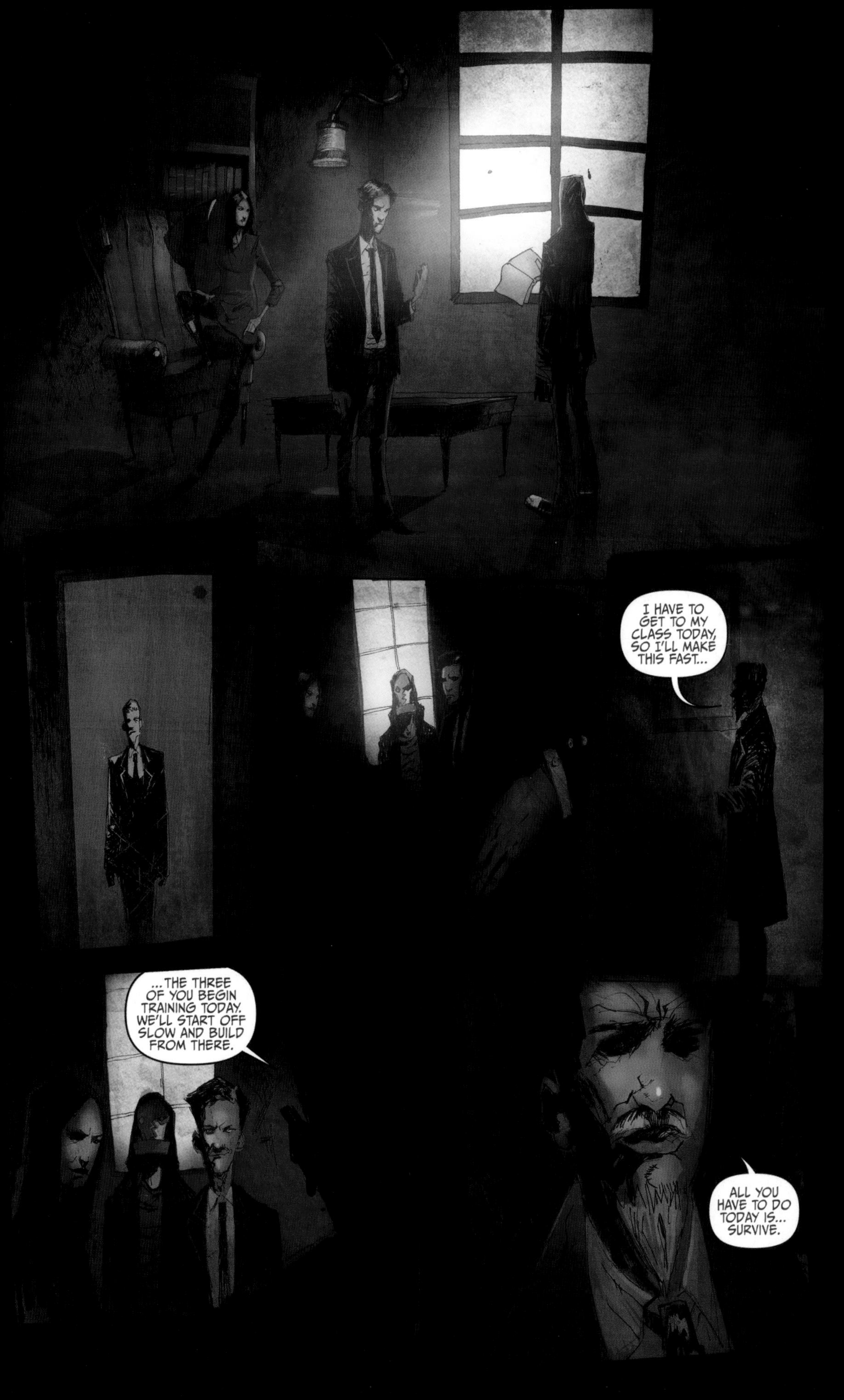
I HAVE TO GET TO MY CLASS TODAY, SO I'LL MAKE THIS FAST...
...THE THREE OF YOU BEGIN TRAINING TODAY. WE'LL START OFF SLOW AND BUILD FROM THERE.
ALL YOU HAVE TO DO TODAY IS... SURVIVE.

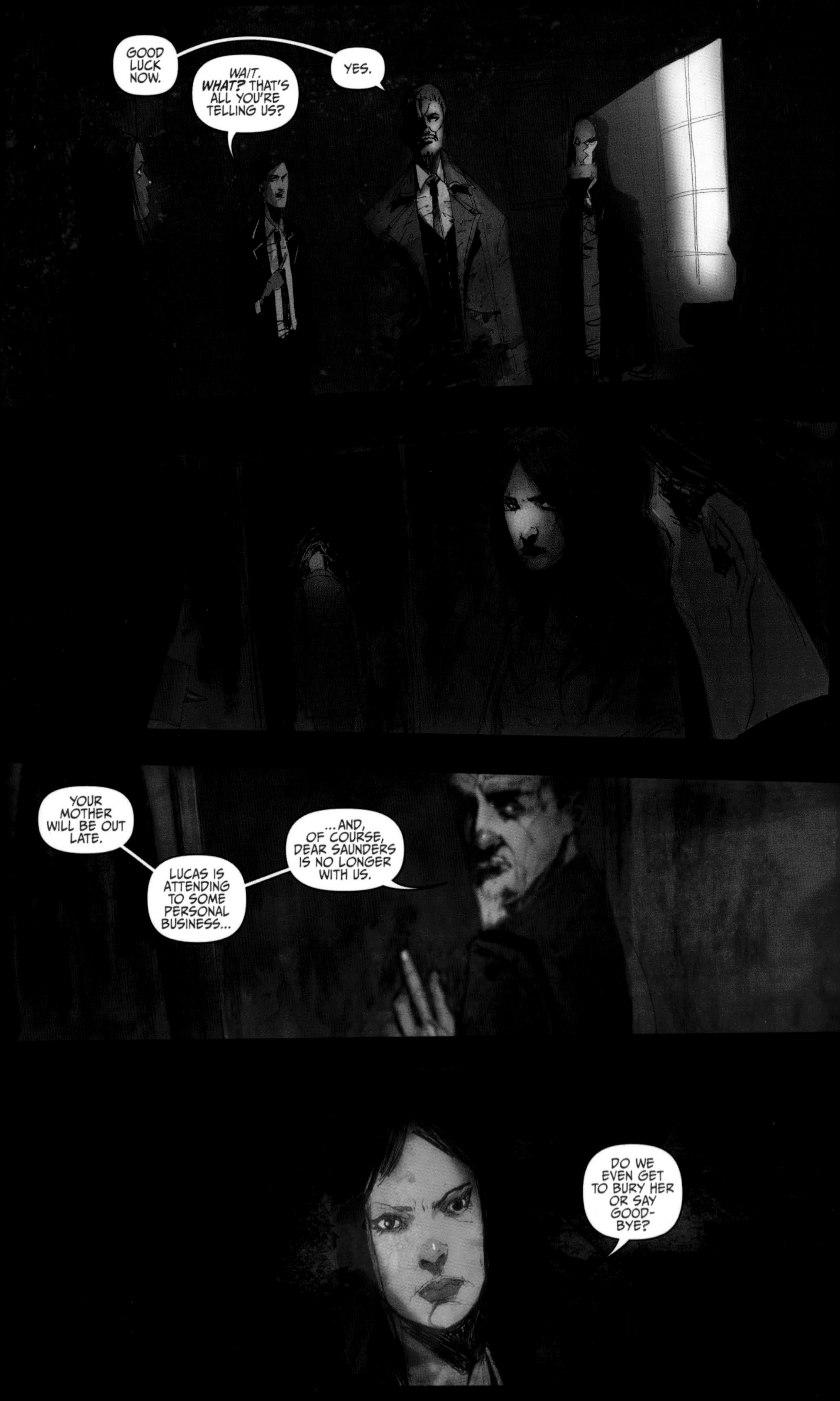
GOOD LUCK NOW.
WAIT. WHAT? THAT'S ALL YOU'RE TELLING US?
YES.
YOUR MOTHER WILL BE OUT LATE.
LUCAS IS ATTENDING TO SOME PERSONAL BUSINESS...
...AND, OF COURSE, DEAR SAUNDERS IS NO LONGER WITH US.
DO WE EVEN GET TO BURY HER OR SAY GOOD-BYE?

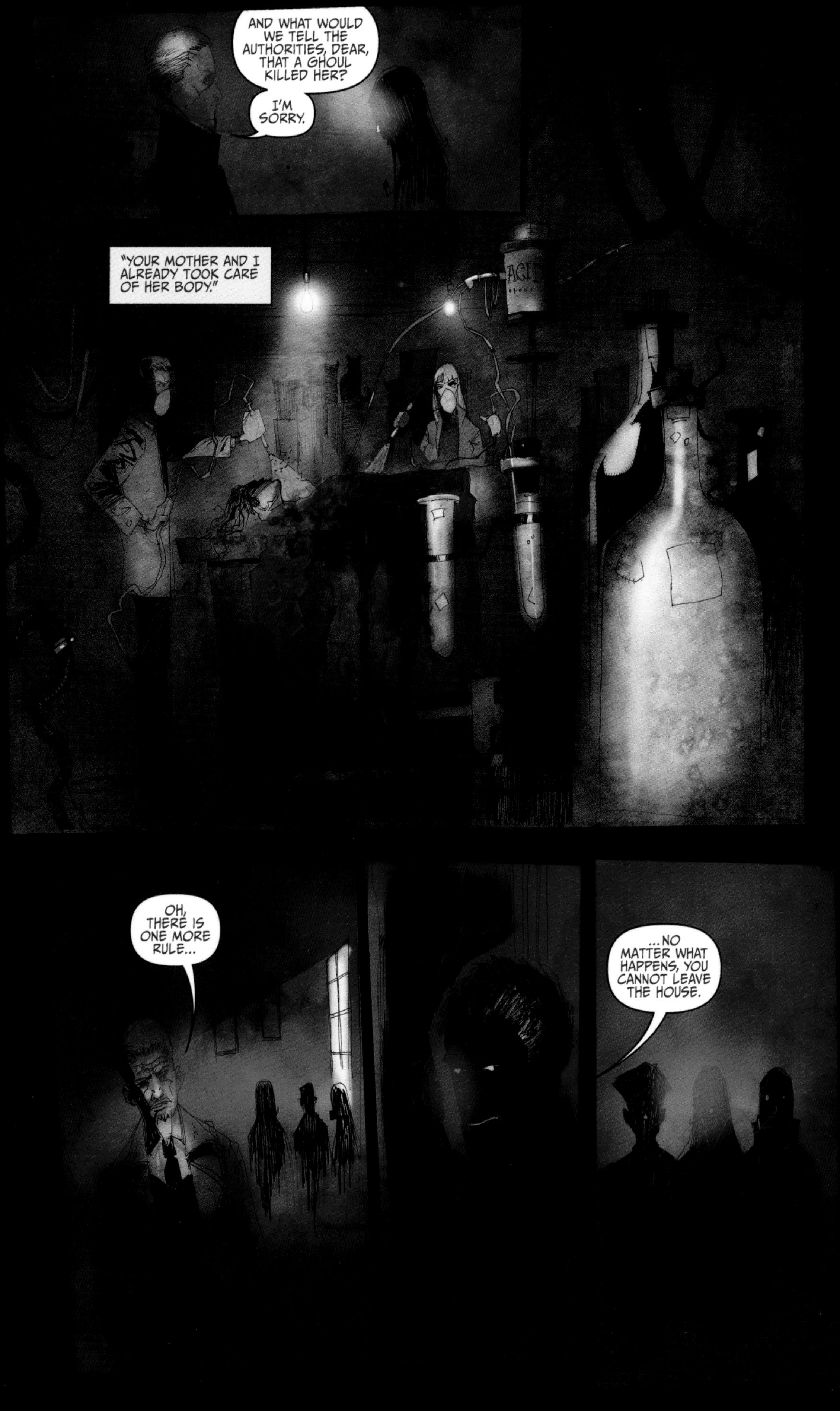
AND WHAT WOULD WE TELL THE AUTHORITIES, DEAR, THAT A GHOUL KILLED HER?
I'M SORRY.
"YOUR MOTHER AND I ALREADY TOOK CARE OF HER BODY."
ACID
OH, THERE IS ONE MORE RULE...
...NO MATTER WHAT HAPPENS, YOU CANNOT LEAVE THE HOUSE.

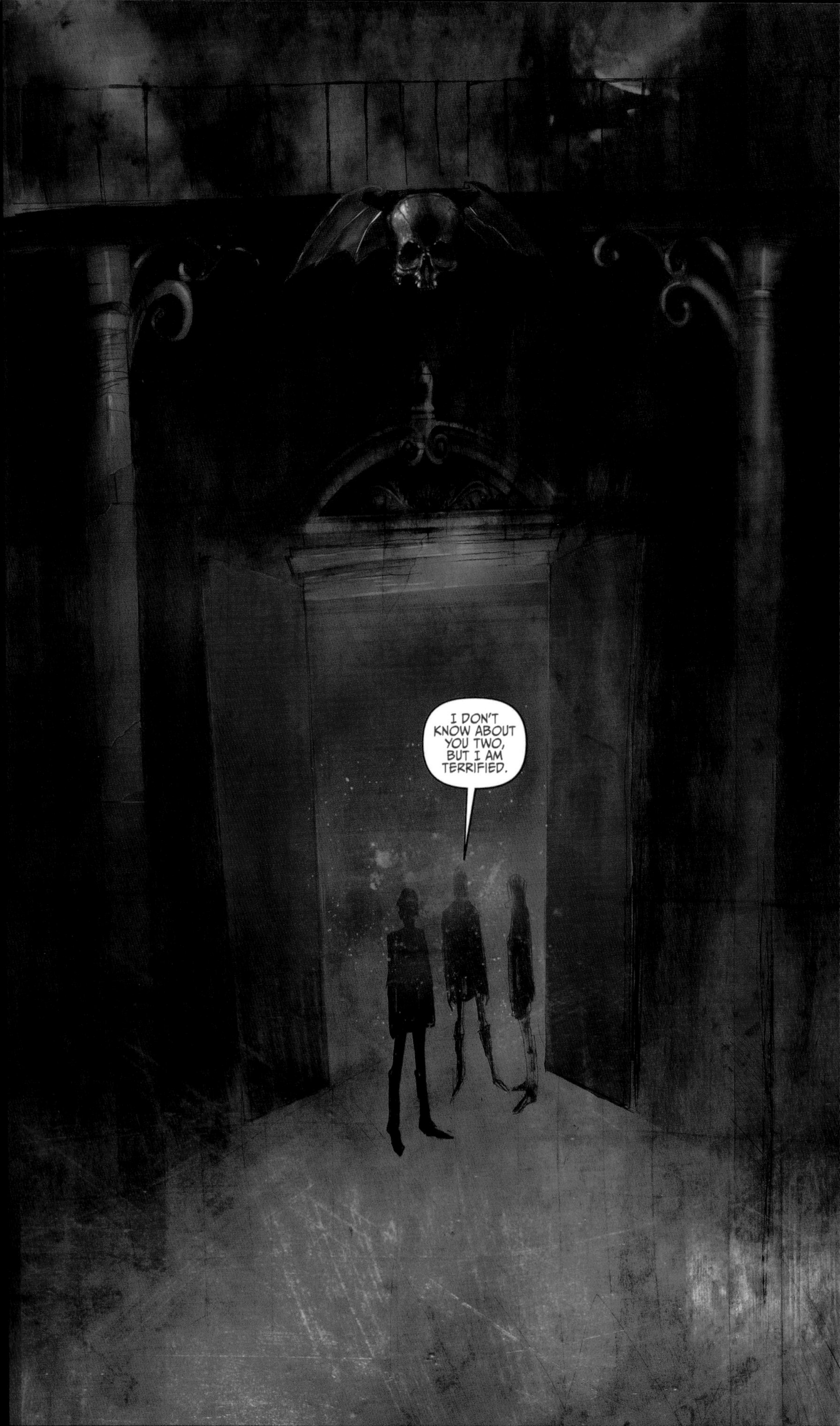
I DON'T KNOW ABOUT YOU TWO, BUT I AM TERRIFIED.

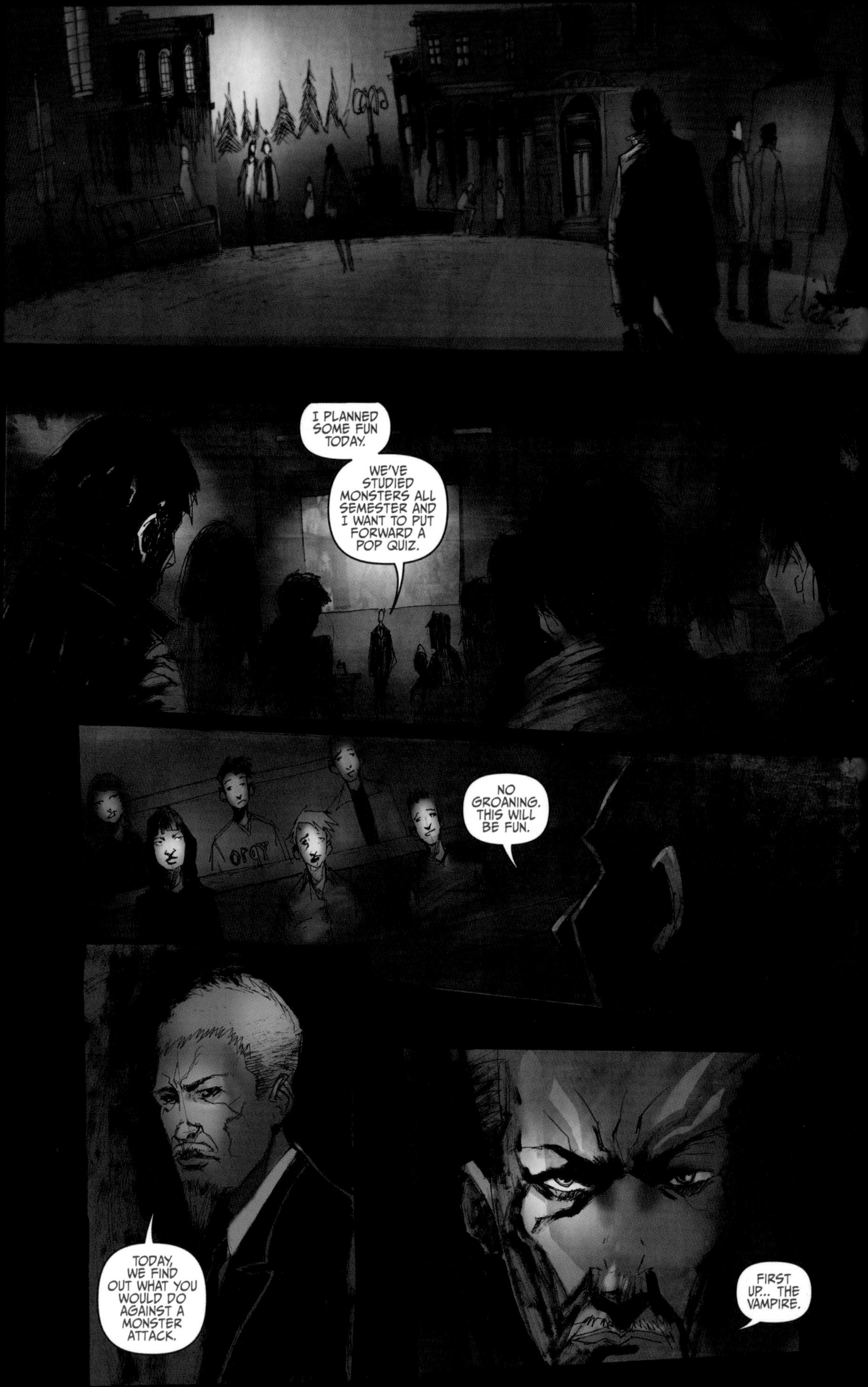
I PLANNED SOME FUN TODAY.
WE'VE STUDIED MONSTERS ALL SEMESTER AND I WANT TO PUT FORWARD A POP QUIZ.
NO GROANING. THIS WILL BE FUN.
TODAY, WE FIND OUT WHAT YOU WOULD DO AGAINST A MONSTER ATTACK.
FIRST UP... THE VAMPIRE.

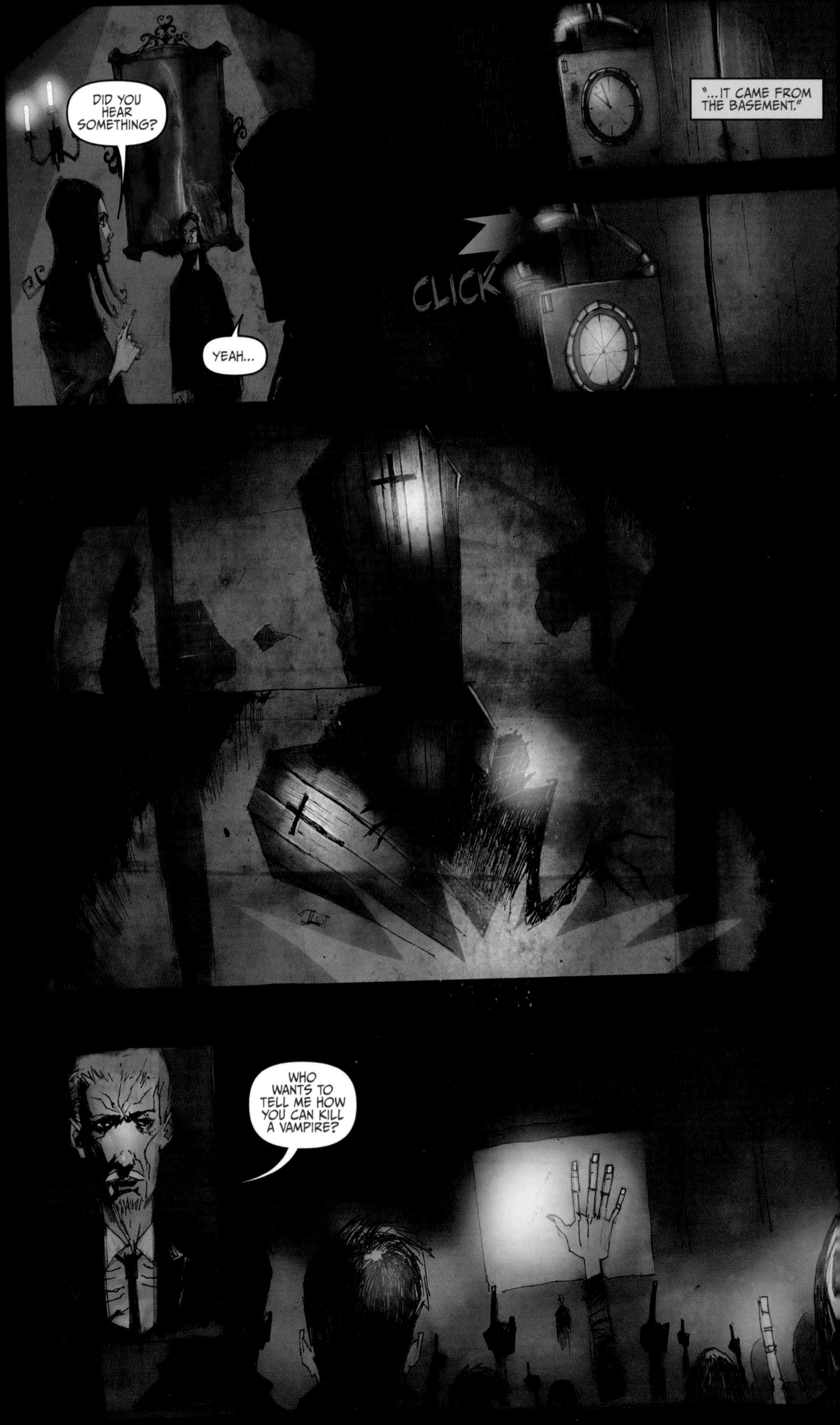
DID YOU HEAR SOMETHING?
YEAH...
CLICK
"...IT CAME FROM THE BASEMENT."
WHO WANTS TO TELL ME HOW YOU CAN KILL A VAMPIRE?

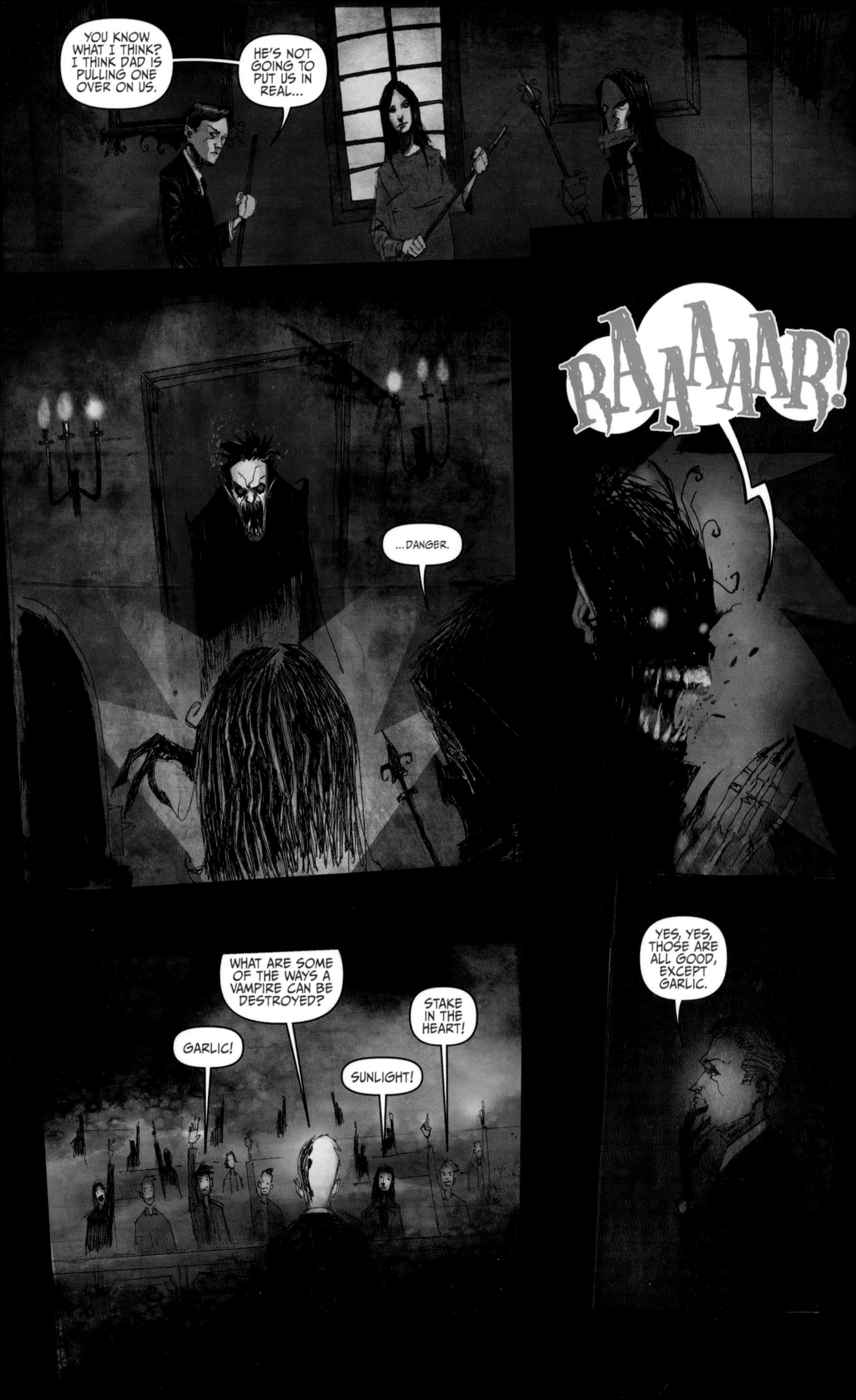
YOU KNOW WHAT I THINK? I THINK DAD IS PULLING ONE OVER ON US.
HE'S NOT GOING TO PUT US IN REAL...
...DANGER.
RAAAAAR!
WHAT ARE SOME OF THE WAYS A VAMPIRE CAN BE DESTROYED?
GARLIC!
SUNLIGHT!
STAKE IN THE HEART!
YES, YES, THOSE ARE ALL GOOD, EXCEPT GARLIC.

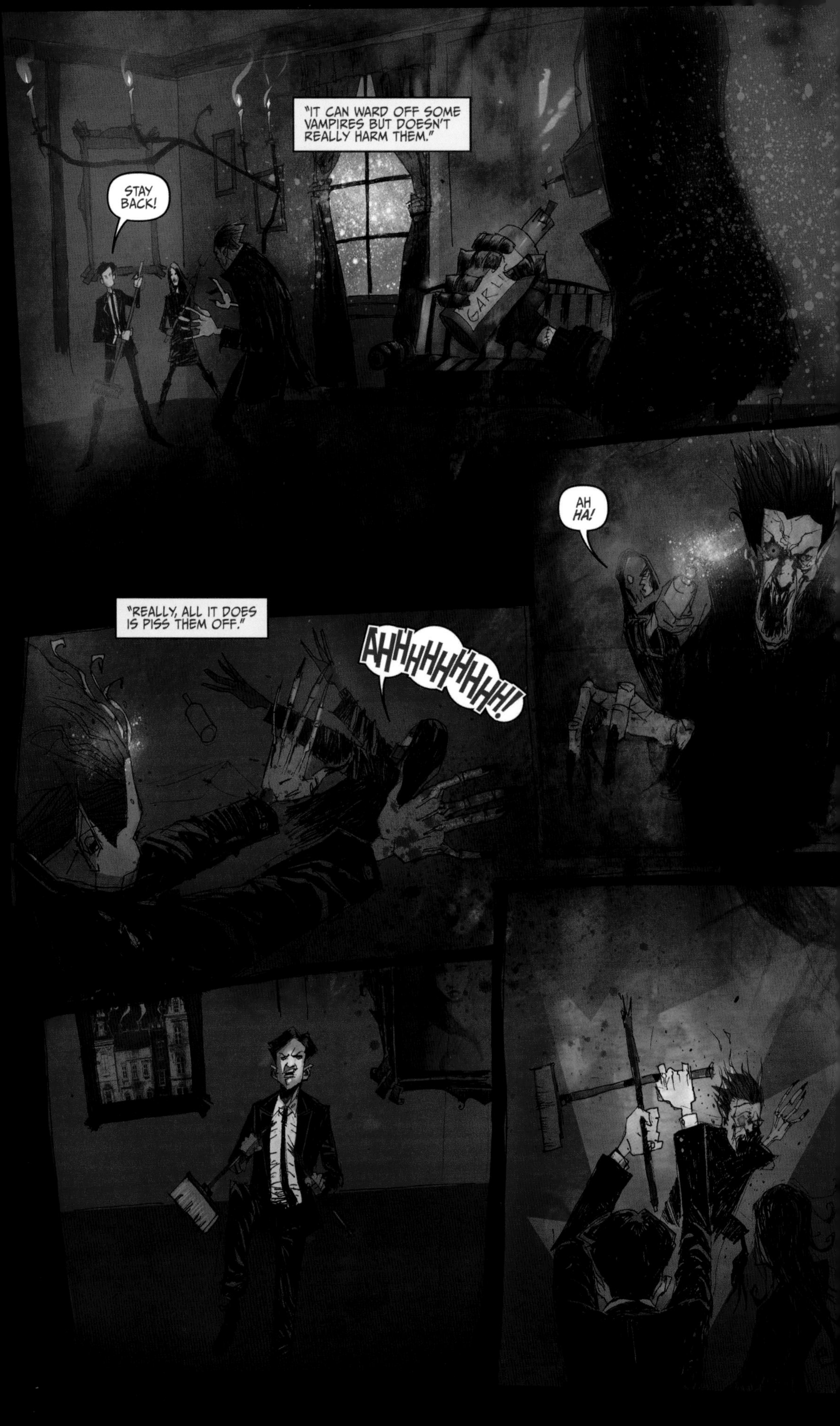
"IT CAN WARD OFF SOME VAMPIRES BUT DOESN'T REALLY HARM THEM."
STAY BACK!
GARLIC
AH HA!
"REALLY, ALL IT DOES IS PISS THEM OFF."
AHHHHHHHHH!

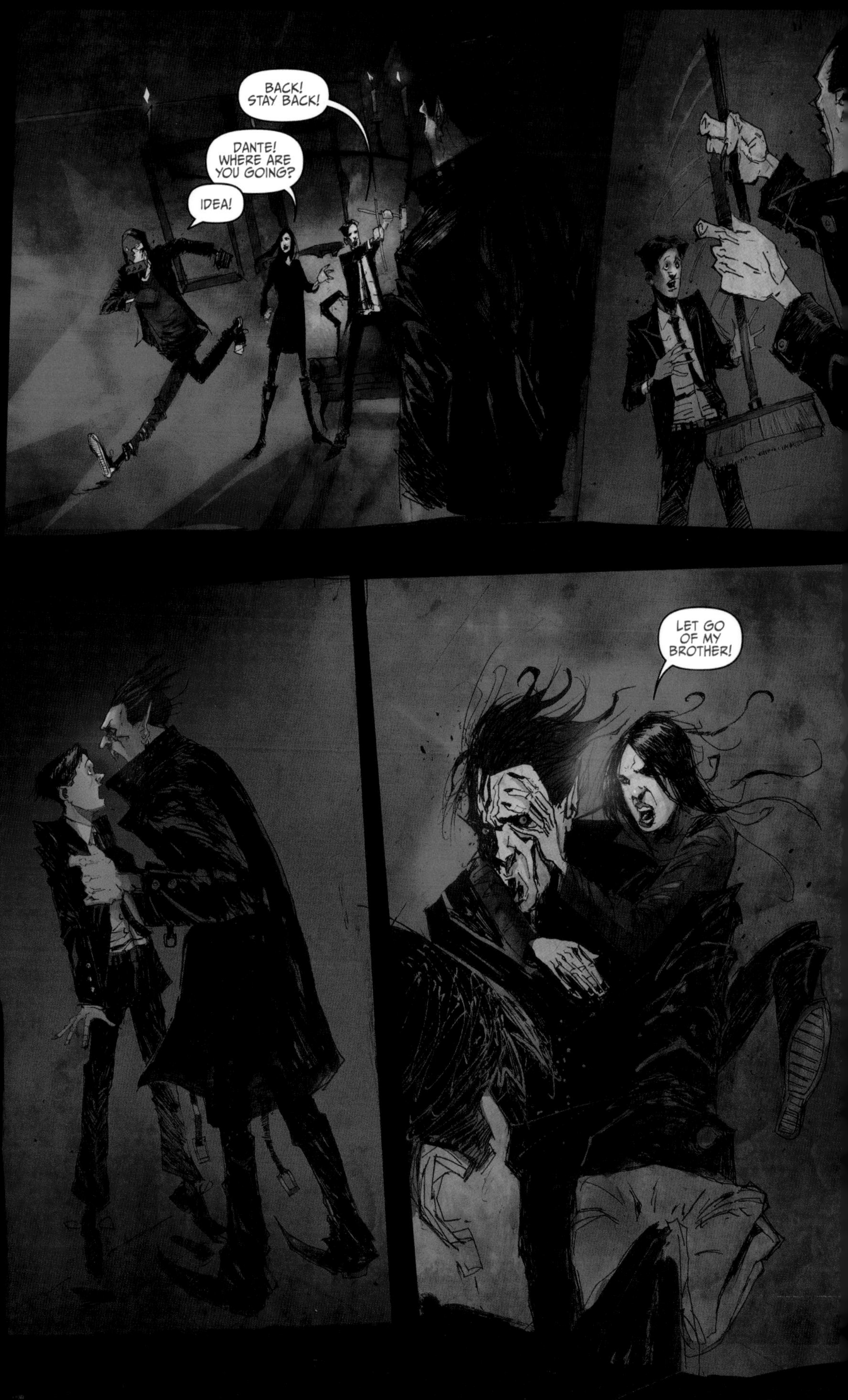
BACK! STAY BACK!
DANTE! WHERE ARE YOU GOING?
IDEA!
LET GO OF MY BROTHER!

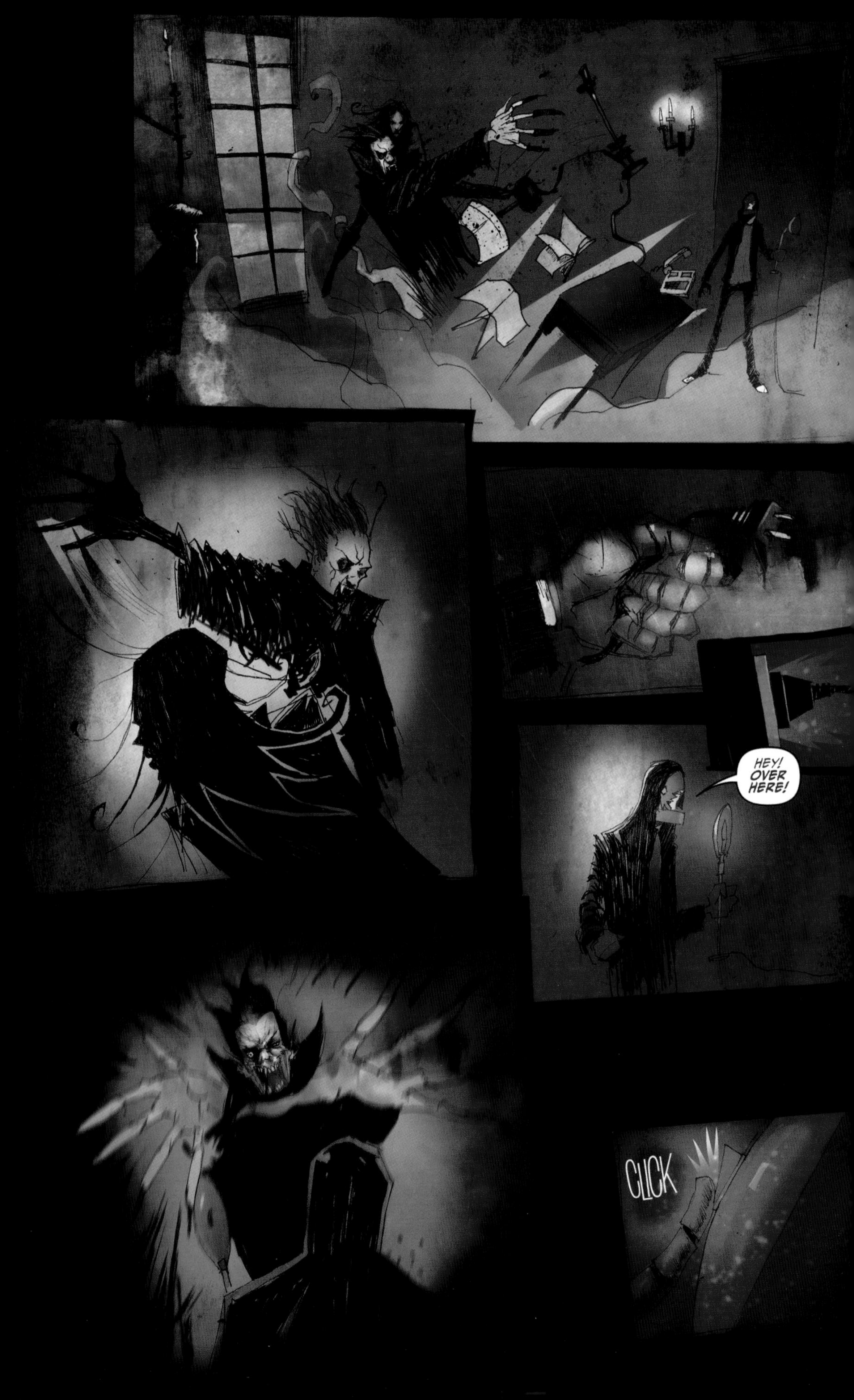
HEY! OVER HERE!
CLICK

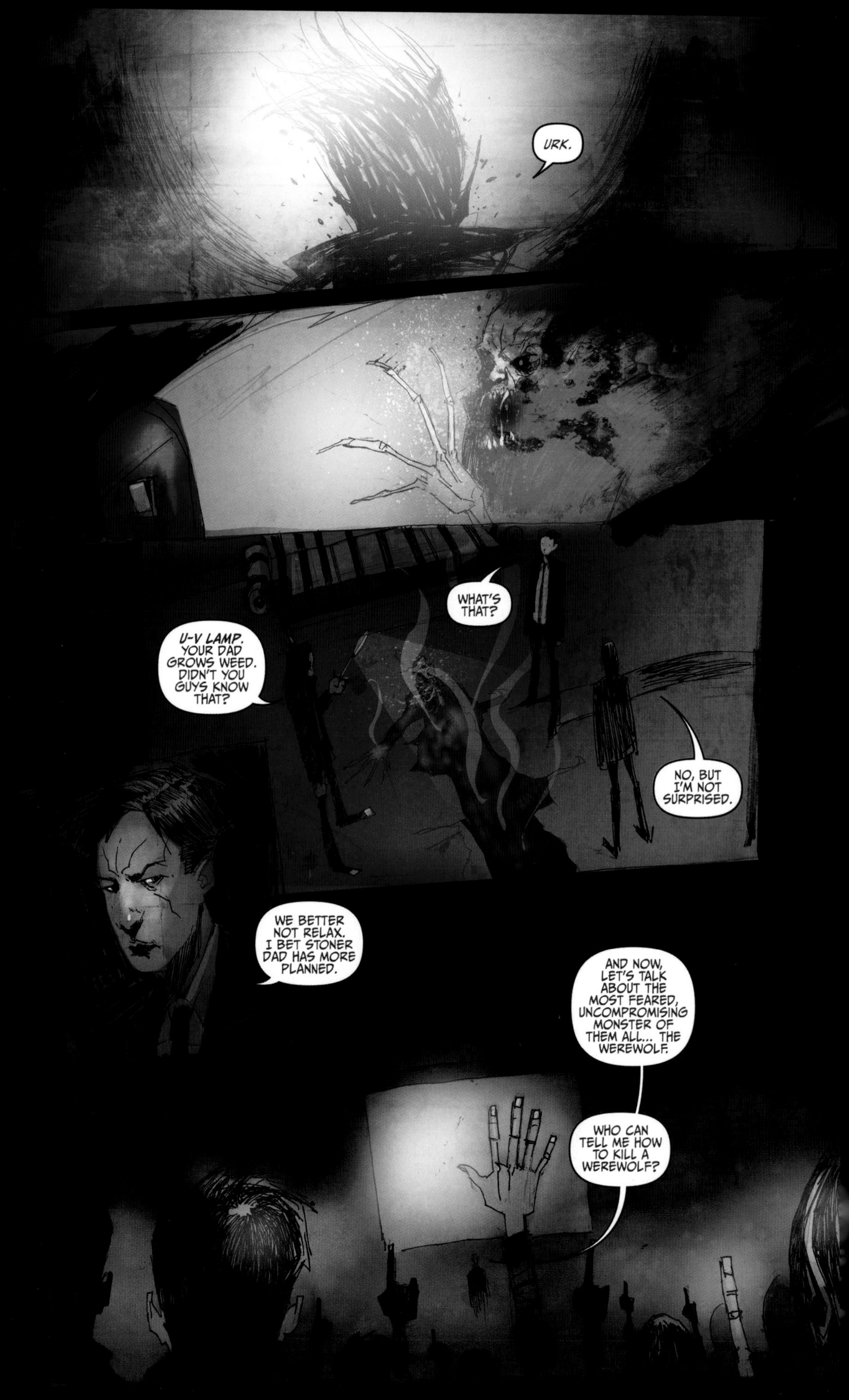
URK.
WHAT'S THAT?
U-V LAMP. YOUR DAD GROWS WEED. DIDN'T YOU GUYS KNOW THAT?
NO, BUT I'M NOT SURPRISED.
WE BETTER NOT RELAX. I BET STONER DAD HAS MORE PLANNED.
AND NOW, LET'S TALK ABOUT THE MOST FEARED, UNCOMPROMISING MONSTER OF THEM ALL... THE WEREWOLF.
WHO CAN TELL ME HOW TO KILL A WEREWOLF?

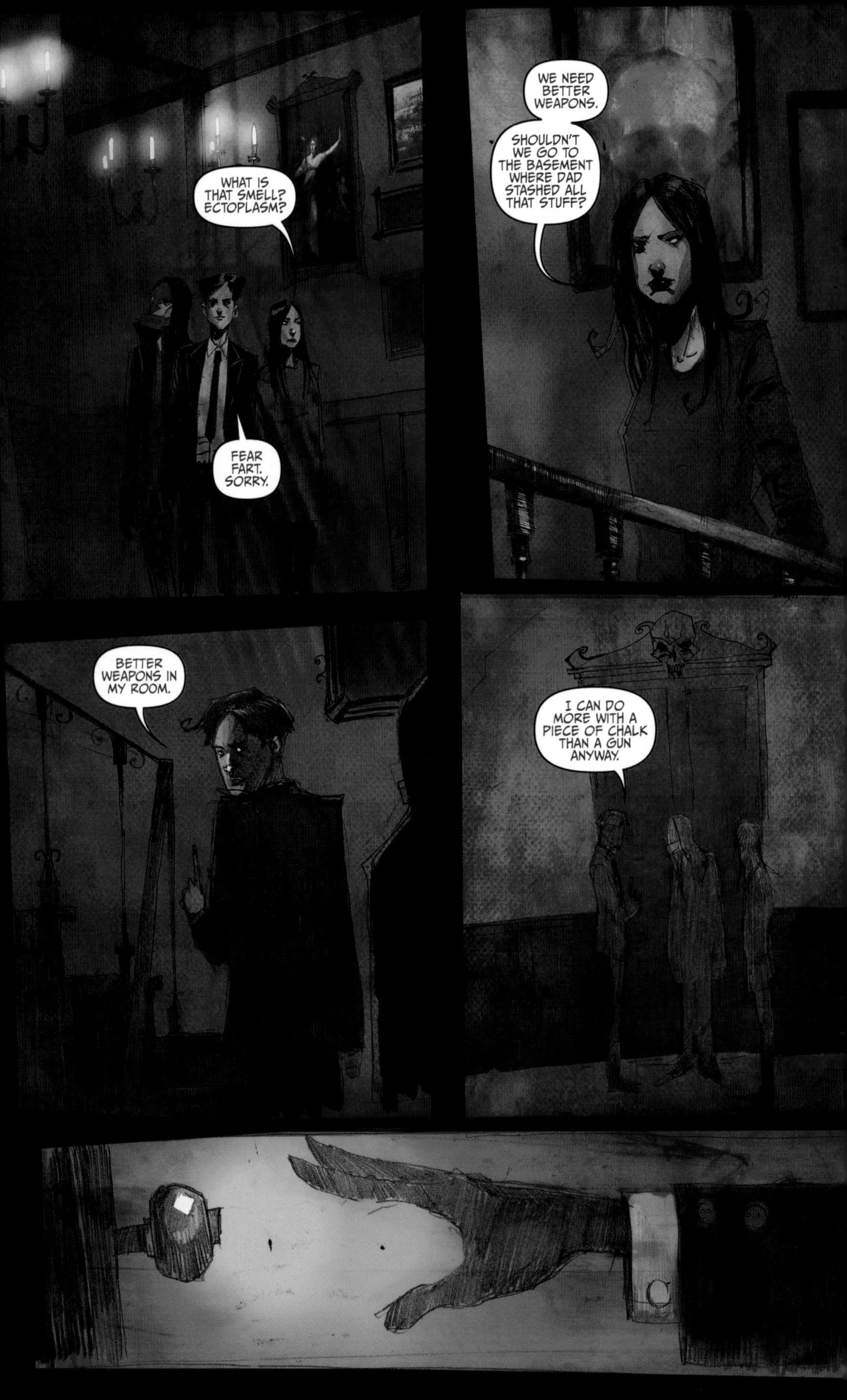
WHAT IS THAT SMELL? ECTOPLASM?
FEAR FART. SORRY.
WE NEED BETTER WEAPONS.
SHOULDN'T WE GO TO THE BASEMENT WHERE DAD STASHED ALL THAT STUFF?
BETTER WEAPONS IN MY ROOM.
I CAN DO MORE WITH A PIECE OF CHALK THAN A GUN ANYWAY.

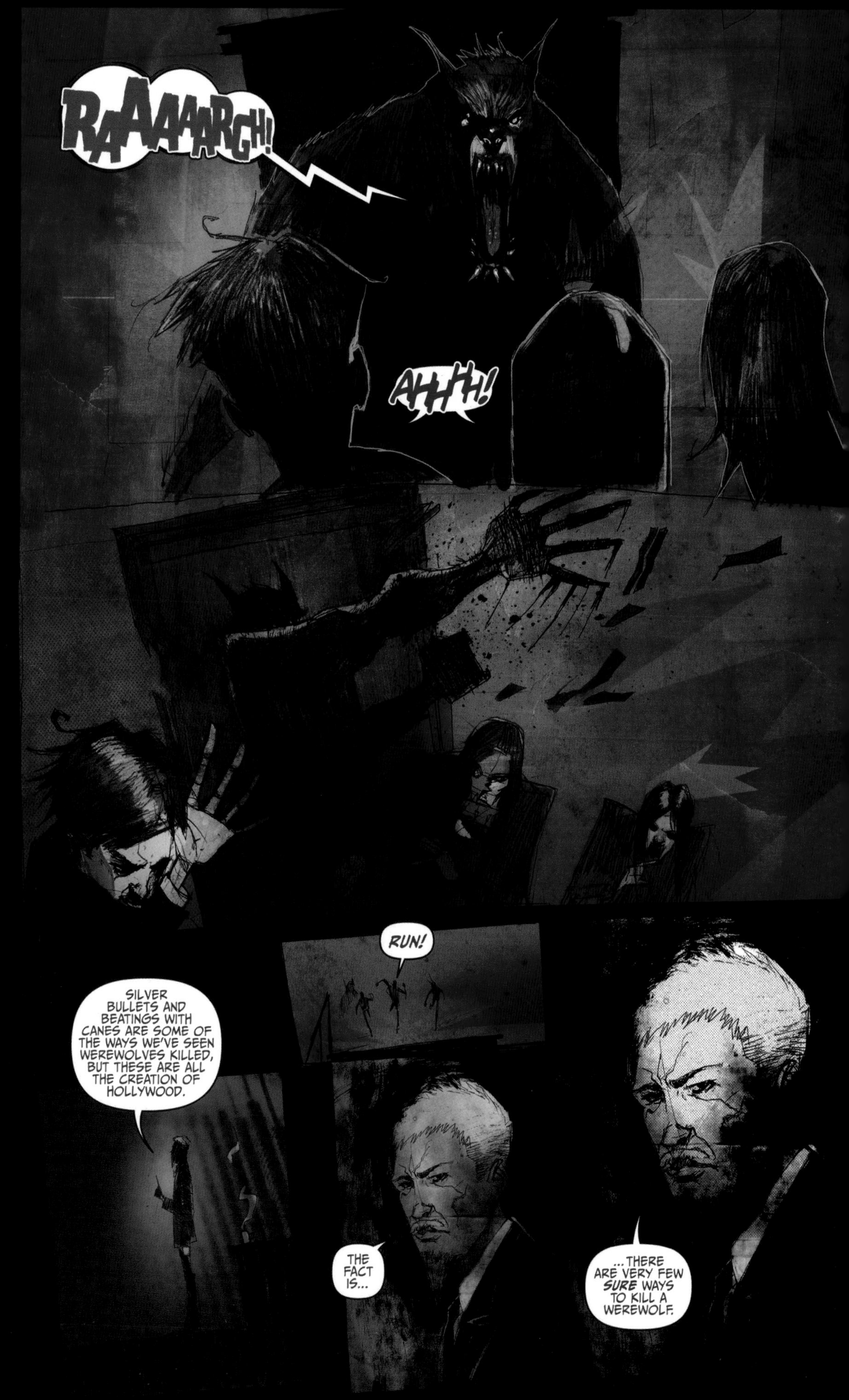
RAAAAARGH!
AHHH!
RUN!
SILVER BULLETS AND BEATINGS WITH CANES ARE SOME OF THE WAYS WE'VE SEEN WEREWOLVES KILLED, BUT THESE ARE ALL THE CREATION OF HOLLYWOOD.
THE FACT IS...
...THERE ARE VERY FEW SURE WAYS TO KILL A WEREWOLF.

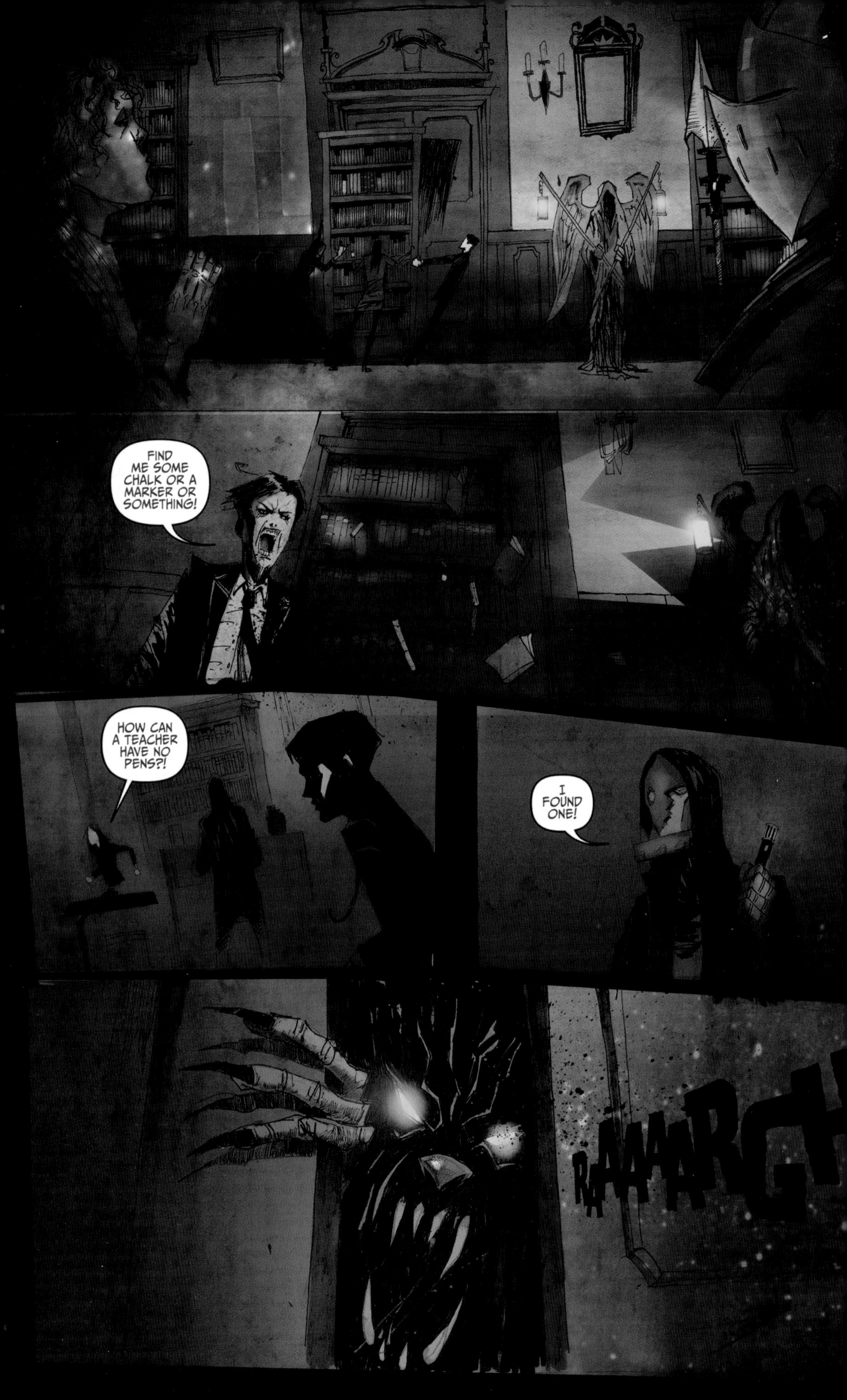
FIND ME SOME CHALK OR A MARKER OR SOMETHING!
HOW CAN A TEACHER HAVE NO PENS?!
I FOUND ONE!
RAAAARGH

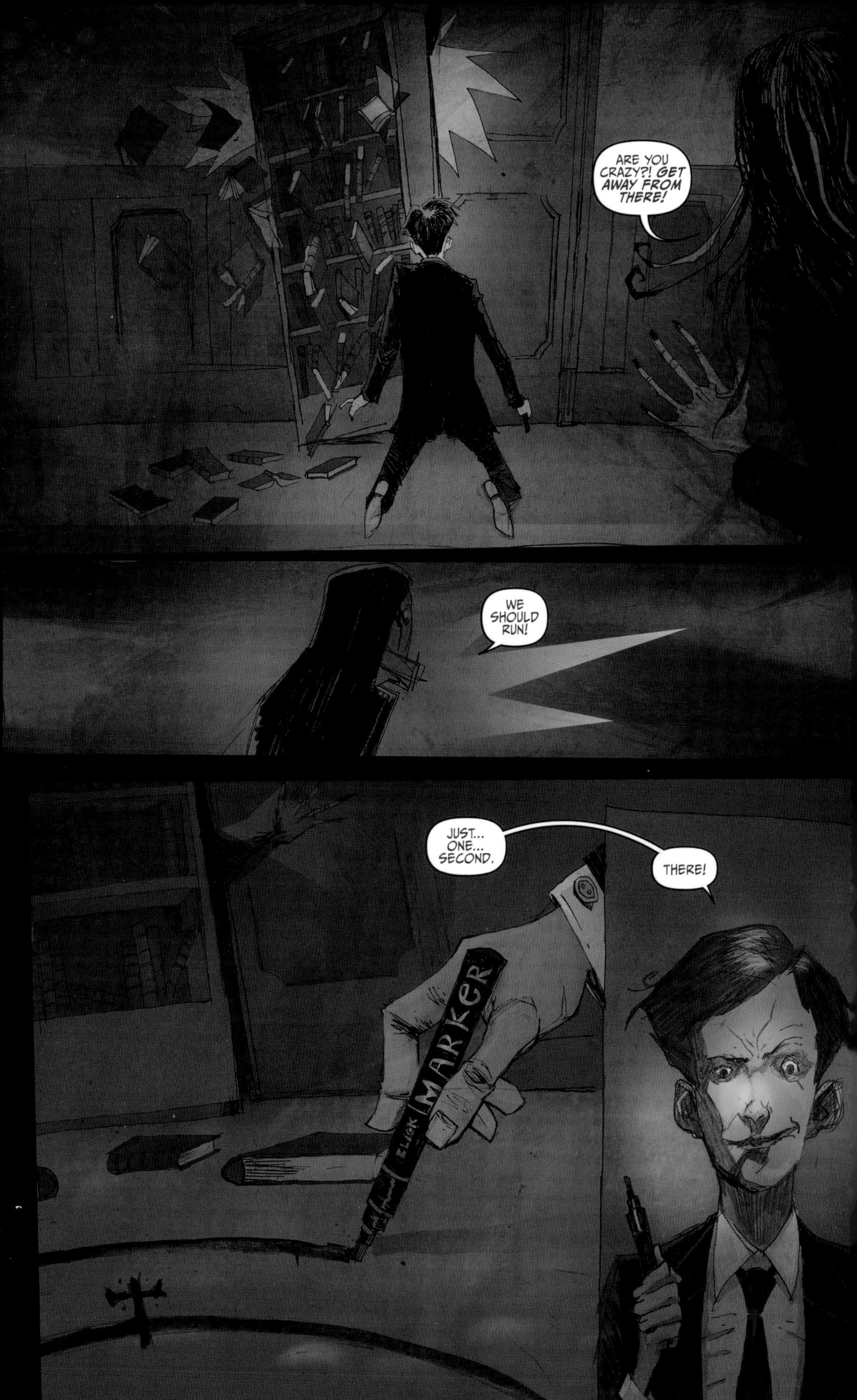
ARE YOU CRAZY?! GET AWAY FROM THERE!
WE SHOULD RUN!
JUST... ONE... SECOND.
THERE!
BLACK MARKER

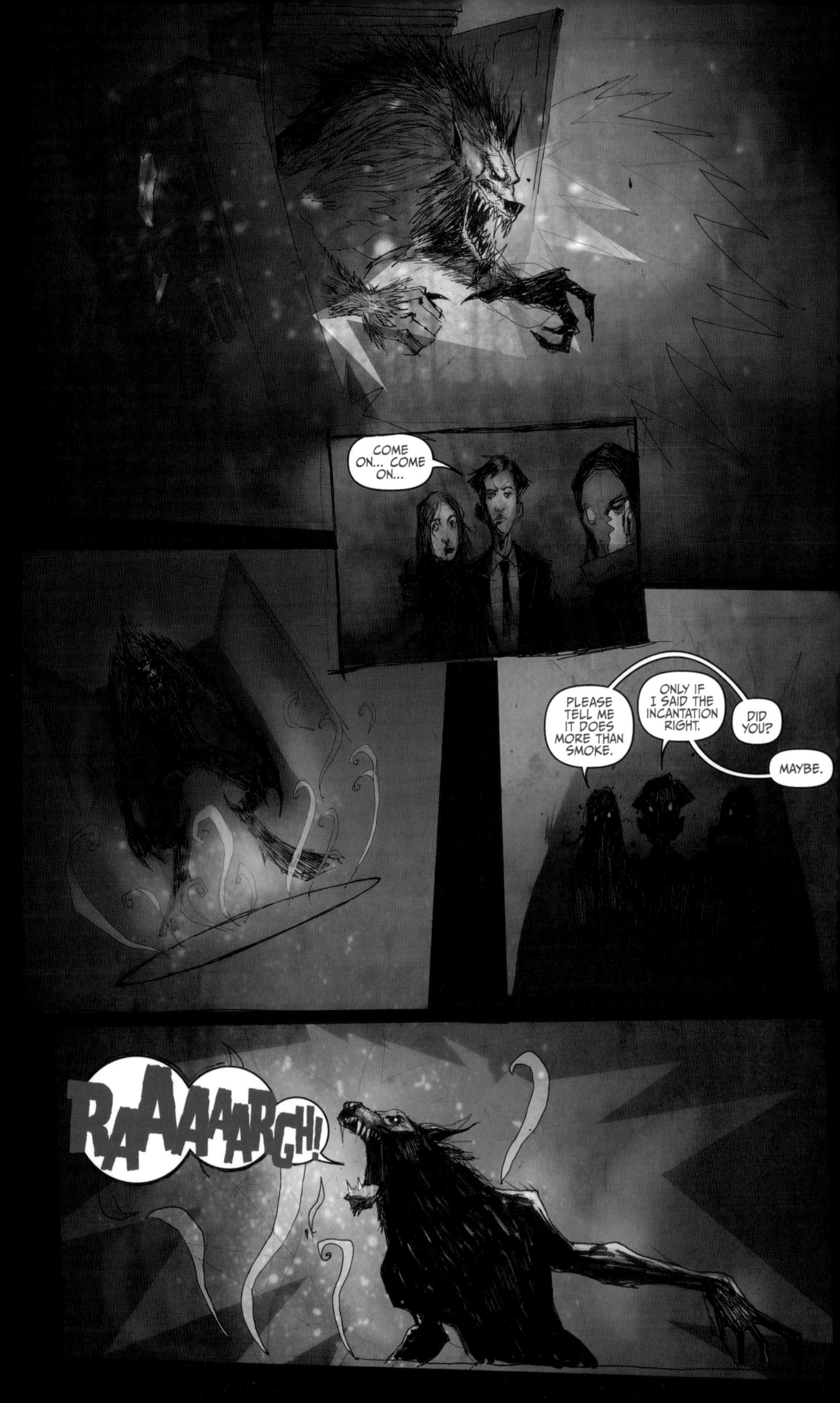
COME ON... COME ON...
PLEASE TELL ME IT DOES MORE THAN SMOKE.
ONLY IF I SAID THE INCANTATION RIGHT.
DID YOU?
MAYBE.
RAAAAARGH!

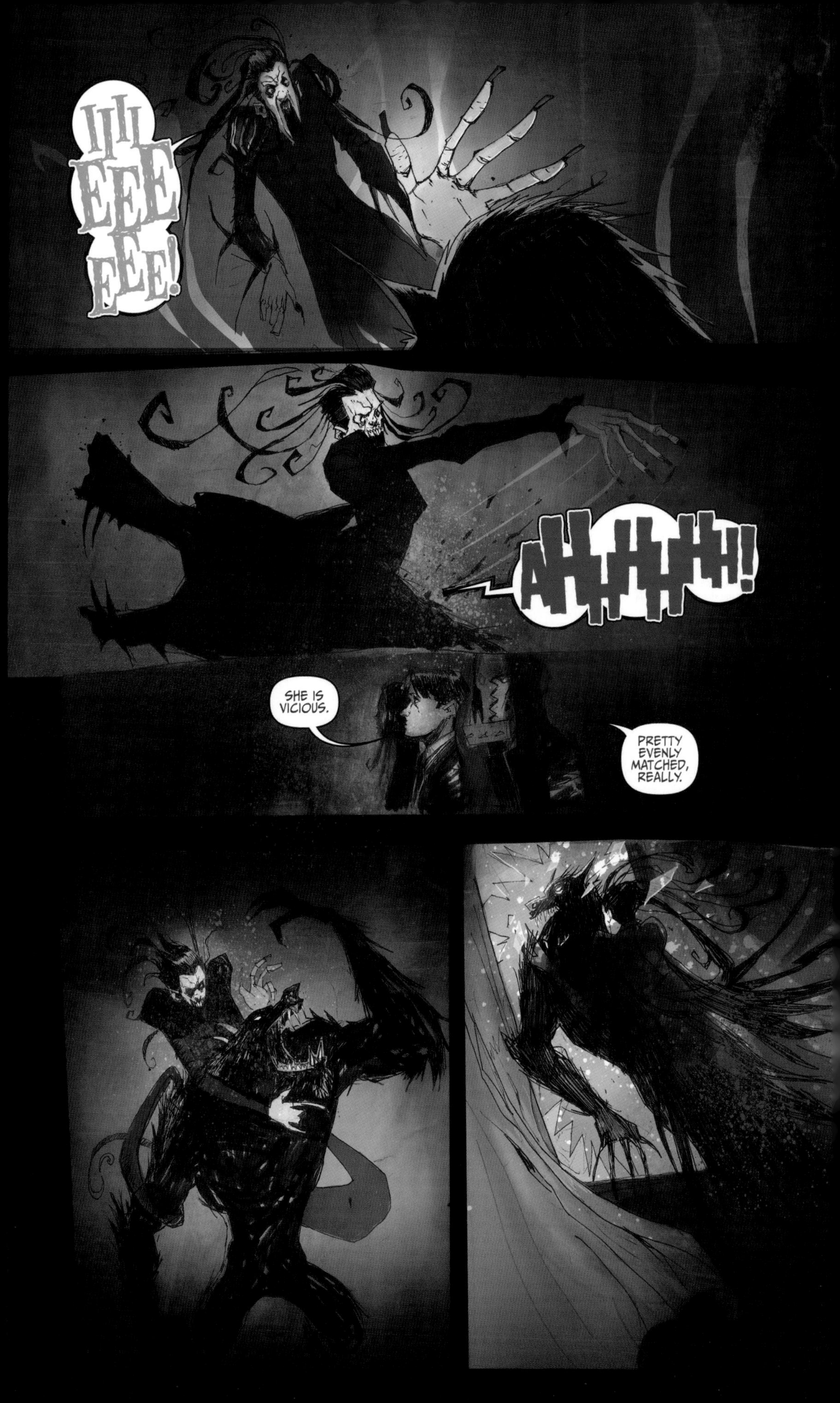
IIII EEE EEE!
AHHHHHH!
SHE IS VICIOUS.
PRETTY EVENLY MATCHED, REALLY.

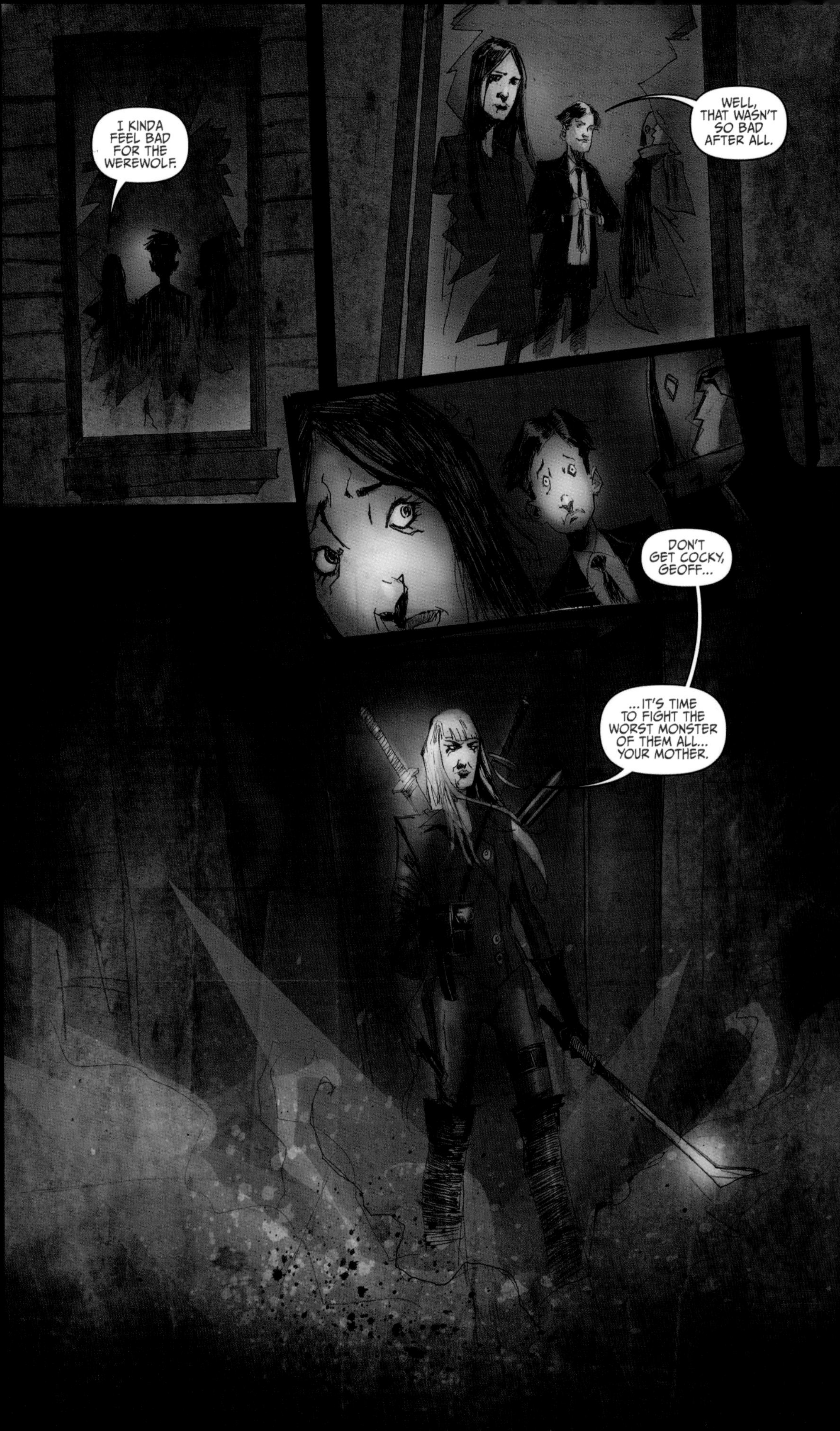
I KINDA FEEL BAD FOR THE WEREWOLF.
WELL, THAT WASN'T SO BAD AFTER ALL.
DON'T GET COCKY, GEOFF...
...IT'S TIME TO FIGHT THE WORST MONSTER OF THEM ALL... YOUR MOTHER.

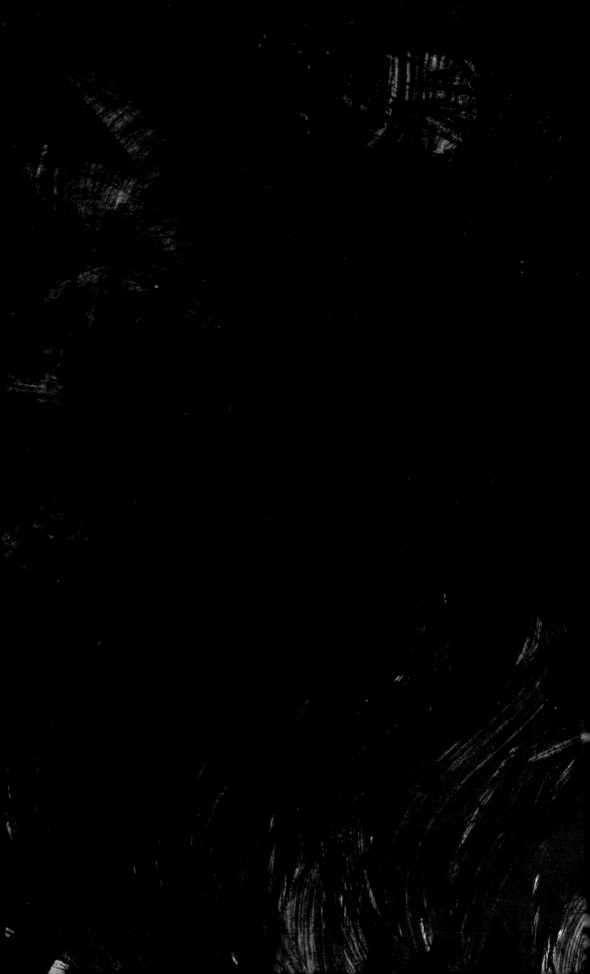

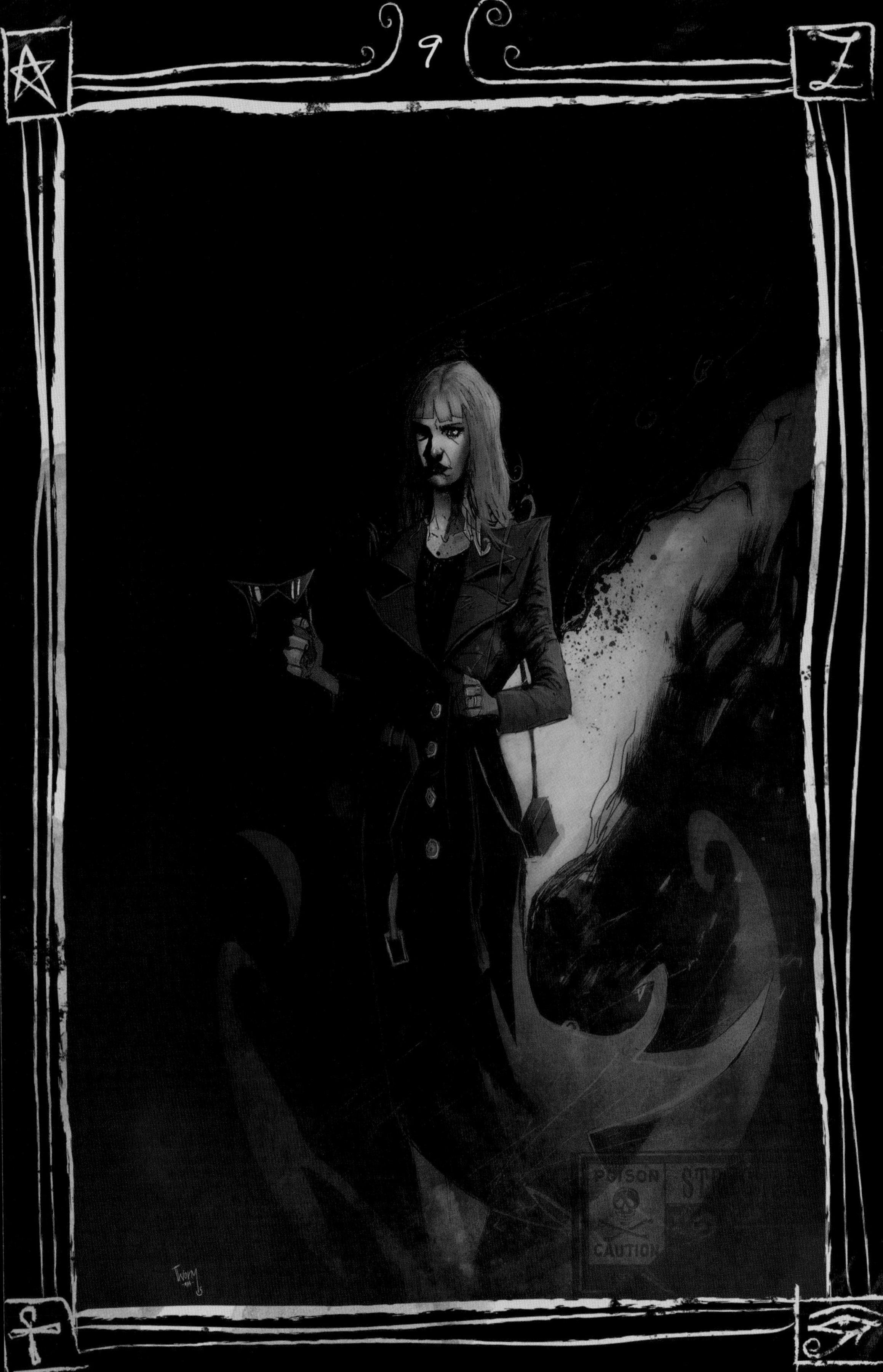
9
POISON
CAUTION

YES, VERY GOOD.

THERE IS A WIDE ARRAY OF METHODS TO KILL JUST ABOUT EVERY MONSTER.

DEMON
DJINN
SUCCUBUS
INCUBUS
GOLEM
BAD SEEDS
SKINWALKER
CHUPACABRA
WENDIGO
GOBLINS
SEA MONSTER
GIL MAN

CENTAUR
TROLL
KRAKEN
KAIJU
MERMEN
ASWANG
WRAITHS
HAG
DYBBUKS

YETI
HOMUNCULUS
KAPPA
KITSUNE
TANUKI
BEKENEKO
AMAITACHI
OKUROBUKI
JIANGSHI
PENANGGALAN
THE POSSESSED
GHOUL

BUT THE TRUTH OF THE MATTER IS, NOTHING—AND I MEAN NOTHING—CAN LIVE WITHOUT A HEAD.

GHOST
DEMON
DJINN
SUCCUBUS
INCUBUS
GOLEM
BAD SEEDS
SKINWALKER
CHUPACABRA
WENDIGO
GOBLINS
SEA MONSTER
GIL MAN.

MEDUSA
CENTAUR
TROLL
KRAKEN
KAIJU
MERMEN
ASWANG
WRAITHS
HAG
DYBBUK

GORGON
SATYR
YETI
HOMUNCULUS
PA
KITSUNE
BEKENEKO
CHI
KI

BEYOND SPIRITS AND DEMONS AND OTHER SUPERNATURAL ENTITIES, IF IT'S MADE OF FLESH, YOU CAN DECAPITATE IT.

THERE IS ONE MONSTER THAT DEFIES ALMOST ALL RULES.

YES, THIS ONE CAN LOSE ITS HEAD, BUT IT IS THE MOST CUNNING OF ALL...

...THE HUMAN MONSTER.

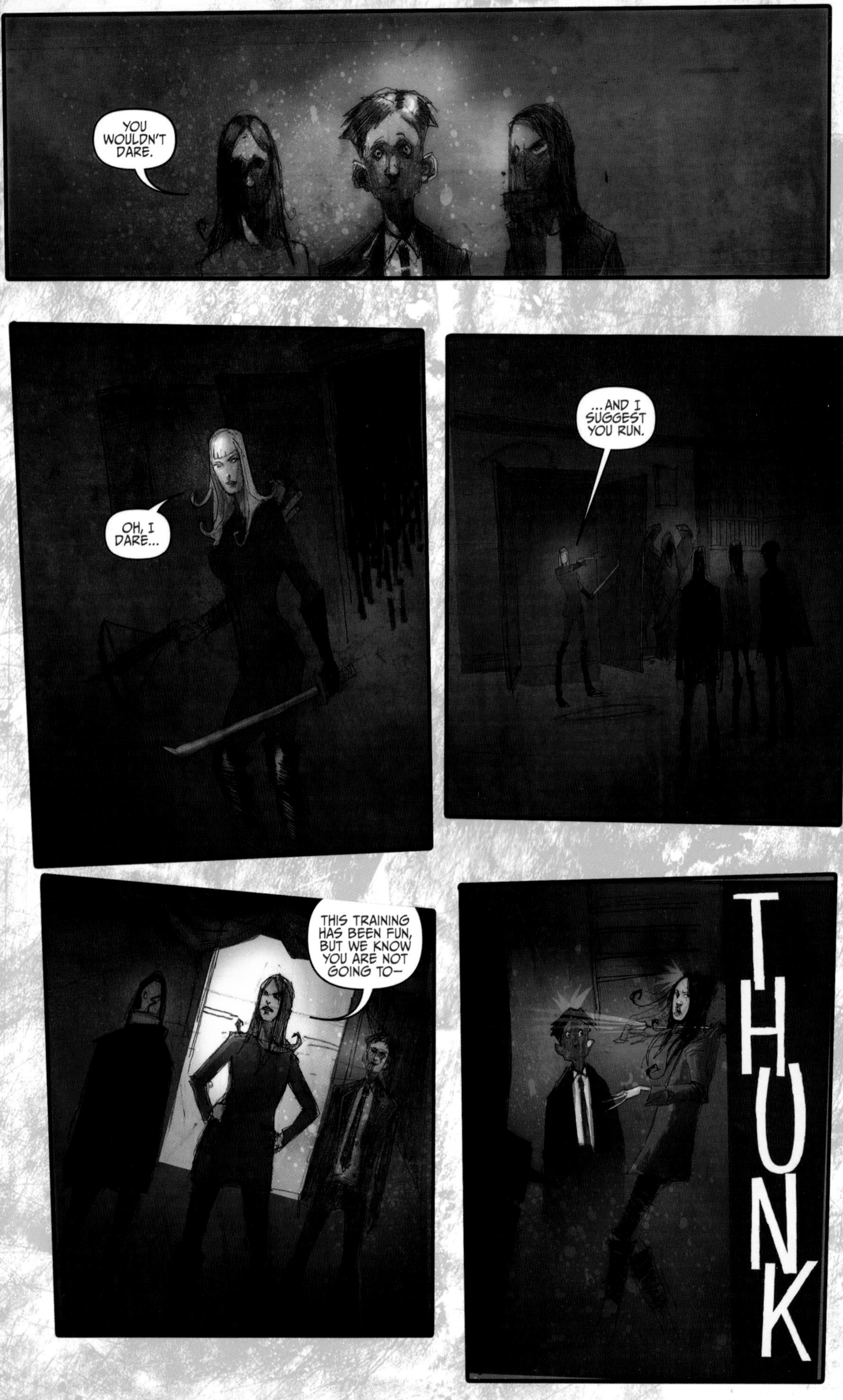
YOU WOULDN'T DARE.
OH, I DARE...
...AND I SUGGEST YOU RUN.
THIS TRAINING HAS BEEN FUN, BUT WE KNOW YOU ARE NOT GOING TO—
THUNK

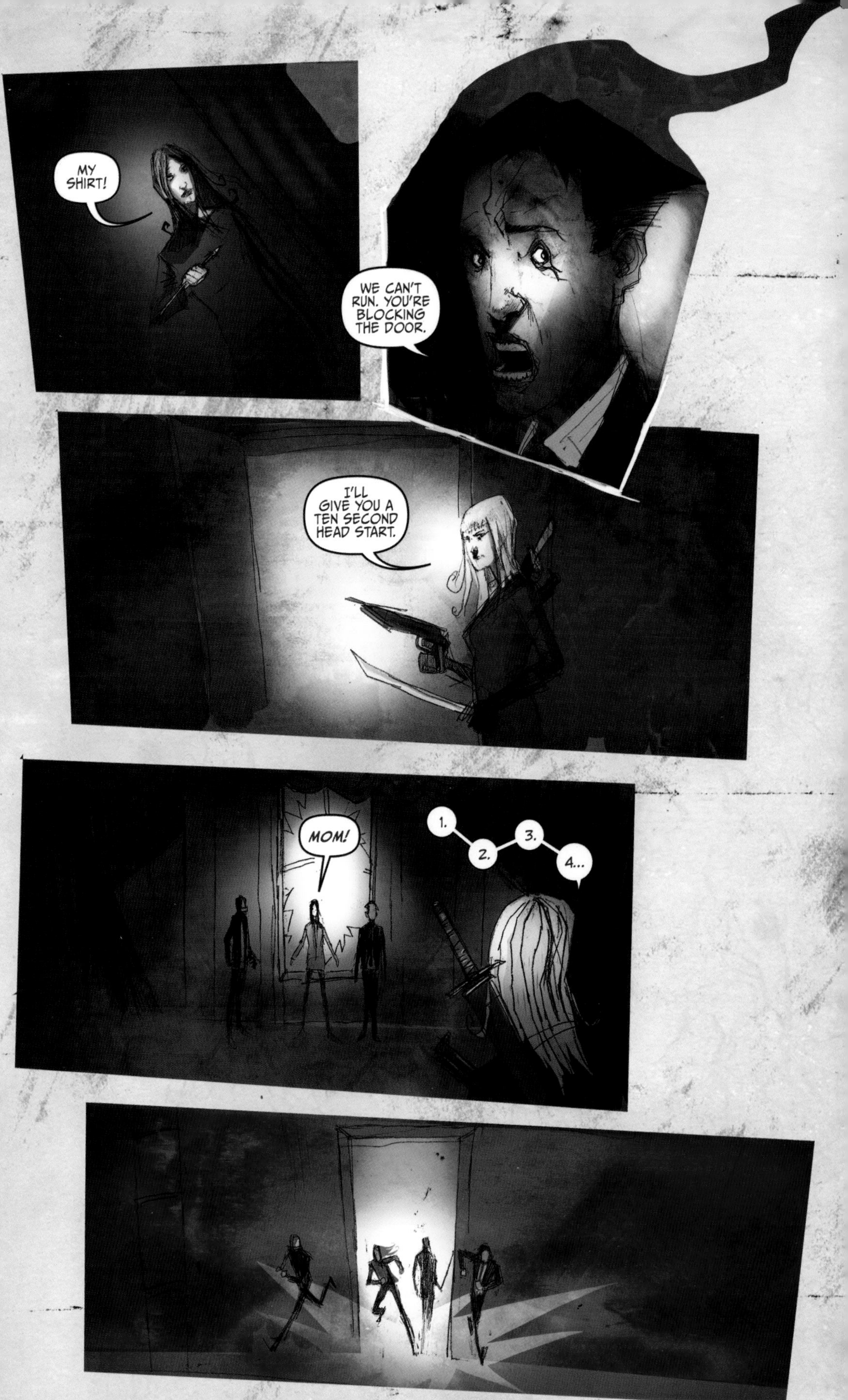
MY SHIRT!
WE CAN'T RUN. YOU'RE BLOCKING THE DOOR.
I'LL GIVE YOU A TEN SECOND HEAD START.
MOM!
1.
2.
3.
4...

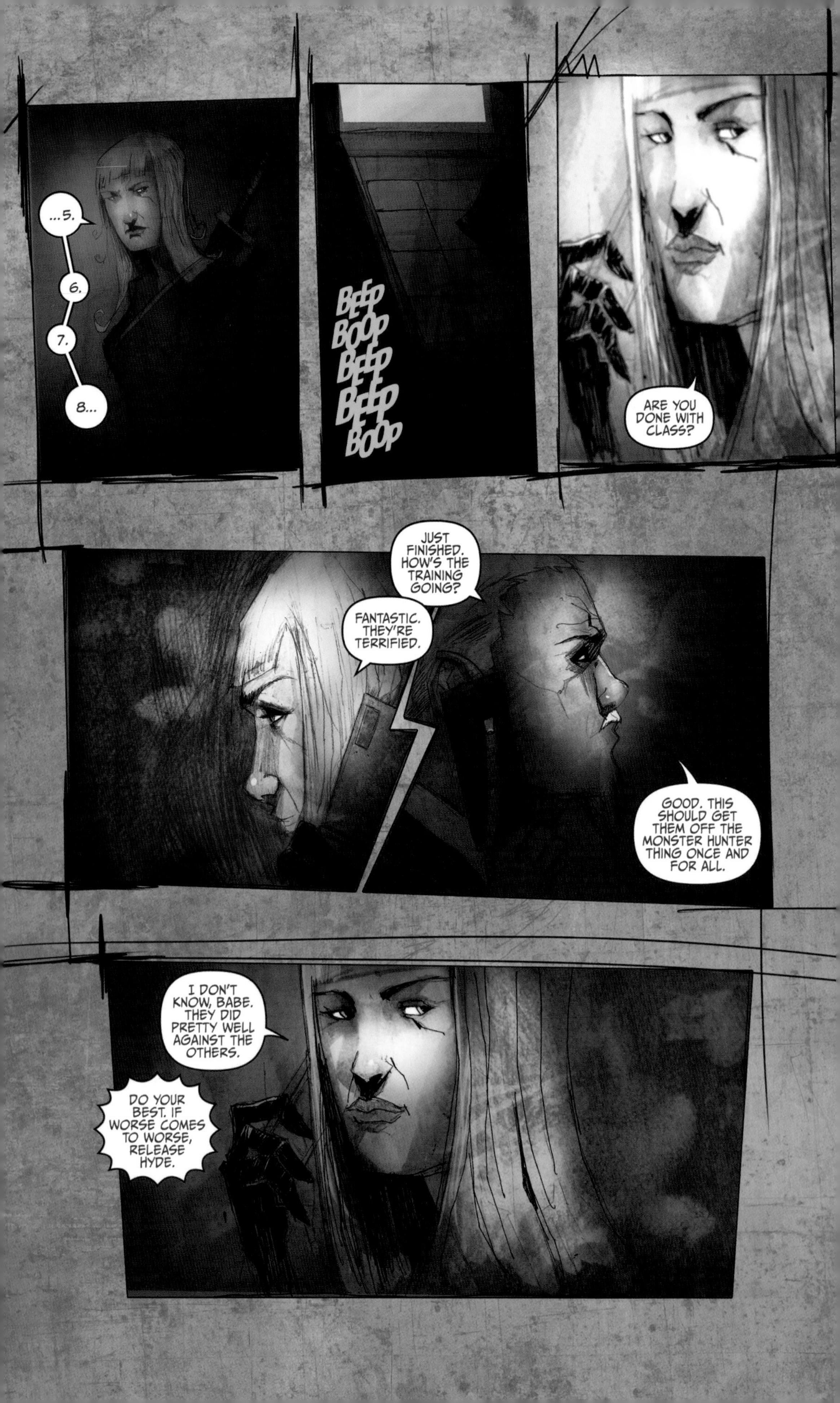

...5.
6.
7.
8...
BEEP BOOP BEEP BEEP BOOP
ARE YOU DONE WITH CLASS?
JUST FINISHED. HOW'S THE TRAINING GOING?
FANTASTIC. THEY'RE TERRIFIED.
GOOD. THIS SHOULD GET THEM OFF THE MONSTER HUNTER THING ONCE AND FOR ALL.
I DON'T KNOW, BABE. THEY DID PRETTY WELL AGAINST THE OTHERS.
DO YOUR BEST. IF WORSE COMES TO WORSE, RELEASE HYDE.

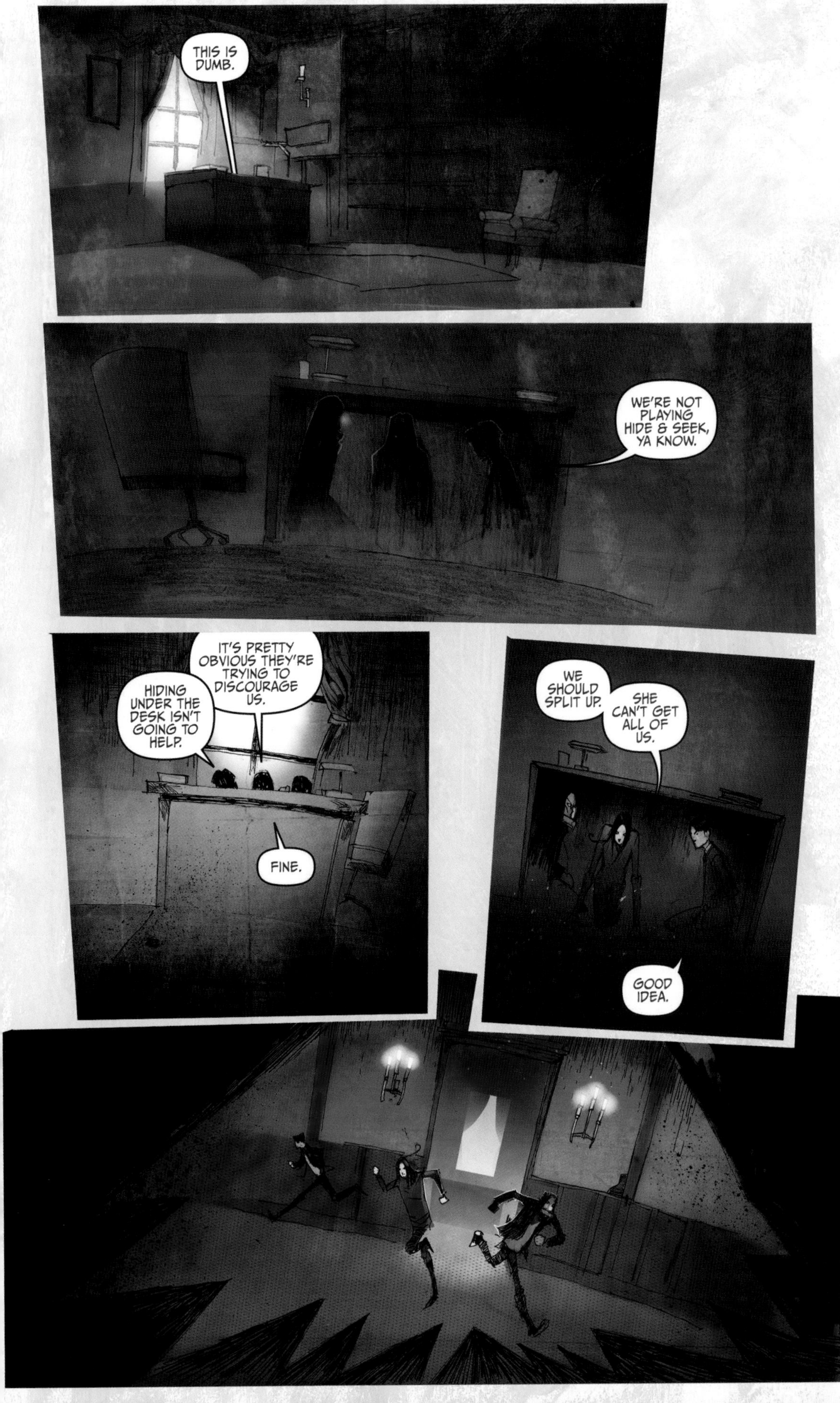
THIS IS DUMB.
WE'RE NOT PLAYING HIDE & SEEK, YA KNOW.
HIDING UNDER THE DESK ISN'T GOING TO HELP.
IT'S PRETTY OBVIOUS THEY'RE TRYING TO DISCOURAGE US.
FINE.
WE SHOULD SPLIT UP.
SHE CAN'T GET ALL OF US.
GOOD IDEA.

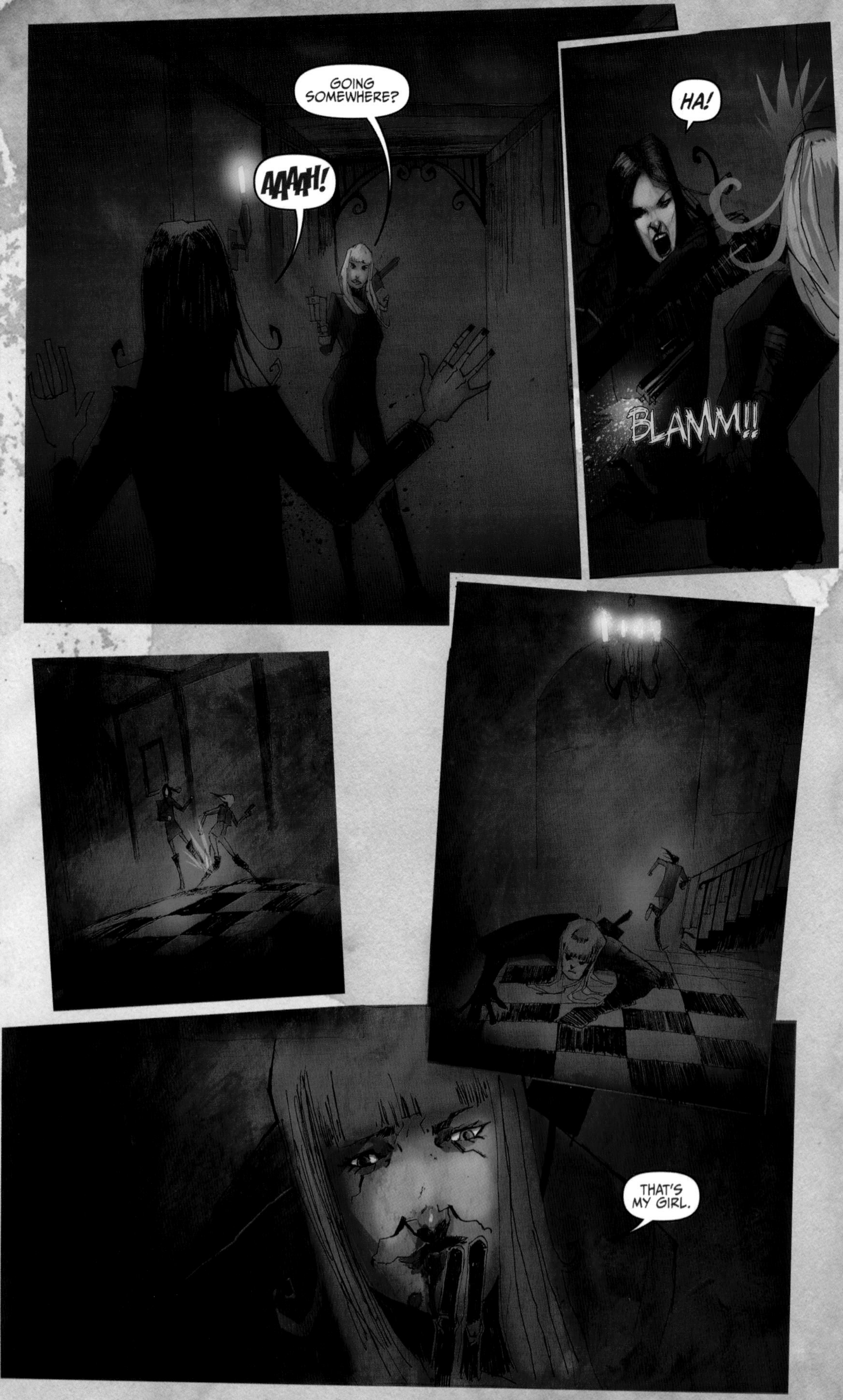
GOING SOMEWHERE?
AAAAH!
HA!
BLAMM!!
THAT'S MY GIRL.

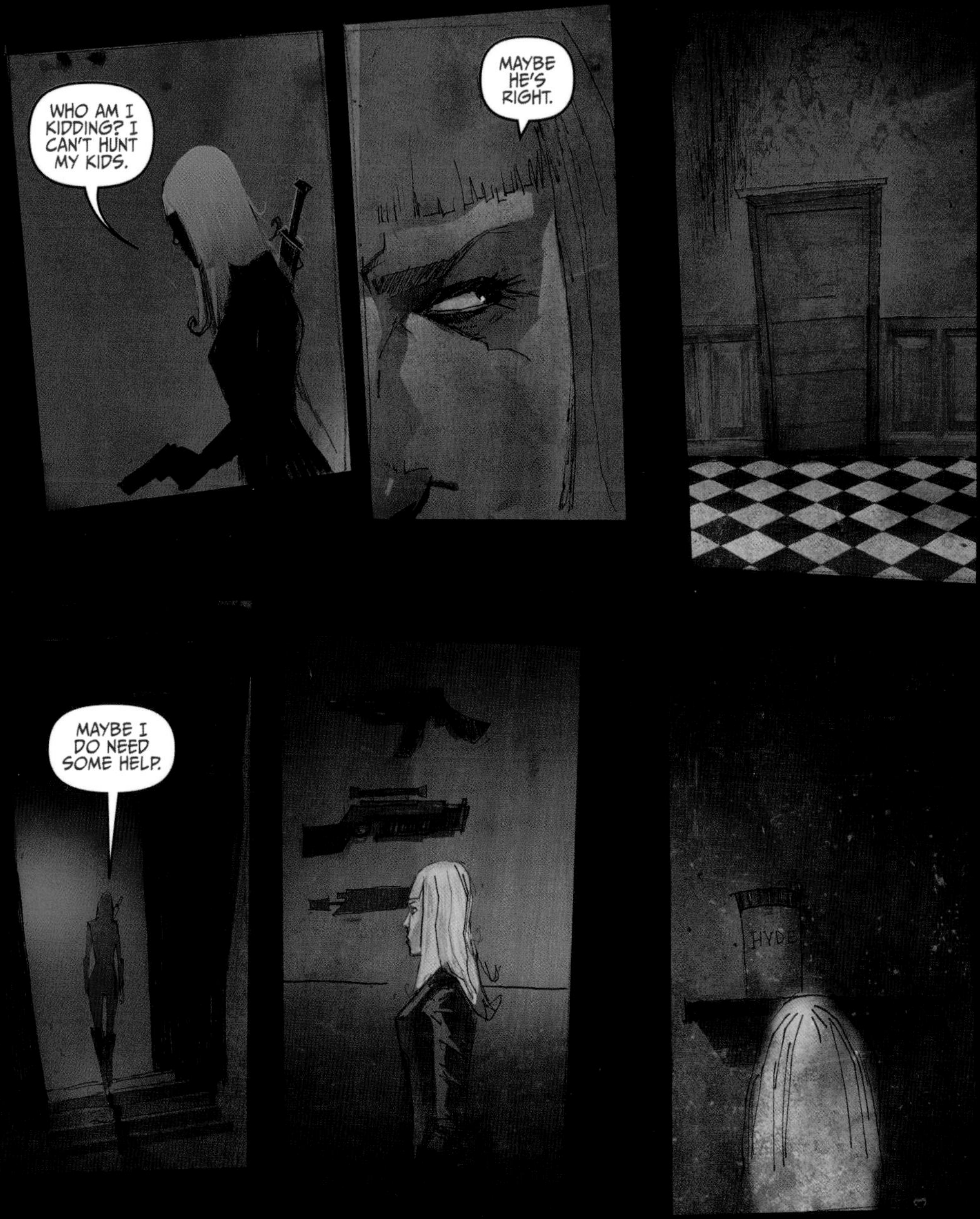
WHO AM I KIDDING? I CAN'T HUNT MY KIDS.
MAYBE HE'S RIGHT.
MAYBE I DO NEED SOME HELP.
HYDE

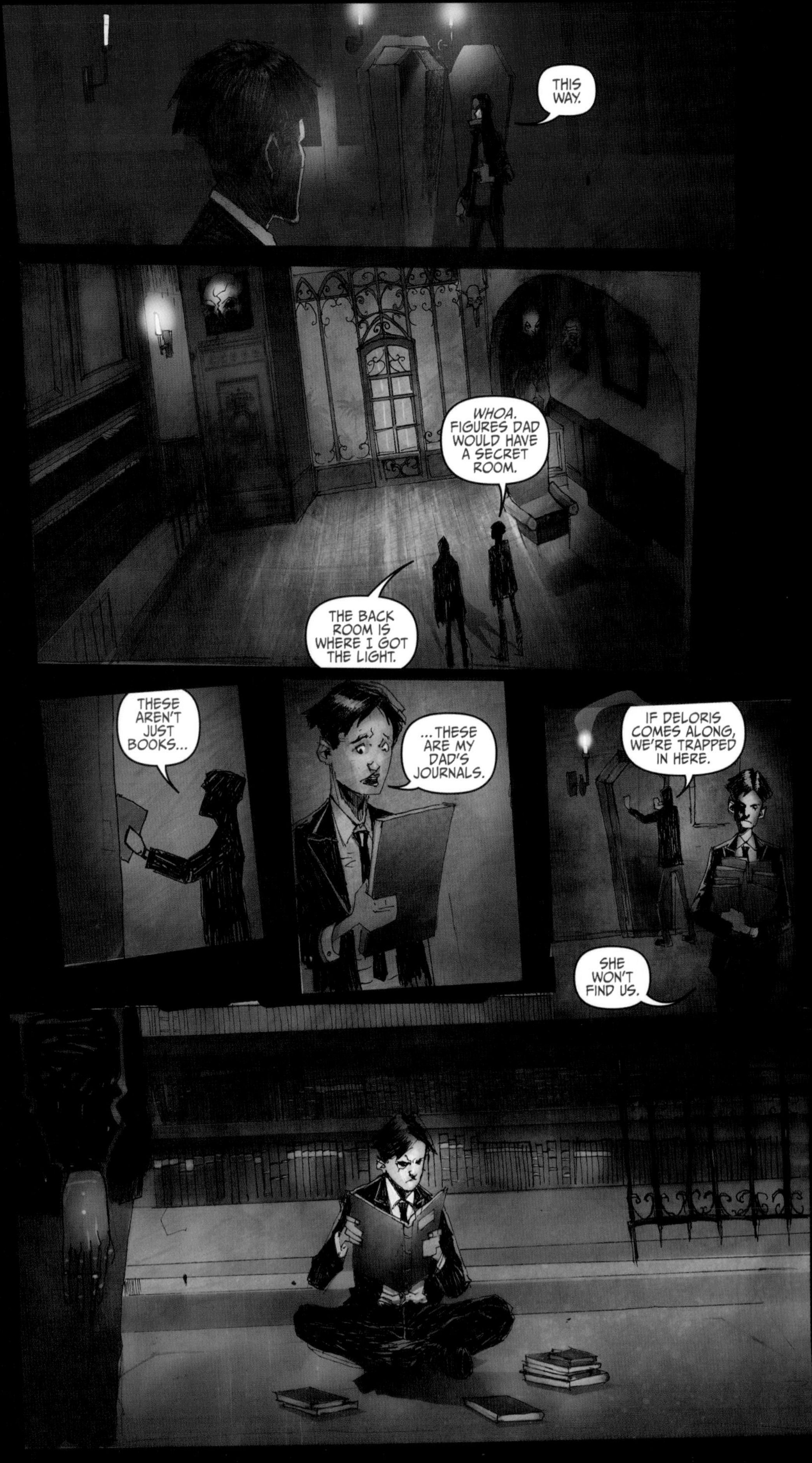
THIS WAY.
WHOA. FIGURES DAD WOULD HAVE A SECRET ROOM.
THE BACK ROOM IS WHERE I GOT THE LIGHT.
THESE AREN'T JUST BOOKS...
...THESE ARE MY DAD'S JOURNALS.
IF DELORIS COMES ALONG, WE'RE TRAPPED IN HERE.
SHE WON'T FIND US.

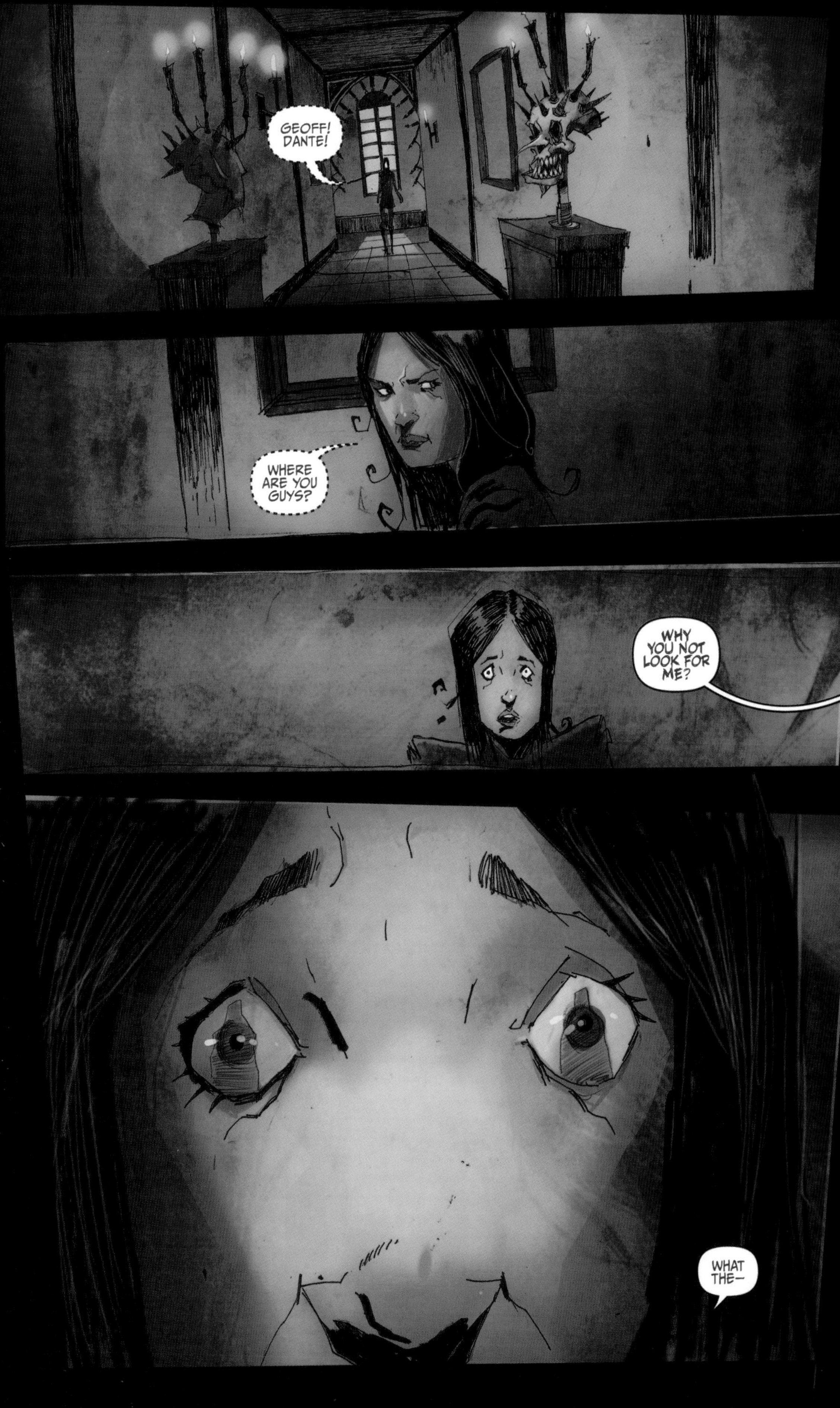
GEOFF! DANTE!
WHERE ARE YOU GUYS?
WHY YOU NOT LOOK FOR ME?
WHAT THE—

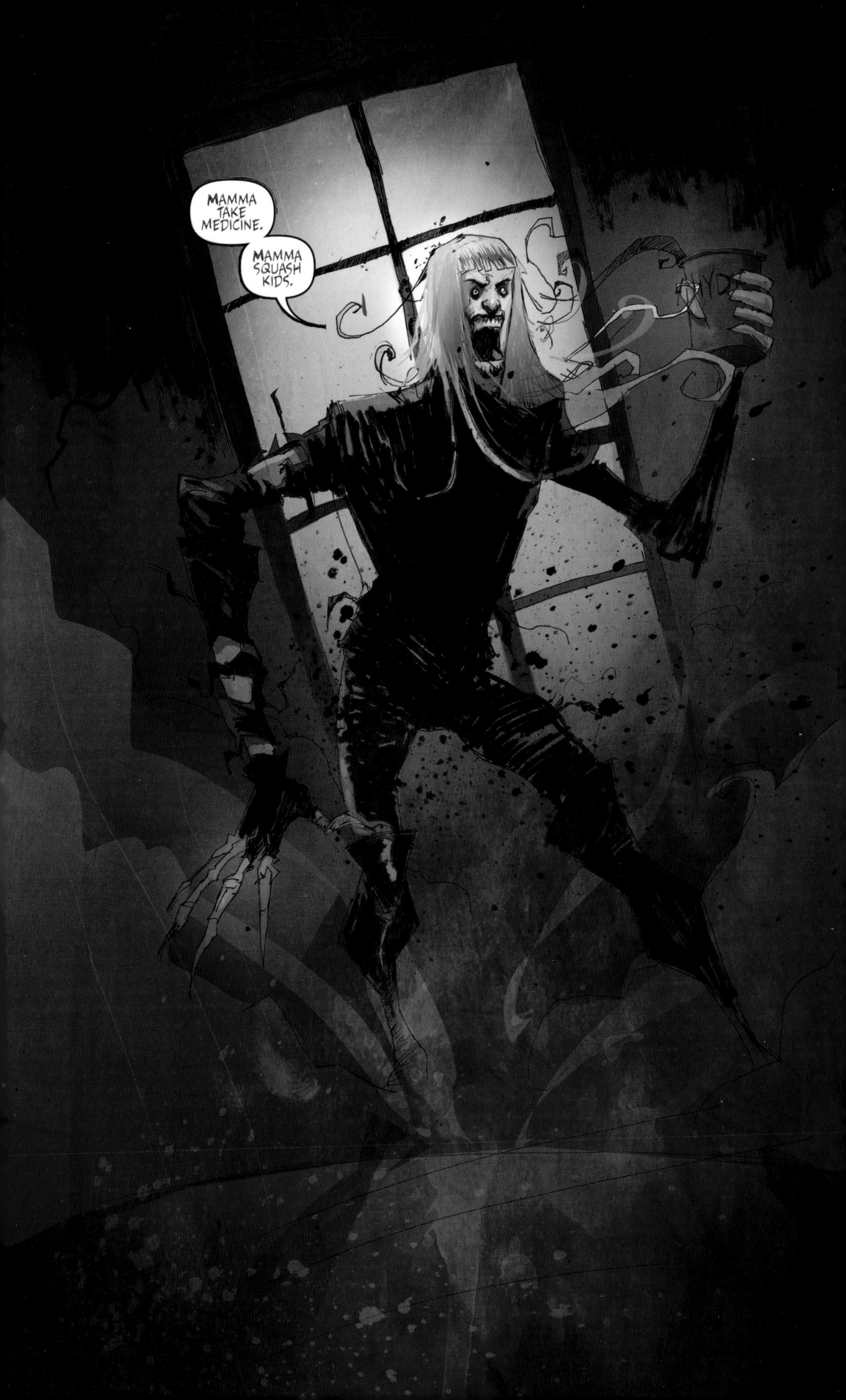
MAMMA TAKE MEDICINE.
MAMMA SQUASH KIDS.

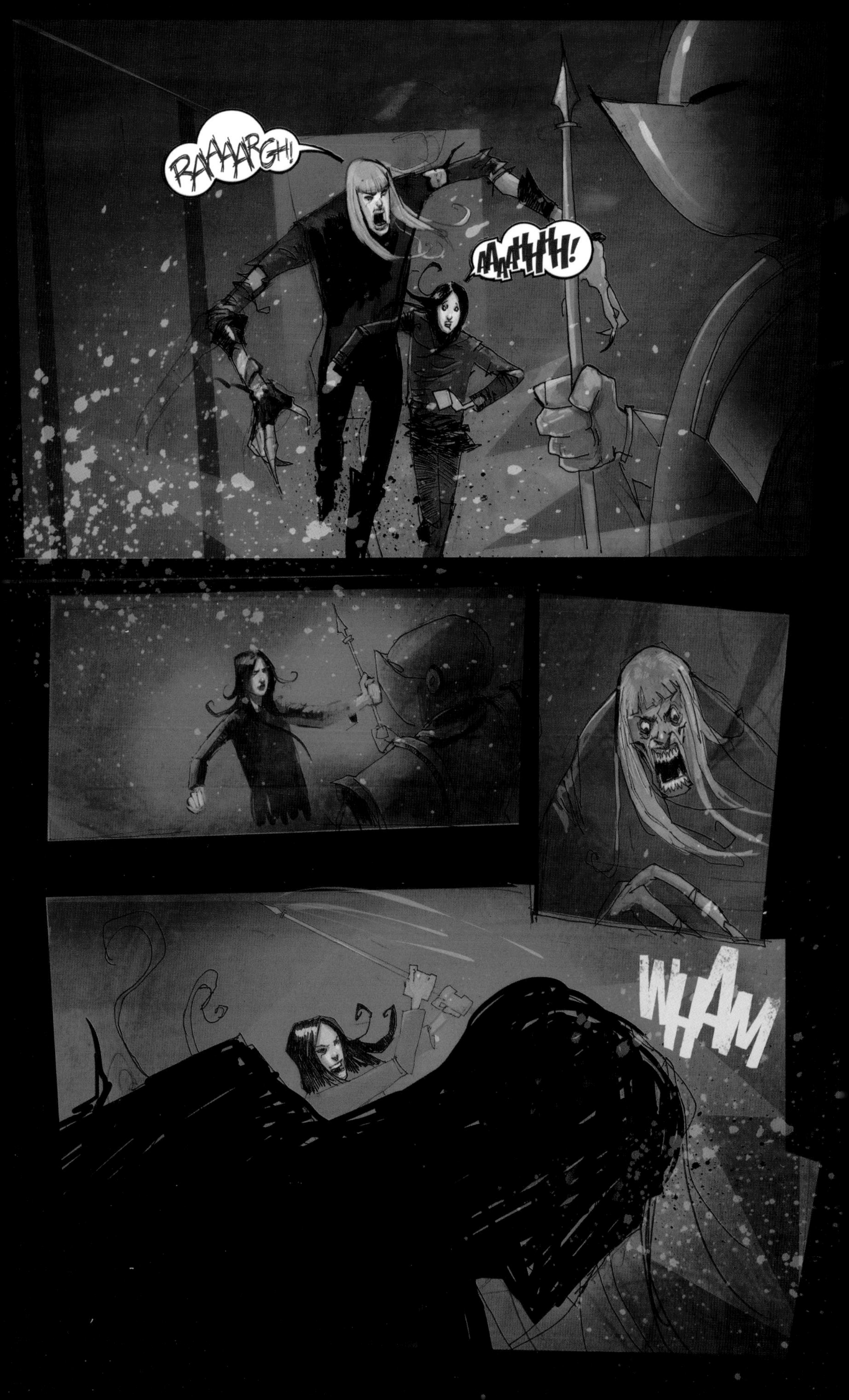
RAAAARGH!
AAAAHHH!
WHAM

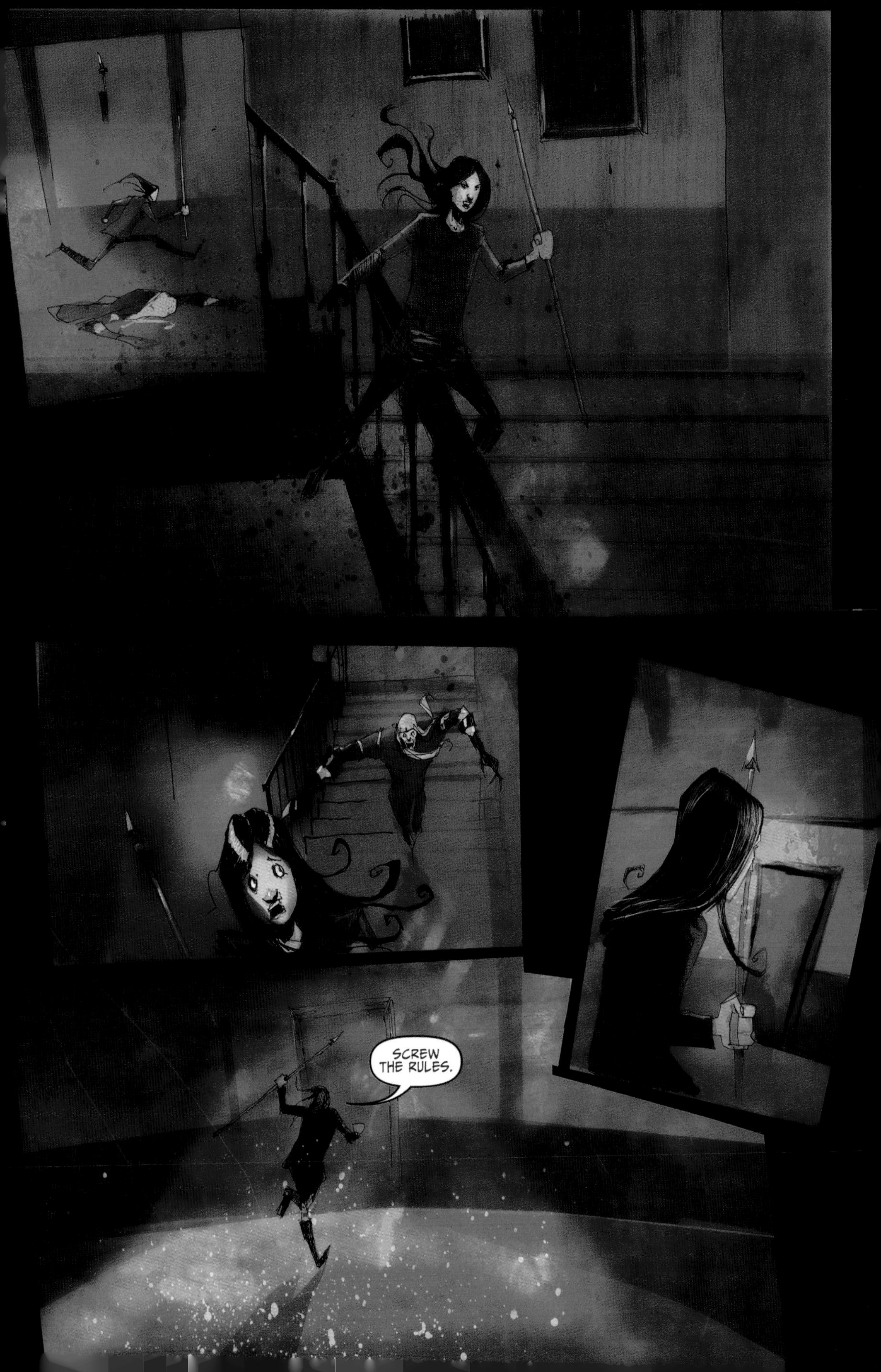
SCREW THE RULES.

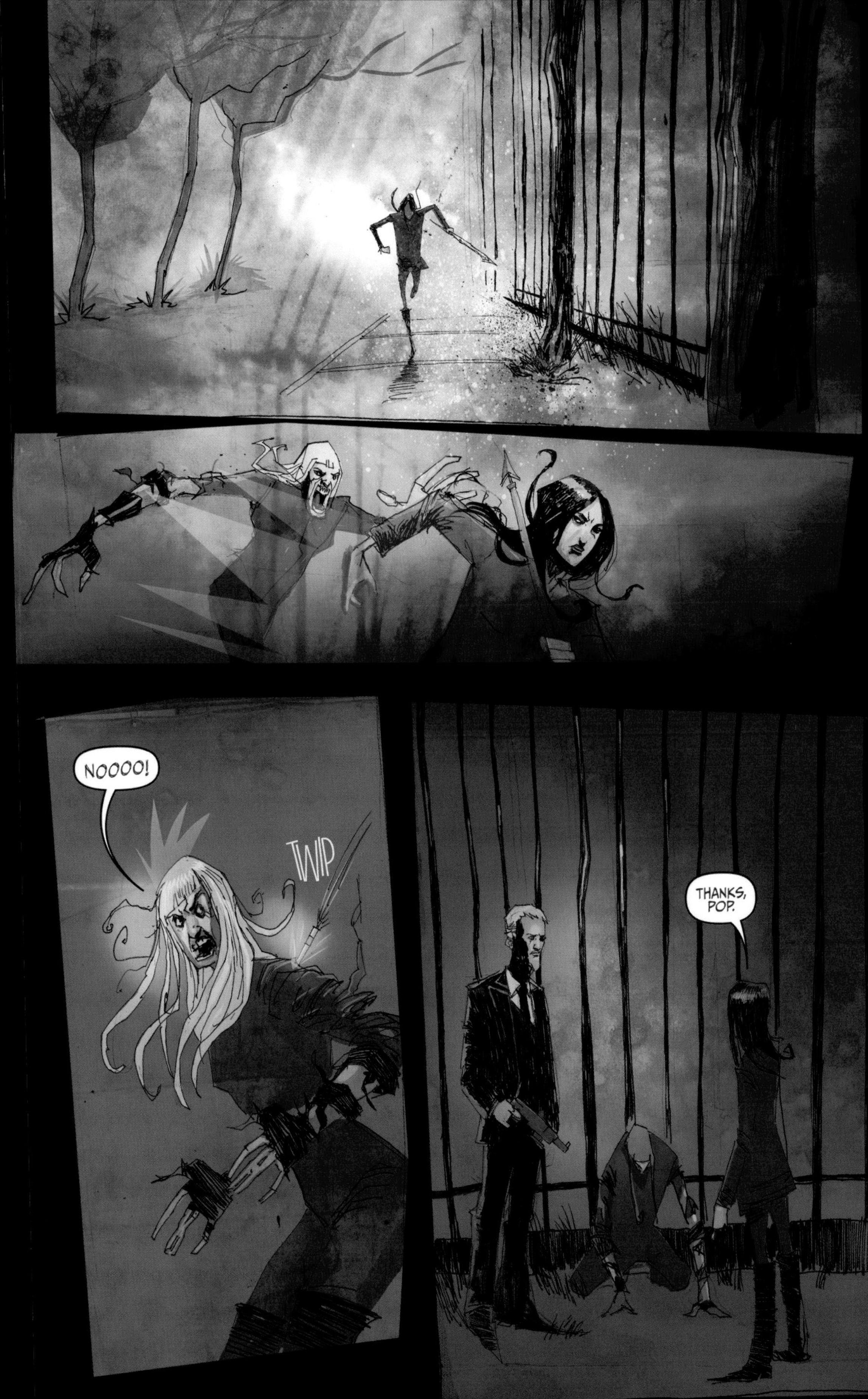
NOOOO!
TWIP
THANKS, POP.

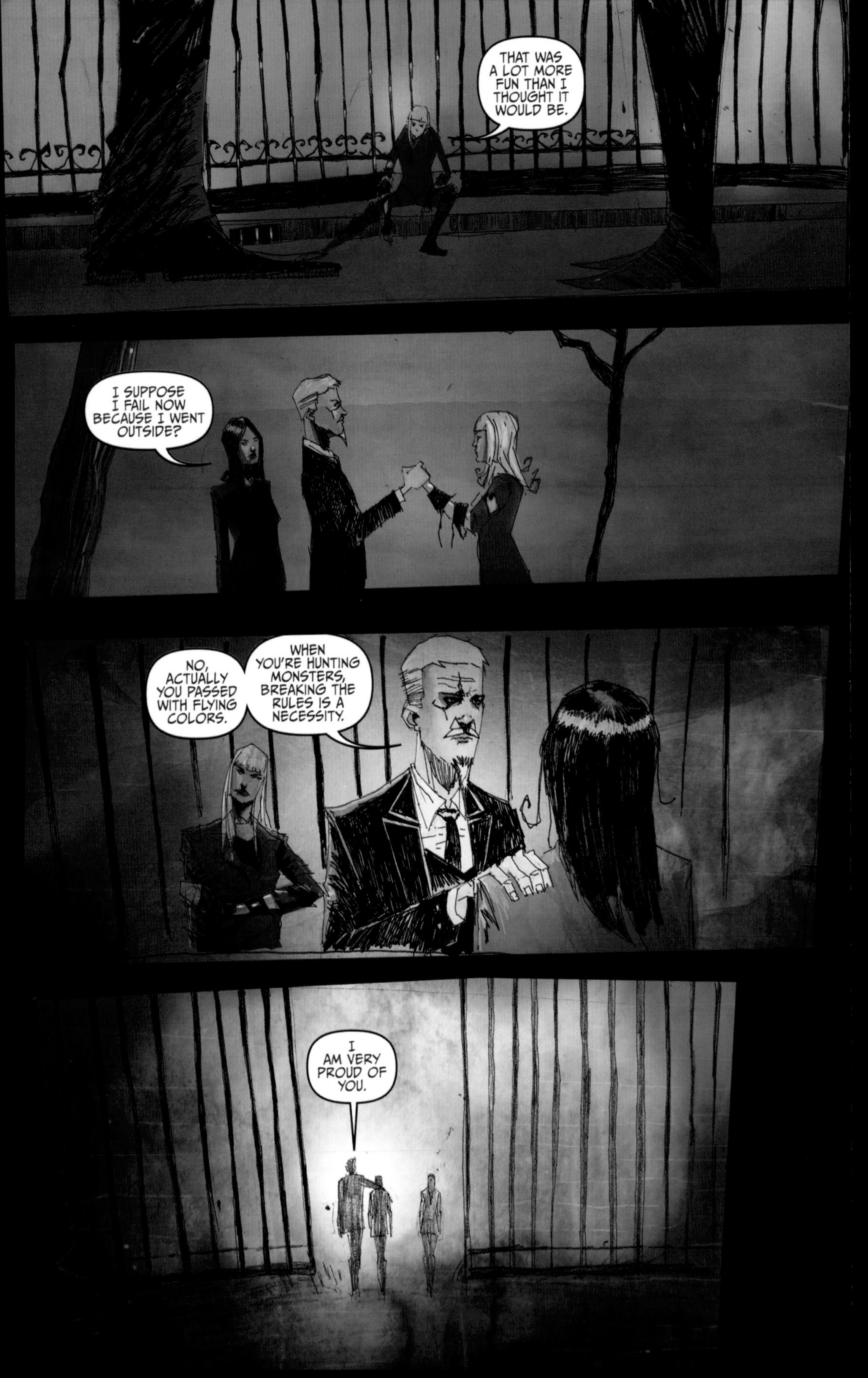
THAT WAS A LOT MORE FUN THAN I THOUGHT IT WOULD BE.
I SUPPOSE I FAIL NOW BECAUSE I WENT OUTSIDE?
NO, ACTUALLY YOU PASSED WITH FLYING COLORS.
WHEN YOU'RE HUNTING MONSTERS, BREAKING THE RULES IS A NECESSITY.
I AM VERY PROUD OF YOU.

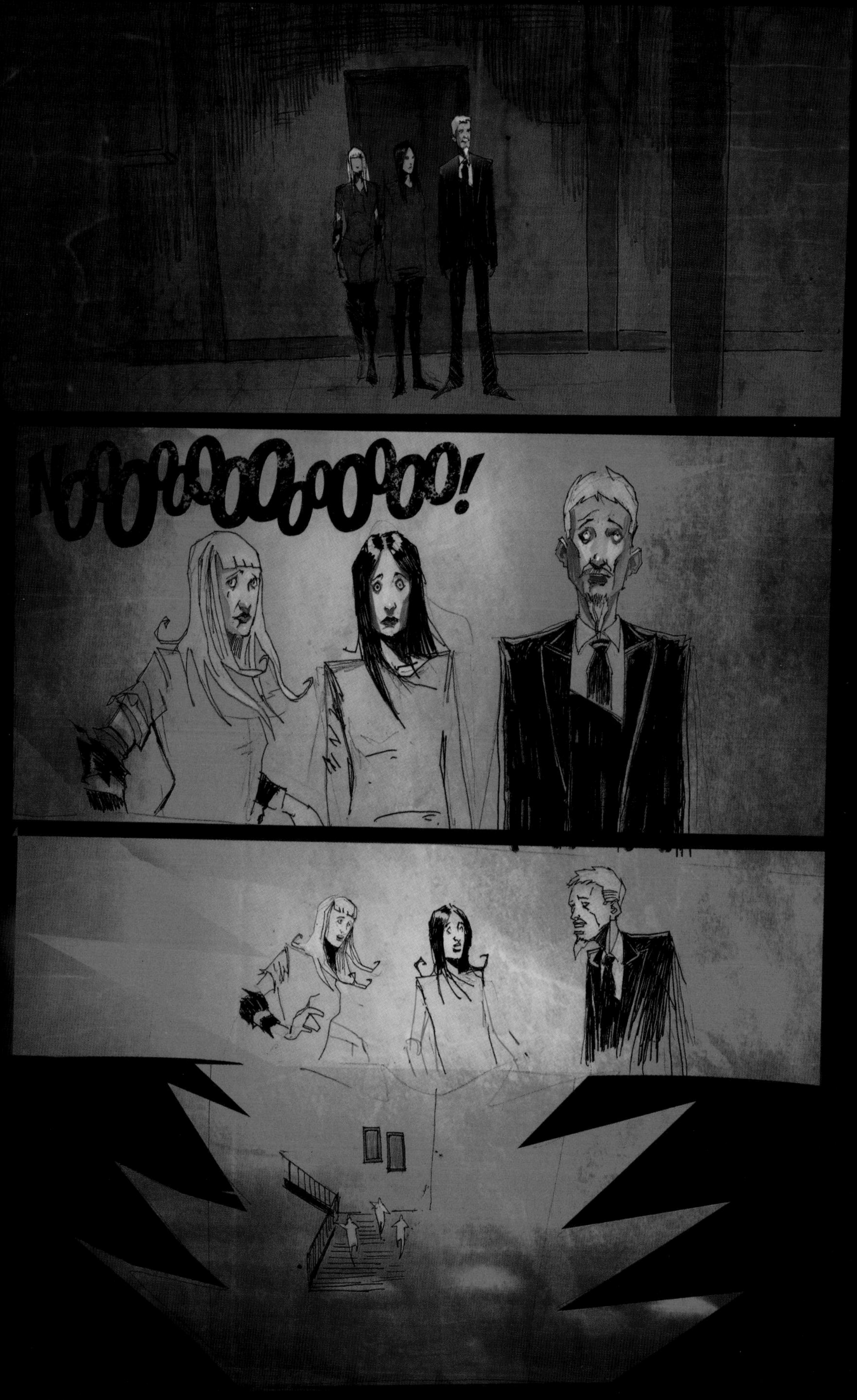
NOOOOOOOOOOOOOO!

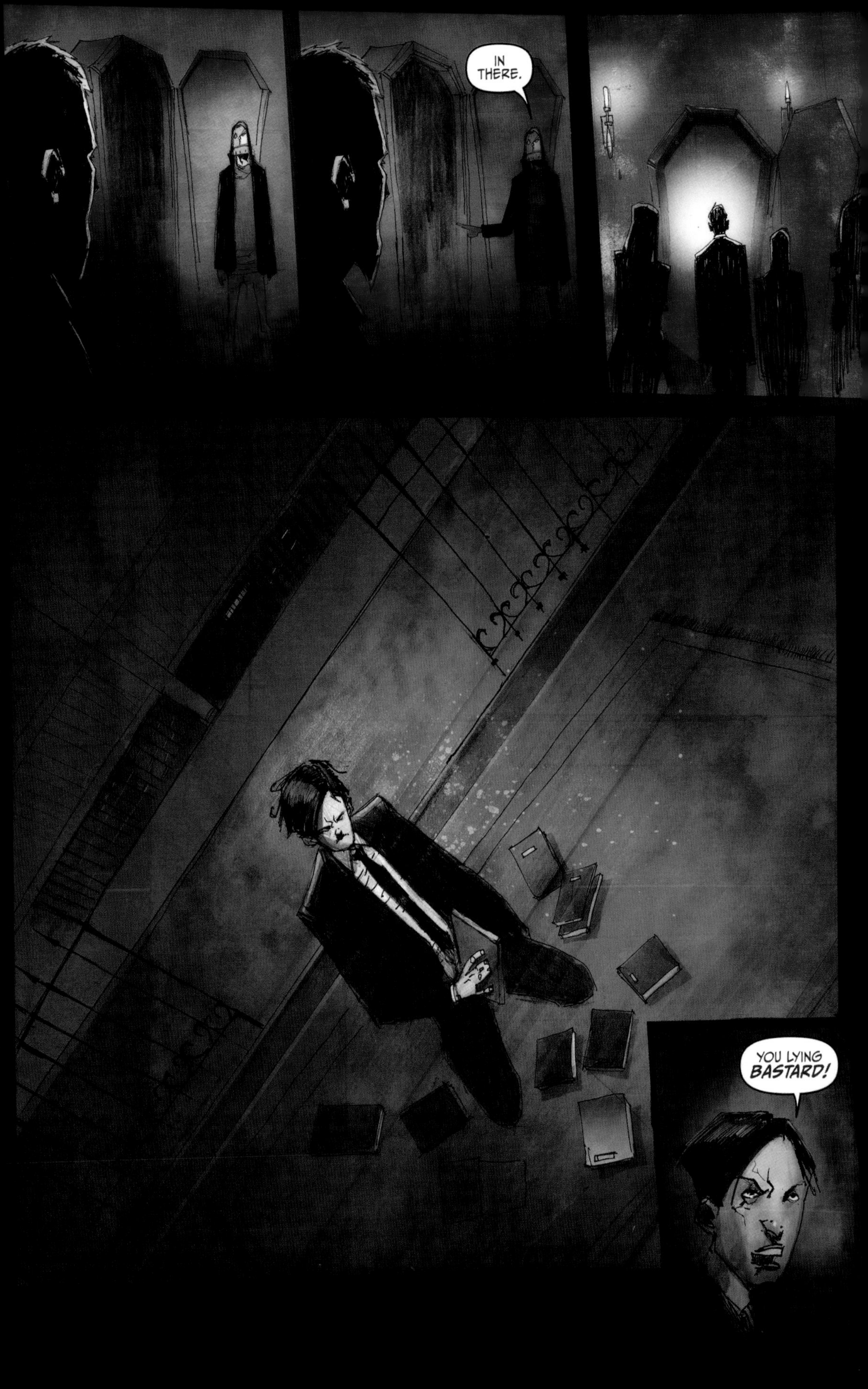
IN THERE.
YOU LYING BASTARD!

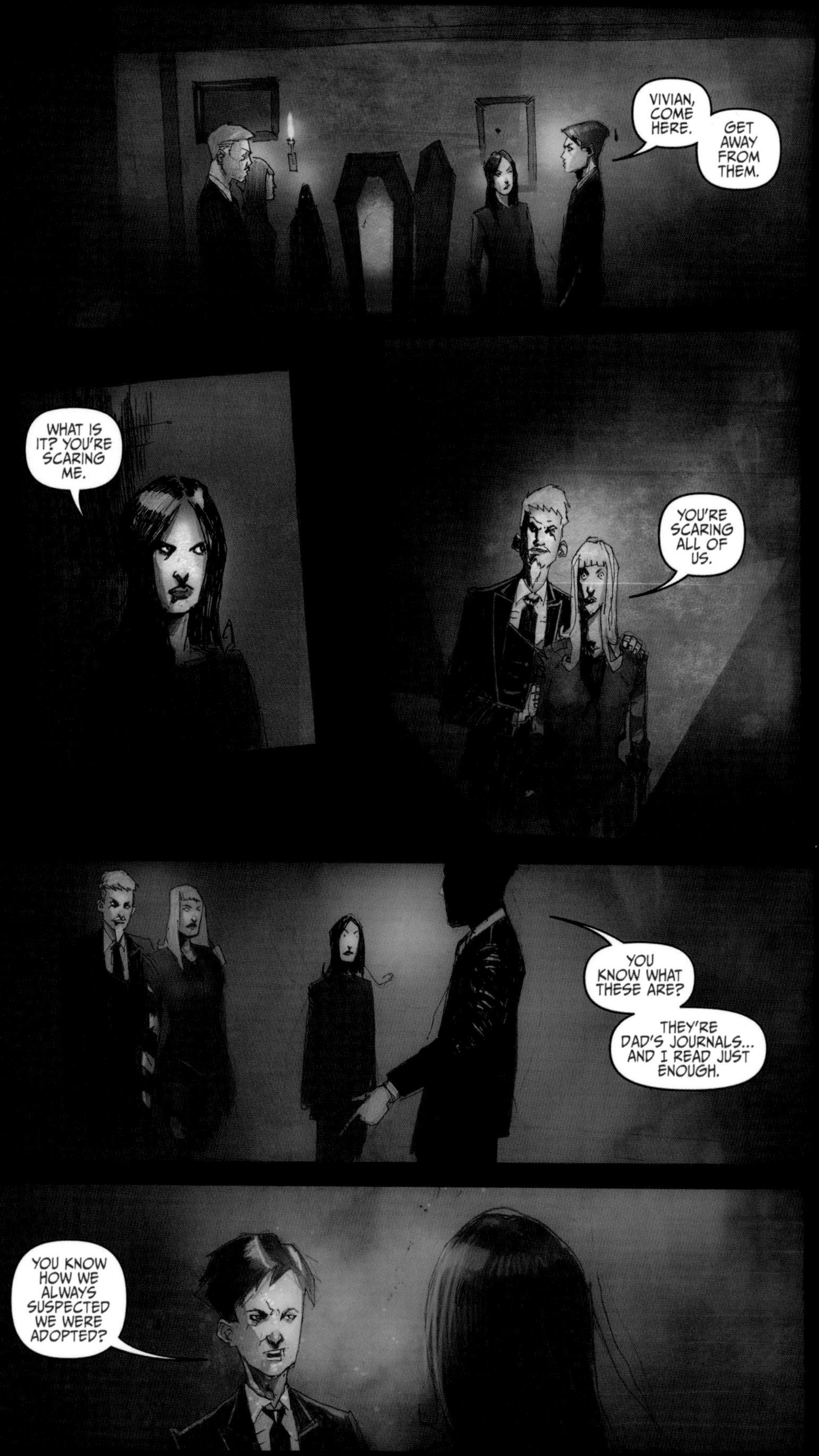
VIVIAN, COME HERE.
GET AWAY FROM THEM.
WHAT IS IT? YOU'RE SCARING ME.
YOU'RE SCARING ALL OF US.
YOU KNOW WHAT THESE ARE?
THEY'RE DAD'S JOURNALS... AND I READ JUST ENOUGH.
YOU KNOW HOW WE ALWAYS SUSPECTED WE WERE ADOPTED?

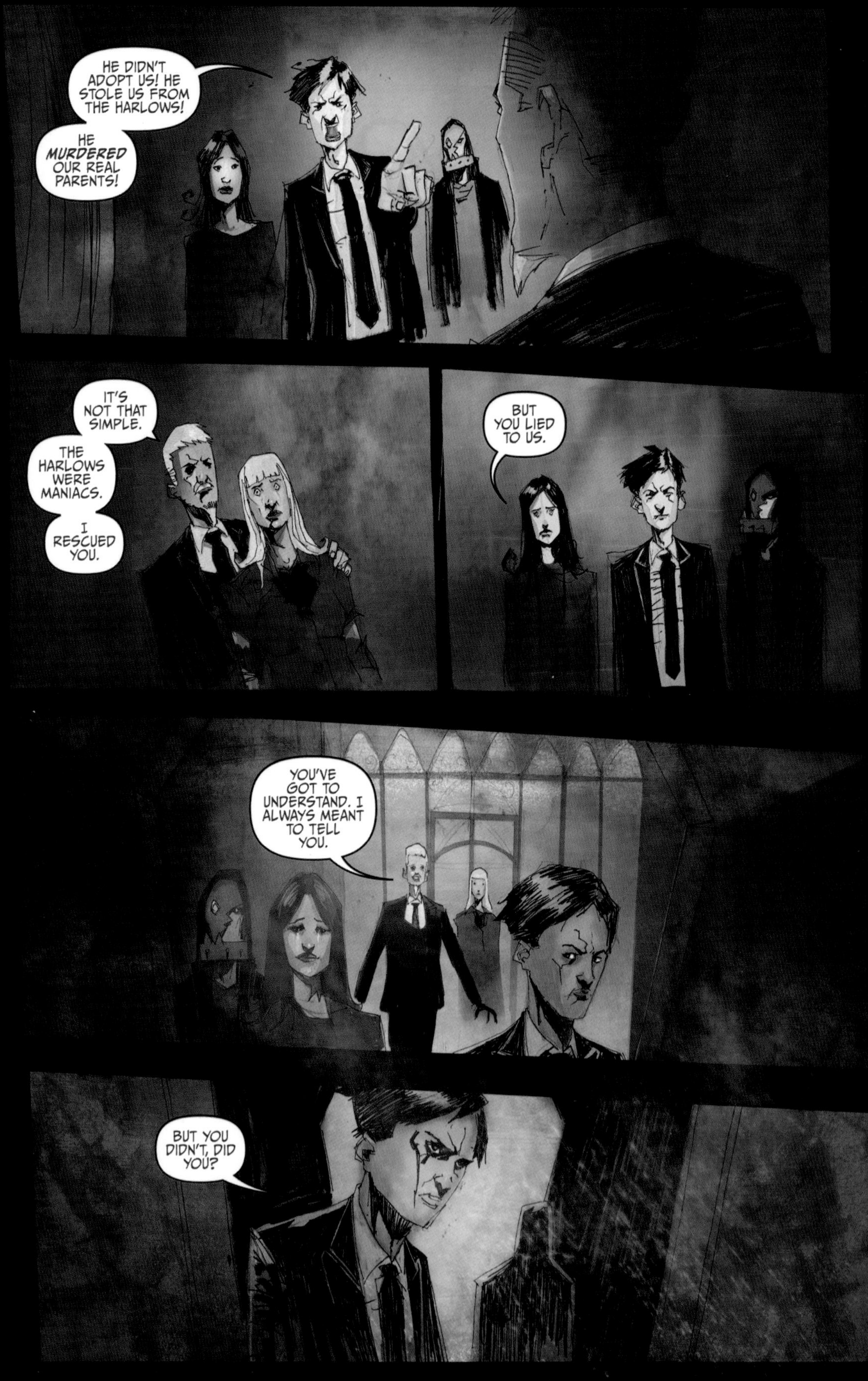
HE DIDN'T ADOPT US! HE STOLE US FROM THE HARLOWS!
HE *MURDERED* OUR REAL PARENTS!
IT'S NOT THAT SIMPLE.
THE HARLOWS WERE MANIACS.
I RESCUED YOU.
BUT YOU LIED TO US.
YOU'VE GOT TO UNDERSTAND. I ALWAYS MEANT TO TELL YOU.
BUT YOU DIDN'T, DID YOU?

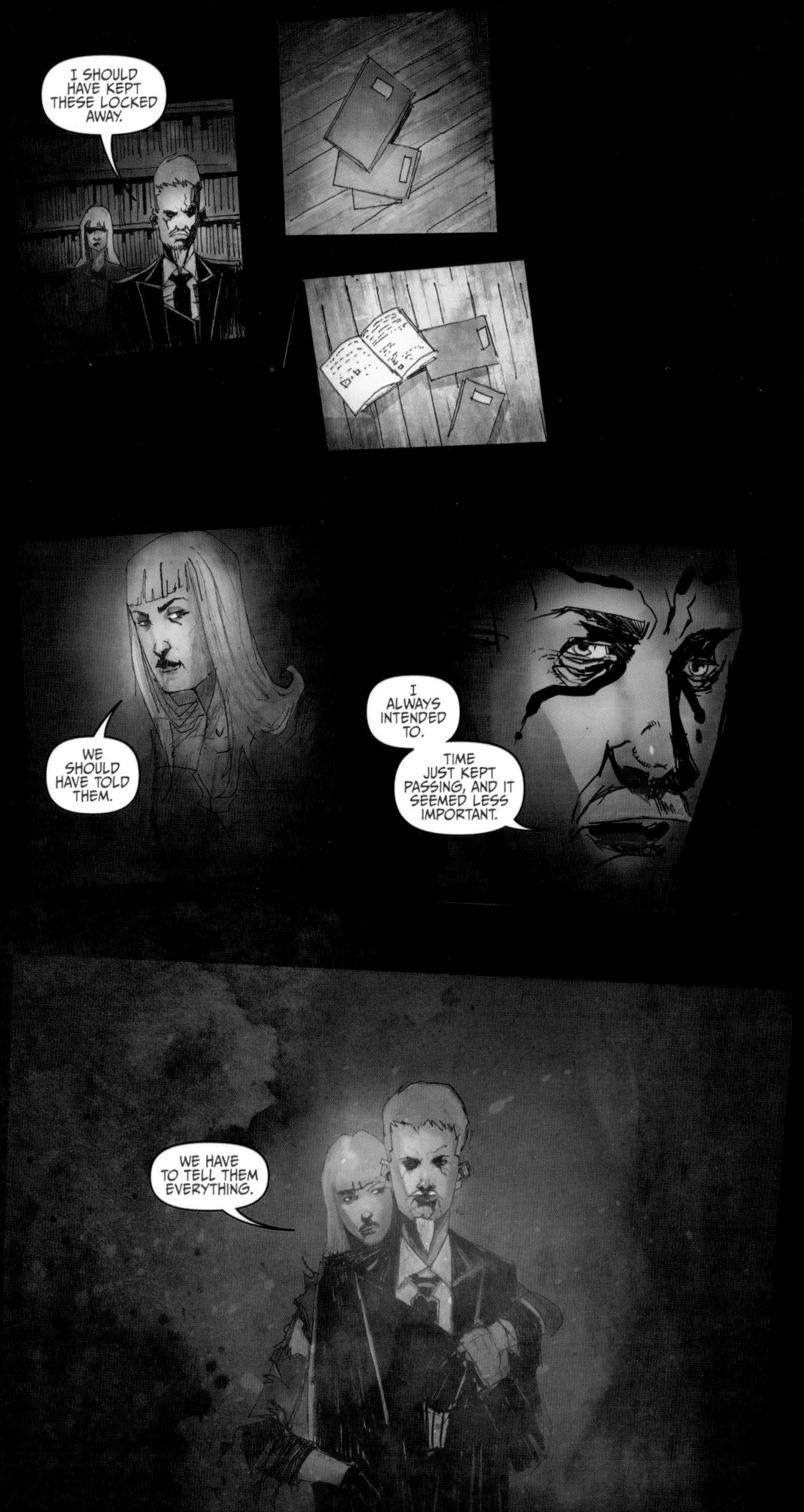
I SHOULD HAVE KEPT THESE LOCKED AWAY.
WE SHOULD HAVE TOLD THEM.
I ALWAYS INTENDED TO.
TIME JUST KEPT PASSING, AND IT SEEMED LESS IMPORTANT.
WE HAVE TO TELL THEM EVERYTHING.

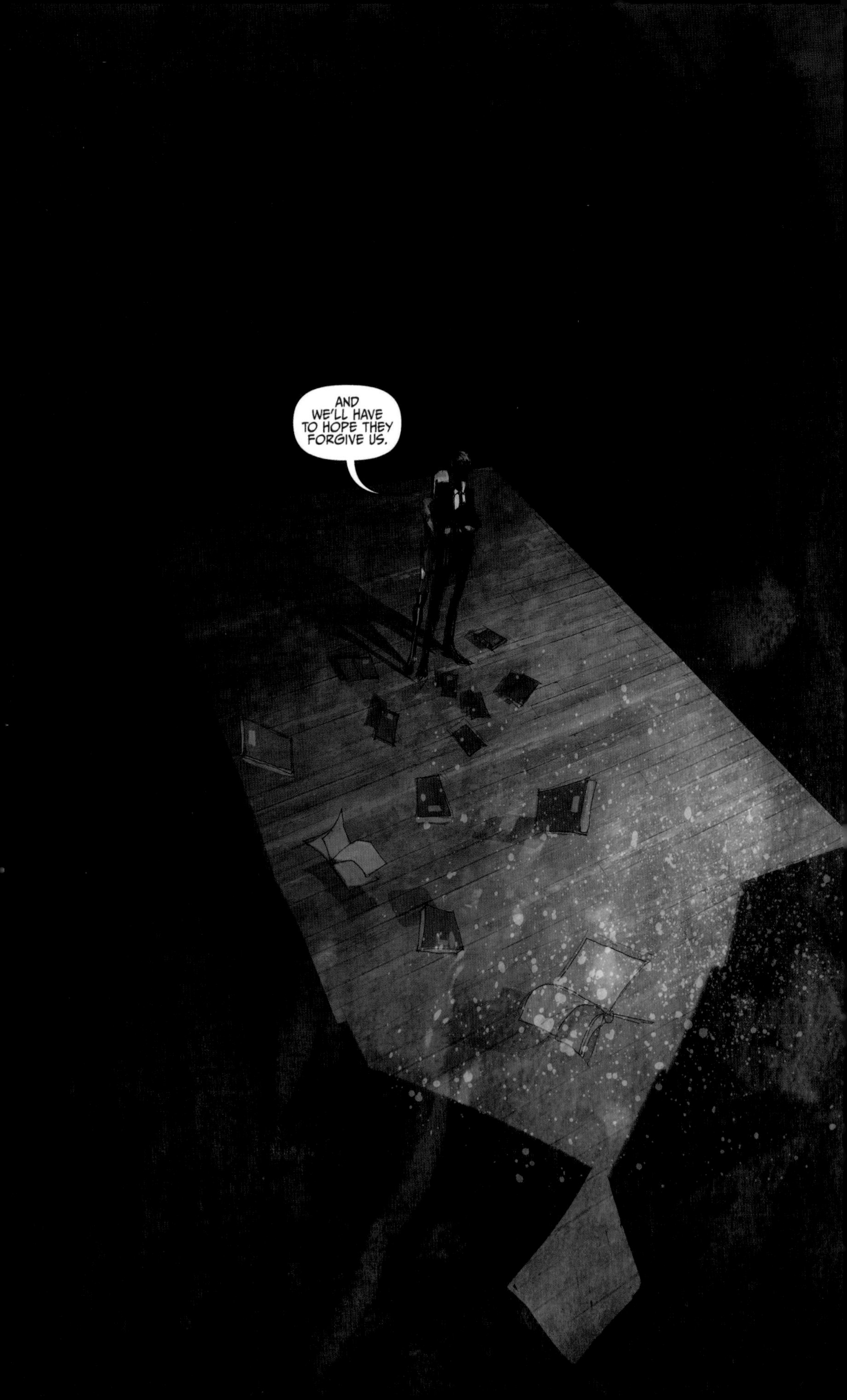
AND WE'LL HAVE TO HOPE THEY FORGIVE US.

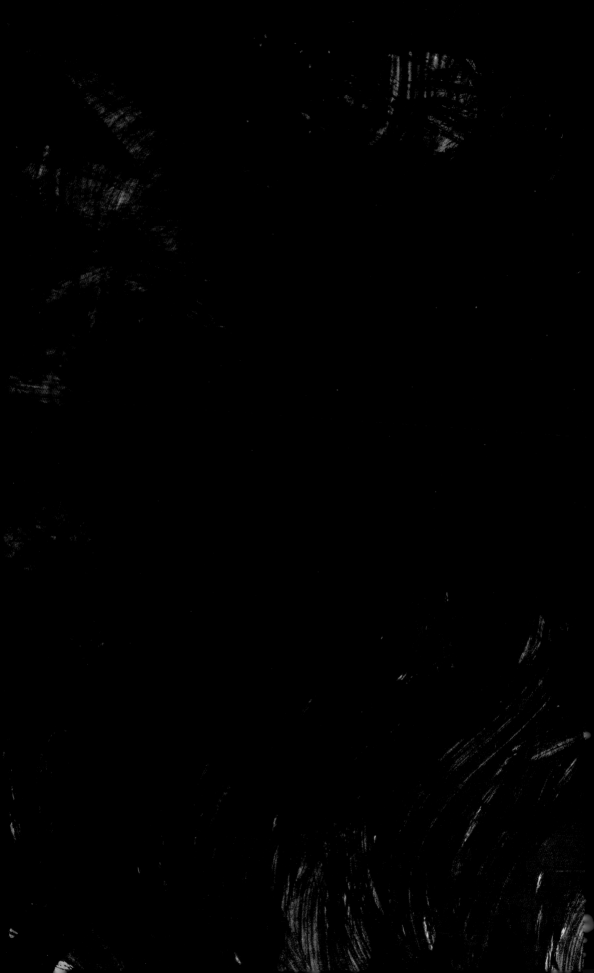

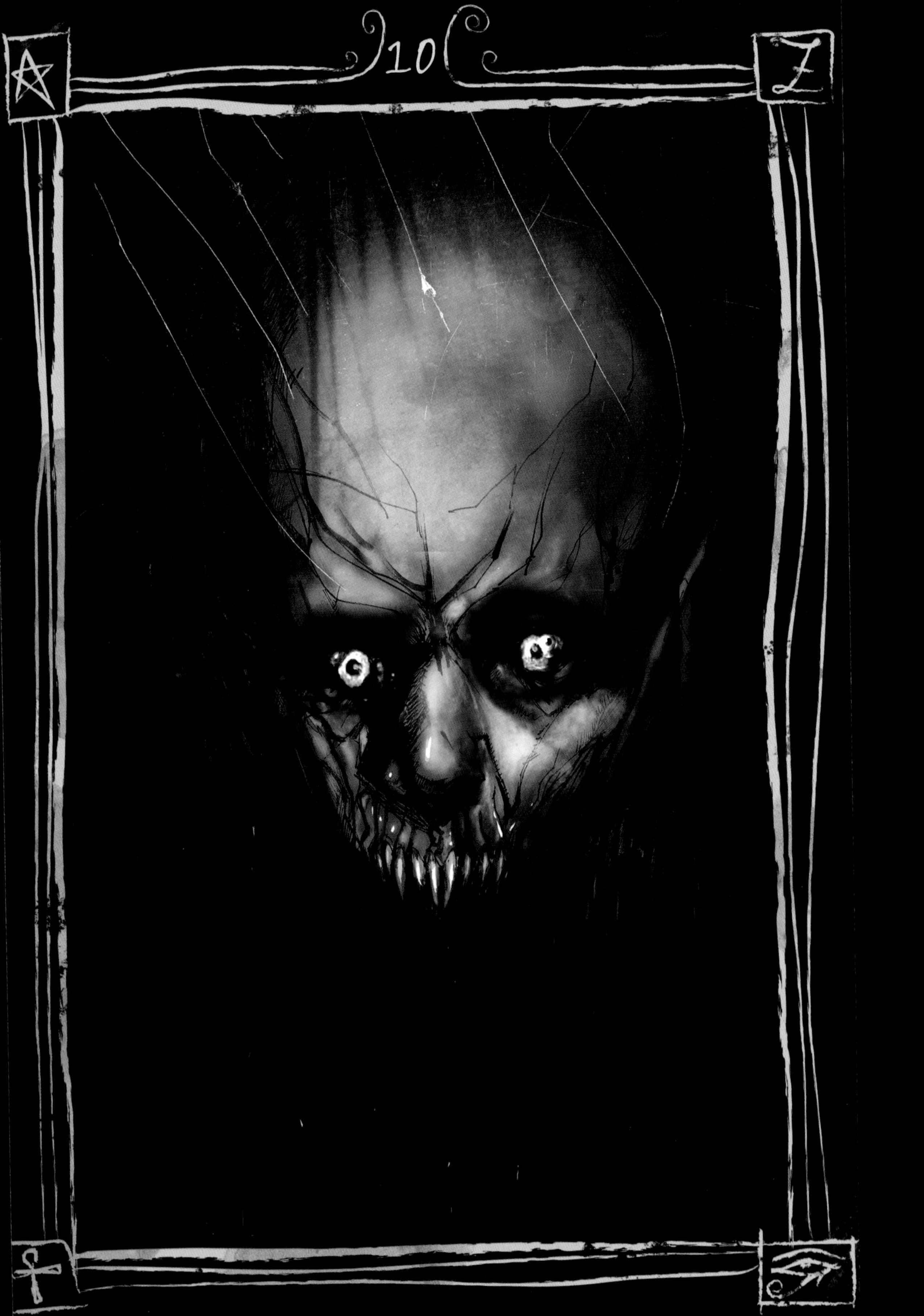
10

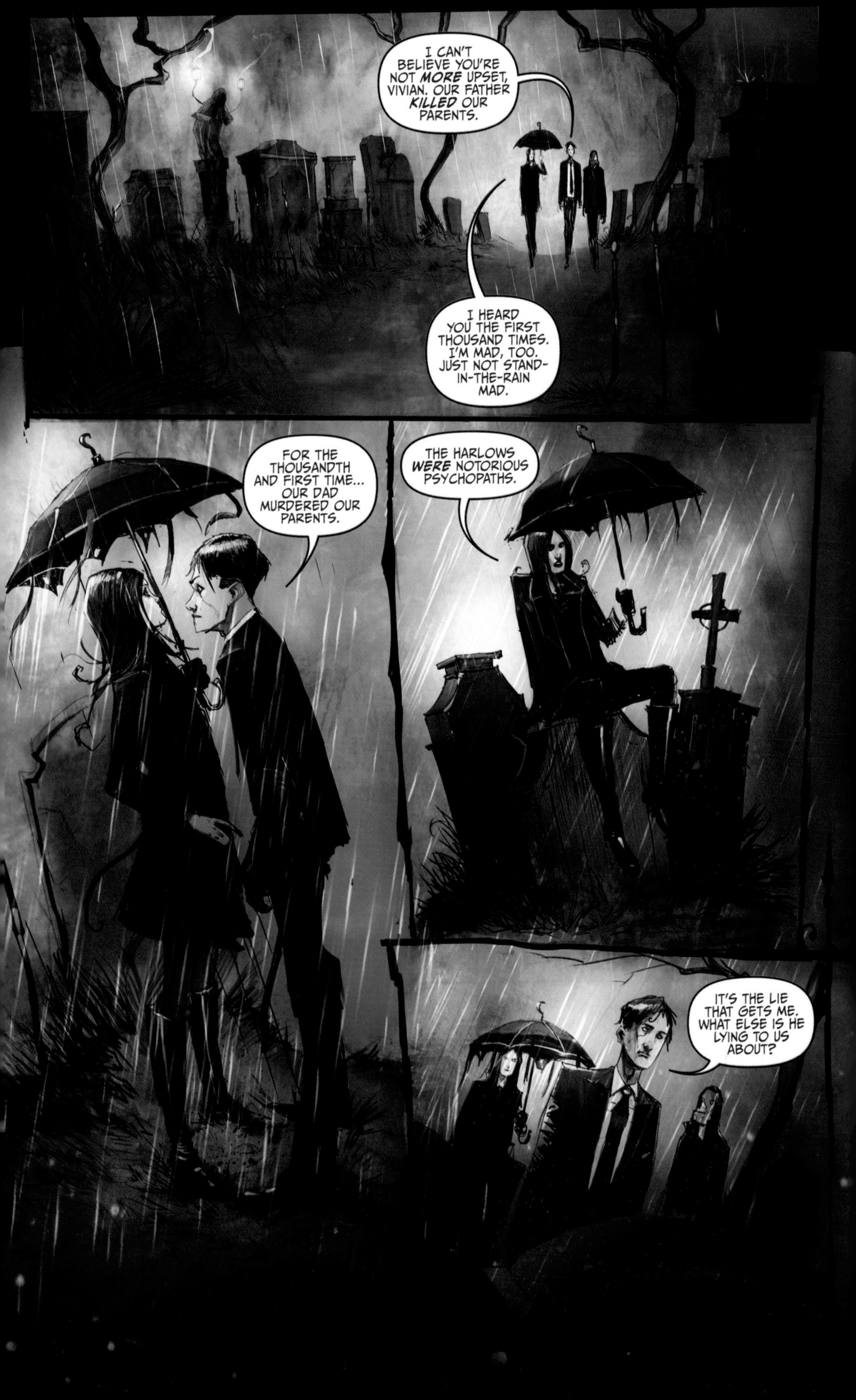
I CAN'T BELIEVE YOU'RE NOT MORE UPSET, VIVIAN. OUR FATHER KILLED OUR PARENTS.
I HEARD YOU THE FIRST THOUSAND TIMES. I'M MAD, TOO. JUST NOT STAND-IN-THE-RAIN MAD.
FOR THE THOUSANDTH AND FIRST TIME... OUR DAD MURDERED OUR PARENTS.
THE HARLOWS WERE NOTORIOUS PSYCHOPATHS.
IT'S THE LIE THAT GETS ME. WHAT ELSE IS HE LYING TO US ABOUT?

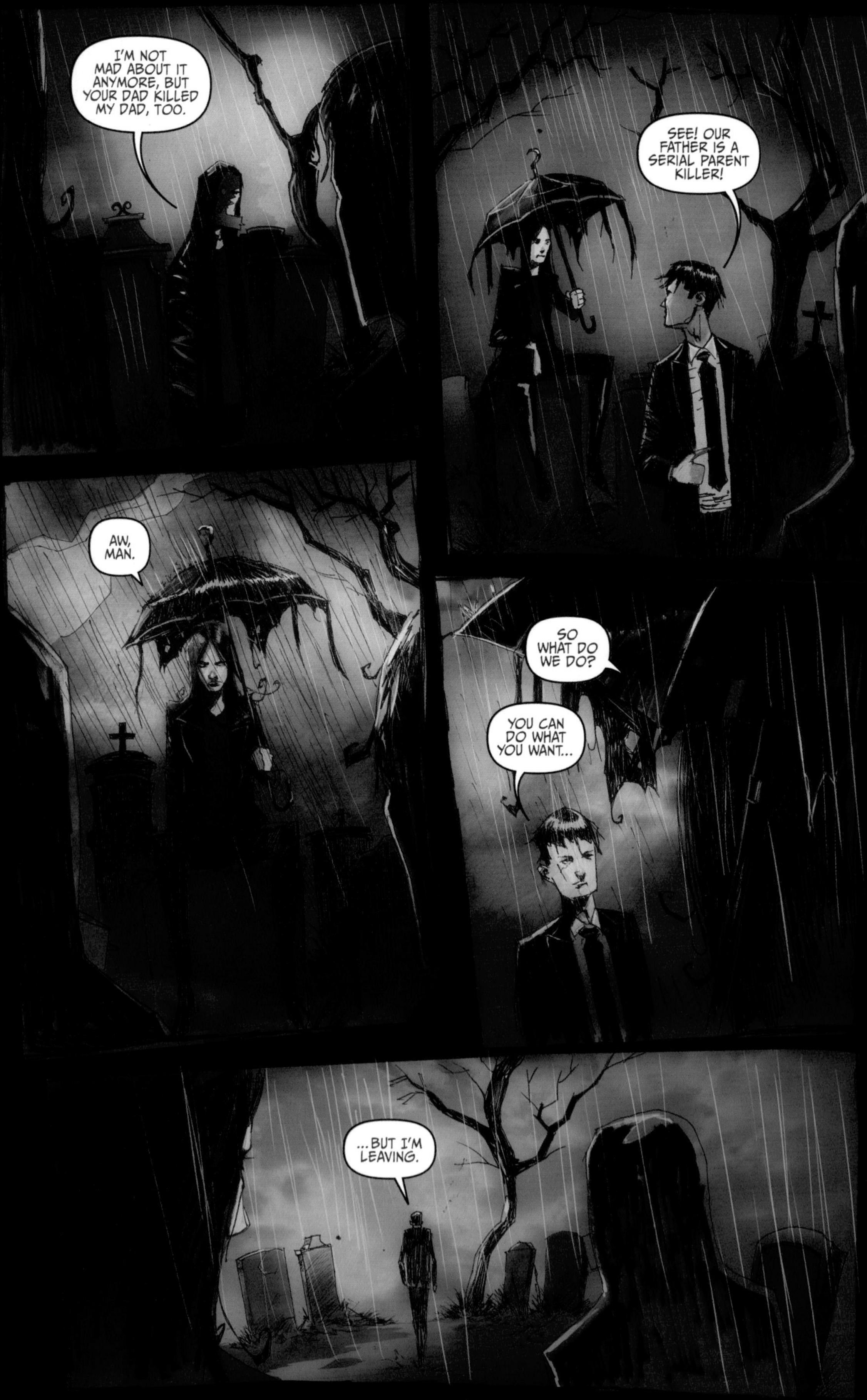
I'M NOT MAD ABOUT IT ANYMORE, BUT YOUR DAD KILLED MY DAD, TOO.
SEE! OUR FATHER IS A SERIAL PARENT KILLER!
AW, MAN.
SO WHAT DO WE DO?
YOU CAN DO WHAT YOU WANT...
...BUT I'M LEAVING.

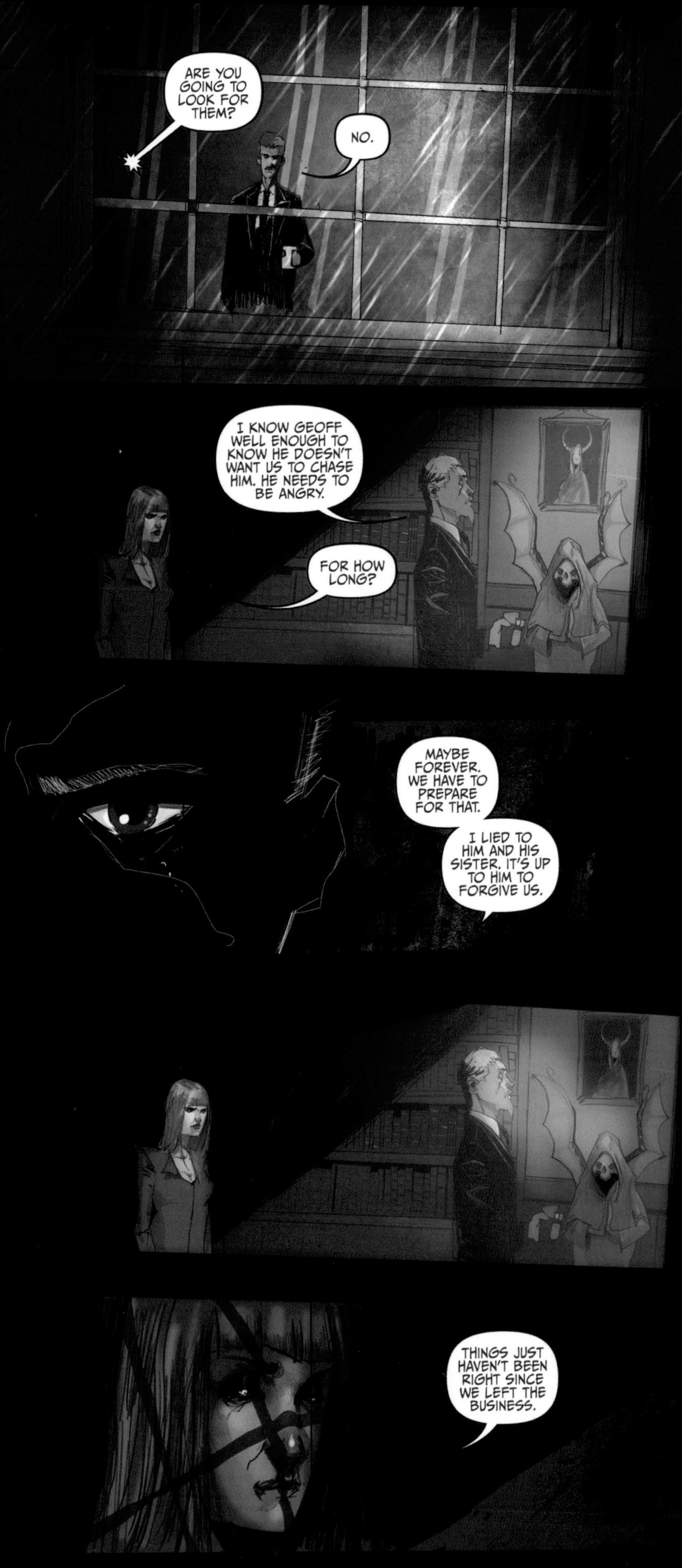
ARE YOU GOING TO LOOK FOR THEM?
NO.
I KNOW GEOFF WELL ENOUGH TO KNOW HE DOESN'T WANT US TO CHASE HIM. HE NEEDS TO BE ANGRY.
FOR HOW LONG?
MAYBE FOREVER. WE HAVE TO PREPARE FOR THAT.
I LIED TO HIM AND HIS SISTER. IT'S UP TO HIM TO FORGIVE US.
THINGS JUST HAVEN'T BEEN RIGHT SINCE WE LEFT THE BUSINESS.

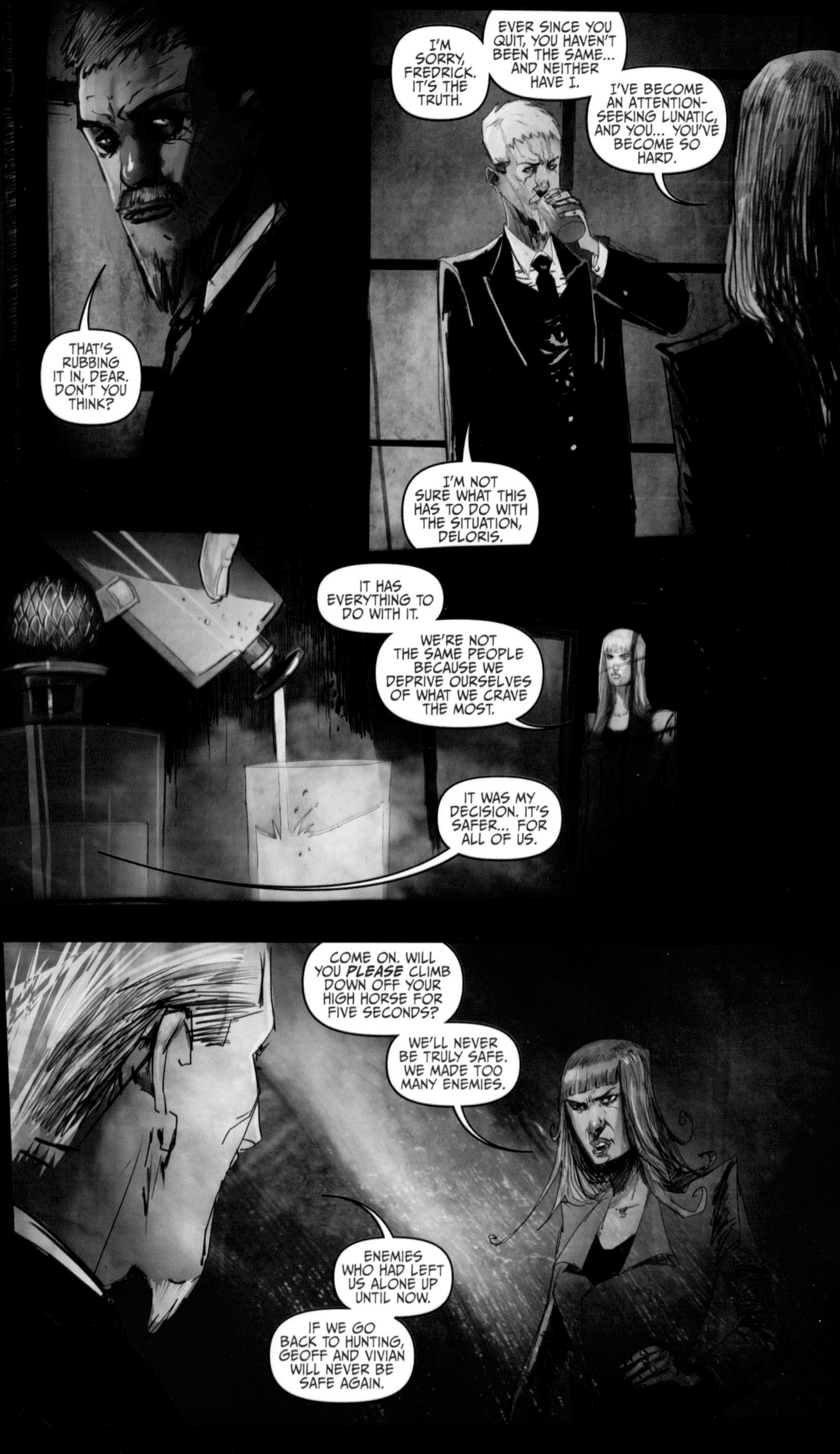

I'M SORRY, FREDRICK. IT'S THE TRUTH.
EVER SINCE YOU QUIT, YOU HAVEN'T BEEN THE SAME... AND NEITHER HAVE I.
I'VE BECOME AN ATTENTION-SEEKING LUNATIC, AND YOU... YOU'VE BECOME SO HARD.
THAT'S RUBBING IT IN, DEAR. DON'T YOU THINK?
I'M NOT SURE WHAT THIS HAS TO DO WITH THE SITUATION, DELORIS.
IT HAS EVERYTHING TO DO WITH IT.
WE'RE NOT THE SAME PEOPLE BECAUSE WE DEPRIVE OURSELVES OF WHAT WE CRAVE THE MOST.
IT WAS MY DECISION. IT'S SAFER... FOR ALL OF US.
COME ON. WILL YOU PLEASE CLIMB DOWN OFF YOUR HIGH HORSE FOR FIVE SECONDS?
WE'LL NEVER BE TRULY SAFE. WE MADE TOO MANY ENEMIES.
ENEMIES WHO HAD LEFT US ALONE UP UNTIL NOW.
IF WE GO BACK TO HUNTING, GEOFF AND VIVIAN WILL NEVER BE SAFE AGAIN.

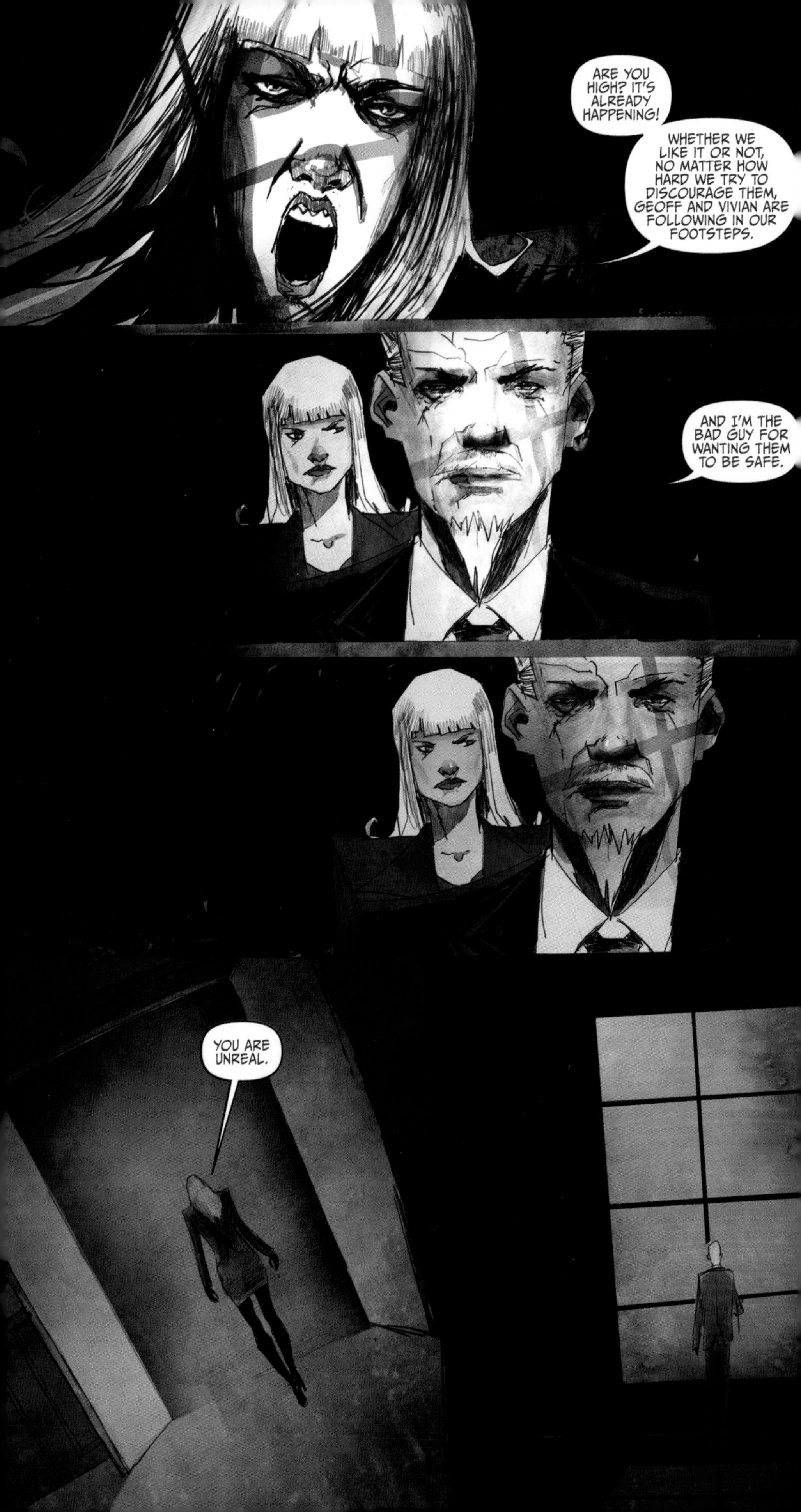
ARE YOU HIGH? IT'S ALREADY HAPPENING!
WHETHER WE LIKE IT OR NOT, NO MATTER HOW HARD WE TRY TO DISCOURAGE THEM, GEOFF AND VIVIAN ARE FOLLOWING IN OUR FOOTSTEPS.
AND I'M THE BAD GUY FOR WANTING THEM TO BE SAFE.
YOU ARE UNREAL.

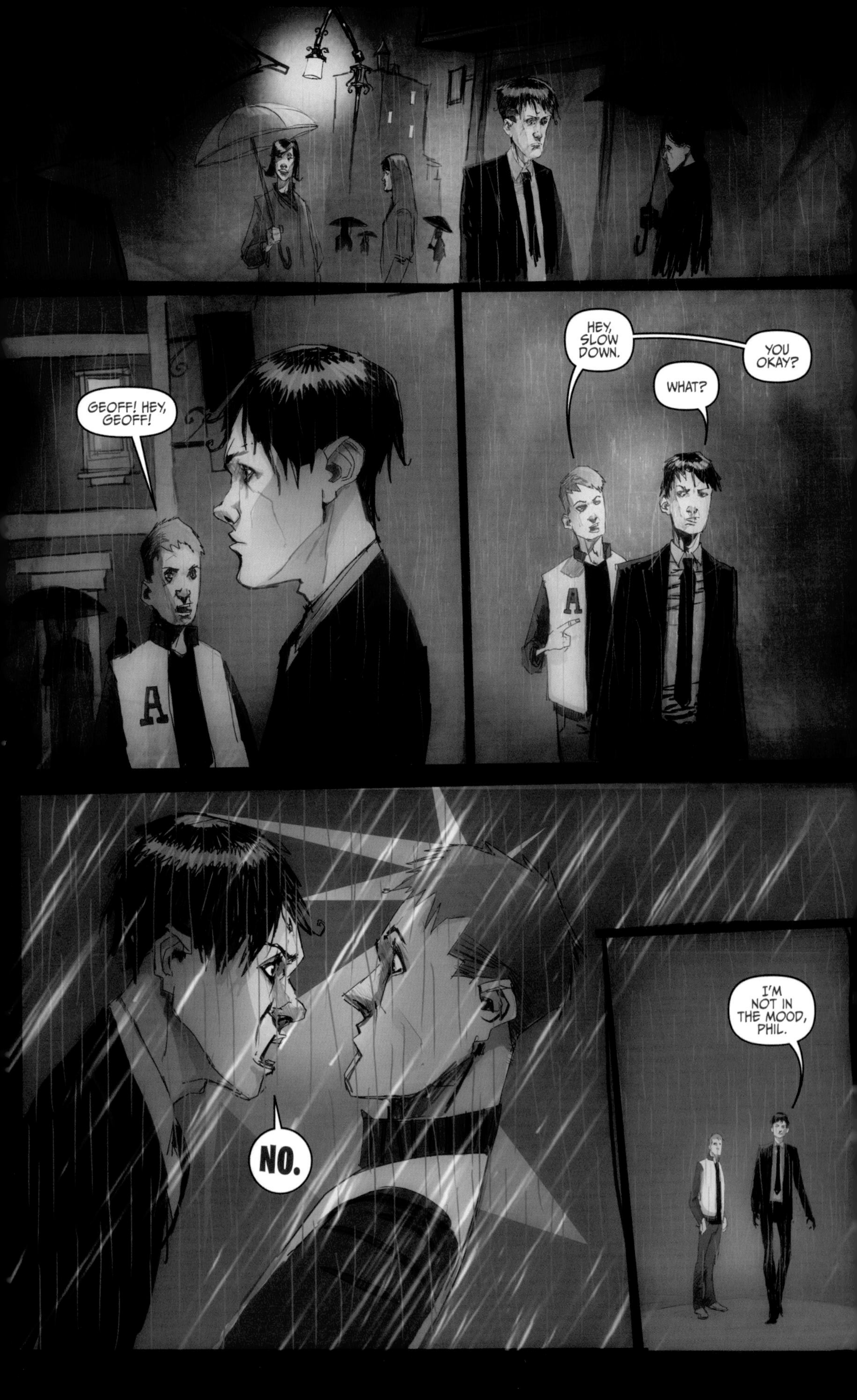
GEOFF! HEY, GEOFF!
HEY, SLOW DOWN.
YOU OKAY?
WHAT?
NO.
I'M NOT IN THE MOOD, PHIL.

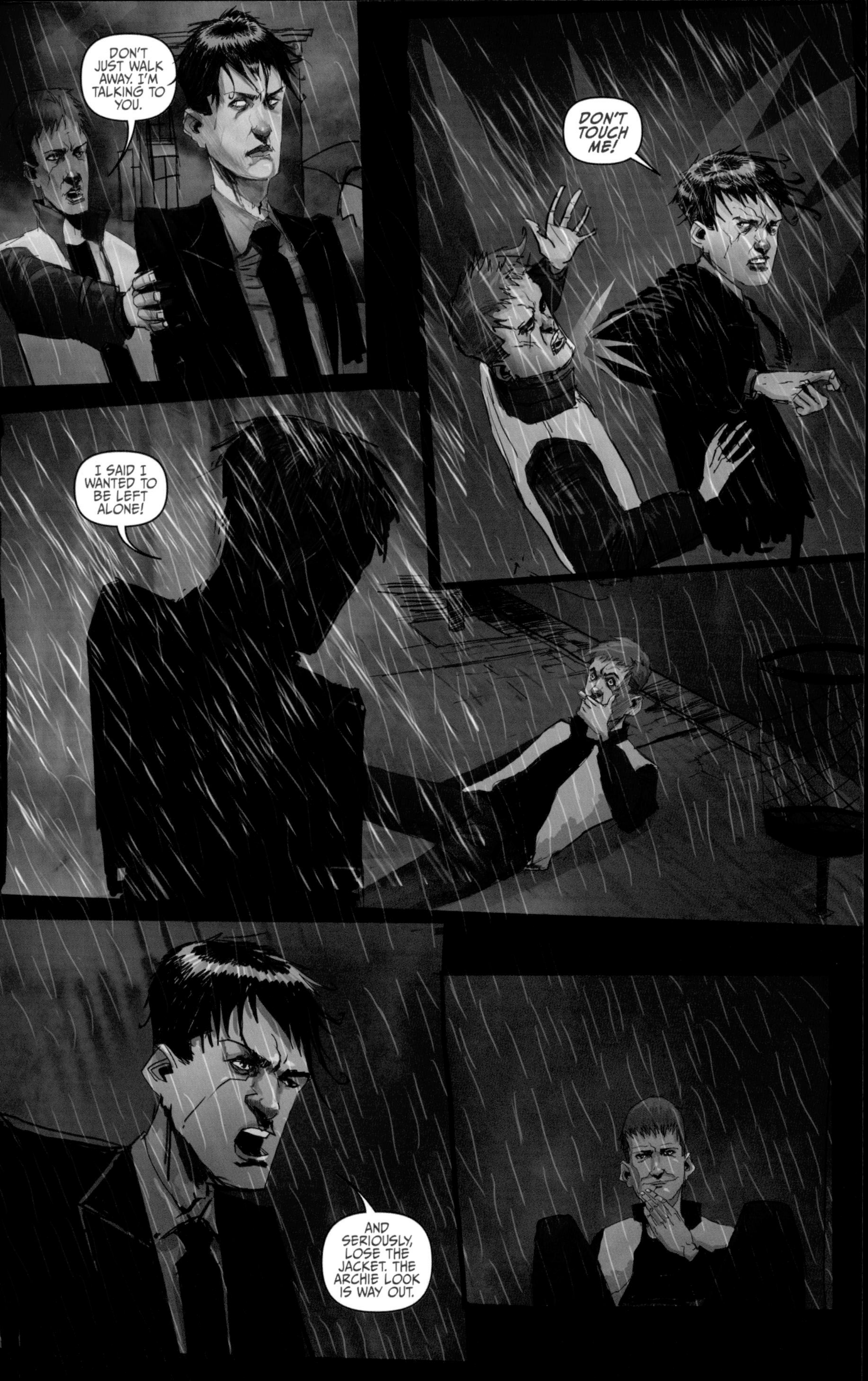
DON'T JUST WALK AWAY. I'M TALKING TO YOU.
DON'T TOUCH ME!
I SAID I WANTED TO BE LEFT ALONE!
AND SERIOUSLY, LOSE THE JACKET. THE ARCHIE LOOK IS WAY OUT.

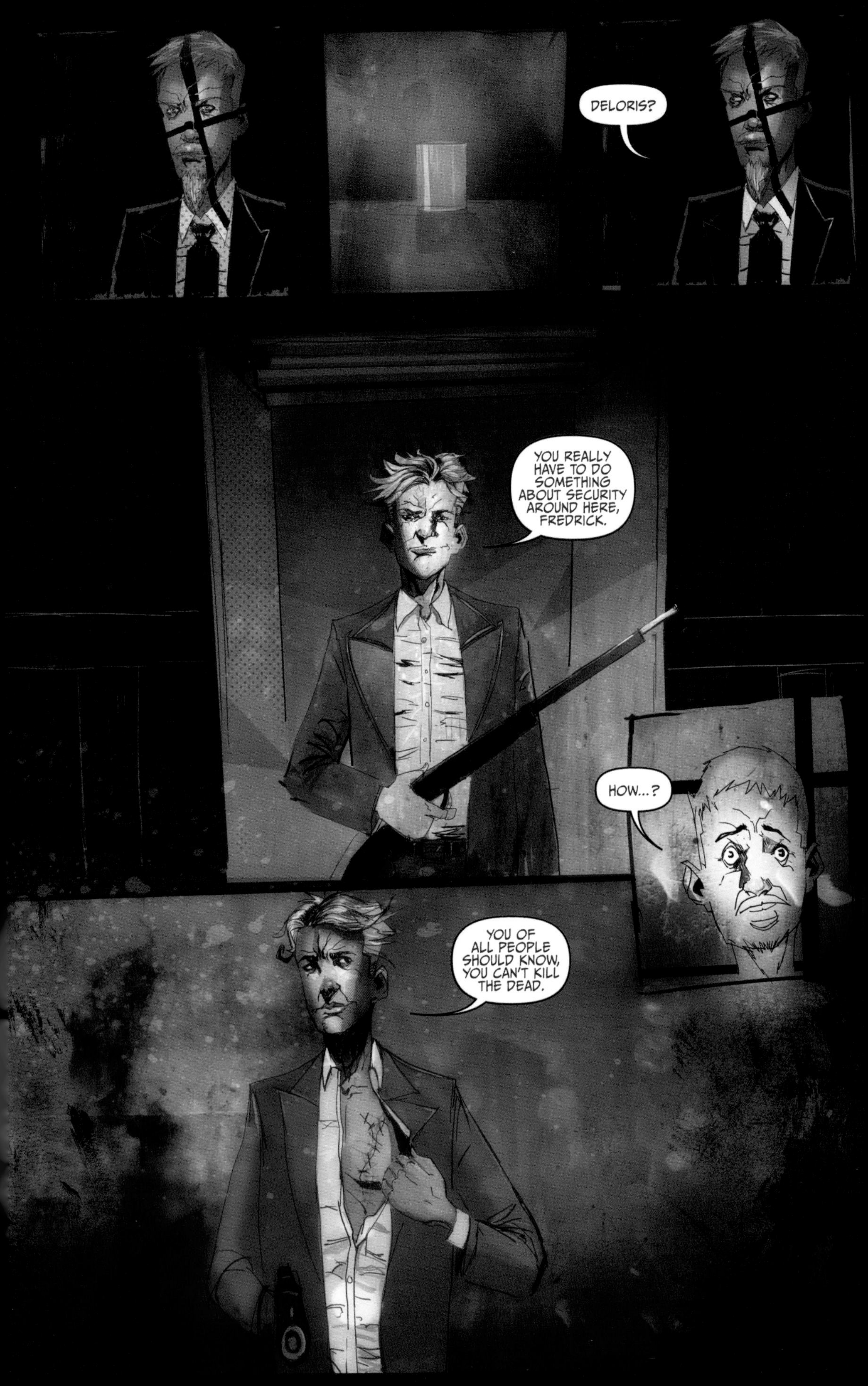
DELORIS?
YOU REALLY HAVE TO DO SOMETHING ABOUT SECURITY AROUND HERE, FREDRICK.
HOW...?
YOU OF ALL PEOPLE SHOULD KNOW, YOU CAN'T KILL THE DEAD.

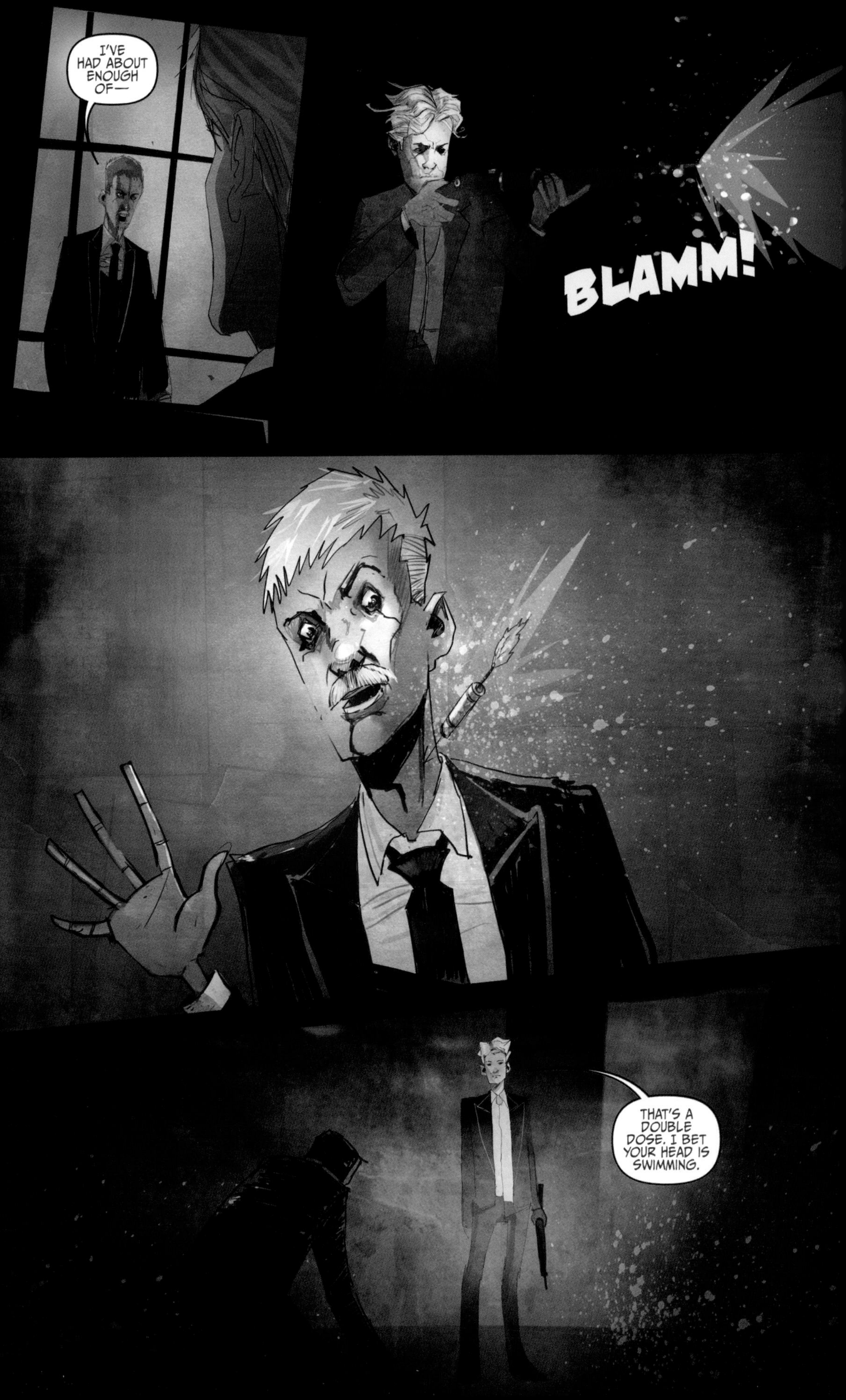
I'VE HAD ABOUT ENOUGH OF—
BLAMM!
THAT'S A DOUBLE DOSE. I BET YOUR HEAD IS SWIMMING.

ALMOST MADE IT.

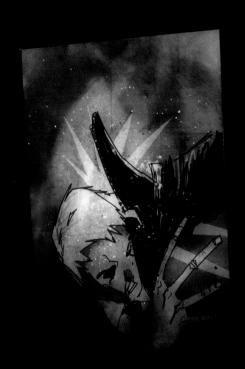

AND DON'T WORRY... I SENT A "DISTRACTION" FOR THE KIDS.

AND THEN YOU'RE GOING TO MEET MOMMA.

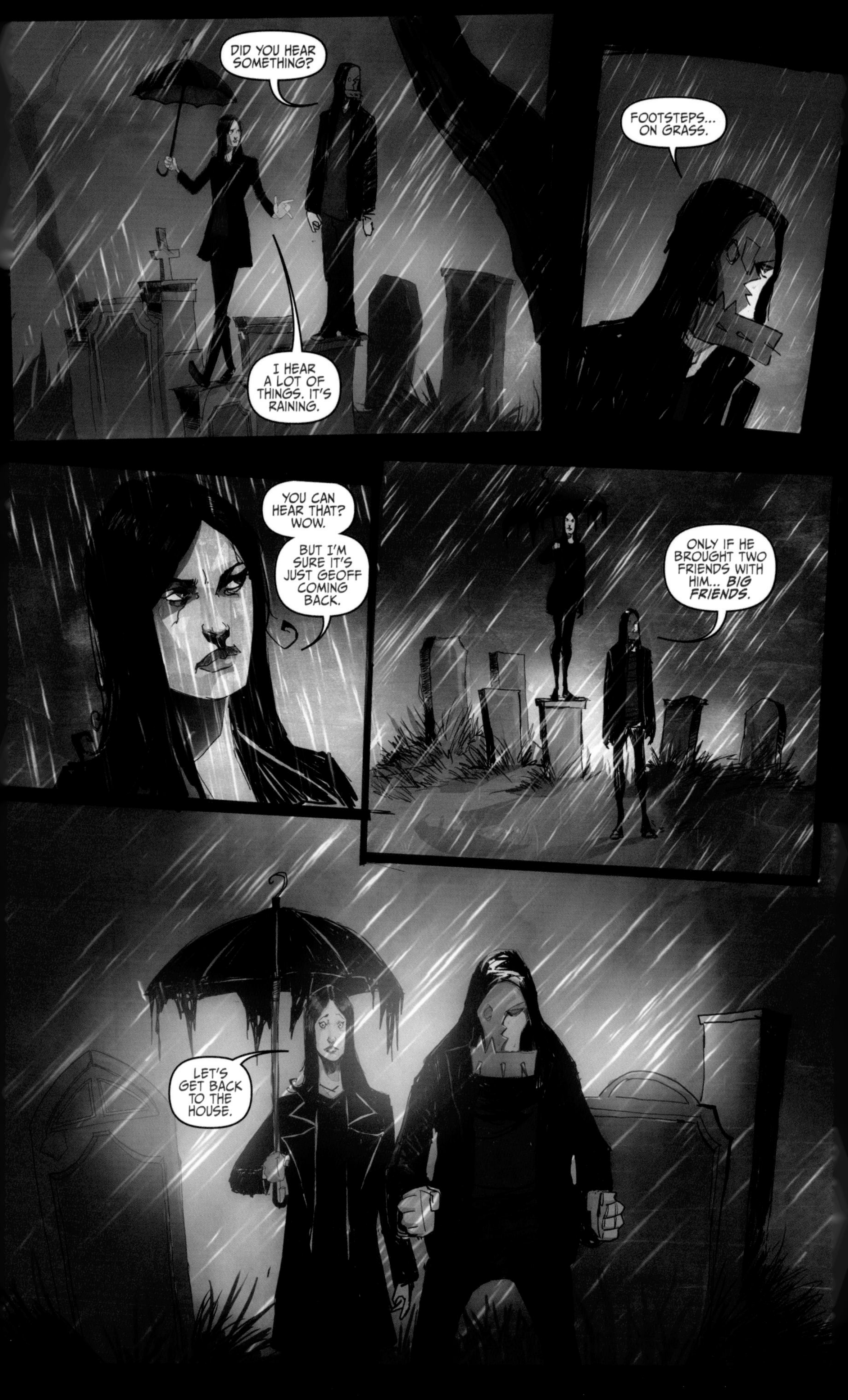
DID YOU HEAR SOMETHING?
I HEAR A LOT OF THINGS. IT'S RAINING.
FOOTSTEPS... ON GRASS.
YOU CAN HEAR THAT? WOW.
BUT I'M SURE IT'S JUST GEOFF COMING BACK.
ONLY IF HE BROUGHT TWO FRIENDS WITH HIM... *BIG FRIENDS*.
LET'S GET BACK TO THE HOUSE.

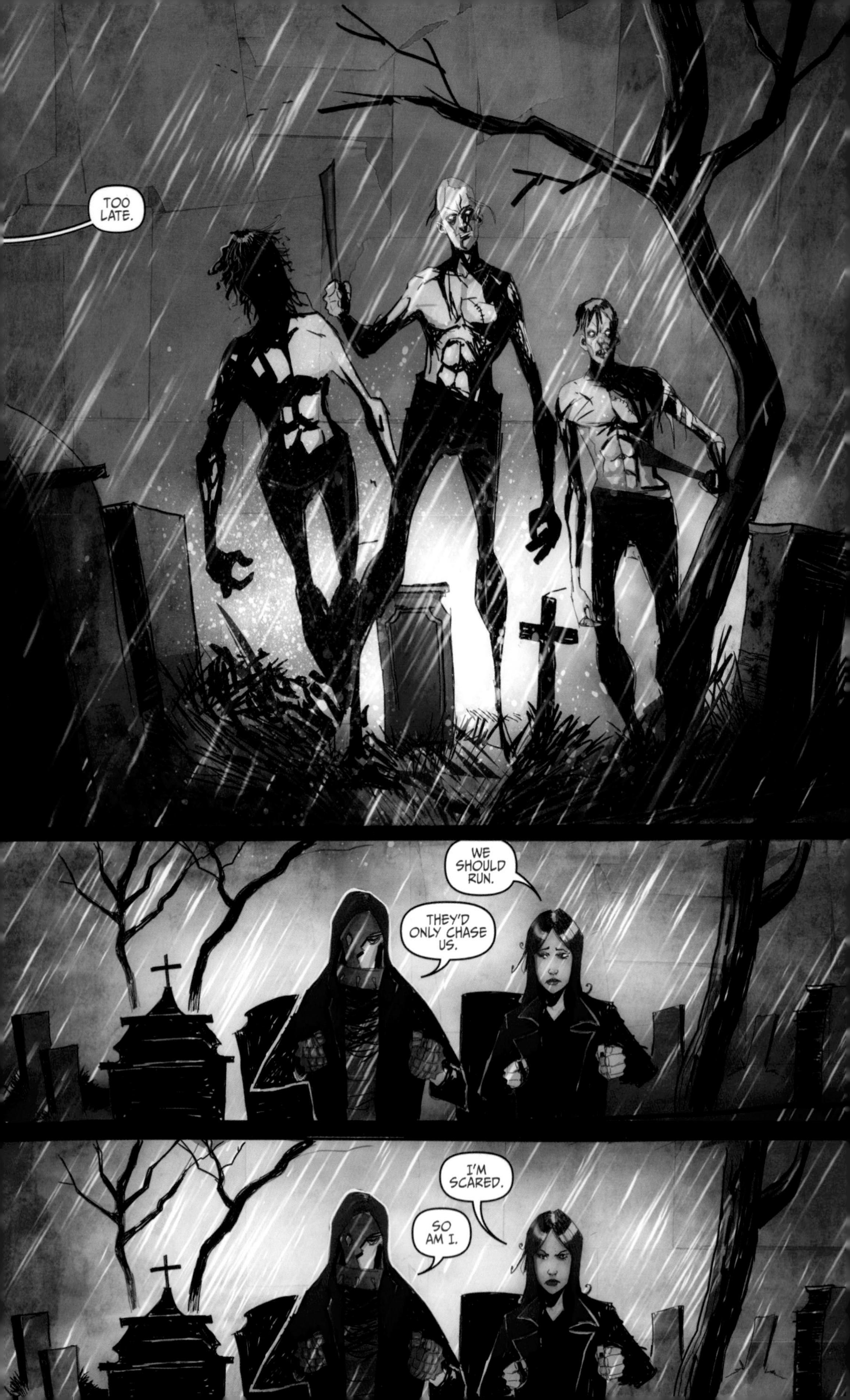
TOO LATE.
WE SHOULD RUN.
THEY'D ONLY CHASE US.
I'M SCARED.
SO AM I.

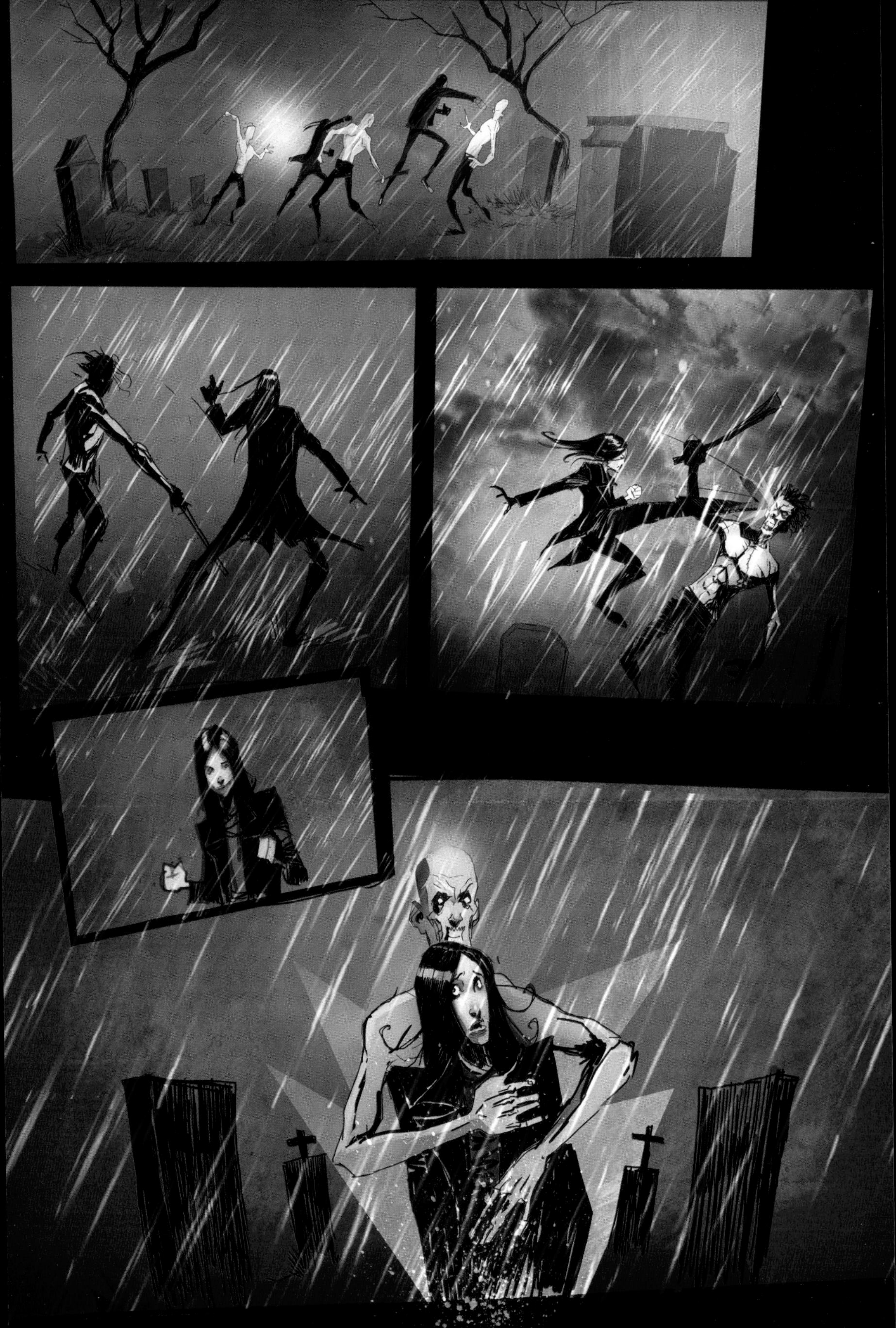

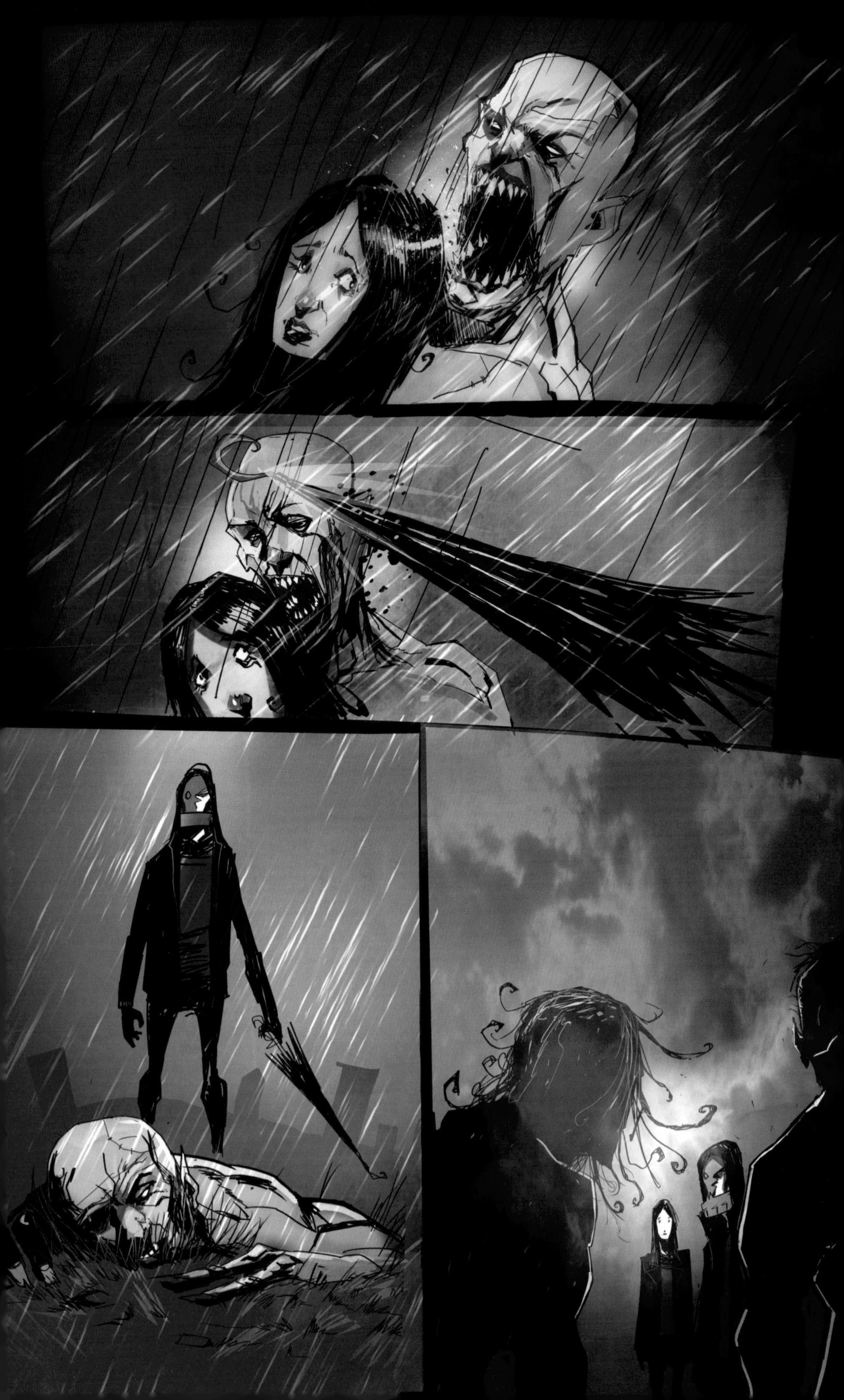

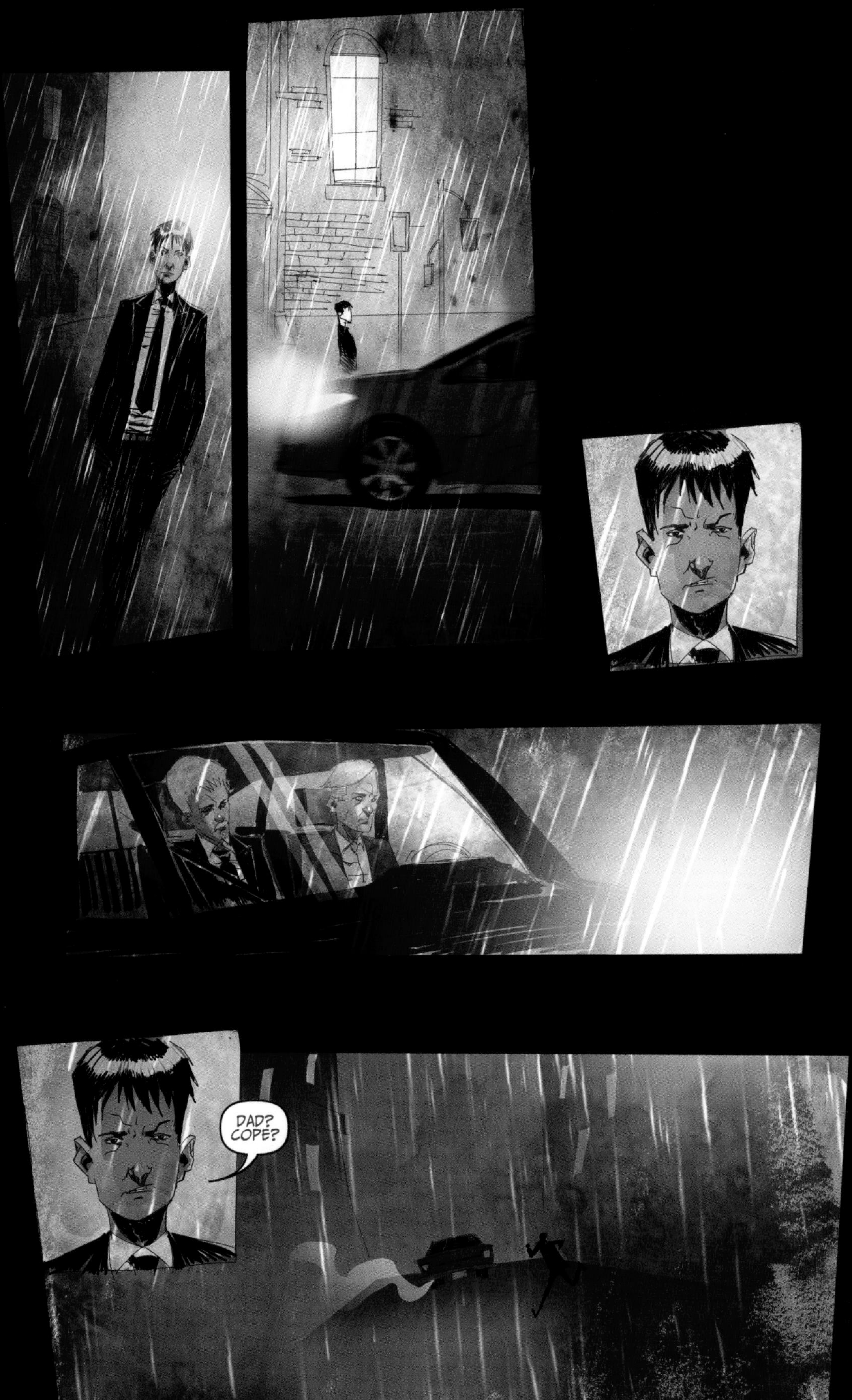
DAD?
COPE?

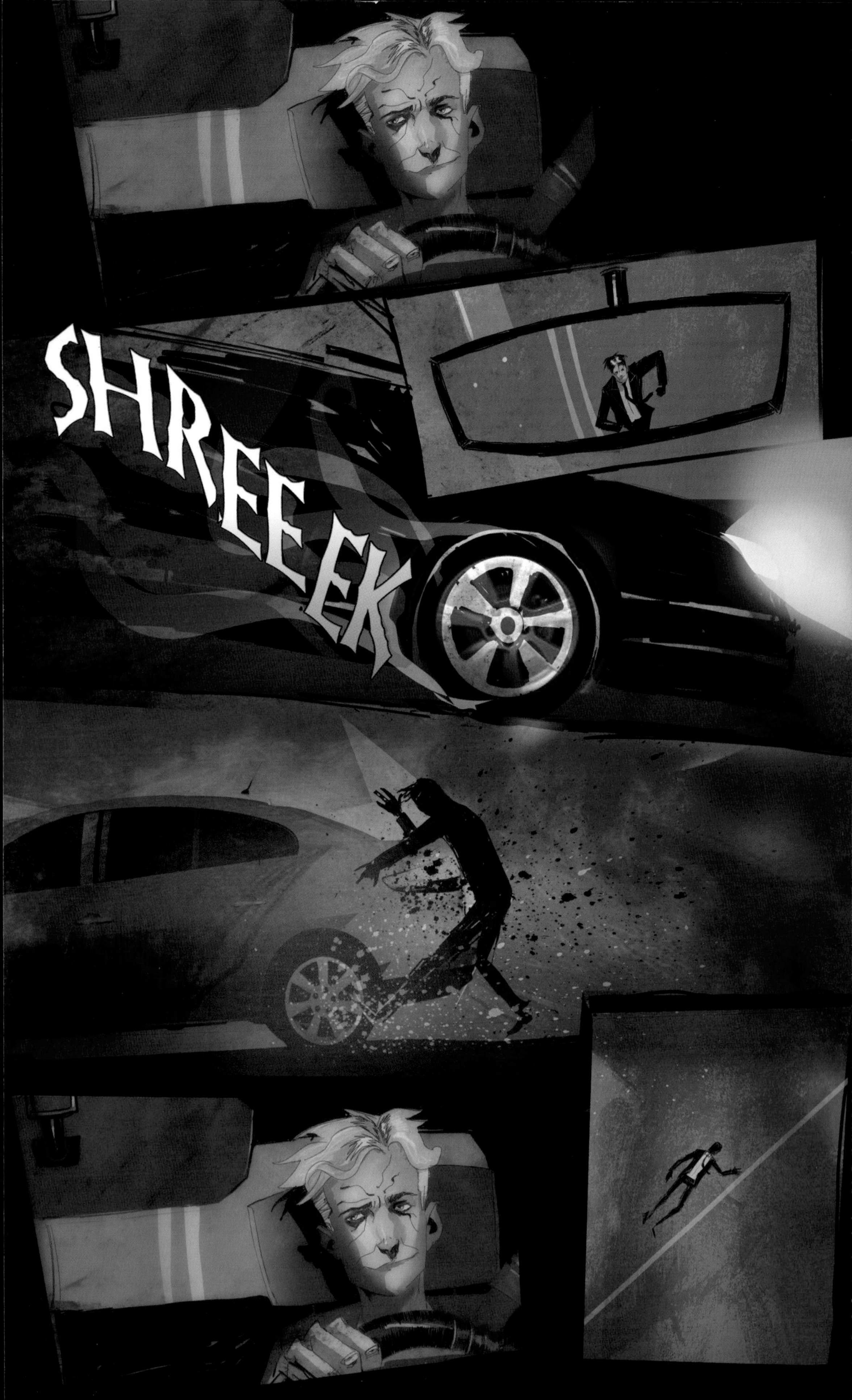
SHREEEK

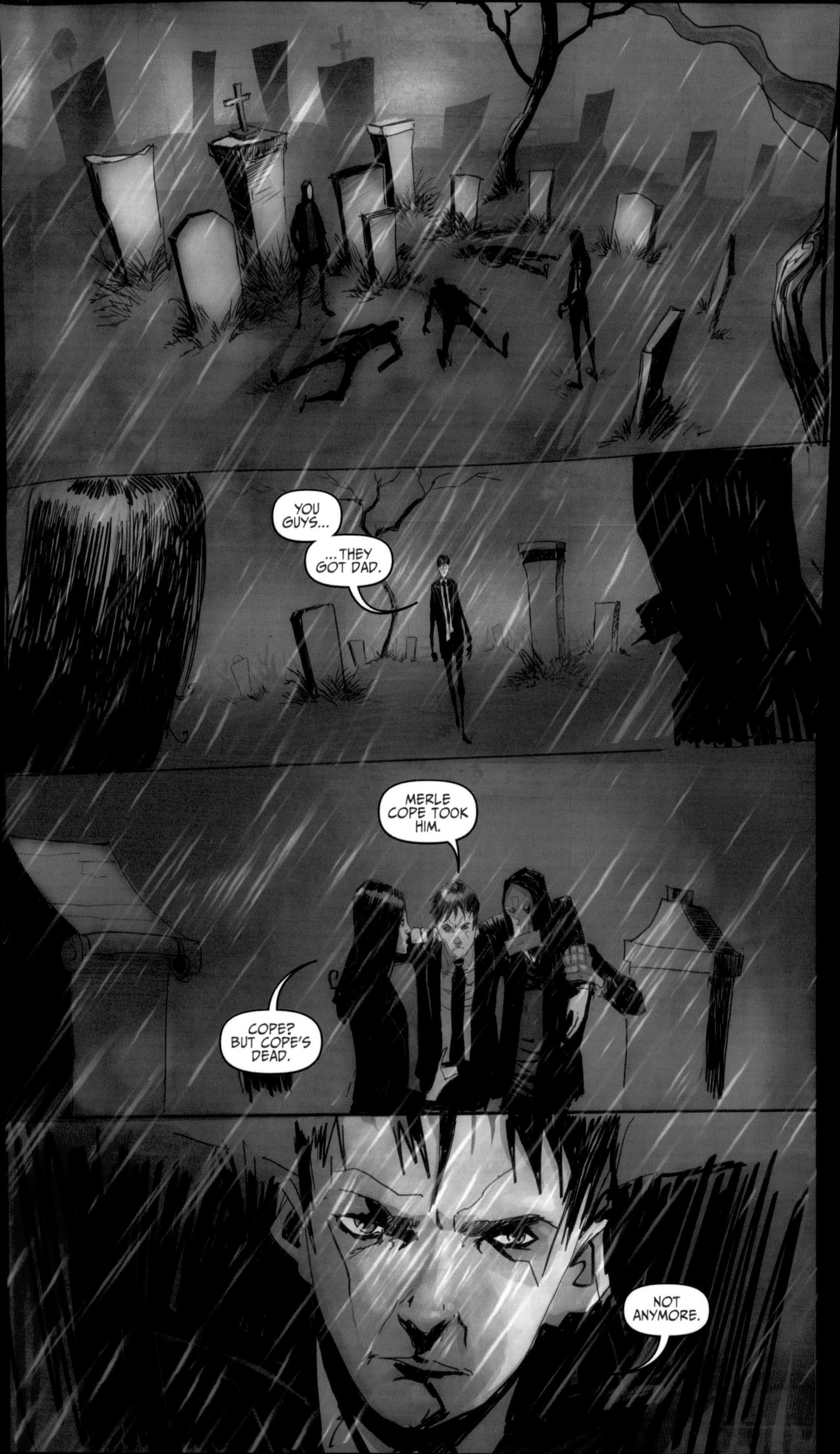
YOU GUYS...
...THEY GOT DAD.
MERLE COPE TOOK HIM.
COPE? BUT COPE'S DEAD.
NOT ANYMORE.

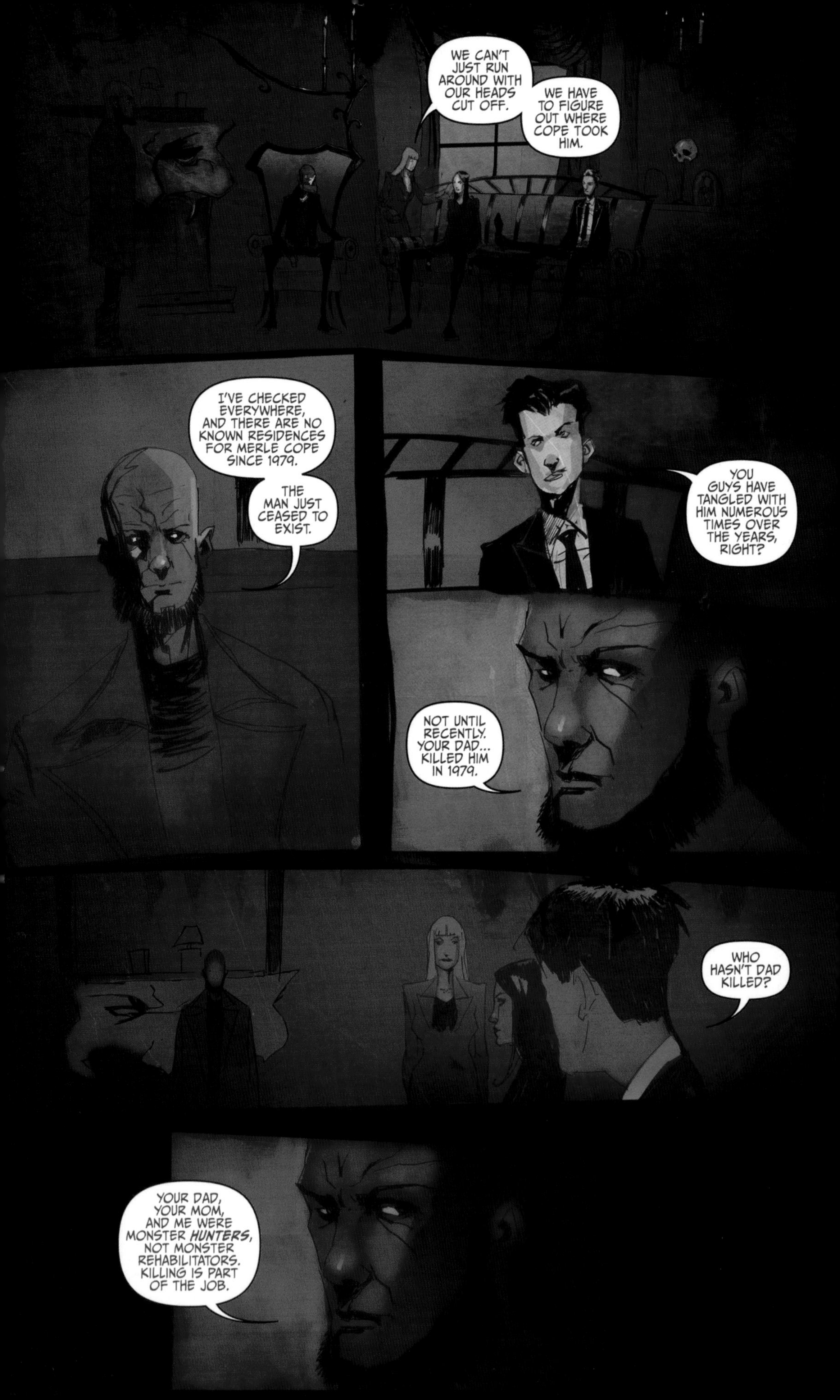
WE CAN'T JUST RUN AROUND WITH OUR HEADS CUT OFF.
WE HAVE TO FIGURE OUT WHERE COPE TOOK HIM.
I'VE CHECKED EVERYWHERE, AND THERE ARE NO KNOWN RESIDENCES FOR MERLE COPE SINCE 1979.
THE MAN JUST CEASED TO EXIST.
YOU GUYS HAVE TANGLED WITH HIM NUMEROUS TIMES OVER THE YEARS, RIGHT?
NOT UNTIL RECENTLY. YOUR DAD... KILLED HIM IN 1979.
WHO HASN'T DAD KILLED?
YOUR DAD, YOUR MOM, AND ME WERE MONSTER *HUNTERS*, NOT MONSTER REHABILITATORS. KILLING IS PART OF THE JOB.

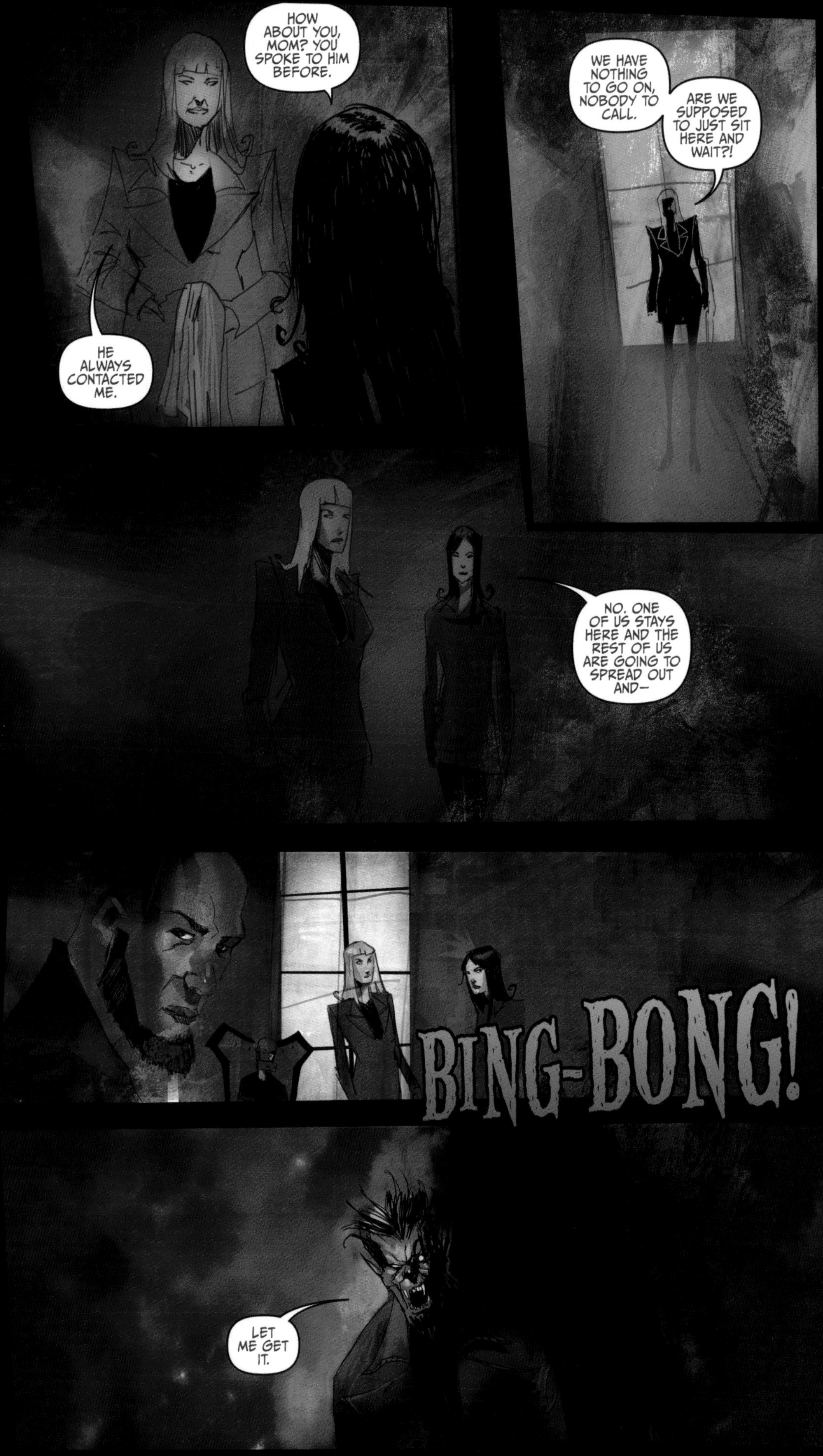
HOW ABOUT YOU, MOM? YOU SPOKE TO HIM BEFORE.
HE ALWAYS CONTACTED ME.
WE HAVE NOTHING TO GO ON, NOBODY TO CALL.
ARE WE SUPPOSED TO JUST SIT HERE AND WAIT?!
NO. ONE OF US STAYS HERE AND THE REST OF US ARE GOING TO SPREAD OUT AND–
BING-BONG!
LET ME GET IT.

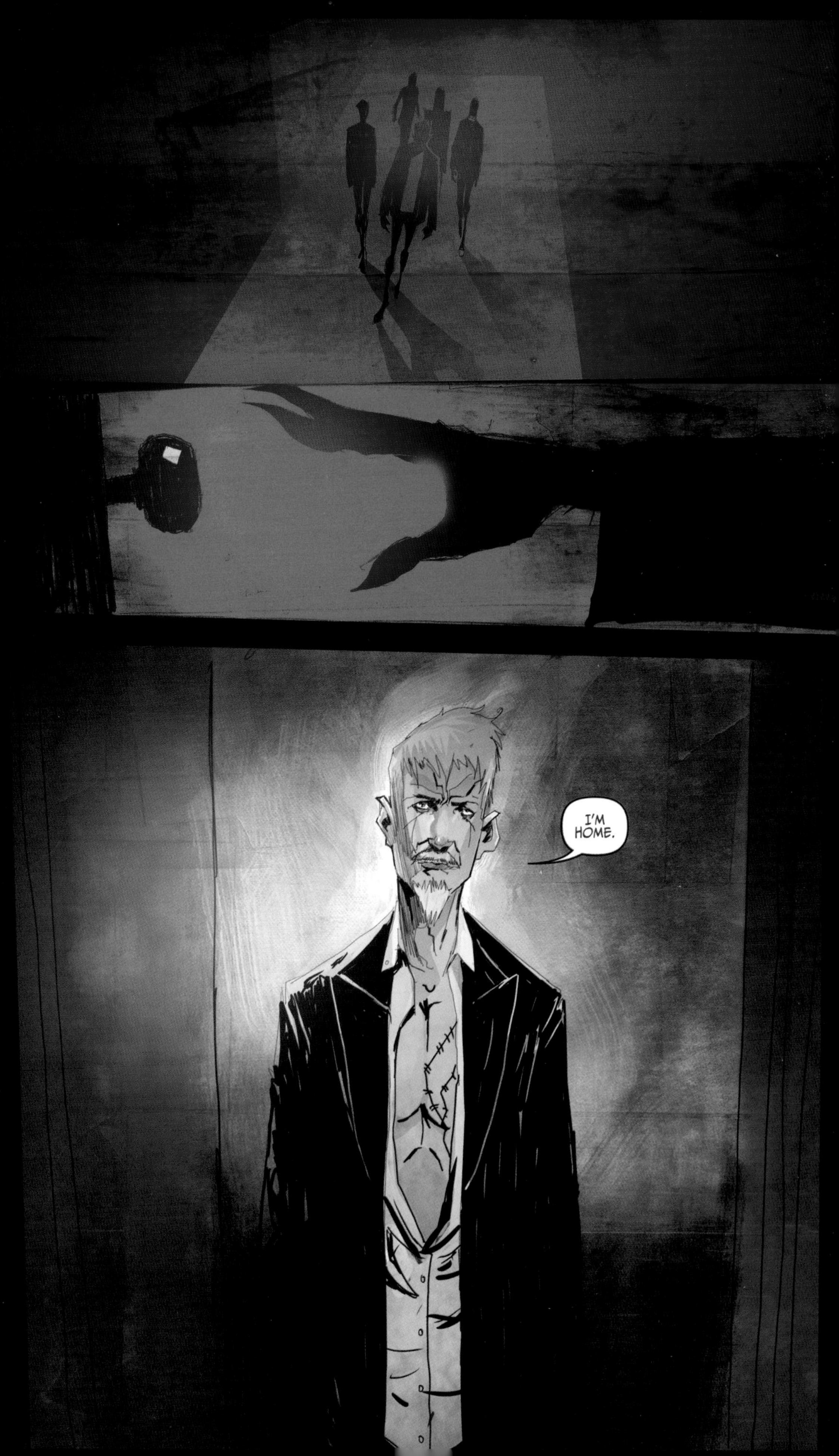
I'M HOME.

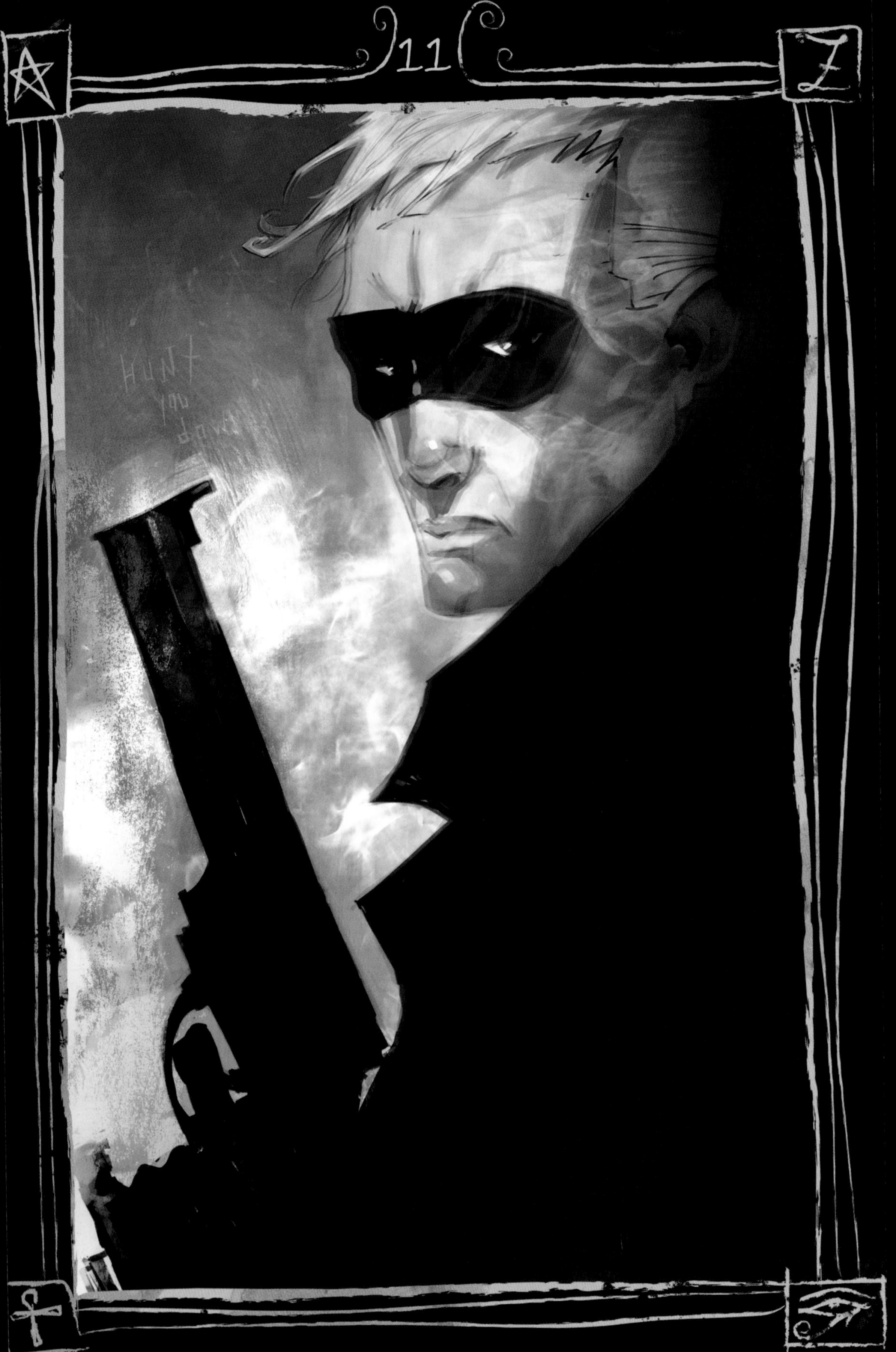
11
HUNT
you

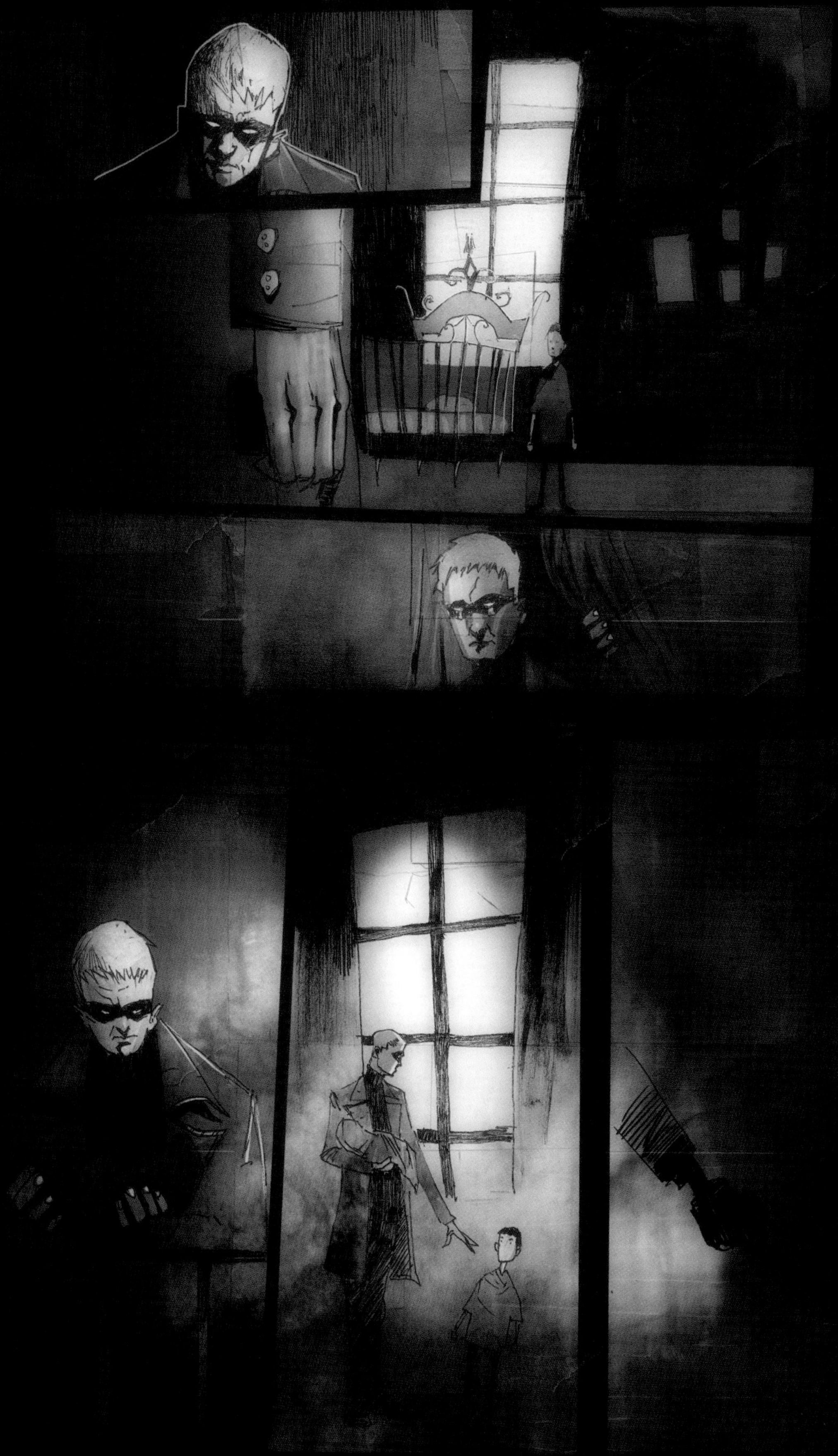

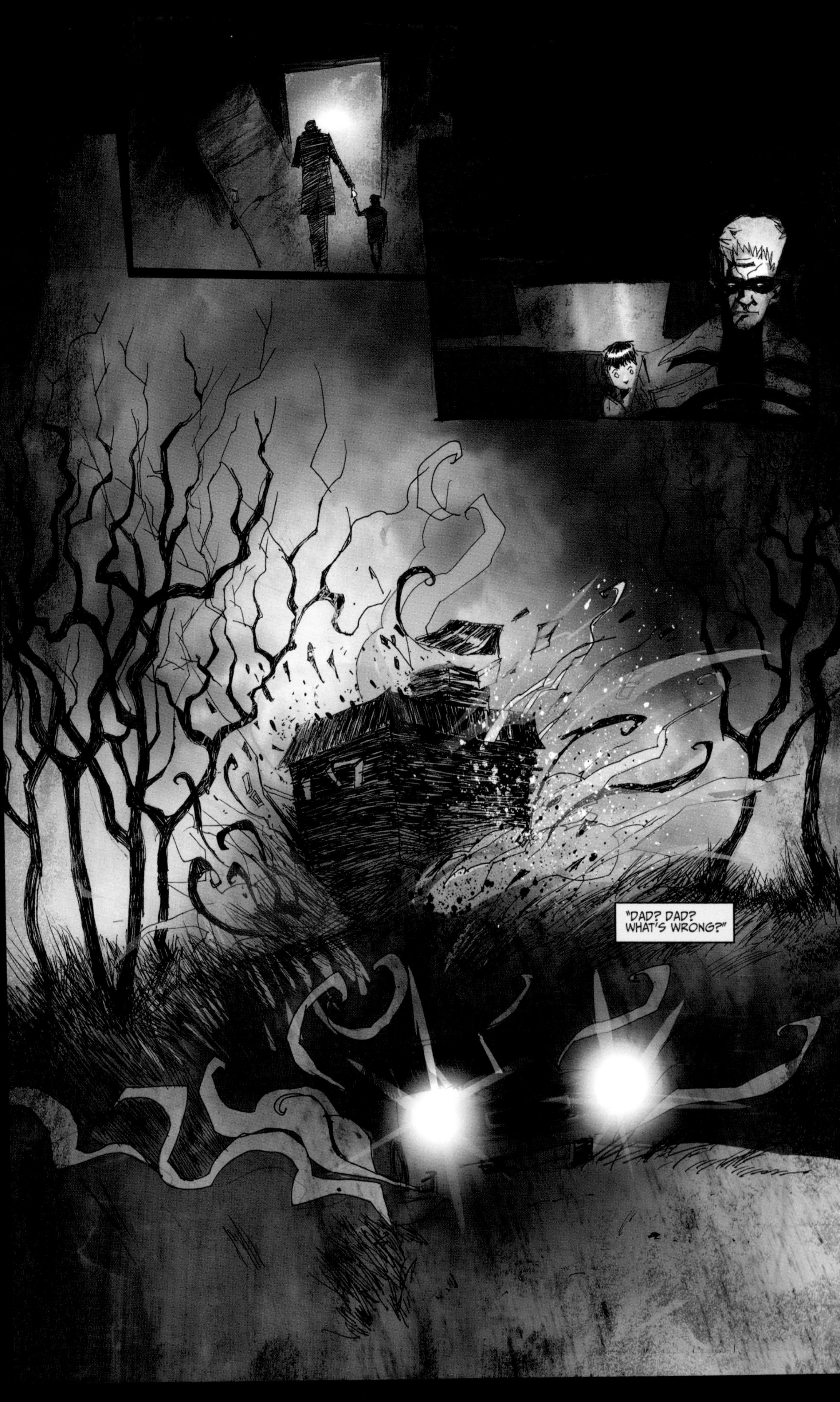
"DAD? DAD? WHAT'S WRONG?"

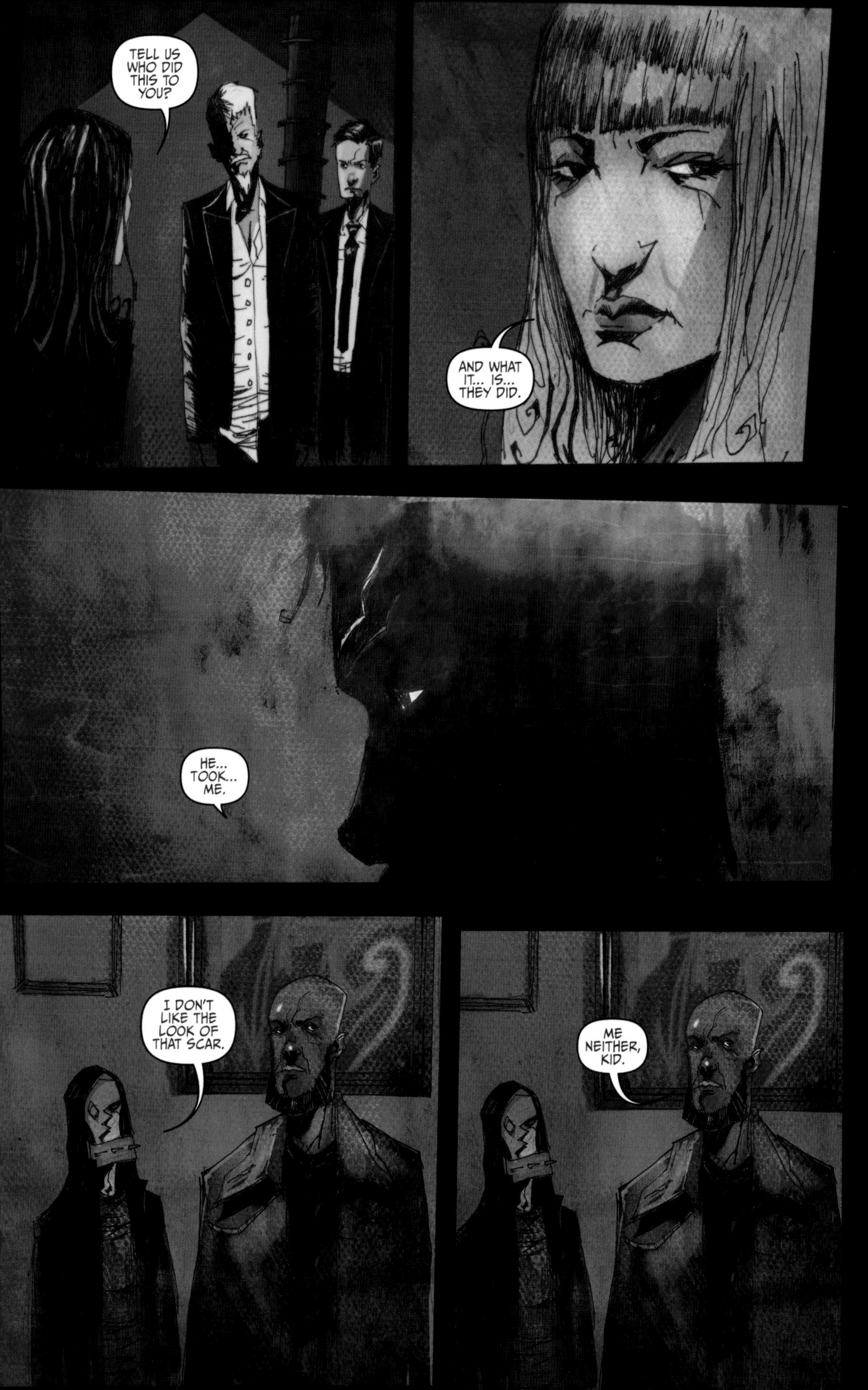
TELL US WHO DID THIS TO YOU?
AND WHAT IT... IS... THEY DID.
HE... TOOK... ME.
I DON'T LIKE THE LOOK OF THAT SCAR.
ME NEITHER, KID.

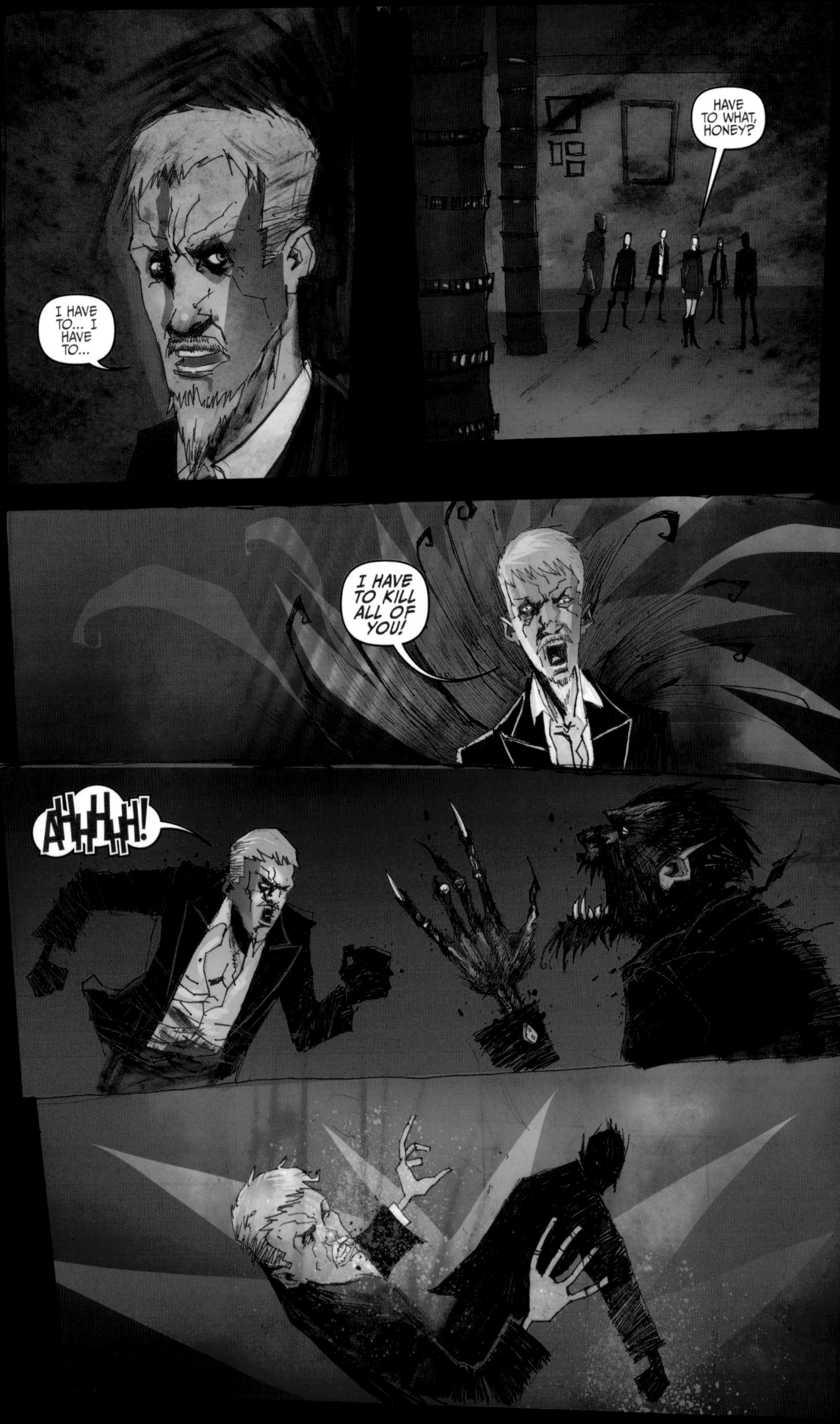
I HAVE TO... I HAVE TO...
HAVE TO WHAT, HONEY?
I HAVE TO KILL ALL OF YOU!
AHHHH!

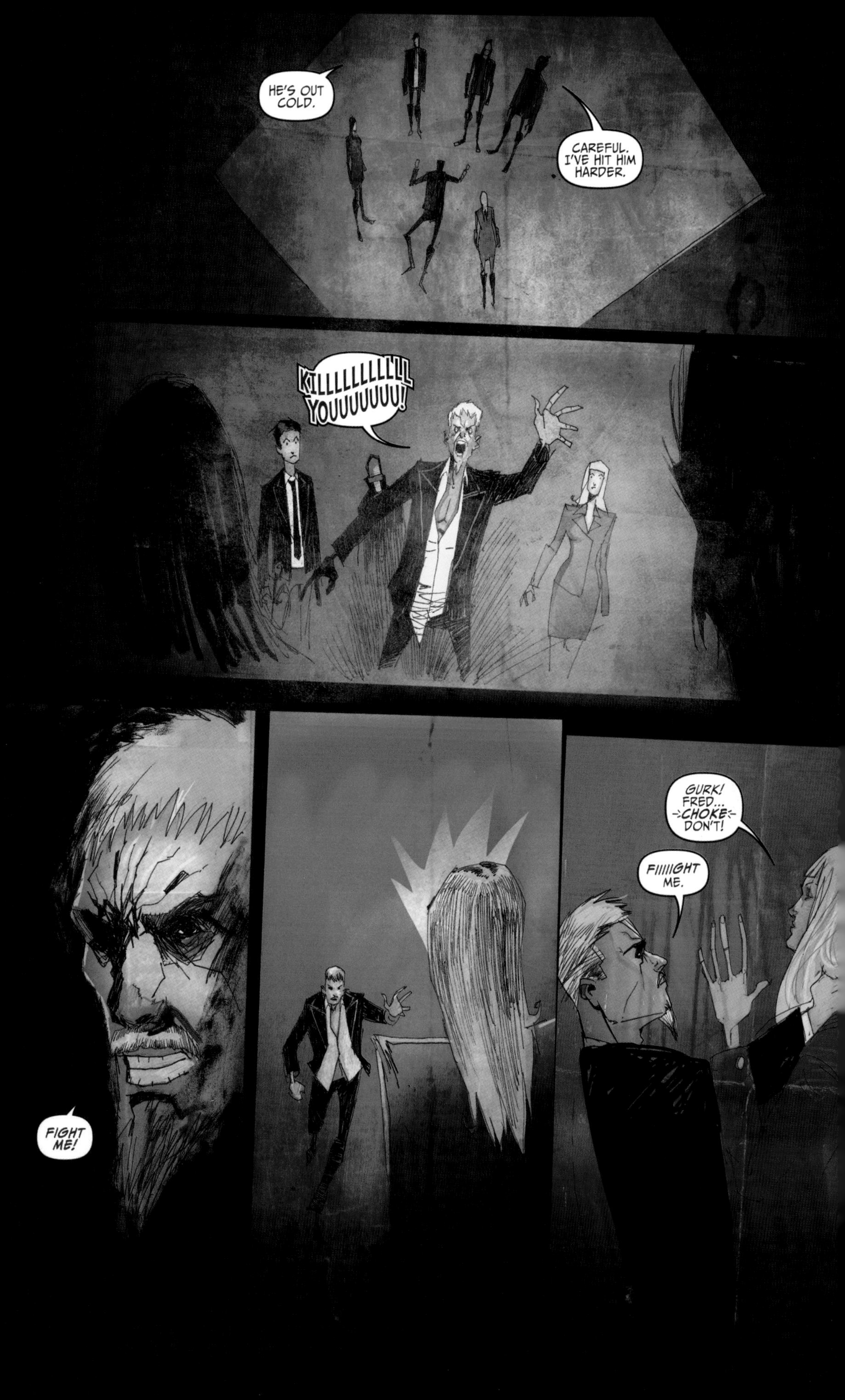
HE'S OUT COLD.
CAREFUL. I'VE HIT HIM HARDER.
KILLLLLLLLLL'LL YOUUUUUUU!
FIGHT ME!
GURK! FRED... -CHOKE- DON'T!
FIIIIIGHT ME.

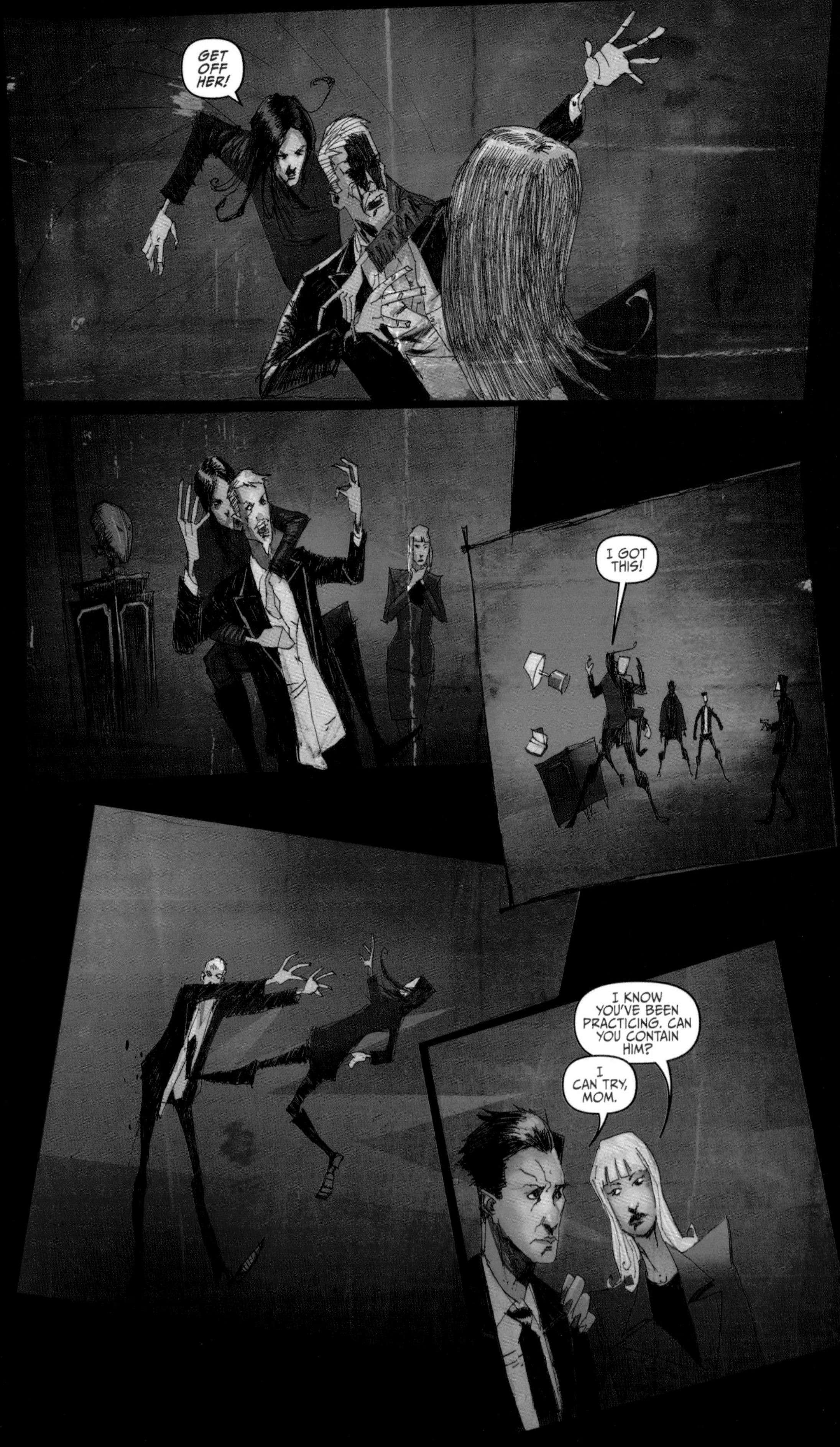
GET OFF HER!
I GOT THIS!
I KNOW YOU'VE BEEN PRACTICING. CAN YOU CONTAIN HIM?
I CAN TRY, MOM.

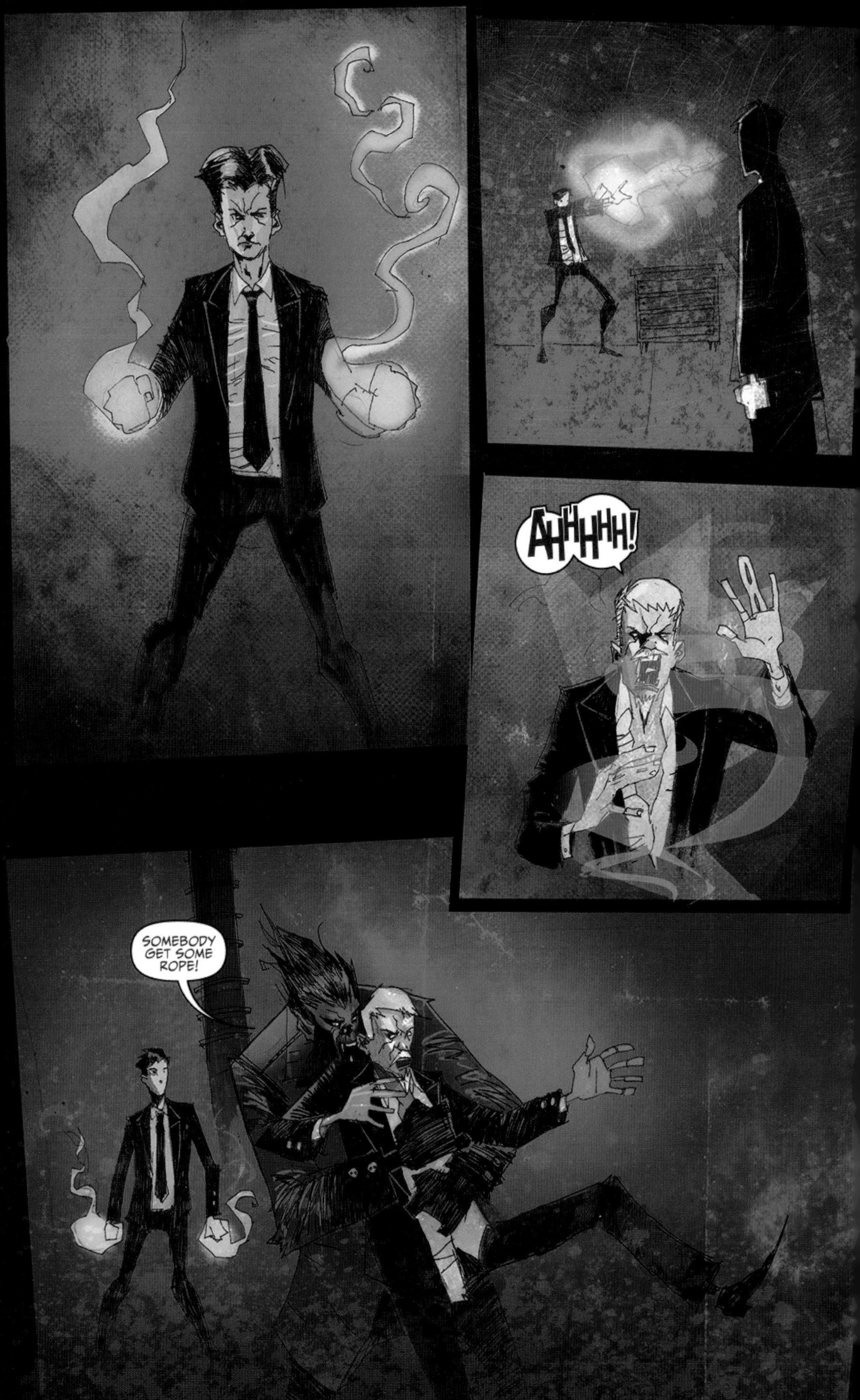

AHHHHH!
SOMEBODY GET SOME ROPE!

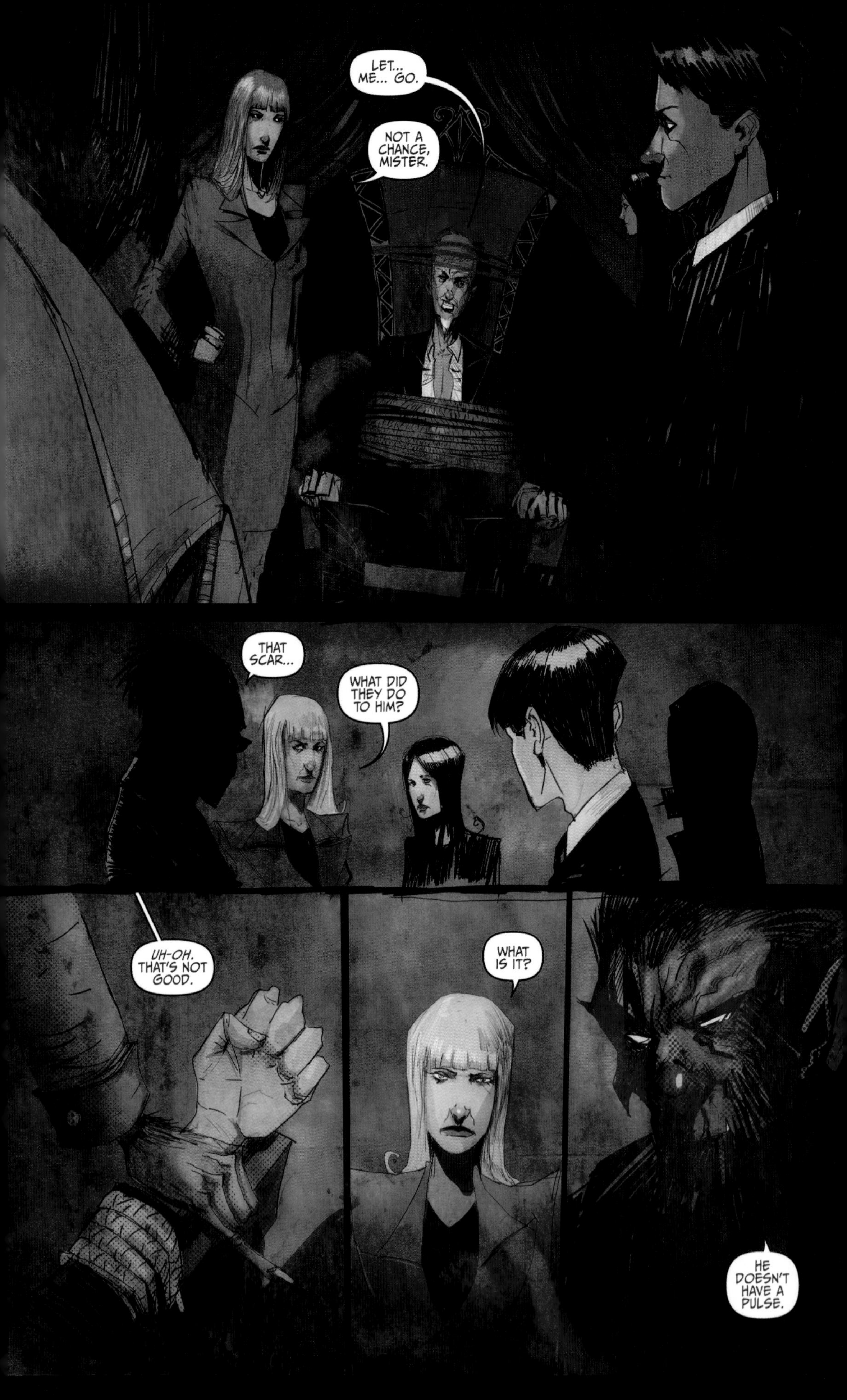
LET... ME... GO.
NOT A CHANCE, MISTER.
THAT SCAR...
WHAT DID THEY DO TO HIM?
UH-OH. THAT'S NOT GOOD.
WHAT IS IT?
HE DOESN'T HAVE A PULSE.

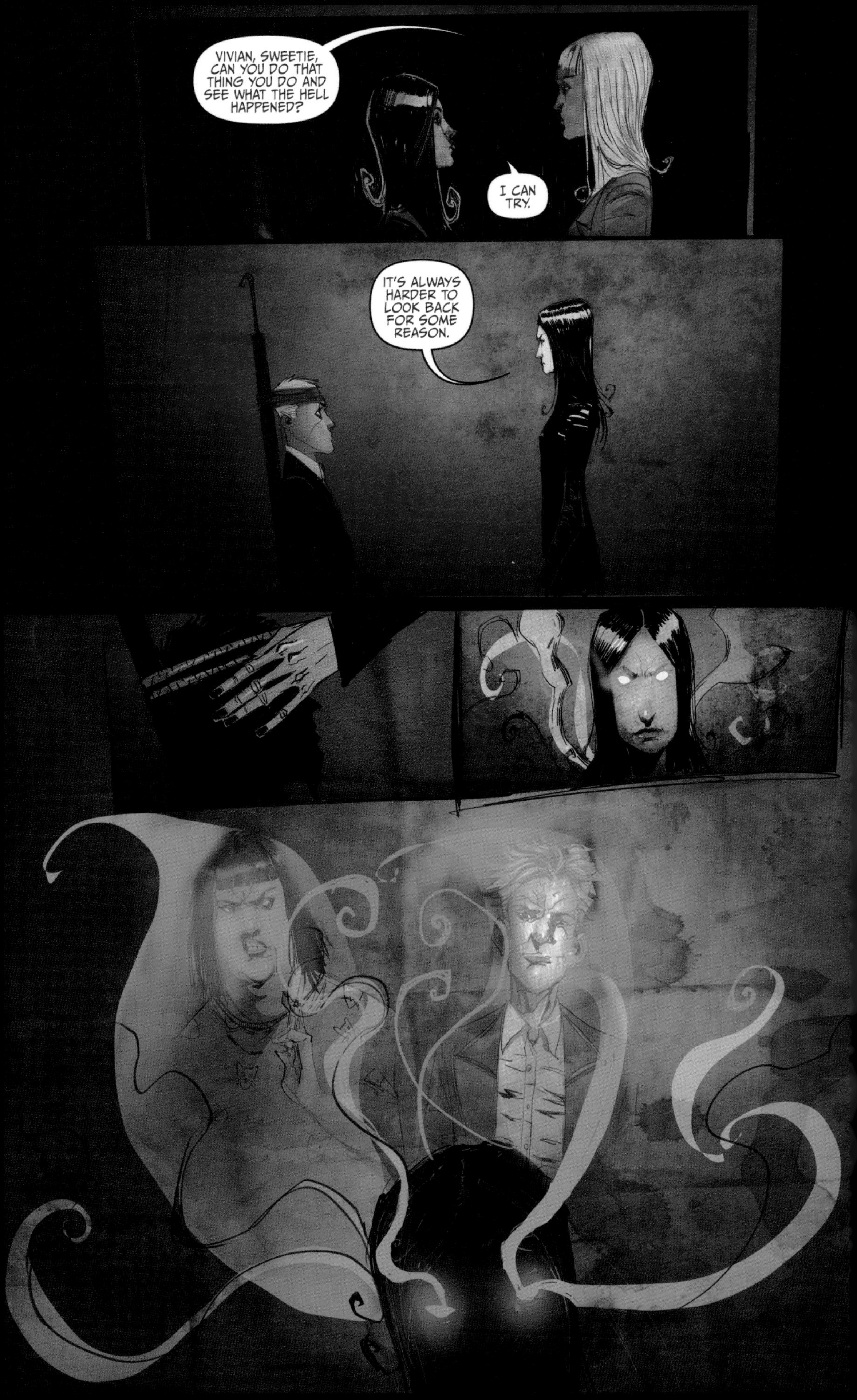
VIVIAN, SWEETIE, CAN YOU DO THAT THING YOU DO AND SEE WHAT THE HELL HAPPENED?
I CAN TRY.
IT'S ALWAYS HARDER TO LOOK BACK FOR SOME REASON.

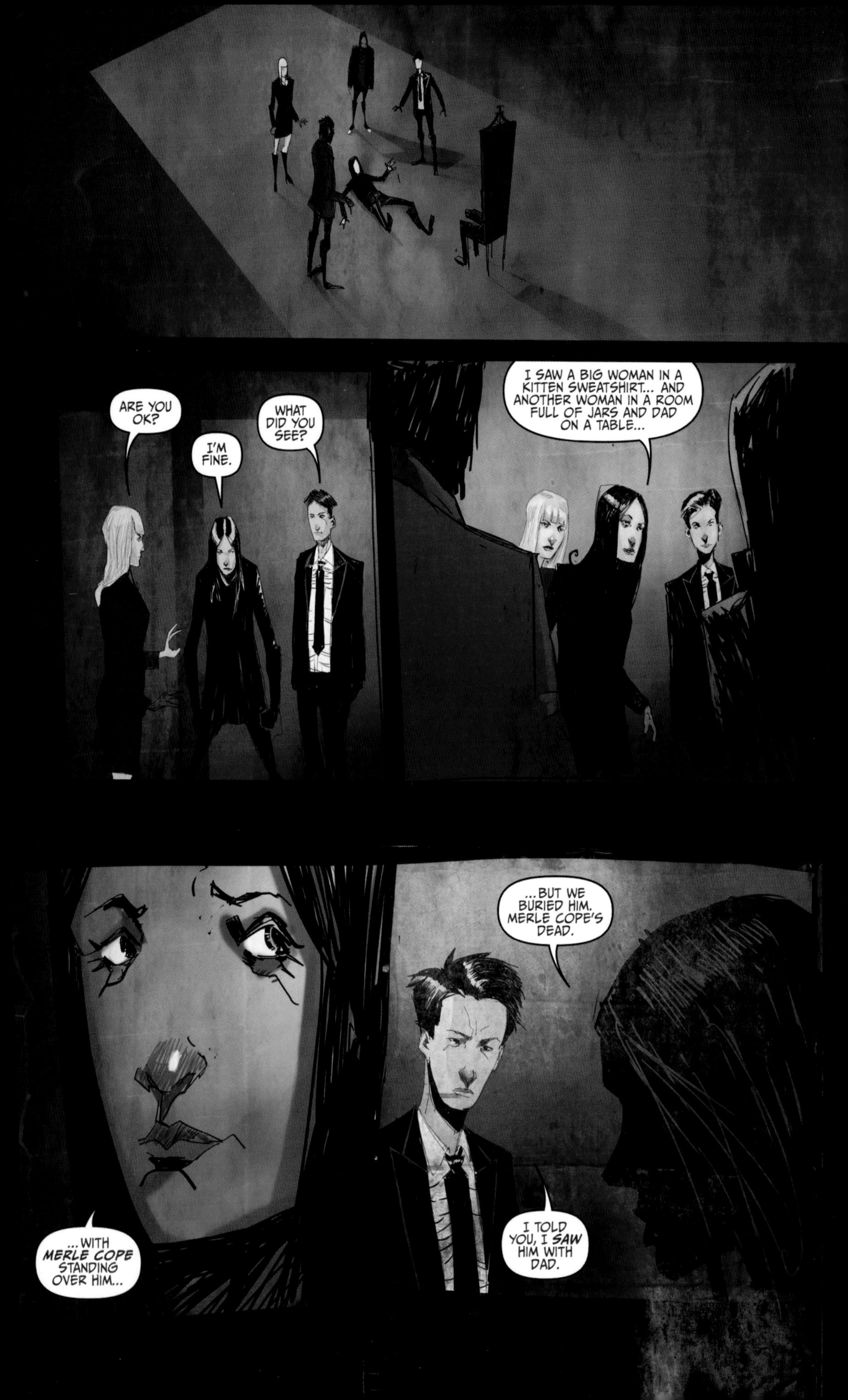
ARE YOU OK?
I'M FINE.
WHAT DID YOU SEE?
I SAW A BIG WOMAN IN A KITTEN SWEATSHIRT... AND ANOTHER WOMAN IN A ROOM FULL OF JARS AND DAD ON A TABLE...
...WITH MERLE COPE STANDING OVER HIM...
...BUT WE BURIED HIM. MERLE COPE'S DEAD.
I TOLD YOU, I SAW HIM WITH DAD.

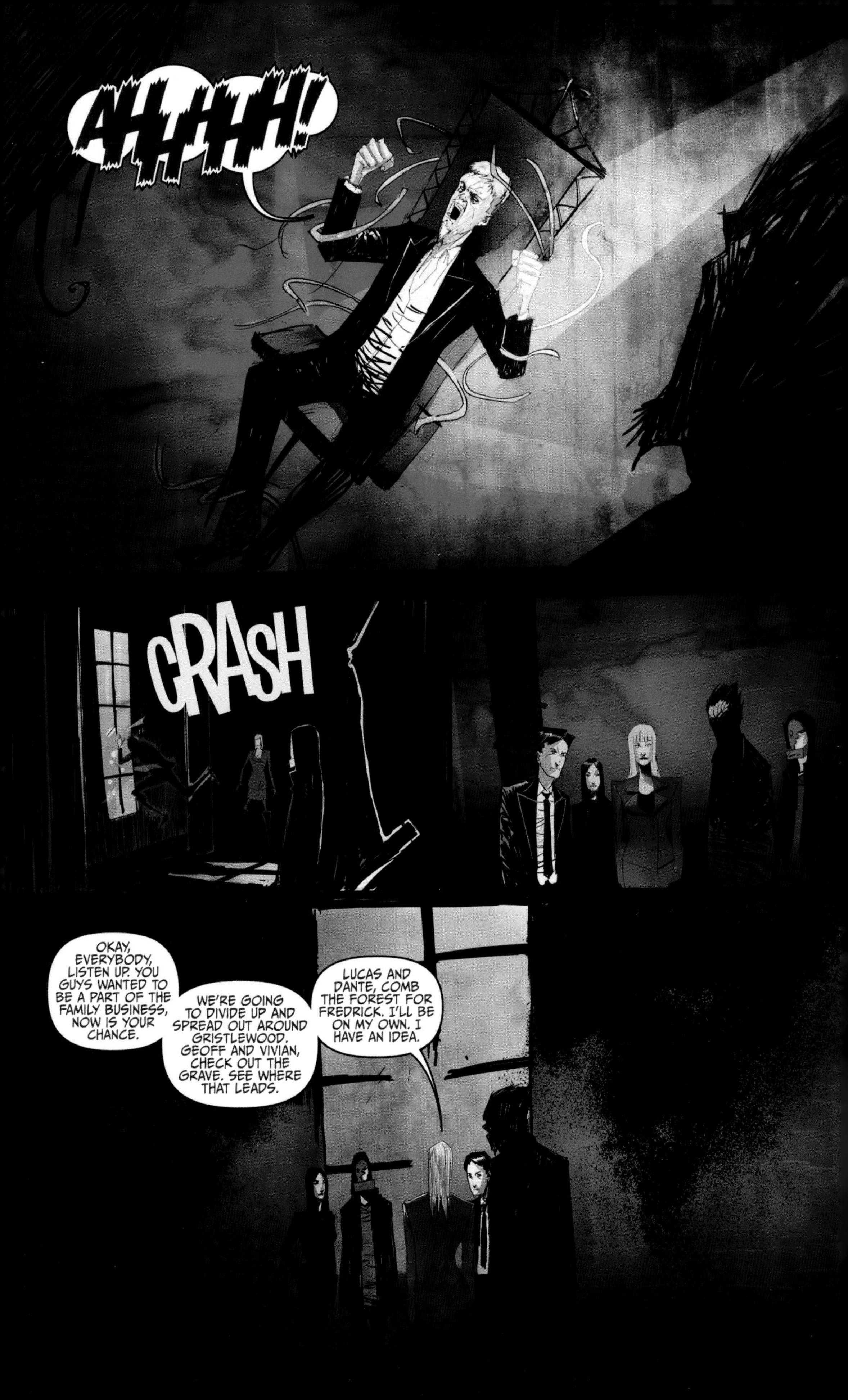
AHHHH!
CRASH
OKAY, EVERYBODY, LISTEN UP. YOU GUYS WANTED TO BE A PART OF THE FAMILY BUSINESS, NOW IS YOUR CHANCE.
WE'RE GOING TO DIVIDE UP AND SPREAD OUT AROUND GRISTLEWOOD. GEOFF AND VIVIAN, CHECK OUT THE GRAVE. SEE WHERE THAT LEADS.
LUCAS AND DANTE, COMB THE FOREST FOR FREDRICK. I'LL BE ON MY OWN. I HAVE AN IDEA.

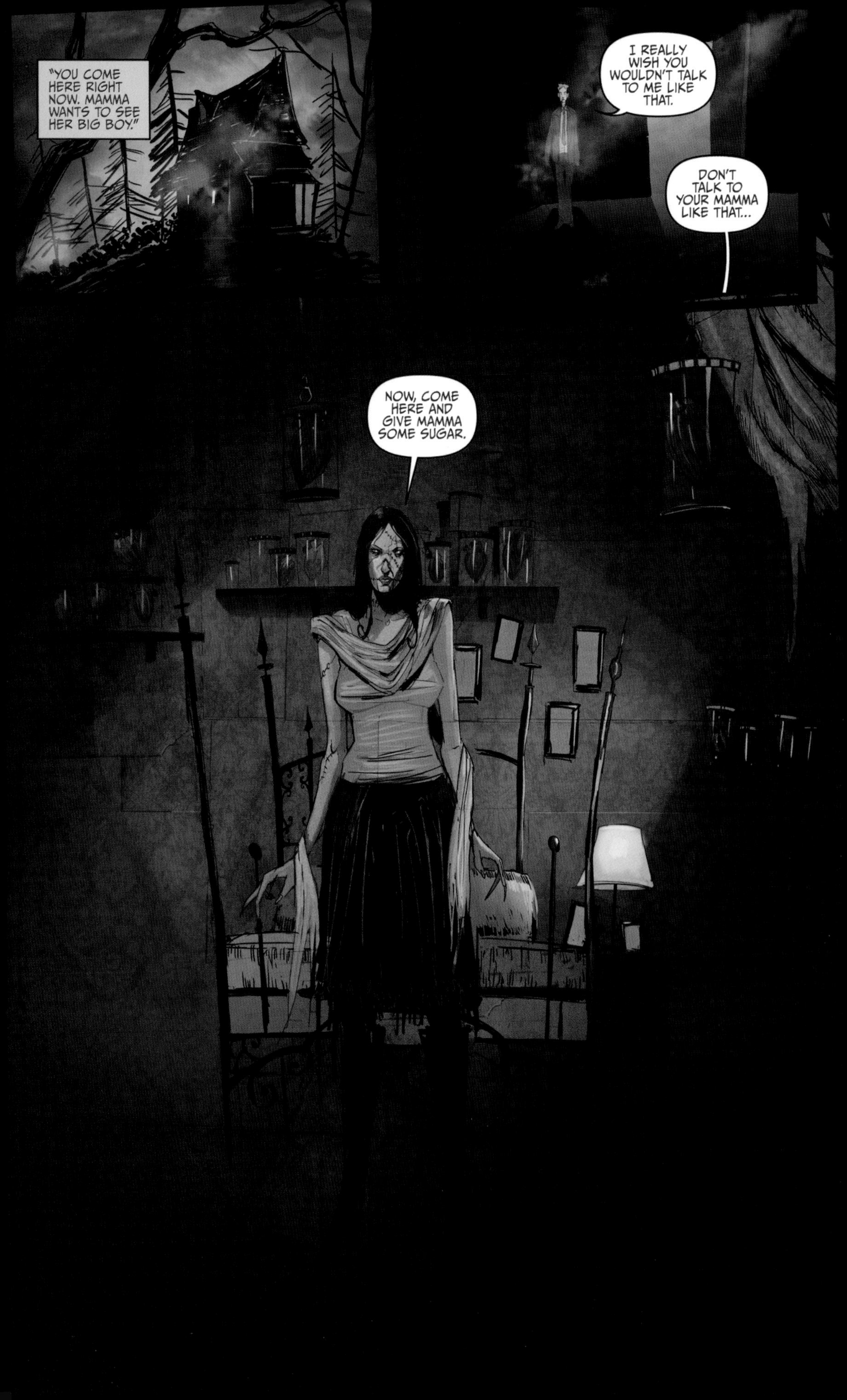
"YOU COME HERE RIGHT NOW. MAMMA WANTS TO SEE HER BIG BOY."
I REALLY WISH YOU WOULDN'T TALK TO ME LIKE THAT.
DON'T TALK TO YOUR MAMMA LIKE THAT...
NOW, COME HERE AND GIVE MAMMA SOME SUGAR.

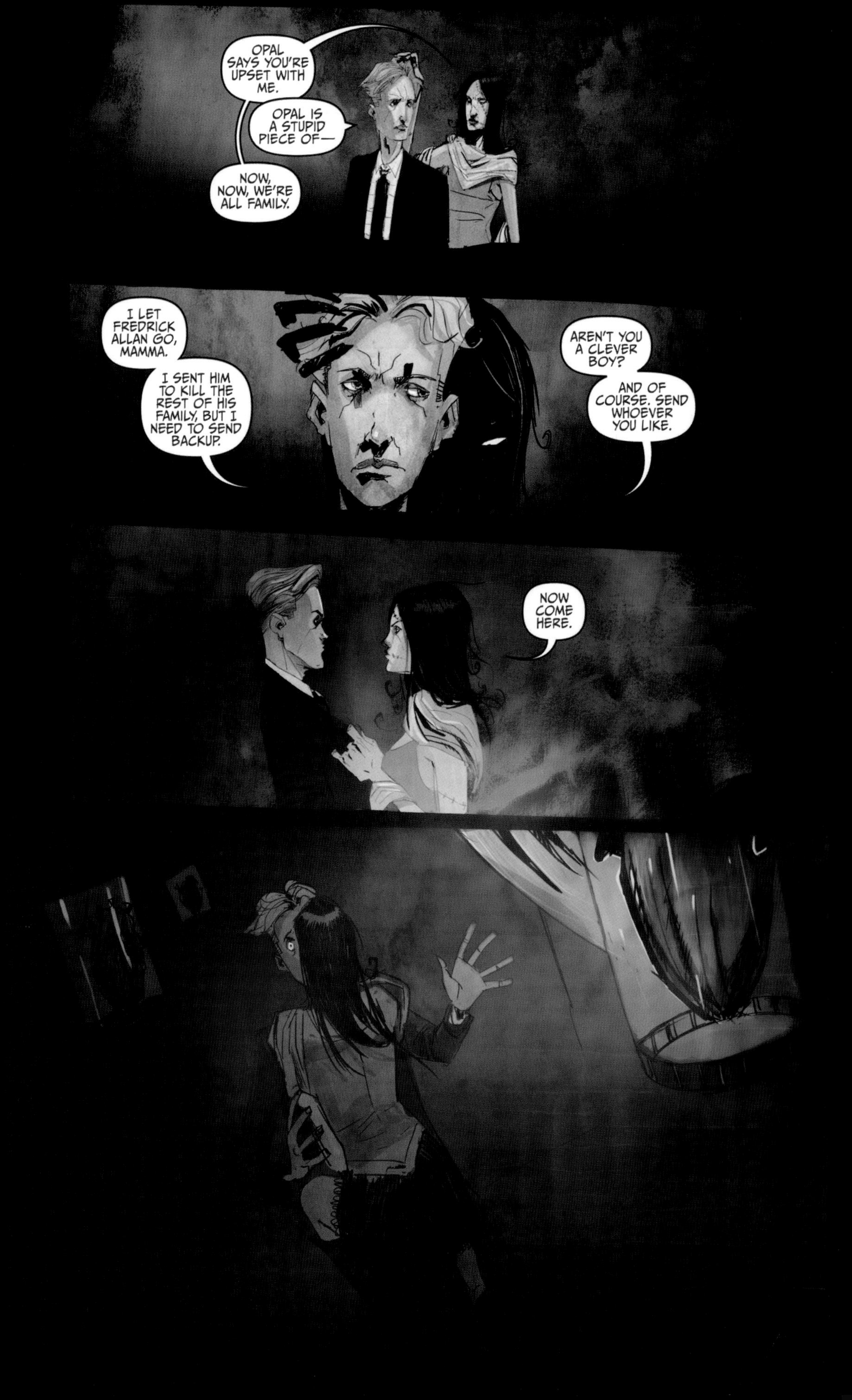
OPAL SAYS YOU'RE UPSET WITH ME.
OPAL IS A STUPID PIECE OF—
NOW, NOW, WE'RE ALL FAMILY.
I LET FREDRICK ALLAN GO, MAMMA.
I SENT HIM TO KILL THE REST OF HIS FAMILY, BUT I NEED TO SEND BACKUP.
AREN'T YOU A CLEVER BOY?
AND OF COURSE. SEND WHOEVER YOU LIKE.
NOW COME HERE.

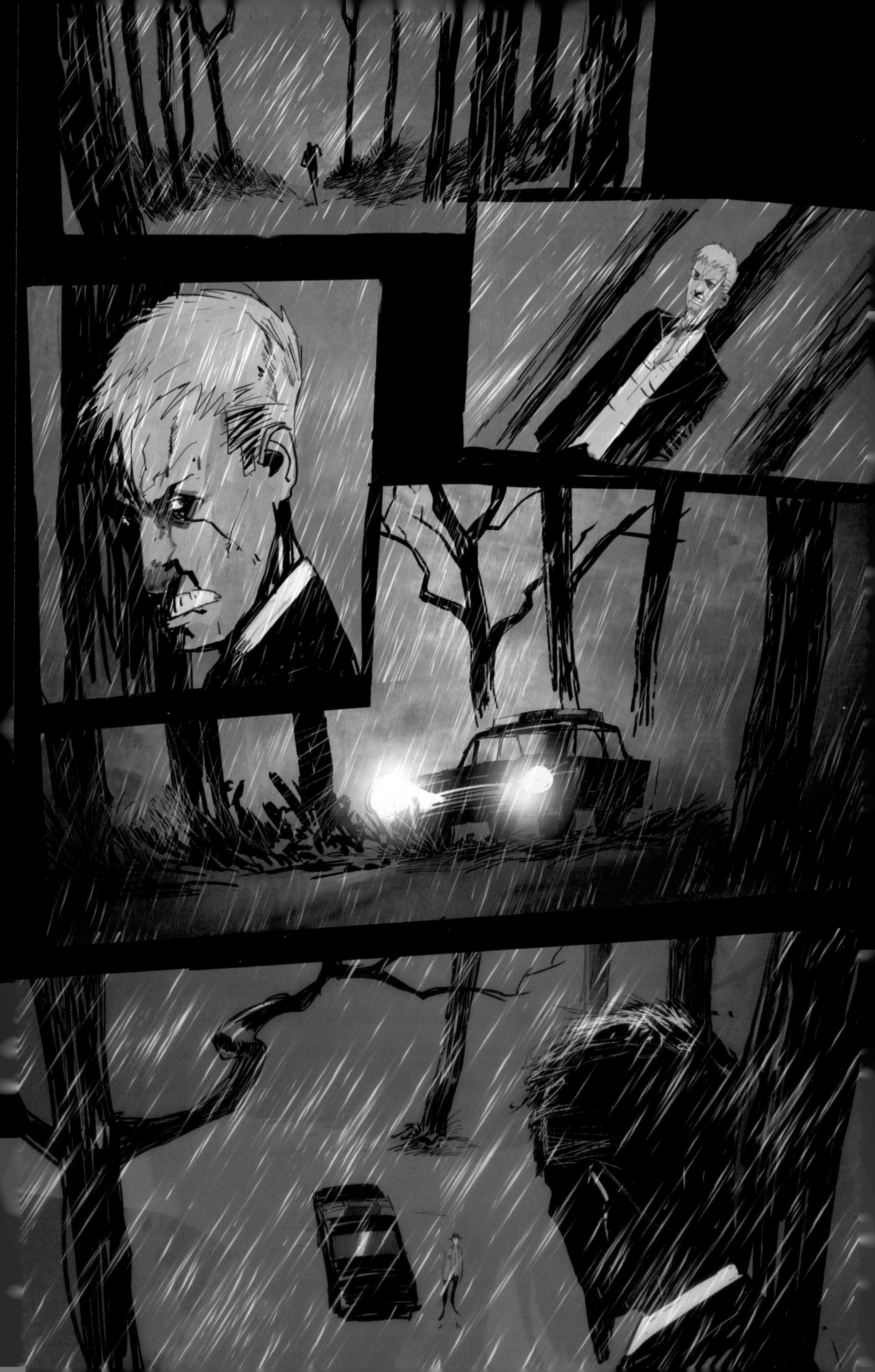

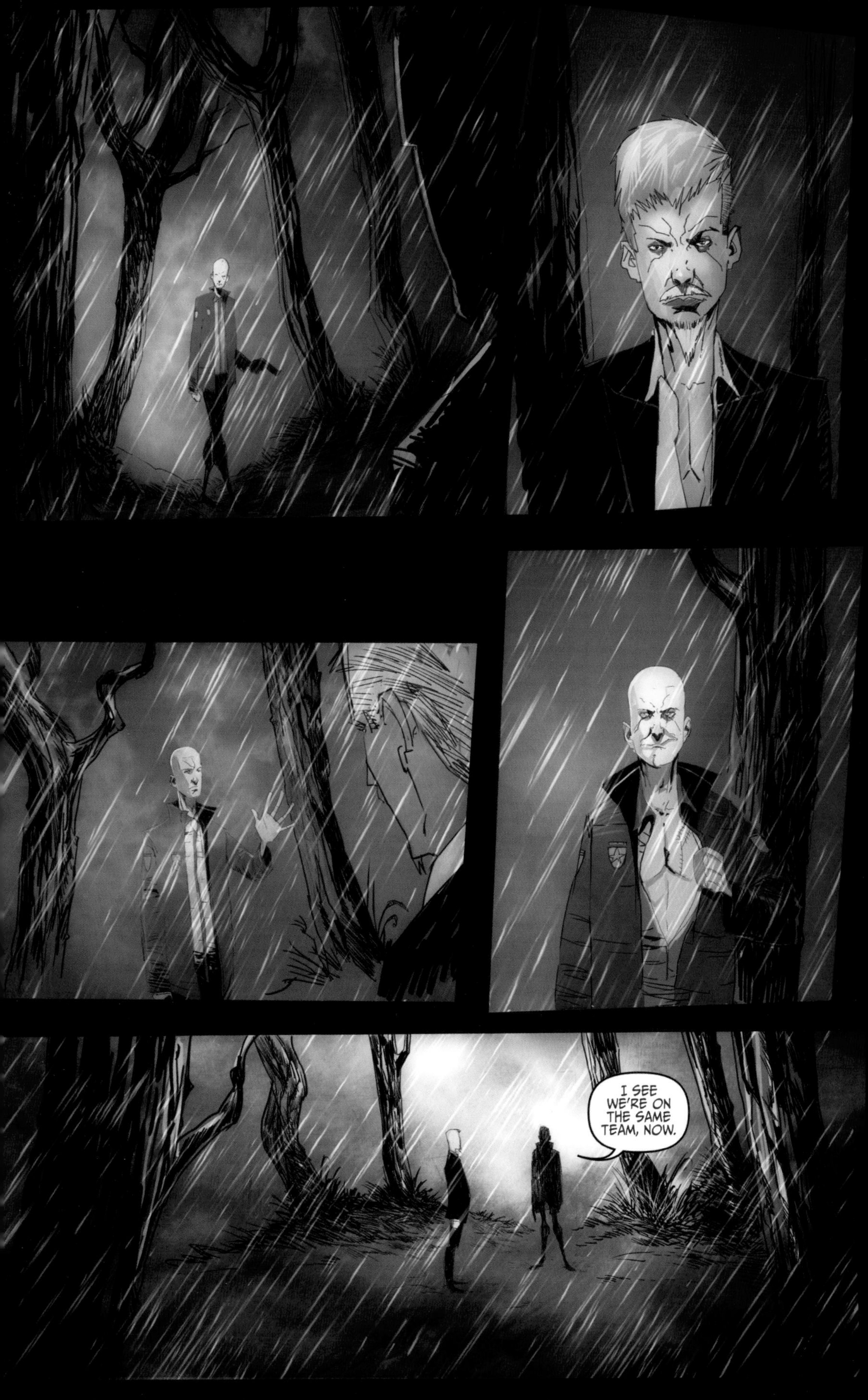
I SEE WE'RE ON THE SAME TEAM, NOW.

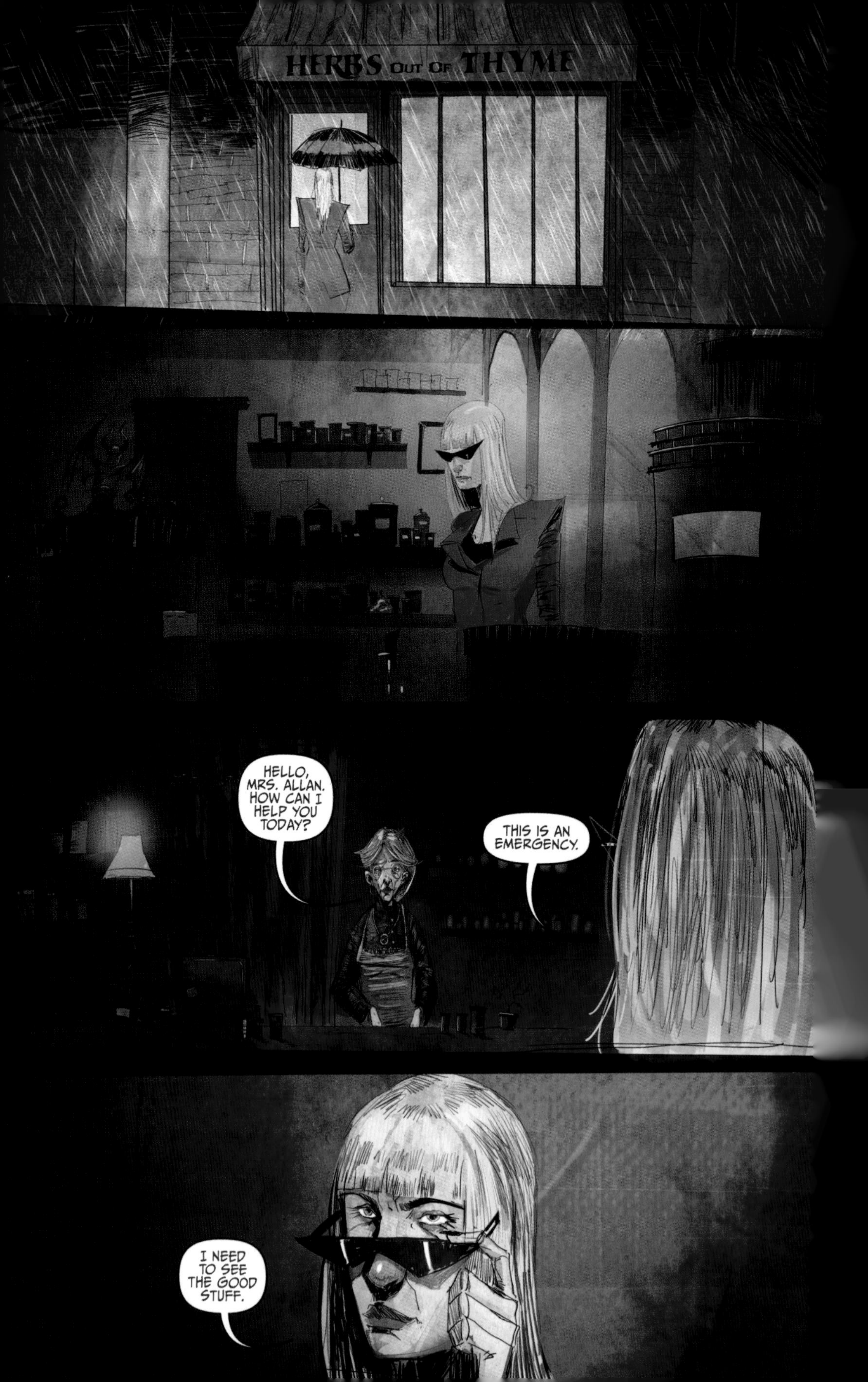
HERBS OUT OF THYME
HELLO, MRS. ALLAN. HOW CAN I HELP YOU TODAY?
THIS IS AN EMERGENCY.
I NEED TO SEE THE GOOD STUFF.

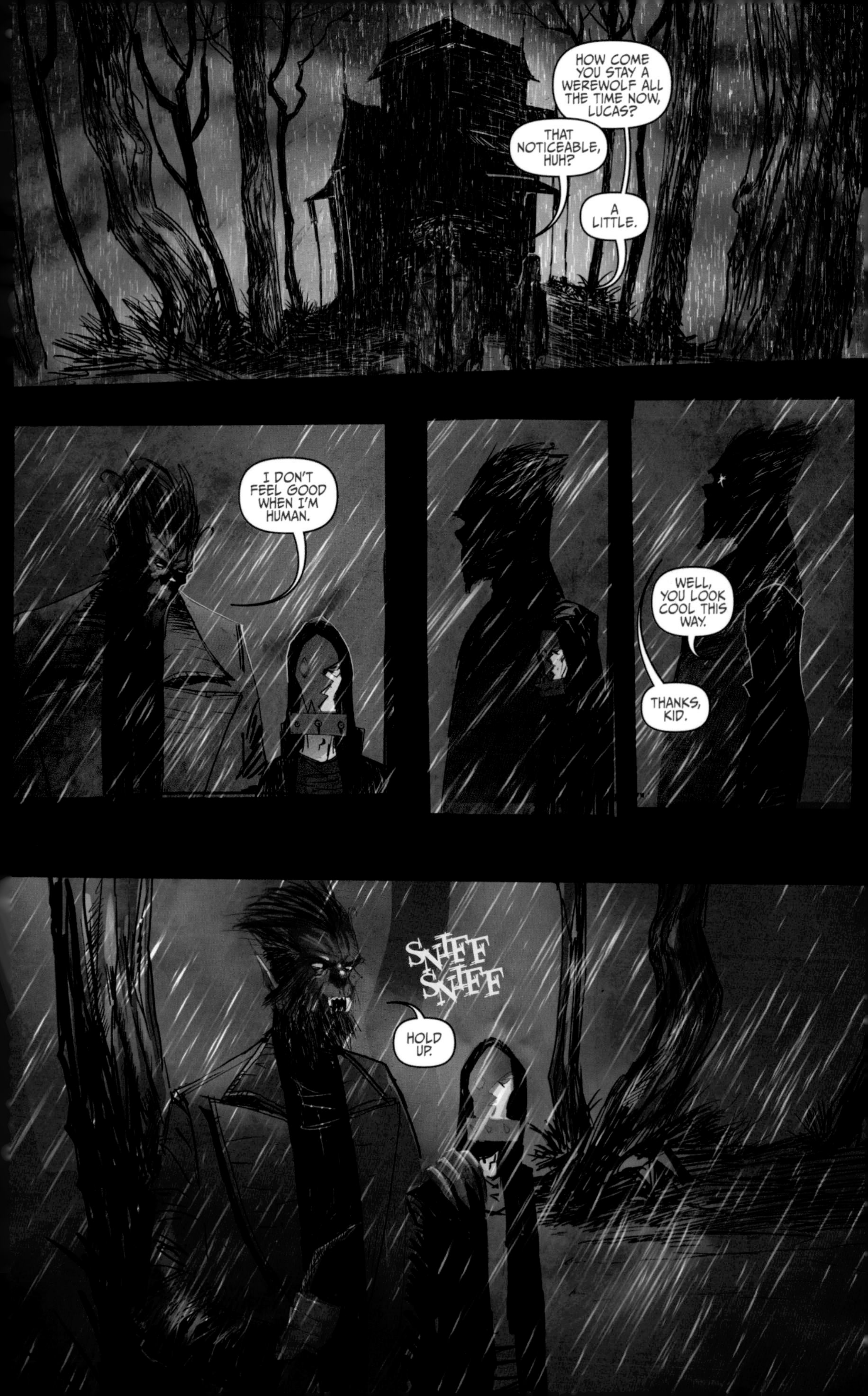
HOW COME YOU STAY A WEREWOLF ALL THE TIME NOW, LUCAS?
THAT NOTICEABLE, HUH?
A LITTLE.
I DON'T FEEL GOOD WHEN I'M HUMAN.
WELL, YOU LOOK COOL THIS WAY.
THANKS, KID.
SNIFF SNIFF
HOLD UP.

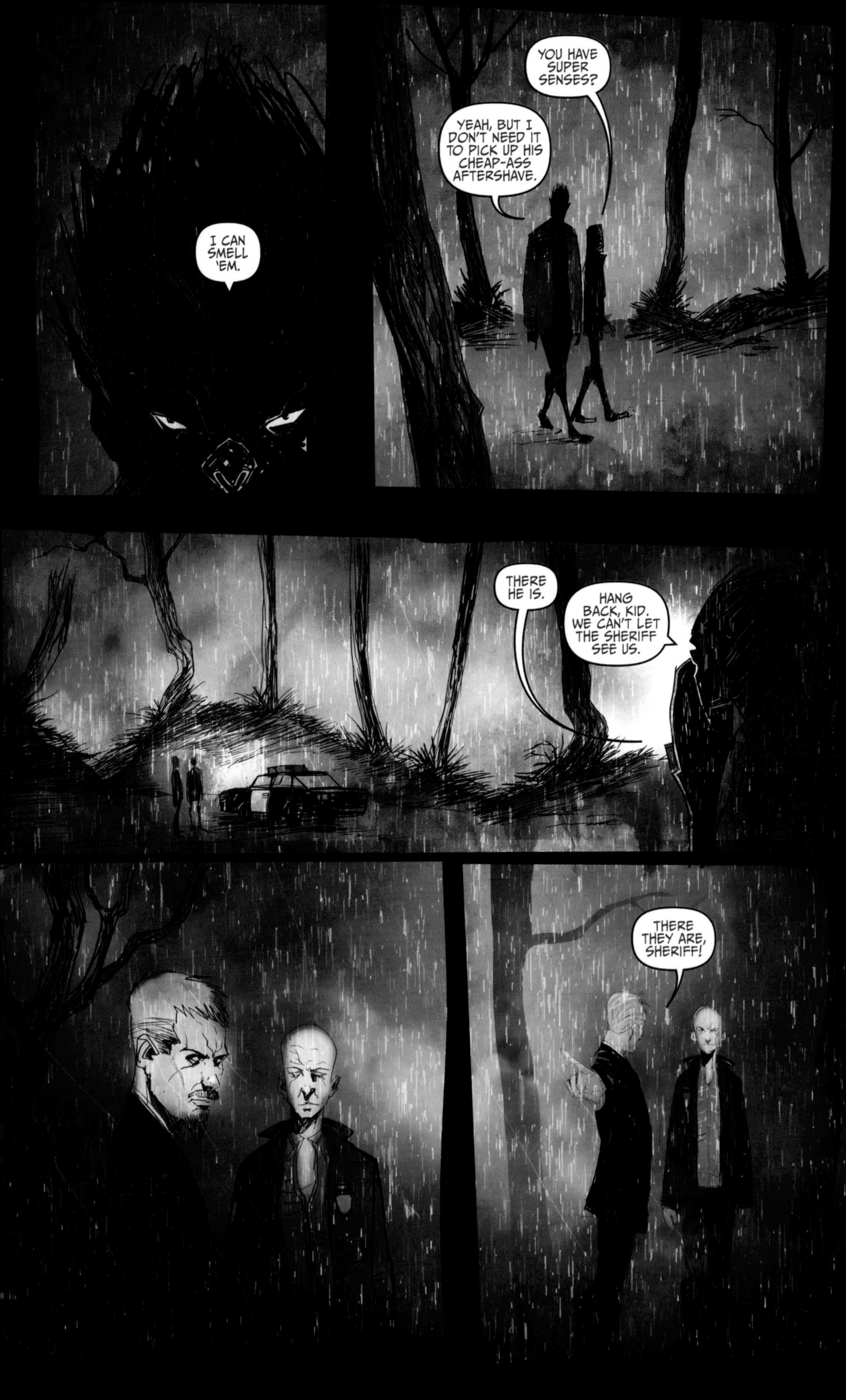
I CAN SMELL 'EM.
YOU HAVE SUPER SENSES?
YEAH, BUT I DON'T NEED IT TO PICK UP HIS CHEAP-ASS AFTERSHAVE.
THERE HE IS.
HANG BACK, KID. WE CAN'T LET THE SHERIFF SEE US.
THERE THEY ARE, SHERIFF!

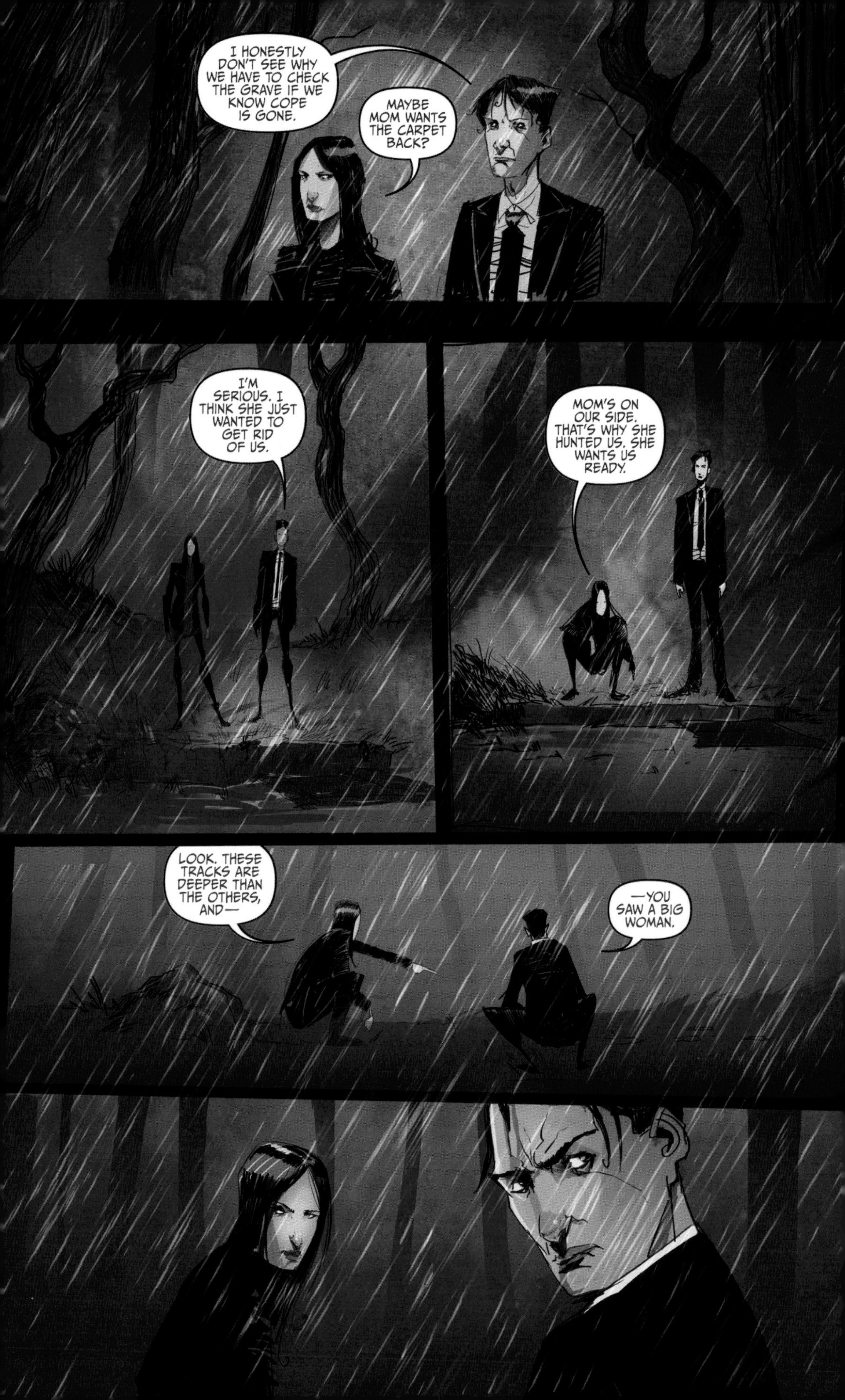
I HONESTLY DON'T SEE WHY WE HAVE TO CHECK THE GRAVE IF WE KNOW COPE IS GONE.
MAYBE MOM WANTS THE CARPET BACK?
I'M SERIOUS. I THINK SHE JUST WANTED TO GET RID OF US.
MOM'S ON OUR SIDE. THAT'S WHY SHE HUNTED US. SHE WANTS US READY.
LOOK. THESE TRACKS ARE DEEPER THAN THE OTHERS, AND—
—YOU SAW A BIG WOMAN.

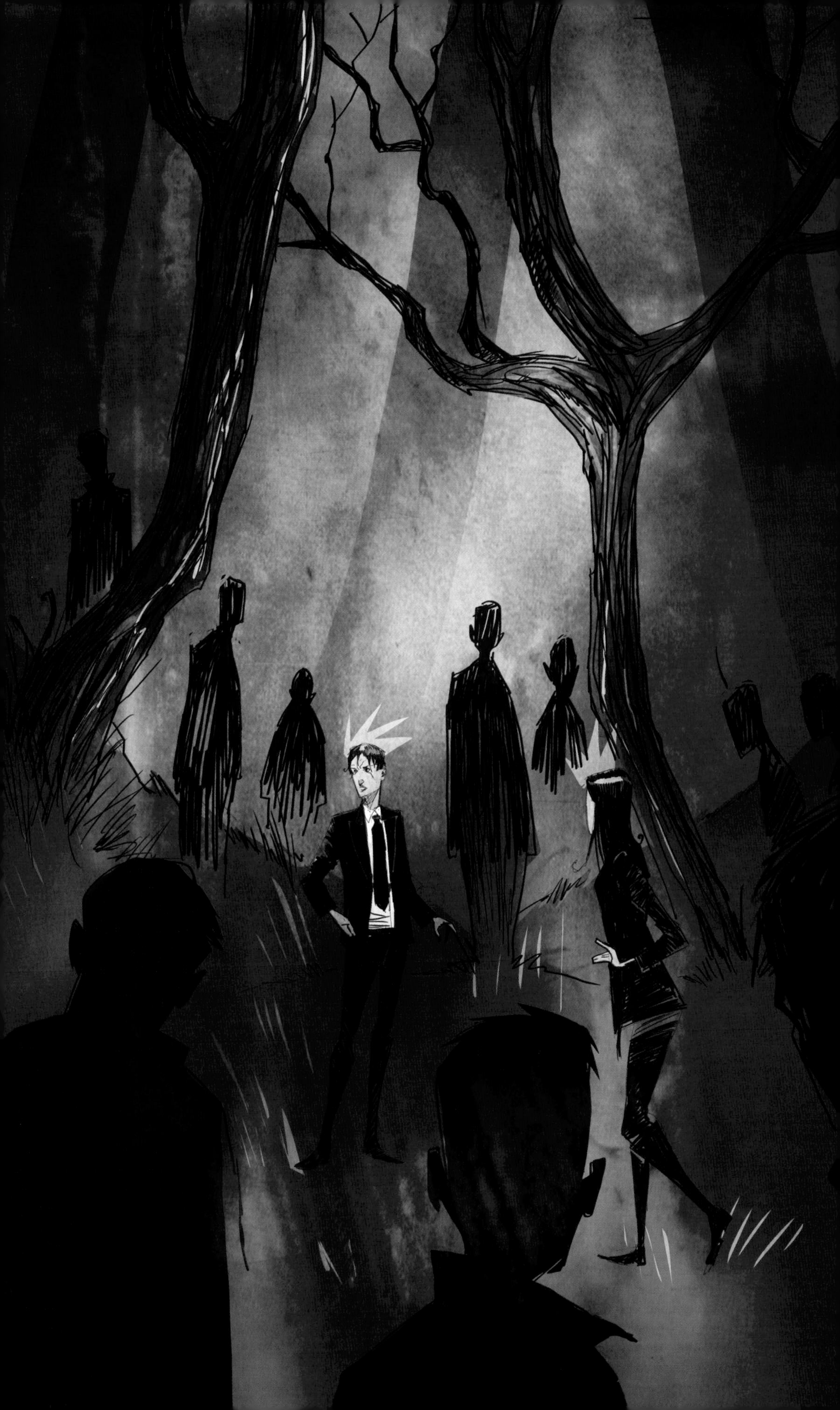

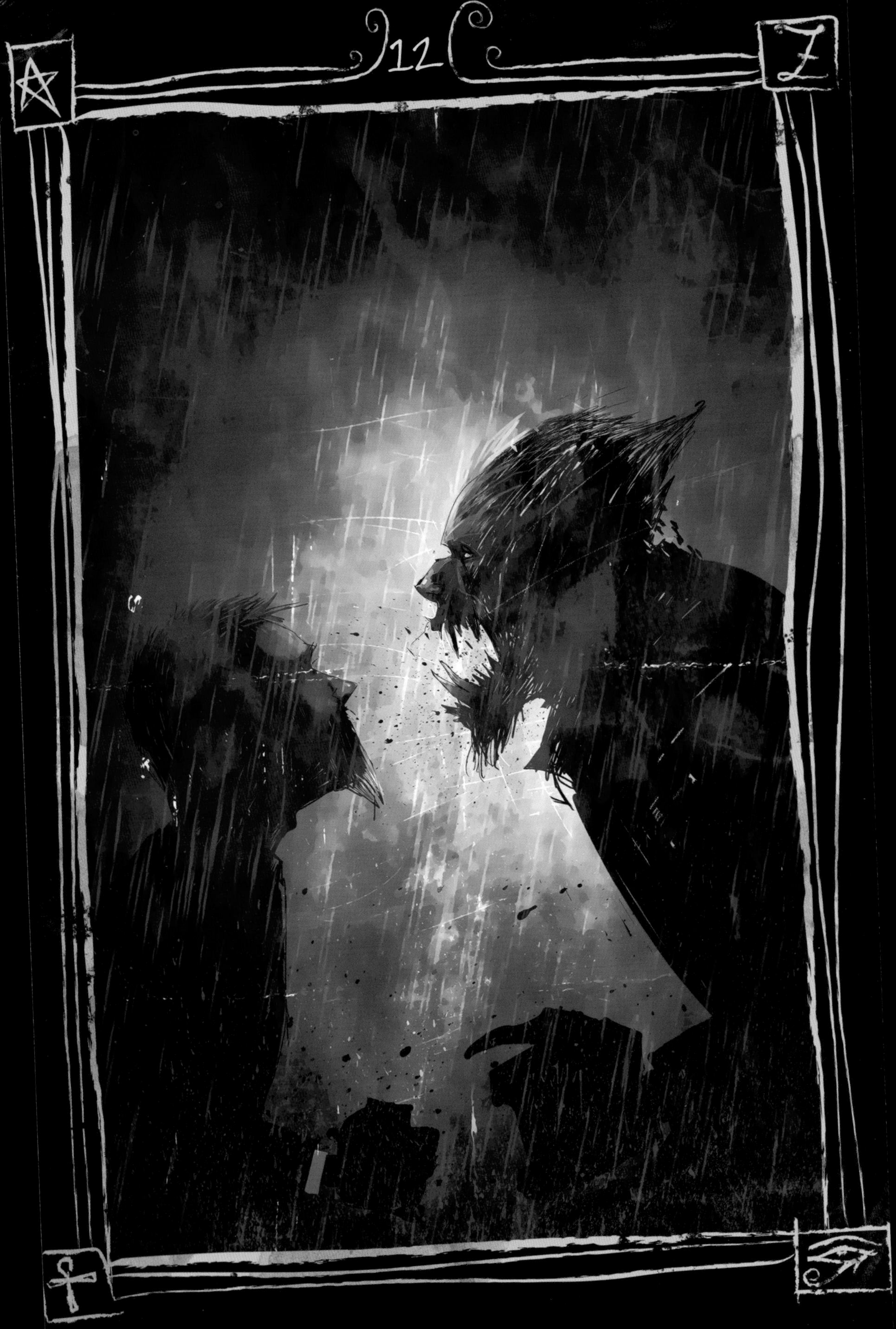
12

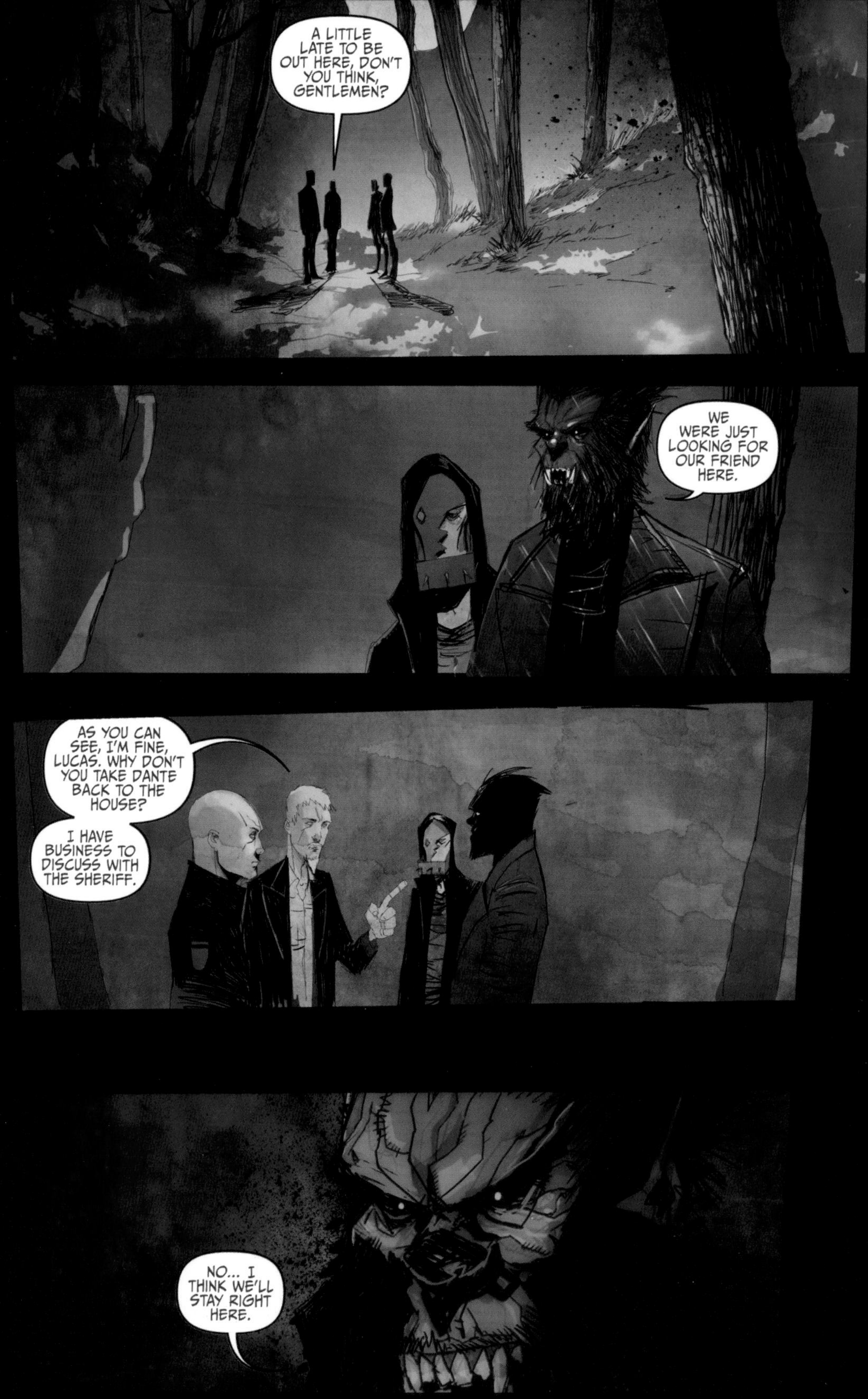
A LITTLE LATE TO BE OUT HERE, DON'T YOU THINK, GENTLEMEN?
WE WERE JUST LOOKING FOR OUR FRIEND HERE.
AS YOU CAN SEE, I'M FINE, LUCAS. WHY DON'T YOU TAKE DANTE BACK TO THE HOUSE?
I HAVE BUSINESS TO DISCUSS WITH THE SHERIFF.
NO... I THINK WE'LL STAY RIGHT HERE.

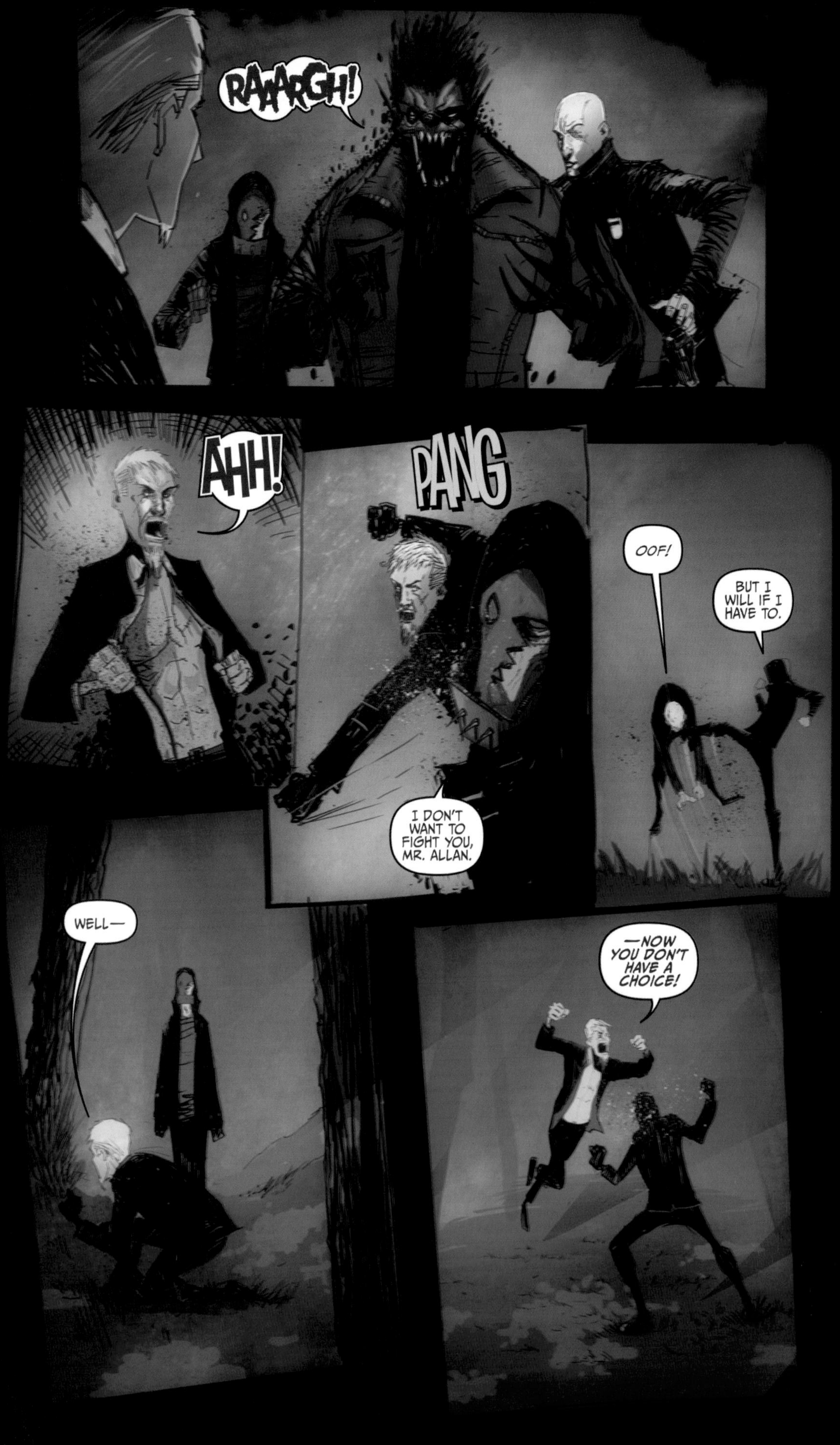
RAAARGH!
AHH!
PANG
I DON'T WANT TO FIGHT YOU, MR. ALLAN.
OOF!
BUT I WILL IF I HAVE TO.
WELL—
—NOW YOU DON'T HAVE A CHOICE!

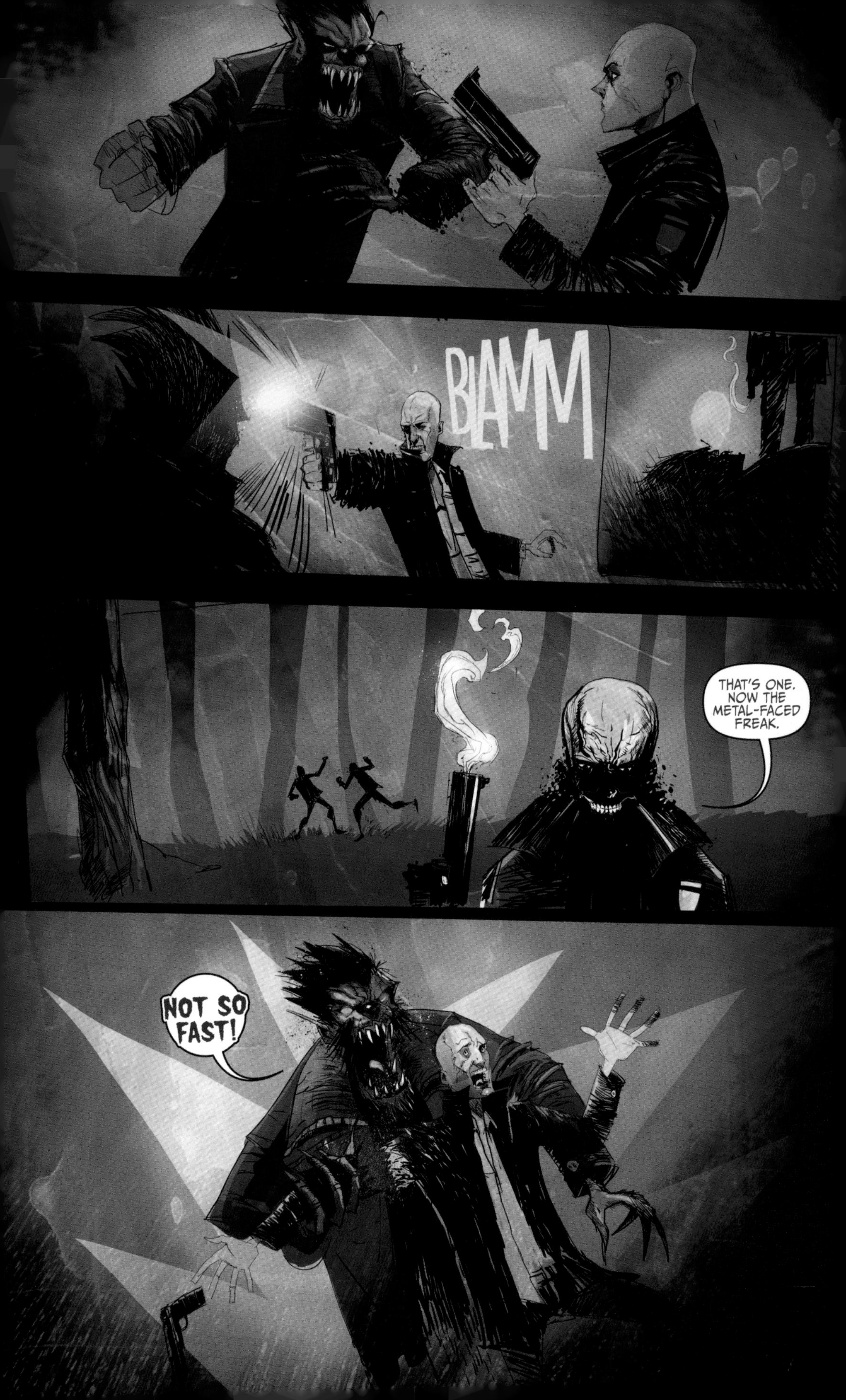
BLAMM
THAT'S ONE. NOW THE METAL-FACED FREAK.
NOT SO FAST!

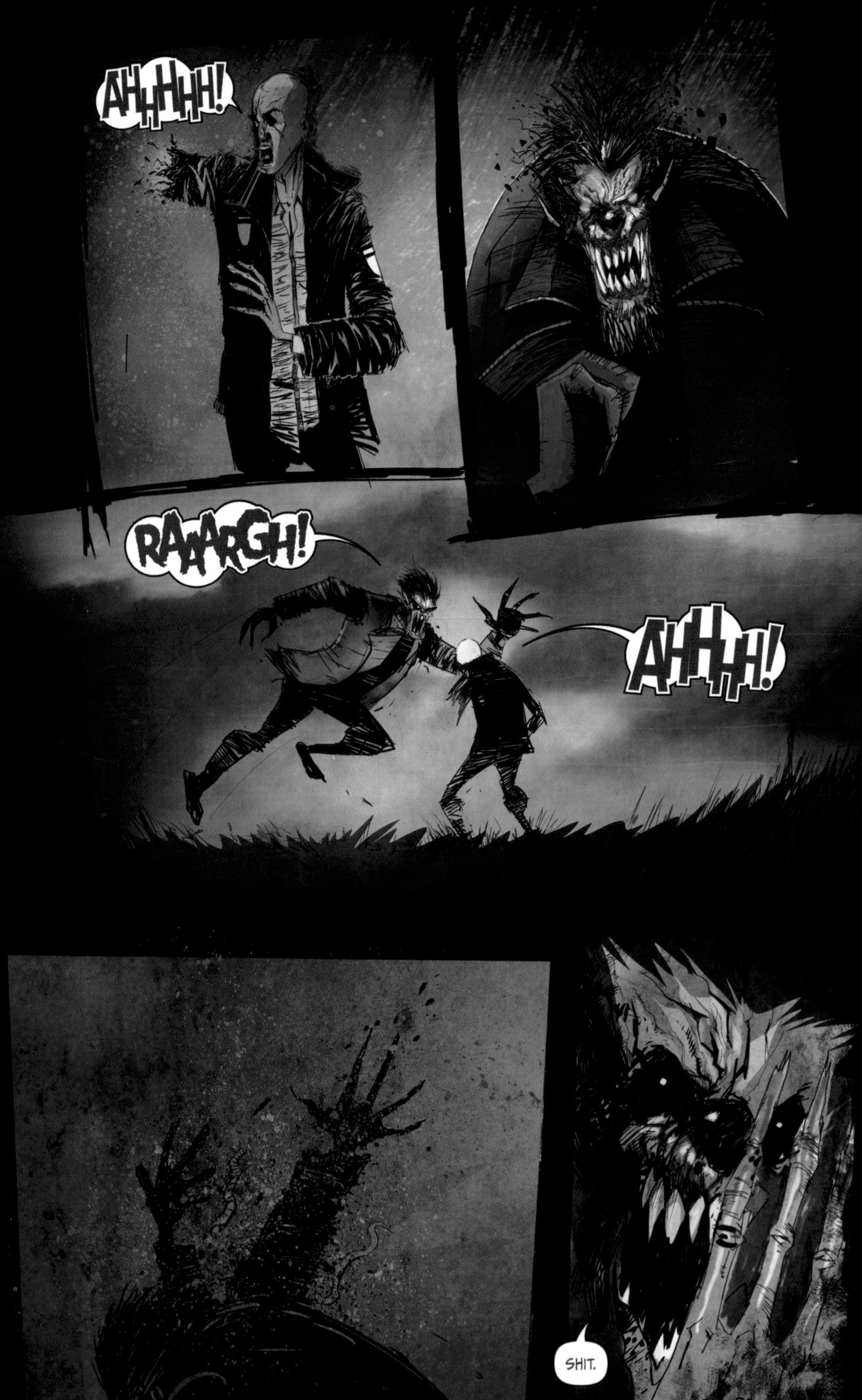
AHHHHH!
RAAARGH!
AHHHH!
SHIT.

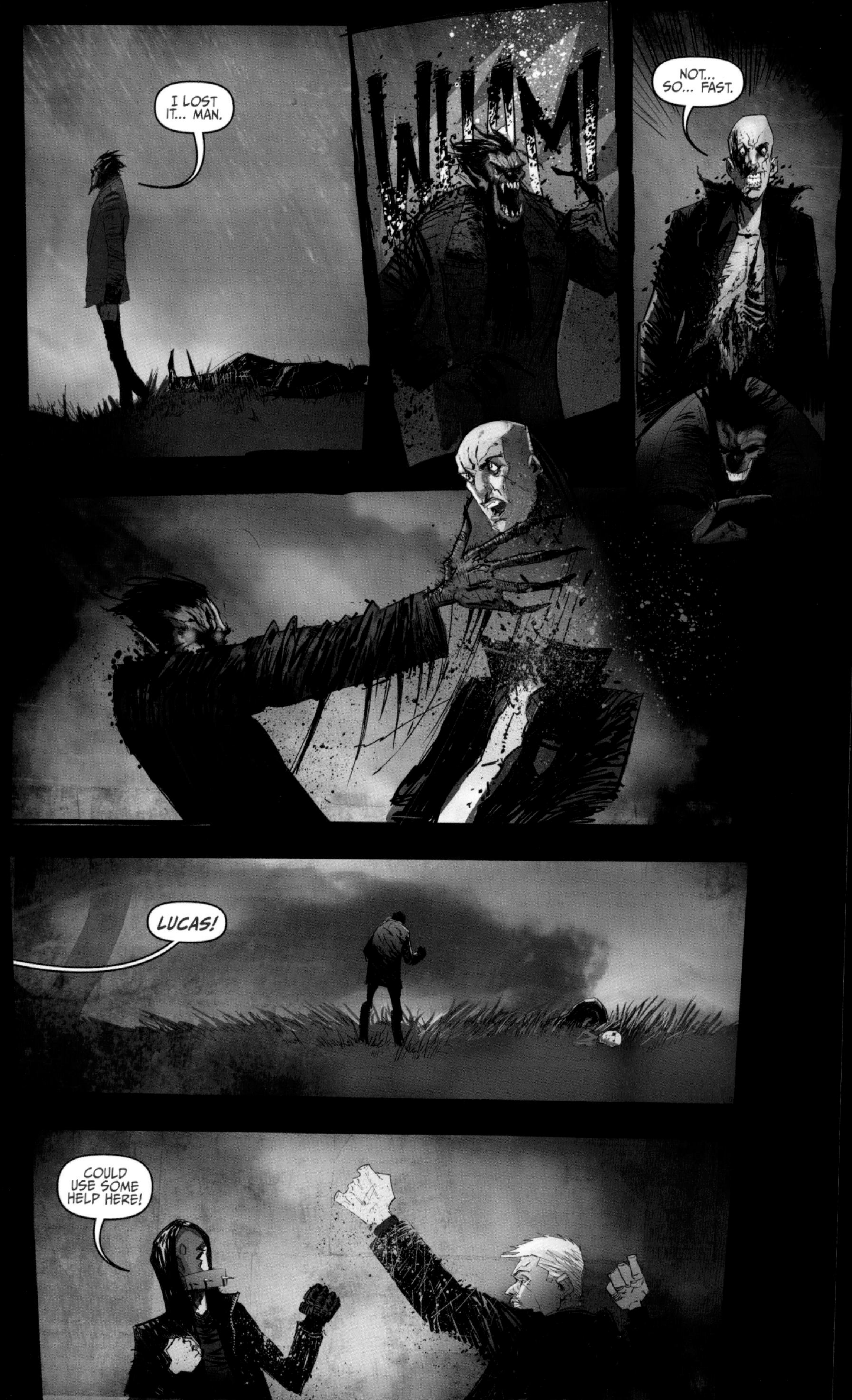
I LOST IT... MAN.
WUMM!
NOT... SO... FAST.
LUCAS!
COULD USE SOME HELP HERE!

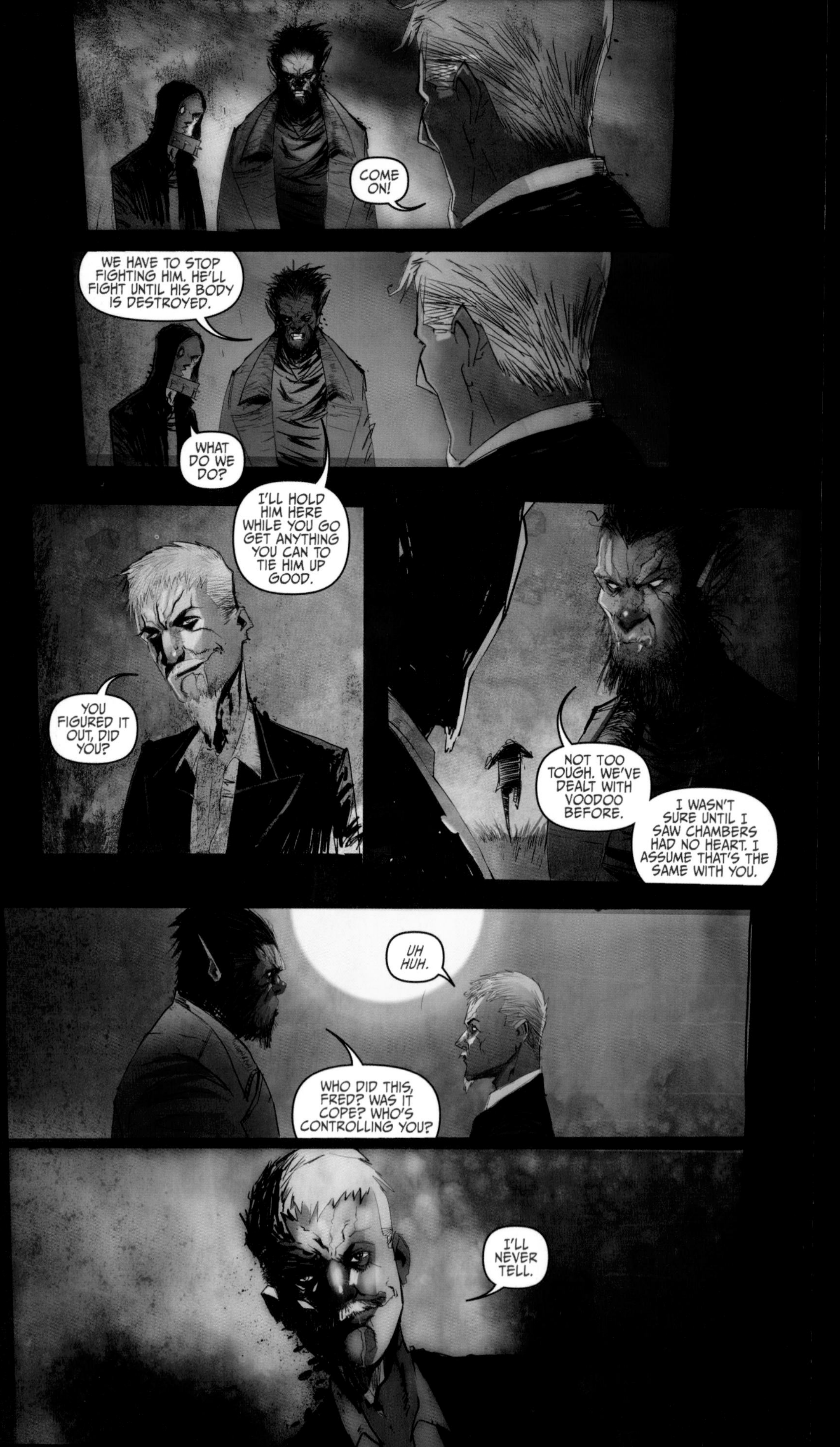
COME ON!
WE HAVE TO STOP FIGHTING HIM. HE'LL FIGHT UNTIL HIS BODY IS DESTROYED.
WHAT DO WE DO?
I'LL HOLD HIM HERE WHILE YOU GO GET ANYTHING YOU CAN TO TIE HIM UP GOOD.
YOU FIGURED IT OUT, DID YOU?
NOT TOO TOUGH. WE'VE DEALT WITH VOODOO BEFORE.
I WASN'T SURE UNTIL I SAW CHAMBERS HAD NO HEART. I ASSUME THAT'S THE SAME WITH YOU.
UH HUH.
WHO DID THIS, FRED? WAS IT COPE? WHO'S CONTROLLING YOU?
I'LL NEVER TELL.

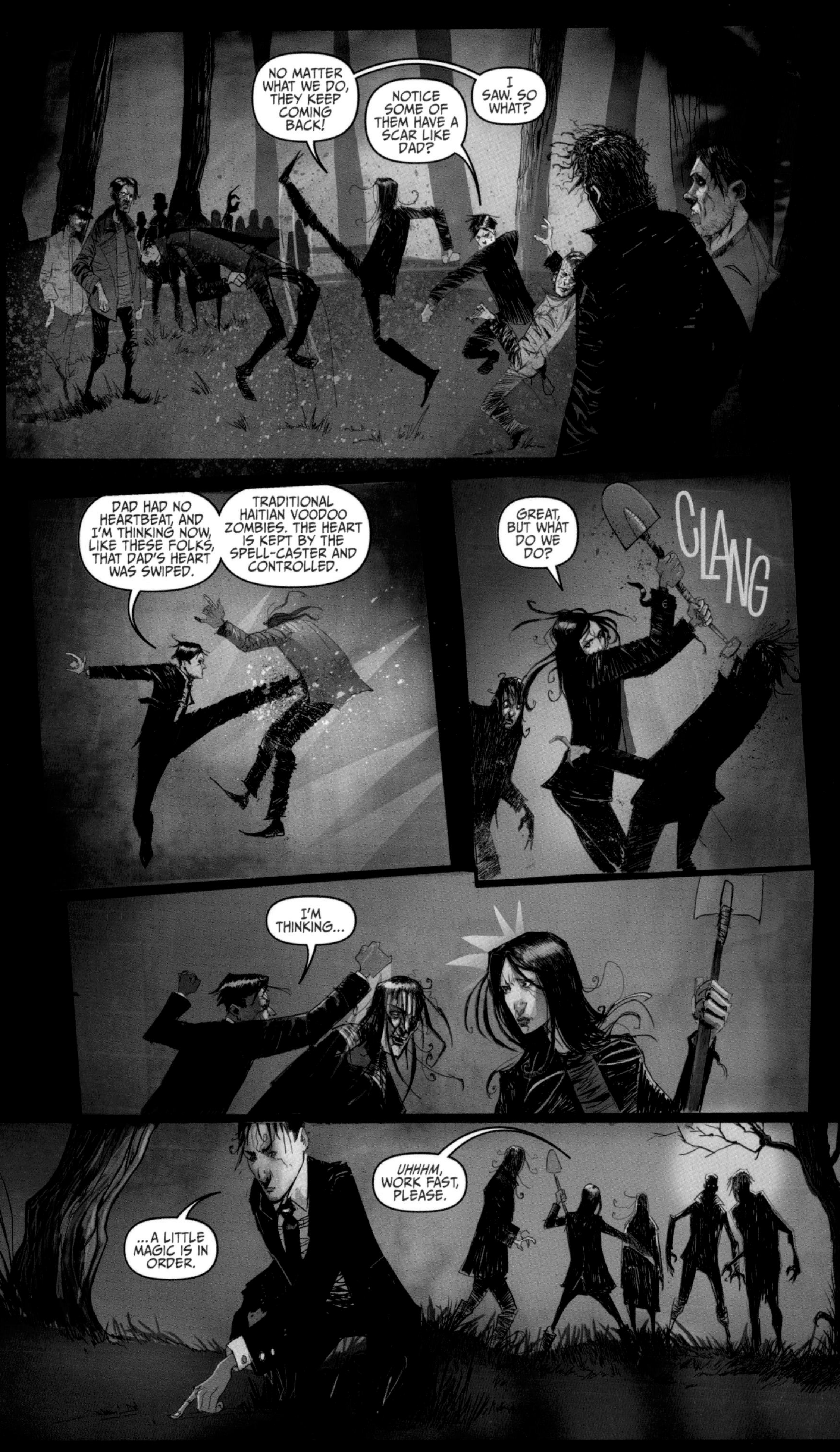
NO MATTER WHAT WE DO, THEY KEEP COMING BACK!
NOTICE SOME OF THEM HAVE A SCAR LIKE DAD?
I SAW. SO WHAT?
DAD HAD NO HEARTBEAT, AND I'M THINKING NOW, LIKE THESE FOLKS, THAT DAD'S HEART WAS SWIPED.
TRADITIONAL HAITIAN VOODOO ZOMBIES. THE HEART IS KEPT BY THE SPELL-CASTER AND CONTROLLED.
GREAT, BUT WHAT DO WE DO?
CLANG
I'M THINKING...
...A LITTLE MAGIC IS IN ORDER.
UHHHM, WORK FAST, PLEASE.

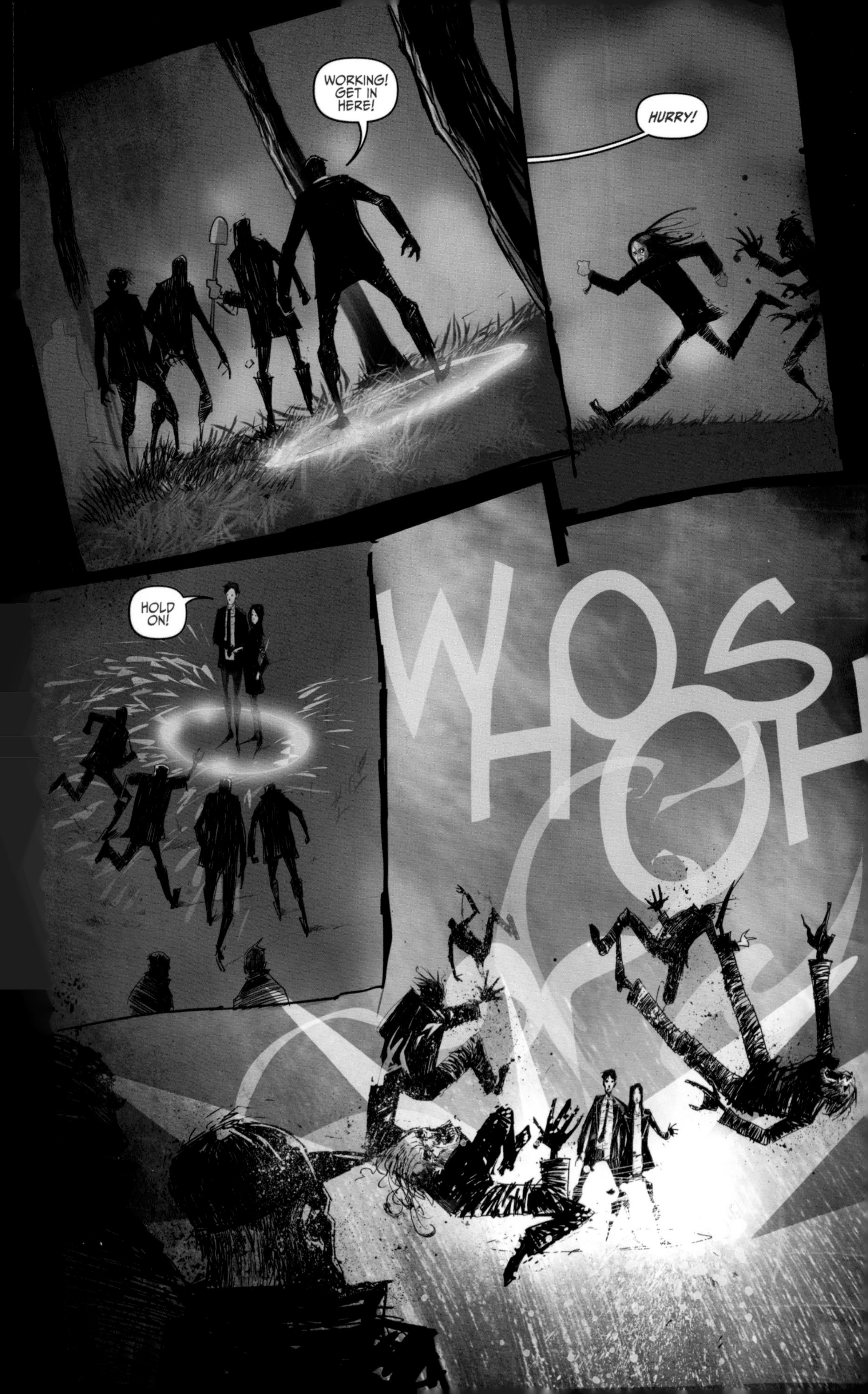
WORKING! GET IN HERE!
HURRY!
HOLD ON!
WHOOSH

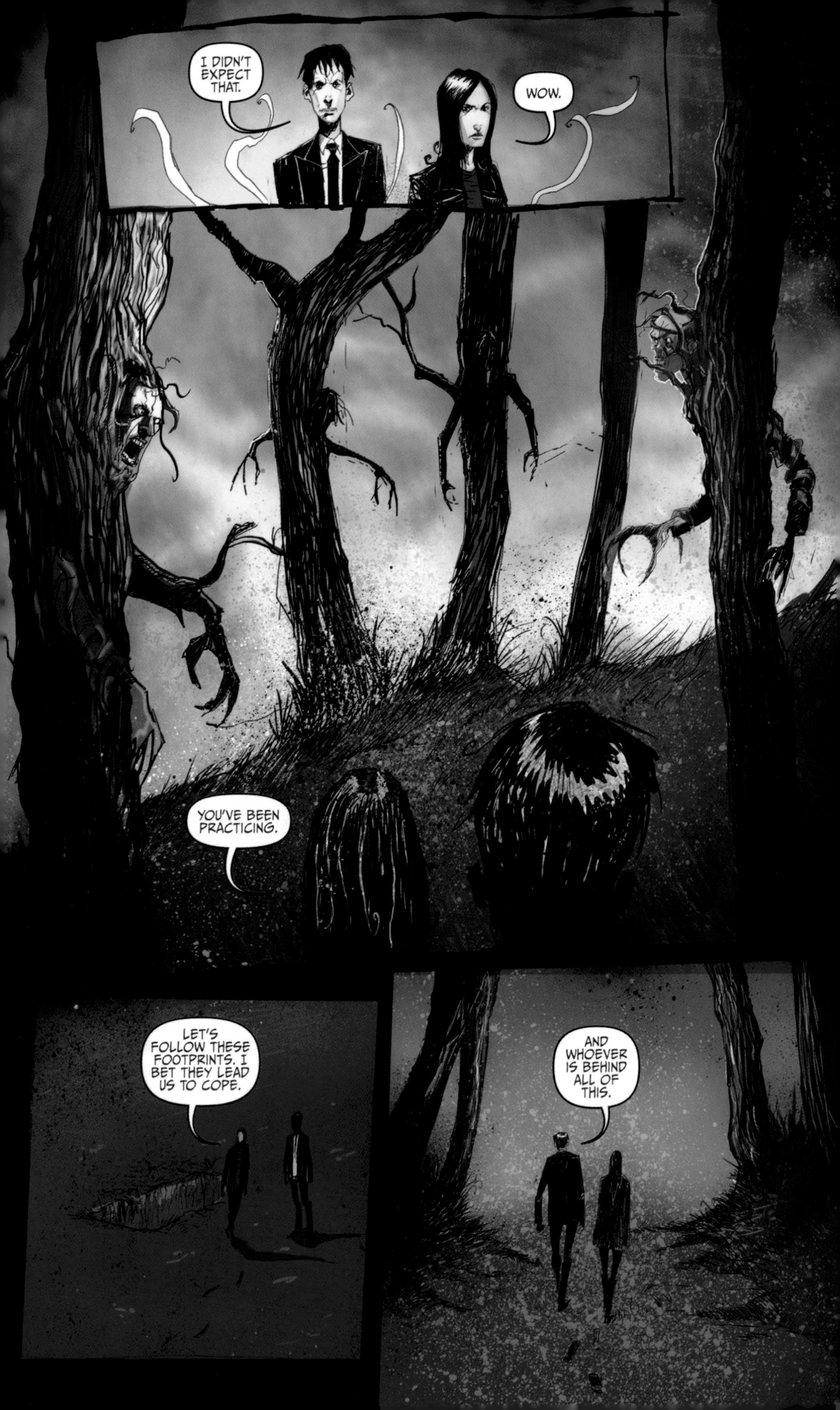
I DIDN'T EXPECT THAT.
WOW.
YOU'VE BEEN PRACTICING.
LET'S FOLLOW THESE FOOTPRINTS. I BET THEY LEAD US TO COPE.
AND WHOEVER IS BEHIND ALL OF THIS.

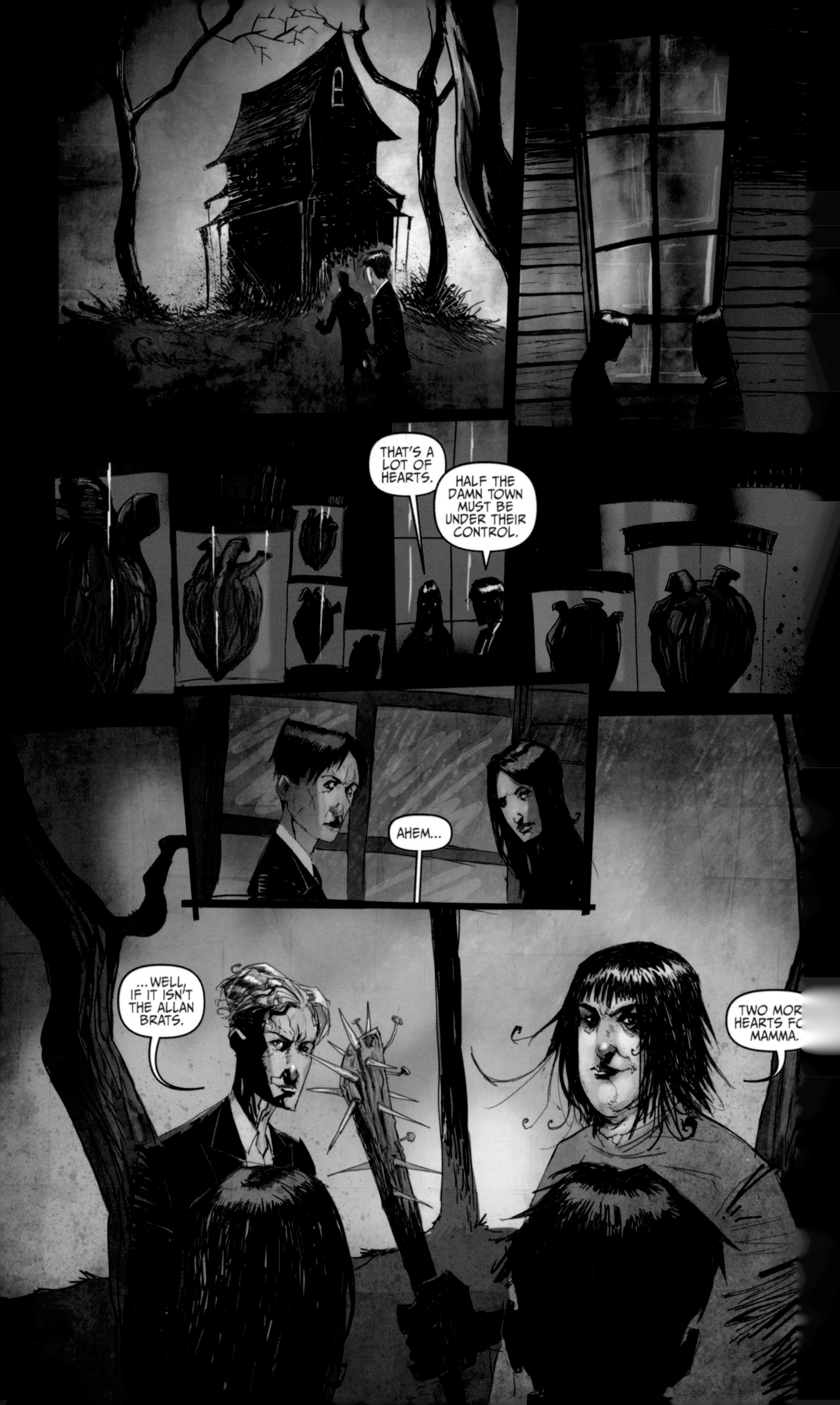
THAT'S A LOT OF HEARTS.
HALF THE DAMN TOWN MUST BE UNDER THEIR CONTROL.
AHEM...
...WELL, IF IT ISN'T THE ALLAN BRATS.
TWO MOR HEARTS FO MAMMA.

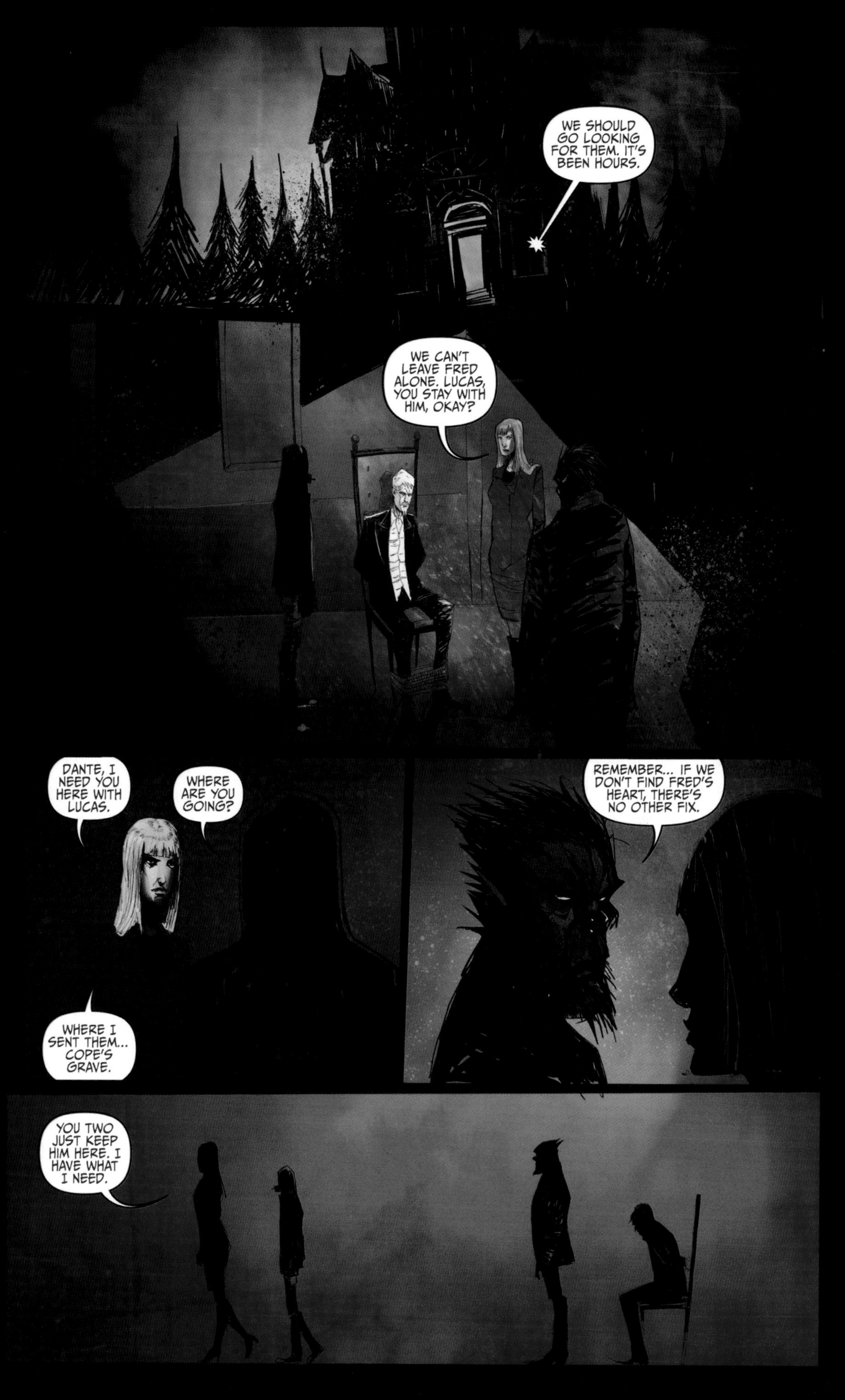
WE SHOULD GO LOOKING FOR THEM. IT'S BEEN HOURS.
WE CAN'T LEAVE FRED ALONE. LUCAS, YOU STAY WITH HIM, OKAY?
DANTE, I NEED YOU HERE WITH LUCAS.
WHERE ARE YOU GOING?
WHERE I SENT THEM... COPE'S GRAVE.
REMEMBER... IF WE DON'T FIND FRED'S HEART, THERE'S NO OTHER FIX.
YOU TWO JUST KEEP HIM HERE. I HAVE WHAT I NEED.

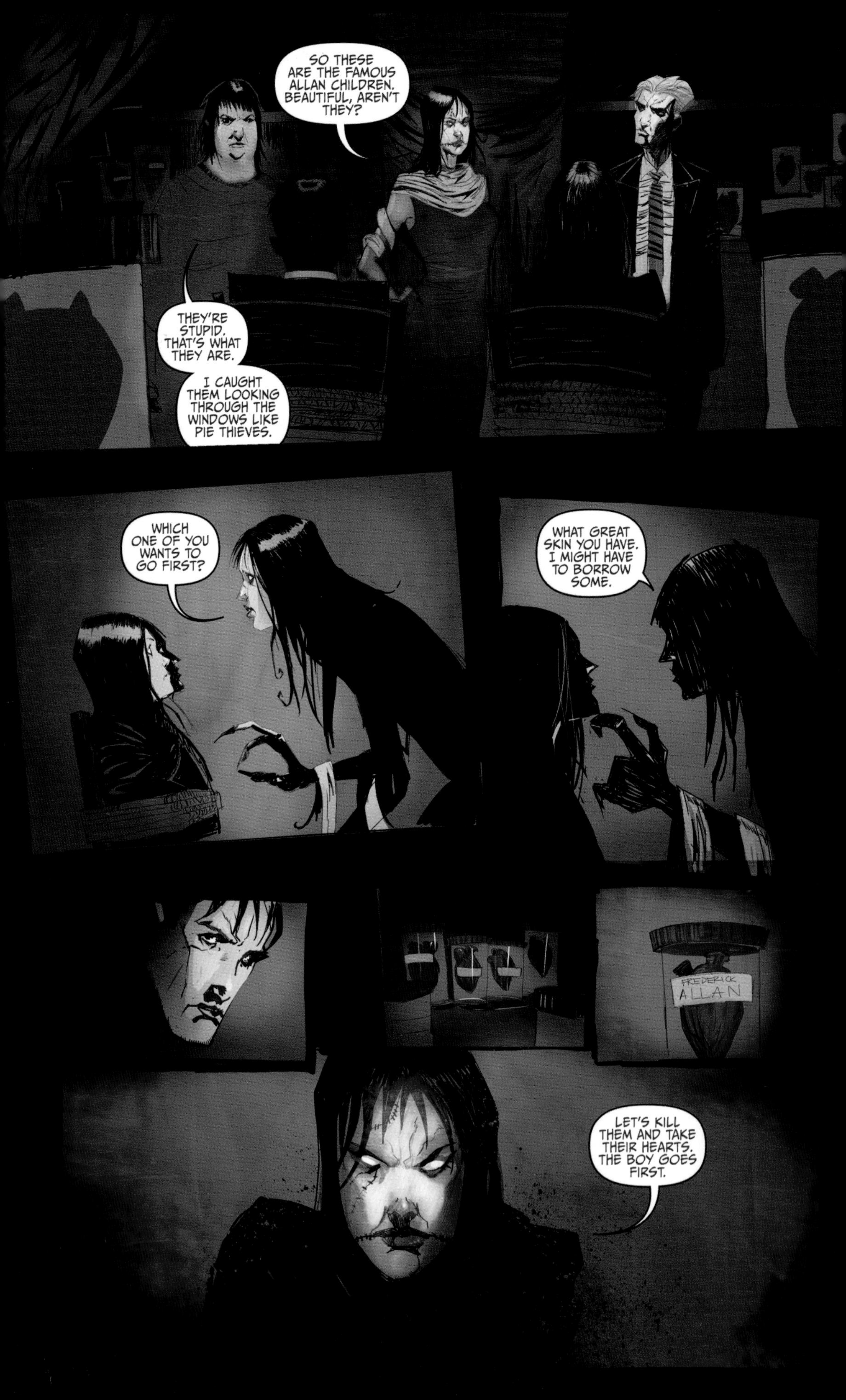
SO THESE ARE THE FAMOUS ALLAN CHILDREN. BEAUTIFUL, AREN'T THEY?
THEY'RE STUPID. THAT'S WHAT THEY ARE.
I CAUGHT THEM LOOKING THROUGH THE WINDOWS LIKE PIE THIEVES.
WHICH ONE OF YOU WANTS TO GO FIRST?
WHAT GREAT SKIN YOU HAVE. I MIGHT HAVE TO BORROW SOME.
FREDERICK ALLAN
LET'S KILL THEM AND TAKE THEIR HEARTS. THE BOY GOES FIRST.

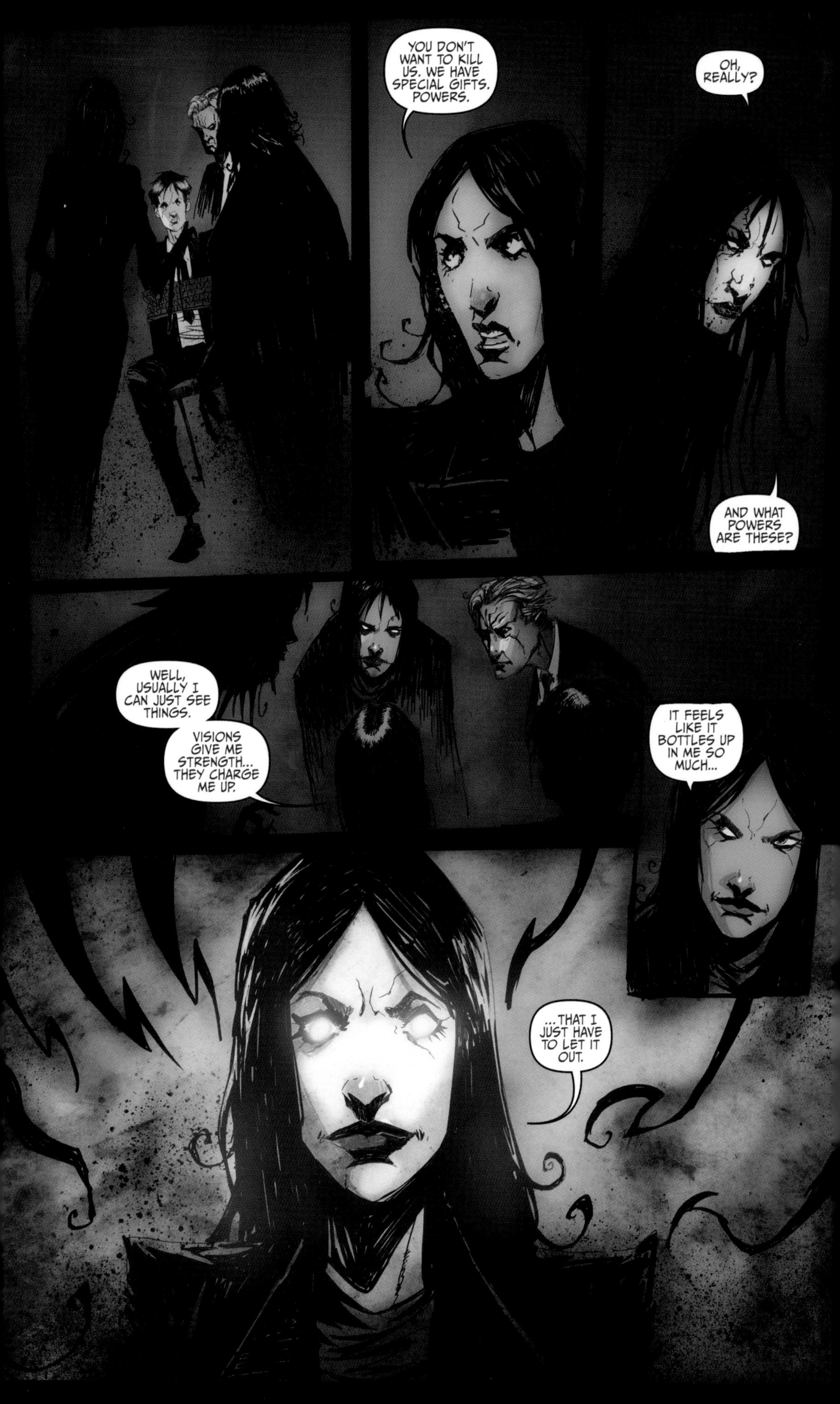
YOU DON'T WANT TO KILL US. WE HAVE SPECIAL GIFTS. POWERS.
OH, REALLY?
AND WHAT POWERS ARE THESE?
WELL, USUALLY I CAN JUST SEE THINGS.
VISIONS GIVE ME STRENGTH... THEY CHARGE ME UP.
IT FEELS LIKE IT BOTTLES UP IN ME SO MUCH...
...THAT I JUST HAVE TO LET IT OUT.

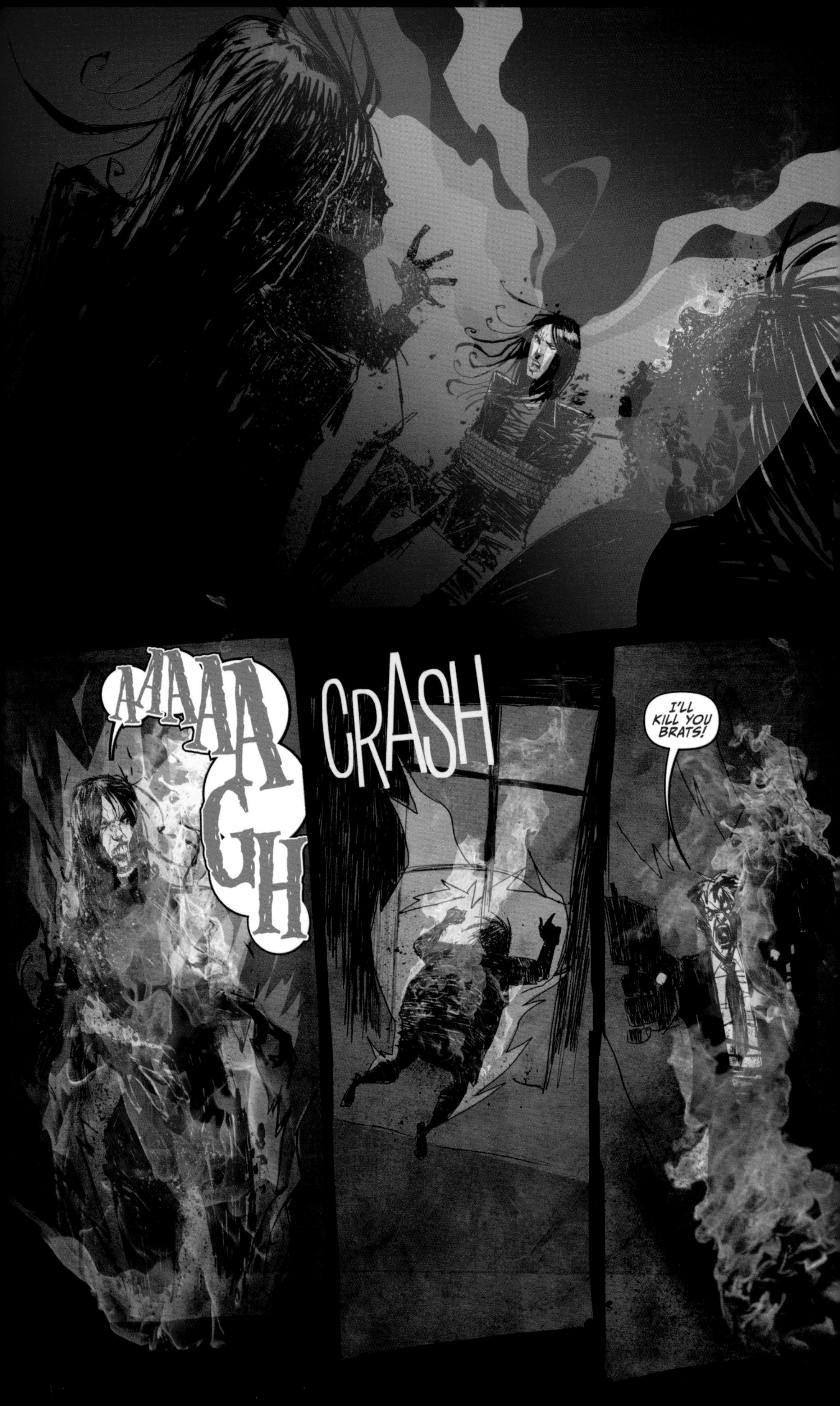
AAAAAAGH
CRASH
I'LL KILL YOU BRATS!

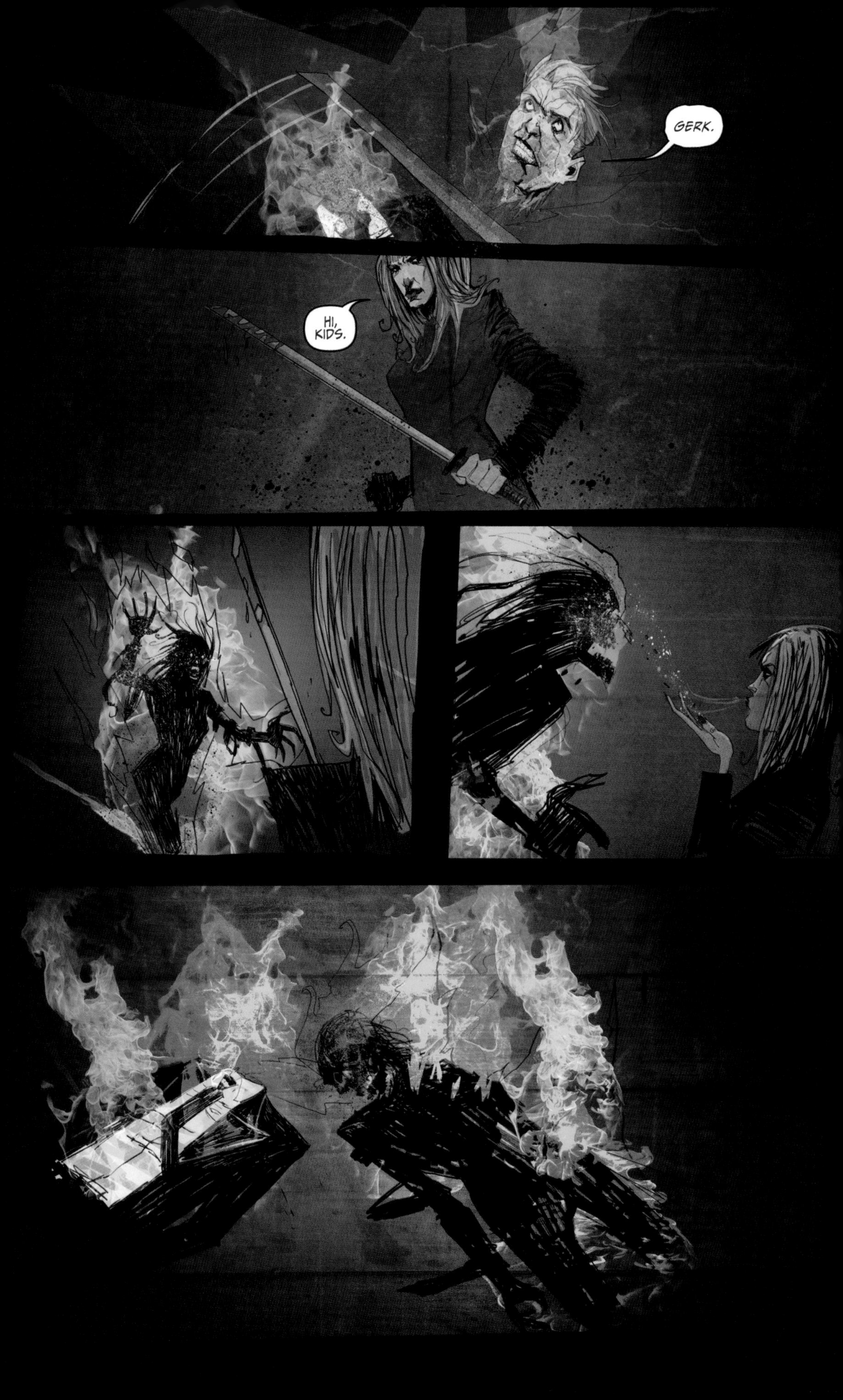
GERK.
HI, KIDS.

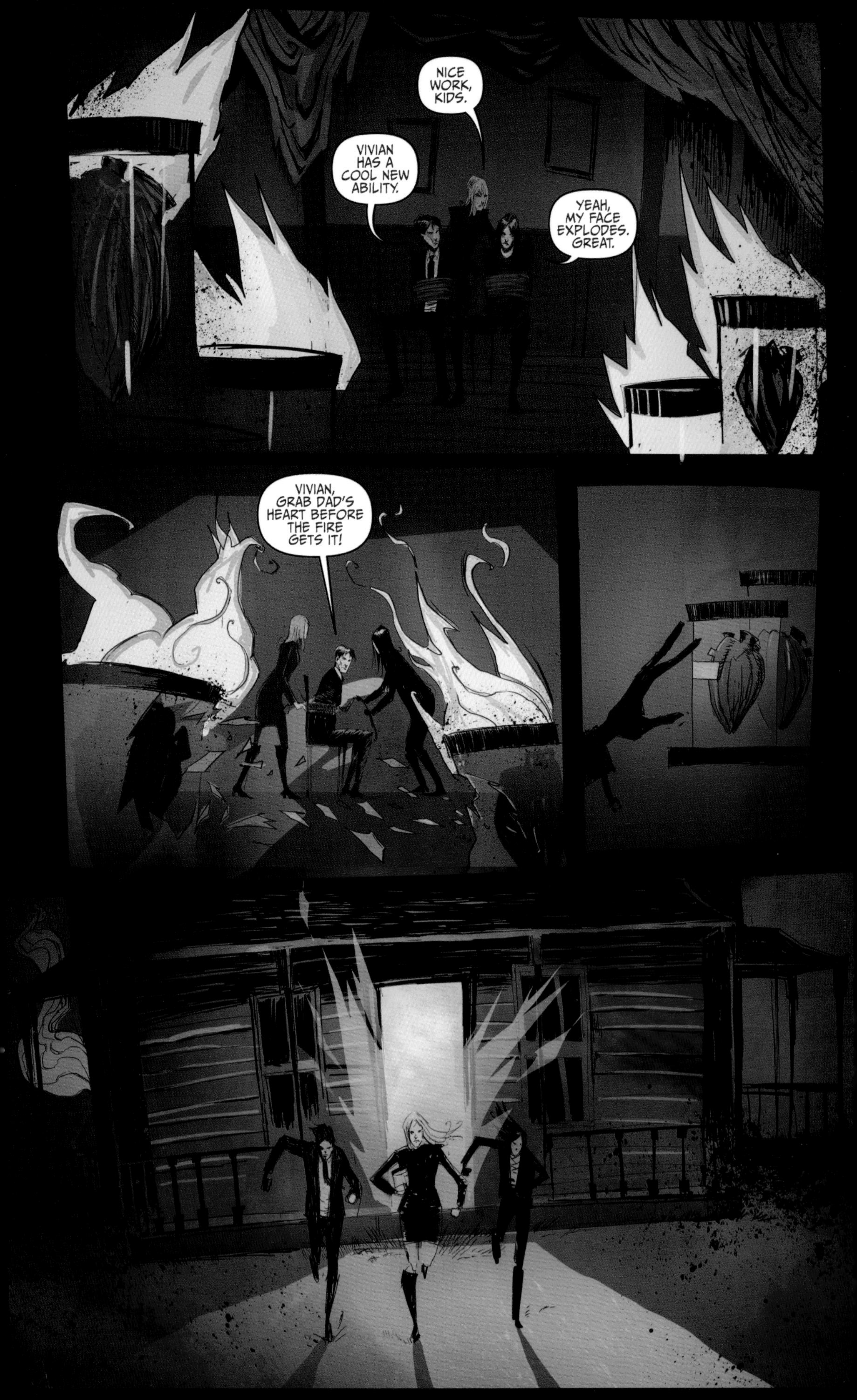
NICE WORK, KIDS.
VIVIAN HAS A COOL NEW ABILITY.
YEAH, MY FACE EXPLODES. GREAT.
VIVIAN, GRAB DAD'S HEART BEFORE THE FIRE GETS IT!

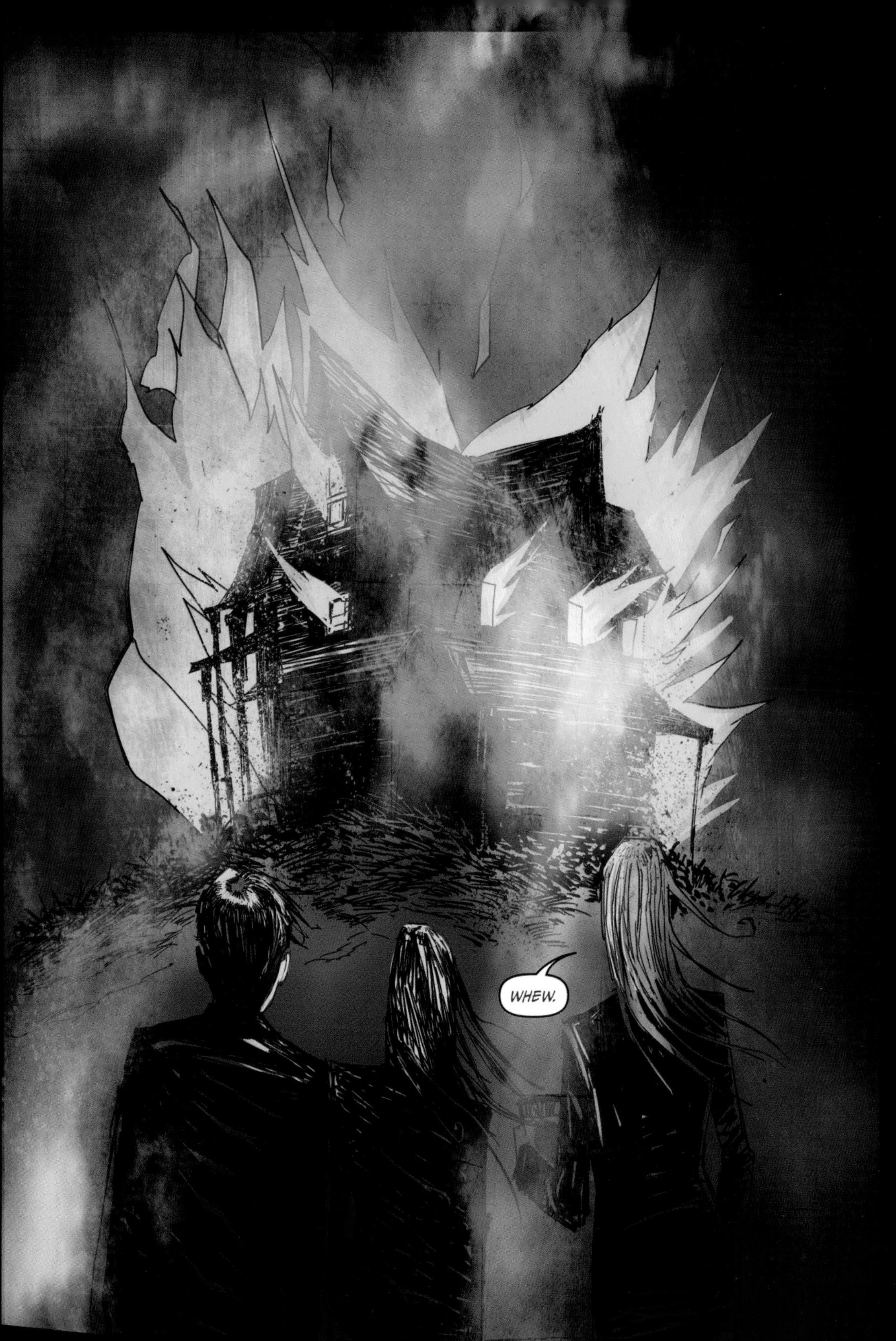
WHEW.

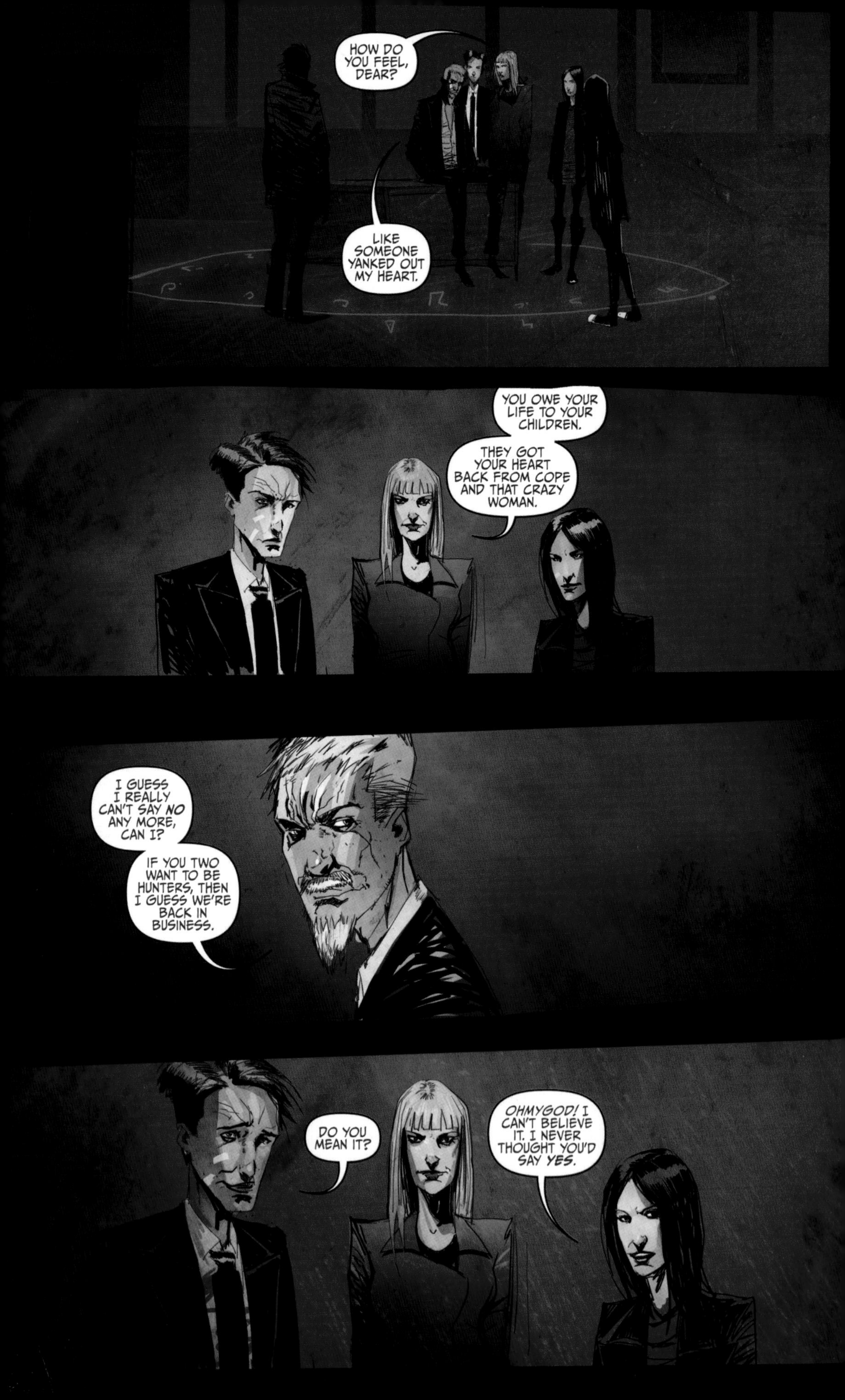

HOW DO YOU FEEL, DEAR?
LIKE SOMEONE YANKED OUT MY HEART.
YOU OWE YOUR LIFE TO YOUR CHILDREN.
THEY GOT YOUR HEART BACK FROM COPE AND THAT CRAZY WOMAN.
I GUESS I REALLY CAN'T SAY *NO* ANY MORE, CAN I?
IF YOU TWO WANT TO BE HUNTERS, THEN I GUESS WE'RE BACK IN BUSINESS.
DO YOU MEAN IT?
OHMYGOD! I CAN'T BELIEVE IT. I NEVER THOUGHT YOU'D SAY ***YES***.

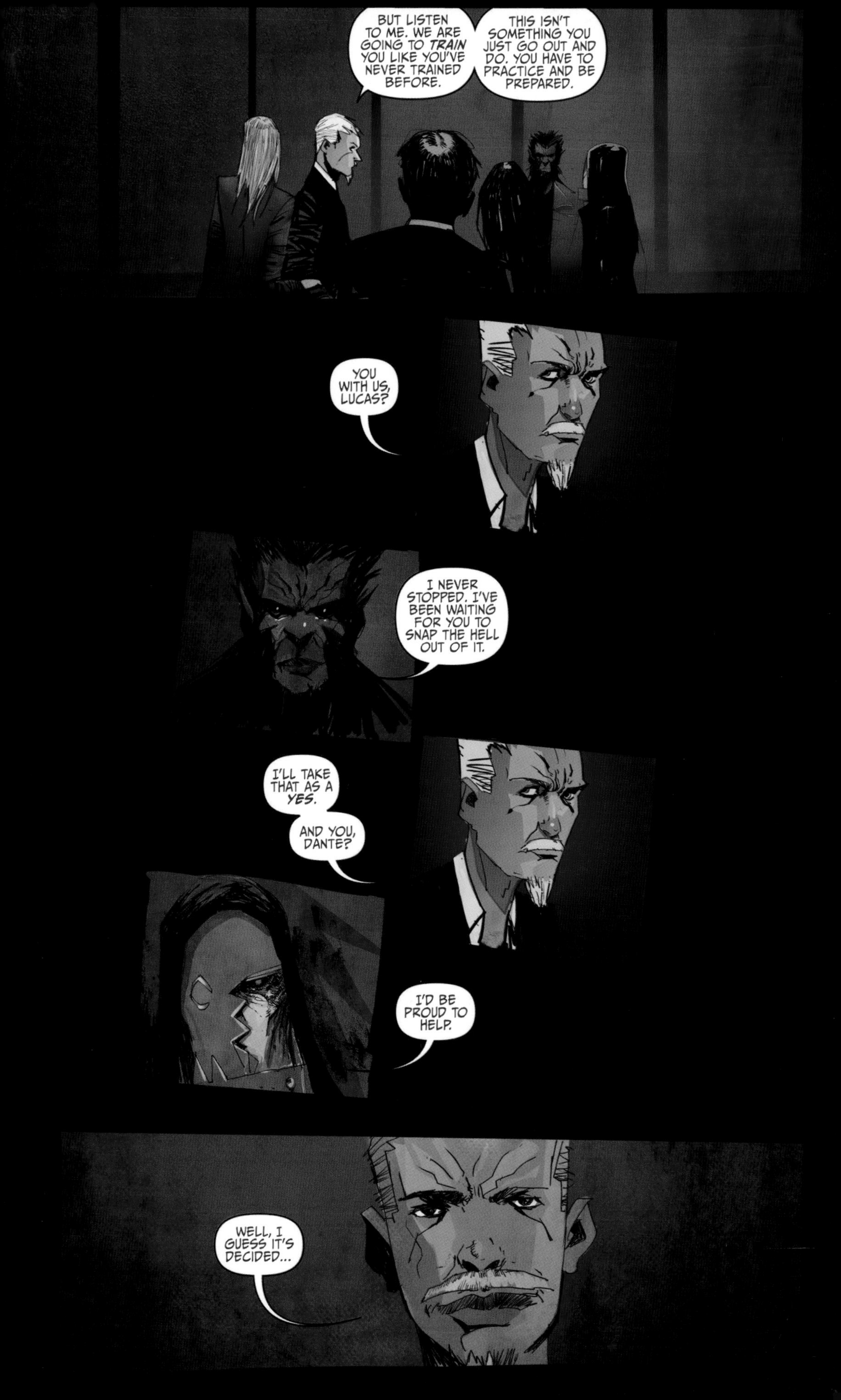
BUT LISTEN TO ME. WE ARE GOING TO TRAIN YOU LIKE YOU'VE NEVER TRAINED BEFORE.
THIS ISN'T SOMETHING YOU JUST GO OUT AND DO. YOU HAVE TO PRACTICE AND BE PREPARED.
YOU WITH US, LUCAS?
I NEVER STOPPED. I'VE BEEN WAITING FOR YOU TO SNAP THE HELL OUT OF IT.
I'LL TAKE THAT AS A YES.
AND YOU, DANTE?
I'D BE PROUD TO HELP.
WELL, I GUESS IT'S DECIDED...

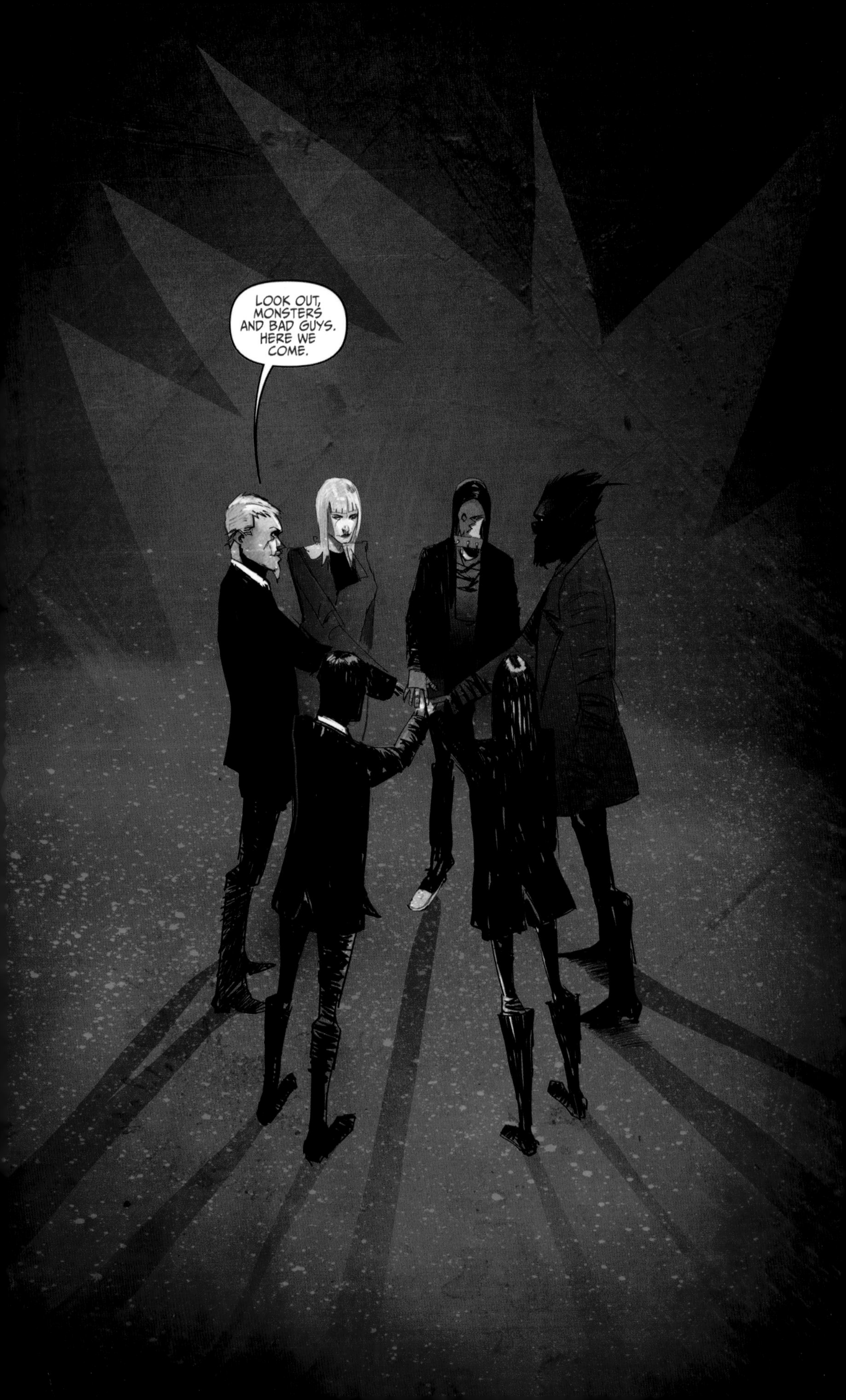
LOOK OUT, MONSTERS AND BAD GUYS. HERE WE COME.

VAMPIRE
WEREWOLF
RANKENSTEIN'S
MUMMY   MONSTER
ZOMBIES
BANSHEE
GHOST
DEMON
DJINN
SUCCUBUS
INCUBUS
GOLEM
BAD SEEDS
SKINWALKER
CHUPACABRA
WENDIGO
GOBLINS
SEA MONSTER
GIL MAN

DRAGON
WITCH
WARLOCK
CTHULHU
DAGON
GHOUL

The
OCTOBER
FACTION

MEDUSA
CENTAUR
TROLL
KRAKEN
KAIJU
MERMEN
HAG
DYBBUKS

YUREY
HARPY
MOTHMAN
ONI
CYCLOPS
SIREN
GORGON
SATYR
YETI
HOMUNCULUS
KAPPA
KITSUNE
TANUKI
BE KENE
KAMAITACHI
ROKUROBU
JIANGSHI
PENANGGALAN
ASWANG
WRAITH
THE POSSESSED
WAR GHOUL

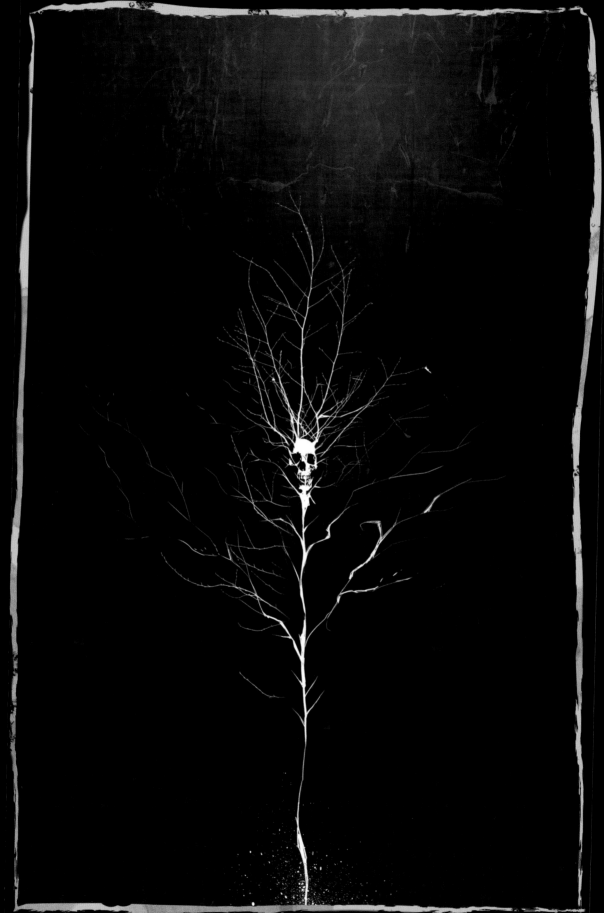

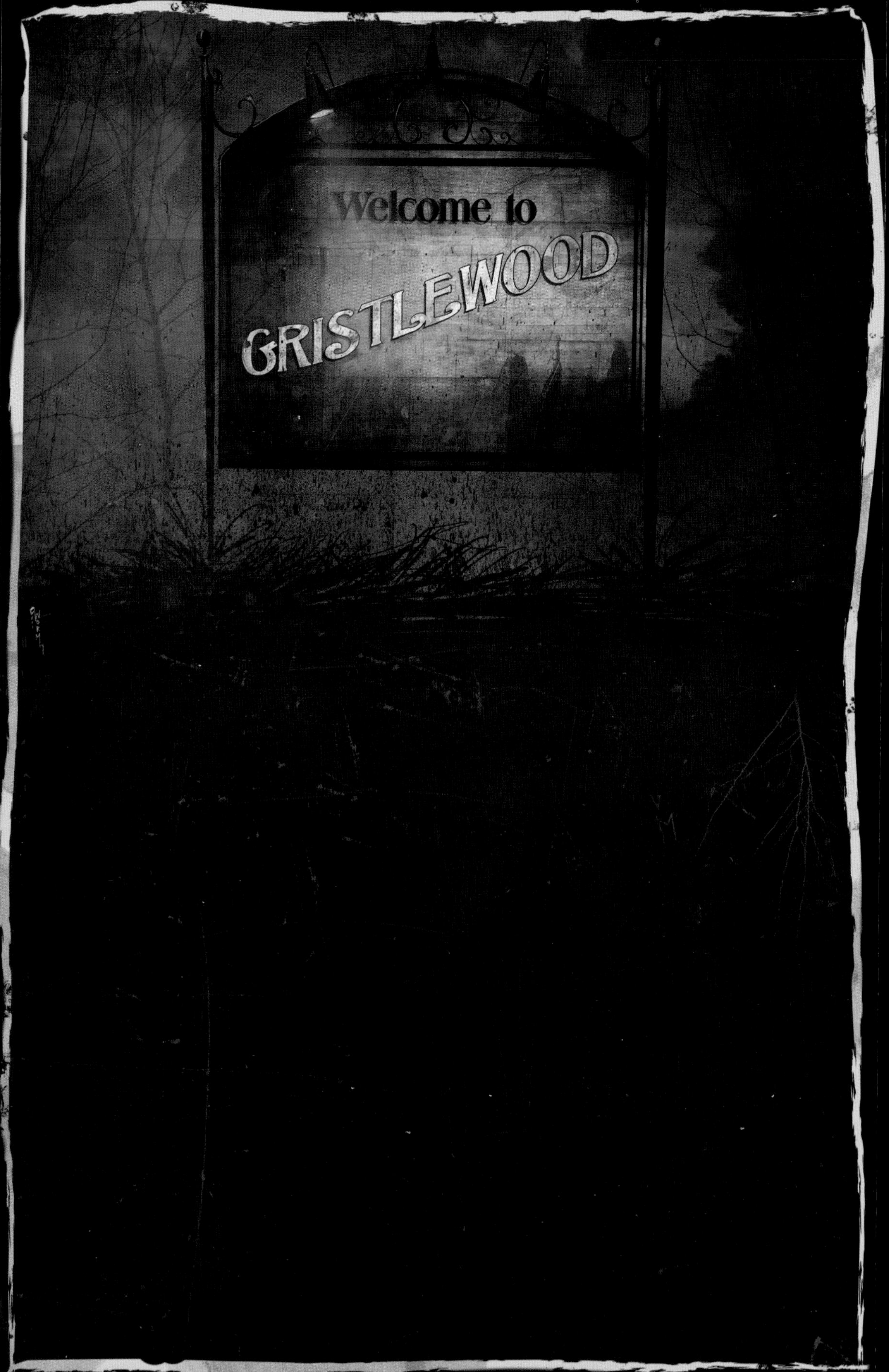

Welcome to
GRISTLEWOOD

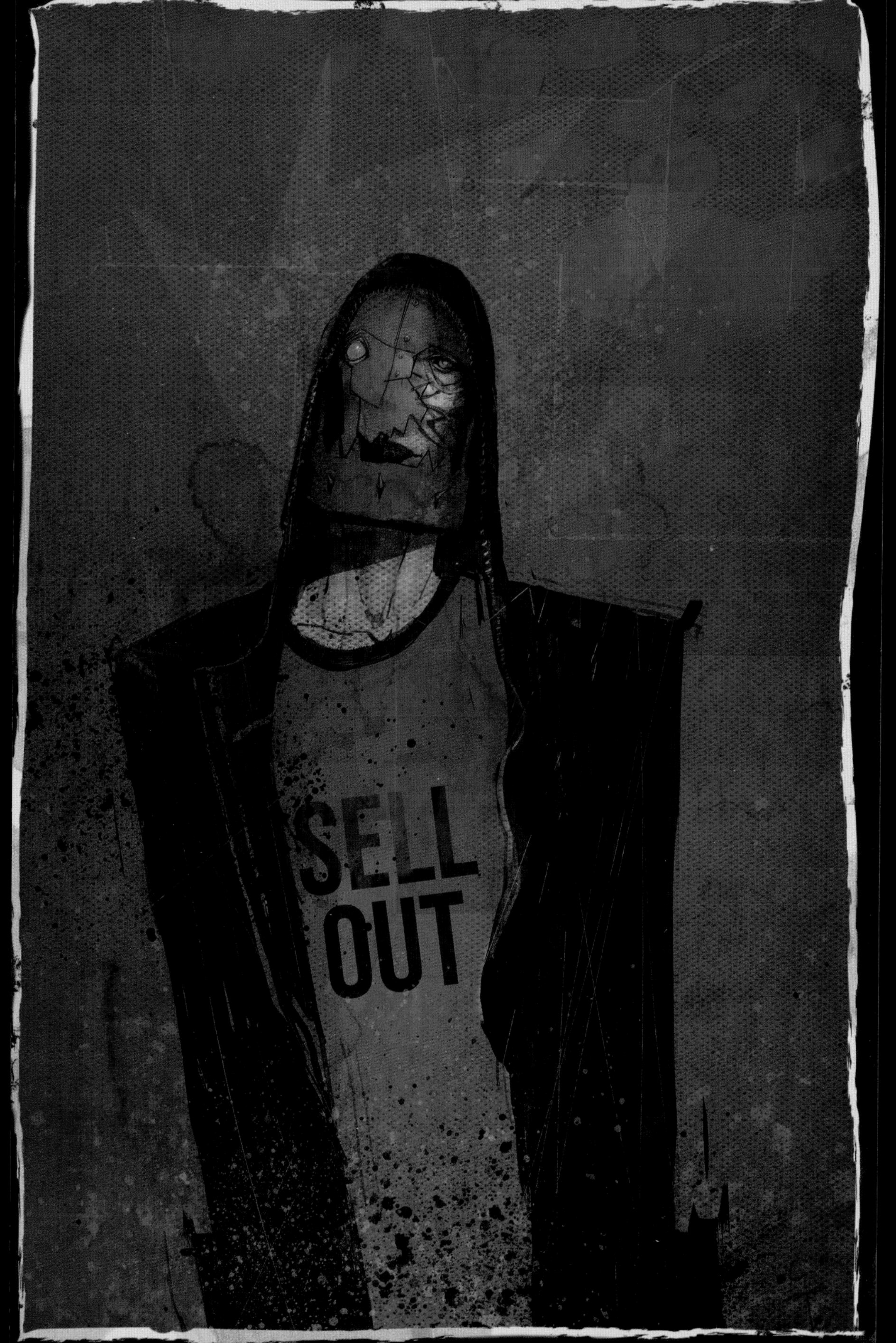
SELL
OUT

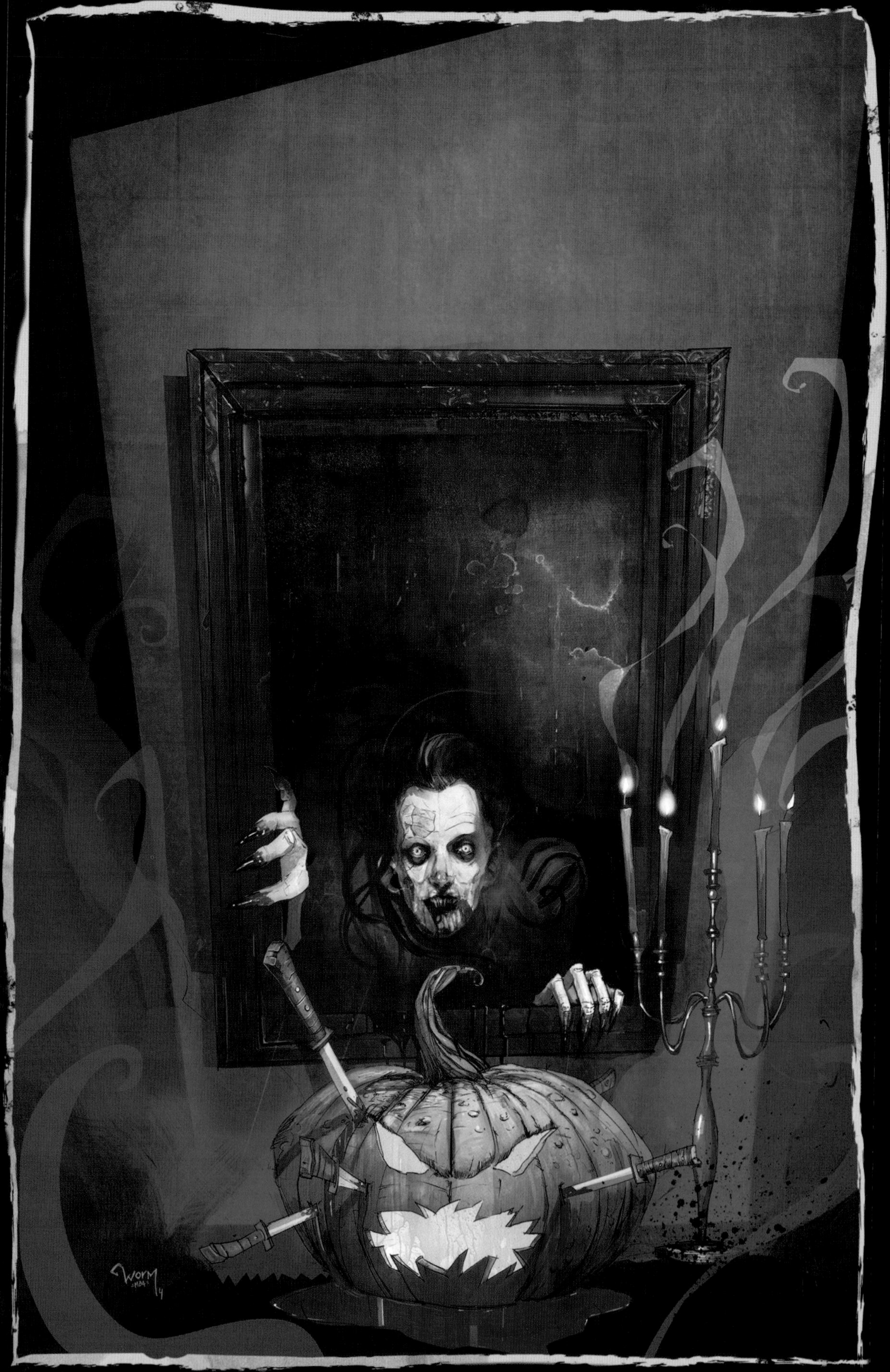

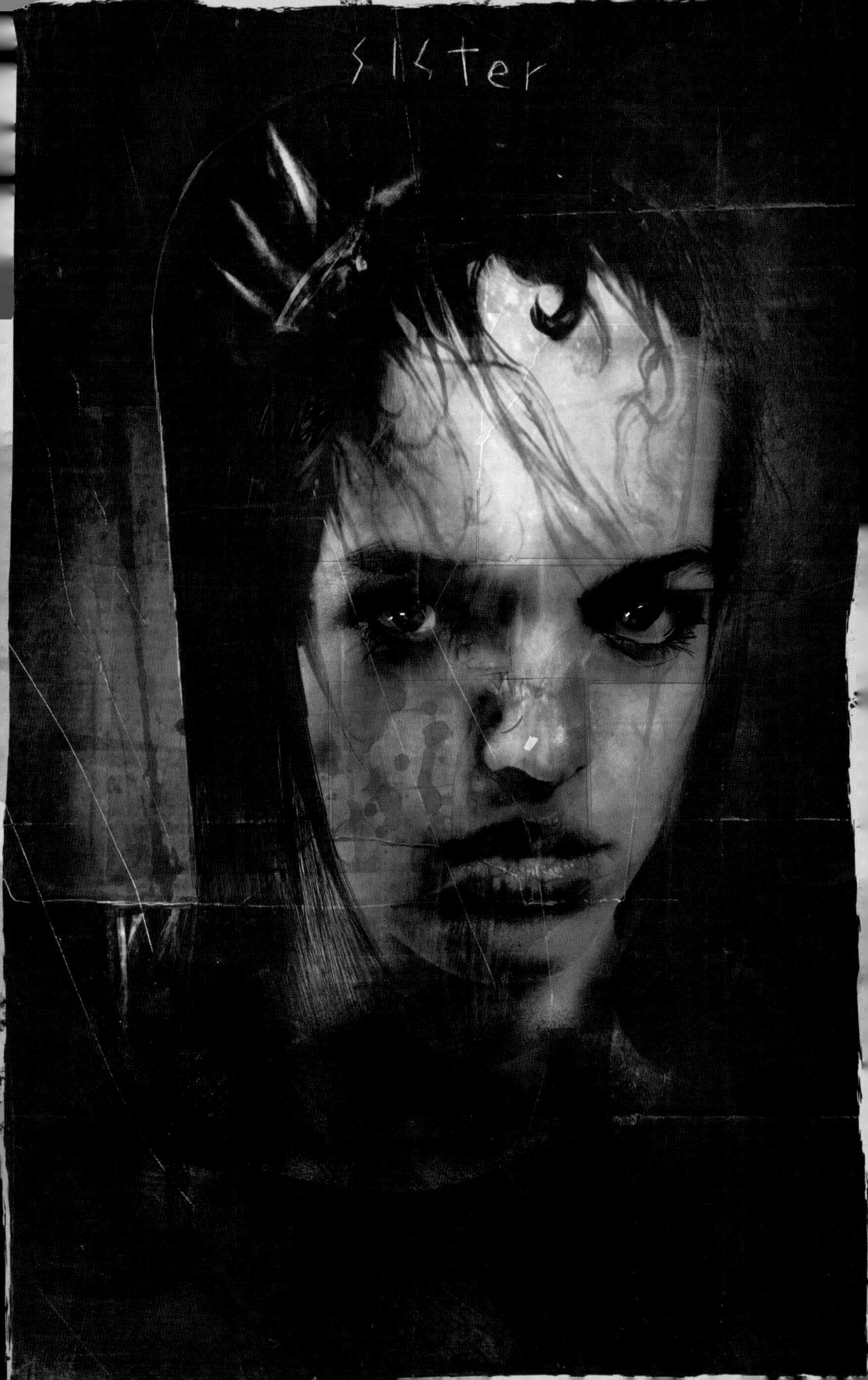
sister

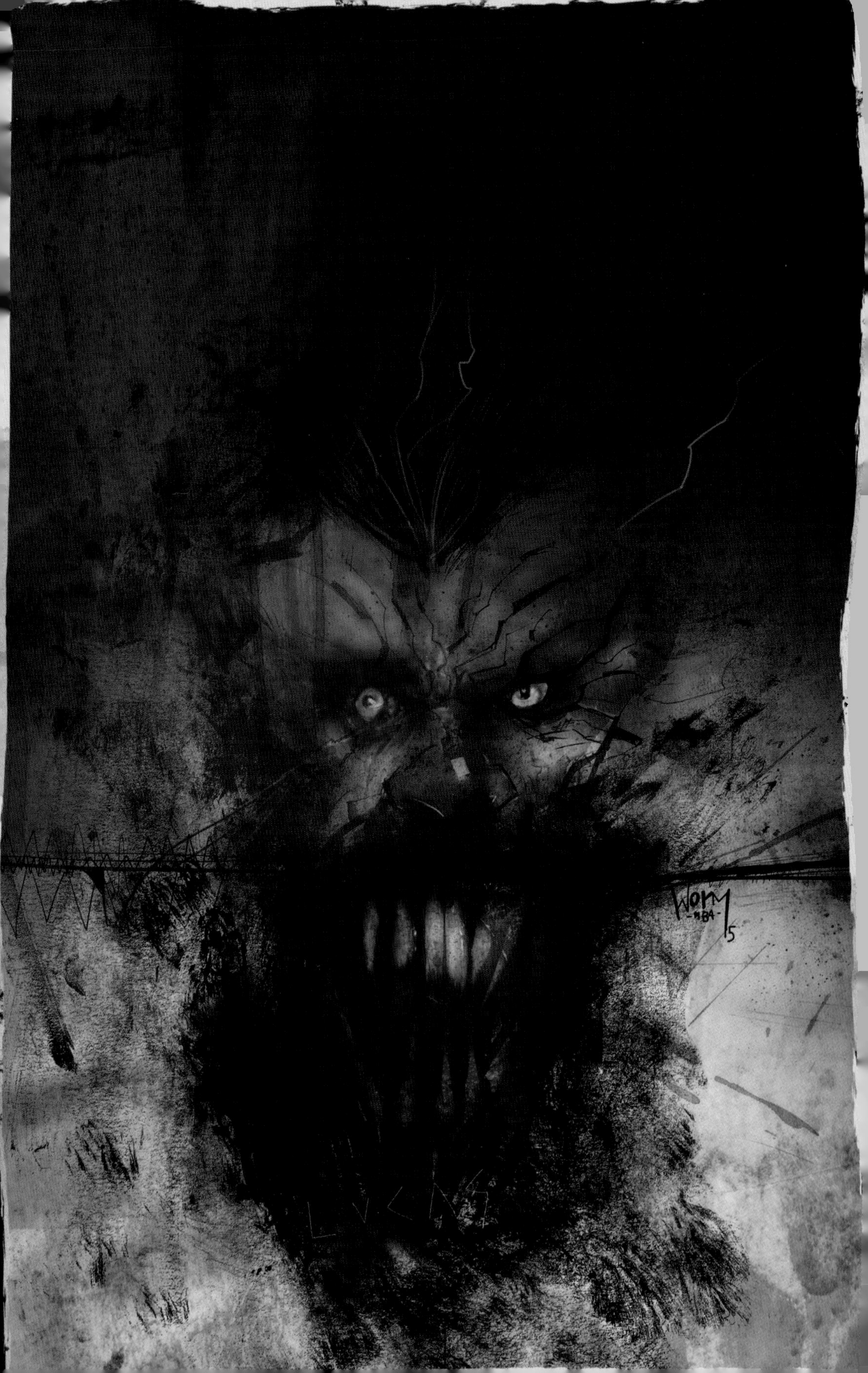

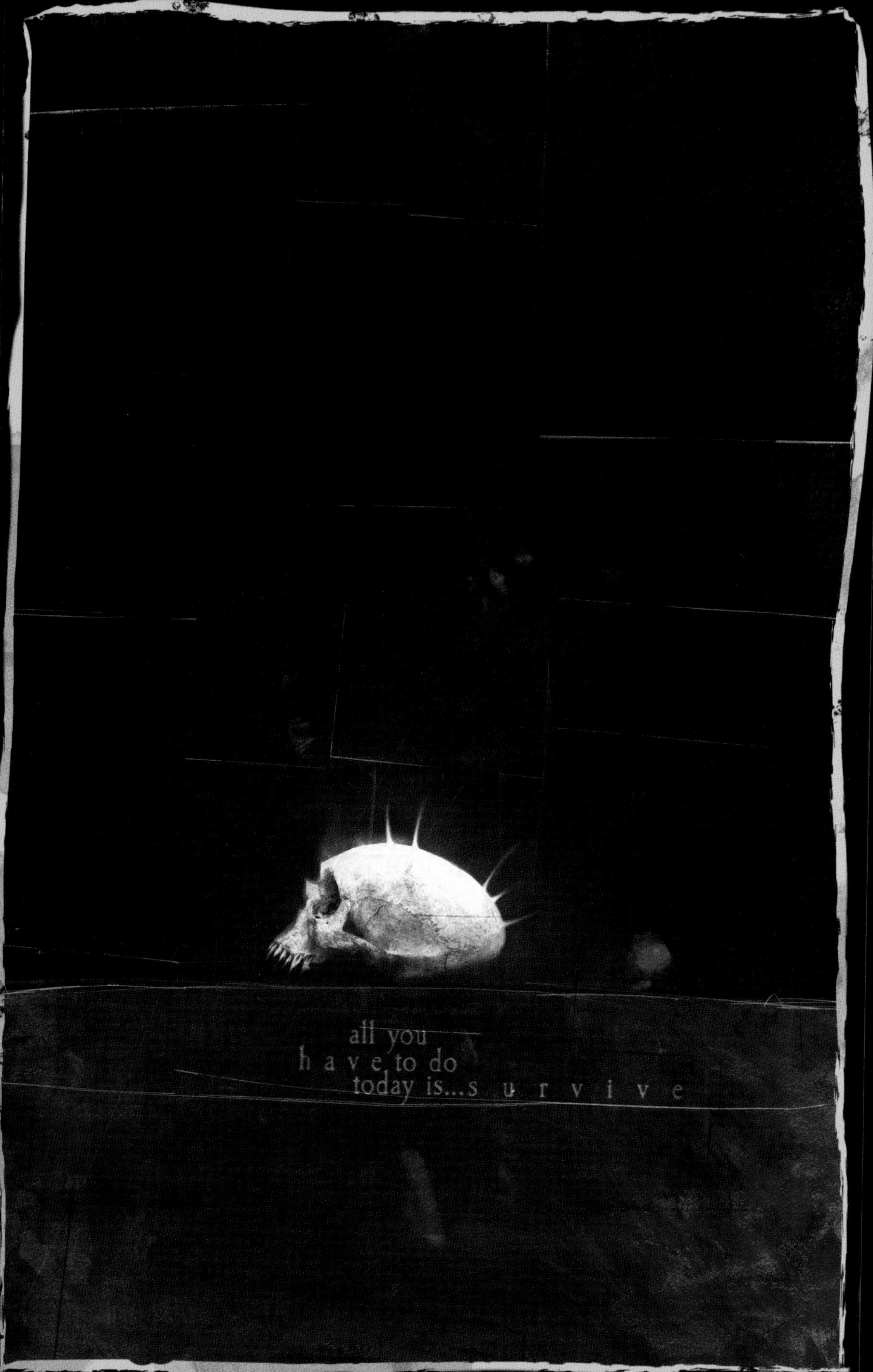
all you
h a v e to do
today is...s u r v i v e

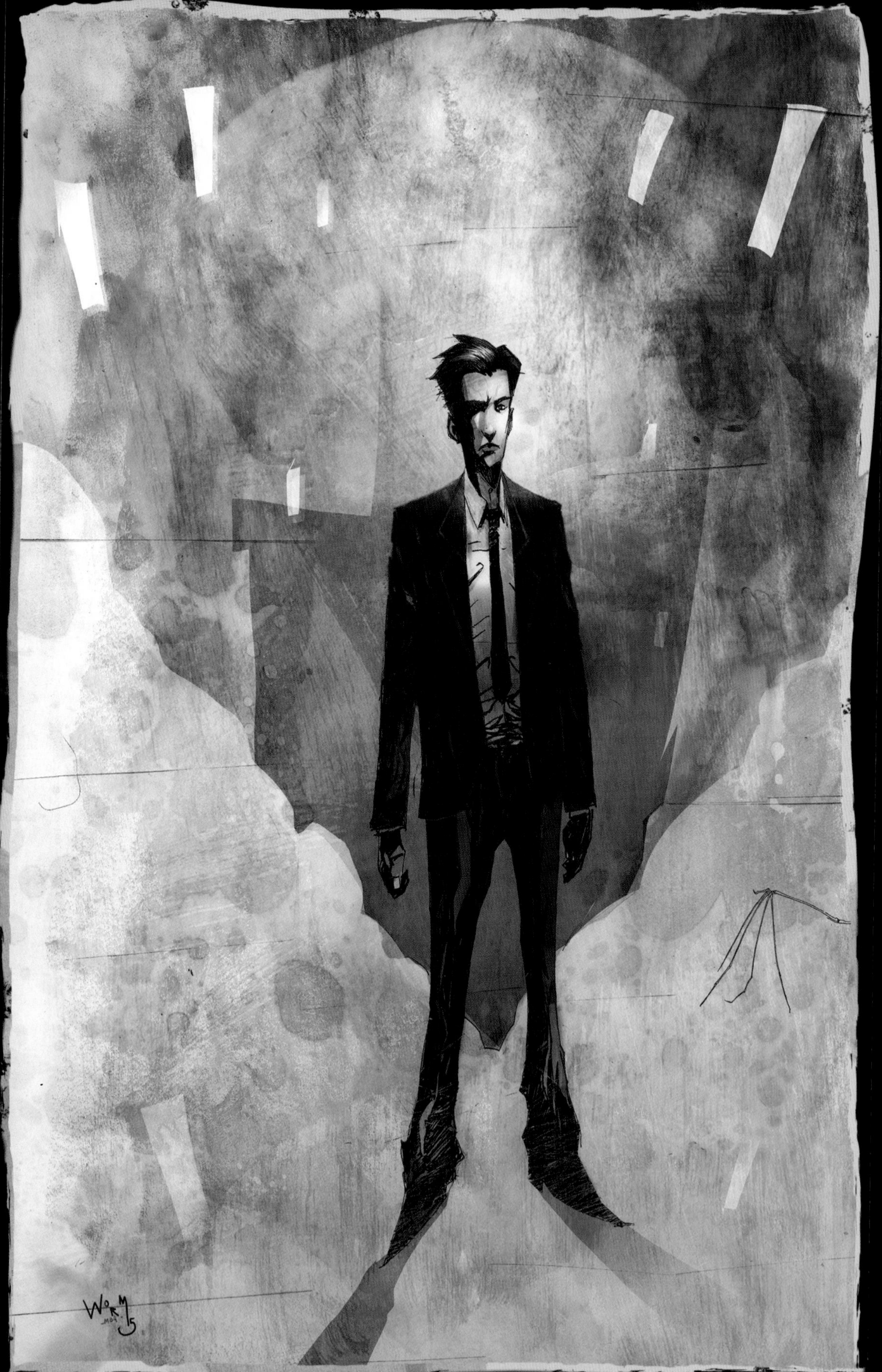

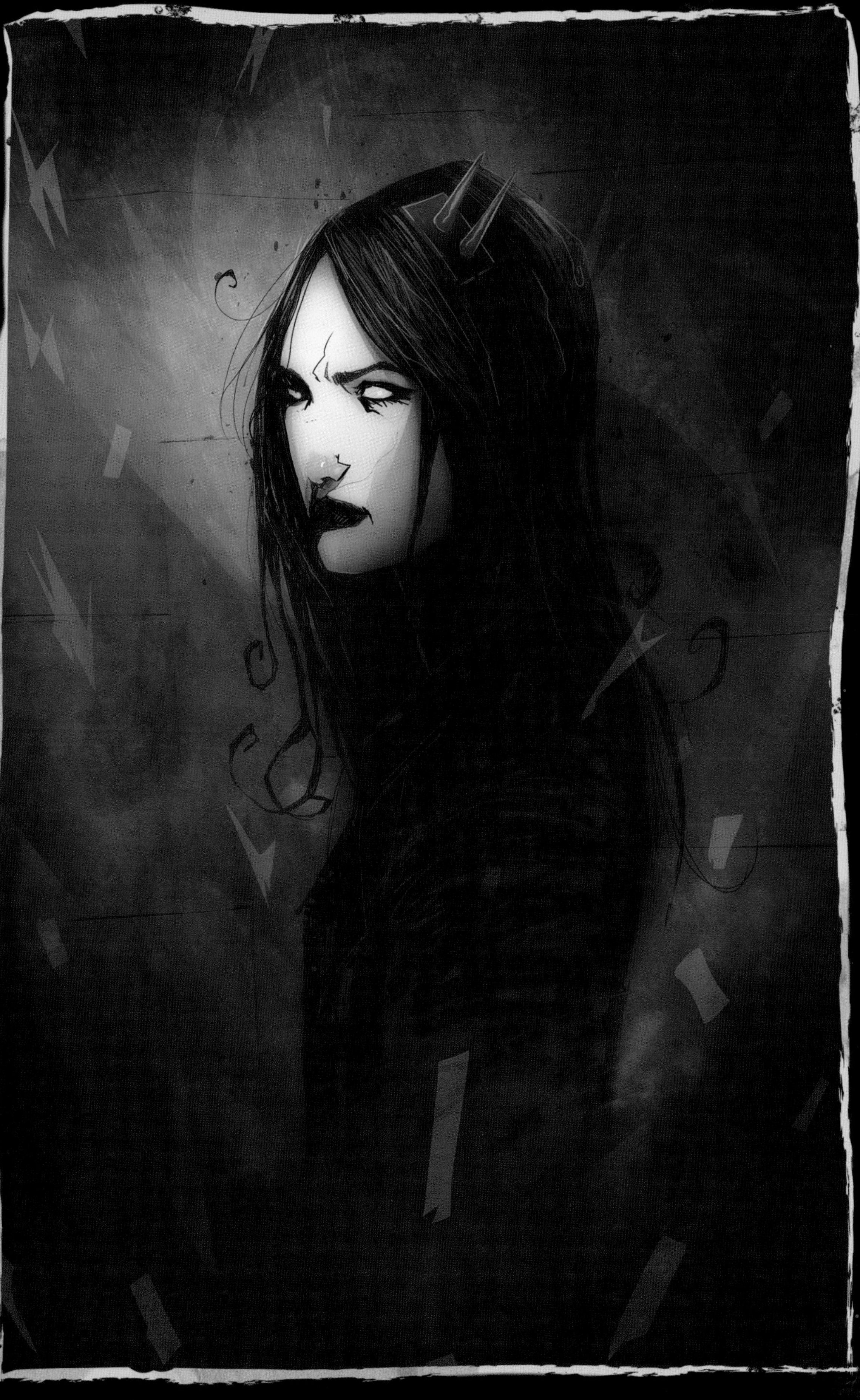

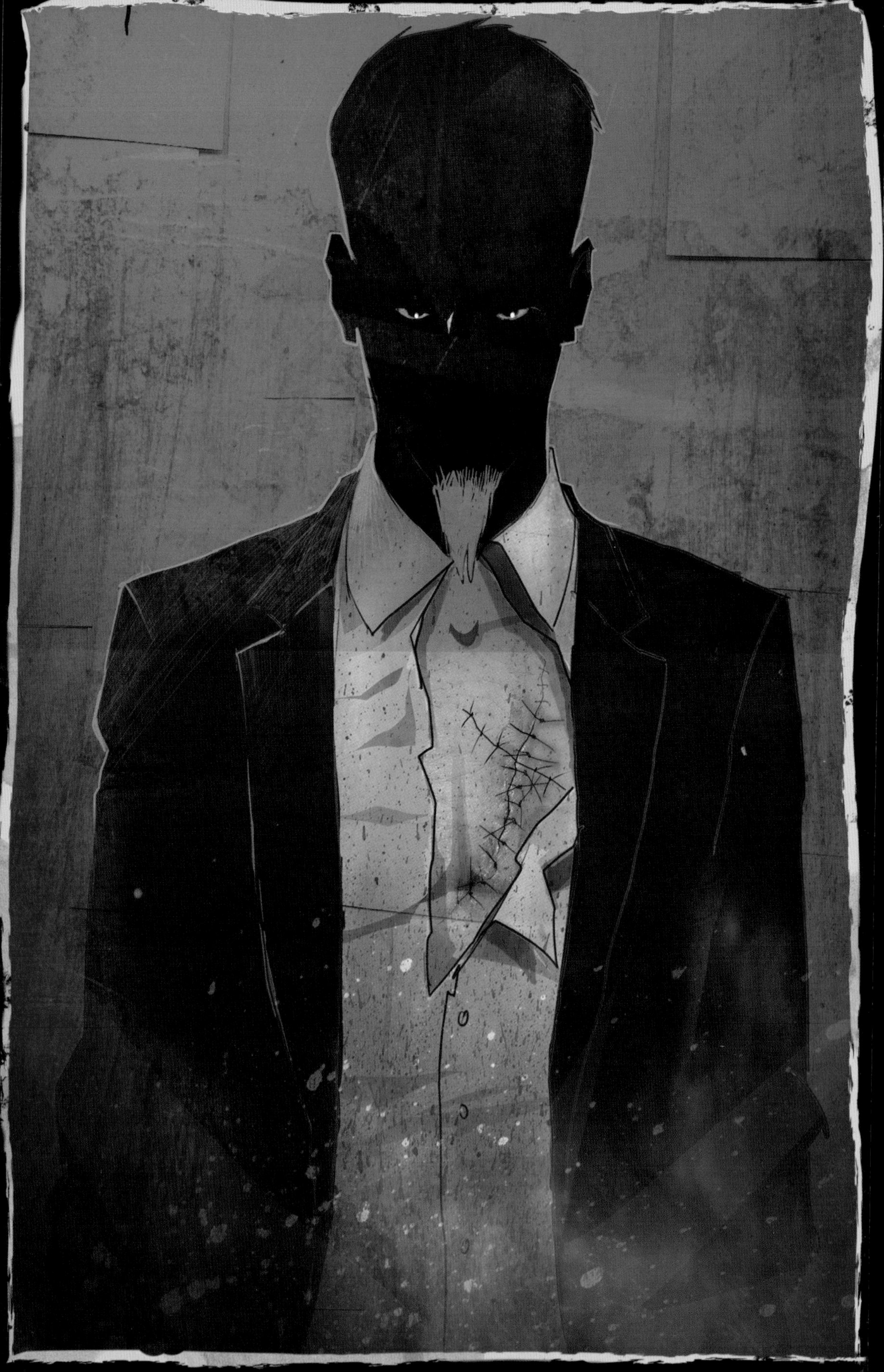

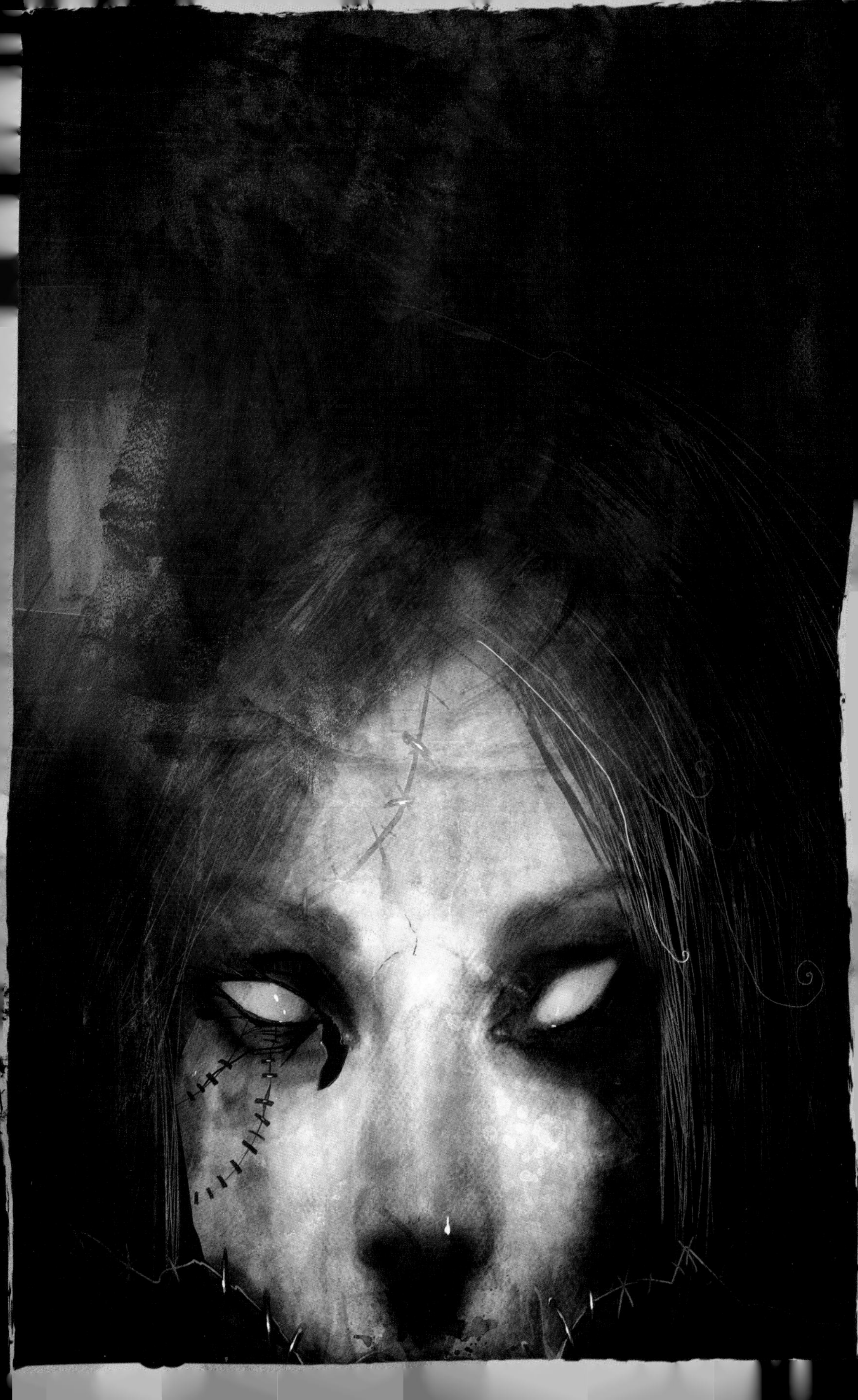

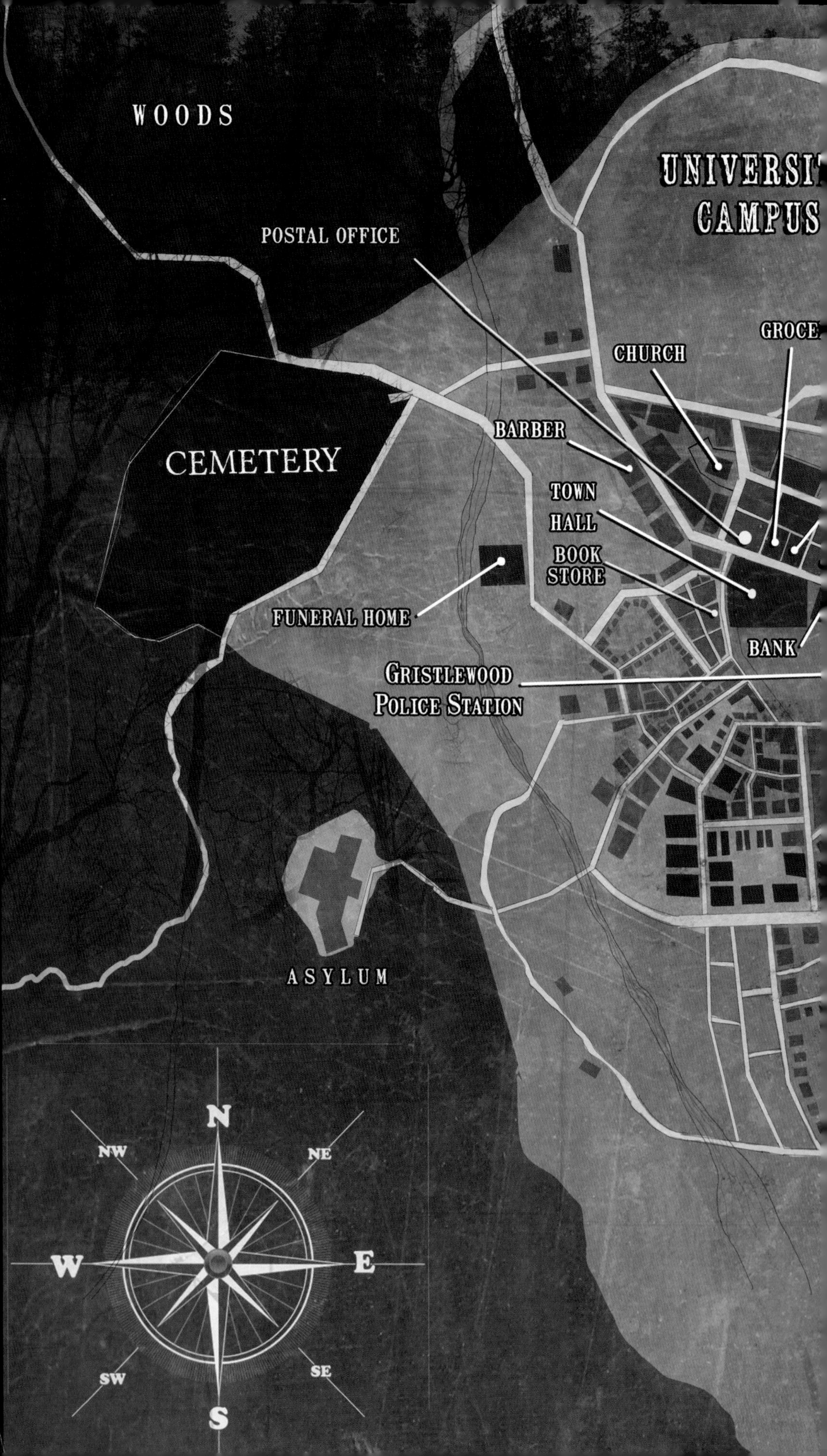
WOODS
UNIVERSIT
CAMPUS
POSTAL OFFICE
GROCE
CHURCH
CEMETERY
BARBER
TOWN
HALL
BOOK
STORE
FUNERAL HOME
BANK
GRISTLEWOOD
POLICE STATION
ASYLUM
N
NW
NE
W
E
SW
SE
S

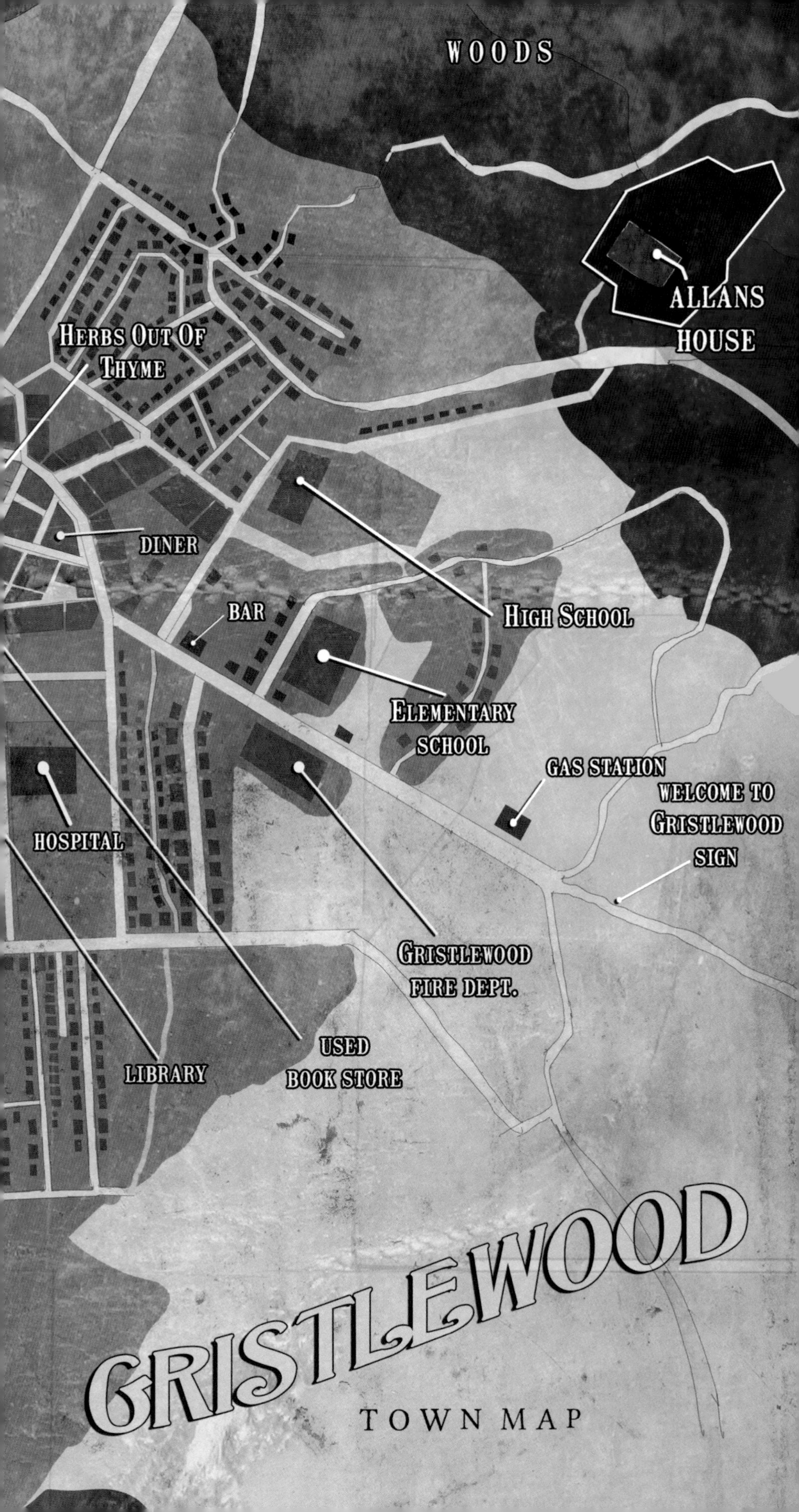
WOODS
ALLANS HOUSE
HERBS OUT OF THYME
DINER
BAR
HIGH SCHOOL
ELEMENTARY SCHOOL
GAS STATION
WELCOME TO GRISTLEWOOD SIGN
HOSPITAL
GRISTLEWOOD FIRE DEPT.
USED BOOK STORE
LIBRARY
GRISTLEWOOD
TOWN MAP

The beginning began like this...:
An interview with Steve Niles and Damien Worm

IDW: Steve, Damien, hello! So happy to have you join us! First off, for fans that are new to *October Faction*, what other comics and projects might they know you from?

Steve Niles (Writer): My other projects include *Criminal Macabre, Mystery Society, Freaks of the Heartland, Frankenstein Alive, Alive*, and many others. I'm probably best known for *30 Days of Night*.

Damien Worm (Artist): Hi! *October Faction* was my second professional work as a comic book artist. Before that, I worked on *Monster & Madman* (Also written by Steve). I've also worked on other titles since like *Dark Souls, The Evil Within* and *Bloodborne*.

IDW: *October Faction* was the second series you did together after the Frankenstein's Monster meets Jack the Ripper thriller, *Monster & Madman*. Can you talk a little bit about that first collaboration?

SN: It all happened pretty fast. I met Damien through Facebook of all places. I saw his art and immediately dropped him a message. I had *Monster & Madman* outlined and we just dove in. I thought Damien did beautiful work on that series.

DW: It was our very first collaboration. And I was so excited because I was going to work with my favorite horror writer on a story about two of my favorite characters. And Steve's story was amazing. It was really dark, intense, and a bit sad. I had so much fun working on it.

IDW: And when did *October Faction* start? Was it something that came up while you guys were working on *Monster & Madman*? Or did it happen later and you just happened to be a great team?

SN: I started developing *October Faction* in 2013 after we'd finished *Monster & Madman*. It was very different at first, very dark and then as I worked, it slowly morphed into the book we have now. Damien was the first choice for the art. He was perfect for this series.

DW: Steve told me about *October Faction* when I was finishing the first issue of *Monster & Madman*. We talked about the story and I was genuinely excited. I started working on character designs between *Monster & Madman* pages.

IDW: One of the major differences between *October Faction* and other horror media (be it comics, books, television, movies, or whatever) is at the core, it's a story about a family. What appealed about doing a story that's more family-focused while also dealing with horrifying monsters?

SN: That was the angle I was going for. I wanted an entire family of monster hunters, but each member with their own personality and talent. I've written monster hunters before and I wanted to find a new way in. For all the horror at its core, *October Faction* is about keeping a family together.

DW: I think the story around the Allans and the other characters is really inviting. Some of them have secrets and problems that threaten them in a way sometimes more horrifying than monsters themselves. And alongside that, they have to deal with some vengeful spirits, vampires... the list is big!

IDW: This new edition of *October Faction* is out just in time for the series' fifth anniversary. Clearly, things have changed a lot in those past few years—most notably, five years ago it was just a comic and not a TV show. What's it like revisiting these early stories now, as opposed to when they were first coming out?

SN: It's fun to look back at the beginning. Things were very different at the start, characters trying to find their place. Now they are a full-blown team.

DW: The story is as great as always! And brings back good memories!

IDW: To build on that a bit more, what's it like seeing the Allan family come to life for television?

SN: I haven't seen the finished versions yet but from what I've seen, it looks great. They've taken the essence of the series and expanded on it. It's a really fun show and all the characters are there, the actors are amazing. I can't wait to see what people think.

DW: It's awesome indeed. The characters that I've been drawing during the last almost five years, they're all real people now.
It's crazy!!

IDW: How involved are you in the show's production? Are you seeing dailies?

SN: They've been great about keeping me in the loop. I got to fly up to Toronto and visit the set, meet the producers and the cast and crew. It was really thrilling seeing the Allans come to life. Just blew me away.

DW: Since I live in Spain, it's complicated to be involved, but Steve keeps me updated about everything.

IDW: Steve, you had a direct connection with EP Damian Kindler throughout the making of the show, can you tell us a bit about working with him and having such close proximity to the process?

SN: I love working with Damian Kindler. He invited me to the writers' room early on and really walked me through the whole process. While visiting the set, we had some time to hang out and I really like the guy and I love his vision of *October Faction*. We write back and forth all the time. I've worked on things where I felt shoved to the side, but with *October Faction* and Damian, I feel very in the loop.

IDW: Steve, are there any moments in the comic that just couldn't make the fit? Anything that got left on the cutting room floor that you wish you could go back and revisit?

SN: They've really managed to capture a lot of the moments. I was very happy.

IDW: Damien, your art style is such a defining feature of the series, but it's also evolving with this increasing crispness and range. What's it like looking back at the first issue and comparing it to some of the later ones?

DW: I really noticed that the art style has evolved during the whole run. I did the first issues with a concrete style. It was very dark and gritty, and more focused on the atmosphere, something similar to what I did on *Monster & Madman*. And then the style slowly changed to something more simple, but the dark feeling is still there.

IDW: Steve, what character do you feel comes most naturally to write?

SN: I really enjoy writing all of the characters, but I love writing the twins, Geoff and Vivian. They even surprise me with some of the things they say and do. The characters just flow out and are a great deal of fun.

IDW: Damien, what character do you feel comes most naturally to draw?

DW: Everyone of the gang... but maybe I should say Vivian, Geoff, and Dante (Robot Face).

IDW: Steve, about how long does it take to write an issue of the series?

SN: I didn't use to outline, so a script could take up to a week while I figured out the story as I went. Now that I do detailed outlines first, I can complete a 20-page script in a couple days.

IDW: Damien, you're doing the full artwork on your own thumbnails, layouts, pencils, inks, and colors! How long does each page take you? Do you have any shortcuts that you use?

DW: Well, every page is a world apart. Sometimes I need a day for one page, and sometimes a day and a half. But being consistent I can finish a page in less than one day. I always start making the rough pencils with no details, and then I start inking, adding details directly with the ink. And after that, the colors, of course!

IDW: There are a ton of different kinds of monsters listed on Fred's chalkboard in the first issue. Have there ever been plans to see all those monsters? Any we definitely won't?

SN: I'd love to check them off one by one. I guess we'll see!

DW: I really hope we can see every monster from the list!

IDW: If you could be a monster, what sort of monster would you be?

SN: Hmmm. That's a tough one. Vampire seems like the best answer because you're still human-ish, but I'd have to go with werewolf. That seems like a great monster to be.

DW: Cthulhu!!

Thank you both for chatting with us! Very excited to see what's next for the Allan family, in print and on streaming!

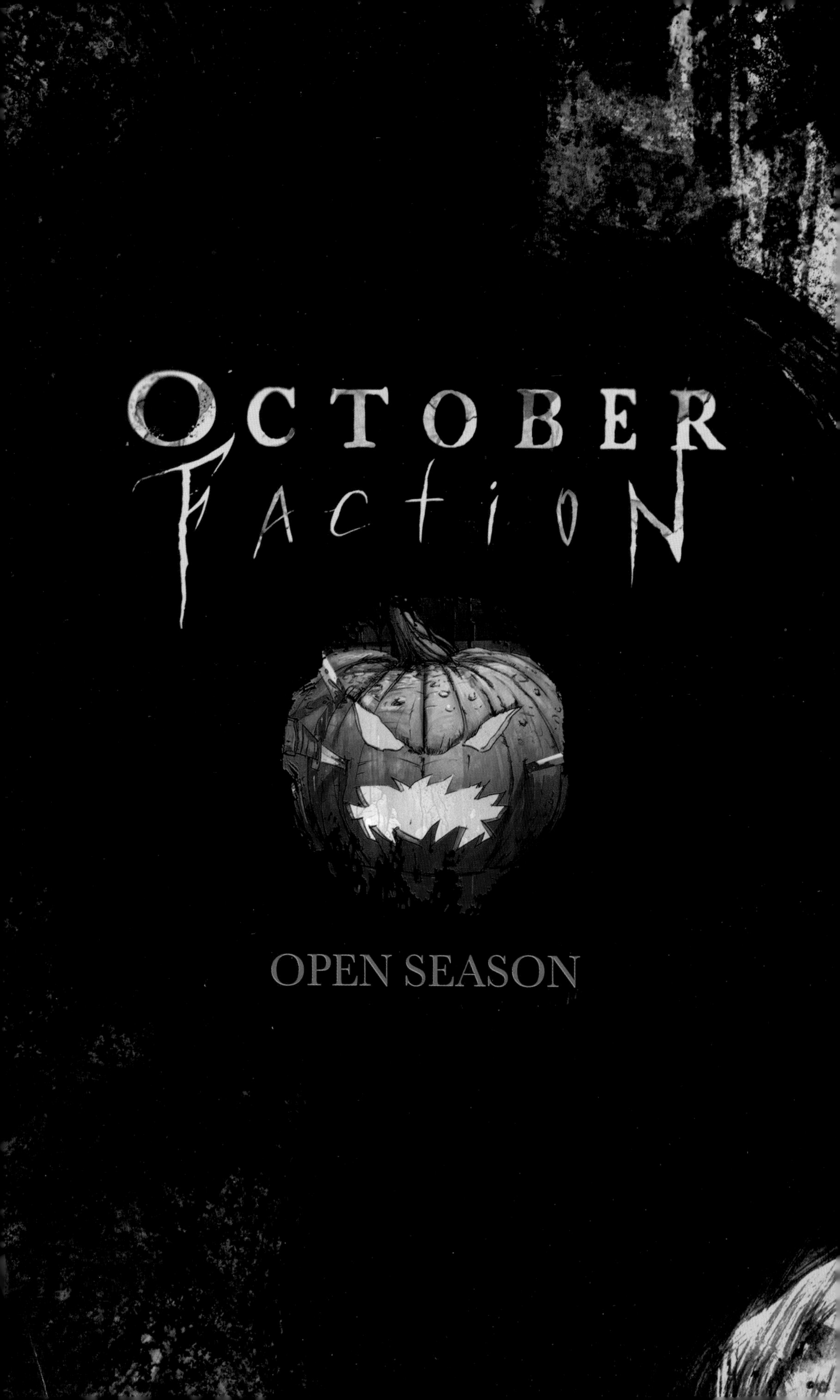
OCTOBER
FACTION
OPEN SEASON